Rick Barry's Pro Basketball Scouting Report

Player Ratings and In-Depth Analysis
on More Than 400 NBA Players and Draft Picks

Rick Barry
and
Jordan E. Cohn

Bonus Books, Inc., Chicago

93   92   91   90   89   5   4   3   2   1

Library of Congress Catalog Card Number: 89–85670

International Standard Book Number: 0–933893–81–7

Bonus Books, Inc.
160 East Illinois Street
Chicago, Illinois 60611

Printed in the United States of America

For Bob Wussler, Ted Turner, and to all of those people at CBS and TBS who have made it possible for me to remain in the sport that has been such an important part of my life.

RB

To my mother: who would have enjoyed this book immensely.

JC

Acknowledgments

This book benefitted enormously from discussions with the following people: Marty Blake, Bob Cousy, Jack McMahon, Tommy Heinsohn, George Blaha, Joe Tait, Curt Pickering, John Sterling, Tom Nissalke, Ailene Voisin, David Aldridge, Glenn Ordway, Terry Foster, Stu Lantz, Sam Smith, Tom Enlund, Dwight Jaynes, Dave Barnett, Kevin Calabro, Rick Majerus, Rod Hundley, Jeff Mullins, Bill Freider, Tom Penders, Ben Jobe, Jerry Pimm, Len Stephens, Boyd Grant, Charlie Coles, Ben Braun, Bill Frieder, Gene Keady, Jim Harrick, C.M. Newton, Billy Hahn, Leonard Hamilton, Billy Tubbs, Tom Scheenman, Pat Kennedy, Tom Davis, Gene Sullivan, Flip Saunders, David Benner, Steve Luhm, and many others around the NBA who offered their opinions.

Special thanks to Margery L. Schwartz of Los Angeles, whose deft editorial touch immeasurably helped the manuscript and Jim LoVerne of RJL Systems of Milford, Connecticut, whose statistical program—*The Basketball Statbook*—was an invaluable aid.

Mitch Kaufman of Hoop 1 Video Productions was a crucial link in this project. Without his service, this book would never have gotten off the ground.

Many thanks to Mike Dunleavey who introduced us to the concept of the true shooting percentage.

We also owe our gratitude to the media relations departments of every NBA team who were consistently helpful. Cari Haught of the Orlando Magic has been a terrific host at the Orlando All-Star Classic the last two years.

And our editor, Larry Razbadouski, who was unfailingly patient, conscientious, and helpful.

Introduction

Is Michael Jordan the best ever? Why has Reggie Williams been such a washout? Did Sedale Threatt have a good season? Is Alvin Robertson overrated? Why did the 76ers pick Kenny Payne? Just who is Haywoode Workman?

Life and death questions? Maybe not. Burning questions for the fanatic fan? Absolutely. Welcome to the first edition of *Rick Barry's Pro Basketball Scouting Report,* the only in-depth analysis available of current and prospective NBA players. Here, at your fingertips, is everything you want to know about a player's game: his repertoire of shots, defensive ability, rebounding prowess, ball handling skills, intangibles, and much more. As the title suggests, this is a scouting report, an evaluation of each player's strengths and weaknesses, combined with a rating system—both of their individual skills and their overall play. The opinions are Rick's but have been supplemented by the views of insiders around the league.

Last season, 353 players played at least one game. For current players, we applied a twofold test to determine who would be included in the book: (a) Each player had to play at least 20 games and/or (b) be reasonably certain to play in the league in the 1989–90 season. The result is a comprehensive analysis of 310 players. We also covered all of the draft picks, the leading undrafted rookies, the foreign players, and the players who were in the CBA, abroad, or did not play last year—and have a reasonable chance of making a team. Because there were only two rounds in this year's draft, many of the free agents are effectively third-round picks and have a chance to make it. We have excluded players who have signed to play in Europe such as Danny Ferry.

There are several things you should know about the format and concept of the book.

A. Every current NBA player is analyzed in six categories: scoring, defense, defensive rebounding (since they are conceptually related, defense and defensive rebounding are grouped together in the text), the floor game, intangibles, and a summary comment. (See paragraph F for a discussion of each category.)

B. Throughout the text, there are numerous references to the commonly used numerical designation for player positions:

> 1—point guard
> 2—shooting guard
> 3—small forward
> 4—power or big forward
> 5—center

C. You will also see numerous references to a player's performance on a *per minute* basis. This is a way of equating the performances of players who play dissimilar minutes. For example, starters will typically accumulate higher totals in all statistical categories than their reserve counterparts but the per minute numbers put them on an equal footing for comparison's sake. Note that the player's per minute numbers are generally compared to others' of his position—and we've created 10 positions (starting 1s, 2s, 3s, 4s, and 5s and backup 1s, 2s, 3s, 4s, and 5s). So when we say Johnny Newman is a below-average defensive rebounder, we mean he is below the norm for starting 3s.

D. We have calculated what we call the *true shooting percentage* for each player, which is listed in the statistical summary as TSP and referred to in the text. The idea is this: Players typically lower their overall shooting percentage when they shoot a lot of three-point attempts because it's a more difficult shot than the two-pointer; but at the same time they are adding an extra point. The true shooting percentage is a way of including the "value added" of that extra point into the overall shooting percentage. For example, Player A, a power forward, shoots 1000 times in a season, makes 450, but attempts no three-pointers. His shooting percentage is 45 percent. Excluding free throws, he has scored 900 points. But consider Player B who also shoots 1,000 times, makes 450, but 100 of his field goals are three-pointers. In the record book, he is also a 45 percent shooter, but he has scored an additional 100 points. So the true shooting percentage translates those 100 points into two-point field goals (50) and adds it to the number of field goals. In effect, Player B has made 500 two-point field goals for a much more impressive 50 percent from the field.

E. The assist-to-turnover ratio is a measure of a player's ball handling efficiency: how many assists he makes relative to the number of turnovers. The ratio varies according to position; for example, point guards have the capacity for the highest ratio because they can generate lots of assists while centers, who don't handle the ball much, have lower ratios.

F. Here is a *sampling* of some of the questions we attempted to answer in each category:

Scoring
—What is his repertoire of shots?
—Does he have any patented shots (i.e., the sky hook)?
—Is he a scorer or pure shooter (or neither)?

—Can he create his own shot?
—Does he exhibit good shot selection?
—Did he have a good year, scoring-wise?
—Is he consistent?
—Does his team look to him to score?

Defense/Defensive Rebounding
—Does he like to play defense?
—What physical skills does he have on defense?
—Does he play good one-on-one defense? Or more effective as team defender?
—Is he a shot blocker?
—Does he steal the ball?
—Does he like to bang the boards?
—What are his per minute defensive rebounding numbers relative to others at his position?
—Is he considered a good defender?
—Why is he a good rebounder? Why not?

The Floor Game
—Does he have good hands?
—Is he a good passer?
—Does he run the floor well?
—Is he a good dribbler?
—What is his assist-to-turnover ratio?
—Does he see the floor?
—Does he move well without the ball?
—Does he make his teammates better?

Intangibles
—Is he a team player?
—Is he a good influence on the team?
—A problem player?
—Is he injury-prone?
—Does he provide leadership?
—Is he consistent?

In Sum
A final comment summarizing his game, his role on the team, his future in the league.

H. Abbreviations:

>   ppg—points per game
>   rpg—rebounds per game
>   apg—assists per game
>   mpg—minutes per game
>   at—assist-to-turnover ratio

THE RATINGS

We have rated every current NBA player (excluding the draft picks and free agents and others entering the league for the first time) on the following skills: scoring, shooting, free throw shooting, ball handling, passing, defense, defensive rebounding, intangibles. Plus there is an overall rating. In addition, there is another category for point guards—playmaking, while power forwards and centers are rated on shot blocking.

Here's what the ratings mean:

>   AAA—Top-of-the-line
>   AA—Big-time
>   A—First-rate
>   B—Middle-of-the-pack
>   C—Mediocre, at best
>   D—Suspect

Here's how we derived the ratings:

Scoring—relies heavily, though not exclusively, on the per minute scoring stats. The comparison is both to all players in the league plus players at his position. But we didn't slavishly adhere to the numbers. Isiah Thomas, for example, would be only an A by the numbers but his ability to take over a game offensively propels him to an AA.

Shooting—Dennis Rodman led the league in shooting percentage, so obviously field goal percentage is only one indicator (or nonindicator as the case may be) of shooting ability. Field goal percentage and true shooting percentage were referenced but consistency, range, and repertoire—among other factors—were also considered.

Free Throw Shooting—strictly by the numbers. No nuances in this category. We evaluated each player's at-the-line 1988–89 performance, not his lifetime effort. Our formula:

>   .880 and above—AAA
>   .879 to .840—AA
>   .839 to .800—A
>   .799 to .750—B
>   .749 to .700—C
>   .699 and below—D

Defense—steals, blocked shots, and fouls per minute were used as references but this was largely a subjective rating.

Defensive Rebounding—per minute numbers comprised the key factor.

Intangibles—obviously subjective.

Shot blocking—per minute numbers were the key criteria.

Playmaking—assist-to-turnover ratios, turnovers per minute, and assists per minute were all considered. This is a combination objective/subjective rating, with leadership and creativity also entering the equation.

Overall—the sum of the parts. Note plusses and minuses (i.e. B +, A –) were used only in this category.

Going back door,

Rick, Jordan.

P.S. We'd love to hear from you. Write us with your opinions and suggestions.

Mark Acres

Birthdate: November 15, 1962
Height: 6-10
Weight: 220
College: Oral Roberts University, Tulsa, Okla.
Drafted: Dallas on second round, 1985 (40th pick).
Positions: Center, Forward
Final 1989 Team: Boston Celtics
Final 1988–89 Statistics:

G	Fg	Fga	Fg%	Ft	Fta	Ft%	Orb	Reb	Ast	Stl	To	Blk	Pts	Ppg
62	55	114	.482	26	48	.542	59	146	19	19	23	6	137	2.2

Three-point goals: 1–1 (1.000)   **TSP:** .487

SCORING

No facing game. No back-to-the-basket moves. No jumper. No hook shot. In a phrase, no offense. In 1988–89, Acres, a two-year pro (both seasons in Boston) and now, as a result of the expansion draft, a member of the Magic, would have barely averaged double figures (10.4) if he played the full 48 minutes. (As it was, he scored 2.2 ppg in 10.2 mpg.) When he does score, it's on the end of the break—he runs well for a 6-10 player—or on the offensive glass (though he doesn't finish well) where he had above-average numbers for a backup center. He's a terrible foul shooter (.542 in 1988–89; .610 lifetime).

DEFENSE/DEFENSIVE REBOUNDING

Defense is Acres' NBA calling card. He'll put his body on the big people and he doesn't back down from anybody. His mobility and hustle made him valuable in the Celtics' new-found trapping defense. Not a particularly good jumper, he'll mix it up on the defensive glass (slightly below average for his position). A tendency to be overly aggressive and foul-prone in his rookie year has given way to a more controlled fury. But at 6-10, he's undersized and more naturally a power forward.

THE FLOOR GAME

As noted, he runs well but his ball handling skills are barely adequate (though he doesn't turn the ball over).

INTANGIBLES

The consensus is that Acres gets the most of his rather limited ability. He has a killer instinct and is willing to put his nose to the grindstone.

IN SUM

With the acquisition of Joe Kleine, Acres was phased out of the rotation. So it was no surprise he was left exposed in the expansion draft. He's strictly a role player—even with an expansion team—again, not as a backup center but as a power forward. But with Orlando hurting for centers, he may end up in the 5 spot again.

RICK'S RATINGS

Scoring: **D**	Defense: **A**
Shooting: **D**	Defensive Rebounding: **B**
Free Throw Shooting: **D**	Shot Blocking: **D**
Ball Handling: **C**	Intangibles: **B**
Passing: **C**	Overall: **D**

Michael Adams

Birthdate: January 19, 1963
Height: 5-11
Weight: 165
College: Boston College, Chestnut Hill, Mass.
Drafted: Sacramento on third round, 1985 (66th pick).
Position: Guard
Final 1989 Team: Denver Nuggets
Final 1988–89 Statistics:

G	Fg	Fga	Fg%	Ft	Fta	Ft%	Orb	Reb	Ast	Stl	To	Blk	Pts	Ppg
77	488	1062	.433	322	393	.819	71	283	490	166	180	11	1424	18.5

Three-point goals: 166–466 (.356)   **TSP:** .507

SCORING

Call it unorthodox, call it ugly, Adams will never win any style awards for his shooting. But as they say, "If it ain't broke, don't fix it." Adams' shot-put-like heaves go in and go in consistently—what better evidence than his incredible streak of hitting three-pointers in a record 79 consecutive games over the last two seasons (the streak finally ended on January 28 against the Nets). Adams is the league's most prolific trifecta shooter—he shot an NBA-record 466 treys last year and canned an NBA-record 166 of them—for a most respectable .356. Overall, he shot only .433 but nowhere is the true shooting percentage more relevant than when applied to Adams (.507). When he was acquired from Washington (with Jay Vincent for Mark Alarie and Darrell Walker in November 1987), no one figured he'd become such a potent scoring threat (18.5 ppg last season). But if he doesn't kill you from beyond the three-point line, he'll hurt you going to the bucket. With his extraordinary quickness, Adams blows by defenders and somehow manages to score amid the trees. Or he'll get fouled (5.1 attempts a game)—only Magic Johnson, Kevin Johnson, and John Stockton went to the line more among starting 1s. Adams shot a decent .819 from the line.

DEFENSE/DEFENSIVE REBOUNDING

Adams is a pest. He'll harass the ball handler and if you're not careful, take it right from you (2.2 steals a game, 11th in the league). Many of his steals also come in help situations, in which Adams is doubling. But at 5-11, he can be posted up or isolated.

THE FLOOR GAME

Adams is the catalyst, the jet who fires Denver's motion offense. He pushes the ball up court in a hurry—he's fast in addition to his quickness—and in the half-court setting, his waterbug style is a perfect mesh for Denver's up-tempo, never-stop-moving system. He's a clever passer—favoring the occasional behind-the-back-pass—and a careful ballhandler. (Vis-á-vis other starting points, his assists, 6.4 a game, were low but he doesn't handle it as much as most 1s.) With Curly Neal-like control, Adams may be the best dribbler in the league, terrific at penetrating, drawing a crowd, and finding the open man.

INTANGIBLES

In a league full of tough hombres, Adams, pound for pound, may be the toughest. He doesn't back down from anyone and is a fearless competitor. You have to admire his persistence. He's a three-time loser (thrice waived—once by Sacramento and twice by Washington) who never gave up on himself. He's also a big-shot guy who has won many a game with his shooting. But he got a little worn out last season (he suffered through a horrendous shooting slump in February) and will be more effective playing fewer minutes (he averaged 36.2 a game).

IN SUM

A few years ago, many thought Adams was a lost cause; now he's one of the premier little men in the league. He's on the right team, and evidently that makes all the difference in the world.

RICK'S RATINGS

Scoring: **AA**	Defense: **A**
Shooting: **AA**	Defensive Rebounding: **B**
Free Throw Shooting: **A**	Playmaking: **A**
Ball Handling: **AA**	Intangibles: **AA**
Passing: **A**	Overall: **A +**

Mark Aguirre

Birthdate: December 10, 1959
Height: 6-6
Weight: 235
College: DePaul University, Chicago, Ill.
Drafted: Dallas on first round as an undergraduate, 1981 (1st pick).
Position: Forward
Final 1989 Team: Detroit Pistons
Final 1988–89 Statistics:

G	Fg	Fga	Fg%	Ft	Fta	Ft%	Orb	Reb	Ast	Stl	To	Blk	Pts	Ppg
80	586	1270	.461	288	393	.733	146	386	278	45	208	36	1511	18.9

Three-point goals: 51–174 (.293) **TSP:** .481

SCORING

His shot attempts went down, his scoring dropped, his minutes decreased, he barely saw the light of day in the fourth quarter. But, at least for now, Mark Aguirre isn't complaining. He has his peace; he has his ring. It was a major-league trade involving major-league scorers. On February 15, the Pistons traded Adrian Dantley (along with a first-round pick in 1991) to the Mavericks in exchange for Aguirre. Why, asked the pundits, did the Pistons want to break up a good thing, to upset the chemistry of a team that had taken the Lakers to the seventh game in the 1987–88 finals and had the second-best record in the league at the time of the trade? And more pointedly, what did they want with Aguirre, a talented fellow but one with a well-known reputation for being moody, unwilling to play in pain, and just plain difficult? For one, the Pistons didn't figure they'd lose much in the way of point production. While Dantley has averaged 25 a game in his 13-year career, Aguirre is the most productive scorer, career-wise, per minute, among starting 3s, a group that includes Charles Barkley, Larry Bird, and Dominique Wilkins. (He averaged 24.6 a game with the Mavs). Then there was the matter of style. Dantley's game is isolation, one-on-one—he's extremely effective, but it eats the clock and leaves teammates out of the picture. Aguirre's pace is snappier; he's a much better passer out of the double-team, runs the court better and unlikely Dantley, has three-point range. Plus, at 29 (he'll be 30 in December), he was four years younger than Dantley. It turned out, too, that Aguirre, always the MAN in Dallas, was willing to become a role player with the Pistons, to submerge his considerable scoring ego and become just another mid-teen scorer (he averaged 15.5 ppg on 12.3 shots in 30.0 mpg with the Pistons, compared to 21.7 ppg, 18.8 shots, and 34.8 minutes with Dallas in 1988–89). And he didn't seem to mind that, particularly during the playoffs, Dennis Rodman finished the game (a scenario Dantley would not have tolerated on a consistent basis). In his limited role, Aguirre remained one of the best post-up players in the league. He sticks that behind of his into defenders and goes to work. His options are numerous and varied: step-back jumpers, pump fakes to draw fouls (he went to the line 4.9 times a game, though he's a below-average foul shooter: .733 last year), power moves off the dribble, turnaround jumpers. But a strength in his game is that he can also go outside and hit from distance, though he's had better seasons (only .293) from beyond the arc. With the Pistons, Aguirre pretty much delivered the goods, though he was occasionally inconsistent.

DEFENSE/DEFENSIVE REBOUNDING

Rodman finished games while Aguirre sat because Piston coach Chuck Daly wanted rebounding and defense down the stretch, rather than scoring. Aguirre is not a bad post defender—with his bulk, he knocks people around and takes them out of their comfort zones in the blocks. But he has definite speed and quickness limitations on the perimeter—he was, many feel, overweight, which isn't news—and gives you nothing in the way of steals, blocked shots, and is a below-average defensive rebounder.

THE FLOOR GAME

Invariably, Aguirre is double-teamed, but he does a fine job of reading it. In fact, he can downright thread the needle in the half-court offense, accumulating as many as 17 assists (with Dallas). But in the transition game—top-of-the-key to top-of-the-key—it's best to keep the ball out of Aguirre's hands altogether. His turnovers were slightly above average.

INTANGIBLES

Almost immediately upon his arrival, Aguirre's teammates made it crystal clear they would not put up with any of his—there's no better way to say it—crap. Aguirre got the message and got it quickly, and he was on his best behavior. You can't argue with the Piston's record after they acquired him: 30-6 (compared to 33-13, pre-Aguirre) during the regular season and an NBA title (though Aguirre disappeared against the Lakers in the finals), which says something about his "chemical effect" on the team.

IN SUM

Ok, the honeymoon is over, and everybody had a good time. Now for the grind of a full season. It will be interesting to see whether Aguirre's model citizenship will last. Of course, Piston coach Chuck Daly has a marvelous way of "controlling" Mark Aguirre: play Dennis Rodman. But let's not forget Aguirre's talent: he's a proven scorer, fine passer, and evidently, meshed as well, if not better, than Adrian Dantley.

RICK'S RATINGS

Scoring: **A**   Defense: **C**
Shooting: **A**   Defensive Rebounding: **C**
Free Throw Shooting: **C**   Intangibles: **B**
Ball Handling: **B**   Overall: **A**
Passing: **A**

Danny Ainge

Birthdate: March 17, 1959
Height: 6-5
Weight: 185
College: Brigham Young University, Provo, Utah
Drafted: Boston on second round, 1981 (31st pick).
Position: Guard
Final 1989 Team: Sacramento Kings
Final 1988–89 Statistics:

G	Fg	Fga	Fg%	Ft	Fta	Ft%	Orb	Reb	Ast	Stl	To	Blk	Pts	Ppg
73	480	1051	.457	205	240	.854	71	255	402	93	145	8	1281	17.5

Three-point goals: 116–305 (.380)   **TSP:** .512

SCORING

In Boston, Ainge was a "satellite" in an offense that revolved around the big guys—Parish, Bird, and McHale. Roaming on the outskirts, he made opponents pay when they double-teamed down low or two-timed Bird. The Celtics rarely ran plays for him, but he managed to put up decent numbers (11.2 ppg for his Celtic career) and he was an All-Star in 1987–88. But in Sacramento (Ainge, along with Brad Lohaus, were exchanged for Joe Kleine and Ed Pinckney right before the 1989 trading deadline) he moved to center stage. Result: more shots (16.5 compared to 13.1), more points (20.3 vs. 15.9), and his own personal high in his fourth game (45 points, tying a mark set earlier in the year against the 76ers). In Boston, the eight-year veteran chafed under criticism that he shot the three-pointer too quickly and too frequently. With the Kings, who are enamored of the three (second in the league in total attempts), Ainge had the green light. And indeed the former Toronto Blue Jay third baseman (good field/no hit) is one of the NBA's most dangerous trifecta shooters: .386 for his career; .380 last year (16th in the league). He can shoot the jumper off the dribble but is best spotting up or coming off picks. He's a good driver and great foul shooter (.854 in 1988–89; .861 lifetime) though he infrequently takes it to the well (only 1.8 free throw attempts a game for his career).

DEFENSE/DEFENSIVE REBOUNDING

Feisty, aggressive, tough—Ainge is an excellent defender who will do anything to stop his man from scoring. As one observer noted, "If he were a salesmen, he'd be calling on you a hundred times a day." He's not extra quick, but he can stop his man from penetrating and is effective as a weak side defender (1.3 steals a game). But he's never been much more than average on the defensive glass.

THE FLOOR GAME

In Boston, Ainge had a penchant for playing under control for 44 minutes and then ushering forth with plays that were out of kilter with the game situation. He's a careful ball handler—his 2.77 assist-to-turnover ratio was third among starting 2s—and a very good passer. While not a pure point, he also has the ability to push the ball on the break. Since he can play both guard spots, he and Kenny Smith can interchange at the 1 and 2, which has freed up Smith's scoring abilities.

INTANGIBLES

Ainge instantly became a leader on the Kings; his two championship rings are a major plus on a team inured to losing. He's vocal on the court, encourages his teammates, and plays hurt. He's an incessant hustler and one of the league's most intense competitors.

IN SUM

Sacramento figures it traded two role players (Kleine and Pinckney) for a role player (Lohaus, now with the Timberwolves) and a star (Ainge). His leadership, hustle, ball handling, and scoring provide a firm foundation as the Kings build toward respectability.

RICK'S RATINGS

Scoring: **AA**	Defense: **A**
Shooting: **AA**	Defensive Rebounding: **B**
Free Throw Shooting: **AA**	Playmaking: **A**
Ball Handling: **A**	Intangibles: **AAA**
Passing: **A**	Overall: **AA**

Mark Alarie

Birthdate: December 11, 1963
Height: 6-8
Weight: 217
College: Duke University, Durham, N.C.
Drafted: Denver on first round, 1986 (18th pick).
Position: Forward

Final 1989 Team: Washington Bullets
Final 1988–89 Statistics:

G	Fg	Fga	Fg%	Ft	Fta	Ft%	Orb	Reb	Ast	Stl	To	Blk	Pts	Ppg
74	206	431	.478	73	87	.839	103	255	63	25	62	22	498	6.7

Three-point goals: 13–38 (.342)   **TSP:** .493

SCORING

After playing mostly mop-up in 1987–88 (12.2 minutes a game)—he was the least used Bullet that year—Alarie, a three-year veteran, finally got some quality time in 1988–89. With the Bullets going nowhere, he became a regular part of the rotation in January and made the most of it. His rep is as a good shooter, and indeed he can stroke with range (.478 overall and an admirable .342 from three-point land). Slow afoot and not quick, Alarie definitely needs help to get his shot. Though he has limited jumping ability (he was a much better jumper in college but hurt his knee at Denver, where he played his rookie year), Alarie is a sneaky rebounder and garnered 1.4 offensive boards a game (which put him in the top one-third among backup 3s). He will occasionally put the ball on the floor, but that's not what he does best. He hit .839 from the line, which was more than 15 percentage points higher than the career 68 percent he was shooting entering the season.

DEFENSE/DEFENSIVE REBOUNDING

Alarie has limitations, athletically, on the defensive end, but he is well-schooled (Krzyzewski's Duke; in fact, Alarie eventually may be best remembered for the clamp job—four points—he did on Danny Manning in the 1986 NCAA semifinals) and knows position defense. Again, he's a surprisingly effective defensive rebounder in spite of his physical drawbacks.

THE FLOOR GAME

Alarie gets up and down the court well and is not uncomfortable passing the ball.

INTANGIBLES

Alarie is a "good kid," and an excellent worker. Early in his career, some said he was soft, but he's gotten a lot tougher under coach Wes Unseld's tutelage.

IN SUM

A disappointment in Denver, with playing time, Alarie showed he can be an effective member of a rotation. His scoring, rebounding, and defense can help at the 7th-8th-man level—and in five games as a starter, he shot .533.

RICK'S RATINGS

Scoring: **B**	Defense: **B**
Shooting: **A**	Defensive Rebounding: **A**
Free Throw Shooting: **A**	Intangibles: **B**
Ball Handling: **B**	Overall: **B**
Passing: **B**	

Steve Alford

Birthdate: November 23, 1964
Height: 6-2
Weight: 185
College: Indiana University, Bloomington, Ind.
Drafted: Dallas on second round, 1987 (26th pick).
Position: Guard
Final 1989 Team: Golden State Warriors
Final 1988–89 Statistics:

G	Fg	Fga	Fg%	Ft	Fta	Ft%	Orb	Reb	Ast	Stl	To	Blk	Pts	Ppg
66	148	324	.457	50	61	.820	10	72	92	45	45	3	366	5.5

Three-point goals: 20–55 (.364)   **TSP:** .488

SCORING

Alford, one of the most heralded ballplayers in Indiana B-Ball history (both in high school—he was "Mr. Basketball"—and in college, where he became Indiana University's leading scorer), has found tougher sledding in his post-Indiana days. First, he had to endure the insult of being drafted in the second round by the Dallas Mavericks in 1987 (he was the fans' choice for the Pacers' No. 1, but Reggie Miller was selected). Then, in his rookie year, Alford sat, and sat, and sat some more (playing in just 28 games for 197 minutes). More, the Mavs felt that Alford, possessor of as sweet a stroke as you'll find anywhere (he's made a successful video detailing his technique), and a pure shooter by birth, was too small (at 6-2) for the 2, so they experimented with him as a 1. The experiment failed, and, piling on another indignity, he was waived by Dallas in December 1988. But Don Nelson, as he is wont to see, had another perspective. If Alford is such a good shooter, why not return him to his natural environs as shooting guard? And there you have it. Alford signed with the Warriors in December 1988 and while he didn't burn up the league (5.5 ppg in 13.7 minutes on .457 shooting)—at least he's in the league, which is more than what some expected of him at this point. And if Alford is going to survive in the NBA, it will be on the basis of his ability to shoot the ball. He has a quick release and deep range—a solid .364 from three-point land. The rap against him is that he has trouble creating his own shot, and while he's best spotting up and getting a pick, he's also clever and knows how to use his dribble to back his man up and then shoot. It doesn't hurt matters that he can shoot foul shots (.820 last year).

DEFENSE/DEFENSIVE REBOUNDING

What made NBA GMs nervous on draft day in 1987 was Alford's lack of lateral quickness. Indeed, he has a problem with quicker and taller opponents, which is just about everybody. But he does play the passing lanes well, knows how to play D, and his weaknesses could be disguised, to a point, since he was usually on the floor with Manute Bol, the league's top shot blocker and intimidator.

THE FLOOR GAME

Moving Alford to the 2 made sense for another reason: he doesn't have great ball handling skills or the blow-by-you ability you want in a point. But he's a solid passer who doesn't make a lot of mistakes.

INTANGIBLES

Bright, friendly, fabulous work ethic. "A quality human being." Alford gets as much as he can out of his physical abilities.

IN SUM

With his limited physical skills, Alford's job will always be precarious. Not a player you want on the floor for 25 minutes a night, he's good for spot duty, if he's shooting the ball well. He may be making it "Back Home Again in Indiana."

RICK'S RATINGS

Scoring: **B**
Shooting: **A**
Free Throw Shooting: **A**
Ball Handling: **B**
Passing: **B**

Defense: **C**
Defensive Rebounding: **B**
Intangibles: **A**
Overall: **C+**

Greg "Cadillac" Anderson

Birthdate: June 22, 1964
Height: 6-10
Weight: 230
College: University of Houston, Houston, Tex.
Drafted: San Antonio on first round, 1987 (23rd pick).
Positions: Forward, Center
Final 1989 Team: San Antonio Spurs
Final 1988–89 Statistics:

G	Fg	Fga	Fg%	Ft	Fta	Ft%	Orb	Reb	Ast	Stl	To	Blk	Pts	Ppg
82	460	914	.503	207	403	.514	255	676	61	102	180	103	1127	13.7

Three-point goals: 0–3 (.000)   **TSP:** .503

SCORING

As long as "Cadillac," who was the Spurs' starting power forward for most of the year and was traded in May with Alvin Robertson to the Bucks for Terry Cummings, stays within 6 feet of the basket, good things happen. His best "shot" is the dunk; next best, the layup. His points come on the break—he's a real thoroughbred, who runs extraordinarily well for a 6-10 man—inside, where he uses his great quickness to spin around his man, lobs, or on the offensive glass (3.1 a game, 22nd in the league on a per minute basis) where he takes advantage of his ability to jump high and quick. Less certain are his other weapons: a developing jump hook and a facing jumper from in close. Anderson, who is entering his third year, had trouble as a rookie defining what his shot was—for example, he'd shoot jumpers beyond his range. But last year, he played within himself more and upped his average (in more minutes) from 11.7 ppg to 13.7. Though he works on it, he still can't shoot free throws; in 1988–89, a pitiful .514, which was worse than his wretched rookie-year .604 performance.

DEFENSE/DEFENSIVE REBOUNDING

When you're 6-10 and can jump the way Anderson does, you'll block some shots. Anderson got 1.2 a game last year. More surprising is his ability to steal the ball (1.2 a game)—with his quick hands, he strips the ball in a pack, rather than playing the passing lanes. But the bottom line is that Anderson has miles to go before he's a good defender. First, he has to learn defensive concepts. Also, he tends to play behind his man, rather than fighting for position. And while he's an average defensive rebounder (8.2 'bounds overall), he hasn't made a habit of blocking opponents off the board.

THE FLOOR GAME

Here, too, Anderson is still in the developmental stage. His passing is suspect; he averaged less than three-quarters of an assist a game in 2401 minutes. You don't want him putting the ball on the floor except for a bounce or two before his own shot. While he's a willing learner, Anderson does not completely comprehend the game.

INTANGIBLES

Anderson is an upbeat, team-oriented player. But he was in coach Larry Brown's doghouse for much of the year due to alleged lack of intensity. So, it was no surprise when he was traded.

IN SUM

At his size and with his ability to run and jump, Anderson should be around a long time. But he needs to refine his game, to pay attention to the game's nuances and subtleties, to harness his considerable athletic talent—in a phrase: learn the game. With Larry Krystkowiak out with a knee injury, pencil in Cadillac as the Bucks starting power forward.

Richard Anderson

Birthdate: November 19, 1960
Height: 6-10
Weight: 240
College: University of California at Santa Barbara, Santa Barbara, Calif.
Drafted: San Diego on second round, 1982 (32nd pick).
Position: Forward
Final 1989 Team: Portland Trail Blazers
Final 1988–89 Statistics:

G	Fg	Fga	Fg%	Ft	Fta	Ft%	Orb	Reb	Ast	Stl	To	Blk	Pts	Ppg
72	145	348	.417	32	38	842	62	231	98	44	54	12	371	5.2

Three-point goals: 49–141 (.348)   **TSP:** .487

SCORING

Anderson has acquired the reputation of being a good shooter, even a pure shooter (the ultimate accolade for a shooter), on his ability to launch from distance. In 1988–89, for example, about 41 percent of his shots were beyond the three-point line. But range, it must be pointed out, is not completely synonymous with shooting ability. Yes, he's a decent three-point shooter (.348 last year and .322 lifetime) but overall, he's abysmal: .417 in 1988–89, .412 for his career, and in a five-year career, a single-season high of .426 (though his true shooting percentage was an OK .487 last season). And only in the last two years has he shot a substantial number of threes (which bring down overall percentages); in his first three seasons, he shot a total of 54 trifectas. Part of the problem is shot selection: Anderson doesn't always take the best shots. Also, when he plays small forward (at 6-10, 240, he plays both forward positions), quicker 3s give him trouble. For that reason, he's more effective against power forwards who won't always go out on the floor to guard him. Otherwise, he runs the floor well for his size but is only a fair offensive rebounder. Anderson is basically a perimeter player who doesn't like contact.

DEFENSE/DEFENSIVE REBOUNDING

Anderson can be outquicked by the 3s and overpowered by the 4s, but he compensates with his intelligence and his understanding of what his opponent will do. He's not physical, doesn't jump well, but through positioning has managed some middle-of-the-pack numbers (per minute) on the defensive boards.

THE FLOOR GAME

Anderson is a fine passer who sees the court well. But you

don't want him putting the ball on the floor against smaller, quicker small forwards.

INTANGIBLES

Anderson may have more than his share of B-Ball smarts but unfortunately, he doesn't always display them. More than once, his mental lapses got him into Mike Schuler's doghouse and he became something of a whipping boy for the former Portland coach. He also moaned about his lack of playing time (15 minutes per). But Rick Adelman, who succeeded Schuler, had a little more confidence in him.

IN SUM

When he keeps his head in the game, Anderson can make a contribution at both forward spots with his shooting and his savvy. But the bottom line is that Portland had a weak bench last year and Anderson was one of its component parts.

RICK'S RATINGS

Scoring: **C**   Defense: **B**
Shooting: **B**   Defensive Rebounding: **B**
Free Throw Shooting: **AA** Intangibles: **C**
Ball Handling: **B**   Overall: **C –**
Passing: **A**

Ron Anderson

Birthdate: October 15, 1958
Height: 6-6
Weight: 215
College: Fresno State University, Fresno, Calif.
Drafted: Cleveland on second round, 1984 (27th pick).
Position: Forward
Final 1989 Team: Philadelphia 76ers
Final 1988–89 Statistics:

G	Fg	Fga	Fg%	Ft	Fta	Ft%	Orb	Reb	Ast	Stl	To	Blk	Pts	Ppg
82	566	1152	.491	196	229	.856	167	406	139	71	126	23	1330	16.2

Three-point goals: 2–11 (.182)   **TSP:** .492

SCORING

Who knows what talent lurks on NBA benches? The 76ers evidently knew about Anderson, who has always been able to score—about a point every two minutes throughout his career—but had languished on NBA benches for four years (first in Cleveland, then in Indiana, where he sat behind Chuck Person and Wayman Tisdale) before the 76ers acquired him for rookie Everette Stephens. The 6-6 small forward finally got his chance and, oh my, did he make the most of it. Off the bench (he also started 12 games), Anderson averaged 16.2 ppg, shot a solid .491, and was one of the league's best sixth men (he received one vote for the award). He also played exceptionally well in the playoff series against the Knicks, scoring 26 in each of the first two games. Anderson can score from outside—he's an excellent jump shooter from 18 to 20 feet (but does not have three-point range), can put the ball on the floor with either hand, and is an exceptional runner of the floor. A superb foul shooter (.856 last year), Anderson also nabbed two offensive caroms a game, and even if he doesn't corral it, tips it to a teammate.

DEFENSE/DEFENSIVE REBOUNDING

The product of a great college defensive tradition (Fresno State), Anderson understands defense: He can deny the ball, gets over screens, but perhaps because he shouldered a lot of offensive responsibility, his defensive effort was sporadic. He's a slightly below-average defensive rebounder.

THE FLOOR GAME

Anderson's ball handling skills are adequate for the 3 spot. He can dribble to get his shots but otherwise he doesn't handle it much. He's a smart player who understands the game.

INTANGIBLES

There isn't a better practice player in the league. With Indiana, for example, Anderson was that rare player, who despite his lack of playing time, would do extra running to stay in shape. He's a dedicated pro who makes everybody better because of his work ethic.

IN SUM

Anderson was one of the NBA success stories of 1988–89, one of the most savvy acquisitions of the year. He's a late bloomer—he didn't play high school basketball—and at 31, he figures he has at least another five years in the league. With only 332 games under his belt (in five seasons), he's probably right.

RICK'S RATINGS

Scoring: **AA**   Defense: **B**
Shooting: **AA**   Defensive Rebounding: **C**
Free Throw Shooting: **AA** Intangibles: **AA**
Ball Handling: **B**   Overall: **A**
Passing: **B**

Willie Anderson

Birthdate: January 8, 1967
Height: 6-8
Weight: 178
College: University of Georgia, Athens, Ga.
Drafted: San Antonio on first round, 1988 (10th pick).
Positions: Forward, Guard
Final 1989 Team: San Antonio Spurs
Final 1988–89 Statistics:

G	Fg	Fga	Fg%	Ft	Fta	Ft%	Orb	Reb	Ast	Stl	To	Blk	Pts	Ppg
81	640	1285	.498	224	289	.775	152	417	372	150	261	62	1508	18.6

Three-point goals: 4–21 (.190)   **TSP:** .500

SCORING

First impressions can be misleading, but that wasn't the case with Willie Anderson, the Spurs' first-round pick in 1988 (10th overall). In the Spurs' opening game of the 1988–89 season, Anderson blitzed the Lakers for 30 points, displaying a repertoire that ran the gamut from jumpers off the dribble, to offensive rebounds, to full-court sprints (and finishes), to easy hoops rewarded for moving without the ball. While his debut was, no doubt, a special game (he scored 30 or more in five games with a high of 36), Anderson's production for the rest of the season indicated he's not a mere flash in the pan. With 18.6 a game, he was the Spurs' highest scorer, made the All-Rookie first team, and even received four votes for Rookie of the Year. Anderson's talents are best displayed in transition, where he can use his speed, quickness, and creativity; but his offensive capabilities suffer in the half-court offense since he's not yet a consistent jump shooter. He can play the 2 and 3 and even some 1, but last year he played mostly at small forward, where he is too quick for most defenders. An exciting player, he seems to come up with a new move every night.

DEFENSE/DEFENSIVE REBOUNDING

Anderson's quickness is a big asset on defense, where he can steal the ball (1.9 a game, 20th in the league) and apply pressure. But at 6-8, 178, he's one of the skinniest players in the league and doesn't have the beef to bang consistently against the bigger small forwards, which is one reason Spur coaches feel he is out of position at the 3. Defensively, as a 2, he matches up better strength-wise. His lack of bulk also hurts on the defensive board, where he relies on his quickness and jumping ability. His 3.3 defensive rebounds a game

(and 5.1 overall) were below average for the position. The feeling is that he is capable of seven boards a night.

THE FLOOR GAME

Anderson played the point for two years at Georgia, so, yes, he can handle it. He's an excellent passer but he also turned the ball over 3.2 times a game, generally because he's often guilty of trying to create something that's not there. As a point, he doesn't have the blow-by-you-with-the-dribble talent that defines the great 1s.

INTANGIBLES

Anderson showed a shortness of fuse on occasion, missed a practice without notifying anybody, and did not always have an easy relationship with coach Larry Brown. Brown likes players who will "go through a wall," but Anderson's game is not predicated on toughness and intensity.

IN SUM

Anderson is one of the bright young talents in the league. He can score, pass, and defend, but he may not maximize his potential until he (a) plays the 2 spot—a likely scenario is Anderson at shooting guard and Sean Elliot at small forward and (b) commits to improving his strength and outside shooting.

RICK'S RATINGS

Scoring: **AA**	Defense: **B**
Shooting: **B**	Defensive Rebounding: **C**
Free Throw Shooting: **B**	Playmaking: **B**
Ball Handling: **C**	Intangibles: **B**
Passing: **B**	Overall: **B +**

John Bagley

Birthdate: April 23, 1960
Height: 5-11
Weight: 192
College: Boston College, Chestnut Hill, Mass.
Drafted: Cleveland on first round as an undergraduate, 1982 (12th pick).
Position: Guard
Final 1989 Team: New Jersey Nets
Final 1988–89 Statistics:

G	Fg	Fga	Fg%	Ft	Fta	Ft%	Orb	Reb	Ast	Stl	To	Blk	Pts	Ppg
68	200	481	.416	89	123	.724	36	144	391	72	159	5	500	7.4

Three-point goals: 11–54 (.204)   **TSP:** .427

SCORING

Bagley had a miserable 1988–89. He shot his usual blah .416 from the field (.436 lifetime), canned only .204 of his three-pointers (.250, career), and lost his starting job to Lester Conner 20 games into the season. He couldn't even make foul shots. A plus-80 percenter for the previous two years, he shot a subpar .724 from the line. His outside shooting comes and goes. He'll take the three-pointer, but that's not really his shot—his range is about 18 feet. He's a spot-up jump shooter but he doesn't create well off the dribble. And he can get by people but has big trouble finishing; he'll throw up a bad shot or get caught in the air for a turnover. His size, 5-11, is part of the problem.

DEFENSE/DEFENSIVE REBOUNDING

Small, not quick, and a little overweight—Bagley's defensive resume is not impressive. Point guards are simply too quick for him, though he's an adequate team defender. He comes up with a lot of long rebounds and he's an average defensive rebounder for his position.

THE FLOOR GAME

One major reason Bagley was relegated to backup duty was that he didn't get the job done as a playmaker. His decision-making is questionable—in particular, as noted, on penetration. This showed up in a mediocre 2.46 assist-to-turnover ratio.

INTANGIBLES

As a point guard, Bagley is not a vocal, take-charge guy, which of course is a definite drawback. These days he's not exactly brimming with confidence.

IN SUM

Bagley is out of his element as a starter. He's basically below average in most categories, which is why some feel he's not even a backup, but rather a backup to a backup. Bagley worked out with the Celtics this past summer, and with the departure of Brian Shaw (to Italy), Boston is desperate for point guard help and Bagley may be their man.

RICK'S RATINGS

Scoring: **D**	Defense: **C**
Shooting: **D**	Defensive Rebounding: **B**
Free Throw Shooting: **C**	Playmaking: **C**
Ball Handling: **C**	Intangibles: **C**
Passing: **C**	Overall: **C –**

Thurl Bailey

Birthdate: April 7, 1961
Height: 6-11
Weight: 222
College: North Carolina State University, Raleigh, N.C.
Drafted: Utah on first round, 1983 (7th pick).
Position: Forward
Final 1989 Team: Utah Jazz
Final 1988–89 Statistics:

G	Fg	Fga	Fg%	Ft	Fta	Ft%	Orb	Reb	Ast	Stl	To	Blk	Pts	Ppg
82	615	1272	.483	363	440	.825	115	447	138	48	208	91	1595	19.5

Three-point goals: 2–5 (.400)   **TSP:** .484

SCORING

Following a 1987–88 season in which he was runner-up for the Sixth-Man Award, averaged 19.6 ppg, and shot .492, Bailey didn't lose a step in 1988–89. He hit for 19.5 a game (second, to Eddie Johnson, among bench players), shot .483 from the field, and again finished second in the balloting (to Eddie Johnson) for the Sixth-Man of the Year. At 6-11, 222 pounds, he's not the prototypical small forward, but his size gives him a huge advantage: He can shoot over people. What makes him difficult to guard, too, is that he is both an inside and outside threat. Bailey has excellent range—about 20 feet, but not three-point—and loves to shoot what is effectively a set shot from the corners. While not a great ball handler, he can take it to the hoop, and with his long stride (he covers a continent with each dribble), he's reminiscent of Connie Hawkins. In the blocks he possesses a nifty right-handed hook and a turnaround jumper. He also runs the floor well and has improved his ability to finish the play. He's been an above-80-percent foul shooter (.825 in 1988–89) for the last five seasons. Bailey, however, was strangely invisible during the Warriors' 3–0 playoff sweep of the Jazz. In games two and three, both of which he not so incidentally started (in 10 games as a starter during 1987–88, he averaged only 13.5 ppg and shot just .396; on the other hand, in the last regular season game of 1988–89 against the Warriors, he scored 24 in a starting role), he scored a *total* of nine points. He had been in single figures only three times during the regular season.

DEFENSE/DEFENSIVE REBOUNDING

Bailey's height comes in handy defensively, too. He's a fine shot blocker for a 3 (1.1 a game). And despite his size, he's quick enough to guard most (but not Chris Mullin!) small forwards. However, because he lacks strength he can at times be overpowered. An average defensive rebounder for a small forward.

THE FLOOR GAME

Bailey is an intelligent player who plays within himself. As noted, he's an adequate ball handler and fair passer, but on a team in which John Stockton has the ball most of the time, it's almost academic. Still, his assist-to-turnover ratio, .66, was ugly.

INTANGIBLES

The Jazz has built its team as much on character as on talent, and Bailey is exhibit No. 1. He's a team player, has improved every year he's been in the league, and he's durable (missed only four games out of a possible 492). In the same vein, he's a steady performer. And he's well-spoken, actively involved in community activities, and won the J. Walter Kennedy Citizenship Award last year (for outstanding community service).

IN SUM

Playing in the shadow of Karl Malone and Stockton (and in Salt Lake City), Bailey doesn't get the recognition he deserves. While he has yet to make the All-Star team, he is clearly that caliber of player.

RICK'S RATINGS

Scoring: **AAA**   Defense: **A**
Shooting: **A**   Defensive Rebounding: **B**
Free Throw Shooting: **A** Intangibles: **AAA**
Ball Handling: **C**   Overall: **AA**
Passing: **B**

———— Charles Barkley ————

Birthdate: February 20, 1963
Height: 6-4½
Weight: 264
College: Auburn University, Auburn, Ala.
Drafted: Philadelphia on first round as an undergraduate, 1984 (5th pick).
Position: Forward
Final 1989 Team: Philadelphia 76ers
Final 1988–89 Statistics:

G	Fg	Fga	Fg%	Ft	Fta	Ft%	Orb	Reb	Ast	Stl	To	Blk	Pts	Ppg
79	700	1208	.579	602	799	.753	403	986	325	126	254	67	2037	25.8

Three-point goals: 35–162 (.216)   **TSP:** .594

SCORING

The elite have unique qualities that set them apart. Michael Jordan has the air game; Magic Johnson, point guard skills in a 6-9 body; Larry Bird, the touch and the vision; Akeem Olajuwon, the quickness and power. Charles

Barkley is that rare combination of strength, quickness, and agility all packed into a no-longer-round-mound 6-4½, 264-pound frame. He has the balance and coordination of a 2, the jumping ability of a 3, and the strength of a 4. And these qualities are best displayed on the offensive board, where he led the league last season with 5.1 offensive caroms a game. He jumps well, but it's his relentlessness—the second and third jump—that makes the difference. Plus, Barkley possesses an unerring sense of where the ball will come off the board, and fantastic hands (which are relatively small). He has a decent jumper, but when opponents give him room to shoot it, Barkley is that rare player who will forego the open shot, preferring instead to put it on the floor, create some contact—he has all manner of spin moves or can beat you with plain power—and get fouled. He was second in the league (to Karl Malone) in free throw attempts with 10.1 per game, though he could improve his foul shooting; his .753 in 1988–89 and .739 lifetime is not commensurate with a player of his stature. Barkley can even shoot the three-pointer, but he shouldn't: .216 in 1988–89; .234 career. Note, too, that he managed to score 25.8 a game, seventh in the league, on a mere 15.3 shots a game; all other top 10 scorers averaged at least 19 shots per game. How does he do it? With all of that inside stuff, Sir Charles doesn't miss much. He was second in the NBA (.579) to Dennis Rodman in field goal percentage.

DEFENSE/DEFENSIVE REBOUNDING

Barkley is equally awesome on the defensive glass; when he gets position, he's not easily nudged out. He was second in the league in rebounding with 12.5 a game. Sixer coach Jimmy Lynam thinks Barkley could make the all-defensive team—if he sets his mind to it. But Barkley has not been so inclined. There are few better defenders when the game is on the line, but Barkley's defensive intensity is not consistent. One-on-one, he'll take a vacation, though he does play the passing lanes (1.6 steals a game). Of course, Philly doesn't want him to get into foul trouble, and he harbors his energy for offense.

THE FLOOR GAME

Barkley initiates the break with his rebounding and then leads it as well. He'll grab a rebound, break out of the pack, and rumble up court (all the while the fans are going nuts). Actually, he makes pretty good decisions as the middle man. But Charles Barkley wouldn't be Charles Barkley if he didn't add a little spice—a behind-the-back pass here, a through-the-legs dribble there—and he's been criticized for overcreating. In 1988–89 he turned the ball over 3.2 times a game. In the half-court setting, Barkley is consistently double-teamed but willingly—and skillfully (4.1 assists a game)—gives it up.

INTANGIBLES

Barkley is the 76ers go-to guy, the Man, and for good reason. When the game is on the line, Barkley shines. He's a ferocious competitor who can single-handedly carry a team. But for reasons that only Charles can explain, he will occasionally vanish, leaving his team rudderless. This was much less common last year; Charles is growing up and emerging as a leader. He reduced his technicals from a league-leading 31 in 1987–88 to 20 last year.

IN SUM

First team, All-NBA.

RICK'S RATINGS

Scoring: **AAA**	Defense: **B**
Shooting: **A**	Defensive Rebounding:
Free Throw Shooting: **B**	**AAA**
Ball Handling: **A**	Intangibles: **AAA**
Passing: **A**	Overall: **AAA**

John Battle

Birthdate: November 9, 1962
Height: 6-2
Weight: 175
College: Rutgers University, New Brunswick, N.J.
Drafted: Atlanta on fourth round, 1985 (84th pick).
Position: Guard
Final 1989 Team: Atlanta Hawks
Final 1988–89 Statistics:

G	Fg	Fga	Fg%	Ft	Fta	Ft%	Orb	Reb	Ast	Stl	To	Blk	Pts	Ppg
82	287	628	.457	194	238	.815	30	140	197	42	104	9	779	9.5

Three-point goals: 11–34 (.324)   **TSP:** .466

SCORING

The Central Division is full of them: gunslinging 2 guards who provide instant offense off the bench. The prototype, of course, is the Pistons' Vinnie Johnson; then there's the Bucks' Ricky Pierce, the Bulls' Craig Hodges (who became a starter), and the youngest of the lot, John Battle, who came into his own in 1987–88 as a legitimate sixth man, averaging 10.6 ppg in only 18.3 minutes a game. Last year, he followed up with similar numbers, though he was slightly less productive on a per minute basis (9.5 ppg in 20.4 mpg). Like his brethren (except for Hodges, who is a three-point specialist), Battle's strength is the mid-range game. He can shoot the three (11 of 34, .324, last year), but what he does best is get into the paint, rise (he has terrific spring), and shoot over the big guys. He's also an excellent pick-and-roll player, and when he turns the

corner, he drives hard to the hoop and can finish the play. And last year, for the first time, he made free throws at a pace (.815) consonant with his shooter's identity (he had never been above .750). But Battle has yet to show the game-in, game-out consistency that his role requires. He is, in a word, erratic. One indication: his .457 from the floor (in four years, his shooting percentage has spanned a remarkably narrow range: .455, .457, .454, and .457). He's been consistently inconsistent.

DEFENSE/DEFENSIVE REBOUNDING

Battle is only a fair defender. Though he is an excellent athlete, he tends to get beat off the dribble. He can swing to the 1, where he matches up better, size-wise, than against many 2s. But he's a poor rebounder for his position, accumulating a mere 1.7 a game last year.

THE FLOOR GAME

Battle has better than average ball handling and passing skills for a 2, OK for a 1. As a point, he can't haul the ball like teammates Doc Rivers or Spud Webb and is vulnerable to pressure. His assist-to-turnover ratio was an adequate 1.89.

INTANGIBLES

Despite signing a three-year contract last year, Battle lacks confidence in his abilities. If he misses a few, it affects his shooting, and ultimately, his whole game. But he plays well down the stretch and doesn't shy from the big shot.

IN SUM

Battle is a solid, if inconsistent, performer who gives the Hawks versatility off the bench, since he can play both guard positions. And he can definitely score. But he's nowhere near the player he could be; once John Battle stops doing "battle" with himself, watch out. Though Reggie Theus is gone to expansion, Battle, by no means, has a lock on a starting job. After all, the Hawks' first-round pick was Roy Marble, a 2. Battle in fact may be more effective as a sixth man.

RICK'S RATINGS

Scoring: **B**	Defense: **C**
Shooting: **B**	Defensive Rebounding: **C**
Free Throw Shooting: **A**	Playmaking: **B**
Ball Handling: **B**	Intangibles: **A**
Passing: **B**	Overall: **B +**

William Bedford

Birthdate: December 14, 1963
Height: 7-1
Weight: 235
College: Memphis State University, Memphis, Tenn.
Drafted: Phoenix on first round as an undergraduate, 1986 (6th pick).
Position: Center

Final 1989 Team: Detroit Pistons
Final 1988–89 Statistics: Did Not Play

SCORING

What a waste. As he approaches his 26th birthday (December 14), Bedford has nothing to show for himself as a professional basketball player. The sixth pick in the 1986 draft (by Phoenix), Bedford had a disappointing rookie season in which he shot .397 and averaged 6.7 a game. The Suns gave up on him quickly and he was traded to the Pistons for a 1989 first-round pick in June 1987. The Pistons weren't enamored of him, either (his 1987–88 Detroit numbers: 38 games, 298 minutes, .436 from the field, 2.7 ppg) and before long, his erratic behavior (missing a practice, for example) raised some doubts. On March 30, 1988 Bedford admitted he had a drug problem and was admitted to the Adult Substance Program in Van Nuys, California. While he played in the summer of 1988 with Piston summer league teams, he was back in the rehab center in October 1988 (he incurred strike No. 2 and now is one strike away from being banned from the league) and spent all of last season there. The sad part is that Bedford is a talent. He's a fine low-post player with a nice touch who can shoot the turnaround from 12 to 15 feet and has started to develop a right-handed hook. He also runs the floor well, though he needs to be more aggressive on the offensive glass and spend a lot of time practicing free throws (.578 in his two years).

DEFENSE/DEFENSIVE REBOUNDING

Bedford had the reputation as a big-time shot blocker coming out of Memphis State, but, like the rest of his game, that element hasn't panned out in the pros. He's more of a finesse player and hasn't learned how to deny low-post position.

THE FLOOR GAME

For a guy his size, Bedford has decent ball handling skills. He's well-coordinated and has good hands.

INTANGIBLES

Bedford is an immature 25-year-old. "Something's missing," said one source. His once atrocious work habits have improved a little since he's been a Piston.

IN SUM

Whether Bedford has the emotional wherewithal to make it back to the NBA is a very iffy proposition. At this stage, he has a long way to go.

RICK'S RATINGS

Scoring: **C**	Defense: **D**
Shooting: **C**	Defensive Rebounding: **B**
Free Throw Shooting: **D**	Shot Blocking: **C**
Ball Handling: **B**	Intangibles: **D**
Passing: **B**	Overall: **D**

Benoit Benjamin

Birthdate: November 22, 1964
Height: 7-0
Weight: 245
College: Creighton University, Omaha, Neb.
Drafted: Los Angeles Clippers on first round as an undergraduate, 1985 (3rd pick).
Position: Center
Final 1989 Team: Los Angeles Clippers
Final 1988–89 Statistics:

G	Fg	Fga	Fg%	Ft	Fta	Ft%	Orb	Reb	Ast	Stl	To	Blk	Pts	Ppg
79	491	907	.541	317	426	.744	164	696	157	57	237	221	1299	16.4

Three-point goals: 0–2 (.000)   **TSP:** .541

SCORING

The Benjamin Clippers fans have come to know and loathe was on display for most of 1988–89: the Benjamin who would dominate one night, disappear the next; the Benjamin who would whet your appetite with big-time shot-blocking, clever passing, and a delicate touch one game and then leave a bitter aftertaste with sleepwalking defense, sloppy passes, and silly shots the next. But then a funny thing happened. Benjamin started to play. Not once a week. Not just at home. But every game, everywhere. In the last 21 games of the season, Benjamin averaged 21 ppg, 11.5 rpg, and 3.7 blocks (compared to 16.4 ppg, 8.8 rpg, and 2.8 bpg overall). Why? Why did this much-maligned (rightly), 7-0, four-year veteran, a player who was (is?), hands down, the most lackadaisical player in the league, decide to work for his money? It wasn't entirely a mystery. First, in January, Gene Shue was fired, and Don Casey, the Clippers assistant for five years, took over. Benjamin didn't like Shue, and the feeling was definitely mutual. On the other hand, Benjamin enjoys playing for Casey, and somehow Casey, evidently a genius of sorts, got Benjamin to play for him. At the same time, Big Ben started to shrink—around the waist. A chronically overweight and out-of-shape player—he would typically start the season with too many pounds and play himself into condition—Benjamin slimmed down to a svelte 245 and he was a different player. For a big guy, Benjamin has always had a nice touch; the problem has been shot selection. On the left block, Casey got Benjamin, for the most part, to eliminate the turnaround to the baseline and concentrate more on turning to the middle for the jump hook or jumper; from 7 to 12 feet, his straightaway shot is quite accurate. On the right block, Benjamin continued with his short jumper where he turns to the middle. Employing this improved judgment, he shot an excellent .541 (compared to his lifetime mark of .496 from the field). These are his two basic moves; he has the capacity to do more—he's well-coordinated for his size—but hasn't reached beyond his comfort zone. Under Casey, he also ran the floor more consistently. But since it takes effort, he's always been, for a 5, a below-average offensive rebounder (2.1 a game in 32.7 minutes last year).

DEFENSE/DEFENSIVE REBOUNDING

The man can block shots. He's been in the top six in the league for each of his four seasons (his 2.8 a game in 1988–89 was 6th the league) and is capable, when he's up to it, of taking over a game defensively. He's learning, à la Bill Russell, to keep his swats in bounds. But defensively, he still relies too much on his shot blocking; he'll allow his man to get good post position rather than denying the block. He's also a better-than-average defensive rebounder.

THE FLOOR GAME

Benjamin is a talented passer, above-average for centers in the league. He has a natural feel for the game and does a nice job of feeding cutters from the post and initiating the Clippers' break. But he's sloppy—three turnovers a game, which, per minute, was third worst among starting centers.

INTANGIBLES

The main rap (at least until Casey took over) against Benjamin, well-supported, is that he simply doesn't come to play every night. The listlessness has been particularly evident on the road, where Benjamin often packs it in early. The Clippers are hoping that he's put all that behind him. Only 20 when he entered the league, at 24 (25 in November), Benjamin may finally be maturing.

IN SUM

Twenty-one games a season does not make. But with a more talented crew surrounding him and a coach he feels cares about him, Benjamin may finally be ready to meet some of the high expectations that have followed him since he was the third pick in the 1986 draft. With Benjamin anchoring the middle, and Charles Smith, Ken Norman, Gary Grant, and a healthy Danny Manning around him the Clippers, finally, can start to realistically think: "playoffs."

RICK'S RATINGS

Scoring: **A**	Defense: **A**
Shooting: **A**	Defensive Rebounding: **A**
Free Throw Shooting: **C**	Shot Blocking: **AAA**
Ball Handling: **C**	Intangibles: **C**
Passing: **A**	Overall: **B +**

Walter Berry

Birthdate: May 14, 1964
Height: 6-8
Weight: 215
College: St John's University, Jamaica, N.Y.
Drafted: Portland on first round as an undergraduate, 1986 (14th pick).
Position: Forward
Final 1989 Team: Houston Rockets
Final 1988–89 Statistics:

G	Fg	Fga	Fg%	Ft	Fta	Ft%	Orb	Reb	Ast	Stl	To	Blk	Pts	Ppg
69	254	501	.507	100	143	.699	86	267	77	29	89	48	609	8.8

Three-point goals: 1–2 (.500)   **TSP:** .508

SCORING

Few players have worn out their welcome(s) faster than Walter Berry. Drafted in the first round by Portland in 1986, he lasted less than two months in Oregon, leaving amid charges of having dogged it. Next stop was San Antonio, where he had a productive two years (17.6 ppg and 17.4). But when Larry Brown took over as the Spurs' coach, Berry was packed off to New Jersey (following Berry's disclosure to Brown that his game "does not consist of the fundamentals") for Dallas Comegys. In Jersey, as a result of scoring ineffectiveness and, again, canine behavior, including alleged feigned injuries, Berry proceeded to play himself out of a starting job. Why then, pray tell, did Houston take a chance on this three-time loser? No mystery here: "The Truth" (as his fans affectionately know him) can score. Consider a few facts: On a historical basis, Berry's a more productive scorer than Chuck Person and James Worthy. In 1987–88, on a per minute basis, he was seventh in scoring among starting 3s. His bread and butter move is . . . well, it's hard to define it. Let's just say Berry knows how to put the ball in the basket. The basic parameters: the ability to change direction with the ball in midair, a sixth sense around the basket, and a soft touch. He is, hands down, the most unorthodox player in the league. It's hard to say what a bad shot (or a good shot, for that matter) is for Berry, but his ugly stuff goes in and goes in consistently (.507 percent in 1988–89). As one wag put it: "He's uniquely oblivious to the time, score, and circumstances on the court." He's also a terrible foul shooter (.699 last year; .638 lifetime).

DEFENSE/DEFENSIVE REBOUNDING

On his fourth team in three years, Berry finally may be

comprehending a fundamental fact of NBA life: You have to play at least a semblance of defense to survive. It's not as if Berry—6-8, wiry strong at 215, and quick—doesn't have assets; it's just he's always had the scorer's mentality to an unhealthy degree. Surprisingly, he can block shots (fourth, per minute, among starting 3s). Similarly, if he puts his mind to it, he can be an effective defensive rebounder (above average for starting small forwards last year).

THE FLOOR GAME

On the court, Berry has tunnel vision; his relationship to the game is Walter Berry and the basket and not much else. Turnover-prone in the past, he did a better job last year taking care of the ball.

INTANGIBLES

Take your pick: head case, problem player, poor work ethic, phantom injuries. Berry has, in a phrase, a bad rep. But Houston saw another side: a come-early, stay-late player who did as told.

IN SUM

Berry evidently saw the handwriting on the wall. If he didn't get his act together in Houston, the next stop was Europe or points beyond. A one-dimensional player who performs that dimension well. There may actually be a light at the end of Berry's "tunnel."

RICK'S RATINGS

Scoring: **A**
Shooting: **A**
Free Throw Shooting: **D**
Ball Handling: **C**
Passing: **D**

Defense: **D**
Defensive Rebounding: **A**
Intangibles: **C**
Overall: **C +**

Larry Bird

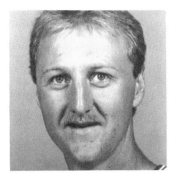

Birthdate: December 7, 1956
Height: 6-9
Weight: 220
College: Indiana State University, Terre Haute, Ind.
Drafted: Boston on first round as junior eligible, 1978 (6th pick).

Position: Forward
Final 1989 Team: Boston Celtics
Final 1988–89 Statistics:

G	Fg	Fga	Fg%	Ft	Fta	Ft%	Orb	Reb	Ast	Stl	To	Blk	Pts	Ppg
6	49	104	.471	18	19	.947	1	37	29	6	11	5	116	19.3

Three-point goals: 0.0 (.000)   **TSP:** .471

SCORING

Remember him? The tall blond with the wispy mustache and the assassin's eyes? Boston fans were in a year-long funk. The league itself suffered by his absence. Only opponents weren't losing any sleep; how could they be anything but delighted they wouldn't have to worry about guarding the 33-year-old (in December). Bird, who, as you undoubtedly know, missed almost the entire 1988–89 season (he played just six games) following surgery in November 1988 to remove bone spurs on both heels. He is, as Hubie Brown would put it, one of the "toughest covers" in the league. Touch. Range. Left-hand. Right-hand. Inside. Outside. Without the ball. With it. His offensive possibilities run the gamut. Let's start from the perimeter. Nobody his size (6-9) has ever shot the ball as well from distance. Since the NBA started keeping track of three-point statistics (1979–80, the year Bird entered the league), only 13 frontcourt players have placed among the leaders for three-point percentage. And only Bird's name has appeared on that list more than once. From 1984–88, he was second, fourth, seventh, and seventh respectively in the league; during that time, he was never under .400 and he's a career .377 (he was also third in 1979–80). To boot, he won the All-Star three-point contest three years in a row (1986–88) (Should Larry's feet fail him, waiting in the wings will be Michael Smith, the Celtics' No. 1 pick in 1989, who, while it might be stretching to call him a Bird clone, is, not coincidentally, 6-10, has three-point range, and can shoot with either hand.) Bird's three-pointer is a set shot. But he's also capable—and it's typically a shorter-range shot, say 15 to 20 feet—of shooting the plain vanilla jumper off the dribble; a natural lefty (he writes and bats left-handed, though he's a right-handed basketball player), it's often off a left-handed dribble. And as he moves in, he's been known to shoot hooks or even inside stuff from close range with his left hand. Get it out of your head that Bird isn't quick. Footspeed he lacks, jumping ability he's without, but quickness, particularly with the ball, he has. Watch him ball-fake and then step back for the three—and make the same move and take it to the hole, with either hand. He's a master at initiating contact, getting the foul, and making the hoop. At the line, you can, as they say, book it; he's a .880 career foul shooter and has led the league three times in free throw percentage (1983–84, 1985–86, and 1986–87). He's expert, too, at moving without the ball and setting his man up by using screens. Once free, he has a marvelous touch around the basket. The free throws, the perimeter game, it all reflects Bird's workaholism—his eye has been honed through countless hours of shooting, his pre-game shooting routine now the stuff of legend. But curiously a goodly portion of his offense derives from shots that he *never* practices, improvisational creations that, as one source described simply, "come in the flow." Bird, like Magic Johnson (and John Stockton, we might add), has that rarefied radar sense of the whereabouts and movements of the other nine players and can adjust his game—and his shots—accordingly. How to defense him? Said one Eastern Conference coach: "Pray he gets sick." More seriously, quicker fellows like Dennis Rodman can give him trouble or perhaps more effectively, make him play defense (opponents isolate him defensively) and outscore him, as say, a Chuck Person might do on a given night.

DEFENSE/DEFENSIVE REBOUNDING

Is Bird a great one-on-one defender? No. Do you want him on the floor with five seconds to play for defensive purposes? Yes. (See game five, 1986–87 Eastern Conference finals; Isiah Thomas taking the ball out of bounds. Bird steals the ball!) What Bird lacks in lateral quickness, he more than makes up for in anticipation. He's a roamer, a one-man zone out there who plays the passing lanes as well as anybody in the league (1.8 steals a game for his career)—the reason he's been named to the All-Defensive second team three times (1981–82, 1982–83, 1983–84). The Bill Russell precept that most rebounds are grabbed six inches below the rim is well supported by Bird's 'bounding prowess; combine his court intelligence, his positioning, and the fact that he's not easily moved and the result is a 10.2 a game rebounder for his career and the best defensive rebounder, lifetime, among starting 3s.

THE FLOOR GAME

Let's explain this oft-repeated truism about Bird: He makes his teammates better. Well, he's a phenomenal passer, clearly the most skilled among current forwards, maybe the best ever (co-author Cohn will put in one vote for co-author Barry on that point). So, in a nutshell, teammates get easy shots they might not ordinarily get. And, oh my, the passes. Bird's a chess player—one, two, three moves ahead of the action—seeing plays before they happen, seeing what others can't perceive. He consistently makes plays that have never been seen before—ah, the joy of watching Larry. Then, too, Bird, who has averaged 25 points a game for his career, attracts lots of attention. To give just one example, last year Kevin McHale had to work much harder for his points (his field goal percentage dropped from .604 in 1987–88 to .546 last year) since defenses could cheat on him without worrying about Bird's bombs from deep.

INTANGIBLES

Another reason for his salutary impact on teammates is that Bird is the team's best player but also its hardest worker. He sets such a high standard of excellence for himself that, as Mike Gorman, a Celtic broadcaster, puts it, "he forces others to play at a level of intensity that may not be natural for them." Perhaps the most telling effect of Bird's absence was manifested in the Celts' road record. They did not win on the road against a .500-plus team. Bird, "the most determined, tough-minded, and competitive player I've ever seen," according to one Eastern Conference coach, has the mind-set that allows you to win on the road.

IN SUM

Bird's back. But is it the Larry Bird we knew? Can he, in other words, play at the level of sustained excellence that he and the Celtics are accustomed? Will his heels (and his back, which he broke this summer) hold up to the pounding? In the out-of-sight, out-of-mind world of the NBA, Bird, in some quarters, has been "evicted" from the penthouse suite occupied by Magic and Michael. Here's praying Larry Bird can still pay the rent.

RICK'S RATINGS

Scoring: **AAA**
Shooting: **AAA**
Free Throw Shooting: **AAA**
Ball Handling: **AA**
Passing: **AAA**

Defense: **A**
Defensive Rebounding: **AAA**
Shot Blocking: **B**
Intangibles: **AAA**
Overall: **AAA**

Uwe Blab

Birthdate: March 26, 1962
Height: 7-1
Weight: 255
College: Indiana University, Bloomington, Ind.
Drafted: Dallas on first round, 1985 (17th pick).
Position: Center
Final 1989 Team: Dallas Mavericks
Final 1988–89 Statistics:

G	Fg	Fga	Fg%	Ft	Fta	Ft%	Orb	Reb	Ast	Stl	To	Blk	Pts	Ppg
37	24	52	.462	20	25	.800	11	44	12	3	14	13	68	1.8

Three-point goals: 0–0 (.000)   **TSP:** .462

SCORING

Blab, who became an unrestricted free agent after the season when the Mavericks didn't offer him a contract, is never going to put a lot of points on the board. In his four years in the league (all with Dallas), he's been a backup, averaging about eight minutes a game; if he played starter minutes, he'd be about a 10-points-a-game scorer. He'll shoot the hook (right-hand only) and can stick the face-up jumper from 15, but lacking aggressiveness, he doesn't do anything on the offensive board (worst among backup 5s, per minute, who played at least 200 minutes). His career shooting percentage is a drab .444 (.462 last year), but he really hasn't played or shot enough (only 329 attempts for his career) to develop any rhythm. Entering 1988–89, he was a .594 free throw shooter, but he shot .800 last year.

DEFENSE/DEFENSIVE REBOUNDING

Blab understands defense—after all, he's a Bobby Knight product—but he doesn't jump well and his lateral movement is limited. His biggest problem, however, is that he plays "soft," he must be more aggressive in battling for defensive position. Nor is he a shot blocker, and he's only going to rebound if the ball is in his area. For defensive rebounding, on a per minute basis, he was in the bottom half of backup centers.

THE FLOOR GAME

Blab has two things going for him: He's a good passer from the high post and he's careful with the ball. He also runs the court decently.

INTANGIBLES

Blab, from West Germany, is still very much a foreign player in instincts and reactions (read: slow). Despite his lack of playing time, he accepts his role and plays hard in practice. But in four years, perhaps because he hasn't been as single-minded as need be, he has shown only marginal improvement.

IN SUM

With Bill Wennington, and/or Roy Tarpley backing up James Donaldson, Blab's minutes got squeezed in 1988–89 (he played more than three times as many in 1987–88) and was not part of the Mavericks' rotation. And it is doubtful he'll ever be part of any team's rotation. The more relevant question is whether he'll ever *play* again on an NBA team. But being 7-0 may keep him around awhile.

RICK'S RATINGS

Scoring: **D**	Defense: **C**
Shooting: **C**	Defensive Rebounding: **B**
Free Throw Shooting: **A**	Shot Blocking: **C**
Ball Handling: **C**	Intangibles: **C**
Passing: **C**	Overall: **C**

Rolando Blackman

Birthdate: February 26, 1959
Height: 6-6
Weight: 194
College: Kansas State University, Manhattan, Kan.
Drafted: Dallas on first round, 1981 (9th pick).
Position: Guard
Final 1989 Team: Dallas Mavericks
Final 1988–89 Statistics:

G	Fg	Fga	Fg%	Ft	Fta	Ft%	Orb	Reb	Ast	Stl	To	Blk	Pts	Ppg
78	594	1249	.476	316	370	.854	70	273	288	65	165	20	1534	19.7

Three-point goals: 30–85 (.353)   **TSP:** .488

SCORING

Blackman is a superb jump shooter, can put it on the floor (going either way), can create his own shot off the dribble, moves well without the ball, has good size (6-6), and is an 80 percent-plus foul shooter—in other words, he's the prototypical 2. He's been killing opponents for years shooting jumpers off double-screens or spotting up to receive a pass from a double-teamed Mark Aguirre or now, Adrian Dantley. But if you take away the jumper, he'll burn you going to the hole; and he's adept at drawing fouls. Blackman is also consistent: Lifetime, he's a .502 shooter, though he shot only .476 last year; his shooting was adversely affected by the mid-season personnel changes (the departure of Aguirre, the injury to James Donaldson, and the arrival of Dantley and Herb Williams) which disrupted Dallas' offensive patterns. And Blackman's a clutch player: "RO" is Dallas's main go-to guy. Never much of a three-point shooter (.202 entering the year), he increased his range with an off-season weight program and shot a solid .353 from trifecta country last year.

DEFENSE/DEFENSIVE REBOUNDING

In one sense, Blackman is not your typical shooting guard: He plays defense. Remember, he came into the league as a defensive specialist (three-time All-Big Eight Defensive Player of the Year) and works hard on the defensive end. He savors the challenge of guarding the likes of Byron Scott and Walter Davis. He doesn't get picked easily and he knows opponents because he studies the scouting reports. Blackman is an average rebounder (3.5 a game) for his position. Dallas coaches would like to see him bulk up even more to counteract the post play of such physical 2s like Dale Ellis and Alvin Robertson.

THE FLOOR GAME

As a ball handler, Blackman is no Joe Dumars, but what shooting guards are? Like most 2s, Blackman handles the ball well in the open floor and when he's making his own play (he's also effective running the pick and roll) but is not as adept against traps and presses. He's made a living moving without the ball and has good overall court sense.

INTANGIBLES

They're all there: Blackman comes to play every night, thrives on pressure, works hard in practice, and hates to lose. He's missed only 26 games in eight years and has worked hard on his game throughout his career.

IN SUM

Blackman is a championship-team-caliber shooting guard. He's a three-time All-Star who will get you 19 a night, makes his man work for his, and consistently hits the big shot. At 30, he shows no signs of slowing down, and with Derek Harper, forms one of the top backcourts in the league.

RICK'S RATINGS

Scoring: **AAA**   Defense: **A**
Shooting: **A**   Defensive Rebounding: **C**
Free Throw Shooting: **AA**   Intangibles: **AAA**
Ball Handling: **B**   Overall: **AA**
Passing: **A**

Muggsy Bogues

Birthdate: January 9, 1965
Height: 5-3
Weight: 140
College: Wake Forest University, Winston-Salem, N.C.
Drafted: Washington on first round, 1987 (12th pick).
Position: Guard
Final 1989 Team: Charlotte Hornets
Final 1988–89 Statistics:

G	Fg	Fga	Fg%	Ft	Fta	Ft%	Orb	Reb	Ast	Stl	To	Blk	Pts	Ppg
79	178	418	.426	66	88	.750	53	165	620	111	124	7	423	5.4

Three-point goals: 1–13 (.077)   **TSP:** .427

SCORING

Look, even in high school ball, a 5-3 player is going to have problems scoring. Unlike his pint-size contemporary, Atlanta's Spud Webb, Bogues doesn't play above the rim. So any time he's in traffic, he has to change his shot. And on the perimeter, where he must rely on the open jumper, the Mugman is, at best, an inconsistent shooter, shooting a miserable .390 in his rookie year (with the Bullets) and .426 last year. Nor does he get fouled much. His best weapon is simply beating the defense down court; in the transition game, Muggsy is a speed merchant.

DEFENSE/DEFENSIVE REBOUNDING

On the plus side: Bogues is a pest; for about 65 feet (from the opponent's end line to just beyond three-point range), he gets in your face—make that beltline—and dogs you. If you're not careful—and you have to be very careful—he'll take it away from you (1.4 steals a game, tops on the Hornets). But once play moves to the scoring area, Bogues is a major liability. For obvious reasons, he can't pressure the shooter or the passer, and is not effective when he doubles down low. While he doesn't get posted up as often as you'd

think (opposition point guards are not typically post-up players), he is vulnerable to the play. His size, again, is disadvantageous on the defensive board.

THE FLOOR GAME

Bogues's natural habitat is the running game. He can uptempo it with the best of them, and he makes things happen on the break. He makes good decisions, has blazing speed with the ball (even to the point of outrunning his teammates; Kelly Tripucka once complained that Muggsy should slow down), and is an excellent passer. He led the league on a 48-minute basis for assists. In the half-court offense, he's something of a minnow out of water. The big drawback: He has trouble passing around opponents and feeding the post. But he takes good care of the ball—an outstanding 5.0 assist-to-turnover ratio, best among all point guards who played more than 300 minutes—and can take the ball anywhere on the floor.

INTANGIBLES

Yes, Bogues works hard; you have to if you're 5-3. He has a good feel for the game and likes to play.

IN SUM

Bogues's major value is revving up the running game, and few do it better. But his scoring and defensive weaknesses can be tolerated only on an expansion/subpar team.

RICK'S RATINGS

Scoring: **D**   Defense: **D**
Shooting: **D**   Defensive Rebounding: **D**
Free Throw Shooting: **B**   Playmaking: **A**
Ball Handling: **AAA**   Intangibles: **A**
Passing: **A**   Overall: **B –**

Manute Bol

Birthdate: October 16, 1962
Height: 7-7
Weight: 225
College: University of Bridgeport, Bridgeport, Conn.
Drafted: Washington on second round as an undergraduate, 1985 (31st pick).

Position: Center
Final 1989 Team: Golden State Warriors
Final 1988–89 Statistics:

G	Fg	Fga	Fg%	Ft	Fta	Ft%	Orb	Reb	Ast	Stl	To	Blk	Pts	Ppg
80	127	344	.369	40	66	.606	116	462	27	11	79	345	314	3.9

Three-point goals: 20–91 (.220)   **TSP:** .398

SCORING

The NBA, the saying goes, is FANtastic! And there isn't a more crowd-pleasing event than Manute Bol shooting—and making—the three. Manute Bol? The 7-7 Dinka tribesman who can touch the basket with his feet flat on the ground? Since Bol only shot .220 from three-land (20-for-91), why, asks the statistically observant fan, does Warrior coach Don Nelson allow him to launch that ugly, from-the-shoulder shot? For one, if the Warriors are playing at home, a Bol-connected three sends fans into paroxysms of joy that can turn a game. More important, it's Nelson's way of saying: "You're just like everybody else, big guy, you're entitled to a taste of the good stuff" (unlike his days as a Bullet, when Washington truly played 4-on-5 on offense, and Bol, positioned 40 feet from the basket, was a forlorn bystander). Otherwise, 'Nute will get an offensive rebound here and there, but his main problem is that he can't hang on to or catch the ball; he has the worst hands in the league. Plus, if you pass him the ball in the post, he is easily knocked around and unable to hold his position. Then again, if he were stronger and could hang onto the ball, they'd have to change the rules. As it is, players like Paul Mokeski, Mark Acres, and Wayne Rollins outscored Bol on a per minute basis (he averaged 3.9 in 22.1 minutes). Most revealing statistic: in his four years, he has never had more points than blocks in a season. And Warriors aficionados don't like to see him on the line (.606 last year; .571 lifetime).

DEFENSE/DEFENSIVE REBOUNDING

Bol is the *ultimate* presence in the middle. Hats off to Mark Eaton, but Bol is the premier shot blocker in the game today. Last year, he lead the league in blocked shots for the second time (4.3 a game), garnering 30 more blocks than Eaton in 1145 less minutes! Bol does precisely what Eaton does—block and alter shots—and last year he did it better, much better. How, then, to explain the fact that he finished as a distant runner-up to Eaton for Defensive Player of the Year? Over their careers, for a full 48, Bol has averaged 9.18 blocks a game and Eaton 6.68. Forget about denying position. Bol lets his man get comfortable—goading him, verbally, to "bring it in here," and then either blocks the shot or alters it or causes a turnover. Team-wise, the Warriors were not a good half-court defensive team last year and Bol allowed them to trap and overplay and not worry about getting beat. One way to counter Bol is to knock him back in the block—get him on his heels—and then shoot it. Note that he improved his defensive rebounding significantly last year.

THE FLOOR GAME

Most revealing fact: when Bol shoots a foul shot, he doesn't dribble the ball. The less he touches the ball, the better. And, no, he can't finish a fast break.

INTANGIBLES

Everybody connected with the Warriors waxes ecstatic when Bol's name is mentioned. His locker room impact can't be underestimated. For one, he's funny. For another, coming from the Sudan where famine is a way of life, he has a unique and refreshing perspective on the "hard life" in the NBA. On the court, he's tough, will put up his dukes in a second, and hates to lose. Consider these comments: "A joy to be around"; he's beautiful"; "a unique human being"; "the best thing to happen to the Warriors franchise in a long time."

IN SUM

Basically a specialist, Bol has elevated his specialty—shot blocking and defense—to new heights (so to speak). And his intangibles are pretty special, too.

RICK'S RATINGS

Scoring: **D**	Defense: **AAA**
Shooting: **D**	Defensive Rebounding: **A**
Free Throw Shooting: **D**	Shot Blocking: **AAA**
Ball Handling: **C**	Intangibles: **AAA**
Passing: **C**	Overall: **A**

Anthony Bowie

Birthdate: November 9, 1963
Height: 6-6
Weight: 190
College: Oklahoma University, Norman, Okla.
Drafted: Houston on third round, 1986 (66th pick).
Position: Guard
Final 1989 Team: San Antonio Spurs
Final 1988–89 Statistics:

G	Fg	Fga	Fg%	Ft	Fta	Ft%	Orb	Reb	Ast	Stl	To	Blk	Pts	Ppg
18	72	144	.500	10	15	.667	25	56	29	18	22	4	155	8.6

Three-point goals: 1–5 (.200)   **TSP:** .503

SCORING

In a limited stint with the Spurs (18 games—he played most of last season in the CBA and was brought up in March), Bowie, a 6-6 off-guard, gave every indication that he belonged. (He was traded to the Rockets for undisclosed terms in August.) His physical skills—running, jumping, quickness—are NBA-caliber, and he showed, too, that he can shoot the ball (a solid .500 from the floor). He's best catching and facing, then using a rocker step to get his shot. He also got the job done on the offensive board (1.4 a game in 24.3 minutes.) While just one-for-five from beyond the arc, the general consensus is that he has three-point range. Needs work on putting the ball on the floor.

DEFENSE/DEFENSIVE REBOUNDING

Bowie, a third-round pick of Houston's in 1986, busted his butt on defense. He played some 3, but he's too thin, too weak, to sustain it at that position. The 2 will thus be Bowie's position. His numbers on the defensive board were average.

THE FLOOR GAME

For a 2, Bowie can certainly handle it, considering that he played some point (though he's really out of position there).

INTANGIBLES

Bowie did everything you would expect of a player fighting for a permanent spot on an NBA roster.

IN SUM

Perhaps not a rotation player, but with his defense and shooting ability, Bowie may stick it out at the 9th to 12th man level.

RICK'S RATINGS

Scoring: **B**   Defense: **B**
Shooting: **B**   Defensive Rebounding: **B**
Free Throw Shooting: **D**   Intangibles: **B**
Ball Handling: **B**   Overall: **B**
Passing: **B**

Sam Bowie

Birthdate: March 17, 1961
Height: 7-1
Weight: 240
College: University of Kentucky, Lexington, Ky.
Drafted: Portland on first round, 1984 (2nd pick).
Position: Center
Final 1989 Team: Portland Trail Blazers
Final 1988–89 Statistics:

G	Fg	Fga	Fg%	Ft	Fta	Ft%	Orb	Reb	Ast	Stl	To	Blk	Pts	Ppg
20	69	153	.451	28	49	.571	36	106	36	7	33	33	171	8.6

Three-point goals: 5–7 (.714)   **TSP:** .474

SCORING

Before we become reacquainted with Bowie, who was traded in June 1989 from Portland to New Jersey along with a first-round pick (which became Mookie Blaylock) for Buck Williams, let's review his sad and now familiar history. The

No. 2 player picked in the 1984 draft (as Portland management will hear to their graves: the No. 3 selection was one Michael Jordan), Bowie, a 7-1 center, made the All-Rookie team in 1984–85, shot .537 from the field, averaged 10 ppg, and was third in the league in blocked shots. A good start. But after playing 38 games in his second year, he had surgery to correct a defect in his left tibia and to remove bone spurs from a big toe and missed the rest of the season. He then broke his right tibia after playing five games in the 1986–87 season, missed the rest of that season, and then rebroke the same tibia during the 1987–88 exhibition season, causing him to miss all of 1987–88. In other words, after his rookie year, he played a total of 43 games over the next three seasons. But in January 1989, after an exhaustive rehabilitation, he made it back into the Portland lineup. But he managed to play in only 20 regular season games (he was back on the injured list for a time with a bad ankle) and all three playoff games against the Lakers. What the Blazers were missing was a dangerous outside shooter who is most comfortable facing the basket. In fact, during his hiatus, it seems that Bowie has extended his range; he had never shot a trey until last year, when he launched seven (and made five!) during the regular season. But overall, he shot only .451 and was inconsistent; right, he was rusty. In the blocks, he can shoot the right-handed hook and is an adequate offensive rebounder, but his is a perimeter, rather than a power game. A below-average foul shooter at .571 last year, .692 lifetime.

DEFENSE/DEFENSIVE REBOUNDING

Bowie will give the Nets what its starting center, Joe Barry Carroll does not: a shot blocking threat in the middle. In 1988–89, he swatted 1.7 a game in only 20.2 minutes per and he also forces opponents to change shots. A fine weak side defender, though one-on-one, he's not the physical presence NBA coaches pray for and really doesn't like to mix it up. For his career, he's an above-average defensive rebounder.

THE FLOOR GAME

Bowie is simply one of the best passing big men in the game, adept from both the high and the low post. He led all backup 5s on a per minute basis in assists last year. He's a fair runner of the floor.

INTANGIBLES

Most players in Bowie's situation, noted one observer, "would have hung it up a long time ago." But he stuck with it, a testament to his mental toughness and depth of character. It goes without saying that's he's a hard worker. Still, there are huge question marks lingering regarding his ability to stay healthy for any substantial period of time.

IN SUM

Assuming he is healthy, the Nets have a big-time shot blocker, a decent outside shooter, and a fine passer who can play either the 4 or 5 in reserve or starting capacities. Though he's not a dominating center in the Ewing/Olajuwon mold, it's not hard to imagine him as a starting center on a good team.

RICK'S RATINGS

Scoring: **B**	Defense: **A**
Shooting: **A**	Defensive Rebounding: **A**
Free Throw Shooting: **D**	Shot Blocking: **AA**
Ball Handling: **A**	Intangibles: **A**
Passing: **AA**	Overall: **B +**

Dudley Bradley

Birthdate: March 19, 1957
Height: 6-7
Weight: 195
College: University of North Carolina, Chapel Hill, N.C.
Drafted: Indiana on first round, 1979 (13th pick).
Positions: Guard, Forward
Final 1989 Team: Atlanta Hawks
Final 1988–89 Statistics:

G	Fg	Fga	Fg%	Ft	Fta	Ft%	Orb	Reb	Ast	Stl	To	Blk	Pts	Ppg
38	28	86	.326	8	16	.500	7	32	24	16	14	2	72	1.9

Three-point goals: 8–31 (.258)   **TSP:** .372

SCORING

Bradley, the ultimate journeyman (seven teams in nine seasons), shot a league-low .357 in 1986–87. So it was no surprise when he checked in last year with an abominable .326 (28 of 86). True, he shoots a lot of threes, but his true shooting percentage was only .372. But Bradley can be a three-point threat if he gets his feet set. He's had several good seasons from trifecta country (including .363 in 1987–88), but last year, .258, was not one of them. Otherwise, he scores on drives but has no in-between game. At North Carolina and in the NBA, he has never averaged more than 10 points a game.

DEFENSE/DEFENSIVE REBOUNDING

The only way you can survive on these anemic shooting percentages is to play defense, very good defense, and indeed Bradley is widely considered a stopper. At 6-7, he has good size, hawks the ball well, steals it (third, per minute, among backup 2s last year), and can guard 2s, 3s, and even 4s. And in 1988–89, he was an above-average defensive rebounder for his position.

THE FLOOR GAME

Bradley is a decent passer and ball handler who takes good care of the ball. He knows how to play.

INTANGIBLES

Bradley missed a substantial chunk of last season with an arthritic knee. He was a negative influence on the Hawks.

IN SUM

Bradley has a limited role—to play defense—but he does that quite well. But at 32, with a bad knee, we may not see Dudley Bradley's name again in an NBA box score.

RICK'S RATINGS

Scoring: **D**	Defense: **AAA**
Shooting: **D**	Defensive Rebounding: **A**
Free Throw Shooting: **D**	Intangibles: **C**
Ball Handling: **B**	Overall: **C**
Passing: **B**	

Adrian Branch

Birthdate: November 17, 1963
Height: 6-7
Weight: 195
College: University of Maryland, College Park, Md.
Drafted: Chicago on second round, 1985 (46th pick).
Position: Forward
Final 1989 Team: Portland Trail Blazers
Final 1988–89 Statistics:

G	Fg	Fga	Fg%	Ft	Fta	Ft%	Orb	Reb	Ast	Stl	To	Blk	Pts	Ppg
67	202	436	.463	87	120	.725	63	132	60	45	64	3	498	7.4

Three-point goals: 7–31 (.226)   **TSP:** .471

SCORING

These truths we hold to be self-evident. The Pope is Catholic, the sky is blue, and Adrian Branch will get his shots. Branch is one of the fastest guns in the league, getting 'em up at about a one-every-two-minutes pace. On some nights, this is indeed a positive force for the world, or at least for the Portland Trail Blazers. He can put points on the board in a hurry. But Branch is streaky, and his jumper, here one night, may be gone the next. (He shot .463 from the field.) He is your basic live body who will work the offensive board, run the lanes on the break, drive to the hoop, and shoot the stationary jumper from 18. Branch is a southpaw, which confuses some defenders—obviously, the bad ones.

DEFENSE/DEFENSIVE REBOUNDING

Defense is not Branch's strong suit. While his quickness helps him guard players on the perimeter, his slightness, 6-7, 195, is a disadvantage in the post. He's a pickpocket (45 steals in 811 minutes) but on the other hand, he often overcommits and gets burned by his man for the easy basket.

THE FLOOR GAME

Fellas, when Branch gets the ball, look for the rebound. He's paid to score, not pass, and is clearly honoring his contract.

INTANGIBLES

Branch is coachable and works hard in practice, but he needs to play more under control.

IN SUM

Branch gives you instant offense off the bench—sometimes—and not much else.

Randy Breuer

Birthdate: October 11, 1960
Height: 7-3
Weight: 263
College: University of Minnesota, Minneapolis, Minn.
Drafted: Milwaukee on first round, 1983 (18th pick).
Position: Center
Final 1989 Team: Milwaukee Bucks
Final 1988–89 Statistics:

G	Fg	Fga	Fg%	Ft	Fta	Ft%	Orb	Reb	Ast	Stl	To	Blk	Pts	Ppg
48	86	179	.480	28	51	.549	51	135	22	9	29	37	200	4.2

Three-point goals: 0–0 (.000)   **TSP:** .480

SCORING

Has anybody seen Randy Breuer lately? Last time he was sighted, the 7-3 center was picking up splinters on the end of the Bucks' bench, a forgotten man in Milwaukee's scheme of things (10.7 minutes a game in 1988–89). Could this be the same Randy Breuer who started 73 games in 1987–88, played 27.9 mpg, averaged 12 ppg and 6.8 rebounds, and then signed a three-year $3 million contract at the beginning of last season? One and the same. With the Bucks' switch to a smaller, quicker lineup (instead of the ponderous Breuer at center and Jack Sikma at power forward, Sikma was moved back to the 5 and Larry Krystkowiak took over at the 4), Breuer was relegated to third-string backup status, giving way to Paul Mokeski, the No. 2 center. Breuer averaged all of 4.2 points a game, played in only 48 games, and was frequently a DNP–CD (did not play—coach's decision). While his moves are mechanical and slow, Breuer is, on a per minute basis, a decent scorer, relying on hook shots with either hand, and facing-up and turnaround jumpers from 15 feet. He's an average offensive rebounder but a poor foul shooter (.549 last year; .655 lifetime).

DEFENSE/DEFENSIVE REBOUNDING

Breuer's deficiencies on defense and defensive rebounding explain why he's sitting the pine. Soft is the best word to describe him. He's not aggressive or a quick reactor on defense, which also hurts him on the defensive glass, where he was below average for backup centers. But he's an above-the-norm shot blocker, though his totals are not when his size is taken into consideration.

THE FLOOR GAME

He may not be a good ball handler but at least Breuer knows to make only the safe pass. He'll run the floor, but he won't beat anybody up court.

INTANGIBLES

Breuer practices hard and plays hard. He has shown a significant commitment to improving his game (for example, he played in the Southern California Summer Pro League in the summer of 1987 and has hit the weights to improve his bulk). But because his contractual situation was unresolved, he didn't put in the same time in the summer of 1988; as a result, he came into camp out of shape, which was one of the reasons why he lost his starting job.

IN SUM

Breuer can score, block a few shots, and has a good attitude. He's a backup on a good team; a possible starter on a less talented club. But with Jack Sikma 34 years old (and looking every bit his age in last year's playoffs), Paul Mokeski nearing the end of his career, and Tito Horford, a project, you have to figure Breuer figures prominently in the Bucks' plans at the 5 spot in the near future.

Frank Brickowski

Birthdate: August 14, 1959
Height: 6-10

Weight: 240
College: Penn State University, University Park, Pa
Drafted: New York on third round, 1981 (57th pick).
Positions: Forward, Center
Final 1989 Team: San Antonio Spurs
Final 1988–89 Statistics:

G	Fg	Fga	Fg%	Ft	Fta	Ft%	Orb	Reb	Ast	Stl	To	Blk	Pts	Ppg
64	337	654	.515	201	281	.715	148	406	131	102	165	35	875	13.7

Three-point goals: 0–2 (.000)   **TSP:** .515

SCORING

Early in his career, first with the Sonics and then with the Lakers, Brickowski's game was like the proverbial bull in a china shop—he was a banger whose offense was limited to putbacks and whose most distinctive trait was the ability to rapidly accumulate fouls. He still is foul-prone, but through a lot of hard work (Pete Newell's tutelage at his Big Man's Camp helped), the five-year veteran has added a large measure of finesse to his game. His bread and butter is taking the ball to the hoop with either hand. His edge? He's a natural power forward playing the 5 spot (but not for long, David Robinson has arrived) who can beat centers off the dribble. He can also outrun them. Inside, he possesses a nice hook with either hand and is an average (2.3 a game) offensive rebounder. Unlike 1987–88, when he was a focal point of the Spurs' offense, Brickowski was asked last year to score less, pass, defend, and rebound more. Plus, he played fewer minutes last season (28.5 vs. 31.8) and took fewer shots (10.2 compared to 11.5). As a result, his ppg dropped from 16.0 a game to 13.7 in 1988–89. A discouraging development also was the decrease in free throw percentage from .768 in 1987–88 to .715 last year. If Brickowski could develop a more consistent outside game, he'd be much more effective.

DEFENSE/DEFENSIVE REBOUNDING

An intelligent defender with a firm grasp of defensive concepts (he rotates well and is a good communicator on D), Brickowski is also very physical (though prone to dumb fouls; he had 10 disqualifications last year, one of six players in the league with 10 or more) and works hard to deny his man position. But he's only 6-10 and is overmatched against bigger centers. And he is not a shot-blocking threat in the middle. His poor defensive rebounding is largely due to lack of concentration because he's clearly strong enough, jumps well enough, and has good enough hands to garner more than his four a game (6.3 rebounds overall).

THE FLOOR GAME

Brickowski is a good passer—third, per minute, among starting centers—but he's not as good as he thinks he is. He tries to make the career pass rather than staying within the confines of the offense. The result is more than his share of turnovers (above average for starting 5s), certainly not the way to get in coach Larry Brown's good graces. He understands basketball.

INTANGIBLES

Brickowski's dramatic improvement (he went from laugh-

able sub to a respected front-line player in one year) is testament to his work ethic. But the Spurs are trying to get him to realize that making the *extra* pass will benefit both Frank Brickowski and the team.

IN SUM

The jury is still out on Brickowski. Basically, he's had one great year (1987–88), one so-so year (1988–89), and three years as a nonentity. When he's playing his natural position, the 4, we may get a better fix on the real Frank Brickowski.

RICK'S RATINGS

Scoring: **A**	Defense: **B**
Shooting: **B**	Defensive Rebounding: **C**
Free Throw Shooting: **C**	Shot Blocking: **C**
Ball Handling: **C**	Intangibles: **B**
Passing: **A**	Overall: **B +**

Scott Brooks

Birthdate: July 31, 1965
Height: 5-11
Weight: 165
College: University of California-Irvine, Irvine, Calif.
Drafted: Free Agent
Position: Guard
Final 1989 Team: Philadelphia 76ers
Final 1988–89 Statistics:

G	Fg	Fga	Fg%	Ft	Fta	Ft%	Orb	Reb	Ast	Stl	To	Blk	Pts	Ppg
82	156	371	.420	61	69	.884	19	94	306	69	65	3	428	5.2

Three-point goals: 55–153 (.359)   **TSP:** .495

SCORING

Brooks, 5-11, may not have textbook form—he looks like he's putting a shot—but as Denver's Michael Adams, another diminutive guard, (who deploys similar technique) has demonstrated conclusively: What's ugly is beautiful if it goes in. Like Adams, who broke an NBA record by making a three in 79 consecutive games, Brooks is a fine three-point shooter, nailing them last season at a .359 clip. Brooks, who was a rookie last year, played most of his college ball at the 2, but for size reasons, he had to make the switch to the 1 in the NBA. Because of his long-range abilities, he makes opponents pay when they double down on Charles Barkley and Mike Gminski. Brooks is less certain when he puts the ball on the floor and tries to shoot among the trees, where his size clearly works against him. He shot only .420 overall, but consider that 42 percent of his shots were from three-point land (for a true shooting percentage of .495). A superb foul shooter at .884.

DEFENSE/DEFENSIVE REBOUNDING

Brooks busts his tail on defense, is expert at harassing the ball handler, and will play his man for 94 feet. He won't hesitate to pick your pocket, either (69 steals in 1,372

Marriott
HOTELS · RESORTS ®

21 So. Penn
Margate 08402

For reservations call toll free **800-228-9290**

what you battled through this
last year or so. You are in
my prayers that this next year
will be much better for you.

Our house is coming along
slowly, but Barbara seems eager
to get everything under control. ~~As~~
~~soon as you feel up to it,~~ We
want you and Casey to come ~~to~~ and
stay with us and relax in the
warmer weather.

As you probably ~~know~~, our
team is having its ups and downs.
But like you, all we can do is
give our best and battle hard

Dear Barbara,

I hope you are feeling better. We all missed seeing you over the holidays. You have always made our Christmas so special because of your generosity.

Because of this crazy job I have, I get so wrapped up in it, I tend to forget what is really important to me and that is family. Barbara and the kids always bring me back to reality and make me appreciate what I have.

Supposedly, I come in contact with a lot of special people. I only wish they had your kindness, character and courage. I can only imagine

God bless you and take care.
Love,
Matty

minutes; in the middle of the pack, per minute, for backup 1s). Of course, his height hurts him if he gets posted up. A subpar defensive rebounder for his position.

THE FLOOR GAME

In Philly's uptempto style, Brooks fits in perfectly. He's a stick of dynamite who can push, push, push the ball and change the tempo of the game. One of his best traits is the ability to accelerate with the ball under control—he had a phenomenal 4.71 assist-to-turnover ratio—almost matching his ultra-careful ex-teammate Maurice Cheeks. (With Cheeks in peak form during the playoffs—a three game loss to the Knicks—Brooks, who averaged 16.7 minutes during the regular season, played only a total of 21 minutes.)

INTANGIBLES

Brooks' high-voltage game is contagious, and his teammates respond well to his energy and enthusiasm. He's a gym rat who loves to play.

IN SUM

If the 76ers acquisition of Ron Anderson (for Everette Stephens) was the deal/steal of the year, their discovery of Brooks, who played in the CBA in 1987–88, was the find of the year. Brooks can shoot, runs the break, plays D, and doesn't turn the ball over. As many NBA teams have found out, good things often come in small packages.

RICK'S RATINGS

Scoring: **C**　　　　　　　Defense: **B**
Shooting: **B**　　　　　　Defensive Rebounding: **C**
Free Throw Shooting:　　　Playmaking: **A**
　AAA　　　　　　　　　Intangibles: **A**
Ball Handling: **A**　　　　Overall: **B**
Passing: **A**

Mike Brown

Birthdate: July 19, 1963
Height: 6-10
Weight: 250
College: George Washington University, Washington, D.C.
Drafted: Chicago on third round, 1985 (69th pick).
Positions: Forward, Center

Final 1989 Team: Utah Jazz
Final 1988–89 Statistics:

G	Fg	Fga	Fg%	Ft	Fta	Ft%	Orb	Reb	Ast	Stl	To	Blk	Pts	Ppg
66	104	248	.419	92	130	.708	92	258	41	25	77	17	300	4.5

Three-point goals: 0–0 (.000)　　**TSP:** .419

SCORING

Brown, who replaced Marc Iavaroni in Utah's starting lineup in late March (and performed the "Iavaroni" role—playing for five to six minutes in the first and third quarters before giving way to Thurl Bailey. He also got minutes as a backup to Karl Malone at power forward and Mark Eaton at center). He's a 6-10, 250-pound 4 who plays the power game. His scoring comes primarily on offensive rebounds (on a per minute basis, slightly better than Karl Malone) and power moves around the basket. He also shoots the 15-foot facing jumper but his isn't reliable. Not fast, he runs the floor fairly well for a man of his bulk. Best way to defend Brown: let him shoot the jumper and block him out on the boards.

DEFENSE/DEFENSIVE REBOUNDING

Like Iavaroni, Brown gives the Jazz a defensive presence. One of his strengths is versatility, the ability to guard 3s, 4s, and 5s. He's a solid low-post defender—extremely physical—though not a shot blocker. However, he is vulnerable to quicker 3s (he usually guards the small forward since Malone takes the power forward. Note: In the last year's playoffs his time was cut to 5.5 minutes a game—compared to 15.9 minutes during the regular season—and he only started one game. One reason: he simply couldn't keep up with Chris Mullin). Not a great jumper, he'll bang the defensive board and on a per minute basis, he was in the middle of the pack for backup 4s (which is what he really is).

THE FLOOR GAME

Brown doesn't hurt you with his ball handling, but he's not a player who can thread the needle, either. He has a working concept of the game and knows how to stay within the Jazz's offensive system. With that big body, he sets a mean screen.

INTANGIBLES

Brown is intelligent, hard working, and is well liked by his teammates.

IN SUM

While limited athletically and skillwise, Brown compensates with his fine work ethic and toughness. He's a competent role player who gives you defense and rebounding every night.

RICK'S RATINGS

Scoring: **D**　　　　　　　Defense: **B**
Shooting: **C**　　　　　　Defensive Rebounding: **B**
Free Throw Shooting: **C**　Shot Blocking: **D**
Ball Handling: **B**　　　　Intangibles: **B**
Passing: **B**　　　　　　　Overall: **C +**

Tony Brown

Birthdate: July 29, 1960
Height: 6-6
Weight: 195
College: University of Arkansas, Fayetteville, Ark.
Drafted: New Jersey on fourth round, 1982 (82nd pick).
Positions: Guard, Forward
Final 1989 Team: Milwaukee Bucks
Final 1988–89 Statistics:

G	Fg	Fga	Fg%	Ft	Fta	Ft%	Orb	Reb	Ast	Stl	To	Blk	Pts	Ppg
43	50	118	.424	24	31	.774	22	44	26	15	17	4	128	3.0

Three-point goals: 4–16 (.250)   **TSP:** .441

SCORING

Brown's a travelin' man. Since being drafted by the Nets on the fourth round in 1982, he's been the property of six teams (including New Jersey twice), has played for five, and last year made three stops, New Jersey, Houston (along with Tim McCormick, Frank Johnson, and Lorenzo Romar, he was traded in November 1988 to Houston for Joe Barry Carroll and Lester Conner), and his final destination—at least for now—Milwaukee. A 2/3 swingman, he's perceived as a good shooter with 20-foot range who uses screens well. But he's a career .446 shooter and in the two years he played substantial minutes (1984–85 with Indiana and 1986–87 with the Nets), he shot a drab .460 and .442, respectively. Nothing much on the offensive glass. Occasionally puts it on the floor going either way.

DEFENSE/DEFENSIVE REBOUNDING

A solid physical defender (as many Arkansas graduates—i.e. Sidney Moncrief, Alvin Robertson—are), Brown stays down well and plays with intelligence. But he's a poor defensive rebounder for his position.

THE FLOOR GAME

Brown is a conservative ball handler and an average passer. Adequate runner of the floor. The fact that he can play both small forward and shooting guard is a nice fit for the Bucks, who like versatile players.

INTANGIBLES

Bad apples don't get six chances. On the contrary, Brown is a team player who works hard.

IN SUM

Milwaukee could do worse than have Tony Brown occupy the 10–12th spot on its roster. A journeyman, jack of many trades, master of none.

RICK'S RATINGS

Scoring: **C**   Defense: **B**
Shooting: **C**   Defensive Rebounding: **D**
Free Throw Shooting: **B**   Intangibles: **A**
Ball Handling: **B**   Overall: **C +**
Passing: **B**

Mark Bryant

Birthdate: April 25, 1965
Height: 6-9
Weight: 240
College: Seton Hall University, South Orange, N.J.
Drafted: Portland on first round, 1988 (21st pick).
Position: Forward
Final 1989 Team: Portland Trail Blazers
Final 1988–89 Statistics:

G	Fg	Fga	Fg%	Ft	Fta	Ft%	Orb	Reb	Ast	Stl	To	Blk	Pts	Ppg
56	120	247	.486	40	69	.580	65	179	33	20	41	7	280	5.0

Three-point goals: 0–0 (.000)   **TSP:** .486

SCORING

As a rookie, Bryant started 32 games at the 4 spot but eventually lost his starting job to Caldwell Jones and was then phased out of the rotation completely (and finished the season on the injured list with a fractured thumb). He showed flashes of offensive potential. He can shoot a jump-hook from the right box or a face-up jumper from 15 feet and in. He shot .486 from the field, not at all shabby for a first-year player. And with his aggressiveness, he's willing to bang on the offensive board (though he was below the norm for starting 4s). But that same aggressiveness was also the source of his lack of productivity (5.0 ppg in 14.3 minutes a game); Bryant never developed any offensive consistency because he was usually in foul trouble, leading starting 4s in personal fouls on a per minute basis. And he's going to have to improve his foul shooting, which was a horrid .580.

DEFENSE/DEFENSIVE REBOUNDING

At 6-9, 240, Bryant has the classic dimensions of an NBA power forward. And he plays accordingly: "Let's Get Physical" is his theme song, but as noted, the refs didn't much care for the tune. His problem was not in the post, where he did a reasonable job of banging and keeping his man from establishing position; but when his man made his move, Bryant would lay his hands on him and invariably the whistle would blow. Unlike many 4s, he has quick feet, enabling him to defend on the perimeter. But, per minute, he was substantially below average for starting power forwards on the defensive boards.

THE FLOOR GAME

Bryant is a competent passer but nothing special as a ball handler. He knows his limitations and won't, for example, force his dribble.

INTANGIBLES

Bryant made a good first impression. He signed early so he could play on the Blazers' summer-league team. Second impressions were equally positive. He's coachable, a hard worker, and has done everything the Portland coaching staff has asked of him.

IN SUM

It's too soon to tell whether Bryant was a wasted draft pick. He had a Marc Iavaroni/Kurt Rambis sort of role in his rookie year: play defense, hit the boards, add a little offense. He needs to reduce his fouls, improve his production on the defensive glass, and, of course, play more. This year he can expect regular, if limited, minutes as Buck Williams' backup.

RICK'S RATINGS

Scoring: **C**	Defense: **C**
Shooting: **C**	Defensive Rebounding: **C**
Free Throw Shooting: **D**	Shot blocking: **D**
Ball Handling: **B**	Intangibles: **B**
Passing: **B**	Overall: **C**

Greg Butler

Birthdate: March 11, 1966
Height: 6-11
Weight: 240
College: Stanford University, Stanford, Calif.
Drafted: New York on second round, 1988 (37th pick).
Positions: Center, Forward
Final 1989 Team: New York Knicks
Final 1988–89 Statistics:

G	Fg	Fga	Fg%	Ft	Fta	Ft%	Orb	Reb	Ast	Stl	To	Blk	Pts	Ppg
33	20	48	.417	16	20	.800	9	28	2	1	17	2	56	1.7

Three-point goals: 0–3 (.000)   **TSP:** .417

SCORING

Butler can flat out shoot the ball from 18 feet and in. He's good as a trailer on the break (think Bill Laimbeer), and he also has a nice step-back move (think Jack Sikma). His low-post game is neglible, nor does he produce on the offensive glass. It doesn't help that he can't jump. And being slow, he has trouble getting his shot.

DEFENSE/DEFENSIVE REBOUNDING

Butler understands defense and is not afraid to bang, though he lacks lateral quickness. He is your basic space eater who can guard both centers and power forwards. Despite his long arms, he is not a shot blocker and needs to become more aggressive on the defensive boards.

THE FLOOR GAME

Well-coordinated, Butler runs fairly well for a big man and

has done a competent job handling the ball from the high post for the Knicks.

INTANGIBLES

Butler loves to play, wants to learn, and works hard. Don't let the Stanford background fool you; he is tough enough to play in the NBA.

IN SUM

A project (Butler played just 33 games and 140 minutes last season). We're not talking about a major talent but there are few big guys who can shoot the ball. This alone could keep Butler employed for a while, though strictly as a third-stringer.

RICK'S RATINGS

Scoring: **C**	Defense: **C**
Shooting: **C**	Defensive Rebounding: **D**
Free Throw Shooting: **A**	Shot Blocking: **D**
Ball Handling: **C**	Intangibles: **B**
Passing: **B**	Overall: **D**

Michael Cage

Birthdate: January 28, 1962
Height: 6-9
Weight: 235
College: San Diego State University, San Diego, Calif.
Drafted: Los Angeles Clippers on first round, 1984 (14th pick).
Position: Forward
Final 1989 Team: Seattle Supersonics
Final 1988–89 Statistics:

G	Fg	Fga	Fg%	Ft	Fta	Ft%	Orb	Reb	Ast	Stl	To	Blk	Pts	Ppg
80	314	630	.498	197	265	.743	276	765	126	92	124	52	825	10.3

Three-point goals: 0–4 (.000)   **TSP:** .498

SCORING

Cage, who was acquired in June 1988 from the Clippers for the draft rights to Gary Grant and a 1989 first-round draft pick, replaced Tom Chambers (an unrestricted free agent who signed with the Suns) in the Sonics lineup. It was anticipated that the exchange would bring Seattle more rebounds (Chambers had averaged 5.9 caroms in his last year in Seattle, while Cage led the league in rebounding in 1987–88 with 13.03) and less points (Chambers scored 20.4 in 1987–88 while Cage went for 14.5). And that's exactly what happened—Cage averaged 10.3 ppg and 9.6 rpg, and took a back seat in Seattle's offense, with only 7.9 field goal attempts a game. But, ironically, 72 games into the season, Cage was benched in favor of the more offensively potent Xavier McDaniel, who proceeded to erupt for 30.5 in the last ten games of the season. To a large extent, Cage has to create his own scoring opportunities, a role that suits him, since he's one of the best offensive rebounders (3.5 a game) in the league (but compare his 5.1 per in 1987–88). He also has a jumper (limited range, 15 feet), which he gets as a trailer on the break or spotting up. Somewhat mechanical in his moves, he can pump fake his man and drive to the basket. In 1988–89, his .743 was his best yet from the line (but he's only a .711 career free throw shooter).

DEFENSE/DEFENSIVE REBOUNDING

Think Michael Cage, and you think rebounding. As noted, he led the league in 1987–88 and finished sixth the previous year. But his defensive rebounding numbers were down last year (from 7.8 a game in 1987–88 to 6.1, and also on a per minute basis), and the Sonics were disappointed he wasn't quite the rebounding machine they had anticipated. Still, he was one of 10 players in the league to pull down more than 9.5 boards a game. He's a master at the controlled rebound, where he'll tip the ball until he's eventually able to snatch it. His edge is that he takes up a lot of space—at least his Mr. America shoulders do—though his lower body doesn't have the same breadth. Defensively, Cage bangs with people, is a solid interior defender, and has the bulk, but not the size, to guard centers (which he did, often at the end of the game).

THE FLOOR GAME

With the Clippers, the concern was that the not-fast-but-not-slow Cage could not play an uptempo game. But Cage is the player who will get the ball off the board and has enough speed to play the trailer role. He's an adequate ball handler and passer and is not turnover-prone.

INTANGIBLES

Cage is your basic lunch-pail player. He brings his hard hat most nights, is always in great shape, and has worked diligently on his game, including work at Pete Newell's Big Man's camp. An intelligent player, he practices hard but had some trouble integrating Seattle's offensive and defensive schemes, resulting in him thinking rather than reacting. His benching threw him and he had some difficulty adjusting to his new role as a reserve.

IN SUM

Seattle wasn't sold a bill of goods, but Cage wasn't exactly a bargain, either. He was not the dominant rebounder the Sonics expected and his offense also didn't measure up. He's

going to have to adapt to fewer minutes off the bench—why would he be returned to the starting lineup?—but he does give you solid rebounding and consistent interior defense.

RICK'S RATINGS

Scoring: **C**
Shooting: **B**
Free Throw Shooting: **C**
Ball Handling: **B**
Passing: **B**
Defense: **A**

Defensive Rebounding: **AA**
Shot Blocking: **C**
Intangibles: **B**
Overall: **B +**

Tony Campbell

Birthdate: May 7, 1962
Height: 6-7
Weight: 215
College: Ohio State University, Columbus, O.
Drafted: Detroit on first round, 1984 (20th pick).
Positions: Forward, Guard
Final 1989 Team: Los Angeles Lakers
Final 1988–89 Statistics:

G	Fg	Fga	Fg%	Ft	Fta	Ft%	Orb	Reb	Ast	Stl	To	Blk	Pts	Ppg
63	158	345	.458	70	83	.843	53	130	47	37	62	6	388	6.2

Three-point goals: 2–21 (.095)   **TSP:** .461

SCORING

There are some players who, regardless of their other talents, are exclusively identified with one skill. Campbell's label is scorer. While his defense has improved, that's not why he's in the league. He was hired to put the ball in the hole, and in his limited minutes, he's had his moments. Brought up from the CBA in the latter stages of the 1987–88 season (after shooting a ridiculous .647 from the field with the Albany Patroons), he averaged 11 points a game (in just 18.6 minutes per) in 13 games on .564 shooting. But last year he was less effective, shooting only .458 and averaging 6.2 a game; he played only 63 games and was only sporadically part of the rotation. However, come NBA finals time, with Magic Johnson and Byron Scott out of the lineup with hamstring injuries, Campbell again got a chance, and he produced (in the finals against the Pistons, he shot a cool .625 and averaged 11 ppg). A 2 or a 3, Campbell has a decent 18-footer (not three-point range), but he's best taking it to the hole. With his low base (a lot like Adrian Dantley), he can shift directions quickly, and he's facile with either hand around the hoop. He's also an effective post-up player and can draw fouls.

DEFENSE/DEFENSIVE REBOUNDING

When he was signed by the Lakers, Campbell had the baggage that often goes with the scorer label: he didn't play defense. But if you play for the Lakers, you *have* to play defense and Campbell showed marked improvement in that part of his game. He has the quick feet, the quick hands, is physical (he's a hard body), but he's a compact, rather than a long (think Thurl Bailey) 6-7, so he's not a shot blocker.

But he still hasn't acquired the rebounder's mentality; he's thinking fast break.

THE FLOOR GAME

Sloppy. Campbell is careless with the ball (significantly above-average turnovers, per minute, for backup 3s). A fair passer, and accustomed to playing with the ball, Campbell is still adjusting to playing without it.

INTANGIBLES

While he kept quiet during the year—winning has a way of silencing disgruntled players—Campbell virtually issued an ultimatum to the Lakers after they lost to the Pistons. "I must play," he said. He will this year, but with Minnesota.

IN SUM

An unrestricted free agent, Campbell, only 27, needs—and probably deserves—substantial minutes. He has the classic trappings of a sixth man, though the Timberwolves could profitably use him as a starter.

RICK'S RATINGS

Scoring: **A**   Defense: **B**
Shooting: **B**   Defensive Rebounding: **C**
Free Throw Shooting: **AA**   Intangibles: **B**
Ball Handling: **C**   Overall: **B**
Passing: **B**

Antoine Carr

Birthdate: July 23, 1961
Height: 6-9
Weight: 240
College: Wichita State University, Wichita, Kan.
Drafted: Detroit on first round, 1983 (8th pick).
Position: Forward
Final 1989 Team: Atlanta Hawks
Final 1988–89 Statistics:

G	Fg	Fga	Fg%	Ft	Fta	Ft%	Orb	Reb	Ast	Stl	To	Blk	Pts	Ppg
78	226	471	.480	130	152	.855	106	274	91	31	82	62	582	7.5

Three-point goals: 0–1 (.000)   **TSP:** .480

SCORING

Though he's averaged only 17 minutes a game in his five-year career, the consensus is that Carr, a power forward, is a major-league offensive talent. As a post-up player, he has few peers, packing quickness, strength, a bundle of fakes, and superb footwork into a 6-9, 240-pound frame. Then, too, Carr can go outside and shoot the standstill jumper from 18 feet. Why, then, is this highly skilled veteran a backup player? When Kevin Willis went out with a foot injury at the beginning of the 1988–89 season, Carr had an opportunity to strut his stuff for the first time on a full-time basis. He started the first 11 games but then lost his job to Cliff Levingston and never regained it. The problem is that he's big—too big. He is, and Carr is the first to admit it, about 10 to 15 pounds overweight. He only plays well in short stretches. One manifestation last year: he shot just .480, the first time he's been under 50 percent for his career. But he did shoot .855 from the line, by far his best performance from the stripe (he's a career .784 foul shooter).

DEFENSE/DEFENSIVE REBOUNDING

Defensively, what unfortunately emerges are the fouls—Carr has been foul-plagued throughout his career. But then there are the shot blocking numbers. With his timing and jumping ability, Carr has consistently been an above-average shot swatter (though his stats, per minute, were down last year compared to his career performance). But he doesn't rebound well, despite his size and strength (Brad Lohaus and Joe Wolf, for instance, did better on the defensive glass). And he's only a fair one-on-one defender; again, lack of stamina is a big part of the problem.

THE FLOOR GAME

Carr is an excellent passer who reads the double-team well and can make the interior play. He runs the court but he can't do it for the entire game.

INTANGIBLES

Carr has never been in good shape, and his weight is the source of the problem. Last year, he issued a "play-me-or-trade-me" ultimatum and, depending on Willis's condition, may be elsewhere this year. He's prone to sulking, doesn't accept criticism well and, as one source put it, "has to be handled with kid gloves." But he practices hard and gives an honest effort.

IN SUM

If only Carr would wake up and realize how good he could be. Until he gets his weight under control, he'll never come close to realizing his vast potential.

RICK'S RATINGS

Scoring: **B**   Defense: **C**
Shooting: **A**   Defensive Rebounding: **D**
Free Throw Shooting: **AA**   Shot Blocking: **AA**
Ball Handling: **A**   Intangibles: **B**
Passing: **AA**   Overall: **B+**

Joe Barry Carroll

Birthdate: July 24, 1958
Height: 7-1
Weight: 255
College: Purdue University, West Lafayette, Ind.
Drafted: Golden State on first round, 1980 (1st pick).
Position: Center
Final 1989 Team: New Jersey Nets
Final 1988–89 Statistics:

G	Fg	Fga	Fg%	Ft	Fta	Ft%	Orb	Reb	Ast	Stl	To	Blk	Pts	Ppg
64	363	810	.448	176	220	.800	118	473	105	71	143	81	902	14.1

Three-point goals: 0–0 (.000)   **TSP:** .448

SCORING

In 1987–88, the Nets won all of 19 games and, among other deficiencies, perhaps their most glaring need was for a low-post player who could score. So when the much-maligned Joe Barry (who had worn out his welcome in Houston) became available, the Nets jumped at the chance of obtaining the eight-year veteran, a proven scorer (18.9 career). Considering former head coach Willis Reed's ability to work with big men and the fact that former Net assistant Lee Rose had coached JBC at Purdue, the acquisition was considered less of a gamble. Unfortunately, Carroll was in and out of the lineup, missed 18 games with an assortment of injuries, scored only 14.1 ppg (second worst in his career), and shot only .448 from the field, his second consecutive sub-45 percent campaign (he's a career .480 shooter). As for his assets, he can draw opposing centers outside with his perimeter jump shooting (18-foot range); and inside he has a nice baby hook, which he shoots spinning into the lane from the left block and on the baseline from the other side; he will even periodically put it on the floor. A below-average offensive rebounder last year, he doesn't run the floor well. His shot selection is dubious at times.

DEFENSE/DEFENSIVE REBOUNDING

Joe Barry has never been a dominating defensive presence, though he does block an occasional shot (1.3 a game). The Nets, however, were happy to have a legitimate 7-footer (he's 7-1) in the middle who at least matches up with the bigger centers. Just a fair defensive rebounder—he'll only get the caroms in his neighborhood.

THE FLOOR GAME

Carroll is a better-than-average passer who sees the floor well and can even dribble decently for his size. In terms of assists and turnovers, per minute, he was in the middle of the pack for starting centers, though sometimes he tends to hold the ball too long. He understands the game.

INTANGIBLES

Lazy. Listless. Laissez-faire. However you describe it, it is a widely held belief that Carroll does not take basketball seriously. As one observer noted: "Basketball is not necessary to fill a void in his life." Also, it's not clear he's ever been in top shape; he still carries too much baby fat.

IN SUM

What Carroll is: an excellent low-post scorer who, when healthy, can be a real asset to a team, though his attitude is antithetical to a winning team. What Carroll is not: a dominating rebounding/shot blocking threat or a player who comes to play every night.

RICK'S RATINGS

Scoring: **A**	Defense: **B**
Shooting: **C**	Defensive Rebounding: **C**
Free Throw Shooting: **A**	Shot Blocking: **B**
Ball Handling: **B**	Intangibles: **D**
Passing: **A**	Overall: **B −**

Bill Cartwright

Birthdate: July 30, 1957
Height: 7-1
Weight: 245
College: University of San Francisco, San Francisco, Calif.
Drafted: New York on first round, 1979 (3rd pick).
Position: Center
Final 1989 Team: Chicago Bulls
Final 1988–89 Statistics:

G	Fg	Fga	Fg%	Ft	Fta	Ft%	Orb	Reb	Ast	Stl	To	Blk	Pts	Ppg
78	365	.768	.475	236	308	.766	152	521	90	21	190	41	966	12.4

Three-point goals: 0–0 (.000)   **TSP:** .475

SCORING

The Bulls acquired Cartwright (from the Knicks for Charles Oakley) for one reason and one reason only: to provide consistent scoring punch from the low post. In his nine-year career, that's what he's done, but during the regular season that's not what he did, having a perplexing and disappointing year. Cartwright, who entering the season was 10th among current NBA players in career field goal percentage (.552), shot only .475 and averaged just 12.4 ppg, well below his 16.2 career mark. The 7-footer was anything but a force in the middle. Part of the problem, at least early in the season, was that Chicago had trouble getting him the ball. And when it was thrown his way, Cartwright much too frequently didn't catch it (it's not clear whether the problem was manual—his hands—or visual—his eyesight). As a result, his teammates lost confidence in him and he averaged only about 10 shots a game. Fact is, with Michael Jordan running the show, Chicago never really made a commitment to the low-post game. But the playoffs were another story. While his points (11.8 ppg) and shooting percentage (.486) were in the same ballpark, he outplayed the Cav's Brad Daugherty in Chicago's 3–2 victory over Cleveland and neutralized Patrick Ewing in the Knick series. Cartwright is a fine inside player. He'll work both blocks, where he fights aggressively for position (he plays with elbows flying; Milwaukee coach Del Harris thinks Cartwright—even if it's unintentional—is one of the most dangerous players in the league), and when he gets the ball, he has a number of options: face-up jumpers, hooks with either hand, power moves to the basket. One of his biggest assets has always been his ability to get to the line (but only 3.9 times last year compared to 5.9 lifetime); and he's a decent foul shooter (.766 last year; .782 lifetime). Though he doesn't jump well and has never been a good offensive rebounder, he makes the effort.

DEFENSE/DEFENSIVE REBOUNDING

Cartwright led the country in rebounding as a college senior, but his NBA numbers have come up short. He ranked in the bottom third, per minute, among starting centers for defensive boards (Dave Hoppen was better!). Cartwright has never been known as much more than an adequate defender (he's not a shot blocker) but he more than held his own in postseason play against Daugherty (who shot .362) and Ewing, who was anything but dominant in the Bulls 4–2 playoff victory.

THE FLOOR GAME

You don't want Cartwright dribbling the ball except for a bounce or two to create his shot. In the past, the book on Cartwright was to double-team him, since he was slow reacting to it and didn't pass well out of the post. He's improved but it remains an issue, and his turnovers were above average for starting centers.

INTANGIBLES

Until recently, the big question about Cartwright was

durability. He missed nearly two entire seasons (1984–85 and 1985–86) but the issue is moot since he's missed only four games in the past two years. Last season, however, Cartwright did have trouble with back-to-back games. He's a team player and a "gem of a person," as one coach put it.

IN SUM

Dave Corzine wasn't the answer. Nor were Jawann Oldham, Artis Gilmore, or Granville Waiters. Cartwright, it was thought, was the missing piece in the puzzle, the low-post meal ticket who would help bring Chicago a title. Well, they didn't quite get that far, but they advanced a round further than they did in 1987–88 (to the Eastern Conference finals where they lost to the Pistons), and Cartwright's postseason contribution had a lot to do with it. From the Bulls' perspective, then, the Cartwright trade was thumbs up.

RICK'S RATINGS

Scoring: **B**	Defense: **B**
Shooting: **B**	Defensive Rebounding: **C**
Free Throw Shooting: **B**	Shot Blocking: **D**
Ball Handling: **C**	Intangibles: **B**
Passing: **C**	Overall: **B**

Terry Catledge

Birthdate: August 22, 1963
Height: 6-8
Weight: 235
College: University of South Alabama, Mobile, Ala.
Drafted: Philadelphia on first round, 1985 (21st pick).
Position: Forward
Final 1989 Team: Washington Bullets
Final 1988–89 Statistics:

G	Fg	Fga	Fg%	Ft	Fta	Ft%	Orb	Reb	Ast	Stl	To	Blk	Pts	Ppg
79	334	681	.490	153	254	.602	230	572	75	46	120	25	822	10.4

Three-point goals: 1–5 (.200)   **TSP:** .491

SCORING

Catledge, who was the Bullets' starting power forward last year, and the fourth player picked by the Magic in the 1989 expansion draft, is a classic "inside player." A look at his shot chart reveals that virtually all of his scoring comes from within a 10-foot radius of the basket. Though he's not an explosive jumper, the four-year veteran is an aggressive banger on the offensive glass (2.9 a game, in the top 20 percent, per minute, among starting power forwards), and many of his points come on put-backs and tip-ins. At 6-8, 235, he runs surprisingly well and scores easy fast break baskets. He has minimal range on his jumper (10 feet, though he occasionally stretched it to 15 last year), which he shoots after posting up or in transition. When he gets on the block, he almost always turns to his right for the jumper. He can even put the ball on the floor after a nice head-and-shoulder fake. He needs to score early or he won't score at all. His foul shooting, however, is horrendous (.619 lifetime; .602 in 1988–89).

DEFENSE/DEFENSIVE REBOUNDING

At 6-8, Catledge is often overmatched, size-wise, as a 4. Lacking size and jumping ability, he won't block shots (only 25 in 2,077 minutes). Nor, for the same reason, is he a particularly good defensive rebounder. But he's strong and works hard to deny position, though in the process he picks up too many fouls; he had a team-high 5 disqualifications last year. The big difference in Catledge's defense in 1988–89 was that he played it: He had weighed in at 245 for most of his pro career but came down to a svelte 235 (his college playing weight), and the lighter weight helped his endurance.

THE FLOOR GAME

Catledge has a knack for coming up with loose balls, and he'll give up his body to the floor for same. He's not a good ball handler and assists are not a big part of his basketball vocabulary (less than one a game). But he doesn't attempt passes that he can't make. He does have trouble catching the ball—you know, bad hands.

INTANGIBLES

The slimmer Catledge was in shape for the first time in his career. A blue-collar player, he gets the most out of his somewhat limited athletic talent. But, he didn't always see eye-to-eye with Coach Unseld and he didn't fit in well with the chemistry of the team.

IN SUM

Catledge tantalizes with some big numbers—he's capable of getting 20 points and 10 rebounds a night—but he's not consistent. He'll play two good games at All-Star pace and then disappear. When he scores big, he rebounds big, but when his point production isn't there, his rebounding generally suffers, too. If he's steadier, Orlando will have one heck of a power forward.

RICK'S RATINGS

Scoring: **C**　　　　　　　Defense: **B**
Shooting: **C**　　　　　　Defensive Rebounding: **B**
Free Throw Shooting: **D**　Shot Blocking: **D**
Ball Handling: **C**　　　　Intangibles: **C**
Passing: **C**　　　　　　　Overall: **C**

Tom Chambers

Birthdate: June 21, 1959
Height: 6-10
Weight: 230
College: University of Utah, Salt Lake City, Ut.
Drafted: San Diego on first round, 1981 (8th pick).
Positions: Forward, Center
Final 1989 Team: Phoenix Suns.
Final 1988–89 Statistics:

G	Fg	Fga	Fg%	Ft	Fta	Ft%	Orb	Reb	Ast	Stl	To	Blk	Pts	Ppg
81	774	1643	.471	509	598	.851	143	684	231	87	231	55	2085	25.7

Three-point goals: 28–86 (.326)　**TSP:** .480

SCORING

After two unhappy stops (in San Diego, from 1981 to 1983, and Seattle, 1983 to 1988), Chambers seems finally to have found a home in Phoenix. Cynics might note that a $9 million, five-year contract (Chambers was an unrestricted free agent at the end of the 1987–88 season) might have something to do with his new-found peace of mind, but it goes beyond financial security. The fact is, he is now a member of a team that won 55 games (and made it to the Western Conference finals), a young team that looked to him to be a leader, and perhaps most importantly, a team that gave him the green light to fire away. After all, Chambers is one hombre who likes to shoot the ball—a predilection that has inspired some to call him a gunner; others to use names that can't appear in family publications. In Seattle, Chambers shared shots with Dale Ellis and Xavier McDaniel, and it was said that one ball was not enough. But in Phoenix, although also a team loaded with scorers (Eddie Johnson, Kevin Johnson, and Armon Gilliam all averaged more than 15 points per game), the chemistry is better, and Chambers never had to worry about getting enough shots; a goodly portion of Phoenix's set plays revolved around him. As a result, he shot a career-high 20.3 times and averaged 25.7 ppg (eighth in the league), also a lifetime best. Of course, it's sound strategy to let Chambers shoot the ball. He's a 6-10 frontcourt player (he can play all three positions but spent most of the year at 3; when Tyrone Corbin replaced Gilliam in the starting lineup in March, he moved over to the 4) who can shoot the three (a respectable .326), runs the floor as well as anybody in the league, can drive with either hand, gets to the line (7.4 attempts last year) where he had an exemplary year (.851) and has a terrific turnaround on the baseline. In other words, he's a scorer, one of the most potent in the league. And what goes along with that territory is an occasional bad shot. He's too big for the 3s to defend effectively and too quick and mobile for the 4s and 5s.

DEFENSE/DEFENSIVE REBOUNDING

In Seattle, as a 4, Chambers was a poor rebounder. For example, in 1987–88, he averaged only 6.0 total rebounds a game. But with Phoenix, he enjoyed far and away his best year on the boards, finishing with 8.4 total rebounds a game (and was third, per minute, among starting 3s for defensive rebounding). This shouldn't come as a complete surprise, since he is 6-10 and can jump out of the building. On the other hand, conceivably he could be even better, but there's a tradeoff between defensive rebounding and getting out on the break, and Chambers, as noted, excels at the latter. Chambers has never been much of a defender; he's vulnerable, in particular, to the quicker players out on the floor. Players with his size and spring are often shot blockers, but he's not (only 55 in 3,002 minutes). But he did an OK job on the weak side (1.1 steals a game) and has done a better job of studying opponents' tendencies.

THE FLOOR GAME

Chambers is known as a non-passer, but he has done a much better job of reading the double-team of late. His 2.9 assists a game last year were above his 2.4 career average. And he can clearly handle the ball.

INTANGIBLES

"Surly and selfish" was the rep that followed Chambers to Phoenix. But Phoenix players, initially wary, saw none of that, and he became a leader on the club. True, he wants to shoot the ball a lot, but he's a ferocious competitor and his priority is winning; he feels, and the numbers seem to bear him out, that his marksmanship is necessary to bringing home a W.

IN SUM

Chambers deservedly made the All-Star team last year for the second time and was also named to the All-League second team (by the players). He was everything Phoenix bargained for—and then some.

RICK'S RATINGS

Scoring: **AAA**	Defense: **B**
Shooting: **A**	Defensive Rebounding: **A**
Free Throw Shooting: **AA**	Shot Blocking: **D**
Ball Handling: **B**	Intangibles: **A**
Passing: **B**	Overall: **AA**

Rex Chapman

Birthdate: October 5, 1967
Height: 6-4
Weight: 185
College: University of Kentucky, Lexington, Ky.
Drafted: Charlotte on first round as an undergraduate, 1988 (8th pick).
Position: Guard
Final 1989 Team: Charlotte Hornets
Final 1988–89 Statistics:

G	Fg	Fga	Fg%	Ft	Fta	Ft%	Orb	Reb	Ast	Stl	To	Blk	Pts	Ppg
75	526	1271	.414	155	195	.795	74	187	176	70	113	25	1267	16.9

Three-point goals: 60–191 (.314)   **TSP:** .437

SCORING

In the exhibition season, Chapman, who was the Hornets' first-round pick in 1988 (eighth overall), shot 29 percent. When the season started—.357 in November—he wasn't much better. The problem, as Hornet coach Dick Harter made clear, was shot selection. Chapman was shooting without conscience, without considering what the defense was giving him, without trying to improve his shot with the dribble. The pundits came out in droves. Had the Hornets made a bad choice? Had Chapman, a would-be junior at Kentucky, come out too early? But as he became acclimated to the NBA game, he learned to use the dribble to get a better shot and to be more discreet with his shot selection. While he finished with .414 from the field (lowest among starting 2s), he shot a respectable .314 from three-land, averaged 16.9 ppg, scored more, per minute, than about three-quarters of the starting off-guards, and made the NBA All-Rookie second team. He also showed the stroke that could, in time, make him a pure shooter. But Chapman has the potential to be an offensive machine, because he can score in myriad ways. He's a great athlete who has superb jumping and running ability. He can get his jumper off the dribble or shoot on the catch. He can take it to the hole and rise over a player and slam it home. And he can also score on the offensive board. But he needs major work on getting to the line; he tends to shy away from contact (only 2.6 attempts a game; starting 2s average 4).

DEFENSE/DEFENSIVE REBOUNDING

At this stage, Chapman is playing your basic matador defense. He has taken his lumps on the defensive end of things and first and foremost needs to get stronger. But he has excellent hands and the athletic ability—there's no reason why he shouldn't be able to hold his own defensively. Similarly, because of his skying prowess, he should be better than a 1.5 a game (2.5 a game overall) defensive rebounder (second worst among starting 2s).

THE FLOOR GAME

Everybody's raving about Chapman's passing ability. While he sometimes tries to do too much, he can make the tough pass. Obviously, coming out two years early, his basketball knowledge is limited.

INTANGIBLES

Chapman showed early on that he's no prima donna. He came to camp and went to work. He is responsive to coaching, as evidenced by his dramatically improved shot selection. His biggest problem is maturity. As a rookie—and this is not unusual—Chapman appeared bewildered by it all—the travel, the media, the incessant schedule.

IN SUM

The word *star* keeps popping up in discussions about Chapman. He's even mentioned in the same breath as Jerry West. But as super scout Marty Blake says, Chapman should be happy being as good as Danny Ainge. Based on his first season, he's within the Ainge range, but has the physical skills to move beyond.

RICK'S RATINGS

Scoring: **AAA**   Defense: **D**
Shooting: **C**   Defensive Rebounding: **D**
Free Throw Shooting: **B**   Intangibles: **A**
Ball Handling: **A**   Overall: **B +**
Passing: **A**

Maurice Cheeks

Birthdate: September 8, 1956
Height: 6-1
Weight: 180
College: West Texas State University, Canyon, Tex.
Drafted: Philadelphia on second round, 1978 (36th pick).

Position: Guard
Final 1989 Team: Philadelphia 76ers
Final 1988–89 Statistics:

G	Fg	Fga	Fg%	Ft	Fta	Ft%	Orb	Reb	Ast	Stl	To	Blk	Pts	Ppg
71	336	696	.483	151	195	.774	39	183	554	105	116	17	824	11.6

Three-point goals: 1–13 (.077)   **TSP:** .483

SCORING

Seventeen feet from the basket, receiving the ball off the rotation, spotting up—nothing but net. When Cheeks shoots, you can, as they say, book it. Entering the 1988–89 season, the venerable Cheeks was a career .532 shooter and only once, at .495 in 1987–88, had he gone under 50 percent. But last year, plagued by a nagging groin injury and a shoulder separation, Cheeks got off to a terrible start (after eight games he was shooting 34 percent), and finished with a career-low .483. Still, when you consider he shot .501 over the last 53 games and had a brilliant playoff series against the Knicks (.512 and 17.7 ppg, compared to his 11.6 regular season average), it was a typical Cheeks year after all. Those out-of-this-world percentages have a lot to do with the fact that Cheeks, who was traded to the Spurs in August (along with Christian Welp and David Wingate for Johnny Dawkins and Jay Vincent), almost never takes a bad shot. Besides the spotting-up jumper, the 11-year veteran is one of the best drivers and finishers (with either hand) in the league. He can beat you off the dribble in the half-court offense or take it all the way to the hole in transition. Scoring, of course, is not his bailiwick—he's a classic point guard—and throughout his career he has never consistently looked for his shot (though he passed the 10,000-point mark last year). Cheeks is a decent foul shooter (.774 last year and .790 lifetime) and is not reluctant to take the big shot.

DEFENSE/DEFENSIVE REBOUNDING

Cheeks is showing signs of slowing down—for the first time in his career he averaged less than two steals a game (1.5 a game)—but he remains one of the league's top defenders. His curriculum vitae is impressive indeed. Four times he's been on the All-Defensive first team, the second team, once. By a huge margin, he's the leader among current NBA players in steals. His thefts are noteworthy because he takes it from the dribbler, so he's not taking chances. Cheeks has total comprehension of team defense and is a dangerous weak side defender—he's almost a designated roamer on D, like a free safety. He's always been a slightly below-average defensive rebounder for his position.

THE FLOOR GAME

Cheeks is the textbook point guard. He knows when to pass, who to pass to, and isn't concerned about his own offense. He won't dazzle you, but that's part of his calling card: His assist-to-turnover ratio consistently has been one of the best among his playmaking peers (4.78 last year, tops among starting 1s). He definitely makes his teammates better and is equally adept in the running of the half-court setting.

INTANGIBLES

A pro's pro. Cheeks is durable and plays hurt. A consummate, though quiet, on-court leader; a coach on the floor.

IN SUM

He may have lost half a step, but so what (and you'd never know it watching last year's playoffs). Cheeks is still one of the premier point guards in the league and could be the quarterback on a championship team. However, that wasn't going to happen in Philadelphia—at least in the near future. In fact, Philly GM Nash said the 76ers wouldn't have traded him if "we were on the verge of a championship." But San Antonio—with Terry Cummings, David Robinson, Willie Anderson, Sean Elliot, and now Cheeks—if not on the verge, is certainly closer than the 76ers to the title round.

RICK'S RATINGS

Scoring: **B**
Shooting: **A**
Free Throw Shooting: **B**
Ball Handling: **AAA**
Passing: **AAA**

Defense: **AAA**
Defensive Rebounding: **C**
Playmaking: **AAA**
Intangibles: **AAA**
Overall: **AAA**

Derrick Chievous

Birthdate: July 3, 1967
Height: 6-7
Weight: 195
College: University of Missouri, Columbia, Mo.
Drafted: Houston on first round, 1988 (16th pick).
Positions: Guard, Forward
Final 1989 Team: Houston Rockets
Final 1988–89 Statistics:

G	Fg	Fga	Fg%	Ft	Fta	Ft%	Orb	Reb	Ast	Stl	To	Blk	Pts	Ppg
81	277	634	.437	191	244	.783	114	256	77	48	136	11	750	9.3

Three-point goals: 5–24 (.206)   **TSP:** .441

SCORING

After he was drafted in the first round in 1988 (16th overall) by the Rockets, Chievous, who does not suffer from excessive modesty, boasted that he could score on "anybody at anytime." And for his first go-around the league, he was a man of his word, blistering away at a .604 pace in November.

But soon after, opponents adjusted, and Chievous struggled the rest of the season to attain the same level of productivity (.437 for the year). What the league discovered was that Chievous liked to drive to the basket virtually every time—which he does exceptionally well—but wasn't as comfortable with his perimeter game. For a while, he was unable to make *his* adjustment and would look to drive. As a result he racked up a bunch of charging calls (1.7 turnovers a game in 19 minutes per). Eventually, he stopped forcing the issue, but his offensive output was inconsistent. He needs to: (a) develop a reliable jumper, (b) improve his shot selection and (c) learn to go left. Otherwise, he has the requisite physical skills—he's the proverbial "live body" who's quick, has excellent body control, a good first step, and can leap—to be a prime-time scorer.

DEFENSE/DEFENSIVE REBOUNDING

Those physical skills are an asset on the defensive side of things, but Chievous has miles to go as an NBA defender. He's OK guarding his own man, but has yet to develop the concept of rotation on the weak side. But he did a nice job on the defensive glass, above average for backup 2s.

THE FLOOR GAME

Chievous played both the small forward and the shooting guard and was lacking at both. His .57 assist-to-turnover ratio was the worst among reserve shooting guards.

INTANGIBLES

The Band-Aid man with a well-earned reputation for eccentricity (and check out the face he makes when he shoots fouls!), Chievous made a lot of NBA teams nervous on draft day. But the fact is, his major asset is his competitiveness and hard-hat attitude. And he's more than willing to take the big shot.

IN SUM

Chievous has a bright future if he develops consistency in his outside game, improves his ball handling, and continues to apply himself on the defensive end.

RICK'S RATINGS

Scoring: **A**
Shooting: **C**
Free Throw Shooting: **B**
Ball Handling: **C**
Passing: **C**

Defense: **C**
Defensive Rebounding: **B**
Intangibles: **B**
Overall: **B –**

Ben Coleman

Birthdate: November 14, 1961
Height: 6-9
Weight: 240
College: University of Maryland, College Park, Md.

Drafted: Chicago on second round, 1984 (37th pick).
Position: Forward
Final 1989 Team: Philadelphia 76ers
Final 1988–89 Statistics:

G	Fg	Fga	Fg%	Ft	Fta	Ft%	Orb	Reb	Ast	Stl	To	Blk	Pts	Ppg
58	117	241	.485	61	77	.792	49	177	17	10	48	18	295	5.1

Three-point goals: 0–0 (.000)   **TSP:** .485

SCORING

Coleman, a backup power forward, is a wide body (6-9, 240) with a surprising array of finesse and power moves around the basket. He can shoot the facing jumper from 15 (he needs to improve his range) or post up and step back to take the shot. Inside, he has an up-and-under move, a baby hook, and does an adequate job on the offensive boards. He knows his range and has always shot for percentage (.521 lifetime, .485 last year).

DEFENSE/DEFENSIVE REBOUNDING

While he's not a great jumper, Coleman gets up quickly and is willing to mix it up. Combine that with his strong but soft hands and the result is a very good defensive rebounder (above average, per minute, for reserve 4s). Defensively, he's physical and knows how to keep his man out of the scoring area. But he's a below-average shot blocker for his position.

THE FLOOR GAME

Many people have praised Coleman for his passing but the record doesn't mirror those opinions. In 1988–89, per minute, he had the fewest assists of backup 4s who played at least 10 games. He runs the floor better than he gets credit for.

INTANGIBLES

Bob Cousy once said Coleman was "a basketball player waiting to happen." The question is: What is Coleman waiting for? His commitment to conditioning has been questioned, he's injury-prone (he missed 24 games last year due to injury), and he remains planets away from his potential. In a word, he's inconsistent.

IN SUM

The 76ers would like to see Coleman be a 12-and-7 man (points and rebounds per game) but his numbers (5.1 ppg, 3.1 rpg in 12.1 mpg) were much less attractive. So far, he's strictly a sub and an underachieving one at that.

RICK'S RATINGS

Scoring: **C**
Shooting: **B**
Free Throw Shooting: **B**
Ball Handling: **C**
Passing: **C**
Defense: **C**

Defensive Rebounding: **AA**
Shot Blocking: **B**
Intangibles: **C**
Overall: **C**

Steve Colter

Birthdate: July 24, 1962
Height: 6-4
Weight: 175
College: New Mexico State University, Las Cruces, N.M.
Drafted: Portland on second round, 1984 (33rd pick).
Position: Guard
Final 1989 Team: Washington Bullets
Final 1988–89 Statistics:

G	Fg	Fga	Fg%	Ft	Fta	Ft%	Orb	Reb	Ast	Stl	To	Blk	Pts	Ppg
80	203	457	.444	125	167	.749	62	182	225	69	64	14	534	6.7

Three-point goals: 3–25 (.120)   **TSP:** .447

SCORING

Colter shot .444 last year but that stat is deceiving. He was shooting 29 percent after the first two months of the season but proceeded to hit about 48 percent of his shots in 1989. Not that he should be confused with a great shooter—he's a career .449, but he can stick the 17-footer if his feet are set, and he has a pet move to the hoop where he changes directions by going behind his back. Strange, however, was his performance, 3–25 (.120), from three-point land; entering the year, he was a respectable .326 from that distance.

DEFENSE/DEFENSIVE REBOUNDING

Colter has good quickness, decent size (6-4), and will get into your jockstrap, full court. But he's skinny, and this lack of strength is a disadvantage when his man gets into the paint. He jumps well and last year was in the top quarter for defensive rebounding, per minute, among backup point guards.

THE FLOOR GAME

Colter doesn't dazzle with his ball handling but he's a solid passer who doesn't turn the ball over much.

INTANGIBLES

A hard worker, Colter provided a spark off the Bullets' bench.

IN SUM

Early on, it looked like Colter had shot himself out of the league. But he had a decent year and is a solid backup who doesn't do anything extraordinarily well. Then again, he doesn't have any major weaknesses.

RICK'S RATINGS

Scoring: **C**
Shooting: **B**
Free Throw Shooting: **C**
Ball Handling: **A**
Passing: **B**
Defense: **B**

Defensive Rebounding: **AA**
Playmaking: **B**
Intangibles: **B**
Overall: **B –**

Dallas Comegys

Birthdate: August 17, 1964
Height: 6-9
Weight: 205
College: DePaul University, Chicago, Ill.
Drafted: Atlanta on first round, 1987 (21st pick).
Position: Forward
Final 1989 Team: San Antonio Spurs
Final 1988–89 Statistics:

G	Fg	Fga	Fg%	Ft	Fta	Ft%	Orb	Reb	Ast	Stl	To	Blk	Pts	Ppg
67	166	341	.487	106	161	.658	112	234	30	42	85	63	438	6.5

Three-point goals: 0–2 (.000)   **TSP:** .487

SCORING

When the Spurs traded Walter Berry to the Nets for Comegys in October 1988, they exchanged a proven scorer (Berry had averaged 17.4 ppg as a Spur in 1987–88) for a player who has yet to show he is anything more than an adequate point producer (6.5 ppg in 16.7 minutes last year and 6.0 lifetime). Comegys, however, has a few things going for him: He has a pogo-stick-like quickness to his jump, which allows him to score down low before his defender can react; better-than-average foot speed so he gets points in the running game; a jump hook, and a turnaround jumper that he likes to shoot off the glass. With his skying ability, Comegys can also get you offensive rebounds (1.7 a game). But he doesn't put the ball on the floor well or have much range (10 to 12 feet) on his shot.

DEFENSE/DEFENSIVE REBOUNDING

Comegys has a speciality: He's a great shot blocker; on a per minute basis, he was second among backup 4s. But he's not a good defender. Part of the problem is physical: He's a 4 in a 3's body (6-9, but ultra skinny at 205) who too easily gives up the post position and lacks the quickness to guard 3s on the perimeter. He also tends to lose track of his man if he doesn't have the ball. And many feel that with his live body, he should be a better defensive rebounder (he was below average on a per minute basis among reserve power forwards).

THE FLOOR GAME

Comegys does not handle the ball well (note his abysmal 0.35 assist-to-turnover ratio). He simply doesn't have a firm grasp of the game, which is a big disadvantage in coach Larry Brown's system, one that depends on reading game situations.

INTANGIBLES

Comegys is a quiet sort—"good people," said one coach.

IN SUM

In his favor: Coach Brown likes him, he can block shots, he's gotten better offensively. Against him: He's the wrong body type for his position, he hasn't defensively rebounded well enough for a 4, and he'll never be much more than an average scorer.

RICK'S RATINGS

Scoring: **B**	Defense: **B**
Shooting: **C**	Defensive Rebounding: **D**
Free Throw Shooting: **D**	Shot Blocking: **AAA**
Ball Handling: **D**	Intangibles: **B**
Passing: **D**	Overall: **C**

Lester Conner

Birthdate: September 17, 1959
Height: 6-4
Weight: 185
College: Oregon State University, Corvallis, Ore.
Drafted: Golden State on first round, 1982 (14th pick).
Position: Guard
Final 1989 Team: New Jersey Nets
Final 1988–89 Statistics:

G	Fg	Fga	Fg%	Ft	Fta	Ft%	Orb	Reb	Ast	Stl	To	Blk	Pts	Ppg
82	309	676	.457	212	269	.788	100	355	604	181	181	5	843	10.3

Three-point goals: 13–37 (.351)   **TSP:** .467

SCORING

Conner was the so-called "throw-in" in the trade that brought Joe Barry Carroll to the Nets last season from Houston (for Frank Johnson, Tim McCormick, Tony Brown, and Lorenzo Romar). But he turned out to be anything but baggage in N.J.'s scheme of things. In December 1988, the six-year veteran took John Bagley's starting point job and proceeded to average 10.3 ppg (his second best), shoot .788 from the line (his best), and .351 in threes (again, his best; he was a .159 trifecta shooter entering the season). And while his .457 overall shooting percentage was nothing to get excited about, the fact is, he was shooting in the high 40s and low 50s for most of the year (.482 after 55 games) but had a horrendous March, which brought down his average. The knock on Conner was that he wasn't a good outside shooter. But he worked hard on his shot in the summer of 1988, and he surprised a lot of people, particularly with his standstill jumper and the pull-up jump shot on the break. Because of his slow release—he almost winds up before he shoots the ball—he can't create for himself off the dribble. And while he can beat players with the dribble in the transition game, that's not what he does in half court.

DEFENSE/DEFENSIVE REBOUNDING

Conner's calling card has always been defense (players with reputations, justified or not, as poor shooters are invariably good defenders). He's strong, has the defensive mind-set, and can steal the ball (he was 10th in the league in steals with 2.2 a game). Conner is also a fine rebounding guard (4.3 a game)—strong hands and good jumping ability are two reasons why.

THE FLOOR GAME

Conner is not a natural 1—or, for that matter, a 2. He is rather, in NBA parlance, a tweener, and at this stage, is not totally comfortable as a point guard. He is not used to, for example, constant communication with the coach. He's more of a make-the-simple-pass-to-get-the-offense-going guy than a penetrator. But he's been careful with the ball; his 3.34 assist-to-turnover ratio was fourth best among starting point guards.

INTANGIBLES

Conner is mentally tough and plays hard. He has somewhat of a thin skin and occasionally goes into a funk when coaches criticize him. Which was certainly the case when his coach, Willis Reed (now in the front office), publicly chastised him for his shortcomings as a playmaker.

IN SUM

Conner is an above-average defender, a playmaker-in-the-making, and can score a few points. After a strong start, he faded at the end of the season. With No. 1 draft pick Mookie Blaylock on board, Conner figures to be his backup—a role more consistent with his talents.

RICK'S RATINGS

Scoring: **C**	Defense: **A**
Shooting: **B**	Defensive Rebounding: **A**
Free Throw Shooting: **B**	Playmaking: **B**
Ball Handling: **B**	Intangibles: **B**
Passing: **B**	Overall: **B**

Michael Cooper

Birthdate: April 15, 1956

Height: 6-7
Weight: 176
College: University of New Mexico, Albuquerque, N.M.
Drafted: Los Angeles on third round, 1978 (60th pick).
Positions: Guard, Forward
Final 1989 Team: Los Angeles Lakers
Final 1988–89 Statistics:

G	Fg	Fga	Fg%	Ft	Fta	Ft%	Orb	Reb	Ast	Stl	To	Blk	Pts	Ppg
80	213	494	.431	81	93	.871	33	191	314	72	94	32	587	7.3

Three-point goals: 80–210 (.381)   **TSP:** .512

SCORING

Gone is the Coop-a-Loop, that breathtaking maneuver where Cooper would burst behind his defender, levitate above the rim, and then receive an expertly thrown Magic Johnson pass for the slam dunk. That's kid stuff, not advised for 33-year-old guards who have been around 11 years and have lost some spring. These days, Cooper's primary offensive weapon comes—more appropriately—with his feet planted firmly on the ground: a set shot for three. Cooper, the NBA all-time playoff leader in trifectas attempted and made (121-for-304, a superb .398), had a terrific year from that distance (.381, 14th in the league). As usual, his overall percentage (.431) was nothing to write home about though his true shooting percentage was an admirable .512. He seems to have recovered from his debacle of a 1987–88 season in which he shot .392 overall and was virtually a disappearing act (.205 from the field) in the finals against the Pistons. Yes, he can still shoot the ball a little (.382 from three-land in the 1988–89 playoffs), but he's never been confused with a pure shooter. Besides the three, he has developed a 15-to-18 foot jumper off the dribble. But Cooper rarely takes the ball to the hoop; in 24.3 minutes last year, he only got to the line 1.2 times, his career low. An excellent foul shooter at .871 last year, .829 for his career.

DEFENSE/DEFENSIVE REBOUNDING

Granted, last year Cooper didn't make either All-Defensive Team (first or second team; it was the first time in nine seasons he didn't). True, he has lost a step and has trouble with smaller guards like Kevin Johnson and Joe Dumars (he's not the only one). But it's not as if Cooper can't defend. At this stage, he's more effective against the bigger players: 2s and 3s. He plays deny defense as well as anybody in the league; he has long arms that are hard to shoot over; and he can make the big defensive play, often a blocked shot. But above all is Cooper's mind set: he doesn't back down from anybody. He'll taunt his opponent verbally, but he has the talent to back it up. He has a good pair of hands, though his defensive rep has not rested on his larceny (0.9 steals a game in 1988–89). And he's an above-average defensive rebounder for his position.

THE FLOOR GAME

Cooper's ball handling skills are often mentioned in the same breath as "turnover." It's a bad rap. He'll get the ball picked clean occasionally—sometimes at inopportune moments—but the man is not turnover-prone. He committed just 1.2 turnovers per game, and his 3.34 assist-to-turnover ratio was way above average. Compare Magic Johnson, who Cooper backs up; in 37.5 minutes, Johnson committed 4.1 turnovers. Right, Magic does more with the ball but that's the point. Cooper, because he's not a natural 1, is a conservative ball handler. The disadvantage is that when the defense gambles, Cooper doesn't exploit the possibilities and explode to the basket—he's not daring—and is content to reset the offense.

INTANGIBLES

Cooper is one tough hombre. His willingness to challenge opponents is a source of inspiration to his teammates. Durable? He played in 455 consecutive games from 1982 to 1988. Last year he ran into a railing after practice before the Lakers first playoff game against the Trail Blazers and suffered a 21-stitch cut. He didn't even consider sitting out that night and handed out eight assists, to go with four rebounds and a three-pointer.

IN SUM

Versatility. Offensively, Cooper's a threat from outside, can handle the ball, and can swing to the 2 or 3. Defensively, he can guards 1s, 2s, and 3s. He can start, if necessary (as he did during the finals last year), or spark the team off the bench. He is a very solid, if aging, backup guard. Cooper has said he wouldn't be surprised if he's traded; if so, he'll be sorely missed.

RICK'S RATINGS

Scoring: **C**	Defense: **A**
Shooting: **B**	Defensive Rebounding: **A**
Free Throw Shooting: **AA**	Playmaking: **B**
Ball Handling: **A**	Intangibles: **AAA**
Passing: **B**	Overall: **B +**

Wayne Cooper

Birthdate: November 16, 1956
Height: 6-10
Weight: 220
College: University of New Orleans, New Orleans, La.

Drafted: Golden State on second round, 1978 (40th pick).
Positions: Forward, Center
Final 1989 Team: Denver Nuggets
Final 1988–89 Statistics:

G	Fg	Fga	Fg%	Ft	Fta	Ft%	Orb	Reb	Ast	Stl	To	Blk	Pts	Ppg
79	220	444	.495	79	106	.745	212	619	78	36	73	211	520	6.6

Three-point goals: 1–4 (.250)   **TSP:** .497

SCORING

In Denver's high-powered offense—they were second in the league in scoring to Phoenix (118 a game)—Cooper, who was signed by the Trail Blazers in July as an unrestricted free agent, played a very minor role. As the starting power forward (72 starts), he managed only 5.6 shots and 6.6 ppg, which of course, was by design; with players like Alex English, Fat Lever, Walter Davis, and Michael Adams in the lineup, the Nuggets were not looking for the 6-10, 11-year veteran to score. He'll shoot the open 15 footer, but it's not a shot Denver's coaches were urging him to shoot—he's just a .459 career shooter. What he does best is bang the offensive glass (2.7 a game in just 23.6 minutes; he was fourth, per minute, among starting 4s, better than Michael Cage, A.C. Green, and Buck Williams) and run the floor.

DEFENSE/DEFENSIVE REBOUNDING

But Denver was counting on the well-traveled Cooper (Portland is his sixth team and this is his second stint with the Blazers) to play the good D, block shots, block out, and rebound. For those tasks, he's well-suited. Healthy after missing 27 games in 1987–88 with a bulging disk in his back, Cooper had a fine year. He was seventh in the league in blocked shots (2.7 a game; second-best in his career). Plus, he was, as one coach described it, "all over the place," helping out. On the defensive board, he was also a monster—finishing 8th in the league, per minute, for defensive rebounding (7.8 total rebounds). He's a physical post defender, though he is known to get in foul trouble (second, per minute, in fouls among starting 4s).

THE FLOOR GAME

As one coach put it, the less Cooper handles the basketball, the better. He had the fewest turnovers per minute among starting 4s, but he rarely is involved in the offense.

INTANGIBLES

Early in his career, Cooper had a reputation for being moody. He's been injury-prone recently and his back, at 33, has to be considered a question mark.

IN SUM

Portland solidified its bench in acquiring Cooper, a quality big man, who is better as a backup because of his limited O, but is a superb shot blocker and rebounder.

RICK'S RATINGS

Scoring: **D**
Shooting: **C**
Free Throw Shooting: **C**
Ball Handling: **C**
Passing: **C**
Defense: **A**

Defensive Rebounding: **AAA**
Shot Blocking: **AAA**
Intangibles: **B**
Overall: **B+**

Tyrone Corbin

Birthdate: December 31, 1962
Height: 6-6
Weight: 222
College: DePaul University, Chicago, Ill.
Drafted: San Antonio on second round, 1985 (35th pick).
Position: Forward
Final 1989 Team: Phoenix Suns
Final 1988–89 Statistics:

G	Fg	Fga	Fg%	Ft	Fta	Ft%	Orb	Reb	Ast	Stl	To	Blk	Pts	Ppg
77	245	454	.540	141	179	.788	176	398	118	82	92	13	631	8.2

Three-point goals: 0–2 (.000)   **TSP:** .540

SCORING

Corbin, who played with Phoenix last year, was the second player picked by Minnesota in the expansion draft. Both sides agree: it was the Suns' loss and the 'Wolves' gain. A backup at the 3 spot for most of the year, Corbin replaced Armon Gilliam in the starting lineup in early March. The move raised a few eyebrows, since Gilliam had been averaging about 18 points a game, while Corbin, in his three previous seasons (with San Antonio, Cleveland, and Phoenix—he came to the Suns along with Kevin Johnson and Mark West for Larry Nance and Mike Sanders in February 1988) had never scored more than 7.4 a game. Well, so much for history. In 22 starts at the end of the season (30 overall), Corbin blistered the nets at a .576 pace (compared to .540 for the season), averaged 10.1 ppg (relative to a regular season 8.2) and added quickness and running ability to a lineup that was already in high gear (the Suns led the league in scoring with 118.6 a game). Not only did Gilliam not get his job back, but he virtually disappeared during the playoffs (126 minutes during three series). Corbin's points come through hustle and activity. He's a superb offensive rebounder (2.3 a game, and second,

per minute, among starting 3s), scores off of steals, and can really run the floor (though he's sometimes an erratic finisher). He's an adequate jump shooter—you can't give it to him—but on the other hand, Phoenix didn't set plays for him. He has limited range (15-foot) and likes to shoot it from the corners or pulling up on the break.

DEFENSE/DEFENSIVE REBOUNDING

Corbin stirs things up defensively. He gets his hands on a lot of balls and can steal it, too (1.1 a game in 21.5 minutes). He works hard, recognizes help situations, and has good lateral quickness. He can guard 2s or 3s. And he's an above-average defensive rebounder. The negatives are that he may gamble too much and gets out of position.

THE FLOOR GAME

Corbin is a decent ball handler who can pass with a solid knowledge of the game.

INTANGIBLES

Corbin's major value is that he makes things happen—be it a steal, an offensive board, recovering a loose ball—often at unexpected times. He's a gambler. An "energy" player.

IN SUM

A pleasant surprise. Phoenix didn't lose a beat with Corbin replacing Gilliam in the lineup and advanced to the Western Conference finals. He's an exceptional offensive rebounder (and solid on the defensive glass), runs well, and plays good defense. And he's obviously capable of starting or coming off the bench. The Suns evidently felt that Tim Perry, their No. 1 pick in the 1988 draft (and seventh overall), was more valuable down the road. That decision will impact quite favorably on the Timberwolves, who are fortunate to have a player of Corbin's caliber.

RICK'S RATINGS

Scoring: **B**
Shooting: **B**
Free Throw Shooting: **B**
Ball Handling: **B**
Passing: **B**

Defense: **A**
Defensive Rebounding: **A**
Intangibles: **A**
Overall: **B+**

Dave Corzine

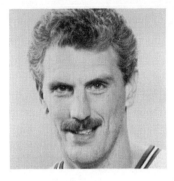

Birthdate: April 25, 1956
Height: 6-11
Weight: 260
College: DePaul University, Chicago, Ill.
Drafted: Washington on first round, 1978 (18th pick).
Position: Center
Final 1989 Team: Chicago Bulls
Final 1988–89 Statistics:

G	Fg	Fga	Fg%	Ft	Fta	Ft%	Orb	Reb	Ast	Stl	To	Blk	Pts	Ppg
81	203	440	.461	71	96	.740	92	315	103	29	93	45	479	5.9

Three-point goals: 2–8 (.250)   **TSP:** .464

SCORING

Corzine, who was traded in June to the Magic for Orlando's second-round draft picks in 1990 and 1992, is a face-the-basket, jump-shooting center, a lot like the Pistons' Bill Laimbeer. Both can drill the 18-footer but have scant inside moves. Corzine is best setting a pick then flaring out for the jumper. It's more problematic when he posts up and shoots the turnaround—he's never been accused of being quick and often has trouble getting his shot off. A pretty good banger on the offensive board (1.1 a game in 1988–89 and average, per minute, among backup 5s, for his career), he relies on tenacity rather than jumping ability. Recently he's developed a nice jump hook.

DEFENSE/DEFENSIVE REBOUNDING

Corzine is a solid defender. He plays good position defense, will fight the big guys for low-post position, and always gives the effort. But he's not much of a shot blocker. Both last year and for his career, he's, per minute, a slightly below-average defensive rebounder, again relying on positioning.

THE FLOOR GAME

In his early days, Corzine was one of the best high-post passers in the league and he remains a solid assist man (fifth, per minute, among backup 5s) and his 1.11 assist-to-turnover ratio was second among his peers. Corzine is in the "running" for the slowest guy in the NBA.

INTANGIBLES

Corzine, an 11-year veteran, is the consummate profes-sional. With Bill Cartwright on board (to whom Corzine lost his starting job) his minutes dropped (from 29.1 in 1987–88 to 18.3 last year). But he accepted it with equanimity. A quiet leader whose intangible contributions cannot be measured, Corzine is only a fair athlete (lacking in quickness, jumping ability, and speed), but he has made the most of his talent. Durable, he once played in 480 consecutive games.

IN SUM

With Corzine as a part-time starter in 1987–88, Chicago won 50 games—good, but not good enough. The problem, the critics railed, was the center. Corzine didn't have the oomph, either as a low-post scorer or as a shot blocker, to move the team to the next level: the NBA title. With Cartwright in the middle, Chicago won fewer games (47) but advanced one round further in the playoffs. So, on the face of it, Corzine's niche would seem to be as a backup, where he's a capable veteran who can shoot a little, defend a little, pass a little, and doesn't hurt you when he's on the floor. But with the Magic, who presently aren't contemplating the playoffs, Corzine is slated to be the starting center.

RICK'S RATINGS

Scoring: **C**	Defense: **C**
Shooting: **B**	Defensive Rebounding: **C**
Free Throw Shooting: **C**	Shot Blocking: **C**
Ball Handling: **B**	Intangibles: **A**
Passing: **A**	Overall: **B –**

Pat Cummings

Birthdate: July 11, 1956
Height: 6-9
Weight: 235
College: University of Cincinnati, Cincinnati, O.
Drafted: Milwaukee on third round as junior eligible, 1978 (59th pick).
Position: Forward
Final 1989 Team: Miami Heat
Final 1988–89 Statistics:

G	Fg	Fga	Fg%	Ft	Fta	Ft%	Orb	Reb	Ast	Stl	To	Blk	Pts	Ppg
53	197	394	.500	72	97	.742	84	281	47	29	111	18	466	8.8

Three-point goals: 0–2 (.000)   **TSP:** .500

SCORING

Cummings has the quintessential scorer's mentality: He

never saw a shot he didn't like, his shot selection is questionable at times, and passing is a foreign language. Still, he's managed to survive 10 years so he must be doing something right. In fact, he's a productive scorer (per minute, he ranked in the top third among backup 4s last year), who combines brute strength with a surprising menu of finesse moves. His jumper, which would make Phil Niekro proud (no rotation whatsoever), is reliable from 15 feet and in. After shooting well under his career percentage the previous three years, Cummings shot .500 in 1988–89, right around his .497 career mark. He can shoot facing up or turning around, put the ball on the floor, and hook with either hand. He'll also hit the offensive glass (almost two a game for his career). At .742 career and .742 last year, Cummings is a slightly below-average foul shooter.

DEFENSE/DEFENSIVE REBOUNDING

He may not jump well, but Cummings works hard on the defensive glass. He's a banger with a capital B and was in the top quarter among backup 4s in 1988–89. But defensively, he has his "shortcummings" (The term is Peter Vecsey's). He's slow, so he can't get to help situations. And with his lack of speed and jumping ability, he's never been a shot blocker. But Cummings does lay his body on his man and will fight him for position. He doesn't back down from anybody.

THE FLOOR GAME

You don't want Cummings's hands on the ball except to shoot it. A "mistake player" and turnover-prone, he's a poor passer and a reluctant one. Nor does he fill the lanes well (again, lack of footspeed), but he will run the court—the effort is there. And he gave Miami versatility up front because he can play both power forward and some backup center.

INTANGIBLES

Cummings has a reputation for being a money player—as in, he's only in it for the money. Maybe so, but he does want to earn his keep and plays hard every night. He's also been accused of being selfish, but, say his defenders, that goes with the territory of being a scorer.

IN SUM

Cummings, who missed the final third of the season with a stress fracture of the tibia and had only a one-year contract with the Heat, provided some much needed scoring punch for Miami both in starting and reserve roles. Ask Pat Cummings to bang both boards, score, and fight his man defensively, and he'll produce. At 33, have we seen the last of Pat Cummings? Probably not.

RICK'S RATINGS

Scoring: **B**
Shooting: **A**
Free Throw Shooting: **C**
Ball Handling: **D**
Passing: **C**
Defense: **C**

Defensive Rebounding: **AA**
Shot Blocking: **D**
Intangibles: **B**
Overall: **B**

Terry Cummings

Birthdate: March 15, 1961
Height: 6-9
Weight: 235
College: DePaul University, Chicago, Ill.
Drafted: San Diego on first round as an undergraduate, 1982 (2nd pick).
Position: Forward
Final 1989 Team: Milwaukee Bucks
Final 1988–89 Statistics:

G	Fg	Fga	Fg%	Ft	Fta	Ft%	Orb	Reb	Ast	Stl	To	Blk	Pts	Ppg
80	730	1563	.487	362	460	.787	281	650	198	106	201	72	1829	22.9

Three-point goals: 7–15 (.467)   **TSP:** .469

SCORING

When you play the word association game and say, "Terry Cummings," there's only one possible response: scorer. This seven-year veteran, who was acquired by the Spurs in May in exchange for Alvin Robertson and Greg Anderson, is one of the league's most prolific point producers, averaging 22.1 a game for his career and only once (and just barely, 19.8 in 1988–89) going below 20 ppg. Cummings has the scorer's multipronged attack: He feasts on the medium-range jumper going to the left (he's right-handed); he posts on the left block and shoots the turnaround, turning to the baseline; and he posts up, faces, and shoots the jumper without a dribble. At 6-9 and playing the 3 spot, he's too big for 3s to handle and too quick for the 4s. With the arrival of Sean Elliot, who is slated to be the Spurs starting small forward, Cummings will move over to the power forward spot. He also runs the court well and can put the ball on the floor going either direction. Cummings has good range, say 18 to 20 feet, but is not a three-point shooter. He is, however, with his strength and size, one of the top offensive rebounders (3.5 a game) among small forwards in the league. Even with all this going for him, Cummings has taken his lumps from the critics. First, he's been accused of being a gunner, unconscious in his shot selection. And yes, he does take some bad shots, but last year he played more within the Bucks' framework. Then there's his inconsistency. While it's true he's not a night-in, night-out percentage shooter (.467 last year), he is a consistent *scorer*. Finally, there's his foul shooting, which until last season was an abominable .695. But in 1988–89, he shot a respectable .787.

DEFENSE/DEFENSIVE REBOUNDING

Cummings has been an excellent defensive rebounder (size and jumping ability help) throughout his career and was above average, per minute, among small forwards in 1988–89. Then there's defense, and more accurately, the absence of same. For Cummings, D has not been a concern, but last year, at least occasionally, he could be called on to play it. But he doesn't have consistent defensive intensity. With his physical ability, there's no reason why he couldn't be a solid defender, though he does have trouble with quicker 3s out on the floor.

THE FLOOR GAME

In the past, the ball usually stopped in Cummings's hands. If he were the first option on a play, that would be the Bucks' only option for that particular possession. Last season, he started to recognize that even if he gave it up, he might get it back and he did a better job of moving the ball. An adequate, safe passer, he doesn't turn the ball over much.

INTANGIBLES

Cummings' commitment to playing team basketball—evidenced by his newly-found D, passing, and improved shot selection—was a major reason for the Bucks' 49-win season as well as his own selection to the All-Star team. And you have to admire his improved foul shooting.

IN SUM

Last year, Cummings moved beyond his scorer's label and became a complete player. Now the test will be whether he can keep up the good work for more than a season. And, more importantly, whether he can adjust to Larry Brown's system.

RICK'S RATINGS

Scoring: **AAA**	Defense: **C**
Shooting: **B**	Defensive Rebounding: **A**
Free Throw Shooting: **B**	Intangibles: **A**
Ball Handling: **B**	Overall: **AA**
Passing: **B**	

Earl Cureton

Birthdate: September 3, 1957

Height: 6-9
Weight: 215
College: University of Detroit, Detroit, Mich.
Drafted: Philadelphia on third round as junior eligible, 1979 (58th pick).
Positions: Forward, Center
Final 1989 Team: Charlotte Hornets
Final 1988–89 Statistics:

G	Fg	Fga	Fg%	Ft	Fta	Ft%	Orb	Reb	Ast	Stl	To	Blk	Pts	Ppg
82	233	465	.501	66	123	.537	188	488	130	50	114	61	532	6.5

Three-point goals: 0–1 (.000)   **TSP:** .501

SCORING

They call him "Earl the Twirl," which is not to be confused with "Earl the Pearl." The latter Earl is, of course, Monroe, late of the Knicks, the backcourt magician with the playground moves. The former Earl, on the other hand, has never made it onto a highlight film (his nickname derives from his baton-twirling ability). He will, however, go down in NBA history as one of the league's truly bad foul shooters: in a nine-year career, Cureton has never shot over 60 percent (.537 last year; .569 high mark). Fortunately, he doesn't get to the line much. Everywhere he's played (Philadelphia, Detroit, Chicago, Los Angeles Clippers), he hasn't generally been involved in the offense. All kidding aside, Cureton does a few things well. For a center/power forward, he runs the court extremely well—and finishes. And with his quickness and jumping ability, he always has been an above-average offensive rebounder. He will even occasionally put the ball on the floor or shoot from outside, but rest assured, those plays do not appear in Charlotte's playbook.

DEFENSE/DEFENSIVE REBOUNDING

Cureton has carved out a career on the strength of his defense and rebounding. His defensive versatility—he can guard 3s, 4s, and 5s—is his biggest asset. He is the closest thing Charlotte has to a shot blocker (61 blocks for the year, high on the Hornets), and his quickness and toughness make him a formidable defender. He started 41 games last year, but at 6-9 he's outsized by the bigger centers. His jumping ability, quickness, and nose for the ball explain his above-average defensive rebounding numbers.

THE FLOOR GAME

In general, keeping the ball out of Cureton's hands is a wise precept. He just doesn't handle it well.

INTANGIBLES

The other reason Cureton has stuck around is his lunch-pail work ethic. He comes to play every night, is aggressive, and is a consummate team player. He's a role player, but he knows it and accepts it.

IN SUM

Because of his versatility, Cureton can fill the gaps when players are hurt. He knows what he does well—defense, rebounding, running the floor—and stays within those limits. But even on an expansion team, he should be playing 17 minutes rather than the 25 a game he averaged in 1988–89.

RICK'S RATINGS

Scoring: **D**
Shooting: **D**
Free Throw Shooting: **D**
Ball Handling: **C**
Passing: **C**

Defense: **A**
Defensive Rebounding: **C**
Shot Blocking: **C**
Intangibles: **A**
Overall: **C +**

Dell Curry

Birthdate: June 25, 1964
Height: 6-5
Weight: 195
College: Virginia Polytechnic Institute and State University, Blacksburg, Va.
Drafted: Utah on first round, 1986 (15th pick).
Position: Guard
Final 1989 Team: Charlotte Hornets
Final 1988–89 Statistics:

G	Fg	Fga	Fg%	Ft	Fta	Ft%	Orb	Reb	Ast	Stl	To	Blk	Pts	Ppg
48	256	521	.491	40	46	.870	26	104	50	42	44	4	571	11.9

Three-point goals: 19–55 (.345)   **TSP:** .510

SCORING

As the first player picked in the expansion draft (as well as the one with the highest scoring average, 10 ppg, in 1987–88), Curry had a virtual lock on a starting job with the Hornets. After two stops, Utah and Cleveland, where he never got the minutes (9.5 a game and 19, respectively), he finally was going to get his chance to show what, most agree, is considerable shooting ability. But in October 1988, he broke his left (nonshooting) wrist, missed the first 19 games, and subsequently was only an intermittent part of the regular rotation. Too bad, because Curry led all backup 2s on a point per minute basis, averaging 11.9 in only 16.9 minutes a game. He's a pure shooter with three-point range (.327 lifetime, .345 in 1988–89) who, like teammate Robert Reid, who took Curry's starting job, needs help to get his shot. Otherwise, he gets the jumper when he pulls up in transition. He's a fair driver—though he seems to have only one speed—who needs to be more forceful going to the hoop. He's an excellent foul shooter (.870 last year; .805 lifetime).

DEFENSE/DEFENSIVE REBOUNDING

Curry makes teammate Kelly Tripucka, who has never been accused of playing defense, look like Michael Cooper. His D essentially consists of waiting around for the Hornets to get the ball back. But he does play the passing lanes well and averaged about a steal a game. Considering his defense, or rather lack thereof, he's a surprisingly effective (long arms help) defensive rebounder.

THE FLOOR GAME

Curry has adequate ball handling skills. He's an above-average passer with average knowledge of the game.

INTANGIBLES

Three teams in three years is not a good sign. Curry's intensity level—he has a lot of "Joe Cool" in him—and work ethic have been questioned and he's been very unhappy with his playing time.

IN SUM

Good shooting will cause a coach to overlook a player's other weaknesses. And indeed Curry has at least one glaring weakness: defense. His attitude isn't a plus, either. With Rex Chapman penciled in as the 2 of the Hornets' future, that leaves limited minutes for Curry. The subject of trade rumors, he's better off elsewhere where he can get significant time.

RICK'S RATINGS

Scoring: **AAA**
Shooting: **AA**
Free Throw Shooting: **AA**
Ball Handling: **B**
Passing: **A**

Defense: **D**
Defensive Rebounding: **A**
Intangibles: **C**
Overall: **B**

Quintin Dailey

Birthdate: January 22, 1961
Height: 6-3
Weight: 200
College: University of San Francisco, San Francisco, Calif.

Drafted: Chicago on first round as an undergraduate, 1982 (7th pick).
Position: Guard
Final 1989 Team: Los Angeles Clippers
Final 1988–89 Statistics:

G	Fg	Fga	Fg%	Ft	Fta	Ft%	Orb	Reb	Ast	Stl	To	Blk	Pts	Ppg
69	448	964	.465	217	286	.759	69	204	154	90	122	6	1114	16.1

Three-point goals: 1–9 (.111)   TSP: .465

SCORING

He's not a pure shooter by any means—streaky is more like it. Nor does he have great range (only 1-for-9 last year from three-land). He's only an average foul shooter (.759 in 1988–89, .784 lifetime). And the rest of his game—defense, rebounding, ball handling, the intangibles—that's not why Dailey is in the league. But make no mistake about it: "Q" can score. In flurries. In bunches. Per minute, he was in the top ten percent in the league and averaged 16.1 a game. He's a 2, but like Ricky Pierce (another off-guard scoring machine), a goodly portion of his offense comes in post-up situations. He thrives in traffic—you can get dizzy watching him pump fake, pump fake, pump fake (it's amazing he doesn't get called for three seconds more often) and somehow get his shot off and draws the foul. He's also adept at coming off screens and shooting immediately on the catch. Those are his tools, and early on, Dailey (who has twice spent time in a drug rehab center) was exploding almost nightly—after 25 games, he was connecting at a .524 clip. But for the rest of the year, he tailed off and finished at .465. His descending percentage had a lot to do with his ascending weight—Dailey didn't just gain weight (about 35 pounds), he had a weight problem. It affected his quickness—down low, for example, he was getting his shot blocked frequently—and it got so bad that the Clippers suspended him briefly in February.

DEFENSE/DEFENSIVE REBOUNDING

The heavier Dailey had trouble playing D—his defense has always been a maybe-I-will, maybe-I-won't proposition anyway—and the added girth affected his stamina. He'd frequently ask to come out of games because he was winded. He lacks lateral quickness, but does an adequate job defending in the post. Not much on the defensive boards; he's a leak-out guy.

THE FLOOR GAME

Dailey will move to get himself open for the ball. At best, he's a fair passer. He's basically a selfish player—a gunner, if you will—which is OK if you're making the shots (which he wasn't in the final two-thirds of the season) and they are good ones (after a while, he had no conscience).

INTANGIBLES

Dailey was co-captain of the Clippers last year, and when he was in shape he seemed to merit the appointment; he was consistent and a go-to guy who produced. But he lost credibility when he gained the weight. There are some real doubts about whether he's a winner.

IN SUM

Dailey is strictly one-dimensional. But he's not a starter—despite what he thinks. If he keeps his weight down, there's no reason why he can't be an instant offense on a good team. Since the Clippers didn't exercise their option, Dailey was a free agent and signed with the Los Angeles Lakers in September.

RICK'S RATINGS

Scoring: **AA**   Defense: **C**
Shooting: **B**   Defensive Rebounding: **B**
Free Throw Shooting: **B**   Intangibles: **C**
Ball Handling: **B**   Overall: **B**
Passing: **C**

Adrian Dantley

Birthdate: February 28, 1956
Height: 6-5
Weight: 210
College: University of Notre Dame, Notre Dame, Ind.
Drafted: Buffalo on first round as hardship case, 1976 (6th pick).
Position: Forward
Final 1989 Team: Dallas Mavericks
Final 1988–89 Statistics:

G	Fg	Fga	Fg%	Ft	Fta	Ft%	Orb	Reb	Ast	Stl	To	Blk	Pts	Ppg
73	470	954	.493	460	568	.810	117	317	171	43	163	13	1400	19.2

Three-point goals: 0–1 (.000)   TSP: .493

SCORING

Dantley, who was acquired from Detroit (along with a first-round pick in 1991) for Mark Aguirre in February 1989, has always been—and continues to be—the prototype scorer. He's been putting points on the board for 13 years—twice he's led the league in scoring, and his 22,458 points places him third among current NBA players. Early in his career, he was primarily a post-up player (at a small 6-5, mind you), but in his later years that's been supplemented with an outside game—an 18-to-20-foot set shot. Throughout, he's had an uncanny, one might say unmatched, ability to get to the line (nine attempts a game for his career), where he's a .819 shooter, though he shot a puzzling .776

with the Mavs. His calling card is the isolation. He likes to set up on the right side, where, for example, he might fake the drive, step back, and shoot the outside shot. Or head fake, dribble to the lane, somehow get his shot off among the trees—and get fouled. These examples just scratch the surface of what is one of the most versatile games in the league. Dantley wants the ball down the stretch and he's the right man for it because of his ability to score and draw fouls.

DEFENSE/DEFENSIVE REBOUNDING

As a scorer extraordinaire, Dantley has never been known for his defense. He picks and chooses his spots—he's shown some surprising defensive focus during playoff time (such as the 1987–88 Piston-Laker series)—but it's the exception rather than the rule. He's generally at a size and quickness disadvantage in guarding small forwards. An adequate defensive rebounder, he is, however, capable of grabbing key rebounds when needed.

THE FLOOR GAME

The rap against Dantley—and one reason Detroit traded him—is that offenses grind to a halt with he touches the ball and begins his elaborate maneuvers to the hoop. The shot clock ticks away, the other players stand around, and offensive continuity is interrupted. On the other hand, good things generally happen—a basket, foul shots or both—when the ball is in his hands. Playing with Adrian Dantley is an adjustment, and the other Mavs haven't yet meshed with him. He will pass the ball out of the invariable double-team, though occasionally he holds it too long.

INTANGIBLES

Dantley is a consummate pro. He keeps himself in phenomenal shape, has excellent work habits, and despite the critics who have labeled him selfish, puts Ws ahead of individual statistics. Unlike a certain small forward who no longer plays in Dallas, you can count on Dantley playing hard every night.

IN SUM

At 33, Dantley remains one of the premier point producers in the NBA. But it remains to be seen whether Dallas *improved* its fortunes by acquiring him.

RICK'S RATINGS

Scoring: **AAA**   Defense: **C**
Shooting: **A**   Defensive Rebounding: **D**
Free Throw Shooting: **A** Intangibles: **A**
Ball Handling: **B**   Overall: **AA**
Passing: **B**

Brad Daugherty

Birthdate: October 19, 1965
Height: 7-1
Weight: 260
College: University of North Carolina, Chapel Hill, N.C.
Drafted: Cleveland on first round, 1986 (1st pick).
Position: Center
Final 1989 Team: Cleveland Cavaliers
Final 1988–89 Statistics:

G	Fg	Fga	Fg%	Ft	Fta	Ft%	Orb	Reb	Ast	Stl	To	Blk	Pts	Ppg
78	544	1012	.538	386	524	.737	167	718	285	63	230	40	1475	18.9

Three-point goals: 1–3 (.333)   **TSP:** .538

SCORING

It may not be as pretty as an Abdul-Jabbar skyhook, but Daugherty's jump hook is fast becoming one of the most reliable weapons in the league. The hook, however, is only one piece of artillery in a multifaceted arsenal. Daugherty, huge at 7-1, 260, is expert at sealing off his man and receiving the pass for an easy duece. He also can go outside—he initiates much of Cleveland's offense from the high-post—and drill the 17-footer, though he has been a somewhat reluctant marksman from that area. Despite his size, he can get up and down the court and will finish the break. And with his back to the basket, Daugherty has an array of power moves that often result in foul shots (his 6.7 foul shots a game was third among starting centers; he's a slightly below-average foul shooter, .737 last year, .718 career). The only shot missing from his repertoire is the offensive put-back. Among starting centers, only Bill Laimbeer and Jack Sikma were worse offensive rebounders. Note that each year Daugherty's scoring average has improved (15.7, 18.7, and 18.9). And consider that he'd certainly score more on other teams, but he's an unselfish player and a member of a team in which the scoring burden is shared (nobody averaged 20 but four were over 17). But Daugherty's All-Star season (his second consecutive selection) was marred by a nightmarish shooting performance (.362, 11 ppg, and three single-digit games) in the 3–2 playoff loss against the Bulls. However, he was injured and obviously it affected his performance.

DEFENSE/DEFENSIVE REBOUNDING

Daugherty is a good defensive rebounder and getting better.

Like his scoring, his totals have increased each year he's been in the league (9.2 total rebounds in 1988–89, 10th in the league). Without the ability to sky, he's a "ground-pounder" who takes up a lot of room. Defensively, he relies on positioning and smarts to get the job done. Coming out of North Carolina, the book on Daugherty was that he was soft. The book was wrong. Following a summer of lifting, he's a horse and doesn't get pushed around by opposition centers. He doesn't block shots (Dave Corzine blocked more!) but, of course, he's teamed with two of the best swatters in the league: John Williams and Larry Nance.

THE FLOOR GAME

Daugherty's extra dimension is his passing. He led all centers in assists for the third consecutive year (3.7 a game), sees the court exceptionally well (Lenny Wilkins, his coach, says he has a point guard's vision), and is willing—maybe too willing at times—to give it up. As is the case with all Dean Smith graduates, he's a heady player.

INTANGIBLES

Daugherty is the consummate team player. He has the desire to be great (for example, he spent time in the summer of 1988 at Pete Newell's Big Man's Camp), and he's getting there. Everybody has nothing but nice things to say about him as a person. But he has failed to produce when it counts: In the last two seasons, the Cavs have lost to the Bulls in the playoffs and Daugherty disappeared in both series. Although, as stated above, he was injured last season.

IN SUM

Daugherty is the cornerstone of Cleveland's franchise. When you talk about the top centers for the 1990s, three names are mentioned in the same breath: Patrick Ewing, Akeem Olajuwon, and Brad Daugherty.

RICK'S RATINGS

Scoring: **AA**	Defense: **A**
Shooting: **A**	Defensive Rebounding: **A**
Free Throw Shooting: **C**	Shot Blocking: **D**
Ball Handling: **A**	Intangibles: **AA**
Passing: **AAA**	Overall: **AAA**

Brad Davis

Birthdate: December 17, 1955
Height: 6-3
Weight: 180
College: University of Maryland, College Park, Md.
Drafted: Los Angeles on first round as undergraduate, 1977 (15th pick).
Position: Guard
Final 1989 Team: Dallas Mavericks
Final 1988–89 Statistics:

G	Fg	Fga	Fg%	Ft	Fta	Ft%	Orb	Reb	Ast	Stl	To	Blk	Pts	Ppg
78	183	379	.483	99	123	.805	14	108	242	48	92	18	497	6.4

Three-point goals: 32–102 (.314)   **TSP:** .525

SCORING

The numbers tell all: Any way you look at it, Davis is a big-league shooter. Consider: He has shot below 50 percent only twice (once was last year, .483) in his 12-year career. A career .519 shooter, he's the only plus-50 percent shooter among backup point guards. For his career, he's shot .329 from three-point land, which equates to almost a 50 percent two-point equivalent. And he's a career .835 foul shooter. Enough said. One reason for Davis' gaudy percentages: He rarely takes a bad shot. And he's tough to guard because he has the outside game but also can get by people with his quickness and finish the play. He loves the pick-and-roll: He'll turn the corner and either find the open man or shoot the jumper. A clutch shooter, Davis won several games for the Mavericks last year.

DEFENSE/DEFENSIVE REBOUNDING

Davis is a heady player and his defense is no exception. A hard-nosed defender, he is willing to take charges, and even at 33 (34 in December), will dive for loose balls. However, at that advanced age (for an NBA guard, that is), he's lost a little quickness which is a disadvantage against the league's jets. They don't pay him to rebound.

THE FLOOR GAME

Rather, he earns his paycheck running the offense, something Davis does—starters and backups included—as well as anybody in the NBA. He can handle the ball against any type of pressure and makes few mistakes. As one coach put it, "He's a veteran who really knows how to play." With his shooting ability, he occasionally plays the 2 with Harper at the point.

INTANGIBLES

Davis can come off the bench (he also started four games when Rolando Blackman was out of the lineup with a broken finger) and have an immediate impact on a game, be it a shot, a pass, or a hustle play. It's hard to keep him out of the lineup; he's missed only 15 games (11 of them in the last two years) in the last eight seasons.

IN SUM

Davis is winding down what has been a solid NBA career.

He can still give you shooting and veteran leadership off the bench. With the departure of Morlon Wiley to Orlando in the expansion draft (who had been touted as Davis' eventual replacement), Davis again will be the third guard in the Mavs' rotation.

RICK'S RATINGS

Scoring: **B**

Shooting: **A**

Free Throw Shooting: **A**

Ball Handling: **A**

Passing: **A**

Defense: **B**

Defensive Rebounding: **B**

Playmaking: **A**

Intangibles: **A**

Overall: **B +**

Charles Davis

Birthdate: October 5, 1958

Height: 6-7

Weight: 215

College: Vanderbilt University, Nashville, Tenn.

Drafted: Washington on second round, 1981 (35th pick).

Positions: Forward, Guard

Final 1989 Team: Chicago Bulls

Final 1988–89 Statistics:

G	Fg	Fga	Fg%	Ft	Fta	Ft%	Orb	Reb	Ast	Stl	To	Blk	Pts	Ppg
49	81	190	.426	19	26	.731	47	114	31	11	22	5	185	3.8

Three-point goals: 4–15 (.267)   **TSP:** .437

SCORING

Davis can play 2 or 3, the two prime scoring positions, but hasn't demonstrated the firepower essential at those spots. He's a career .457 shooter with an adequate jumper (off of picks) and limited ability to create off the dribble or drive it to the basket. A good jumper, he did an excellent job on the offensive glass (one a game) last year. He'll shoot the trey occasionally, but why? For his career, he's 12-for-87, a miserable .137. He even sees some time at the 4, but at 6-7, 215, he is truly out of position there.

DEFENSE/DEFENSIVE REBOUNDING

Davis is a physical defender, who will fight over screens but lacks lateral quickness. For his career, he's an above-average defensive rebounder.

THE FLOOR GAME

Davis runs the lanes well and is an adequate ball handler.

INTANGIBLES

A class act, a nice guy—Davis brings a positive attitude to any team. He knows the game, which is one reason he's stuck around for seven years.

IN SUM

Davis is a tease: He'll show you stuff that makes you think

he can really play, but there's no consistency to his game. Still, he's a smart veteran who can be effective as a spot player.

RICK'S RATINGS

Scoring: **C**

Shooting: **C**

Free Throw Shooting: **C**

Ball Handling: **B**

Passing: **B**

Defense: **B**

Defensive Rebounding: **B**

Intangibles: **B**

Overall: **C**

Walter Davis

Birthdate: September 9, 1954

Height: 6-6

Weight: 200

College: University of North Carolina, Chapel Hill, N.C.

Drafted: Phoenix on first round, 1977 (5th pick).

Positions: Forward, Guard

Final 1989 Team: Denver Nuggets

Final 1988–89 Statistics:

G	Fg	Fga	Fg%	Ft	Fta	Ft%	Orb	Reb	Ast	Stl	To	Blk	Pts	Ppg
81	536	1076	.498	175	199	.879	41	151	190	72	132	5	1267	15.6

Three-point goals: 20–69 (.290)   **TSP:** .507

SCORING

Denver won 54 games in 1987–88 but there was a missing piece: a perimeter threat off the bench. What better candidate than Davis, who in 11 seasons with the Suns (six of them as an All-Star) established himself as one of the game's premier pure shooters. The "Greyhound" (an unrestricted free agent, he signed a two-year deal in July 1988) is still sleek, still smooth, and can still shoot, hitting .498 last year (right around his career .518 mark). However, while he provided the requisite instant offense off the bench, often it was more like absent offense: Davis was up and down, inconsistent, streaky. Consider, for example, his shooting stats in a six-game stretch beginning on January 7: 11–14, 3–15, 8–15, 9–22, 5–16, 10–18. When he's on, he can carry a team; when he's not, he's best left on the pine because his game is scoring and scoring only. One of his specialties is the pull-up jumper on the break. He's also solid coming off picks and is one of the few Nuggets who can create off the dribble. He can shoot the three, but it's a here one-year, gone-the-next affair. Last year, it was more of the latter (.290). He keeps defenses honest by taking it to the hole—usually after his patented head-and-shoulder fake. A superb foul shooter (.879 last year; .844 lifetime).

DEFENSE/DEFENSIVE REBOUNDING

Davis, who played mostly small forward for the Nuggets, after spending the bulk of his career as a 2, has trouble keeping pace with his nightly matchup. He's always been offensive-minded, which was certainly the case with the Nuggets. Working so hard in Denver's motion offense—a physically taxing system—he often had little left for D. He's OK on the ball but doesn't offer much help off the ball. Nor did he go to the boards much (1.9 rebounds in 22.9 minutes), nor has he ever.

THE FLOOR GAME

While he consistently has put up big numbers in the scoring column (20 a game for his career), Davis has also accumulated some nice assist totals: 4.2 a game lifetime and 2.3 per game last year. A good ball handler, he can run all day.

INTANGIBLES

Davis, of course, came to the Nuggets with a blemished rep as a result of his involvement with the drug scandal that wracked the Phoenix Suns two years ago. But he's put that behind him and is now exhibiting the leadership and work ethic—he still religiously hones his jumper—that we've come to expect of him.

IN SUM

Davis provided scoring off the bench—much of the time. This is the last year of his contract and will likely be the final year of an outstanding career, marked by its consistent productivity.

RICK'S RATINGS

Scoring: **AAA**   Defense: **C**
Shooting: **A**   Defensive Rebounding: **C**
Free Throw Shooting: **AA**   Intangibles: **A**
Ball Handling: **B**   Overall: **B +**
Passing: **A**

———— Johnny Dawkins ————

Birthdate: September 28, 1963
Height: 6-2
Weight: 175
College: Duke University, Durham, N.C.
Drafted: San Antonio on first round, 1986 (10th pick).
Position: Guard
Final 1989 Team: San Antonio Spurs
Final 1988–89 Statistics:

G	Fg	Fga	Fg%	Ft	Fta	Ft%	Orb	Reb	Ast	Stl	To	Blk	Pts	Ppg
32	177	400	.443	100	112	.893	32	101	224	55	111	0	454	14.2

Three-point goals: 0–4 (.000)   **TSP:** .443

SCORING

Dawkins may play the point but he's a 2 at heart (his position at Duke). And, yes, he can score. He started the 1988–89 season like gangbusters, having an all-star November (19.1 ppg). But his production tailed off and then he suffered a rare injury—palsy of the peroneal nerve in his left leg—which caused him to miss 49 games. Dawkins, who was traded to the 76ers in August (along with Jay Vincent for Maurice Cheeks, Christian Welp and David Wingate), is more of a scorer than a pure shooter (.443 from the field last year). His jumper, which he can create off the dribble or pulling up on the break (he has three-point range, .297 lifetime, though he was 0–4 last year) is erratic. He's best in transition, where he uses his exceptional quickness (is there anybody quicker?) to get by opponents—which he can also do in half-court. Dawkins also gets many of his points on steals. And he's one of the top foul shooters in the league (.893 last year, which would have placed him fifth had he had the minimum 125 attempts).

DEFENSE/DEFENSIVE REBOUNDING

There are doubts about Dawkins's defense. He hasn't done a good job pressuring the ball, tending to mirror his man rather than forcing him to do what he doesn't want to do. His lack of strength—he's 6-2 and all of 175—also is a drawback. But he's beginning to use his quickness more effectively—entering last season he had only 1.1 steals a game which he improved to 1.7 per in 1988–89. A below-average defensive rebounder for a starting 1.

THE FLOOR GAME

Dawkins is learning the point, and the consensus is that he has a lot to learn. For example, he'll simply pass the ball, rather than getting the shooter the ball at the precise moment he can use it. His decisions on the break—when to give it up, when to shoot it—have also been questioned. But with his intelligence and work habits, it appears that he can master the position.

INTANGIBLES

Dawkins has a can't-miss attitude: upbeat, works hard, thinks "team," and is fun to be around. He's also a graduate of one of the finest programs, Duke, in the country.

IN SUM

OK, maybe Dawkins is not All-Star caliber. With his attitude and his physical skills, however, Johnny Dawkins will be around for at least a decade. Which is the major reason the 76ers traded for him: Cheeks has two, maybe three years left while Dawkins has a career ahead of him. He has big shoes to fill in Philadelphia but, for now, he has a lot of growing to do as a 1 before those shoes will fit.

RICK'S RATINGS

Scoring: **B**	Defense: **B**
Shooting: **C**	Defensive Rebounding: **C**
Free Throw Shooting:	Playmaking: **C**
AAA	Intangibles: **AA**
Ball Handling: **B**	Overall: **B +**
Passing: **B**	

Vinny Del Negro

Birthdate: August 9, 1966
Height: 6-5
Weight: 185
College: North Carolina State University, Raleigh, N.C.
Drafted: Sacramento on second round, 1988 (29th pick).
Position: Guard
Final 1989 Team: Sacramento Kings
Final 1988–89 Statistics:

G	Fg	Fga	Fg%	Ft	Fta	Ft%	Orb	Reb	Ast	Stl	To	Blk	Pts	Ppg
80	239	503	.475	85	100	.850	48	171	206	65	77	14	569	7.1

Three-point goals: 6–20 (.300)   **TSP:** .481

SCORING

While most rookie guards were mired in the low 40s or high 30s (Kevin Edwards: .425, Rex Chapman: .414, Morlon Wiley: .404), Del Negro shot a respectable .475, proof positive that he can shoot the basketball. (Only two rookie guards, Kevin Gamble and Tom Garrick, shot better.) He is a pure shooter, with classic form, who can create his own shot off the dribble from 20 feet. He was an excellent three-point shooter in college (.447) and showed some potential (6–20, .300) from NBA three-point range. At 6-5, Del Negro has deceptive quickness and is talented with the ball,

but his ability to finish is still evolving. At .850, he's a top-notch foul shooter.

DEFENSE/DEFENSIVE REBOUNDING

Del Negro has sound defensive instincts. He does the little things—gets over screens, takes charges—that coaches love. His only drawback is his strength; he hardly weighs anything (185) and is currently on a weight program. But he has had trouble with smaller, quicker guards. With his size, he's a fine rebounder; he was in the top third among backup point guards on a per minute basis.

THE FLOOR GAME

Del Negro has a real feel for the game. Not surprisingly, he made the smooth transition from shooting guard in college to the point. His play-calling and decision-making have been beyond reproach, and while his assist-to-turnover ratio was only average, this reflected (relative to other point guards) fewer assists (the Kings were a low-scoring team) but few turnovers. With his shooting ability, Del Negro can also play the off-guard.

INTANGIBLES

Del Negro is a quick learner, tough, and willing to pay his dues. He will only get better.

IN SUM

Sacramento made a terrific pick when it drafted Del Negro on the second round (29th player overall). He stepped right in and provided competent backup help: on a per minute basis, he ranked better than Kenny Smith (who he played behind) in rebounding and steals. He reminds some people of the Suns' Jeff Hornacek, a fine shooter who will get after you and can play both guard positions. Whether or not Del Negro is an NBA starter remains to be seen. But Sacramento coaches are high on him.

RICK'S RATINGS

Scoring: **C**	Defense: **B**
Shooting: **AA**	Defensive Rebounding: **B**
Free Throw Shooting: **AA**	Playmaking: **B**
Ball Handling: **AA**	Intangibles: **A**
Passing: **A**	Overall: **B**

Fennis Dembo

Birthdate: January 24, 1966
Height: 6-5
Weight: 210
College: University of Wyoming, Laramie, Wyo.
Drafted: Detroit on second round, 1988 (30th pick).
Position: Guard
Final 1989 Team: Detroit Pistons

Final 1988–89 Statistics:

G	Fg	Fga	Fg%	Ft	Fta	Ft%	Orb	Reb	Ast	Stl	To	Blk	Pts	Ppg
31	14	42	.333	8	10	.800	8	23	5	1	7	0	36	1.2

Three-point goals: 0–4 (.000)   **TSP:** .333

SCORING

Here we enter the realm of speculation . . . In his rookie season, Dembo, Detroit's second-round pick in 1988, played the fewest minutes of a player who was with a club for an entire season (74 minutes in 31 games; at his contract price, $150,000, that works out to be about $2,000 a minute—beats working). Part of the problem was not of his making. Dembo was playing behind the best guard rotation in the league (Isiah Thomas, Joe Dumars, and Vinnie Johnson). On the other hand, Dembo was making the transition from the 3 to the 2, and the adjustment wasn't smooth. It's not clear whether he can create for himself off the dribble, and he tends to be a streaky shooter. His strength so far has been his post-up game—more familiar territory. A physical guard (6-5, 210).

DEFENSE/DEFENSIVE REBOUNDING

Dembo arrived in the Pistons' camp with no clue about D—coach Chuck Daly even asked at one point: "Hasn't anybody ever talked to this guy about playing defense?" He has pretty good lateral quickness, but he didn't know how to employ it. Potentially, then, he's an adequate defender. And with his jumping ability, you can say the same about his defensive rebounding.

THE FLOOR GAME

Dembo's ball handling skills are underdeveloped. He needs work on putting the ball on the floor.

INTANGIBLES

Despite the heavy dose of pine time, Dembo managed to maintain his competitiveness and confidence.

IN SUM

Daly made another telling comment about Dembo: "Fennis Dembo's impact in this league is down the road, if ever." He has a great NBA physique but how is he going to get the minutes with the Pistons to see if there's anything more to him than just that "pro body?"

RICK'S RATINGS

Scoring: **D**   Defense: **D**
Shooting: **D**   Defensive Rebounding: **B**
Free Throw Shooting: **A**   Intangibles: **B**
Ball Handling: **C**   Overall: **D**
Passing: **C**

James Donaldson

Birthdate: August 16, 1957
Height: 7-2
Weight: 260
College: Washington State University, Pullman, Wash.
Drafted: Seattle on fourth round, 1979 (73rd pick).
Position: Center
Final 1989 Team: Dallas Mavericks
Final 1988–89 Statistics:

G	Fg	Fga	Fg%	Ft	Fta	Ft%	Orb	Reb	Ast	Stl	To	Blk	Pts	Ppg
53	193	337	.573	95	124	.766	158	570	38	24	83	81	481	9.1

Three-point goals: 0–0 (.000)   **TSP:** .573

SCORING

What he takes he makes—among active players Donaldson is the NBA career leader in shooting percentage with .587 (.573 last season)—but he is not offensive-minded. A typical night: 3 for 5. Career average: 9.1 ppg. Dallas would like him to be more "selfish" and score, say, 10 to 15 a game. Donaldson, who suffered a potentially career-threatening knee injury in March, is a deliberate player who lacks quickness and therefore occasionally has trouble getting his shot off. But he has developed a workable repertoire: a left-handed hook in the lane, a turnaround jumper on the baseline, and offensive rebounds (three a game in 1988–89). Practicing the martial art Tae Kwando has helped his mobility on the offensive boards (and overall). Early in his career, Donaldson's foul shooting left much to be desired (under 70 percent the first three seasons) but he's been over 76 percent in each of last four (.766 in 1988–89).

DEFENSE/DEFENSIVE REBOUNDING

This is *big* James Donaldson (7-2, 260), and he exploits that size on the defensive board. He's doesn't venture far from the basket so he's usually in position for the carom. Per minute, his 7.8 defensive rebounds a game (10.8 overall) placed him third among starting centers. Defensively, he holds up well against centers who camp in the post, but he's not consistent in denying players position. Donaldson's a laid-back, easygoing guy and that temperament often works against him. He also has trouble with centers who play outside, like Denver's Danny Schayes. Donaldson can block shots (1.5 a game) but, lacking quickness, he too often lets opposing guards get layups down the middle.

THE FLOOR GAME

Donaldson will not finish many fast breaks—he's slow afoot—but surprisingly he doesn't get beat defensively by centers running the court. His assists (0.7 a game) and turnovers (1.6 a game) are a reflection of his minimal offensive role.

INTANGIBLES

Donaldson's lack of offensive "ego" mirrors his unselfishness; he's a team player all the way. At one time, he was criticized for being too much the Gentle Giant, too mild-mannered to make it in the NBA. While he's clearly more aggressive than when he came into the league, his lack of consistent machismo hurts him defensively.

IN SUM

Yes, he has offensive limitations, but Dallas isn't hurting for scorers. Donaldson gives the Mavericks big-time rebounding consistently and solid defense more often than not. But the big question is when—if ever—James Donaldson, 32, will play another NBA game?

RICK'S RATINGS

Scoring: **D**
Shooting: **B**
Free Throw Shooting: **B**
Ball Handling: **B**
Passing: **C**
Defense: **A**

Defensive Rebounding: **AAA**
Shot Blocking: **B**
Intangibles: **A**
Overall: **B +**

Greg Dreiling

Birthdate: November 7, 1963
Height: 7-1
Weight: 250
College: University of Kansas, Lawrence, Kan.
Drafted: Indiana on second round, 1986 (26th pick).
Position: Center
Final 1989 Team: Indiana Pacers
Final 1988–89 Statistics:

G	Fg	Fga	Fg%	Ft	Fta	Ft%	Orb	Reb	Ast	Stl	To	Blk	Pts	Ppg
53	43	77	.558	43	64	.672	39	92	18	5	39	11	129	2.4

Three-point goals: 0–0 (.000)   **TSP:** .558

SCORING

Dreiling simply hasn't gotten the opportunity to show what he can do. Last year, he averaged 7.5 minutes a game and 2.4 ppg. He was caught up in a numbers game; Indiana was loaded with centers (Rik Smits, the now-departed Stuart Gray, and LaSalle Thompson, who doubles at power forward and was acquired from Sacramento in February; they also had Herb Williams until they traded him to Dallas for Detlef Schrempf). On a per minute basis, the three-year veteran has been an average scorer in the pros, though he didn't put up big numbers at Kansas (highest ppg was 13.1). He's a better-than-average offensive rebounder, has an OK hook, and can power it to the basket for a dunk.

DEFENSE/DEFENSIVE REBOUNDING

Dreiling will bang but he suffers from (a) lack of quickness, (b) lack of foot speed and (c) foul trouble. His defensive rebounding and shot blocking numbers are subpar.

THE FLOOR GAME

Dreiling is one of the best pick-setters in the league. He'll level guys out—legally. He's a decent passer but doesn't run the floor well.

INTANGIBLES

Dreiling has an excellent attitude: Though he accepts his role, he's not satisfied with it. He'll do whatever it takes to win and doesn't care about his points.

IN SUM

A limited talent who will stick around for a time because of his attitude and the fact that there's a premium on individuals who are 7-1. With Gray gone to Charlotte, Dreiling, as the backup to Rik Smits, should finally get a chance to play regular minutes.

RICK'S RATINGS

Scoring: **C**
Shooting: **B**
Free Throw Shooting: **D**
Ball Handling: **B**
Passing: **B**

Defense: **C**
Defensive Rebounding: **D**
Shot Blocking: **C**
Intangibles: **A**
Overall: **C –**

Clyde Drexler

Birthdate: June 22, 1962
Height: 6-7
Weight: 215
College: University of Houston, Houston, Tex.
Drafted: Portland on first round as an undergraduate, 1983 (14th pick).
Positions: Guard, Forward

Final 1989 Team: Portland Trail Blazers
Final 1988–89 Statistics:

G	Fg	Fga	Fg%	Ft	Fta	Ft%	Orb	Reb	Ast	Stl	To	Blk	Pts	Ppg
78	829	1672	.496	438	548	.799	289	615	450	213	250	54	2123	27.2

Three-point goals: 27–104 (.260)   **TSP:** .504

SCORING

He flies, he swoops, he floats. . . . Clyde the Glide is one of the most gifted and graceful athletes in the league. Leaping ability, size, huge hands, speed, body control—nothing's missing. The six-year pro is now one of the league's most potent point producers, encoring a 27.0 ppg showing in 1987–88 (sixth in the league) with a 27.2 ppg performance (fourth) last season. His talent is best displayed in the transition game: He's a superb passer off the dribble as the middleman on the break, and as a finisher his acrobatic dunks are the stuff of highlight films. In the half-court setting, he's by far the best offensive rebounder among 2s (3.7 a game). Drexler can get to the hole with a great first step, get fouled (a hefty seven attempts per game) and convert—he shot a decent .799 from the line in 1988–89. And then there's his jump shot. Say this: it's gotten better. But he's still a streaky shooter. He's fine if he's squared to the basket and has his legs under him, but Drexler doesn't shoot the same way every time and he's often on the move when he fires. He'll take an occasional bad shot and even miss shots and try for the offensive rebound. His inconsistency as an outside shooter has really hurt Portland in the playoffs, which tend to be half court battles rather than up-and-down sprints. For example, in the 1987–88 playoff series against the Jazz, Drexler shot an abysmal .386; and while he shot .507 in the Laker playoff series last year, he nary hit a jump shot. But under coach Rick Adelman, Drexler has added a new wrinkle: Playing the 3 spot, he's becoming an extremely effective post player, which is a healthy substitute for his jumper.

DEFENSE/DEFENSIVE REBOUNDING

Drexler plays the passing lanes as well as anybody in the league. He averaged 2.7 steals a game, fifth in the league, and he has a career average of 2.3 steals a game. He is a constant threat to create havoc in the opposing team's offense. But Clyde the Glide is not sound defensively. His mind will wander when he guards his man one-on-one, and he doesn't consistently take care of the little things—such as getting around picks—that good defenders do. But he's an excellent defensive rebounder, fourth, per minute, among starting 2s.

THE FLOOR GAME

As noted, Drexler is one of the premier creators on the break. In the half court, he's not as comfortable, which is reflected in his assist-to-turnover ratio, an OK 1.80, and his turnovers, 3.2 a game. But he's unselfish and in his new-found post role, has been very effective making interior passes to cutters.

INTANGIBLES

Drexler, a quiet guy, is not a leader in the usual sense, but when he's playing well, he definitely provides an inspiration. He does not like to practice (a situation that has irked many of his teammates) though he did so rather vigorously after Adelman took over from deposed coach Mike Schuler. Despite his erratic shooting, he has yet to fully commit himself to becoming an effective jump shooter. To some extent, Drexler is gliding on his talent.

IN SUM

The 1988–89 Blazers were "Team Turmoil" and Drexler's relationship with Mike Schuler was one of the root causes. Well, Schuler got fired, the Blazers barely made the playoffs (qualifying on the last day of the season), and were swept by the Lakers in the playoffs. Whatever Portland's problems—and there were a multitude—it's hard to find fault with Drexler's All-Star year. If he'd only work on his shooting.

RICK'S RATINGS

Scoring: **AAA**   Defense: **B**
Shooting: **B**   Defensive Rebounding:
Free Throw Shooting: **B**   **AA**
Ball Handling: **B**   Intangibles: **B**
Passing: **AA**   Overall: **AA +**

Kevin Duckworth

Birthdate: April 1, 1964
Height: 7-0
Weight: 270
College: Eastern Illinois University, Charleston, Ill.
Drafted: San Antonio on second round, 1986 (33rd pick).
Position: Center
Final 1989 Team: Portland Trail Blazers
Final 1988–89 Statistics:

G	Fg	Fga	Fg%	Ft	Fta	Ft%	Orb	Reb	Ast	Stl	To	Blk	Pts	Ppg
79	554	1161	.477	324	428	.757	246	635	60	56	200	49	1432	18.1

Three-point goals: 0–2 (.000)   **TSP:** .477

SCORING

Even as a 300-pound-plus behemoth (in college and his first

year in the league, which was split between San Antonio and Portland), Duckworth had the soft hands and nimble feet. Combine those natural assets with a weight program (he's now a svelte 270), a Larry Bird-like work ethic, and the result is one of the emerging offensive forces in the league. In the space of three years, Duckworth has gone from backup center on a lousy team (5.4 ppg in his rookie year), to All-Star center (18.1 ppg) in 1988–89. Duckworth's unusual mix of bulk and well-honed moves makes him tough to guard. He's huge but he's smooth, relying on a sweet right-handed hook (along with a less effective left-handed counterpart), a turnaround jumper (from the left block where he turns right), and a least-effective-of-all face-up jumper from 15 feet. He bangs the offensive boards consistently and effectively (3.1 a game last year) and can even get out on the break. However, Duckworth is no longer a secret. Last year, he had a tougher time scoring because he was often double and triple-teamed (opponents took away his hook) and the Blazers didn't have an outside game to counter it. Note, for example, his poor performance in the playoffs against the Lakers where he shot 40 percent and averaged only 11.3 ppg.

DEFENSE/DEFENSIVE REBOUNDING

Duckworth works at it but defense remains the weakest part of his game. He's not a quick or explosive jumper and is not blessed with long arms. Result: He doesn't block shots, a mere 49 in 2662 minutes. He needs to learn to use his size to deny his opponent position. His defensive rebounding isn't much better—lower, on a per minute basis, than nonbounders like Bill Cartwright and Dave Hoppen. His lack of jumping ability and tendency to not pursue the ball are two explanations.

THE FLOOR GAME

He'll get better but right now Duckworth is not a good passer, only 60 assists for the year and an ugly 0.30 assist-to-turnover ratio (only Rony Seikaly was worse among starting centers). When he gets it, he shoots it. He has a tendency to rush his game, which often results in bad shots and turnovers.

INTANGIBLES

Duckworth was voted the most improved player in the league in 1987–88, a testament to his extraordinary work habits. Portland rewarded him with a fat contract ($16 million over eight years, which incidentally, included a weight clause) but he didn't take the money and run. In fact, he made the All-Star team for the first time.

IN SUM

Duckworth's offense is in place. He just needs now to channel that tremendous desire to improve into defense and rebounding, and before long, Portland should have a fine all-around center—perhaps not in the same echelon as Patrick Ewing, Brad Daugherty, and Akeem Olajuwon, but just a notch below.

Chris Dudley

Birthdate: February 22, 1965
Height: 6-11
Weight: 245
College: Yale University, New Haven, Conn.
Drafted: Cleveland on fourth round, 1987 (75th pick).
Positions: Center, Forward
Final 1989 Team: Cleveland Cavaliers
Final 1988–89 Statistics:

G	Fg	Fga	Fg%	Ft	Fta	Ft%	Orb	Reb	Ast	Stl	To	Blk	Pts	Ppg
61	73	168	.435	39	107	.364	72	157	21	9	44	23	185	3.0

Three-point goals: 0–1 (.000)   **TSP:** .435

SCORING

Dudley is a Yalie (the only current NBA player from the Ivy League), but he plays like he's out of the Big Ten. His game is bang, smash, crash—Cleveland broadcaster Joe Tait calls it "ugly but strong"—and he utilizes his strength (6-11, 245) well on the offensive board, where, on a per minute basis, he led all backup 5s (he can also play power forward). He'll get the rebound, knock three guys to the ground, and power his way to the hoop. Otherwise, he's currently developing a hook; he doesn't have much of a jump shot. But the real fun starts when Dudley goes to the line. For a while there, Dudley made Kim Hughes, the legendary foul line brickmaster (.275 from the line in 1976–77 with the Nets), look like, well, Magic Johnson (who, with .911, led the league in free throw percentage last year). Dudley made a stupefying 4 of his first 25 (.160), fewer than many NBA guys can make blindfolded. In his defense, Dudley was learning an entirely new way of shooting. But his .364 for the year is a convincing argument not to have him on the floor at the end of games. He's a prime candidate for my underhand style.

DEFENSE/DEFENSIVE REBOUNDING

Dudley is not a leaper but his brute power serves him on the defensive boards, though he was slightly below the norm, per minute, among reserve centers. He also has great hands and once he gets his paws on the ball, it's his. He has some shot blocking ability (23 blocks in 544 minutes) but still doesn't get the benefit of the doubt from referees and has been foul-plagued in his two years in the league.

THE FLOOR GAME

Dudley can run the floor, but you don't want to give him any leeway in terms of dribbling the ball when he receives it. He is slightly turnover-prone but generally makes the safe, rather than the career, pass.

INTANGIBLES

Dudley is a fast and willing learner. He has paid his dues the last two summers at Peter Newell's Big Man's camp. Here's a player who nobody thought—Dudley himself had doubts—would make it in the league. And last June he was on Cleveland's protected list!

IN SUM

Dudley, it goes without saying, needs to improve his foul shooting, as well as expand his offensive repertoire. Otherwise, Cleveland loves his hustle, his rebounding, and his every-time-out intensity. But he's still a project and as evidenced by his splinter accumulation during last year's playoffs (a 3–2 loss to Chicago), when he played all of four minutes (Tree Rollins was the backup center), he can't yet be counted on when it counts.

RICK'S RATINGS

Scoring: **C**	Defense: **B**
Shooting: **C**	Defensive Rebounding: **B**
Free Throw Shooting: **D**	Shot Blocking: **A**
Ball Handling: **C**	Intangibles: **B**
Passing: **C**	Overall: **C**

Joe Dumars

Birthdate: May 24, 1963
Height: 6-3
Weight: 190
College: McNeese State University, Lake Charles, La.
Drafted: Detroit on first round, 1985 (18th pick).
Position: Guard
Final 1989 Team: Detroit Pistons
Final 1988–89 Statistics:

G	Fg	Fga	Fg%	Ft	Fta	Ft%	Orb	Reb	Ast	Stl	To	Blk	Pts	Ppg
69	456	903	.505	260	306	.850	57	172	390	63	178	5	1186	17.2

Three-point goals: 14–29 (.483)   **TSP:** .513

SCORING

Underrated—no more! Four splendid games in June against

the Lakers, and what had not been a very well-kept secret among basketball cognoscenti, is out: Joe Dumars is one of the best all-around guards in the league. With his NBA finals MVP-winning performance against the Lakers—he sizzled at a .576 pace and averaged 27.3 ppg—the four-year veteran showed that he can fill it up with the best of them. The irony is that Dumars, still the 17th leading scorer in collegiate history (for McNeese State), has for most of his career taken a backseat, scoring-wise, to teammates like Adrian Dantley (now a former teammate who plays for the Mavericks) and his backcourt partner, Isiah Thomas. But each year Dumars has become a little more assertive on offense and 1988–89 was his best scoring (17.2 ppg, compared to 13 ppg lifetime) and shooting year—from all distances (.505 overall, .483 from three-land on 14-for-29, and .850 from the line—his career numbers: .488, .376 and .806, respectively). James Worthy, who tried without any success to guard Dumars in the finals, can vouch for the fact that Joe is extremely dangerous off the dribble. He can manufacture his jumper with the ball, or with his deceptive quickness take it strong to the hoop. He particularly loves a right-to-left crossover dribble, and he then finishes with a reverse layup. But he also can face and shoot without the dribble and is effective floating around on the outskirts and receiving passes from, say, a double-teamed Aguirre for the 18-footer. Last year, Dumars seemed to have overcome an oft-heard rap against him: inconsistency.

DEFENSE/DEFENSIVE REBOUNDING

A major component of that all-around label is Dumar's defense, and last year he got his long overdue due. He was named to the NBA All-Defensive first team, the first time he's been selected to an all-defensive team. Michael Jordan, who was matched against Dumars in last season's playoffs, can attest to Dumars' considerable defensive prowess. In a few games, Dumars actually "contained" Jordan. (In the 1987–88 Bulls-Pistons series, he came close to stopping him.) Against Air, Dumars played glove to Jordan's hand, displaying basic in-your-jockstrap defense that requires superb lateral movement, tenacity, and total concentration. Dumars also may be the best at getting through picks in the league—an activity that requires the absorption of much punishment—but he's a well-built 6-3, 190 and can take the pounding. Also, nobody guards 1s *and* 2s as well as Dumars. But he's not a steal guy (only 0.9 a game), and mark these words, he actually has a weakness: he is a terrible defensive rebounder, the worst among starting 2s (only 2.5 total rebounds a game in 1988–89).

THE FLOOR GAME

Dumars can play the 2 to Isiah's 1 (that's the Pistons' starting scenario). Or 1 to Isiah's 2. Or 1 to Vinnie Johnson's 2. Or even 2 to Vinnie's 1. Now that's flexibility. As a point guard, Dumars is a steady ball handler, who gets the job done with a reasonable amount of turnovers (average for 2s) and pinpoint passing (5.7 assists a game). He runs the floor exceptionally well and, as noted, knows how to position himself for the open jumper.

INTANGIBLES

Dumars is a joy to coach. Coach Chuck Daly has likened him to Maurice Cheeks, another consummate pro who goes about his business quietly and unselfishly. Until recently, he lived in the huge shadow cast by Isiah, but he never complained—he eschews the limelight—about his lack of star status. (Obviously, he's now a star.)

IN SUM

Last season was the coming-out party for Joe Dumars. And there was a lot to celebrate: prime-time scoring, all-pro defense, expert ball handling. All for a quality fellow they just call Joe, the good 'ol boy amid the Bad Boys.

RICK'S RATINGS

Scoring: **A**	Defense: **AAA**
Shooting: **AAA**	Defensive Rebounding: **D**
Free Throw Shooting: **AA**	Playmaking: **AA**
Ball Handling: **AA**	Intangibles: **AAA**
Passing: **AA**	Overall: **AAA**

T.R. Dunn

Birthdate: February 1, 1955
Height: 6-4
Weight: 192
College: University of Alabama, University, Ala.
Drafted: Portland on second round, 1977 (41st pick).
Position: Guard
Final 1989 Team: Phoenix Suns
Final 1988–89 Statistics:

G	Fg	Fga	Fg%	Ft	Fta	Ft%	Orb	Reb	Ast	Stl	To	Blk	Pts	Ppg
34	12	35	.343	9	12	.750	30	60	25	12	6	1	33	1.0

Three-point goals: 0–0 (.000)   **TSP:** .343

SCORING

Dunn has never made much noise on the offensive end and, over the last couple of years, he's been downright mum. In 1987–88, for example, while with the Nuggets, (where he played from 1980–88; he sat out the 1988–89 season until the Suns signed him in February), he was the least productive scorer in the league, averaging just 2.2 a game (in 18.7 minutes) and an anemic 6.4 a game if he played the full 48. Last year, he put up similar numbers: 1.0 ppg in 9.4 minutes (in 34 games). To say that he is reluctant to shoot is an understatement. Strangely, he can knock down the open 15-to-17 footer and, historically, has been a good offensive rebounder.

DEFENSE/DEFENSIVE REBOUNDING

Dunn's raison d'être, of course, is defense. He's a three-time All-Defensive player (second team) who has made his living making life uncomfortable for opponents. His assets: excellent hands (1.4 steals a game for his career), the D mentality,

strength, quickness, and smarts—his game reflects his 12 years in the league. He's also a fine defensive rebounder for his position. Dunn is that rare 'bounder who, with his vision and timing, can get the carom even though he's boxed out.

THE FLOOR GAME

Dunn, primarily a 2, doesn't turn the ball over much. In 1988–89, he had an outstanding 4.17 assist-to-turnover ratio, tops among backup 2s, though he doesn't handle it much, what with Kevin Johnson as his running mate. And while not a creator, you won't take it from him.

INTANGIBLES

Dunn has been remarkably durable. From 1978 to 1988, he missed only 6 of 820 games. He knows his limitations and strengths as well as anybody in the league.

IN SUM

Dunn is a classic role player who gives his team major league defense and rebounding. But at 34, his NBA days are waning.

RICK'S RATINGS

Scoring: **D**	Defense: **AA**
Shooting: **D**	Defensive Rebounding: **A**
Free Throw Shooting: **B**	Intangibles: **A**
Ball Handling: **A**	Overall: **B –**
Passing: **B**	

Ledell Eackles

Birthdate: November 24, 1966
Height: 6-5
Weight: 220
College: University of New Orleans, New Orleans, La.
Drafted: Washington on second round, 1988 (36th pick).
Position: Guard
Final 1989 Team: Washington Bullets
Final 1988–89 Statistics:

G	Fg	Fga	Fg%	Ft	Fta	Ft%	Orb	Reb	Ast	Stl	To	Blk	Pts	Ppg
80	318	732	.434	272	346	.786	100	180	123	41	128	5	917	11.5

Three-point goals: 9–40 (.225)   **TSP:** .441

SCORING

Microwave II? A young Vinnie Johnson? Eackles has the same instant-offense capabilities as the veteran Detroit guard. In only 18.2 minutes a game, he averaged 11.5 ppg, which placed him in the top 10 percent of the league in points per minute and the best among rookies. Like the older model, Eackles is built like a halfback and is not at all shy about putting them up. He mixes the jumper (he has three-point range but shot only .225) with aggressive drives that often conclude with highlight-film dunks: for he can sky and has great body control. His ventures to the basket are extremely productive; he led all backup 2s with 4.3 foul shots a game (and he shot .786 from the line). He can also offensive rebound (1.3 a game). But his shot selection—he shot only .434 from the field—needs work.

DEFENSE/DEFENSIVE REBOUNDING

It comes as no surprise that Eackles has a long way to go on D. On the ball, he does an adequate job, but he tends to lose his concentration after the ball leaves his man's hands. Nor has he shown much ability for thievery. With his strength and jumping prowess, Eackles should be a much better defensive rebounder than he is (just one a game).

THE FLOOR GAME

Though his role is as a scorer, Eackles is an excellent passer who can make the play. A superb athlete, he runs the floor exceptionally well.

INTANGIBLES

Eackles, playing at about 260, was never in shape in college. Questions about his discipline were one reason he slipped to the second round (36th player picked) in the 1988 draft. But when the Bullet coaching staff browbeat him to a sleek 220, Eackles took his boot-camp treatment in stride.

IN SUM

Washington figures it made the steal of the draft when they landed Eackles in the second round. He has a bright future if he keeps his weight down, improves his defense, and becomes a more consistent outside shooter. He is, by all accounts, a major league talent.

RICK'S RATINGS

Scoring: **AA**	Defense: **D**
Shooting: **B**	Defensive Rebounding: **D**
Free Throw Shooting: **B**	Intangibles: **B**
Ball Handling: **A**	Overall: **B**
Passing: **B**	

Mark Eaton

Birthdate: January 24, 1957
Height: 7-4
Weight: 290
College: University of California at Los Angeles, Los Angeles, Calif.
Drafted: Utah on fourth round, 1982 (72nd pick).
Position: Center
Final 1989 Team: Utah Jazz
Final 1988–89 Statistics:

G	Fg	Fga	Fg%	Ft	Fta	Ft%	Orb	Reb	Ast	Stl	To	Blk	Pts	Ppg
82	188	407	.462	132	200	.660	227	843	83	40	142	315	508	6.2

Three-point goals: 0–0 (.000)   **TSP:** .462

SCORING

Among current NBA players, Eaton had the lowest scoring average as a college senior—1.3 ppg at UCLA. He hasn't been much more productive as a pro. In 30.2 minutes a game over seven years, the 7-4, 290-pound Eaton (the heaviest player in the league) has averaged 7 ppg and only twice shot over 45 percent (including last year's .462). Eaton scores in three ways, none of which are pretty: a left or right-handed hook close to the basket (we're not talking sky hook; this is a 3-to-5 foot job); putbacks (he's an average offensive rebounder for his position); and dunks that are a direct result of Stockton's penetration. He's a lousy foul shooter (.660 last year; .649 career).

DEFENSE/DEFENSIVE REBOUNDING

Utah was the best defensive team in the league in 1988–89 (both in terms of points allowed and field goal percentage), and it doesn't take a genius to figure out that Eaton, who was named Defensive Player of the Year for the second time, is the prime reason. He is THE FORCE in the middle who completely disrupts opposing offenses. Not only does he block shots—he led the league in blocked shots four times and was second (to Manute Bol) last year (3.8 a game)—but alters the trajectories of countless others. He knows how to "stay home," and, of course, he can't jump a lick anyway. And in Bill Russell-like fashion, Eaton keeps the ball in play instead of swatting it out of bounds. Opponents counter Eaton by trying to get him into foul trouble, but the big guy isn't foul-prone. But he is vulnerable to quicker, perimeter-shooting centers who can take him away from the basket (or simply centers who stay away from the hoop such as Golden State's Larry Smith or Manute Bol. During last year's playoffs, with Smith and Bol on the outskirts, the Warriors neutralized Eaton's shot blocking potency—he had all of two blocks in the three games and Utah didn't win a game). An average rebounder for most of his career, Eaton, for the first time last season, had more than 10 'bounds a game (10.3 a game in 1988–89 and 11 per in the playoffs). Once he gets position, nobody is going to move him.

THE FLOOR GAME

Eaton rarely handles the ball though he does have good hands. He's a superb outlet passer; he simply takes the rebound, puts it high above his head, and snaps it out to Stockton.

INTANGIBLES

In a league of prima donnas, Eaton is just a regular guy. Talk about a hard worker: while at UCLA, Eaton was the guy left behind (coach's decision) for an NCAA tournament game; last year, he made the NBA All-Star team.

IN SUM

While Utah fans have booed him mercilessly over the years (though less so last year), teammates—and opponents—have long recognized how Eaton can dominate a game defensively. He's invaluable, and a key cog in Utah's emergence as an NBA power.

RICK'S RATINGS

Scoring: **D**
Shooting: **D**
Free Throw Shooting: **D**
Ball Handling: **C**
Passing: **A**
Defense: **AAA**

Defensive Rebounding: **AAA**
Shot Blocking: **AAA**
Intangibles: **A**
Overall: **A +**

James Edwards

Birthdate: November 22, 1955
Height: 7-1
Weight: 252
College: University of Washington, Seattle, Wash.
Drafted: Los Angeles on third round, 1977 (46th pick).
Position: Center

Final 1989 Team: Detroit Pistons
Final 1988–89 Statistics:

G	Fg	Fga	Fg%	Ft	Fta	Ft%	Orb	Reb	Ast	Stl	To	Blk	Pts	Ppg
76	211	422	.500	133	194	.686	68	231	49	11	72	31	555	7.3

Three-point goals: 0–2 (.000)   **TSP:** .500

SCORING

They are not easy to find. Just go down the list. Jerome Whitehead? No way. Mike Smrek? Don't be silly. How about Joe Kleine, Dave Corzine, Tim McCormick, Randy Breuer, and Eric Leckner? Sometimes. What we are looking for are quality backup centers who can score. There's Mychal Thompson (who likely will be a starter this season), and the best of the lot—at least in terms of point-producing ability— James Edwards. Just how rare—and valuable—Mr. Edwards is was highlighted by the Pistons' failure to protect Rick Mahorn in the expansion draft. Beyond Mahorn's back problems, one reading on this surprising move was that the Pistons could more readily replace Mahorn, their *starting* power forward (they have John Salley but rookie Anthony Cook signed in Italy) than find a big guy who could come off the bench and put points on the board like Edwards can. And do it at crunch time. Edwards, after all, has been a steady NBA scorer for the last 12 years (career average: 14.3 ppg). Last year, in fact, was the first time in his career he didn't average in double figures (7.3 ppg). And he had a rather unobstrusive regular season. But come playoff time, particularly during the Bulls series and against the Lakers, there was Edwards doing what he does best: shooting the feathery fadeaway on the right baseline or the same shot from 8 to 10 feet in the paint. Otherwise, he occasionally shoots the hook as he turns to the middle from the left block or, even more infrequently, takes it all the way to the basket off the dribble. Despite his touch, he's never been a good foul shooter (.686 last year, .689 lifetime).

DEFENSE/DEFENSIVE REBOUNDING

Edwards is a big center—7-1, 252—a space eater, if you will. But beyond his physique, his defensive assets are minimal. He's inconsistent in denying low-post position, doesn't block shots (less than one a game for his career in 26.8 minutes), is occasionally foul-prone, and is a below-average defensive rebounder—on a per minute basis, Will Perdue, John Shasky, and Scott Hastings outrebounded him.

THE FLOOR GAME

Edwards is a scorer; the Pistons are not looking for him to make the play. Doesn't run the floor well.

INTANGIBLES

Edwards is an easy fellow to get along with, one of the most "polite" players on the Pistons, as one source put it. At this advanced stage of his career (he turns 34 in November) he's not moaning and groaning about minutes; he accepts his limited role (16.5 mpg in 1988–89).

IN SUM

Can the Pistons repeat? Part of the answer depends on the continued clutch productivity from the man they call Buddha.

RICK'S RATINGS

Scoring: **AA**
Shooting: **A**
Free Throw Shooting: **D**
Ball Handling: **B**
Passing: **B**

Defense: **C**
Defensive Rebounding: **D**
Shot Blocking: **C**
Intangibles: **B**
Overall: **A –**

Kevin Edwards

Birthdate: October 30,1965
Height: 6-3
Weight: 200
College: DePaul University, Chicago, Ill.
Drafted: Miami on first round, 1988 (20th pick).
Position: Guard
Final 1989 Team: Miami Heat
Final 1988–89 Statistics:

G	Fg	Fga	Fg%	Ft	Fta	Ft%	Orb	Reb	Ast	Stl	To	Blk	Pts	Ppg
79	470	1105	.425	144	193	.746	85	262	349	139	246	27	1094	13.8

Three-point goals: 10–37 (.270) **TSP:** .430

SCORING

Edwards had a typical rookie-guard year from the field, misfiring at a .425 clip. But that number disguises the fact that after the All-Star break, he came into his own, shooting 45 percent, averaging 16.3 ppg, and ending up as the Heat's leading scorer with 13.8 ppg. The consensus is that the 6-3, 200-pound Edwards—with his impressive technique (he squares himself well to the basket)—will indeed be a fine shooter. He has good range, though he's not quite a three-point threat—yet (only 10 of 37, 27 percent). The first-round pick (20th overall) likes to come off screens and shoot off the catch, but can also create off the dribble. Early in the season, he'd blow by players with a quick first step, but couldn't decide between taking it all the way or passing. The result: a hard to make pass or a difficult shot. Later, he became more decisive—and tougher to stop. He's a slightly below-average foul shooter at .746.

DEFENSE/DEFENSIVE REBOUNDING

Edwards has the tools to be a quality defender. He's quick, likes to play defense, and has great hands (1.8 steals a game). As a rookie, his only weakness was a tendency to lose concentration, particularly on the ball, and would often go for steals rather than play good position defense. Since he can sky, he ought to garner more than 3.3 rebounds a game.

THE FLOOR GAME

Edwards is a decent ball handler for a 2, and even saw some time at the point. He sees the court and is more than willing to give up the ball to a teammate who has a better shot (a healthy 4.4 assists per game). Sometimes, he's unselfish to a fault—and will give up the open jumper when he should take it. Edwards moves well without the ball and can finish the break. He needs work, however, on ball handling in the open court, and his turnovers per minute numbers were the worst among starting 2s.

INTANGIBLES

Edwards is a quick learner and determined to make a good career, but he's prone to getting down on himself when he makes a mistake. Everybody has nothing but nice things to say about him as a person.

IN SUM

Edwards, who made the All-Rookie second team, is one of the warm spots in the Heat's future. He has a huge upside once he becomes a more consistent shooter and defender. He'll be in the league for a long time.

RICK'S RATINGS

Scoring: **A**
Shooting: **C**
Free Throw Shooting: **C**
Ball Handling: **D**
Passing: **A**

Defense: **B**
Defensive Rebounding: **B**
Intangibles: **A**
Overall: **B +**

Craig Ehlo

Birthdate: August 11, 1961
Height: 6-7
Weight: 185

College: Washington State University, Pullman, Wash.
Drafted: Houston on third round, 1983 (48th pick).
Positions: Guard, Forward
Final 1989 Team: Cleveland Cavaliers
Final 1988–89 Statistics:

G	Fg	Fga	Fg%	Ft	Fta	Ft%	Orb	Reb	Ast	Stl	To	Blk	Pts	Ppg
82	249	524	.475	71	117	.607	100	295	266	110	116	19	608	7.4

Three-point goals: 39–100 (.390)   **TSP:** .512

SCORING

Ehlo is the Cavs' Mr. Fix-It. On a given night, he might be asked to score or to make the play or to be a stopper. Since his role is constantly changing—he plays the 1, 2, and 3, though he's primarily the backup to Ron Harper at the 2—scoring is not always his main responsibility. Ehlo is a three-point threat (he shot an excellent .390 in 1988–89, 12th in the league), will bang the offensive board (1.2 a game in 22.8 minutes), and is a kamikaze driver. More of a set shooter than a pure jump shooter, Ehlo is most effective when his feet are set. Cleveland wants him to take the long one to give its big people operating room in the middle. He's never been a good foul shooter (.668 career), but last year things got out of hand and he finished at .607.

DEFENSE/DEFENSIVE REBOUNDING

At 6-7, Ehlo's all-purpose size comes in handy on D. He matches up against the smaller 3s (such as Dominique Wilkins) and uses his height advantage to bother the guards. He deflects a lot of balls, comes up with steals (1.3 a game in 1988–89), and is constantly hustling. Whether you call him a guard or a forward, he's a top-notch defensive rebounder (in the top 20 percent, per minute, among backup 2s).

THE FLOOR GAME

As a 2 or a 3, Ehlo is a fine ball handler. He also can get the job done as a 1, but he has trouble with the quicker players such as Isiah Thomas. He had a solid 2.29 assist-to-turnover ratio.

INTANGIBLES

This is another NBA success story. Ehlo was plucked from the CBA in 1987 (he had been waived by Houston in 1986) and here he is, two years later, an integral member of a championship-caliber team. His never-say-die attitude is the primary reason he's in the league.

IN SUM

Michael Jordan's buzzer-beater in the fifth and deciding playoff game against the Cavs last year deprived Ehlo, who three seconds earlier had made a spectacular give-and-go basket and had scored *15 points* in the fourth quarter, of some much deserved attention. He's a blue-collar player whose offensive and defensive versatility fills the gaps as needed. A perfect seventh or eighth player in a rotation.

Dale Ellis

Birthdate: August 6, 1960
Height: 6-7
Weight: 215
College: University of Tennessee, Knoxville, Tenn.
Drafted: Dallas on first round, 1983 (9th pick).
Position: Guard
Final 1989 Team: Seattle Supersonics
Final 1988–89 Statistics:

G	Fg	Fga	Fg%	Ft	Fta	Ft%	Orb	Reb	Ast	Stl	To	Blk	Pts	Ppg
82	857	1710	.501	377	462	.816	156	342	164	108	218	22	2253	27.5

Three-point goals: 162–339 (.478)   **TSP:** .549

SCORING

It's not hard to make the case that Ellis is one of the league's most potent shooters and scorers. The numbers tell all: For the third consecutive year, he shot more than 50 percent (.501). His plus-50 percent shooting is all the more distinctive considering that more than 19 percent of his shots were from three-point land. Of course, what keeps his overall percentage high is that he shot .478 from three-point country (second in the league; to boot, he won the three-point shootout at the All-Star game). His "true" shooting percentage was an excellent .549 percent. He scored 27.5 ppg, third in the league. And he shot .816 from the line (the first time he's been over the 80 percent mark). Case closed! Ellis makes his living shooting jumpers off picks; with his extraordinarily quick release, nobody is better catching and shooting. Opponents would rather have him dribble a few times—because he's not a good ball handler and he's better without the dribble. He puts the ball on the floor sporadically, but that's not his strength. A forward at Tennessee, Ellis also has a dangerous post-up game (at 6-7, he's a *big* guard) and with his quickness to the ball, he can get the offensive rebound (1.9 per game, fifth among starting 2s). But he had a subpar playoff year, shooting .450 and averaging only 22.9 ppg in the two playoff series against the Rockets and the Lakers.

DEFENSE/DEFENSIVE REBOUNDING

Expending all of that energy on offense doesn't leave a whole lot left for defense. Ellis will occasionally lose concentration on D and is vulnerable to quicker 2s. But for the most part, he's a decent defender who takes pride in his defense and plays the passing lanes well (he was second on the Sonics in steals with 108). A better offensive than defensive rebounder, Ellis placed in the bottom third for starting 2s on a per minute basis for defensive boards.

THE FLOOR GAME

Ellis' major weakness is his ball handling skills. He is neither a good dribbler nor a good passer, and he has trouble creating for himself off the dribble. He averaged only two assists a game (of course, his role is to shoot) and his .45 assist-to-turnover ratio was the worst among starting shooting guards.

INTANGIBLES

Ellis gets the job done in crunch time. He seems to thrive on pressure, on the plays where he's backed against the wall. He takes great pride in his game and has improved his scoring average for the last four years (his off-season regimen is Larry Bird-like). Though he has had off-court contractual and marital difficulties, they haven't discernably affected his performance (he recently signed a six-year $7.8 million contract). Quiet, not a leader-type.

IN SUM

Ellis made the All-Star team for the first time in 1988–89. Is there a better shooter in the league?

RICK'S RATINGS

Scoring: **AAA**	Defense: **B**
Shooting: **AAA**	Defensive Rebounding: **D**
Free Throw Shooting: **A**	Intangibles: **AA**
Ball Handling: **C**	Overall: **AA**
Passing: **C**	

Alex English

Birthdate: January 5, 1954
Height: 6-7
Weight: 190
College: University of South Carolina, Columbia, S.C.
Drafted: Milwaukee on second round, 1976 (23rd pick).
Position: Forward
Final 1989 Team: Denver Nuggets
Final 1988–89 Statistics:

G	Fg	Fga	Fg%	Ft	Fta	Ft%	Orb	Reb	Ast	Stl	To	Blk	Pts	Ppg
82	924	1881	.491	325	379	.858	148	326	383	66	198	12	2175	26.5

Three-point goals: 2–8 (.250)   **TSP:** .492

SCORING

English continues to amaze with his production. At an age, 35 (he'll be 36 in January), when most basketball players have slowed down, or retired, the 6-7 small forward hasn't lost a step. Wilt Chamberlain couldn't do it, nor could Oscar Robertson, George Gervin, or Jerry West, but last season English became the first NBA player to score 2,000 or more points in eight seasons—and he did it in consecutive years. In 1988–89, he was the most productive scorer, per minute, among starting small forwards, a group that includes, Chris Mullin, Dominique Wilkins, Tom Chambers, Charles Barkley, James Worthy, and Xavier McDaniel; fifth in scoring (26.5 ppg), the ninth year in a row English was one of the top ten scorers. He is, in fact, the leading scorer in the NBA in the 1980s; last year he scored in double figures in all 82 games and with Denver (he started his career with Milwaukee) has hit for 10 or more in 751 of 756 games. Amazing—and not at all bad for a second-round pick! And even more so, considering that the slender (190 pounds) English doesn't overwhelm opponents with his physical skills: he lacks, for example, the quickness of a Worthy, the explosiveness of a Wilkins, or the sheer power of a Barkley. Instead, he relies on superb body control, an extended-arm shot that is difficult to block, a delicate touch, and an ability to know how to get his shot. His are "quiet" points—not the "film at 11" variety—and with a dancer's grace, English makes the hard shot look easy. He's completely at home in the corners, is best coming off a pick, and is not a guy who is going to beat you to the basket off the dribble from the perimeter. When he drives, he'll pull up for the short-range jumper. An excellent foul shooter at .858 (.830 lifetime).

DEFENSE/DEFENSIVE REBOUNDING

Not a great defender, not a bad defender, English can, for the most part, hold his own defensively, but his lack of lateral quickness makes it tough for him against players like Derrick McKey or Xavier McDaniel. Not physical, not a jumper, better off running the lane—all reasons why English is a way below-average defensive rebounder.

THE FLOOR GAME

As is often the case with scorers, English's passing skills go unnoticed, but the fact is, he's an underrated passer. He may not be a thread-the-needle type, but he'll make the right play. In Denver's motion offense, he relentlessly hits a cutting Fat Lever for easy baskets. Note the numbers: English was fourth, per minute, among starting 3s in assists.

INTANGIBLES

You could write a book here, but we only have a paragraph. So let's begin with the durability factor: English was the only Nugget to play all 82 games last year, and has missed just five games over the last nine seasons. Then there's his competitiveness, which Denver coaches feel is his most distinctive asset. To these attributes we add his extensive off-court charity work and we ask: Is there a better role model in the league?

IN SUM

23,417 points and still going strong. A sure Hall of Famer. Entering his 13th season, English remains one of the most potent scorers in the league. How long can it last? Look for him to play fewer than the 36.5 minutes a game he logged last year.

RICK'S RATINGS

Scoring: **AAA**
Shooting: **AAA**
Free Throw Shooting: **AA**
Ball Handling: **B**
Passing: **A**

Defense: **B**
Defensive Rebounding: **D**
Intangibles: **AAA**
Overall: **AAA**

Patrick Ewing

Birthdate: August 5, 1962
Height: 7-0
Weight: 240
College: Georgetown University, Washington, D.C.
Drafted: New York on first round, 1985 (1st pick).
Position: Center
Final 1989 Team: New York Knicks
Final 1988–89 Statistics:

G	Fg	Fga	Fg%	Ft	Fta	Ft%	Orb	Reb	Ast	Stl	To	Blk	Pts	Ppg
80	727	1282	.567	361	484	.746	213	740	188	117	266	281	1815	22.7

Three-point goals: 0–6 (.000)   **TSP:** .567

SCORING

Who would have thunk it? When he came into the league

(1985–86 season), Ewing was likened to Bill Russell, a player who'd score points but whose presence would be felt most conspicuously on the defensive end. But Ewing has emerged as an offensive stud, a dominating center who is virtually unstoppable.

For starters, he works hard to get good position on the blocks—with his strength (7-0, 240) he's not easily denied. Once he catches the ball, Ewing has a ton of moves. He can shoot the turnaround jump shot, the jump hook, or he'll fake the jumper and convert an up-and-under move. What makes him so tough to guard is that he can turn either way. On the right box, using his exceptional quickness, he'll spin baseline for the jam. On the left block, he'll shoot the jump hook in the middle or turn the other way for the jumper. Ewing has simply become one of the best short-range jump shooters in the league (.567 from the floor, fourth in the NBA). He overpowers smaller opponents and outmaneuvers players his size. Ewing also gets to the line a lot (6.1 attempts per game in 1988–89), but he's still a below-average foul shooter (.728 career, though last year's .746 was his career-high). On the offensive glass, he was slightly below average for starting centers, with 2.7 a game. Unfortunately, during the playoffs, he was anything but dominant or unstoppable, shooting a drab .486 and averaging only 19.9 ppg compared to his regular season 22.7. Many reasons: foul trouble, he wasn't getting the ball, defenses were pushing him farther out on the blocks, he just plain missed the shots.

DEFENSE/DEFENSIVE REBOUNDING

Leaping ability + timing + pride = premier shot blocker. Ewing has been third in the league the last two seasons (three a game in 1987–88 and 3.5 a game last season). He is the Knicks' final weapon—and an intimidating one—when opponents pass out of the trap. He's also a bothersome figure when he's one of the trappers. He even steals the ball (1.5 a game, second on the Knicks). But Ewing's been plagued by foul trouble throughout his career—picking up many cheap fouls by being overly aggressive. But last year, mindful of the Knicks' scant backup help, he was more conservative, reducing his fouls from 332 in 1987–88 to 311. But, as evidenced by the playoffs, it's still an issue.

Leaping ability + timing + pride = premier defensive rebounder. But despite these qualities, Ewing has never been more than an average defensive rebounder. (On a career basis, per minute, Joe Kleine and David Hoppen are better.) Strange. In 1988–89, however, he had his best year on the defensive glass (though still below average for starting centers) and snagged more than nine rebounds a game for the first time in his career. Charles Oakley must be contagious.

THE FLOOR GAME

The great ones add a little something to their game every year. Ewing's new dimension in 1988–89 was his passing prowess from the post. No more "black hole" post play: What goes in, now comes out—to spotting-up three-point shooters or cutters through the lane. Still, he is turnover-prone—second worst among starting centers—and his hands (which are small for his size) remain suspect, even if they are improved. He runs the court as well as any center in the league.

INTANGIBLES

Ewing's desire to win is almost palpable. While he's clearly the Knicks' main man, he thinks *we* not *I*. The doubts regarding durability, once an issue (he missed 51 games in his first two years), have been laid to rest since Ewing has missed just two games in the last two years. Surly to some, his teammates and coaches love him.

IN SUM

You're starting a team. First pick: Akeem Olajuwon. Second pick: Patrick Ewing. Enough said.

RICK'S RATINGS

Scoring: **AAA**	Defense: **AAA**
Shooting: **AAA**	Defensive Rebounding: **B**
Free Throw Shooting: **C**	Shot Blocking: **AAA**
Ball Handling: **B**	Intangibles: **AAA**
Passing: **A**	Overall: **AAA**

Jim Farmer

Birthdate: September 23, 1964
Height: 6-4
Weight: 190
College: University of Alabama, University, Ala.
Drafted: Dallas on first round, 1987 (20th pick).
Position: Guard
Final 1989 Team: Utah Jazz
Final 1988–89 Statistics:

G	Fg	Fga	Fg%	Ft	Fta	Ft%	Orb	Reb	Ast	Stl	To	Blk	Pts	Ppg
37	57	142	.401	29	41	.707	22	55	28	9	26	0	152	4.1

Three-point goals: 9–20 (.450)   **TSP:** .433

SCORING

Farmer, a 2 (but a 3 at Alabama), has suffered from a malady that afflicts many young players: lack of playing time. The first-round pick of the Dallas Mavericks in 1987 (20th overall), Farmer warmed the bench behind Derek Harper, Rolando Blackman, and Brad Davis as a rookie, playing all of 157 minutes. Last year, after a poor preseason, he was waived by the Mavericks, sat at home, and then joined the Jazz in January when Bobby Hansen suffered a broken jaw (courtesy of a New Year's party punch by teammate Bart Kofoed). He was immediately thrust into the rotation, where he did an adequate job, averaging 5.9 ppg but shooting only 39 percent until Hansen returned—at which point he was once again relegated to mini-minutes. Then he broke his wrist in March, came back in April, but played little. Selected by the Magic in the expansion draft, he did not sign with Orlando and played on Chicago's team in the Southern California Summer Pro League. Minnesota was impressed enough to sign him in late August. Still, in

his limited minutes (412 for the year) Farmer showed that he might have a future in the league. He has excellent range (9 of 20, .450 from three-point country, but just .401 overall), can get his own shot off the dribble, and can go to the hole.

DEFENSE/DEFENSIVE REBOUNDING

Farmer is not blessed with an enormous amount of quickness, but he compensates with aggressiveness—maybe too much aggressiveness; he has a tendency to foul a lot. As a former small forward, he's willing to hit the boards, too.

THE FLOOR GAME

As a rookie, Farmer had trouble handling the ball in transition. And last year his assist-to-turnover ratio was a subpar 1.08. But Utah insiders felt that Farmer is nevertheless a promising passer and ball handler.

INTANGIBLES

Confidence: After Dallas waived him, Farmer refused to entertain offers to play in the CBA. He feels he belongs in the league.

IN SUM

Farmer has some scoring potential and is willing to play D. He certainly has the talent and attitude to make an NBA team.

RICK'S RATINGS

Scoring: **C**	Defense: **B**
Shooting: **D**	Defensive Rebounding: **B**
Free Throw Shooting: **C**	Intangibles: **B**
Ball Handling: **C**	Overall: **C**
Passing: **B**	

Rolando Ferreira

Birthdate: May 24, 1964
Height: 7-1
Weight: 240
College: University of Houston, Houston, Tex.
Drafted: Portland on second round, 1988 (20th pick).
Position: Center
Final 1989 Team: Portland Trail Blazers
Final 1988–89 Statistics:

G	Fg	Fga	Fg%	Ft	Fta	Ft%	Orb	Reb	Ast	Stl	To	Blk	Pts	Ppg
12	1	18	.056	7	8	.875	4	13	1	0	6	1	9	.08

Three-point goals: 0–0 (.000)   **TSP:** .056

SCORING

If you're 7-1 and can shoot, you probably will be able to find a job in the NBA—at least for a while. And the consensus is that the Brazilian-born and bred Ferreira (he played on the

Brazilian Olympic team) has NBA-level offensive talent: good range, a hook shot with both hands, decent hands, and both a facing and a turnaround jumper. But he lacks strength (he's 240 and on a weight program) and is easily pushed out of the post. Like many rookies, Ferreira had trouble getting the shot he wanted and tended to rush his offense. Of course, we actually know little of what he can do, since he played only 12 games (34 minutes) and spent most of the year on the injured list with tendinitis of the right knee.

DEFENSE/DEFENSIVE REBOUNDING

Defensively, Ferreira's lack of muscle also hurts. He's not at all physical—a requisite for his position—and has a tendency to back off when his man catches the ball. With his size, he has potential as a shot blocker. And in time, he could be a competent defensive rebounder because of his timing and willingness to pursue the ball.

THE FLOOR GAME

Ferreira's basketball instincts are more advanced than most foreign players. He understands the game, sees the court, and is a better-than-average passer. He even runs the floor well.

INTANGIBLES

Ferreira is a quick and willing learner. The feeling is that when he gets the minutes, he'll improve rapidly.

IN SUM

Of course, the question remains: Will he get to play? On the theory that big men take longer to develop, he'll be around for a couple/three years (he has two years remaining on his contract). He's a project, no doubt, but an intriguing one because of his offensive skills.

RICK'S RATINGS

Scoring: **D**   Defense: **C**
Shooting: **C**   Defensive Rebounding: **C**
Free Throw Shooting: **AA**   Shot Blocking: **B**
Ball Handling: **B**   Intangibles: **C**
Passing: **B**   Overall: **D**

Duane Ferrell

Birthdate: February 28, 1965
Height: 6-7
Weight: 209
College: Georgia Institute of Technology, Atlanta, Ga.
Drafted: Free Agent
Positions: Forward, Guard
Final 1989 Team: Atlanta Hawks
Final 1988–89 Statistics:

G	Fg	Fga	Fg%	Ft	Fta	Ft%	Orb	Reb	Ast	Stl	To	Blk	Pts	Ppg
41	35	83	.422	30	44	.682	19	41	10	7	12	6	100	2.4

Three-point goals: 0–0 (.000)   **TSP:** .422

SCORING

Ferrell, a 6-7 small forward/shooting guard, is a self-described "scorer not a shooter" but if he wants to stick, he'll have to develop into more of the latter. Right now, his jumper is shaky, and he relies on his athletic ability—Ferrell, no doubt, can jump and run, which is a nice fit for the Hawks who like the transition game. As a rookie last season, he played mop-up minutes and was effectively the 12th man. With his jumping ability, he can go to the offensive board and will drive to the hoop but needs to develop an outside game off the dribble.

DEFENSE/DEFENSIVE REBOUNDING

If he wants playing time, Ferrell must improve his perimeter defense and his consistency in terms of defensive intensity. He has the potential to be a solid defensive rebounder.

THE FLOOR GAME

Ferrell runs the floor well, but his ball handling and passing skills are not up to par for a 2 or a 3.

INTANGIBLES

When Ferrell, undrafted, made the Hawks, coach Mike Fratello said: "Here you see the virtue of hard work." The intangibles are there: the work ethic, the acceptance of his role, the cooperative spirit.

IN SUM

Ferrell could journey around the league for a while on his athletic talent. But if he wants to make a bigger contribution—and a career for himself—he should spend hours shooting jump shots.

RICK'S RATINGS

Scoring: **B**   Defense: **C**
Shooting: **D**   Defensive Rebounding: **A**
Free Throw Shooting: **D**   Intangibles: **A**
Ball Handling: **C**   Overall: **D**
Passing: **B**

Vern Fleming

Birthdate: February 4, 1961
Height: 6-5

Weight: 195
College: University of Georgia, Athens, Ga.
Drafted: Indiana on first round, 1984 (18th pick).
Position: Guard
Final 1989 Team: Indiana Pacers
Final 1988–89 Statistics:

G	Fg	Fga	Fg%	Ft	Fta	Ft%	Orb	Reb	Ast	Stl	To	Blk	Pts	Ppg
76	419	814	.515	243	304	.799	85	310	494	77	192	12	1084	14.3

Three-point goals: 3–23 (.130)   **TSP:** .517

SCORING

Fleming, a five-year veteran, has shown remarkable offensive consistency, never averaging less than 12 ppg and hitting his career best, 14.3, in 1988–89. He has shown similar stability from the field and has been under 50 percent only once; last year he shot .513, near his career mark of .504. Which is not to say that Fleming is a great shooter since he gets the majority of his points on penetration drives—at 6-5, he's reasonably quick and can overpower opponents getting to the hoop. He got to the line four times a game last year and shot .799. He's particularly good taking it to the hole in transition. Befitting a converted forward, he produces on the offensive glass (1.1 a game). Then there's Flemings' jumper, which is not exactly a work of art—for you old-timers, a Hoyt Wilhelm job (no rotation)—but it's pretty accurate when he's pulling up on the break or spotting up, though he has limited range (16 feet).

DEFENSE/DEFENSIVE REBOUNDING

Fleming is a quality defender (he was honorable mention All-Defensive team in 1985–86) who has long arms and takes up a lot of space. He's particularly adept in trapping situations, but because of his size, he's vulnerable to quicker guards. He's consistently been an above-average defensive rebounder for his position. But he only had one steal a game last year and he was the worst "thief," per minute, among starting point guards.

THE FLOOR GAME

Fleming is making the near-impossible switch from college forward to pro point and the results have been decidedly mixed. Yes, he has gotten better, but he doesn't have jet speed, is not creative at all (his 6.5 assists a game placed him in the bottom third, per minute, among starting 1s), has trouble seeing the left side of the floor, and is sometimes indecisive at game's end. Plus, on the break he often thinks shot rather than pass and doesn't read his teammates' actions well.

INTANGIBLES

You have to respect Fleming's work ethic—he constantly is improving his game. But he has yet to provide the leadership his position requires.

IN SUM

Fleming is a solid player, giving the Pacers defense, rebounding, and scoring. But he is not the answer—at least as a starter—at the point.

Sleepy Floyd

Birthdate: March 6, 1960
Height: 6-3
Weight: 175
College: Georgetown University, Washington, D.C.
Drafted: New Jersey on first round, 1982 (13th pick).
Position: Guard
Final 1989 Team: Houston Rockets
Final 1988–89 Statistics:

G	Fg	Fga	Fg%	Ft	Fta	Ft%	Orb	Reb	Ast	Stl	To	Blk	Pts	Ppg
82	396	893	.443	261	309	.845	48	306	709	124	253	11	1162	14.2

Three-point goals: 109–292 (.373)   **TSP:** .504

SCORING

To shoot or not to shoot? That is the question Sleepy Floyd wrestles with every night. The problem is that Floyd is a 1 with a 2's mentality. He can dazzle with his scoring—who can forget his 51-point explosion as a Warrior against the Lakers in the 1986 playoffs—but he's a point guard whose role is to distribute. During the 1987–88 season, according to the loud voice of teammate Akeem Olajuwon, Floyd had "resolved" his inner struggle by shooting too much. ("He's a shooter, not a playmaker," the Dream said.) So when Don Chaney took over the Houston coaching reins last year, he made it clear to the seven-year veteran that if he wanted to stick around, he'd have to reverse the roles. So early in the season, in the half-court setting, Floyd's points came on open jumpers when Otis Thorpe or Olajuwon were double-teamed. He maintained freedom, however, to create on the break, where he's a superb driver and finisher. But as the season progressed, he had the hot hand from the outside, particularly from beyond the three-point line (he made threes in 23 consecutive games and shot an excellent .373 from trifecta-land, 16th in the league), so he started to look for his shot more. Overall, he finished with only .443 from the field, but until a late-season slump he was shooting in the high 40s (.476 after 57 games) and scored 14.2 per game. He's a terrific foul shooter, .845 last year and .830 lifetime.

DEFENSE/DEFENSIVE REBOUNDING

One-on-one, Floyd is a only a fair defender, but he does a fine job on the weak side. He understands defensive rotation and knows how to push his man toward help. In the defensive rebounding category, he was slightly above-average among his playmaking peers.

THE FLOOR GAME

John Stockton he isn't, nor will he ever be. As one observer noted, "Floyd isn't a situation creator." No, he's only an adequate ball handler (watching Floyd dribble makes one realize that palming is a rule in theory only), isn't particularly fast with the ball, and is vulnerable to pressure. But he sets up the plays and runs the options. In 1987–88, he had a poor 2.44 assist-to-turnover ratio, which he improved last year to an average 2.80. He also finished tied for sixth in the league in assists with 8.6 a game.

INTANGIBLES

For the most part, Floyd has stayed within the parameters established by Chaney at the onset of the season and has made the considerable adjustment that entailed. Although he has grown increasingly vocal on the court, he remains, at heart, a reluctant playmaker.

IN SUM

Floyd did an adequate job at the point, but in a league where a top-notch 1 is critical to playoff advancement, adequate isn't enough. A talented ballplayer, his skills would be better utilized primarily at the 2 spot.

RICK'S RATINGS

Scoring: **A**	Defense: **B**
Shooting: **A**	Defensive Rebounding: **B**
Free Throw Shooting: **AA**	Playmaking: **B**
Ball Handling: **B**	Intangibles: **B**
Passing: **A**	Overall: **B +**

Tellis Frank

Birthdate: April 26, 1965
Height: 6-9
Weight: 225
College: Western Kentucky University, Bowling Green, Ky.
Drafted: Golden State on first round, 1987 (14th pick).
Positions: Forward, Center
Final 1989 Team: Golden State Warriors
Final 1988–89 Statistics:

G	Fg	Fga	Fg%	Ft	Fta	Ft%	Orb	Reb	Ast	Stl	To	Blk	Pts	Ppg
32	34	91	.374	39	51	.765	26	61	15	14	29	6	107	3.3

Three-point goals: 0–1 (.000)   **TSP:** .374

SCORING

So far, not so good. In his two years, Frank, the Warriors first-round pick in 1987 (14th overall), has been a bust. A 6-9 3/4/5 combo, Frank has adapted poorly to the NBA. He hasn't discovered what a good shot is and he's been inconsistent, shooting just .374 last year, following .428 in his rookie year. Allegedly, he's a good shooter with decent range—he shot well at Western Kentucky, and his stroke is fine. In his favor are a quick first step—he handles fairly well for a guy his size—and he has the ability to finish in traffic. Last year, he was a nonentity (32 games for 245 minutes) and after injuring his shoulder in March, was effectively sent home and finished the year on the injured list.

DEFENSE/DEFENSIVE REBOUNDING

Two reasons Frank appeared so far down the Warriors depth chart were his deficiencies on D and the boards. He's a well-schooled defender, but when he got a chance to play, he didn't do the little things like blocking out. A below-average defensive rebounder for a backup 4. As one observer said: "He doesn't think rebounding."

THE FLOOR GAME

Despite an abominable 0.52 assist-to-turnover ratio (remember his extremely limited minutes), Frank can pass and has a good feel for the game.

INTANGIBLES

Lots of negatives here. Work ethic is questionable. Intensity level is not what it should be. Had trouble picking up Don Nelson's system.

IN SUM

Frank has NBA-level talent, particularly as a scorer. And with a little effort, he could be an up-to-speed defender and rebounder. But he's basically wasted two years. Now's the time, Tellis.

RICK'S RATINGS

Scoring: **B**	Defense: **D**
Shooting: **C**	Defensive Rebounding: **C**
Free Throw Shooting: **B**	Shot Blocking: **C**
Ball Handling: **B**	Intangibles: **D**
Passing: **B**	Overall: **C –**

Anthony Frederick

Birthdate: December 7, 1964
Height: 6-7
Weight: 205
College: Pepperdine University, Malibu, Calif.
Drafted: Denver on sixth round, 1986 (133rd pick).
Position: Guard

Final 1989 Team: Indiana Pacers
Final 1988–89 Statistics:

G	Fg	Fga	Fg%	Ft	Fta	Ft%	Orb	Reb	Ast	Stl	To	Blk	Pts	Ppg
46	63	125	.504	24	34	.706	26	52	20	14	34	6	152	3.3

Three-point goals: 2–5 (.400)   TSP: .512

SCORING

Frederick, a small forward who barely played (313 minutes) last season, scored big in the CBA (21.7 in 1987–88) and has excellent athletic ability. He is lightning quick on the break, though he has trouble finishing. He can sky, and will get you an offensive rebound here and there. He can also beat his man off the dribble in the half-court offense. Though he hit two of five three-pointers last year, he's not a player who will hurt you with his perimeter game.

DEFENSE/DEFENSIVE REBOUNDING

In college Frederick was defensive-minded, but in the NBA his D has been suspect. His footwork and body positioning need work. Also, as a collegian, he had some shot-blocking ability, which he has yet to display in the pros. A below-average defensive rebounder for his position.

THE FLOOR GAME

Frederick's ball handling, baseline to baseline, needs work. He's not a guy you want to handle the ball against traps. Among backup 3s, he had the second-worst turnover rate per minute.

INTANGIBLES

With his marginal stature in the league, Frederick should be working exceptionally hard, but he hasn't.

IN SUM

Frederick seemingly has the tools but hasn't been able to harness them. He'll have to work harder.

RICK'S RATINGS

Scoring: **B**   Defense: **C**
Shooting: **C**   Defensive Rebounding: **D**
Free Throw Shooting: **C**   Intangibles: **C**
Ball Handling: **D**   Overall: **D**
Passing: **C**

Corey Gaines

Birthdate: June 1, 1965
Height: 6-3
Weight: 195
College: Loyola Marymount University, Los Angeles, Calif.
Drafted: Seattle on third round, 1988 (65th pick).
Position: Guard

Final 1989 Team: New Jersey Nets
Final 1988–89 Statistics:

G	Fg	Fga	Fg%	Ft	Fta	Ft%	Orb	Reb	Ast	Stl	To	Blk	Pts	Ppg
32	27	64	.422	12	16	.750	3	19	67	15	20	1	67	2.1

Three-point goals: 1–5 (.200)   TSP: .430

SCORING

It's not as if Gaines, who came to the Nets from the CBA in February 1989 can't shoot—he averaged 17.4 a game as a Loyola Marymount senior, including 50 percent from three-point land. But as he attempted to adapt to his NBA role, specifically, point guard, Gaines focused on playmaking to the exclusion of his offense and launched a measly two shots a game. (He went 27 of 64 for .422 in 32 games.) So it's hard to get a read on whether he can be an NBA-level shooter. He showed, at least in practice, that he can put the ball on the floor, but it's likely he doesn't have the quickness to create the shot off the dribble.

DEFENSE/DEFENSIVE REBOUNDING

Gaines is a solid athlete—strong, with good lateral quickness—so the tools are there for him to become a competent defender. And in his limited time (10.5 mpg), he did a decent job for the Nets.

THE FLOOR GAME

Gaines is not a natural 1, and the big question about him is whether he has the ball handling skills essential to make it in the league as a point. Can he, in other words, readily get to spots on the floor when harassed by quicker points? His 3.35 assist-to-turnover ratio was one encouraging sign.

INTANGIBLES

Coachable, a hard worker, just happy to be in the league, Gaines has an excellent attitude.

IN SUM

Gaines is on the bubble: He doesn't have the firepower to be a 2 and may not have the handling skills to make it as a 1.

RICK'S RATINGS

Scoring: **D**   Defense: **C**
Shooting: **D**   Defensive Rebounding: **D**
Free Throw Shooting: **B**   Playmaking: **D**
Ball Handling: **C**   Intangibles: **B**
Passing: **C**   Overall: **D**

Kevin Gamble

Birthdate: November 13, 1965
Height: 6-5
Weight: 215
College: University of Iowa, Iowa City, Ia.
Drafted: Portland on third round, 1987 (63rd pick).

Positions: Guard, Forward
Final 1989 Team: Boston Celtics
Final 1988–89 Statistics:

G	Fg	Fga	Fg%	Ft	Fta	Ft%	Orb	Reb	Ast	Stl	To	Blk	Pts	Ppg
44	75	136	.551	35	55	.636	11	42	34	14	19	3	187	4.3

Three-point goals: 2–11 (.182)   TSP: .559

SCORING

Call it "A Tale of Two Kevin Gambles." In installment No. 1 our main character, up from the CBA in December 1988, experiences the NBA almost exclusively in a sitting position. Since being brought up, he has been DNP–CD 17 times by Celtic coach Jimmy Rodgers, and when he manages to log some time, it's strictly garbage. Gamble's putting up the usual scrub numbers: .367 from the field, 1.4 a game in 38 games. You know, just another CBA player up for, in his case, a rather extended cup of coffee. But on the night of April 14, our man replaces the injured Dennis Johnson in the starting lineup. Dramatically, without warning, Gamble, a powerfully built 6-5 2/3 (who was used mostly at the 2), transforms himself into a 20-a-night (22.8 to be exact) scorer. He starts with 20 against Cleveland, follows with 25 against Charlotte, then 18 versus the Bullets, 16 against the Knicks, 27 versus the Pacers, and the coup de grace, 31 points against the Hornets in the season finale. The Celtics take notice and rip up one protected list (the one that included Kelvin Upshaw) and draw up another (the one with Kevin Gamble on it). Actually, Gamble's efforts were not produced by some deus ex machina; he did score big in the CBA and he has tools: he's a superb driver (explosive first step) who likes to challenge the defense and can make the tough shot in traffic; he runs the floor well, hits the offensive glass and showed a consistency from the outside (at least in those six games) that many thought was lacking.

DEFENSE/DEFENSIVE REBOUNDING

While he made the effort, Gamble's D has a ways to go before it catches up with his offense. He often got lost on screens. In essence, he has a lot to learn. He jumps well and has the potential to be a decent defensive rebounder.

THE FLOOR GAME

Gamble's ball handling in half court was sound. He showed an ability to manufacture his own shot off the dribble and reliably fed the post. But in transition situations, he's not real smooth.

INTANGIBLES

Even when he wasn't playing, Gamble was a good practice player—"a pleasure to work with," said one coach. "Intense competitor, hungry athlete," said another.

IN SUM

Has any NBA player come so far so quickly? But hold on—where is Gamble going to get minutes this year? We have a healthy Larry Bird, backed up by No. 1 pick, Michael Smith, at small forward. We have Reggie Lewis moving to the 2 with Dennis Johnson in reserve. (This, of course, is one of several possibilities for the rotation.) Does Gamble take time from DJ? Stay tuned.

RICK'S RATINGS

Scoring: **A**	Defense: **B**
Shooting: **B**	Defensive Rebounding: **B**
Free Throw Shooting: **D**	Intangibles: **B**
Ball Handling: **B**	Overall: **B**
Passing: **B**	

Winston Garland

Birthdate: December 19, 1964
Height: 6-2
Weight: 170
College: Southwest Missouri State University, Springfield, Mo.
Drafted: Milwaukee on second round, 1987 (40th pick).
Position: Guard
Final 1989 Team: Golden State Warriors
Final 1988–89 Statistics:

G	Fg	Fga	Fg%	Ft	Fta	Ft%	Orb	Reb	Ast	Stl	To	Blk	Pts	Ppg
79	466	1074	.434	203	251	.809	101	328	505	175	187	14	1145	14.5

Three-point goals: 10–43 (.233)   TSP: .439

SCORING

Befitting a converted 2—he averaged almost 19 a game as a college player—the strength of Garland's game is his scoring ability. As one source put it, "He has a 1's body (6-2, 170) and a 2's mentality." As the Warriors' starting point guard, entering his third season, Garland is a solid jump shooter off the dribble (going either right or left) and has good range, though he didn't shoot well from beyond the arc last year (.233; compared to .333 in his rookie year). He's particularly tough taking it into the paint and shooting the jumper from 8-to-10-foot range. From that distance, it's usually a contested shot, which in part explains his less-than-impressive shooting percentage (.434)—he's taking difficult shots. But despite that, he's one of the Warriors go-to guys and savors—and consistently makes—the clutch shot. His offensive growth will come in learning to take the ball

all the way to the hoop for layups, to draw fouls, or to dish the ball to the big guys. A decent foul shooter at .809.

DEFENSE/DEFENSIVE REBOUNDING

Garland's a feisty defender who isn't afraid to get his pants dirty. His harassing tactics often result in deflected passes and steals (2.2 a game, 10th in the league). He also understands help defense and takes his defensive commitment seriously. Not the fastest guy in the world, he can be hurt by such quicker points as Kevin Johnson. While his defensive rebounding numbers were average, he's capable of grabbing the tough carom in traffic.

THE FLOOR GAME

To some extent, Garland is really a point guard in name only. In the Warriors' passing offense, which utilizes the point forward concept (where the entry pass is by a forward, generally Chris Mullin), the ball handling chores are shared. For his part, Garland has improved his court awareness, but he doesn't have blow-by-you ability. He's not turnover-prone, but he's not a particularly clever passer.

INTANGIBLES

If Garland is not the leader on the court, he clearly has gained the respect of his teammates. As noted, he thrives in the fourth quarter. And you have to admire the stick-to-it-iveness of a player who has been cut twice by NBA teams (once by Milwaukee, who drafted him, and once by the Warriors, in 1987) and then comes back to earn a starting job.

IN SUM

Garland scores, defends, and is tough, but he's only an adequate playmaker. While he was a starter on a good team last year, that might not be his role—though he'd certainly be a contributor—on a serious contender. He has a solid career ahead of him.

RICK'S RATINGS

Scoring: **A**   Defense: **A**
Shooting: **B**   Defensive Rebounding: **B**
Free Throw Shooting: **A**   Playmaking: **B**
Ball Handling: **B**   Intangibles: **A**
Passing: **B**   Overall: **B +**

Tom Garrick

Birthdate: July 7, 1966
Height: 6-2
Weight: 185
College: University of Rhode Island, Kingston, R.I.
Drafted: Los Angeles Clippers on second round, 1988 (45th pick).
Position: Guard
Final 1989 Team: Los Angeles Clippers
Final 1988–89 Statistics:

G	Fg	Fga	Fg%	Ft	Fta	Ft%	Orb	Reb	Ast	Stl	To	Blk	Pts	Ppg
71	176	359	.490	102	127	.803	37	156	243	78	116	9	454	6.4

Three-point goals: 0–13 (.000)   TSP: .490

SCORING

It's always a bonus when your second-round pick—and a low one at that (45th overall)—can make a contribution and even join the rotation. Garrick, a combo 1/2—"a bastard 1," as one wag put it—is a muscular 6-2, 185 (he was recruited by Penn State out of high school to play football), started 20 games but was used mostly as a backup to Gary Grant at the point and Quintin Dailey at the shooting guard. He'll shoot the 18-footer (he likes the corners) and is explosive with the ball going to the hoop. But his .490 from the field is a little deceiving; many of his points came on layups and Clippers insiders felt his shooting was somewhat inconsistent. One problem: he had trouble getting his shot because he doesn't have a quick release. A good foul shooter at .803.

DEFENSE/DEFENSIVE REBOUNDING

Garrick is your basic blue-collar defender. He'll apply pressure full court, has terrific hands (1.1 steals in 21.1 minutes), and is willing to mix it up on the defensive boards (above average for a backup 1). He's quick enough to handle the points but sufficiently physical, if a little small, to body the 2s. He thinks defense and takes pride in it.

THE FLOOR GAME

Garrick, who played primarily at 2 at Rhode Island, is a "push" guy—speedy, he can blow by people in transition. In half court, he's a distributor but not a creator or threader of needles. His vision, as good 1s go, is limited.

INTANGIBLES

Tom Penders, Garrick's college coach, called him, "a coach's player." "A special person" said one source; "unquestionably has an extraordinary work ethic," said another.

IN SUM

Garrick, as one coach described it, is the Clippers' Michael Cooper (without the range), giving versatility off the bench. A solid player, he'll never make an all-star team, never be a regular starter, but he can definitely help an NBA team.

RICK'S RATINGS

Scoring: **C**   Defense: **A**
Shooting: **B**   Defensive Rebounding: **A**
Free Throw Shooting: **A**   Playmaking: **B**
Ball Handling: **B**   Intangibles: **A**
Passing: **B**   Overall: **B**

Ben Gillery

Birthdate: September 19, 1965
Height: 7-0
Weight: 235
College: Georgetown University, Washington, D.C.
Drafted: Free Agent
Position: Center
Final 1989 Team: Sacramento Kings
Final 1988–89 Statistics:

G	Fg	Fga	Fg%	Ft	Fta	Ft%	Orb	Reb	Ast	Stl	To	Blk	Pts	Ppg
24	6	19	.316	13	23	.565	7	23	2	2	5	4	25	1.0

Three-point goals: 0–0 (.000)   **TSP:** .316

SCORING

Gillery has the dubious distinction of having the second-lowest scoring average as a college senior (2.1 ppg at Georgetown; Mark Eaton's 1.3 at UCLA was the worst) among current NBA players. His offensive skills are negligible, though he's working on a half hook. He has no jump shot.

DEFENSE/DEFENSIVE REBOUNDING

At 7-1, Gillery is a quick jumper and *potentially* could block some shots. He has the physique to be able to put his body on people.

THE FLOOR GAME

Gillery runs the floor very well for a big man. He is in general an outstanding athlete (good hands, good jumper) though his ball handling skills are poor.

INTANGIBLES

The biggest strike against Gillery is his inexperience. He hardly played at Georgetown (less than 10 minutes a game

---

for his career), so it's hard to see him competing in the NBA. He's not lazy, but on the other hand, he's not exactly been what you call a workhorse in developing his game.

IN SUM

Gillery's major pluses are his height and his athletic ability. Some attribute his presence in the NBA to the Bill Russell (the Kings' general manager)-John Thompson (coach of Georgetown) connection. But connections aside, with his limited skills and minimal experience, he has a slim chance of sticking as a backup center.

RICK'S RATINGS

Scoring: **D**   Defense: **C**
Shooting: **D**   Defensive Rebounding: **B**
Free Throw Shooting: **D**   Shot Blocking: **B**
Ball Handling: **D**   Intangibles: **C**
Passing: **D**   Overall: **D**

Armon Gilliam

Birthdate: May 28, 1964
Height: 6-9
Weight: 230
College: University of Nevada at Las Vegas, Las Vegas, Nev.
Drafted: Phoenix on first round, 1987 (2nd pick).
Position: Forward
Final 1989 Team: Phoenix Suns
Final 1988–89 Statistics:

G	Fg	Fga	Fg%	Ft	Fta	Ft%	Orb	Reb	Ast	Stl	To	Blk	Pts	Ppg
74	468	930	.503	240	323	.743	165	541	52	54	140	27	1176	15.9

Three-point goals: 0–0 (.000)   **TSP:** .503

SCORING

Gilliam, the second player picked in the 1987 draft, combines the unusual: brute power—he's 6-9, 230 and very, very strong—with a soft touch. He's effective from both blocks with turn-arounds, power moves off the dribble, and jump hooks with either hand. He's confusing to guard because he doesn't seem to favor one hand or the other. A decent face-up shooter from about 15 feet, he's often the trailer on the break. With that body and strength, he should be more of an offensive rebounding force (2.2 a game, which puts him in the bottom third, per

---

minute, among starting power forwards), but his tendency is to run back on D instead of fighting for position on the offensive glass. Though he can run the floor, he doesn't do so with any consistency. Still, despite these limitations, Gilliam was, per minute, the sixth-most productive scorer among starting power forwards last season, averaging 15.9 ppg, and shooting .503 from the field. But then again, he lost his starting job to Tyrone Corbin three-quarters of the way through the season and was a "forgotten man" as the Suns advanced to the Western Conference finals (he barely saw the light of day against the Nuggets and the Warriors though he did play some—14.5 mpg a game—against the Lakers). His foul shooting showed considerable improvement from .675 in his rookie year to .743 last year.

DEFENSE/DEFENSIVE REBOUNDING

Again, Gilliam has the physical ability to play bang 'em defense, but he needs to compete more consistently on D. He will, for example, let his man flash into good post position. Plus he doesn't change ends well, despite the fact he doesn't do a lot of offensive rebounding. And he is nonexistent as a shot blocker. Then, too, he's a barely above-average defensive rebounder. As his coach, Cotton Fitzsimmons, once put it, "He's satisfied getting one rebound."

THE FLOOR GAME

Gilliam had the worst assist-to-turnover ratio among starting 4s, which reflects that (a) he's a scorer; when he gets it, he goes to the hole, (b) he's not a good passer, and (c) when he puts the ball on the floor, opponents often steal it.

INTANGIBLES

How does a player averaging 17.8 points a game (Gilliam's ppg when Corbin took over for him) lose his job? True, Corbin added an element—quickness—that Gilliam couldn't provide. But the fact is, Gilliam's lackadaisical attitude toward rebounding and defense didn't help his case at all. Gilliam was involved in arguably the year's ugliest incident when he slugged Miami's Pearl Washington in the locker room *after* an on-court confrontation.

IN SUM

We know he can score. But there is major room for improvement in Gilliam's defense, passing, and rebounding. And his intensity level will have to pick up if he wants to become the player he could be—if not an All-Star, then close to it. He's been the subject of numerous trade rumors.

RICK'S RATINGS

Scoring: **AA**	Defense: **C**
Shooting: **A**	Defensive Rebounding: **B**
Free Throw Shooting: **C**	Shot Blocking: **D**
Ball Handling: **D**	Intangibles: **C**
Passing: **D**	Overall: **B +**

Mike Gminski

Birthdate: August 3, 1959
Height: 6-10
Weight: 280
College: Duke University, Durham, N.C.
Drafted: New Jersey on first round, 1980 (7th pick).
Position: Center
Final 1989 Team: Philadelphia 76ers
Final 1988–89 Statistics:

G	Fg	Fga	Fg%	Ft	Fta	Ft%	Orb	Reb	Ast	Stl	To	Blk	Pts	Ppg
82	556	1166	.477	297	341	.871	213	769	138	46	129	106	1409	17.2

Three-point goals: 0–6 (.000) **TSP:** .477

SCORING

In this world of uncertainty, it's nice to know you can count on a few things: One is that Mike Gminski, the "G-Man," will score 16 to 17 points a game. He's done so (16.5, 16.4, 16.9, 17.2) the last four years, which must be some kind of NBA record for scoring consistency. The other is that the G-Man will not miss a free throw—well, hardly ever: He shot .871 in 1988–89, tied for eighth in the league, following a .906 performance in 1987–88. (Philly fans, however, will not soon forget Gminski's strange 11-16, .688 free throw shooting during last year's playoffs against the Knicks). He is a versatile offensive performer. He can take his man outside and shoot the 19-footer (on the catch), but he also has an inside game, which consists primarily of hooks with both hands. For a player who can barely jump up to the curb, Gminski garners his share of offensive rebounds (2.6 a game in 1988–89). He is the initiator rather than the finisher on Philly's fast break.

DEFENSE/DEFENSIVE REBOUNDING

Gminski's record makes the case that defensive rebounding is not a function of jumping ability or even size. He's an unathletic 6-10 who grabbed 9.4 rebounds a game, tied for eighth in the league (after averaging 10 a game in 1987–88)—6.8 of which were on the defensive board. The ingredients are timing, positioning, and a sure sense of where the ball is coming off the board. Defensively, he relies on positioning and knowledge of opponents to compensate for lack of strength, mobility, and jumping ability. With New Jersey (where he played for just over seven seasons), Gminski had trouble in defensive transition and would often get beat up court by opposing centers. A lot of that had to do with the fact that he was overweight. But in the summer of 1988, he lost 20 pounds and is now better able to change ends. He's not what you call an intimidating presence in the middle—a fact the Knicks exploited effectively in the playoffs—but he'll occasionally block a shot (on the weak side, not on his own man; 1.3 a game).

THE FLOOR GAME

Gminski triggers the 76ers' fast break with his defensive rebounding and outlet passing. He'll take a rebound and without bringing the ball below his shoulders, flick it out to the point guards. With the Nets, he didn't handle the ball well, but last year he had only 2.3 turnovers per game, which, per minute, was the second best among starting centers. He's well-schooled in all phases of the game—a Duke product all the way.

INTANGIBLES

The word "professional" always seems to come up in discussions about Gminski. "Bright guy, positive attitude," said one coach. And he plays hurt.

IN SUM

Gminski will get you 17 points and nine rebounds every night. He's not an "elite" center (like Akeem Olajuwon, Patrick Ewing, Robert Parish, Brad Daugherty), but he's clearly one of the "best of the rest." Could the 76ers win a championship with Gminski? The answer is a qualified *yes*. He needs a strong supporting cast and a physical shot blocking backup. Unfortunately, the 76ers have some but not all of the former, and none of the latter.

RICK'S RATINGS

Scoring: **AA**
Shooting: **A**
Free Throw Shooting: **AA**
Ball Handling: **A**
Passing: **A**
Defense: **B**

Defensive Rebounding: **AA**
Shot Blocking: **C**
Intangibles: **A**
Overall: **AA**

Ron Grandison

Birthdate: July 9, 1964
Height: 6-8
Weight: 217
College: New Orleans University, New Orleans, La.
Drafted: Denver on fifth round, 1987 (100th pick).
Position: Forward
Final 1989 Team: Boston Celtics
Final 1988–89 Statistics:

G	Fg	Fga	Fg%	Ft	Fta	Ft%	Orb	Reb	Ast	Stl	To	Blk	Pts	Ppg
72	59	142	.415	59	80	.738	47	92	42	18	36	3	177	2.5

Three-point goals: 0–10 (.000)   **TSP:** .415

SCORING

Grandison, a 6-8 small forward who can also play the 4 spot, isn't looked to—and doesn't look to—score (2.5 ppg in 7.3

minutes with the Celtics last year). He's a garbage player, his points coming on hustle on the offensive boards and running the floor, which he does well. He will occasionally put it on the floor, but his outside shot is the weakest element of his game.

DEFENSE/DEFENSIVE REBOUNDING

Grandison won a job through his aggressiveness and all-out play on defense and the boards. He has the quickness to guard players on the perimeter and can play physical in the post. But his per minute defensive rebounding numbers were, in a word, lousy.

THE FLOOR GAME

Grandison does a better than adequate job handling the ball in both half court and in transition. You can count on him not to make a lot of mistakes with the ball.

INTANGIBLES

Grandison made the Celtics because he exemplifies everything a coach wants in a non-rotation player: he's a hard worker, practices hard, and doesn't make waves.

IN SUM

Grandison, who became an unrestricted free agent (he was in an Orlando Magic tryout camp and played on the Atlanta Hawks team in the Southern California Pro Summer League this past summer), is a marginal talent who can play defense and rebound a little. His intensity level is a big plus, and if he can enlarge his offensive repertoire, he might last long enough to collect a few more NBA paychecks.

RICK'S RATINGS

Scoring: **C**
Shooting: **D**
Free Throw Shooting: **C**
Ball Handling: **A**
Passing: **A**

Defense: **B**
Defensive Rebounding: **D**
Shot Blocking: **D**
Intangibles: **B**
Overall: **C –**

Gary Grant

Birthdate: April 21, 1965
Height: 6-3

Weight: 195
College: University of Michigan, Ann Arbor, Mich.
Drafted: Seattle on first round, 1988 (15th pick).
Position: Guard
Final 1989 Team: Los Angeles Clippers
Final 1988–89 Statistics:

G	Fg	Fga	Fg%	Ft	Fta	Ft%	Orb	Reb	Ast	Stl	To	Blk	Pts	Ppg
71	361	830	.435	119	162	.735	80	238	506	144	258	9	846	11.9

Three-point goals: 5–22 (.227)   TSP: .438

SCORING

NBA championship blueprints these days necessarily include a point guard who can score. And the Clippers—with Grant at the helm—have mapped out their future accordingly. The 15th player picked in the 1988 draft, Grant is a gifted 6-3, 195-pound athlete with multiple offensive skills (11.9 ppg in 27.1 minutes) who is quick, strong, and capable of accelerating with the ball. In his rookie year he was most effective taking the ball to the hoop in transition or in half court; early on, he had trouble finishing, but he was putting it down regularly as the year progressed. Grant, who for most of the year shared the starting playmaking duties with Norm Nixon (until Nixon retired from the NBA, which was the best thing to happen to both Grant and Nixon—Stormin' Norman had lost it), is also a jump shooter with excellent range (but just 5-for-22 from three-point-land) and is quite capable of creating it for himself off the dribble. But as with many rookie guards, Grant was erratic, canning them at only a .435 pace. That low percentage reflected, to some extent, poor shot selection. But when he was handed the starting job in March, he made better decisions with the ball. Then, too, he'll sneak in and grab an offensive rebound (1.1 a game, 5th among starting 1s). But in a reversal of what usually happens, his foul shooting (.735) was worse than it was in his college days (.790 for his career).

DEFENSE/DEFENSIVE REBOUNDING

Even if he couldn't score, Grant could land a job in the league with his D (as T.R. Dunn and Elston Turner have done). His quick and active hands are larcenous; per minute, he was second in the league (to John Stockton) in steals and averaged two steals a game, 15th in the league. His strength, size, and willingness to compete are his biggest assets. An average defensive rebounder for his position.

THE FLOOR GAME

In the early part of the season, Grant had too much "stuff," too much playground in his game—he wanted to make the "big" play at the expense of the safe one. Result: too many turnovers. For the season, Grant led all 1s (by far!) in turnovers per minute. But by year's end, he had toned it down considerably and also was thinking more like a true point. The Clippers are a better team when Grant focuses on pushing, distributing, and penetrating and kicking rather than looking for the shot first; his points should come in the flow of the offense.

INTANGIBLES

He plays hard and he plays hurt. One rap against Grant in college, however, was that he disappeared in big games—but it was au contraire last year in the NBA. A leader by example.

IN SUM

He can score, he can defend, he can make the play. Most encouraging was his dramatic improvement as the year progressed. And he should only get better. The Clippers' fortunes will be closely connected with his progress.

RICK'S RATINGS

Scoring: **B**	Defense: **AA**
Shooting: **C**	Defensive Rebounding: **B**
Free Throw Shooting: **C**	Playmaking: **B**
Ball Handling: **B**	Intangibles: **A**
Passing: **B**	Overall: **B**

Harvey Grant

Birthdate: July 4, 1965
Height: 6-9
Weight: 205
College: University of Oklahoma, Norman, Okla.
Drafted: Washington on first round, 1988 (12th pick).
Position: Forward
Final 1989 Team: Washington Bullets
Final 1988–89 Statistics:

G	Fg	Fga	Fg%	Ft	Fta	Ft%	Orb	Reb	Ast	Stl	To	Blk	Pts	Ppg
71	181	390	.464	34	57	.596	75	163	79	35	28	29	396	5.6

Three-point goals: 0–1 (.000)   TSP: .464

SCORING

Grant looks like Bob McAdoo, he's the same size (6-9), though much skinnier (205) than the 'Doo and, yes, has the same feathery touch from 18 feet and in as the three-time scoring champion who now slings his shots in the Italian League. And Grant, the Bullets' first-round pick in 1988 (12th overall), got off to a McAdoo-like start in 1988–89, shooting an incredible .577 after 11 games. Then he suffered an avulsion fracture in his right foot, missed eight games, and while it took him a while to settle back into the same shooting groove, he ended the season with a respectable (for a rookie) .466. In college he was an inside player, but with his rail-thin frame and lacking strength, Grant, unlike his twin brother Horace (Bulls), couldn't play anything but a 3 in the NBA. While he can shoot from outside, he needs major work on creating his own shot off the dribble, as well as putting the ball on the floor—standard repertoire for small forwards. Grant can jump, but he didn't do much on the offensive board.

DEFENSE/DEFENSIVE REBOUNDING

Grant is quick, has long arms, moves his feet—all requisites of a good defender. But he was ineffective on the defensive glass because he's easily pushed out of position. He knows it, and he hit the weight room hard this past summer, to add 20 to 25 pounds of brawn.

THE FLOOR GAME

Grant can run all day. In college he could play full-out for 40 minutes. His ball handling skills, as noted, need work, though he is not a mistake player. Excluding Tom Tolbert (who only played 117 minutes), Grant's 2.82 assist-to-turnover ratio was tops in the league among backup 3s.

INTANGIBLES

Grant is a terrific competitor who is not afraid to take the big shot. He has good work habits and has shown he wants to be a Player.

IN SUM

Anybody who can shoot the rock like Grant has a bright future in the league. Once he beefs up, and gains experience, he could be a key part of Washington's rebuilding program. (Bullets finished strong at 40–42 last season.)

RICK'S RATINGS

Scoring: **C**   Defense: **B**
Shooting: **B**   Defensive Rebounding: **D**
Free Throw Shooting: **D**   Intangibles: **B**
Ball Handling: **A**   Overall: **B –**
Passing: **B**

Horace Grant

Birthdate: July 4, 1965
Height: 6-9

Weight: 220
College: Clemson University, Clemson, S.C.
Drafted: Chicago on first round, 1987 (10th pick).
Position: Forward
Final 1989 Team: Chicago Bulls
Final 1988–89 Statistics:

G	Fg	Fga	Fg%	Ft	Fta	Ft%	Orb	Reb	Ast	Stl	To	Blk	Pts	Ppg
79	405	781	.519	140	199	.704	240	681	168	86	128	62	950	12.0

Three-point goals: 0–5 (.000)   **TSP:** .519

SCORING

Grant's repertoire consists of a little bit of this and a little bit of that. He'll shoot the turnaround jumper, jump hook shots from either box, fill the lane on the break, and crash the offensive board (three a game last year). This multidimensional quality was one of the reasons why the Bulls felt Grant could fill the shoes of Charles Oakley, who doesn't have the same offensive diversity. Grant, a two-year veteran, is a superb athlete: He's a slashing kind of player who knifes his way in for offensive rebounds, jumps out of the building (and gets up quickly), and can run all day. At this stage, he has trouble creating his own shot off the dribble—fake, two dribbles, and shoot would be a nice addition. Plus, he's not much of a post-up player because at 6-9, 220, he can be pushed out of the blocks by larger 4s. Which is why Chicago doesn't go to him often (or as frequently as Grant thinks they should; he has complained a few times about not getting enough shots). As it was, last season he averaged about 10 shots a game, 12 ppg, and shot .519. He's still a pretty bad foul shooter (.704, which was an improvement from .626 in his rookie year).

DEFENSE/DEFENSIVE REBOUNDING

Trading Oakley meant finding a player to replace 13 rebounds a game. Grant, who is quick to the board, competitive, and, as noted, can jump, took up some of the slack, averaging 8.6 total rebounds, though he was slightly below average for starting 4s. But he picked it up during the playoffs, averaging a hefty 9.8 a game. As a defender, his strengths are quickness and activity, which makes it tough to post him, since he can go around his man for a steal. On the other hand, he's giving away 20 to 30 pounds a night, and can be knocked back in the post. Grant's lack of lateral quickness is a liability when he guards players on the perimeter.

THE FLOOR GAME

Grant is a surprisingly good passer (2.1 assists per game), which is always a plus for a 4, and Chicago is not hesitant to run plays through him. He understands the game, moves well without the ball, and doesn't turn the ball over. His 1.31 assist-to-turnover ratio was second best among starting 4s.

INTANGIBLES

A great competitor, Grant works hard and gets along with his teammates. He's his own worst critic, constantly analyzing his performance and willing to pay the price to improve. Still, he doesn't always show up and isn't yet an every-night performer. Chicago definitely missed Oakley's enforcer qualities; alas, Grant doesn't have an ounce of bad boy in him. And, as noted, he was an unhappy camper because he felt he wasn't getting the ball enough.

IN SUM

Grant is more of a 3.5 than a true 4 and lacks the machismo and bulk that characterize most power forwards. Which is why one school of thought feels his varied talents may be better displayed as a combo 3/4 off the bench, playing substantial minutes. On the other hand, if he can maintain his playoff pace, he may in fact be the Bulls answer at the 4 spot.

RICK'S RATINGS

Scoring: **C**	Defense: **B**
Shooting: **B**	Defensive Rebounding: **B**
Free Throw Shooting: **C**	Shot Blocking: **B**
Ball Handling: **B**	Intangibles: **B**
Passing: **A**	Overall: **B +**

Stuart Gray

Birthdate: May 27, 1963
Height: 7-0
Weight: 245
College: University of California at Los Angeles, Los Angeles, Calif.
Drafted: Indiana on second round as an undergraduate, 1984 (29th pick).
Position: Center
Final 1989 Team: Indiana Pacers
Final 1988–89 Statistics:

G	Fg	Fga	Fg%	Ft	Fta	Ft%	Orb	Reb	Ast	Stl	To	Blk	Pts	Ppg
72	72	153	.471	44	64	.688	84	245	29	11	48	21	188	2.6

Three-point goals: 0–1 (.000)   TSP: .471

SCORING

Gray, who was traded to the Hornets in June for the draft rights to Dyron Nix, is rather inconspicuous on the offensive end of things. Consider: Chuck Nevitt, Earl Cureton, and Keith Lee are more productive scorers on a per minute basis for their careers. Over Gray's five-year career his highest average has been 3 ppg and he has never averaged more than 2.6 shots a game. All of this verifies that Gray has limited, if any, offensive moves. Passing the ball to him can be an adventure—he has trouble catching it. Most of his points come on putbacks—on a per minute basis, he's an above-average offensive rebounder. He also runs the floor well, but finishing is problematic.

DEFENSE/DEFENSIVE REBOUNDING

What Gray does best is rebound on the defensive glass. He was in the top 10 percent among backup 5s on a per minute

basis last year. Defensively, he's not afraid to put his body on people but don't count on him for shot blocking.

THE FLOOR GAME

As noted, his ball handling, particularly his ability to catch the ball, is shaky.

INTANGIBLES

Gray has worked hard to make himself an NBA ballplayer. But he seems to have an overinflated opinion of himself and feels—not an uncommon view among NBA players—that he should be getting more minutes. He tends to forget play sets.

IN SUM

Gray takes up space on defense and does a nice job on the defensive board. That's about it. On the Hornets, a team with arguably the least talented centers in the league last season, Gray figures to do more playing and less complaining.

RICK'S RATINGS

Scoring: **D**	Defensive Rebounding:
Shooting: **D**	**AAA**
Free Throw Shooting: **D**	Shot Blocking: **C**
Ball Handling: **D**	Intangibles: **C**
Passing: **D**	Overall: **D**
Defense: **B**	

Sylvester Gray

Birthdate: July 8, 1967
Height: 6-6
Weight: 230
College: Memphis State University, Memphis, Tenn.
Drafted: Miami on second round as an undergraduate, 1988 (35th pick).
Position: Forward
Final 1989 Team: Miami Heat
Final 1988–89 Statistics:

G	Fg	Fga	Fg%	Ft	Fta	Ft%	Orb	Reb	Ast	Stl	To	Blk	Pts	Ppg
55	167	398	.420	105	156	.673	117	286	117	36	102	25	440	8.0

Three-point goals: 1–4 (.250)   TSP: .421

SCORING

Most NBA players take a year or two (and big guys often longer) to find themselves on the offensive end of the court. Gray, a 21-year-old rookie (now 22), had typical first-year difficulties (.420 from the field), but he had to overcome an additional handicap: He played only 39 games as a collegian, since he was disqualified from NCAA play when he talked to an agent five games into his sophomore year. In effect, he's still learning to play. He's a tremendous athlete, with a Charles Barkley-like body—6-6, 230—whose combination of speed, strength, and jumping ability are indeed comparable to the 76ers star. He's acrobatic, exciting, and will break a backboard or two before his career is over. Gray scores at the end of the break, on offensive rebounds (2.1 a game), and with an occasional jumper. But he lacks the consistent outside shooting and ball handling skills he'll need to be a big-league 3. He flashed signs of brilliance but couldn't sustain it. Improving his foul shooting (.673) is also a priority.

DEFENSE/DEFENSIVE REBOUNDING

Miami has no complaints about Gray's defense. He's physical enough to guard 4s (though he gives away a few inches) and is quick enough to play opponents on the perimeter. As a rebounder, he relies on his great jumping ability (5.2 a game in only 22.2 minutes) and will obviously improve when he learns such techniques as blocking out.

THE FLOOR GAME

Gray is Miami's best passer. He's unselfish, sees the floor, and is creative. He can run and finish and is fearless going to the hoop. But he'll have to be more careful with the ball; his turnovers were above-average.

INTANGIBLES

Until Miami coach Ronnie Rothstein got hold of him, Gray had never really been in shape. Rothstein rode him hard in training camp, and now Gray can run all day. He's the type of player who needs a good kick in the pants or his concentration wavers. He gets down on himself easily. If he doesn't start a game with a quick basket or rebound, he can take himself right out of the contest dwelling on his mistakes. His biggest drawback, of course, is inexperience, exacerbated last year by the fact that he missed 17 games with torn tendons in his right thumb. However, the injury was a blessing in disguise. During his rehabilitation, he lost 15 pounds, worked on his game, and came back a more confident player.

IN SUM

Because of his age and inexperience, Gray is a project. A raw talent, his progress will depend on his work ethic during the off season. He needs a more consistent outside game and improved going-to-the-basket moves.

RICK'S RATINGS

Scoring: **C**	Defense: **A**
Shooting: **D**	Defensive Rebounding:
Free Throw Shooting: **D**	**AA**
Ball Handling: **A**	Intangibles: **B**
Passing: **A**	Overall: **C**

Jeff Grayer

Birthdate: December 17, 1965
Height: 6-5
Weight: 220
College: Iowa State University, Ames, Iowa.
Drafted: Milwaukee on first round, 1988 (13th pick).
Positions: Guard, Forward
Final 1989 Team: Milwaukee Bucks
Final 1988–89 Statistics:

G	Fg	Fga	Fg%	Ft	Fta	Ft%	Orb	Reb	Ast	Stl	To	Blk	Pts	Ppg
11	32	73	.438	17	20	.850	14	35	22	10	19	1	81	7.4

Three-point goals: 0–2 (.000)   **TSP:** .438

SCORING

Milwaukee is looking to build a more athletic team, and Grayer, who was the Bucks first-round pick in 1988 (13th overall), is a case in point. At 6-5, 220, he's an extremely strong shooting guard/small forward who runs and jumps well. But he had a tough rookie year, contracting chicken pox at the beginning of the season and then hurting his knee; he played in only 11 games (200 minutes). But even in his limited time, he gave indications that he could be the Bucks' best draft pick since Sidney Moncrief (1979). He's probably best suited for the 2 spot where, with his size, he can post up smaller players. He also likes to get into the paint, lean on his man, and then shoot jumpers over him. Other Grayer assets include an ability to drive or take the pull-up jumper on the break. He doesn't yet have three-point range and must prove he can score from outside.

DEFENSE/DEFENSIVE REBOUNDING

Grayer has the potential to be a big-time defender. Selected for the All-Big Eight defensive team each of his four years (in his senior year, he showed his versatility by guarding Danny Manning, Harvey Grant, and Mitch Ritchmond). With his long arms, jumping ability, and timing, he can block shots and be a force on the defensive board (he was second in the Big Eight in rebounding in his senior year).

THE FLOOR GAME

One of Grayer's many strengths is his ability to see the floor. He could play point, since he feeds the post well and can bring the ball up against pressure. He also moves well without the ball.

INTANGIBLES

For a rookie, Grayer was extremely poised. He's quiet, unassuming, willing to learn, and has excellent work habits. The big question is the status of his knee. His name came up several times in trade talks, which put the league on notice that his knee might be a major impediment to his playing 100 percent.

IN SUM

Grayer can do many things well: score, pass, defend, and rebound. There's a big upside here, assuming, of course, the knee is healthy.

RICK'S RATINGS

Scoring: **B**	Defense: **B**
Shooting: **B**	Defensive Rebounding: **A**
Free Throw Shooting: **AA**	Intangibles: **B**
Ball Handling: **B**	Overall: **B**
Passing: **B**	

A.C. Green

Birthdate: October 4, 1963
Height: 6-9
Weight: 224
College: Oregon State University, Corvallis, Ore.
Drafted: Los Angeles Lakers on first round, 1985 (23rd pick).
Position: Forward
Final 1989 Team: Los Angeles Lakers
Final 1988–89 Statistics:

G	Fg	Fga	Fg%	Ft	Fta	Ft%	Orb	Reb	Ast	Stl	To	Blk	Pts	Ppg
82	401	758	.529	282	359	.786	258	739	103	94	119	55	1088	13.3

Three-point goals: 4–17 (.235)   **TSP:** .532

SCORING

Effort. Energy. Intensity. Nobody works harder than Green, the Lakers starting power forward, a fourth-year pro whose 13.3 ppg last year was his best yet and marked a continued upward progression from 6.4 in his rookie year. As usual,

Green did a stellar job on the offensive glass (3.1 a game). He's a good, though not great, leaper. What sets him apart is his relentlessness; the Lakers grade their players on rebounding *attempts* and A.C. goes after it most of the time. He occasionally has trouble converting, because he's only a fair two-legged jumper, but he's learned to grab the rebound on one side and, using the basket as an ally, shoot on the opposite side. Speedy, he's also a superb runner of the floor. His added productivity last year, however can be traced to the consistency in his outside game. Early in his career, he was a reluctant and erratic perimeter player, but he's gradually increased both his confidence and his range (20 feet). Of course, it helps that the Lakers had three prime-time post-up players (James Worthy, Kareem Abdul-Jabbar, and Magic Johnson), who were constantly double-teamed. Result: Green got wide-open shots—shots he might not get on a lesser team—but to his credit, he took full advantage and knocked them down regularly. Off the double-team, he also slices to the basket for layups—his hands are not the greatest but he's improved his ability to catch the ball and finish the play. He was, relative to his regular season performance, a no-show during last year's playoffs, shooting a dismal .412 and averaging 10.1 ppg in the four series (compared to .529 and 13.3 ppg in the regular season).

DEFENSE/DEFENSIVE REBOUNDING

His coach, Pat Riley, is the originator of the "No rebounding, no rings" maxim, and A.C. has taken this piece of wisdom to heart. Last season he had his best year ever on the boards, averaging 9.0 a game overall, 11th in the league (there were only 19 players who averaged nine or more rebounds a game) and per minute, his defensive rebounding numbers put him in the same ballpark as Rick Mahorn, Karl Malone, and Michael Cage. Again, the work ethic is the prime explanation because at 6-9, 224, (he may be more like 6-8), Green doesn't have exceptional size—in fact, defensively, he really doesn't match up well with players like Malone or Kevin McHale (which is why Mychal Thompson is so valuable). So, Green is not a shot blocker but a decent defender who is vulnerable to quicker players (say, Seattle's Derrick McKey) out on the floor.

THE FLOOR GAME

Laker insiders think Green is an excellent ball handler. Indeed, he often handles the ball against pressure and has the ability to clear the rebound with the dribble and then pass it to Magic. But he has yet to show much ability to create off the dribble.

INTANGIBLES

Green is a coach's dream. He does the dirty work—banging both boards, diving for loose balls, playing aggressive defense—that championships are made of. A deeply religious man, he plays with an equal amount of commitment. But there are still some questions hanging about his ability to play in crunch time as his playoff woes suggest.

IN SUM

Not an upper-echelon 4, in the realm of a Malone or a McHale or a Larry Nance, Green is now a card carrying member of the next bunch (including Otis Thorpe, Sam Perkins, Horace Grant). His name has been mentioned in trade talks periodically but where are you going to find a power forward who gets you nine rebounds a night, runs the floor like a 3, hits the open jumper, and comes to play every night?

RICK'S RATINGS

Scoring: **B**
Shooting: **A**
Free Throw Shooting: **B**
Ball Handling: **A**
Passing: **B**
Defense: **B**

Defensive Rebounding: **AA**
Shot Blocking: **C**
Intangibles: **AAA**
Overall: **A**

Sidney Green

Birthdate: January 4, 1961
Height: 6-9
Weight: 220
College: University of Nevada at Las Vegas, Las Vegas, Nev.
Drafted: Chicago on first round, 1983 (5th pick).
Position: Forward
Final 1989 Team: New York Knicks
Final 1988–89 Statistics:

G	Fg	Fga	Fg%	Ft	Fta	Ft%	Orb	Reb	Ast	Stl	To	Blk	Pts	Ppg
82	194	422	.460	129	170	.759	157	394	76	47	125	18	517	6.3

Three-point goals: 0–3 (.000) **TSP:** .460

SCORING

Green, a six-year veteran who last year played with the Knicks, has never been much of a scorer (he's averaged over 10 points a game just once; 8.1 ppg for his career); now that he's a member—and a likely starter—with the expansion Orlando Magic, it will be interesting to see whether his career pattern changes. He'll shoot the 15-foot jumper, but won't hit it with any consistency (.460 from the field in 1988–89; .433 playoffs; .456 lifetime). But last year, one significant advance in his game was the refinement of his low-post moves (a spin, a jump hook, an up-and-under). Still, Green's major offensive tool is

offensive rebounding, for which, per minute, he was 10th in the league (of players who played more than 500 minutes) and second among backup power forwards (an awesome 1.9 a game in only 15.6 minutes). One slight problem, however, he'll get the ball but he doesn't always complete the play. The same goes for when he fills the lane on the break. In years past, Green, who also logged substantial minutes as Patrick Ewing's backup, was arguably the worst finisher in the league, but he was better last year. His foul shooting, which had plummeted each year from 1984–85 (.806) to 1987–88 (.663), improved to .759 in 1988–89.

DEFENSE/DEFENSIVE REBOUNDING

Green is a big-time defensive rebounder (in the top 20 percent, per minute, among backup 4s)—the prime reason he was the first player picked overall in the expansion draft. He's strong, aggressive, and has a nose for the ball. Defensively, he's a solid low-post defender who knows how to put his body on people. He's equally adept guarding 4s and 5s, though at 6-9 he usually gives away several inches to the centers. Lacking lateral quickness, Green does have trouble guarding people on the perimeter.

THE FLOOR GAME

In the Knicks' offense, the power forward handled the ball at the high post; and there Green did a good job (above-average assists for his position). But he is turnover-plagued (1.5 a game). He runs the floor OK, but again, he doesn't always make the layup.

INTANGIBLES

Ill winds followed Green to New York, but he was a model citizen in the Big Apple, working hard on his game (low post in particular) and seemingly accepting his role as a support player.

IN SUM

On the Knicks, Green found his niche as a backup player who played hard on D, banged both boards, but didn't score with any consistency. In that capacity, he was a valuable member of the Knicks' potent second unit. With the Magic, however, he'll get substantial minutes; whether he can remain productive in that role remains to be seen.

RICK'S RATINGS

Scoring: **C**
Shooting: **C**
Free Throw Shooting: **B**
Ball Handling: **C**
Passing: **B**
Defense: **A**

Defensive Rebounding: **AAA**
Shot Blocking: **D**
Intangibles: **B**
Overall: **B**

David Greenwood

Birthdate: May 27, 1957
Height: 6-9
Weight: 225
College: University of California at Los Angeles, Los Angeles, Calif.
Drafted: Chicago on first round, 1979 (2nd pick).
Position: Forward
Final 1989 Team: Denver Nuggets
Final 1988–89 Statistics:

G	Fg	Fga	Fg%	Ft	Fta	Ft%	Orb	Reb	Ast	Stl	To	Blk	Pts	Ppg
67	167	395	.423	132	176	.750	140	402	96	47	91	52	466	7.0

Three-point goals: 0–0 (.000)   **TSP:** .423

SCORING

These days, any points you get from Greenwood, a 10-year veteran who in January 1989 was traded from the Spurs to the Nuggets (along with Darwin Cook for Jay Vincent and Calvin Natt), are a bonus. For his career, he's averaged 11.2 ppg and .477 from the field, but his numbers last year, 7.0 ppg and .423, were, respectively, his second-to-worst and career-worst. Of course, injuries (he ruptured his left Achilles tendon in March 1988) and age (32), have slowed him and he's rarely 100 percent physically. Greenwood is a power forward who likes to post up and then turn and face for the 12-to-15 foot jumper. He's still pretty quick and has a nice first step going to the hole. Career-wise, he's been an effective offensive rebounder and that continues to be the case: 2.1 a game in 20.9 minutes last year.

DEFENSE/DEFENSIVE REBOUNDING

Greenwood's current value now rests on his defense and rebounding. He's a student of the game and has a solid grasp of defensive concepts. He's quick enough to guard the 3s and strong enough to play the 4s and even smaller 5s. He's averaged about one block a game for his career but is essentially a position defender. He's always been an excellent defensive rebounder (averaging as many as 10 total rebounds a game—10.1 in 1983–84— and has been over nine a game four times), but his physical problems have cut into his per minute productivity.

THE FLOOR GAME

Greenwood's ability to run the floor has, again, been com-

promised by his injuries. He's an adequate passer who doesn't turn the ball over.

INTANGIBLES

Durability is the big issue here. How much more pounding can David Greenwood take? He's a team player and a pro who, even though he didn't play for a long stretch when he first joined the Nuggets, kept himself ready. And when he saw some quality time, he held his own.

IN SUM

Greenwood gives you versatility off the bench because he can guard players at three positions. He's in the twilight of his career but his defense and rebounding may keep him in the league a little longer. An unrestricted free agent, as of this writing he has not come to an agreement with any team.

RICK'S RATINGS

Scoring: **C**
Shooting: **C**
Free Throw Shooting: **B**
Ball Handling: **B**
Passing: **B**

Defense: **A**
Defensive Rebounding: **A**
Shot Blocking: **B**
Intangibles: **B**
Overall: **C +**

Darrell Griffith

Birthdate: June 16, 1958
Height: 6-4
Weight: 190
College: University of Louisville, Louisville, Ky.
Drafted: Utah on first round, 1980 (2nd pick).
Position: Guard
Final 1989 Team: Utah Jazz
Final 1988–89 Statistics:

G	Fg	Fga	Fg%	Ft	Fta	Ft%	Orb	Reb	Ast	Stl	To	Blk	Pts	Ppg
82	466	1045	.446	142	182	.780	77	330	130	86	141	22	1135	13.8

Three-point goals: 61–196 (.311)   **TSP:** .476

SCORING

Griffith's trademark, of course, is that hit-the-ceiling (does anybody's have a higher arc?) three-pointer. His form is perfect: body squared to the basket, rotation true, the rainbow arc, and finally the follow-through. The results are pretty impressive as well. Entering 1988–89, the eight-year veteran was second only to Larry Bird for most three-point field goals made and attempted, led the league in three-point percentage in 1983–84 and 1984–85, and last year hit an OK .311 (career, .323) from that distance. But overall, Griffith had a disappointing season. Though he started the season with a bang—he was averaging 19.3 ppg and shooting .481 after 19 games—he was inconsistent for most of the year and eventually lost his starting job to Bobby Hansen. He finished at 13.8 ppg (his second worst), shot .446 (which was in the same zone he was the previous two years, .429 and .446 respectively), and played poorly in the playoff loss to Golden State (.408). Griffith is basically a spot-up shooter (and he's fortunate to have John Stockton as a backcourt mate) who moves well without the ball and will pull up in transition for the jumper. He will on occasion put it on the floor and can finish acrobatically (his old nickname is Dr. Dunkenstein), but he doesn't get to the line much (only 2.2 attempts a game). One oddity in Griffith's game is foul shooting. Widely hailed as a pure shooter, last year was the first season (.780) he shot over .725 from the stripe.

DEFENSE/DEFENSIVE REBOUNDING

Griffith has never been known for his defense—he doesn't have a good feel for it—but he wasn't a total liability last year, either. He does a decent job playing the passing lanes (one steal a game). Like his scoring, Griffith started last year strong rebounding-wise (5.5 after 19 games), but he tailed off, finishing with 4 per, slightly above his 3.7 career average.

THE FLOOR GAME

Griffith doesn't handle the ball well, particularly in transition. But in 1988–89 he did a better job of getting the ball to somebody—i.e., John Stockton—who does (his assist-to-turnover ratio was .92, second worst among starting 2s).

INTANGIBLES

Nobody wants the clutch shot as much as Griffith. He craves the shot and he'll make it, too. He's well liked by his teammates, is coachable, and a fierce competitor.

IN SUM

A dangerous long-range threat, Griffith can be an explosive scorer. But if he's not shooting well, he doesn't contribute much to the total game. His career, a good one, is on its downward arc.

RICK'S RATINGS

Scoring: **A**   Defense: **C**
Shooting: **B**   Defensive Rebounding: **A**
Free Throw Shooting: **B**   Intangibles: **A**
Ball Handling: **C**   Overall: **B**
Passing: **C**

Jack Haley

Birthdate: January 27, 1964
Height: 6-10
Weight: 240
College: University of California at Los Angeles, Los Angeles, Calif.
Drafted: Chicago on fourth round, 1987 (79th pick).
Position: Forward
Final 1989 Team: Chicago Bulls
Final 1988–89 Statistics:

G	Fg	Fga	Fg%	Ft	Fta	Ft%	Orb	Reb	Ast	Stl	To	Blk	Pts	Ppg
51	37	78	.474	36	46	.783	21	71	10	11	26	0	110	2.2

Three-point goals: 0–0 (.000)   **TSP:** .474

SCORING

Haley's not in the league for his scoring prowess. He barely scored in college (3.7 ppg at UCLA) and his prospects for point production in the pros are no more promising. He will pound the offensive glass but needs to pick and choose his spots better. His limited repertoire includes a couple of back-to-the-basket moves, but his jumper is uncertain at best. He runs well, so he'll pick up points in the transition game.

DEFENSE/DEFENSIVE REBOUNDING

Haley is a hard-nosed and aggressive defender—at this stage, too aggressive—and tends to pick up lots of fouls in little time. He's primarily a power forward but can also guard centers. Tenacious and blessed with good hands, he's a decent defensive rebounder.

THE FLOOR GAME

Haley will do the little things—dive for loose balls, set good picks—that teams need to win. He doesn't get much opportunity to handle the ball, nor does he handle it well.

INTANGIBLES

Haley is a self-styled enforcer. "If somebody tries to hurt Michael Jordan or anyone else," he once said, "I'm going to be there." His gung-ho intensity earned him a job.

IN SUM

Haley knows his role—play defense, rebound, hustle—and he relishes it. He's a limited talent with a great work ethic who needs seasoning. An ideal 12th man.

RICK'S RATINGS

Scoring: **D**   Defense: **B**
Shooting: **D**   Defensive Rebounding: **A**
Free Throw Shooting: **B**   Shot Blocking: **D**
Ball Handling: **C**   Intangibles: **A**
Passing: **C**   Overall: **D**

Bob Hansen

Birthdate: January 18, 1961
Height: 6-6
Weight: 195
College: University of Iowa, Iowa City, Iowa.
Drafted: Utah on third round, 1983 (54th pick).
Position: Guard
Final 1989 Team: Utah Jazz
Final 1988–89 Statistics:

G	Fg	Fga	Fg%	Ft	Fta	Ft%	Orb	Reb	Ast	Stl	To	Blk	Pts	Ppg
46	140	300	.467	42	75	.560	29	128	50	37	43	6	341	7.4

Three-point goals: 19–54 (.352)   **TSP:** .498

SCORING

Hansen, a shooting guard, had a tough year. At the onset of the season he missed 21 games with a broken hand, returned for nine games, and then had his jaw broken by teammate Bart Kofoed at a New Year's eve party (who quickly became an ex-teammate when the Jazz released him) and missed another 16 games. As a result, his play was inconsistent, hitting .467 from the floor, which actually was close to his career stats (.479) but down from 1987–88 (.517). And he bombed out (a miserable .314) in the 3–0 playoff loss against the Warriors. Never a good foul shooter (.696 career), he plummeted to .560. To get his shot, Hansen either needs a pick or moves without the ball; he works well with John Stockton who can deliver it. Then, too, if Hansen sees an opening in the defense, he takes it hard to the hole. He's also effective running the lanes on the break, usually the right side. He rarely takes a bad shot. And he has great range (.352 from three-point land in 1988–89) and is the NBA playoff career leader for three-point percentage (50 percent; he shot three of nine against the Warriors).

DEFENSE/DEFENSIVE REBOUNDING

Hansen's biggest plus is his defensive skills. Hard-nosed, with good size (6-6), he more than holds his own against some of the Western Conference's toughest hombres such as Magic Johnson and Dale Ellis. He gets in your face and stays there all night. He's a hustle player who comes up with loose balls and will take the charge. He's also a better-than-average defensive rebounder.

THE FLOOR GAME

Hansen plays with reckless abandon and sometimes out of control. He's an adequate passer and ball handler.

INTANGIBLES

Hansen gives Utah toughness on D, just like his coach, Jerry Sloan, did for the Chicago Bulls.

IN SUM

Hansen is a superb defender who can hit the open jumper. That combination should keep the five-year veteran in the league for another five years. He had an off-year but keep in mind he suffered two serious injuries.

RICK'S RATINGS

Scoring: **C**
Shooting: **B**
Free Throw Shooting: **D**
Ball Handling: **B**
Passing: **B**

Defense: **AA**
Defensive Rebounding: **A**
Intangibles: **A**
Overall: **B**

Bill Hanzlik

Birthdate: December 6, 1957
Height: 6-7
Weight: 200
College: University of Notre Dame, Notre Dame, Ind.
Drafted: Seattle on first round, 1980 (20th pick).
Positions: Forward, Center
Final 1989 Team: Denver Nuggets
Final 1988–89 Statistics:

G	Fg	Fga	Fg%	Ft	Fta	Ft%	Orb	Reb	Ast	Stl	To	Blk	Pts	Ppg
41	66	151	.437	68	87	.782	18	93	86	25	53	5	201	4.9

Three-point goals: 1–5 (.200)   **TSP:** .440

SCORING

At Notre Dame, Hanzlik averaged less than six points a game (5.9). In his nine-year pro career he's hit for less than eight an outing (7.4 ppg). The last time he shot over 45 percent he was playing for Seattle, way back in 1981–82. He's a career .432 shooter and shot .437 last year. Per minute, he was the least productive scorer among backup small forwards in 1988–89. No, Hanzlik, who has undergone two back surgeries in the last two years (he started last season on the injured list, played only 41 games, and didn't get substantial minutes until February), has not hung around this long on the strength of his scoring and shooting.

But, interestingly, when he's played significant minutes (such as in 1985–86 and 1986–87 and during last year's 3–0 playoff loss to Phoenix, in which he started every game), he's averaged double figures. So he's not totally inconsequential on offense. But basically his role isn't scoring and he knows it. He'll get his points off angled cuts in Denver's motion offense—he moves well without the ball—on pull-up jumpers on the break (definitely not off the dribble), or on opportunistic drives to the basket. He doesn't have three-point range (.216 lifetime) and is inconspicuous on the offensive glass. But he's a decent foul shooter at .782 last year, .785 lifetime.

DEFENSE/DEFENSIVE REBOUNDING

Hanzlik, who made the second team All-Defensive Team in 1985–86, makes his living playing D. Biggest asset: he's an uncanny post defender—*uncanny* since he's only 6-7, 200, and regularly gives away significant pounds and inches to the 4s and 5s he frequently guards. He simply can't be backed down (excellent balance has something to do with it). He's tough, a nuisance, aggressive—a walking advertisement for the proper defensive mind set. Versatile, too, since he can guard *anybody*, though his specialized niche is guarding players much larger than himself. A below-average defensive rebounder.

THE FLOOR GAME

Hanzlik is turnover-prone, particularly off the dribble. He garners lots of assists in Denver's offense (he was third, per minute, among backup 3s) and knows how to rotate the ball to hit the open man. A heady player.

INTANGIBLES

A role player who accepts his role unreservedly, Hanzlik is extremely competitive. He works so hard it's contagious. A player coaches love to have around.

IN SUM

Hanzlik's impact is not reflected in his numbers. He gives the Nuggets a defensive toughness and provides a spark off the bench. His skills, except his defense, are average or even below average, but the sum of his playing parts is valuable indeed. An unrestricted free agent, he'll likely be in a Denver uniform this year, muscling, elbowing, pushing, antagonizing, and frustrating opponents.

RICK'S RATINGS

Scoring: **D**   Defense: **AA**
Shooting: **D**   Defensive Rebounding: **C**
Free Throw Shooting: **B**   Intangibles: **AAA**
Ball Handling: **C**   Overall: **B**
Passing: **A**

Derek Harper

Birthdate: October 13, 1961
Height: 6-4
Weight: 203
College: University of Illinois, Champaign, Ill.
Drafted: Dallas on first round as an undergraduate, 1983 (11th pick).
Position: Guard
Final 1989 Team: Dallas Mavericks
Final 1988–89 Statistics:

G	Fg	Fga	Fg%	Ft	Fta	Ft%	Orb	Reb	Ast	Stl	To	Blk	Pts	Ppg
81	538	1127	.477	229	284	.806	46	228	570	172	205	41	1404	17.3

Three-point goals: 99–278 (.356)   **TSP:** .521

SCORING

Steady progress: 5.7, 9.6, 12.2, 16.0, 17.0, 17.3. Harper, a six-year veteran, has improved his scoring average each year he's been in the league, quite a feat on a team where the go-to guys are Rolando Blackman and Adrian Dantley (and previously, Mark Aguirre). Harper can hurt you from three-point range (a solid .356 in 1988–89, .330 lifetime), jumpers from 15 to 18 feet (either off the dribble or on the catch), or driving to the basket. He has tremendous explosiveness to the hoop, and with his long arms, the ball is usually in the basket before it can be blocked. Harper likes to take—and makes—the pressure shot. He has won numerous games for the Mavs over the last several years with last-second shots. However, after three consecutive years of shooting over 50 percent, Harper dropped to a mediocre .459 in 1987–88 and .477 last year. But he finally shot well from the line, his .806 in 1988–89 comparing favorably with a .743 career mark.

DEFENSE/DEFENSIVE REBOUNDING

Harper, who was selected to the NBA All-Defensive second team in 1986–87, has all the defensive tools: exceptionally quick hands, the aforementioned long arms, and lateral agility. Dallas likes to pressure guards high—really go after them—and Harper fits the bill perfectly. He was 13th in the league in steals in 1988–89 (2.1 a game) and can break games open with his thievery. His one weakness is in the post (on those rare times he is taken inside), where he tends to be cute, rather than put a body on people. He also is a below-average rebounder at the point, usually looking for the outlet pass, rather than being in position for the long rebound.

THE FLOOR GAME

Harper is not a true point guard—look first, shoot second—in the John Stockton mold. He still has a little 2 in him (the position he played in college). So, when he penetrates, it's almost always to the hoop rather than for the dish. His decision-making—when to pull up, when to take it all the way, who to pass it to—could be improved in transition. He is not a particularly clever passer, but he would likely generate more than seven assists a game (as he did in 1988–89) if Dallas were a running team. His assist-to-turnover ratio was an adequate 2.78 in 1988–89.

INTANGIBLES

Dallas coaches love this guy. He's a pleasure to coach, an enthusiastic, cheerleader type who simply loves the game. Durable, he's played 483 out of a total 492 regular season games. Clearly a prime-time player, Harper long ago recovered from his rookie season faux pas, Harper's Folly, when he held the ball with the score tied against the Lakers in the playoffs.

IN SUM

As an elite point guard, Harper's stock has fallen slightly with the emergence of players like Mark Jackson, Mark Price, John Stockton, and Kevin Johnson. But he's still in the upper echelon and at 28 (in October) is at the peak of his career.

RICK'S RATINGS

Scoring: **A**	Defense: **AAA**
Shooting: **A**	Defensive Rebounding: **D**
Free Throw Shooting: **A**	Playmaking: **B**
Ball Handling: **A**	Intangibles: **A**
Passing: **B**	Overall: **A**

Ron Harper

Birthdate: January 20, 1964
Height: 6-6
Weight: 205
College: Miami University, Oxford, O.
Drafted: Cleveland on first round, 1986 (8th pick).

Position: Guard
Final 1989 Team: Cleveland Cavaliers
Final 1988–89 Statistics:

G	Fg	Fga	Fg%	Ft	Fta	Ft%	Orb	Reb	Ast	Stl	To	Blk	Pts	Ppg
82	587	1149	.511	323	430	.751	122	409	434	185	230	74	1526	18.6

Three-point goals: 29–116 (.250) **TSP:** .523

SCORING

Harper has been called the poor man's Michael Jordan, and to a large extent, the comparison is apt. Both fly and soar and play above the rim. Both can create something out of nothing and beat you with their sheer athleticism. And both have the ability to break down defenses with the dribble in the half-court game. The big difference is that Jordan is a deadeye jump shooter, while Harper's jumper is inconsistent, though improving. He shot .511 last year, compared to .458 coming in, an increase due, in large part, to superior shot selection, which had been a problem in the past. Note, too, the slight jump in three-point percentage (from .202 in 1987–88, to .250 last season; he was shooting .316 after 44 games but a post All-Star slump killed his average for the year). But Harper's game is still the open floor, where he can dribble or run by his man and swoop in for one of his patented finger rolls or Slam Dunk Contest-caliber jams. He can also get to the line (5.2 per game in 1988–89) and like the rest of his shooting, his foul-line performance improved to .751, his best year yet.

DEFENSE/DEFENSIVE REBOUNDING

Harper has all the tools—long arms, excellent anticipation, good lateral quickness—that make for a quality defender. But he needs to improve his defensive consistency, to be focused night-in, night-out. He's ranked in the top 10 in steals in two of his three years (2.3 a game in 1988–89, eighth in the league) and can even block shots (his 74 blocks were tops among starting shooting guards), though after breaking his foot during the 1987–88 season blocking a shot, he vowed to leave the shot blocking to teammates Larry Nance, John Williams, and Tree Rollins. He's an above-average rebounder for his position (five per game last year), but Cleveland insiders feel that with his jumping ability and size he could do better and do it more consistently.

THE FLOOR GAME

As a rookie, Harper almost led the league in turnovers. He was a wild horse, he needed taming. He's still turnover-prone—his 1.89 assist-to-turnover ratio in 1988–89 was a bare improvement on the previous year's 1.78—but he's an excellent passer.

INTANGIBLES

Harper had been the "Man" while at Miami of Ohio, and in his first two years in Cleveland, but a measure of his maturity has been his willingness to submerge his individual talent and to play within the team concept. In the past he felt compelled to out "Jordanize" opponents, but now he stays within the Cavs game plan. He is a pressure player.

IN SUM

If Harper improved his outside shooting, he'd be an automatic All-Star. Even without it, he's that level; if it weren't for the All-Star selection process (which requires two backup players for each position), he would have made the team in 1988–89.

RICK'S RATINGS

Scoring: **AA**

Shooting: **B**

Free Throw Shooting: **B**

Ball Handling: **B**

Passing: **A**

Defense: **A**

Defensive Rebounding: **A**

Intangibles: **AA**

Overall: **AA**

Scott Hastings

Birthdate: June 3, 1960

Height: 6-10

Weight: 235

College: University of Arkansas, Fayetteville, Ark.

Drafted: New York on second round, 1982 (29th pick).

Position: Center

Final 1989 Team: Miami Heat

Final 1988–89 Statistics:

G	Fg	Fga	Fg%	Ft	Fta	Ft%	Orb	Reb	Ast	Stl	To	Blk	Pts	Ppg
75	143	328	.436	91	107	.850	72	231	59	32	68	42	386	5.1

Three-point goals: 9–28 (.321)   **TSP:** .450

SCORING

One way to look at Scott Hastings's 1988–89 season is to say: "He blew it." After all, here's a player who has basically sat on NBA benches (mostly with Atlanta) for six years (only once playing more than 1000 minutes for the year, 1983–84) finally getting his chance with an expansion team. So what does he do? He spends most of the year mired in a shooting slump (.376 after 57 games). Finally, in the last third of the season he picked it up, and he finished at .436, which included 55 percent as a starter in the last six games. Hastings managed to play 1,206 minutes, his career high, but he would have played more had he merited it. With Atlanta, Hastings was an afterthought on offense with much of his scoring coming on garbage. In Miami, there wasn't much garbage to be had, and Hastings, it was hoped, would be an integral part of the attack. Unfortunately, he didn't live up to expectations. He's basically a stationary shooter (it's almost a set shot; he has three-point range, .321 last year) with a jump hook with either hand, but he doesn't run the floor well or bang much on the offensive board.

DEFENSE/DEFENSIVE REBOUNDING

Hastings is not a shot blocker (he can't jump) and can be overpowered by bigger, quicker centers (he's only 6-10 and slow). But he's a smart defender who has a good feel for the pushing, shoving, elbowing, and grabbing known as post defense. He's a pretty good defensive rebounder, blocking out diligently.

THE FLOOR GAME

"Intelligent" is a word most often used to describe Hastings' play. He understands the game, and with Atlanta and Miami, he's been used in last-minute situations for in-bounds passing.

INTANGIBLES

Another word that describes Hastings is "funny." He has a terrific sense of humor, which partially explains why he's lasted seven years with limited talent. He accepts his role and realizes he's not the second coming of Akeem Olajuwon. Or as he once put it: His name is often used in the same breath as Larry Bird—as in "he's not another Larry Bird."

IN SUM

Early in the season, Hastings made a comment, half-serious, half-joking, regarding Miami's personnel. "It's scary. I think I'm the best player here." Well, it turns out, for most of the year, he was one of the worst. Hastings is better suited for spot duty on a veteran team. Which is precisely what the Pistons were thinking when they signed him in July.

RICK'S RATINGS

Scoring: **C**

Shooting: **C**

Free Throw Shooting: **AA**

Ball Handling: **A**

Passing: **A**

Defense: **B**

Defensive Rebounding: **D**

Shot Blocking: **D**

Intangibles: **A**

Overall: **C +**

Hersey Hawkins

Birthdate: September 29, 1965

Height: 6-3

Weight: 190

College: Bradley University, Peoria, Ill.

Drafted: Los Angeles Clippers on first round, 1988 (6th pick).

Position: Guard

Final 1989 Team: Philadelphia 76ers
Final 1988–89 Statistics:

G	Fg	Fga	Fg%	Ft	Fta	Ft%	Orb	Reb	Ast	Stl	To	Blk	Pts	Ppg
79	442	971	.455	241	290	.831	51	225	239	120	158	37	1196	15.1

Three-point goals: 71–166 (.428)   **TSP:** .492

SCORING

The 76ers acquired Hawkins, the leading collegiate scorer in 1988 (36.3 at Bradley), to fill a gaping hole at the shooting guard spot. In the process, they passed up Charles Smith, the 6-9 forward from Pittsburgh who showed enormous promise with the Clippers. But Philadelphia can indeed feel comfortable with its choice. While some of his numbers were not impressive (.455 percent from the field and an absolutely horrid 3 of 24 playoff performance against the Knicks), few doubt that Hawkins will be a big-time scorer for years to come. He is, first of all, a pure shooter with excellent technique who can stroke it from three-point land (an outstanding .428, fourth in the league), and his 15.1 ppg was fourth best among NBA rookies. Adept at moving without the ball and working off screens, Hawkins is best spotting up and shooting it on the catch. He can also shoot it off the dribble, though he's not yet as smooth or proficient in that area. But he's not strictly a jump shooter; he can take it to the hole with either hand, though Philly's coaches would like to see him get to the line at least six times (compared to 3.7 in 1988–89) a game. He also needs work on getting a good shot once he penetrates. A very good foul shooter (.831), Hawkins finishes well on the fast break and will hit the big shot.

DEFENSE/DEFENSIVE REBOUNDING

By no means does Hawkins have the typical scorer's mentality. In other words: He plays defense. He gets over screens and is focused on defense, but while he has the makings of a good defender, he's not there yet. In the Knick series, for example, the quicker Gerald Wilkins continually got by the slower-footed Hawkins. He comes by his share of steals (1.5 a game), but he's going to have to stick his nose into the mix and become a better defensive rebounder (only 2.2 a game, below average for starting 2s, and 2.8 overall).

THE FLOOR GAME

Despite his reputation as a scorer, Hawkins is not a gunner. On the move, he's a superb interior passer and in fact the Philly coaching staff have often urged him to shoot more. Interesting stat: He averaged 36.3 a game at Bradley on only 23 shots a game.

INTANGIBLES

There's a quiet pride about Hawkins that translates to "winner." He's an intelligent basketball player who responds well to coaching and is completely dedicated to team basketball.

IN SUM

Hawkins will score a lot of points over a long career. But he's

also a multidimensional player who plays both ends of the court. His playoff invisibility was more a slump—a rookie's first-time-in-the-playoff blues—than a reflection of fundamental flaws in his game. He's the type of 2 coaches dream about.

RICK'S RATINGS

Scoring: **A**   Defense: **B**
Shooting: **A**   Defensive Rebounding: **C**
Free Throw Shooting: **A**   Intangibles: **A**
Ball Handling: **B**   Overall: **A –**
Passing: **A**

Gerald Henderson

Birthdate: January 16, 1956
Height: 6-2
Weight: 180
College: Virginia Commonwealth University, Richmond, Va.
Drafted: San Antonio on third round, 1978 (64th pick).
Position: Guard
Final 1989 Team: Philadelphia 76ers
Final 1988–89 Statistics:

G	Fg	Fga	Fg%	Ft	Fta	Ft%	Orb	Reb	Ast	Stl	To	Blk	Pts	Ppg
65	144	348	.414	104	127	.819	17	68	140	42	73	3	425	6.5

Three-point goals: 33–107 (.308)   **TSP:** .461

SCORING

It was a down year for Henderson, a 10-year veteran. Down went his shooting percentage, as it has for the last four years—from .482 to .442 to .428 to .414—his career-low. Down went his three-point percentage, from a superb .423 in 1987–88 (fourth in the league) to a subpar .308. Down went his scoring average, to 6.5, continuing a five-year slide from a career high 13.4 ppg in 1984–85. Only his foul shooting picked up--from .812 in 1987–88 to .819 last year. But when fans think of Henderson's charity work in 1988–89, they'll ignore those numbers and concentrate on those two missed free throws in the final seconds against the Knicks in the third game of the playoffs. All of which is to say that Henderson, who backed up Hersey Hawkins at the 2, may be employed elsewhere this year (if at all). He can shoot the trifecta spotting up or off the dribble. He can also get to the line since he's one of the best "floppers" in the league and consistently gets bailed out when he drives to the hoop.

DEFENSE/DEFENSIVE REBOUNDING

Henderson is a gritty defender. He chases after loose balls, takes the charge, and doesn't back down from anybody. He also can make the steal (who can forget his theft of a James Worthy pass in the second game of the 1983–84 Celtic-Laker championship that turned the series around?), but he has never been a good defensive rebounder for his position.

THE FLOOR GAME

Because of his sloppy ball handling (above-average turnovers per minute last year) and because he doesn't always use the best judgment when he penetrates or on the break, the 76ers have used Henderson more as a 2 than a 1. He's more of a guard, period, than a true point or a prototype 2.

INTANGIBLES

Henderson is a feisty competitor. He has two championship rings to his credit and that experience is a valuable asset on any team.

IN SUM

At 32, Henderson is on the downside of his career. He can play the D, but he'll have to shoot better if he wants to continue playing with the big boys.

RICK'S RATINGS

Scoring: **B**
Shooting: **C**
Free Throw Shooting: **A**
Ball Handling: **C**
Passing: **B**

Defense: **A**
Defensive Rebounding: **D**
Intangibles: **B**
Overall: **C**

Rod Higgins

Birthdate: January 31, 1960
Height: 6-7
Weight: 205
College: Fresno State University, Fresno, Calif.
Drafted: Chicago on second round, 1982 (31st pick).
Position: Forward
Final 1989 Team: Golden State Warriors
Final 1988–89 Statistics:

G	Fg	Fga	Fg%	Ft	Fta	Ft%	Orb	Reb	Ast	Stl	To	Blk	Pts	Ppg
81	301	633	.476	188	229	.821	111	376	160	39	76	42	856	10.6

Three-point goals: 66–168 (.393)   **TSP:** .528

SCORING

Warrior coach Don Nelson, who knows a few things about maximizing a player's strengths, took one look at Rod Higgins' game and instructed: fire away—from a distance. Shoot the trey. It was an excellent piece of advice considering Higgins was coming off a year in which he blistered the nets from beyond the arc at a .487 pace. But he shot only 39

three-pointers (making 19) in 1987–88. Last year, Higgins, a small forward, attempted more trifectas (168) and made more (66) than he had in his first six years in the league—and hit for a sizzling .393, 11th in the league. Higgins fit in well with the Warriors open-court style. While he has a quick release, he needs room to shoot—he's not much creating off the dribble—and a familiar sight last season was Higgins pulling up in transition and launching. His put-it-on-the-floor skills are below average but he's a sneaky offensive rebounder (1.4 a game in 23.3 minutes).

DEFENSE/DEFENSIVE REBOUNDING

Higgins is solid defensively, an intelligent defender (another Boyd Grant, Fresno State trained product) who won't hurt you on D. If he has a limitation, it's that he's not a tremendously gifted athlete—quickness and strength are in short supply—and he's vulnerable to high-powered 3s. Nobody seems to think Higgins is anything more than an average defensive rebounder, but his numbers last year were above average for his position.

THE FLOOR GAME

Higgins is not going to beat you with his passing or dribbling. He's a fair ball handler, not a mistake player. He can run the floor, but he doesn't use his speed as well as he should; in other words, he paces himself.

INTANGIBLES

A quality person. "An extremely nice guy." Somebody you want in your organization. Plays hard and likes to play. While he started in 1987–88 and was the team's leading scorer (15.5 ppg), he readily accepted his reserve role and lesser offensive contribution (10.6 ppg) last year. Persistent: Higgins played on four NBA teams in 1985–86.

IN SUM

Solid sums him up. Perfect as a 7th-9th man. Can kill opponents with his outside shooting, and the rest of his game is good enough. Gives the Warriors firepower off the bench.

RICK'S RATINGS

Scoring: **B**
Shooting: **AA**
Free Throw Shooting: **A**
Ball Handling: **B**
Passing: **B**

Defense: **B**
Defensive Rebounding: **A**
Intangibles: **A**
Overall: **B +**

Roy Hinson

Birthdate: May 2, 1961
Height: 6-9
Weight: 220
College: Rutgers University, New Brunswick, N.J.
Drafted: Cleveland on first round, 1983 (20th pick).
Positions: Center, Forward
Final 1989 Team: New Jersey Nets
Final 1988–89 Statistics:

G	Fg	Fga	Fg%	Ft	Fta	Ft%	Orb	Reb	Ast	Stl	To	Blk	Pts	Ppg
82	495	1027	.482	318	420	.757	152	522	71	34	165	121	1308	16.0

Three-point goals: 0–2 (.000) **TSP:** .482

SCORING

Hinson had an excellent season, leading the Nets in scoring with 16 a game, his second best average in a six-year career, and he was the team's most consistent offensive performer. This was a considerable accomplishment, considering he didn't really have a position: He started and played a reserve role at center and both forward slots. Now that's versatility. The 6-9, 220-pound Hinson owns a fine turn-around jumper from the baseline, can put the ball on the floor (invariably to his left, though he is right-handed) and displayed a nifty left-handed hook. He's a fair runner of the floor and an OK offensive rebounder (1.9 a game but, per minute, way below average; players like Russ Schoene and Blair Rasmussen were better). With his superb jumping ability and quickness, the feeling is that Hinson could do more. He's been a slightly below-average foul shooter for his career (.736) and last year (.757) was no exception.

DEFENSE/DEFENSIVE REBOUNDING

On the positive side, Hinson is a top-notch shot blocker (1.5 a game). Which is not to say he is a good defender. For starters, he has a tendency to play off his man and wait for him to come to him. And he'll get called for goaltending. And whether Hinson's guarding 3s, 4s, or 5s, he encounters problems. The small forwards give him trouble because of quickness (Hinson tends to play D straight-legged, rather than bending his knees); the 4s, such as the Knicks' Charles Oakley, have their way with him because of the strength differential; and the 5s are simply too big. He's a slightly below-average defensive rebounder (6.4 total rebounds a game).

THE FLOOR GAME

For a player of his stature, Hinson has one glaring defi-

ciency: passing. He accumulated only 71 assists in 2,542 minutes. And his assist-to-turnover ratio was a dismal 0.43.

INTANGIBLES

Hinson's resume is complete: He plays hurt, has an excellent work ethic, wants to improve, and is well-liked and well-respected by his teammates. A pro.

IN SUM

Great things—i.e., All-Star status—have been predicted for Hinson since his splendid 1985–86 showing in Cleveland when he averaged 19.6 ppg and 7.8 rpg. But he has been plagued by inconsistency—not showing the game-to-game dominance that merits that acclaim. He did better last season and, no doubt, is a quality NBA player, but his defense and ball handling skills are not yet up to snuff.

RICK'S RATINGS

Scoring: **AA**	Defense: **B**
Shooting: **B**	Defensive Rebounding: **B**
Free Throw Shooting: **B**	Shot Blocking: **AAA**
Ball Handling: **D**	Intangibles: **A**
Passing: **D**	Overall: **A**

Craig Hodges

Birthdate: June 27, 1960
Height: 6-2
Weight: 195
College: California State University at Long Beach, Long Beach, Calif.
Drafted: San Diego on third round, 1982 (48th pick).
Position: Guard
Final 1989 Team: Chicago Bulls
Final 1988–89 Statistics:

G	Fg	Fga	Fg%	Ft	Fta	Ft%	Orb	Reb	Ast	Stl	To	Blk	Pts	Ppg
59	203	430	.472	48	57	.842	23	89	146	43	57	4	529	9.0

Three-point goals: 75–180 (.417) **TSP:** .559

SCORING

If it wasn't quite a match made in basketball heaven, it was at least a comfortable fit. On the one hand, there was Hodges, perhaps the ultimate spot-up shooter in the league, and on the other, Michael Jordan, certainly the ultimate drawer of double-(and triple)-teams. The Bulls' progress (they advanced to the Eastern Conference final before losing to the Pistons) last season had a lot to do with two critical lineup moves: Air's switch from shooting guard to the point in March and, a few games later, the insertion of Hodges, who was acquired by the Bulls in December from the Suns (where he had languished on the bench) for Ed Nealy, into the starting lineup, to play the 2 to Michael's 1. Nothing fancy there. Jordan would penetrate, the defense would collapse, Jordan would kick it out to Hodges, waiting in his familiar spot beyond the three-point line. And Hodges, as he has done for most of his career, would nail a high percentage of the three-pointers. He is, of course, one of the league's premier trifecta specialists—twice he's led the league in three-point percentage (.451 in 1985–86 and .491 in 1987–88), and last season he stroked at a .417 pace, fifth in the league (note his true shooting percentage: .559). He tends to be streaky—consider, for example, his 24 point effort on 10-for-18 shooting against the Knicks in playoff game No. 1, which was followed by 10-for-37 in the next four games—but you can never ignore him. Otherwise, he rarely takes it to the basket (only one free throw attempt in 20.4 minutes), though he is an excellent foul shooter (.842 last season, .891 in 1986–87). He has a problem finishing the play when, as one coach put it, there is "confrontation" around the hoop.

DEFENSE/DEFENSIVE REBOUNDING

Hodges, offensively a 2, is usually matched up against the 1s on defense. (At 6-2, he is simply too small to guard most shooting guards). While there's no question about his tenacity, he has trouble keeping up with the Mark Prices and the Isiah Thomases of the league. A way below-average defensive rebounder for his position.

THE FLOOR GAME

For a 2, Hodges is a more-than-adequate ball handler (in 1988–89, a solid 2.56 assist-to-turnover ratio and above-average assists—2.5 a game). In a pinch, he can even play the point, but while a good "push" man, he's less skilled in getting a team into an offense.

INTANGIBLES

Possesses some on-court leadership ability. Team player. Solid citizen. Hodges fit in well with the mood and chemistry of the Bulls.

IN SUM

Hodges has a specialty, and he's very good at it. But his defense is adequate at best, and he's somewhat inconsistent. Which is to say, that despite Chicago's success with him as a starter, the 29-year-old is not the Bulls' long-term answer at the 2 spot (of course, that may be academic if Jordan moves back to shooting guard). Either way, with his long-range bombs, he can still make a significant contribution off the bench.

Michael Holton

Birthdate: August 4, 1961
Height: 6-5
Weight: 185
College: University of California at Los Angeles, Los Angeles, Calif.
Drafted: Golden State on third round, 1983 (53rd pick).
Position: Guard
Final 1989 Team: Charlotte Hornets
Final 1988–89 Statistics:

G	Fg	Fga	Fg%	Ft	Fta	Ft%	Orb	Reb	Ast	Stl	To	Blk	Pts	Ppg
67	215	504	.427	120	143	.839	30	105	424	66	119	12	553	8.3

Three-point goals: 3–14 (.214)   **TSP:** .430

SCORING

Charlotte doesn't run plays for Holton, who started 60 games at point guard, and it's no wonder, He's a streaky shooter (.427 in 1988–89; .440 lifetime) who can shoot the jumper off the dribble from 18 and in. In defense of his talents, a good percentage of his shots come when the clock is running down, so he does not always get the best shots. He'll also take the pull-up jump shot on the break or get spot-up shots in the offense. Holton shoots the three-pointer, but not accurately (.214 last season and .257 lifetime). At 6-5, Holton has good size for a guard, is physical, and can get to the hole, though he's an erratic finisher. A good foul shooter (.839 last year, .808 for his career), he occasionally swings to the 2 spot.

DEFENSE/DEFENSIVE REBOUNDING

Holton gets the job done on defense. He's quick for his size, has excellent hands, and has the desire and work ethic that characterize good defenders. If there's a weakness, it's that he doesn't pressure the ball consistently. And he's a poor rebounder (1.6 a game)—next to worst among starting point guards.

THE FLOOR GAME

Holton has done a nice job running Charlotte's offense. He makes the steady, rather than the spectacular pass—reflected in a stellar 3.56 assist-to-turnover ratio—but he doesn't have the "push" ability of his teammate, Muggsy Bogues. On the other hand, he's not an aggressive leader, which of course you'd like from that position.

INTANGIBLES

Where ever he's been—and he's been around (four NBA teams and three CBA teams), Holton has been a positive force. He's coachable, a team player, liked by his teammates, and tough.

IN SUM

Holton doesn't dazzle but his defense, playmaking, and attitude constitute a plus on any team. Of course, on a good club, he's a backup, but expansion teams can't be choosy.

RICK'S RATINGS

Scoring: **C**	Defense: **A**
Shooting: **D**	Defensive Rebounding: **D**
Free Throw Shooting: **A**	Playmaking: **B**
Ball Handling: **A**	Intangibles: **A**
Passing: **A**	Overall: **B –**

Dave Hoppen

Birthdate: March 13, 1964
Height: 6-11
Weight: 235
College: University of Nebraska, Lincoln, Neb.
Drafted: Atlanta on third round, 1986 (65th pick).
Position: Center
Final 1989 Team: Charlotte Hornets
Final 1988–89 Statistics:

G	Fg	Fga	Fg%	Ft	Fta	Ft%	Orb	Reb	Ast	Stl	To	Blk	Pts	Ppg
77	199	353	.564	101	139	.727	123	384	57	25	77	21	500	6.5

Three-point goals: 1–2 (.500)   **TSP:** .565

SCORING

In a starting role, Hoppen put up a mere five shots a game (he lost his starting job in December to Earl Cureton and didn't get it back until March), but the consensus is that for a center he possesses a decent touch with excellent range (18 feet). He's basically a "facing" center with limited back-to-the-basket moves. His other offensive asset is his ability to run the floor and finish. He also possesses a turnaround jumper and jump hook. Statistically, he was an average offensive rebounder. Unfortunately, he has zero ability to create his own shot.

DEFENSE/DEFENSIVE REBOUNDING

At this stage, Hoppen's game includes a heavy dose of the "S" word: He's soft. When he's up against centers like New York's Patrick Ewing or Boston's Robert Parish, he is almost awestruck and doesn't play physical enough. For a center, he had some truly Lilliputian shot blocking numbers: in roughly the same number of minutes, Dennis Hopson, Ricky Berry, and Derek Smith (guards and small forwards all) blocked more shots. But he's young and really just learning how to play one-on-one defense. At Golden State, where he played in 1987–88, he was a terrific rebounder. He hasn't shown the same aptitude with the Hornets.

THE FLOOR GAME

Hoppen is an above-average passer and dribbler for a center and doesn't turn the ball over. His knowledge of the game is still evolving; after all, this is a player who has played only 116 NBA games.

INTANGIBLES

Hoppen works hard in practice, but he hasn't shown the required come-early, stay-late mentality. He got his butt kicked a lot last season but hasn't yet mustered the retaliatory verve to return the favor.

IN SUM

But for expansion, Hoppen would be considered an advanced project. Thrust into a starting role, he didn't cut it. He's still at least a couple of years away. His touch and running ability are the positives; defense and rebounding are the negatives.

RICK'S RATINGS

Scoring: **C**	Defense: **D**
Shooting: **B**	Defensive Rebounding: **B**
Free Throw Shooting: **C**	Shot Blocking: **D**
Ball Handling: **A**	Intangibles: **C**
Passing: **A**	Overall: **D**

Dennis Hopson

Birthdate: April 22, 1965
Height: 6-5

Weight: 200
College: Ohio State University, Columbus, O.
Drafted: New Jersey on first round, 1987 (3rd pick).
Position: Guard
Final 1989 Team: New Jersey Nets
Final 1988–89 Statistics:

G	Fg	Fga	Fg%	Ft	Fta	Ft%	Orb	Reb	Ast	Stl	To	Blk	Pts	Ppg
62	299	714	.419	186	219	.849	91	202	103	70	102	30	788	12.7

Three-point goals: 4–27 (.148)   **TSP:** .422

SCORING

Hopson, the third player picked in the 1987 draft, was a huge disappointment in his rookie year, shooting a horrible .404 from the field, and playing as if he didn't belong. He also missed 21 games with a sprained ankle and was beset by nagging injuries throughout the season. To right himself, he played in several pro summer leagues and worked on his jumper. But misfortune again struck in preseason when he again injured his ankle and missed the first four regular season games. Finally, he worked himself back into the rotation and eventually into the starting lineup in January and showed flashes of why the Nets drafted him so high. While his shooting percentage was still rather dreary (.419), he displayed some decent scoring ability (12.7 ppg and a point about every two minutes, which put him in the middle of the pack for starting 2s). For now, at least, he's more a scorer than a pure shooter; for a 2, he has a strange shot—almost a push shot with a slow release. Hopson is fond of taking the ball to the basket and can make off-balance shots, though Net coaches would like to see him power, rather than finesse, his way to the hoop. A converted forward, he also can get you points on the offensive board (1.5 caroms a game). But he can't make the three (4 of 27 last year); his range is more like 18 feet. His .849 from the line was a dramatic improvement over his rookie year's .740.

DEFENSE/DEFENSIVE REBOUNDING

Hopson's defense is a concern. Both his effort and his concentration level must improve. He got taken to the cleaners by the league's 2s on a consistent basis. And he doesn't completely understand defensive positioning. Despite his size and his background as a forward, he didn't get the job done on the defensive glass.

THE FLOOR GAME

While he can create some off the dribble, and handles it OK on the break, Hopson needs major work on his ball handling. He had a glaring 1.01 assist-to-turnover ratio and also needs to pay more attention to his non-scoring duties, such as setting picks, not picking up his dribble too fast, and overdribbling.

INTANGIBLES

Some have questioned: (a) Hopson's willingness to play in pain and (b) his devotion to team as opposed to Dennis

Hopson and his scoring totals. Then, too, his durability is an issue, having missed 43 games in two seasons. But at least he seems to have regained his confidence.

IN SUM

Hopson has shown he can be a better-than-adequate NBA scorer. But a more consistent jumper and significant strides in his ball handling and defense are essentials before it can be confirmed that he's there.

RICK'S RATINGS

Scoring: **A**	Defense: **C**
Shooting: **D**	Defensive Rebounding: **C**
Free Throw Shooting: **AA**	Intangibles: **C**
Ball Handling: **C**	Overall: **C**
Passing: **C**	

Tito Horford

Birthdate: January 19, 1966
Height: 7-1
Weight: 245
College: University of Miami, Coral Gables, Fla.
Drafted: Milwaukee on second round as an undergraduate, 1988 (39th pick).
Position: Center
Final 1989 Team: Milwaukee Bucks
Final 1988–89 Statistics:

G	Fg	Fga	Fg%	Ft	Fta	Ft%	Orb	Reb	Ast	Stl	To	Blk	Pts	Ppg
25	15	46	.326	12	19	.632	9	22	3	1	15	7	42	1.7

Three-point goals: 0–0 (.000)   **TSP:** .326

SCORING

At 7-1, 245, Horford, Milwaukee's second-round pick in 1988 (39th overall), has the proverbial pro body and NBA-level jumping and running ability. He even has a decent face-up jumper and an improving hook shot. But while these basic tools are present, the ability to apply them is not. He is as raw a talent as the NBA has seen in a while and is just learning to play. For example, Horford is easily confused by changing defenses and his shot selection is, how shall we say it, off-beat at times. With that body, he should be a better offensive rebounder. And he's a terrible foul shooter (.565 at Miami and .632 last season).

DEFENSE/DEFENSIVE REBOUNDING

Because of his athletic ability and size, Horford has the potential (underline that word!) to be a competent shot blocker. Otherwise, he's a slow reactor on D and doesn't sum up situations well.

THE FLOOR GAME

Horford can run the floor but ball handling is another weak area.

INTANGIBLES

Horford's inexperience is the major drawback and he didn't get much time last year (25 games and 112 minutes; and from March 9 on, he was on the injured list with a hammertoe condition for which he had surgery). Then, too, in college he was not what you call a workaholic but has improved his work ethic under the tutelage of Buck assistant Mack Calvin and now has a better grasp of what it takes to be an NBA center.

IN SUM

The term project was invented to describe Horford. The Bucks figured he was worth the risk as the 39th pick. But a project he is, and a project he will remain.

RICK'S RATINGS

Scoring: **D**	Defense: **C**
Shooting: **D**	Defensive Rebounding: **C**
Free Throw Shooting: **D**	Shot Blocking: **B**
Ball Handling: **D**	Intangibles: **B**
Passing: **D**	Overall: **D**

Jeff Hornacek

Birthdate: April 3, 1963
Height: 6-4
Weight: 190
College: Iowa State University, Ames, Ia.
Drafted: Phoenix on second round, 1986 (46th pick).
Position: Guard
Final 1989 Team: Phoenix Suns
Final 1988–89 Statistics:

G	Fg	Fga	Fg%	Ft	Fta	Ft%	Orb	Reb	Ast	Stl	To	Blk	Pts	Ppg
78	440	889	.495	147	178	.826	75	266	465	129	111	8	1054	13.5

Three-point goals: 27–81 (.333)   **TSP:** .510

SCORING

Like many NBA players, Hornacek hit his stride in his third year as a pro. In 1988–89, he scored 13.5 ppg (his previous best was 9.5), shot .333 from three-point land, and a solid .495 overall. The Suns' starting shooting guard who also backs up Kevin Johnson at the point, Hornacek is a superb jump shooter (particularly when he has room) who gets his

shots coming off picks, pulling up on the break, or off Kevin Johnson's penetration. Not the quickest guy, Hornacek is not adept at creating the jumper off the dribble, but he can get to the hoop (using a crossover dribble), where he has an uncanny ability to make tough shots over the big guys. And when he gets fouled, he makes the shots (.826 last year from the line). Best way to defend him: Crowd him and make him put the ball on the floor going left.

DEFENSE/DEFENSIVE REBOUNDING

While he sacrifices quickness and strength, and occasionally size (he's 6-4, 190), Hornacek is a decent defender. He's active, has good hands, and averaged 1.7 steals a game in 1988–89. He's hardworking and will take a charge or hit the floor for a loose ball. His defensive rebounding numbers are slightly below average for a starting 2.

THE FLOOR GAME

One of Hornacek's assets is the fact that he can play both guard positions. He's a good passer, who takes excellent care of the ball (a starting-2-best 4.19 assist-to-turnover ratio). As a point, he's a get-the-offense-going quarterback rather than a penetrate-and-dish guy. Occasionally, he's vulnerable to pressure.

INTANGIBLES

"Hard-nosed," "full of basketball savvy," "courageous," "great practice player." It says something that Hornacek is the only remaining member of the scandal-wrecked Phoenix team of two years ago.

IN SUM

Hornacek is a solid all-around player who comes to play every night and gets the most out of his abilities. Though he is not a "scoring machine 2," he doesn't have to be on a team that features point producers such as Eddie Johnson, Kevin Johnson, and Tom Chambers. Hornacek, in a word, is underrated.

RICK'S RATINGS

Scoring: **B**	Defense: **B**
Shooting: **A**	Defensive Rebounding: **B**
Free Throw Shooting: **A**	Playmaking: **A**
Ball Handling: **A**	Intangibles: **A**
Passing: **A**	Overall: **B +**

Eddie Hughes

Birthdate: May 26, 1960
Height: 5-10
Weight: 164
College: Colorado State University, Fort Collins, Colo.
Drafted: San Diego on seventh round, 1982 (140th pick).

Position: Guard
Final 1989 Team: Denver Nuggets
Final 1988–89 Statistics:

G	Fg	Fga	Fg%	Ft	Fta	Ft%	Orb	Reb	Ast	Stl	To	Blk	Pts	Ppg
26	28	64	.438	7	12	.583	6	19	35	17	11	2	70	2.7

Three-point goals: 7–22 (.318)   **TSP:** .492

SCORING

Hughes, a tiny (5-10, 164) CBA journeyman, has had two cups of coffee in the NBA, an 11-game stint with Utah in 1987–88 (where he also played in seven playoff games) and a 26-game stretch with the Nuggets last year. He's been banging around the CBA since 1982 and spending a lot of time in Jazz training camps (he's been waived by Utah four times). Hughes is lightening quick (his nickname: Quick), who is most effective scoring in transition. In the CBA, he's been a major league three-point threat and in the NBA last season was an OK 7–22. When he penetrates in half court, he hasn't shown an ability to finish the play.

DEFENSE/DEFENSIVE REBOUNDING

Hughes will get after you defensively. Guys his size have to play pressure D for 94 feet and that's exactly what he does. Stronger than his frame suggests, he has good hands and moves well laterally.

THE FLOOR GAME

Hughes' value is pushing the ball on the break. The drawback is that he will occasionally play out of control. He's good at drawing and kicking.

INTANGIBLES

Anybody who has been "tapped on the shoulder" as often as Hughes and is still at it, is, if nothing else, persistent. Works extremely hard and is coachable.

IN SUM

Good CBA player.

RICK'S RATINGS

Scoring: **D**	Defense: **B**
Shooting: **C**	Defensive Rebounding: **C**
Free Throw Shooting: **D**	Playmaking: **C**
Ball Handling: **B**	Intangibles: **B**
Passing: **B**	Overall: **D**

——— Jay Humphries ———

Birthdate: October 17, 1962
Height: 6-3
Weight: 185
College: University of Colorado, Boulder, Colo.
Drafted: Phoenix on first round, 1984 (13th pick).
Position: Guard
Final 1989 Team: Milwaukee Bucks
Final 1988–89 Statistics:

G	Fg	Fga	Fg%	Ft	Fta	Ft%	Orb	Reb	Ast	Stl	To	Blk	Pts	Ppg
73	345	714	.483	129	158	.816	70	189	405	142	160	5	844	11.6

Three-point goals: 25–94 (.266)   **TSP:** .501

SCORING

Humphries gave the Bucks double figures every night (11.6 ppg), shot for the good percentage (.483), and made over 80 percent (.816) from the line—nice numbers for a point guard or, for that matter, anybody. A model of consistency throughout his five-year career, he's averaged below 10 per game only once (8.8 in his rookie year), with last year's ppg his high; and he's shot under .477 only in his rookie year (.446), with a top mark of .528 in 1987–88. He's an excellent mid-range jump shooter off the dribble or on the catch, though his three-point range is suspect (.266 in 1988–89). While not exceptionally fast or quick, Humphries is a fine driver with either hand (he's one of the most purely ambidextrous players in the league; right-handed, he may even favor his left) who uses his body well and owns an array of shots to finish (including the dunk, though he's doing less of that these days). He takes good shots and is not reluctant to attempt the clutch shot. The Bucks also swing Humphries to the 2, when Paul Pressey plays the point.

DEFENSE/DEFENSIVE REBOUNDING

Humphries is a first-rate defender. He has strength, good enough speed, and is hard-nosed. He can apply pressure on the ball, knows how to keep it away from the middle, and anticipates well (1.9 steals, 17th in the league). There are few better defensive combos when he's teamed with Pressey in the backcourt. Humphries is an adequate defensive rebounder for his position.

THE FLOOR GAME

Humphries, who was traded to the Bucks for Craig Hodges

in February 1988, is a solid floor leader: nothing flashy, not real creative. He makes good decisions as the middleman on the break and runs Milwaukee's offense ably (and was far more comfortable last season with a complete season with the team under his belt). He is slightly turnover-prone.

INTANGIBLES

The dreaded S word, *soft*, had been used to describe Humphries in Phoenix, but those in the know in Milwaukee didn't find that to be the case at all. Humphries, it turns out, doesn't back down from anybody. His teammates like him and he has a fine work ethic. Nor had he any qualms about coming off the bench early in the season (which he did when Sidney Moncrief was healthy), because he still got substantial minutes (30.4 a game).

IN SUM

One of the key chapters of Milwaukee's surprising success story last season, whether as a starter or a reserve (he's a *luxury* coming off the bench), Humphries is a solid all-around point guard who can score, defend, and distribute, as well as give you quality minutes as a 2.

RICK'S RATINGS

Scoring: **B**　　　　　Defense: **A**
Shooting: **A**　　　　Defensive Rebounding: **D**
Free Throw Shooting: **A**　Playmaking: **A**
Ball Handling: **A**　　Intangibles: **A**
Passing: **A**　　　　Overall: **A**

Mark Jackson

Birthdate: April 1, 1965
Height: 6-3
Weight: 205
College: St. John's University, Jamaica, N.Y.
Drafted: New York on first round, 1987 (18th pick).
Position: Guard
Final 1989 Team: New York Knicks
Final 1988–89 Statistics:

G	Fg	Fga	Fg%	Ft	Fta	Ft%	Orb	Reb	Ast	Stl	To	Blk	Pts	Ppg
72	479	1025	.467	180	258	.698	106	341	619	139	226	7	1219	16.9

Three-point goals: 81–240 (.338)　　**TSP:** .507

SCORING

Jackson's the name, penetration's his game. Quick? Not particularly. Fast? A half-step slow or slower. But Jackson gets into the paint at will (deception and the ability to spin are two reasons), where he is *dangerous*. He has the uncanny ability to score in a crowd, over outstretched arms, kissing it high off the glass for the hoop. You can't teach that—it's all feel, all playground moxie, a commodity Jackson has an ample supply of.

And his jumper? Let's just say it's good enough to keep the defense honest, but opposing coaches would much prefer to see Jackson shooting 18-footers all night (.467 last year). He can shoot it standing still or off the dribble—either way, he's inconsistent. But—and it's a big but—he'll drill it when the Knicks really need it, because Jackson is a money ballplayer—a guy you want to have the ball come crunch time, even if it's to shoot jump shots. He's now shooting the trey—in 1987–88, it was a veritable heave (a shabby .254), but last year, when the Knicks made the trifecta the focal point of their offense, he improved to .338. Jackson's also added a post-up game, where he shoots a baby hook. For a point guard, he's a superb offensive rebounder (1.5 a game), and many come at crucial junctures. Oh, yes, his foul shooting and that familiar cupped-hand, pointed-fingers, finger routine. Face it, Mark: It doesn't work. He shot .698 from the line last season, second worst among starting point guards—who collectively average over 80 percent—and down significantly from his rookie year's .774.

DEFENSE/DEFENSIVE REBOUNDING

On the plus side, Jackson has great anticipation—in the Knicks' trapping defense, he's good off the ball and comes up with a lot of steals (1.9 a game; 18th in the league). But as a trapper (on the ball), he's below average and is vulnerable, quickness-wise, to the Mark Prices of the world. In the half-court D, he is learning to use space and strength against the quicker guards. With 3.3 defensive rebounds a game, he was sixth, on a per minute basis, among his playmaking peers.

THE FLOOR GAME

Stylistically, Jackson is cut from the Magic Johnson mold: the no-look pass, see-what-nobody-else-sees, give-'em-their-money's worth style of playmaking. Pizzazz. Flair. Élan. Call it what you want, it turns on the fans, and, for the most part, it works. But Jackson has taken the heat because he's a shoot-first, look-second quarterback. The Knicks, say his critics, are better off when Jackson gets 14 points and 14 assists rather than 24 points and 4 assists. In other words, he shoots too much. A point well taken. How is it, for example, that Patrick Ewing, who shot .567 from the field, averaged only 16 shots a game while Jackson, who was 10 percentage points worse, took 14? And indeed last year, compared to his rookie season, Jackson had fewer assists (10.6 vs. 8.6) and his assist-to-turnover ratio dropped from a stellar 3.36 in 1987–88 to a mediocre 2.74.

INTANGIBLES

Ewing is the "man," but Jackson is the heart and soul of the

Knicks. Mentally tough, self-assured, hates to lose, a pressure player—Jackson has the whole package.

IN SUM

Rookie of the Year in 1987–88. An All-Star in 1988–89. For Jackson to reach a higher plateau, he will have to improve his shooting, both from the field and the foul line as well as think pass first, shot second, more often. As for team achievements, with Mark Jackson, Patrick Ewing, and Charles Oakley in place, the Knicks have laid a solid foundation for a championship in the 1990s.

RICK'S RATINGS

Scoring: **A**
Shooting: **B**
Free Throw Shooting: **D**
Ball Handling: **A**
Passing: **AA**

Defense: **B**
Defensive Rebounding: **B**
Playmaking: **A**
Intangibles: **AAA**
Overall: **A +**

Avery Johnson

Birthdate: March 25, 1965
Height: 5-11
Weight: 175
College: Southern University, Baton Rouge, La.
Drafted: Free Agent
Position: Guard
Final 1989 Team: Seattle Supersonics
Final 1988–89 Statistics:

G	Fg	Fga	Fg%	Ft	Fta	Ft%	Orb	Reb	Ast	Stl	To	Blk	Pts	Ppg
43	29	83	.349	9	16	.563	11	24	73	21	18	3	68	1.6

Three-point goals: 1–9 (.111)   **TSP:** .355

SCORING

As a rookie, in limited minutes (6.8 a game)—which makes it difficult to accurately gauge shooting ability—Johnson shot a horrible .349, including 1-for-9 in trifectas. But he's a backup guard whose role is to push the ball and get it to others in the half-court offense, rather than score himself. Still, he's going to have to hit the open jumper when others are double-teamed to have a future in the league. He will drive to the hoop and then fade, and he has the ability to lob it off the glass with either hand; he is not, however, a consistent finisher.

DEFENSE/DEFENSIVE REBOUNDING

One reason Johnson, 5-11, made the Sonics (over veteran Danny Young) was that it was felt that he could guard the likes of Denver's Michael Adams (who destroyed the Sonics in the 1987–88 playoffs) and John Stockton. Johnson moves well laterally, can pressure the ball full court and improved his position defense as the year progressed. He's not going to get defensive rebounds.

THE FLOOR GAME

Another reason Johnson made the team was his ability to

push the ball and also to find people in the half-court offense. At Southern University, he led the country in assists in both his junior and senior years. He has fantastic peripheral vision and can thread the needle, though he will occasionally opt for the spectacular over the simple pass. His assist-to-turnover ratio, 4.06, was way above average.

INTANGIBLES

Johnson has a lot going for him. He's intelligent, willing to work on his game, and as his college coach, Ben Jobe, put it, "He's the sanest player I've ever coached."

IN SUM

In a league where small points are increasingly becoming the norm, Johnson may stick, though he's strictly a backup because of his lack of firepower.

RICK'S RATINGS

Scoring: **D**
Shooting: **D**
Free Throw Shooting: **D**
Ball Handling: **A**
Passing: **A**

Defense: **B**
Defensive Rebounding: **D**
Playmaking: **B**
Intangibles: **A**
Overall: **C**

Buck Johnson

Birthdate: January 3, 1964
Height: 6-7
Weight: 200
College: University of Alabama, University, Ala.
Drafted: Houston on first round, 1986 (20th pick).
Position: Forward
Final 1989 Team: Houston Rockets
Final 1988–89 Statistics:

G	Fg	Fga	Fg%	Ft	Fta	Ft%	Orb	Reb	Ast	Stl	To	Blk	Pts	Ppg
67	270	515	.524	101	134	.754	114	286	126	64	110	35	642	9.6

Three-point goals: 1–9 (.111)   **TSP:** .525

SCORING

Johnson is a converted center playing the 3 spot—and as players like Kenny Walker and Brad Sellers can attest—the transition is not without its rough edges. Unlike most 3s, Johnson isn't an explosive scorer (second worst, per minute, among starting 3s) and, in fact, at this stage of his career he doesn't have the requisite small forward tools—in particular, a solid jumper or a going-to-the-basket game. After starting the first 31 games, he missed 15 games with a thigh bruise. He was then periodically a starter for the rest of the year. His weakness: he couldn't drill the jumper consistently, which allowed opponents to relentlessly double-team Akeem Olajuwon. Johnson's major assets are his jumping ability, speed, and quickness—he runs the break well—and he is active on the offensive glass (1.7 a game in 27.6 minutes). He has limited range (15 feet) and likes to shoot the jumper in the paint, but he can't easily manufacture his own shot.

DEFENSE/DEFENSIVE REBOUNDING

With the departure of Rodney McCray (to Sacramento), one of the league's top defenders, the question was whether Johnson could guard the likes of James Worthy and Alex English with any facility. One concern was whether Johnson, rail-thin at 6-7, 190, would get pushed around. But he gained 10 pounds in the summer of 1988. Add his quickness, ability to deny the ball, and good hands, and the results were satisfactory. Still, he needs to get tougher and more tenacious. He's below average on the defensive board, but that may be academic since his frontcourt mates are Akeem Olajuwon (1st in the league in rebounding) and Otis Thorpe (7th).

THE FLOOR GAME

In light of his background as a center, it's not surprising that Johnson needs work on his passing and ball handling skills. His knowledge of the game is improving.

INTANGIBLES

Johnson is a solid citizen, is well liked by his teammates, and has shown a tremendous desire to improve. A starter for the first time in 1988–89 (he's a three-year veteran), his confidence has ebbed and flowed.

IN SUM

Johnson is still a player in the making. He brings energy and movement to the Rockets' offense and solid effort to the defense. But his offensive skills could stand some refining, his jumper in particular. His skill level is that of a sub rather a starter.

RICK'S RATINGS

Scoring: **C**	Defense: **B**
Shooting: **C**	Defensive Rebounding: **C**
Free Throw Shooting: **B**	Intangibles: **A**
Ball Handling: **B**	Overall: **C +**
Passing: **B**	

Dennis Johnson

Birthdate: September 18, 1954
Height: 6-4
Weight: 200
College: Pepperdine University, Malibu, Calif.
Drafted: Seattle on second round as hardship case, 1976 (29th pick).
Position: Guard
Final 1989 Team: Boston Celtics
Final 1988–89 Statistics:

G	Fg	Fga	Fg%	Ft	Fta	Ft%	Orb	Reb	Ast	Stl	To	Blk	Pts	Ppg
72	277	638	.434	160	195	.821	31	190	472	94	175	21	721	10.0

Three-point goals: 7–50 (.140)   **TSP:** .440

SCORING

Beset by nagging injuries and age (he's 35 and 1989–90 is his final campaign), last season was DJ's worst as a Celtic. He scored only 10 a game, his lowest ppg since his rookie year, and his .434 from the field—Johnson is a notoriously below-average percentage shooter (.446 lifetime)—was his Boston low. The book on Johnson has always been that he's not a good outside shooter, but he'll kill you at crunch time. To a large extent, that's still true and he won four games for Boston last year with pressure shots. However, with no Larry Bird to relieve the pressure on McHale and Parish, Johnson's inefficiency from outside became more glaring. Compounding his ineffectiveness was his lack of productivity taking it to the hole. He didn't go as much (an Achilles' heel injury was the major reason), and when he did, he couldn't finish like he used to (when he was healthy, which was only briefly, there were vestiges of the old DJ). As for his perimeter game, he generally gets the open jumpers because of a double-team down low. Johnson is a poor three-point shooter (.140 last year; .180 lifetime) but a solid foul shooter (.821 in 1988–89; .796 for his career).

DEFENSE/DEFENSIVE REBOUNDING

Johnson, of course, has long been one of the league's most feared stoppers (he's been on the NBA All-Defensive first team six times—as recently as 1986–87—and the second team three times). His trademark: poking the ball away from the dribbler with his right hand at critical junctures (though he's never been in the top 10 steals or averaged more than 1.8 steals a game). But these days, he's vulnerable to quicker guards and has been called for a lot of reaching fouls coming from behind the ball handler.

THE FLOOR GAME

In the Celtics' move to the up-tempo game, Johnson was a bit out of his element (which is one reason he was switched to the 2 spot, while Brian Shaw took over at the point). He's never been fast and clearly has lost a step. He's a decent passer, if not a creative one, who makes the sound, rather than the spectacular, play. Lacking quickness and speed has forced him to be a cautious ball handler.

INTANGIBLES

The effort is there, but Johnson simply can't do it on a night-in, night-out basis. He can still make the big play, just not as consistently. But this past season, he provided veteran leadership and was particularly helpful with rookie Shaw, who will make a $1,000,000 playing in Italy.

IN SUM

Johnson heads into the last year of a glorious career, a career that nobody could imagine would last this long and be so productive. If he plays fewer minutes than last year (32.1 a game), he'll be more effective.

RICK'S RATINGS

Scoring: **D**   Defense: **A**
Shooting: **C**   Defensive Rebounding: **C**
Free Throw Shooting: **A** Playmaking: **B**
Ball Handling: **A**   Intangibles: **AAA**
Passing: **A**   Overall: **B**

Eddie Johnson

Birthdate: May 1, 1959
Height: 6-8
Weight: 218
College: University of Illinois, Champaign, Ill.
Drafted: Kansas City on second round, 1981 (29th pick).
Position: Forward
Final 1989 Team: Phoenix Suns

Final 1988–89 Statistics:

G	Fg	Fga	Fg%	Ft	Fta	Ft%	Orb	Reb	Ast	Stl	To	Blk	Pts	Ppg
70	608	1224	.497	217	250	.868	91	306	162	47	122	7	1504	21.5

Three-point goals: 71–172 (.413)   TSP: .526

SCORING

Johnson has a lot in common with Lamar Mundane. You know Lamar, the legendary playground whiz who "plays" for Reebok, the sharpshooter who shoots 35-footers raining out of the sky—layup. Well, move Eddie Johnson in about 12 to 15 feet, and it's the same—an automatic two. The eight-year veteran is as pure a shooter as there is in the league. And in 1988–89, Johnson, whose instant offense was one of the major reasons for Phoenix's dramatic turnaround, led all bench scorers with a 21.5 average (and won the Sixth Man Award) and shot career-bests from the field (.497) and three-point country (.413, sixth in the league). He doesn't put the ball on the floor well, so the obvious strategy is to deny him the ball. But Johnson is cagey and knows how to use picks, to play "possum" (acting like he's not involved in the play), and then move to get free. Once he has the ball, his quick release makes it extremely difficult to stop him. And when he's hot, call the fire department. In a game against the Clippers in November 1988, he scored 43 points—in a half! He can also play the post up game (he's 6-9, according the *NBA Register*, 6-7 says the Phoenix Suns media guide; the truth is likely somewhere in between) and will surprise you with an offensive rebound (1.3 a game). He's a terrific foul shooter (.868, ninth in the NBA). The only down note in his otherwise scintillating season was his playoff dropoff: 17.8 ppg and 41.3 percent from the field in three series.

DEFENSE/DEFENSIVE REBOUNDING

Johnson has had an all-O, no-D rep since he was a rookie, but he played a little defense last year. His drawbacks on defense are that he lacks quickness and doesn't move his feet that well. More of a runner than a 'bounder, he's a slightly below-average defensive rebounder who will forget to block out.

THE FLOOR GAME

Nobody confuses Johnson with say, Bernard King or Larry Bird, probably the best passers among 3s in the league. No, Johnson's a shooter all the way, but his passing is good enough (2.3 assists a game) that, if you run at him, he'll give it up. Just a fair ball handler, but he doesn't make many mistakes.

INTANGIBLES

A pro is a player who constantly improves his game. While maintaining his usual high offensive standards, Johnson made a commitment to playing D last year. He's a veteran who has helped the younger Suns on the court and is actively involved in charity work off the court.

IN SUM

Johnson's Sixth Man Award pretty much sums it up.

RICK'S RATINGS

Scoring: **AAA**
Shooting: **AAA**
Free Throw Shooting: **AA**
Ball Handling: **B**
Passing: **B**

Defense: **C**
Defensive Rebounding: **C**
Intangibles: **A**
Overall: **A +**

Frank Johnson

Birthdate: November 23, 1958
Height: 6-3
Weight: 185
College: Wake Forest University, Winston-Salem, N.C.
Drafted: Washington on first round, 1981 (11th pick).
Position: Guard
Final 1989 Team: Houston Rockets
Final 1988–89 Statistics:

G	Fg	Fga	Fg%	Ft	Fta	Ft%	Orb	Reb	Ast	Stl	To	Blk	Pts	Ppg
67	109	246	.443	75	93	.806	22	79	181	42	102	0	294	4.4

Three-point goals: 1–6 (.167)   **TSP:** .445

SCORING

Johnson, who backed up Sleepy Floyd at the point in Houston last season, has shown some decent scoring ability in an eight-year career (9.5 lifetime average and above average for backup 1s on a per minute basis), but his role in Houston's offense was to distribute rather than shoot. Which is appropriate as Johnson's eye has seen better days: Since shooting a career-high .489 with Washington in 1984–85, Johnson has put up some rather drab numbers: in 1985–86 .448, followed by .461, .434, and .443 last year. In 1988–89, he averaged a career-low 4.4 ppg in 879 minutes. Which is one reason he was considered expendable by the Rockets in the expansion draft—he was selected by Orlando. He relies on the pull-up jumper (he's good off the break) and penetrating moves—he's still very quick—to the hoop. Johnson is also expert at running the pick-and-roll and gets open off the screen or makes the pass for the easy deuce. He's been above 80 percent from the line the last two years (.806 in 1988–89 after never having been above .751).

DEFENSE/DEFENSIVE REBOUNDING

Quick and aggressive, Johnson is a decent defender who adjusts well to his opponent's abilities and follows the defensive system according to plan. For his position, he's an adequate defensive rebounder.

THE FLOOR GAME

Some feel Johnson's a better 2 than 1 (he's played both in his career) because he doesn't run the break that efficiently and tends to get ahead of himself with the ball. Last year, he had a less-than-impressive 1.77 assist-to-turnover ratio and didn't inspire confidence from his teammates. Actually he played better in the half-court game, where he got his teammates the ball and did the little things, like rewarding players (with the ball, that is) who had made a good defensive play.

INTANGIBLES

"A classy veteran who loves to compete," said one coach. And it's a promising sign that his fragile feet—stress fractures have forced him to miss major portions of three seasons (from 1985 to 1987 he played only 78 games)—have held up for the last two seasons.

IN SUM

Johnson was a disappointment in 1988–89. He shot poorly and his playmaking was below average. With three fairly talented point guards (there may be more) on Orlando's roster—Sam Vincent, Morlon Wiley, and Scott Skiles—Johnson will have trouble making the team.

RICK'S RATINGS

Scoring: **C**
Shooting: **D**
Free Throw Shooting: **A**
Ball Handling: **B**
Passing: **B**

Defense: **B**
Defensive Rebounding: **B**
Playmaking: **C**
Intangibles: **A**
Overall: **C –**

Kevin Johnson

Birthdate: March 4, 1966
Height: 6-1
Weight: 180
College: University of California, Berkeley, Calif.
Drafted: Cleveland on first round, 1987 (7th pick).
Position: Guard
Final 1989 Team: Phoenix Suns
Final 1988–89 Statistics:

G	Fg	Fga	Fg%	Ft	Fta	Ft%	Orb	Reb	Ast	Stl	To	Blk	Pts	Ppg
81	570	1128	.505	508	576	.882	46	340	991	135	322	24	1650	20.4

Three-point goals: 2–22 (.091)   **TSP:** .506

SCORING

When the Cavaliers drafted Kevin Johnson on the the first round (seventh pick overall) in 1987, a commonly heard refrain was: "Who's he?" And in his rookie year, first with the Cavs, and then with Phoenix (he was traded with Mark West and Tyrone Corbin for Larry Nance and Mike Sanders—draft picks were also exchanged—in February 1988) Kevin Johnson wasn't exactly a household name, either (9.2 ppg and 5.5 assists). But as he enters his third year, everybody with at least a passing interest in the NBA knows about KJ, as he is nicknamed. It's hard to be a secret after putting up these numbers: 20.4 ppg, 12.2 apg (third in the league), .505 from the field (up from .461), and .882 from the line (sixth in the league)—a masterful performance that earned him the Most Improved Player of the Year award. Johnson became only the fifth player in NBA history to score 20 or more points a game and average 10 or more assists per outing, joining an elite group comprised of Oscar Robertson, Isiah Thomas, Nate Archibald, and Magic Johnson. He has a game that leaves you awestruck at first glance—and on subsequent viewings, too. The 6-1, 180-pound point guard is a defender's nightmare: If you play off him, he'll destroy you with his stop-on-a dime jumper from 15 to 19 feet (he shot 2 of 22 from three-point land). And if you play him close, he'll blow by you with either hand—his left may be as strong as his right (he's right-handed)—and he is exceptionally quick to the rim. Fearless and strong despite his size, Johnson will draw the contact and get to the line (7.1 attempts a game), second only to Magic Johnson among starting 1s. Best way to "defend" Kevin Johnson: Deny him the ball early so he can't set the tempo of the game. Good luck! With his jumper and drive-either-way arsenal, he's basically unstoppable.

DEFENSE/DEFENSIVE REBOUNDING

Johnson is a fair defender and will get better. He's a ball hawk—his 1.7 steals a game led the Suns—but he needs to pick and choose his spots better. He does a good job of pressuring the ball, but his size hurts against bigger point guards and he tends to lose concentration when his man doesn't have the ball. A great leaper, he was third among starting points in defensive rebounding and averaged a solid 4.2 rebounds overall.

THE FLOOR GAME

For the Suns, the bottom line is to have the ball in Kevin Johnson's hands most of the time. He has the freedom to do pretty much as he pleases, and there isn't much he can't do. In the running game, few can accelerate under control like KJ; in the half-court setting, he penetrates and dishes as well as anybody in the league, though he might also decide to take it all the way or pull up for the shorter-range jumper. He's not a classic point—he's definitely looking to score—but, as noted, he was third in the league in assists and managed to keep gunslingers Eddie Johnson, Tom Chambers, and Armon Gilliam happy. He commits a lot of turnovers (four a game), but of course he has the ball most of the game and his assist-to-turnover ratio was an above-average 3.08.

INTANGIBLES

Johnson has become a quiet leader for the Suns. He's extraordinarily determined, plays hard, and is a complete team player. He's bright, coachable, and has already shown marked improvement in his two years in the league—a testament to his work ethic.

IN SUM

When Magic Johnson pulled a hamstring and couldn't play in the All-Star game, Kareem Abdul-Jabbar was selected in his place. Nice gesture, but come on, Kevin Johnson merited the selection based on *performance*. Johnson, however, will not be ignored too many times in the future. Phoenix has its point guard—one of the most talented and entertaining players in the league—for the 1990s.

RICK'S RATINGS

Scoring: **AA**
Shooting: **AAA**
Free Throw Shooting:
  AAA
Ball Handling: **AAA**
Passing: **AAA**

Defense: **B**
Defensive Rebounding: **B**
Playmaking: **AAA**
Intangibles: **AAA**
Overall: **AAA**

Magic Johnson

Birthdate: August 14, 1959
Height: 6-9
Weight: 226
College: Michigan State University, East Lansing, Mich.
Drafted: Los Angeles on first round as an undergraduate, 1979 (1st pick).
Position: Guard
Final 1989 Team: Los Angeles Lakers
Final 1988–89 Statistics:

G	Fg	Fga	Fg%	Ft	Fta	Ft%	Orb	Reb	Ast	Stl	To	Blk	Pts	Ppg
77	579	1137	.509	513	563	.911	111	607	988	138	312	22	1730	22.5

Three-point goals: 59–188 (.314)   **TSP:** .535

SCORING

He goes through you or around you. Over the top or down low. And he spends a lot of time at the line. In other words, he beats you every which way. Some of the pieces he's had from the get-go, others he added and refined as he's borne more of the Lakers' scoring responsibility. Until recently,

Johnson, entering his 11th season, had always been more comfortable in the classic playmaking role—getting teammates involved first, thinking about his points later. But at the beginning of the 1986–87 season, acknowledging the wear and tear on Kareem and the fact that the offense had become too predictable (sky hook, sky hook, sky hook), Laker coach Pat Riley structured the offense around Johnson, a reluctant scorer. He responded with a career-high 23.9 ppg, won the MVP award for the first time (the scuttlebutt was that Johnson never won the MVP because he didn't score enough), and led the Lakers to their fourth title in the 1980s. In 1987–88, his average dipped a bit (19.5 ppg), but last year, he had his second-best scoring year (22.5) and, not so coincidentally, won his second MVP. From the start, he's been a master at getting to the hole. He's a man of many moves—and oh, what moves! If you overplay him to the left, he'll spin right, attack the basket—nobody dribbles better in traffic—and jam it home. Or he'll go end to end: grab a rebound (he's the best defensive rebounder among starting 1s—both last season and lifetime), charge up court, and toss up one of those dipsy-doos or simply overpower his man to the hoop and get fouled (7.3 free throw attempts a game; although to say that Magic gets the benefit of the doubt on calls is a major understatement). And last year—typical of the ever-evolving Magic man—he was the top foul shooter in the league (.911). Recently, we've also seen the full flowering of his post-up game, in particular a Jabbar-clone that Magic calls "the junior, junior, sky hook." At 6-9, he's never had trouble getting the shot over his invariably smaller defender. But as he's moved in, he's also moved out. Early in his career, his perimeter game was suspect; later, he improved his accuracy from 16 to 20 feet. And in 1988–89, for the first time, he became a legitimate three-point threat (entering the season, he had made 58 threes for his career and shot a dismal .192; last year, he was 59-for-188, an OK .314, slightly below the league average of .323). His is a set shot; a rare sight is Magic shooting the jumper off the dribble.

DEFENSE/DEFENSIVE REBOUNDING

Defense is not Johnson's natural habitat. He doesn't move well laterally—he's vulnerable to quicker, small guards—but the problem is mitigated because his backcourt partner, Byron Scott, can play the points and James Worthy matches up well against many 2s, leaving Magic to guard 4s and even some 5s (such as Bill Laimbeer). But he's a savvy team defender and plays the passing lanes well. Little-remembered stat: Johnson led the league in steals in 1981–82 and 1982–83 and had a team-leading 138 last year. Johnson's uniqueness is revealed by a statistic that's been synonymous with his name: the triple double (double figures in points, assists, and rebounds). Quality point guards regularly have 10 or more points and assists but rarely that many rebounds. Johnson, big enough to play both forward positions (and even center, as he did in that memorable title-clinching game in 1980 against the 76ers), has averaged as many as 9.6 rebounds a year and had 17 triple doubles last year, tops in the NBA. Little-recognized stat (except by the Laker coaching staff): Johnson hadn't pulled down more than 392 defensive rebounds in the past five seasons; he grabbed 496 in 1988–89, his second-highest total in the pros.

THE FLOOR GAME

A 6-9 point guard? Magic is one-of-a-kind just by virtue of his size and the position he plays. But, of course, his "magic" is founded on a lot more than his dimensions. For one, there is his extraordinary court awareness, that special intuitive sense of where players are and where they are going to be. But as Bob Cousy, who had a similar sixth sense, once noted, it's not enough to have great vision; you need the tools and the willingness to get the ball to your teammates. And Johnson has an extensive repertoire of passes—the no-look pass, the baseball pass, the touch pass, the bowling pass, something different every night. And he's also well aware that it's his responsibility to keep his teammates happy by getting them the ball. He's frequently paid the ultimate basketball compliment: he makes his teammates better. And they are never more efficient than when Johnson takes the outlet pass and leads one of the most exciting weapons in basketball: the Laker fast break. He's an excellent dribbler in the open court and is expert at dishing off at precisely the right time to the right man. There's an aura of unpredictability about what he's going to do—which is why he's so much fun to watch—but his decisions are consistently the right ones. He turns the ball over frequently (4.1 times a game last season though he had a solid 3.17 assist-to-turnover ratio), but that's expected since he takes chances and handles the ball so much.

INTANGIBLES

Magic is about the fourth quarter, crunch time, buzzer beaters, wins, division championships, rings. He's the best momentum stopper in the league; nobody has a keener sense of when his team needs a boost—and nobody so unfailingly produces when it counts. On and off the court, he's one of the *world's* most respected athletes—charismatic, genuine, accessible.

IN SUM

Since we've already given the nod to Michael Jordan as the best ever, where does that leave Magic Johnson? His coach, Riley, is fond of saying that you have to distinguish *best* player from *most valuable* (and two awards should be given accordingly). Last year, Magic was MVP and Jordan placed second, and you could make a cogent argument that the award should have been shared. But Johnson has no competition when it comes time to picking the MVP of the decade. Five championships in ten years—with Magic running the Show(time)—is very persuasive evidence.

RICK'S RATINGS

Scoring: **AAA**   Defense: **B**
Shooting: **AA**   Defensive Rebounding:
Free Throw Shooting: **AAA**
  AAA   Playmaking: **AAA**
Ball Handling: **AAA**   Intangibles: **AAA**
Passing: **AAA**   Overall: **AAA**

Steve Johnson

Birthdate: November 3, 1957
Height: 6-10
Weight: 235
College: Oregon State University, Corvallis, Ore.
Drafted: Kansas City on first round, 1981 (7th pick).
Positions: Center, Forward
Final 1989 Team: Portland Trail Blazers
Final 1988–89 Statistics:

G	Fg	Fga	Fg%	Ft	Fta	Ft%	Orb	Reb	Ast	Stl	To	Blk	Pts	Ppg
72	296	565	.524	129	245	.527	135	358	105	20	140	44	721	10.0

Three-point goals: 0—0 (.000)   **TSP:** .524

SCORING

Johnson, a center/power forward who played with the Trail Blazers the last three years and was selected by Minnesota in the expansion draft, is one of the best low-post players in the league. He has a bundle of moves, great footwork, and an excellent touch around the basket. He also has a knack for sealing off his defender, receiving the ball, and then making it all look so easy as he spins to the hoop. Johnson almost always gets the shot he wants, which is often a layup. Not surprisingly, he's consistently one of the top percentage shooters in the league: He shot .524 last year, has been over 60 percent three times, is a lifetime .574 shooter, and his .746 as a senior at Oregon State is still the NCAA record. He also relies on a jump hook. Johnson has never been a good offensive rebounder (not quick, not a leaper), though he did a nice job (1.9 a game) last year. His Achilles' heel is foul shooting. He draws fouls but he's a dreadful .635 for his career, shot .527 in 1988–89, has thrice been under 60 percent (and in 1982–83 his field goal percentage, .624, was higher than his free throw percentage, .574).

DEFENSE/DEFENSIVE REBOUNDING

Johnson will get *his* and the Timberwolves can only hope that his man doesn't get *his*. Like many scorers, he doesn't have the defensive mind-set; never has, and now, after eight years in the league, it's safe to say he never will. He's been in foul trouble since his career began. As a result, he backs off his man, playing "softer" than he has to. Johnson has never had more than 100 blocks in a season and is an average defensive rebounder, who relies on positioning rather than jumping ability.

THE FLOOR GAME

When he's healthy, Johnson runs the floor wide and hard. He's a fair passer who has improved his passing from the post when he's double-teamed, but he won't remind anybody of Brad Daugherty. With almost two turnovers a game (in only 20.5 minutes), Johnson makes too many mistakes.

INTANGIBLES

The big if with Johnson is his health. He's 32 and missed 10 games last year (and 39 the previous year) because of an assortment of injuries; he is rarely 100 percent physically. Then there's his mood: If Johnson is playing and contributing, all's right with the world. When he's not, he's a completely different person. While he volunteered at the beginning of last season to come off the bench, he was not happy with his playing time. That shouldn't be an issue this year as he is targeted as Minnesota's starting center.

IN SUM

Johnson is a proven scorer—and a center—a rare combination for an expansion club. When he's on, he's basically unstoppable; when he's not, his defensive weaknesses can hurt a team. Along with Tyrone Corbin and Ricky Mahorn, he forms a frontcourt that is considerably more competitive than most expansion combos.

RICK'S RATINGS

Scoring: **A**
Shooting: **AA**
Free Throw Shooting: **D**
Ball Handling: **C**
Passing: **C**

Defense: **C**
Defensive Rebounding: **C**
Shot Blocking: **B**
Intangibles: **C**
Overall: **B –**

Vinnie Johnson

Birthdate: September 1, 1956
Height: 6-3
Weight: 200
College: Baylor University, Waco, Tex.
Drafted: Seattle on first round, 1979 (7th pick).
Position: Guard
Final 1989 Team: Detroit Pistons

Final 1988–89 Statistics:

G	Fg	Fga	Fg%	Ft	Fta	Ft%	Orb	Reb	Ast	Stl	To	Blk	Pts	Ppg
82	462	996	.464	193	263	.734	109	255	242	74	105	17	1130	13.8

Three-point goals: 13–44 (.295)   **TSP:** .470

SCORING

His secret is out. Johnson, alias the Microwave, takes ginseng, a Chinese herb believed to have medicinal properties, both before and during games. Helps his conditioning, he says. Whatever turns you on, Vinnie, whatever turns you on. Johnson, of course, has made the phrase, "heats up in a hurry" a part of the basketball lexicon. His role is to provide instant offense, and last season—after an off 1987–88, when he shot a career low .443—more often than not the 33-year-old Microwave was on. He is, by all accounts, streaky; a career .474 shooter, Johnson has been over 47 percent (.473 in 1983–84) only once in the last six seasons and is a career .449 shooter in the playoffs. But when he's firing on all cylinders, he's unstoppable. You can get in his face; you can leave him alone; he'll score. VJ is the quintessential playground player, a consummate one-on-one artist who can most definitely create for himself off the dribble (he likes to go behind his back or through his legs) but also has made a living coming off of baseline screens for his hard-to-block jumper. When the jump shot isn't there, he can take it to the hole (either hand), and with that strong body (6-3, 200), take the contact and finish the play. And his missed shots often end up in his own hands; he's an effective offensive rebounder for his position (1.3 caroms in 25.9 minutes). He shoots three-pointers, but not accurately (.295 last year, his career high; .241 lifetime); his game is midrange. Not a particularly good foul shooter, either: .734 last year; .759 lifetime.

DEFENSE/DEFENSIVE REBOUNDING

The offensive-minded Johnson has never focused on D (which is one of the reasons he's not a starter) but he's improved considerably in the last few years. As one source explained it, "He plays defense at a level you can win championships with." His assets are strength and his knowledge of the game; his weakness is that he doesn't have particularly good technique and his decision-making in transition defense (i.e., he might not give the good hard foul that will stop the basket) has been questioned. A below-average defensive rebounder, for a 2.

THE FLOOR GAME

Like his backcourt mates, Joe Dumars and Isiah Thomas, Johnson is an interchangeable guard and can play both the 1 and the 2. In other words, he's a fine ball handler and an underrated passer (three assists a game in 1988–89).

INTANGIBLES

When Johnson is scoring and shooting well, his whole game picks up: defense, rebounding, passing. The flip side is that when he's off, the rest of his game also suffers. He needs his minutes and he needs his shots; otherwise he tends to get moody. Johnson is a delight be around: he's funny, charming, a stimulating conversationalist.

IN SUM

At his age, any traces of slowing down are cause for concern. But last year, Johnson gave every indication that the heat indeed is still on.

RICK'S RATINGS

Scoring: **AAA**
Shooting: **B**
Free Throw Shooting: **C**
Ball Handling: **A**
Passing: **A**

Defense: **B**
Defensive Rebounding: **C**
Intangibles: **A**
Overall: **A+**

Anthony Jones

Birthdate: September 13, 1962
Height: 6-6
Weight: 195
College: University of Nevada, Las Vegas, Las Vegas, Nev.
Drafted: Washington on first round, 1986 (21st pick).
Position: Guard
Final 1989 Team: Dallas Mavericks
Final 1988–89 Statistics:

G	Fg	Fga	Fg%	Ft	Fta	Ft%	Orb	Reb	Ast	Stl	To	Blk	Pts	Ppg
33	29	79	.367	14	16	.875	14	28	17	11	5	3	78	2.3

Three-point goals: 4–16 (.250)   **TSP:** .392

SCORING

Jones, who backed up Rolando Blackman at the 2 for part of the year (since the Mavs used a three-guard rotation—Blackman, Derek Harper, and either Brad Davis or Morlon Wiley—that didn't provide Jones with many minutes, 5.9 a game), has bounced around since being drafted in the first round by the Bullets in 1986. He played 16 games with the Bullets, was cut, then caught on with the Spurs where he averaged 5.8 points in 49 games. But at the end of the season, the Spurs waived him. He played the 1987–88 season in the CBA, which was followed by a stint with the 6-5 and under World Basketball League. In 1988–89, he started the season with the Chicago Bulls, lasted eight games, went back to the CBA, and was picked up by the Mavericks in February. Perhaps he's finally found a basketball home, because Dallas insiders like his range (three-point), his quickness, and his ability to run the floor. Of course, he only shot .367 but, and you've heard this before: he didn't get many shot opportunities (29-for-79). He likes to pull up in transition, will jam the offensive rebound, and can get to the hole, particularly on the baseline.

DEFENSE/DEFENSIVE REBOUNDING

Jones, say those same insiders, is a pretty good defender. He moves his feet well and gets after people, though he lacks strength. Nothing exceptional as a defensive rebounder.

THE FLOOR GAME

In very limited minutes, Jones registered a superb 3.40

assist-to-turnover ratio. He knows how to play. With its relatively ponderous first team (Adrian Dantley, Sam Perkins, and James Donaldson), Dallas is looking to get speed off the bench, and Jones could help.

INTANGIBLES

He's hungry, he picks things up quickly, but a few sources said his mental toughness is an issue.

IN SUM

Seemingly, the physical tools are there. But he probably won't get the minutes he needs in Dallas.

RICK'S RATINGS

Scoring: **B**
Shooting: **C**
Free Throw Shooting: **AA**
Ball Handling: **A**
Passing: **A**

Defense: **B**
Defensive Rebounding: **B**
Intangibles: **C**
Overall: **C**

Bill Jones

Birthdate: March 18, 1966
Height: 6-7
Weight: 180
College: University of Iowa, Iowa City, Ia.
Drafted: Free Agent
Positions: Forward, Guard
Final 1989 Team: New Jersey Nets
Final 1988–89 Statistics:

G	Fg	Fga	Fg%	Ft	Fta	Ft%	Orb	Reb	Ast	Stl	To	Blk	Pts	Ppg
37	50	102	.490	29	43	.674	20	47	20	17	18	6	129	3.5

Three-point goals: 0–1 (.000)   **TSP:** .490

SCORING

If Jones, who came to the Nets from the CBA in January, wants a steady job in the NBA, he will have to improve both his outside shooting and his ability to put the ball on the floor. A 6-7 small forward who can swing to the off-guard—of course, at either the 2 or the 3, the description of the prototype model includes scoring punch. Jones shot a decent percentage, .490, last season but for now his is a slow release and he tends to shoot straight-legged, from limited range. One asset: he runs the floor well.

DEFENSE/DEFENSIVE REBOUNDING

You've heard this before: the offense is suspect, the defense is A-OK. New Jersey likes Jones' D. He can deny the ball, takes a charge, and has excellent anticipation (tied for third, per minute, among backup 3s in steals. He played 37 games and 307 minutes). But at 180 pounds, he's entirely too skinny and doesn't match up well against bulkier 3s for extended minutes. A below-average defensive rebounder for his position.

THE FLOOR GAME

Jones can and will pass the ball. His basketball IQ is more than adequate.

INTANGIBLES

"A superkid, responsive to coaching," said one coach.

IN SUM

Jones needs major surgery on his offense. But his D and his attitude are two reasons you may periodically see him on the end of an NBA bench.

RICK'S RATINGS

Scoring: **C**
Shooting: **B**
Free Throw Shooting: **D**
Ball Handling: **B**
Passing: **B**

Defense: **A**
Defensive Rebounding: **C**
Intangibles: **B**
Overall: **C**

Caldwell Jones

Birthdate: August 4, 1950
Height: 6-11
Weight: 225
College: Albany State College, Albany, Ga.
Drafted: Philadelphia on second round, 1973 (32nd pick).
Positions: Center, Forward
Final 1989 Team: Portland Trail Blazers
Final 1988–89 Statistics:

G	Fg	Fga	Fg%	Ft	Fta	Ft%	Orb	Reb	Ast	Stl	To	Blk	Pts	Ppg
72	77	183	.421	48	61	.787	88	300	59	24	83	85	202	2.8

Three-point goals: 0–1 (.000)   **TSP:** .421

SCORING

Well, he scored in the ABA! Yes, Jones goes back that far, back to 1973 when he started his professional career with none other than the San Diego Conquistadores (Trivia question: Who was the player/coach of that outfit? Answer: Wilt Chamberlain). Jones, who with the retirement of Kareem Abdul-Jabbar, becomes the oldest player (39) in the league (by far) actually averaged 15.8 a game for his three seasons in the ABA. (Moses Malone is the only other active NBA player to have seen ABA action.) But he's been a single-digit guy ever since; in 13 NBA seasons, he's come close to double figures several times (9.3, 9.5, and 9.9), but no cigar. This eschewing of the scoring function is evidently in the bloodline, since his brother, Charles Jones of the Bullets (2.6 ppg in 21.8 minutes in 1988–89), has also carved out a career in which making baskets is not a central part of the equation. In the NBA, Caldwell, who signed with the Spurs in July as an unrestricted free agent, simply has never looked to score—8.3 shots a game are the most he's ever attempted. Word is he was once a pretty fair jump shooter, but these days he'll score on putbacks (1.2 offensive rebounds a game last season), a little hook, and layups from guard penetration.

DEFENSE/DEFENSIVE REBOUNDING

Jones has made a very nice living for himself because he plays defense. The component parts include intelligence, lateral quickness (still), shot blocking ability (still; 1.2 a game last year in 17.8 minutes) and versatility—he can guard all frontcourt players (he has, historically, given fits to players such as Adrian Dantley). He's not physical—reed-like at 6-11, 225—but difficult to drive around. He's also been a solid defensive rebounder for his career (in 1988–89, he was above average for backup 4s).

THE FLOOR GAME

Decent passer, obviously he'll give it up. He even runs the floor.

INTANGIBLES

Teammates respect and admire Jones just for being out there. He fulfills the veteran role to a T, offering advice to younger players, serving as a role model for all. Nothing but a team player.

IN SUM

He can't play big minutes, but you couldn't imagine a better player to teach David Robinson about life in the NBA.

RICK'S RATINGS

Scoring: **D**	Defense: **A**
Shooting: **D**	Defensive Rebounding: **A**
Free Throw Shooting: **B**	Shot Blocking: **A**
Ball Handling: **B**	Intangibles: **A**
Passing: **B**	Overall: **B**

Charles Jones

Birthdate: April 3, 1957
Height: 6-9
Weight: 215
College: Albany State College, Albany, Ga.
Drafted: Phoenix on eighth round, 1979 (165th pick).
Positions: Center, Forward
Final 1989 Team: Washington Bullets
Final 1988–89 Statistics:

G	Fg	Fga	Fg%	Ft	Fta	Ft%	Orb	Reb	Ast	Stl	To	Blk	Pts	Ppg
53	60	125	.480	16	25	.640	77	257	42	39	39	76	136	2.6

Three-point goals: 0–1 (.000)   **TSP:** .480

SCORING

The story goes that when Charles Jones and his brother Caldwell (now a Spur) would play one-on-one, nobody would score! Caldwell, whose highest average was 9.9 ppg, is a veritable scoring machine compared to Charles, who doesn't have an ounce of offense in his stickly 6-9, 215-pound frame. To say that he's not offensive-minded is putting it mildly: In 21.8 minutes a game, he averaged all of 2.6 ppg, hands-down the least "offensive" numbers for starters (he started 45 games at center for the Bullets) in the league. He reportedly has a 15-footer, but it hasn't been sighted since he graduated from Albany State. Jones runs the court well but nobody can remember him finishing a play. He's an adequate offensive rebounder and, what a surprise, he rarely gets to the line (only 25 foul shots in 1,154 minutes).

DEFENSE/DEFENSIVE REBOUNDING

If Jones is inconspicuous on the offensive end, the same can't be said for his defense. He has survived three NBA teams, three CBA teams, a year in Italy, a year in France, (not to mention being waived five times), all on the strength of his defense. He's a premier shot blocker (1.4 a game last year; career-wise, third, per minute, among starting centers), particularly from the weak side, who is quick, has excellent timing, can jump, and moves well laterally. He can guard both 4s and 5s, though he's usually overmatched by the bigger centers in the league. However, he's a below-average rebounder.

THE FLOOR GAME

Jones does the dirty work—sets picks, blocks out, plays

defense—that coaches rave about. A fair passer who doesn't take chances with the ball, he shouldn't put the ball on the floor except to create a better passing angle.

INTANGIBLES

Jones is a team player, almost to a fault, since he'd be more effective if he shot the ball more. He's a coach's player who works hard both during games and in practice.

IN SUM

Jones has a specialty: defense. Because of his limited O, it's easy to say that he's a backup center. But consider: After missing 24 games (from December to February) with a torn ligament in his knee, Jones played one game as a reserve and then returned to the starting lineup on February 18. The Bullets, 18–30 at that point, proceeded to go 22–12 the rest of the year. Of course, whether Washington could sustain that pace for an entire year with Jones at center is another question. Any way you look at it, however, it's obvious that Jones' D and attitude are invaluable to the Bullets.

RICK'S RATINGS

Scoring: **D**
Shooting: **D**
Free Throw Shooting: **D**
Ball Handling: **C**
Passing: **B**

Defense: **AA**
Defensive Rebounding: **D**
Shot Blocking: **AA**
Intangibles: **AA**
Overall: **B**

Charles A. Jones

Birthdate: January 12, 1962
Height: 6-8
Weight: 215
College: University of Louisville, Louisville, Ky.
Drafted: Phoenix on second round, 1984 (36th pick).
Position: Forward
Final 1989 Team: Washington Bullets
Final 1988–89 Statistics:

G	Fg	Fga	Fg%	Ft	Fta	Ft%	Orb	Reb	Ast	Stl	To	Blk	Pts	Ppg
43	38	82	.463	33	53	.623	54	140	18	18	22	16	110	2.6

Three-point goals: 1–3 (.333) **TSP:** .470

SCORING

If you read your Bullets box scores carefully last year, you know that Washington had cornered the market on Charles Joneses. There was C. Jones, the center. And power forward C.A. Jones, the subject at hand. This Charles Jones, attended Louisville, was drafted by Phoenix in 1984, played there for two seasons, moved onto Portland for one, and is not part of the Caldwell/Charles/Major Jones family, all of whom have played in the NBA. Now that you have him clearly placed in your mind, note that both Charles Joneses are notorious non-scorers; Charles Jones, the center, averaged 2.6 ppg in 21.8 minutes while this C.J. would barely have averaged 10 if he played the entire game. His one

major asset he brings to the game is his work on the offensive glass, in a mere 12 minutes a game, he averaged 1.3 offensive caroms.

DEFENSE/DEFENSIVE REBOUNDING

Jones, a 4, has 'tweener size at 6-8, 215; he's physical but he just isn't big enough or strong enough to be much of a presence. He's an adequate shot blocker and defensive rebounder.

THE FLOOR GAME

A fair ball handler and passer. Same goes for his ability to run the floor.

INTANGIBLES

"Nice kid, soft-spoken, good practice player," said one source.

IN SUM

A 12th man, easily replaceable, with limited skills, and undersized, to boot. Jones is free to negotiate with any team, and was in Miami's free agent camp this past summer.

RICK'S RATINGS

Scoring: **D**
Shooting: **D**
Free Throw Shooting: **D**
Ball Handling: **B**
Passing: **B**

Defense: **C**
Defensive Rebounding: **B**
Shot Blocking: **B**
Intangibles: **B**
Overall: **C –**

Shelton Jones

Birthdate: April 6, 1966
Height: 6-9
Weight: 210
College: St. John's University, Jamaica, N.Y.
Drafted: San Antonio on second round, 1988 (27th pick).
Position: Forward
Final 1989 Team: Philadelphia 76ers
Final 1988–89 Statistics:

G	Fg	Fga	Fg%	Ft	Fta	Ft%	Orb	Reb	Ast	Stl	To	Blk	Pts	Ppg
49	90	204	.441	58	80	.725	30	111	40	18	46	15	238	4.9

Three-point goals: 0–1 (.000) **TSP:** .441

SCORING

Shelton Jones, where are you? Jones, a second-round pick of the Spurs in 1988, led the league last year in addresses. He opened in San Antonio (nine games). Next stop was Golden State (he was traded to the Warriors for Jerome Whitehead), where he lasted two games. After the Warriors waived him, on to Philadelphia, where he finished the season. And finally, Minnesota, who selected him in the expansion draft. In Philly, where he got the most playing time (42 games), he played the old Iavaroni role: start the game, play six minutes (giving way to Ron Anderson), sit the rest of the half, start the third quarter, another six minutes, and then the bench for the duration. Tough way to develop any offensive rhythm, but the fact is three NBA teams have already passed on Jones because they discovered that the 6-9 small forward provides little punch from a position that requires it. His jumper is erratic at best and while he's an excellent jumper and runner—his athletic ability is what's keeping him in the league—he was an inconsistent finisher. You'd think with that live body he'd get some offensive rebounds but he didn't.

DEFENSE/DEFENSIVE REBOUNDING

Jones showed an ability to guard 3s on the perimeter—but his concentration was poor. Pretty good numbers on the defensive glass. He was an excellent shot blocker at St. John's and showed some potential in that area last year.

THE FLOOR GAME

Jones needs an open-court, transition team because his game is running the court. His handling and passing skills are adequate.

INTANGIBLES

In San Antonio, they questioned his mental toughness; in Philadelphia, his work ethic and consistency. A good kid but he doesn't yet understand what it takes to be an NBA player.

IN SUM

Might hang for awhile because he's a live body. Needs some offense and more diligence defensively.

RICK'S RATINGS

Scoring: **D**	Defense: **B**
Shooting: **D**	Defensive Rebounding: **B**
Free Throw Shooting: **C**	Intangibles: **C**
Ball Handling: **B**	Overall: **C –**
Passing: **B**	

Michael Jordan

Birthdate: February 17, 1963
Height: 6-6

Weight: 195
College: University of North Carolina, Chapel Hill, N.C.
Drafted: Chicago on first round as an undergraduate, 1984 (3rd pick).
Position: Guard
Final 1989 Team: Chicago Bulls
Final 1988–89 Statistics:

G	Fg	Fga	Fg%	Ft	Fta	Ft%	Orb	Reb	Ast	Stl	To	Blk	Pts	Ppg
81	966	1795	.538	674	793	.850	149	652	650	234	290	65	2633	32.5

Three-point goals: 27–98 (.276)   **TSP:** .546

SCORING

Maybe the best way to approach this is to ask: What *doesn't* he do well? For one, he was a subpar three-point shooter, .276, in 1988–89 (which was, however, a dramatic improvement over his .132 in 1987–88). Next, well there is no "next." As Kings coach Jerry Reynolds put it, "He's so good it's a joke."

Nobody has ever played in the air better: Jordan's dunks, his aerodynamics, his body control (not to mention his tongue!) already are the stuff of legend. If Dominique Wilkins is the "Human Highlight Film," Michael Jordan is an entire collection.

But first he has to get to the hoop. He's absolutely devastating off the dribble. Like the great running back he could have been (could still be?), he needs only a crack in the defense—nobody has a better first step—and he's gone. The result: a hoop, a hoop and a foul, or two shots; he was third in the league in free throw attempts (9.8 a game) and at .850, is an excellent foul shooter.

Air Jordan thrives on the drive, but you can't concede the jumper. Once a streaky shooter, it's now automatic (a guard-leading .538 from the field; tied with John Stockton) and impossible to stop because, à la Jerry West, Jordan stops on a dime and is up quickly. He's the best one-on-one player in the league. For that matter, he's the best one-on-two player (the double-team is essential to even conceive of stopping him) in the league. In fact, as the Pistons showed in the 1987–88 playoffs, the only way to stop Jordan is to triple-team him and force him to give up the ball: after all, even Michael Jordan can't score without the ball. He is the most dominant offensive player since Wilt Chamberlain and the first to win three consecutive scoring championships (32.5 ppg last year) since George Gervin did it from 1978–80.

DEFENSE/DEFENSIVE REBOUNDING

Wonder of wonders, in 1987–88, Jordan won the scoring title *and* the Defensive Player of the Year award. This may seem to be a contradiction in terms, but Michael Jordan is making up the rules as he goes along. The mere fact that he even plays defense—he was selected to the all-defensive first team last year—is to his credit. After all, in 1988–89 he led the league in minutes played (40.2 a game) and expends tremendous energy on offense. His major defensive assets include: his ability to create turnovers via steals—his 2.9 steals a game last season were third in the league—and blocks (65); transition defense—there are few better in the league; and his ubiquitous presence on the weak side. And it should come as no surprise that he's now one of the top rebounding guards in the league (eight a game in 1988–89).

THE FLOOR GAME

One of Jordan's goals in 1988–89 was to shoot less, pass more. With Bill Cartwright now in the middle, and a maturing Scottie Pippen, Horace Grant, and Brad Sellers, it was thought best, following the 1987–88 playoff debacle with Detroit (where the Bulls were exposed as a one-man team), to spread the offense around. But for most of the year Jordan's assists remained essentially the same, about seven a game, and observers felt that he simply didn't pass the ball enough. But then, in March, in what was undoubtedly the most heralded position switch in NBA history (sports history?), Jordan was switched to the 1 (for several reasons: Sam Vincent wasn't doing the job; to reduce the double and triple-teams on Jordan; to better exploit Chicago's perimeter players, in particular Craig Hodges; because Jordan likes a challenge; and to restore offensive balance—Jordan often found himself under the basket as a shooting guard and his man would leak out for an easy two). In the past, when Jordan went to work, the other Bulls had a tendency to stand and admire; now they were more involved in the play. It was a brilliant move and all very simple: Jordan penetrates—which he can do at will; Hodges, John Paxson, or Scottie Pippen spot up; and Jordan, with his see-the-whole-court vision, either finishes the play (short jumper, air dunk, what have you) or delivers the ball—and, oh, can he thread the needle. How about his ability to handle the ball against pressure? Ask the Knicks, who saw their vaunted press/trap defense shredded by Jordan's prestidigitation. Yes, his assist total increased to 10.7 a game, while playing the position during the regular season, and 7.6 a game in the playoffs. But the bottom line is that the Bulls advanced to the Eastern Conference finals.

INTANGIBLES

No shortage of superlatives here, either. Jordan is a remarkably ferocious competitor and clutch player (see fifth game, Cleveland vs. Chicago series, three seconds left) who hates to lose, plays hurt, provides on and off the court leadership. A once in a lifetime person and player.

IN SUM

The best ever? Until that fateful day in March, naysayers could argue Jordan didn't make his teammates better. But that argument lost its potency when Jordan became a point guard and showed that other Bulls can indeed thrive even though Jordan is the SHOW. Doubters could also contend that Jordan has competition on the offensive end—Oscar Robertson, as the cognoscenti have pointed out, *averaged* a triple double his second year in the league. But what sets Jordan apart, beyond his clear stylistic edge (which really doesn't make him better, just more fun to watch) is the mix of offense *and* defensive prowess. That combination has never been matched.

RICK'S RATINGS

Scoring: **AAA**
Shooting: **AAA**
Free Throw Shooting: **AA**
Ball Handling: **AAA**
Passing: **AAA**
Defense: **AAA**

Defensive Rebounding: **AAA**
Playmaking: **AAA**
Intangibles: **AAA**
Overall: **AAA**

Tim Kempton

Birthdate: January 25, 1964
Height: 6-10
Weight: 245
College: University of Notre Dame, Notre Dame, Ind.
Drafted: Los Angeles Clippers on sixth round, 1986 (124th pick).
Positions: Center, Forward
Final 1989 Team: Charlotte Hornets
Final 1988–89 Statistics:

G	Fg	Fga	Fg%	Ft	Fta	Ft%	Orb	Reb	Ast	Stl	To	Blk	Pts	Ppg
79	171	335	.510	142	207	.686	91	304	102	41	121	14	484	6.1

Three-point goals: 0–1 (.000)   **TSP:** .510

SCORING

Who knew? In his four years at Notre Dame, Kempton's scoring average *declined* each year (from 10.6 in his freshman year to 6.5 in his senior year). The Clippers' sixth-round pick in 1986, he averaged 4.4 ppg in limited action in his rookie year but couldn't stick with a team that won 12 games. Then he went abroad (Europe), got some seasoning, worked on his moves, and showed last year that he can score in the NBA (6.1 a game and above-average on a per minute basis among backup centers). His specialty is driving to the basket (either hand), which is distinctive considering he's a 6-10 center. With that size, he's quicker than most of the players he's up against. Kempton can also get to the line (third among backup 5s with 2.62 attempts a game) though he shot only .686 from the stripe. If he could drill his outside jumper consistently (range is 10 to 12 feet), he could be downright dangerous; instead, he tends to look for the drive every time.

DEFENSE/DEFENSIVE REBOUNDING

While his size is a benefit on offense, on defense Kempton usually gives away two inches or more a night. He has particular trouble with bigger, quicker centers. He is not a shot blocker (a mere 14 blocks in 1,341 minutes), and his defensive rebounding—which was slightly above average for backup centers—depends on positioning and blocking out. He's only a fair jumper.

THE FLOOR GAME

Kempton is turnover-prone and has a tendency to force the action. But he runs the floor well.

INTANGIBLES

Kempton is another blue-collar player who has to overcome his physical liabilities by sheer hustle. A classic NBA overachiever.

IN SUM

Kempton's above-average scoring ability and hell-bent-for-leather attitude are marketable assets that could keep him in the league for a while. He was traded to Denver in September for a second-round pick.

RICK'S RATINGS

Scoring: **C**   Defense: **C**
Shooting: **C**   Defensive Rebounding: **B**
Free Throw Shooting: **D**   Shot Blocking: **D**
Ball Handling: **D**   Intangibles: **A**
Passing: **C**   Overall: **D**

Steve Kerr

Birthdate: September 27, 1965
Height: 6-3
Weight: 175
College: University of Arizona, Tucson, Ariz.
Drafted: Phoenix on second round, 1988 (50th pick).
Position: Guard
Final 1989 Team: Phoenix Suns
Final 1988–89 Statistics:

G	Fg	Fga	Fg%	Ft	Fta	Ft%	Orb	Reb	Ast	Stl	To	Blk	Pts	Ppg
26	20	46	.435	6	9	.667	3	17	24	7	6	0	54	2.1

Three-point goals: 8–17 (.471)   **TSP:** .522

SCORING

Leave Kerr open at your peril. He's a Craig Hodges/Jon Sundvold type: a smallish 2, 6-3 (who can also play the point), with downtown range. Consider that last season, his rookie year, he took only 46 shots (in 26 games; he was on the injured list twice with tendinitis in his left ankle) but 17 were threes, of which he canned eight for an eye-popping .471. And in his senior year at Arizona, he netted 114 of 199 trifectas for .573. (Further note: Kerr shot *65* percent in his senior year in high school.) But he needs room to shoot, since quickness is not his game nor can he create much off the dribble. And driving to the hoop is not part of his repertoire. In other words, he's a spot-up shooter.

DEFENSE/DEFENSIVE REBOUNDING

The pluses: He's smart, understands help defense, comes from a quality program. The minuses: he's slow, his lateral quickness is questionable, and he's not at all physical.

THE FLOOR GAME

While he's still adjusting to the pro point position, Kerr takes good care of the ball, sees the court, and can deliver the ball to the open man. But he lacks explosiveness to the hoop; he's not a penetrator.

INTANGIBLES

Kerr is a coach-on-the-floor sort. He's Mr. Solid Citizen, one of the most beloved players in Arizona basketball history.

IN SUM

Kerr, traded to Cleveland, will have to get by in the league on his brains and his desire and his shooting, because his physical skills are marginal, at best.

RICK'S RATINGS

Scoring: **C**   Defense: **C**
Shooting: **A**   Defensive Rebounding: **B**
Free Throw Shooting: **D**   Intangibles: **A**
Ball Handling: **A**   Overall: **C**
Passing: **A**

Jerome Kersey

Birthdate: June 26, 1962
Height: 6-7
Weight: 222
College: Longwood College, Farmville, Va.
Drafted: Portland on second round, 1984 (46th pick).
Position: Forward
Final 1989 Team: Portland Trail Blazers
Final 1988–89 Statistics:

G	Fg	Fga	Fg%	Ft	Fta	Ft%	Orb	Reb	Ast	Stl	To	Blk	Pts	Ppg
76	533	1137	.469	258	372	.694	246	629	243	137	167	84	1330	17.5

Three-point goals: 6–21 (.286)   **TSP:** .471

SCORING

First, he took his job. Then he had to fill his shoes. During the 1987–88 season, Kersey replaced Kiki Vandeweghe, one of the NBA's most prolific scorers (22.8 ppg), in the Blazers lineup when Vandeweghe went down with a back injury. Vandeweghe never got his job back. Kersey, a five-year veteran filled in ably, scoring 19.2 a game and shooting .499 from the field. Last year, with Vandeweghe hurt for the first two months of the season and pining for a trade (he was eventually dealt to the Knicks for a 1989 first-round draft pick), Kersey was expected to take up where he left off.

While he put up similar, though slightly depressed, numbers (17.5 ppg on .469 shooting), the fact is Portland desperately missed Kiki's outside and, in particular, three-point shooting. True, Kersey, through a lot of hard work, has improved his shot since he's been in the league, but he's inconsistent and doesn't have Kiki's range (only 6 of 21 trifectas last year). No, Jerome's talents are best displayed in the running game where he can use his speed, quickness, and jumping ability; he is one of the best finishers (read: dunkers) in the league. In the half-court offense, he's a superb offensive rebounder (3.2 a game) and decent driver, though opponents have given him room to shoot the jumper, which makes it tougher for him to get to the hoop. His foul shooting is a problem; only .694 last year.

DEFENSE/DEFENSIVE REBOUNDING

The Kersey-for-Vandeweghe switch had much to do with Kersey's ability as a defender and rebounder. Vandeweghe provided negligible input in those areas, while Kersey, to a large extent, gets the job done. Defensively, Kersey uses his athleticism for steals (1.8 a game) and blocks (1.1 a game) and to recover readily from any mistakes—for example, he tends to play too close to his man—he should make. A trademark: He can catch up to players in the open court and block layups. He's an active, aggressive defender who gets into foul trouble (six disqualifications in 1988–89). His jumping ability has helped him become a very good defensive rebounder (five a game and 8.3 overall).

THE FLOOR GAME

Kersey is not a great ball handler, but unlike many 3s, he will pass the ball (3.2 feeds a game). Still, in the open court, he's better receiving the pass than making the play.

INTANGIBLES

Besides his athletic skills, what sets Kersey apart is his work ethic—both on and off the court. A relentless player, he is always working, always on the move, and never gives up on a play.

IN SUM

Kersey has made himself into a quality player. *How good* is the question. One school of thought, looking at his athletic skills and desire to improve, figures he'll blossom into an All-Star. Another focuses on his deficiencies as a shooter and believes he's an overrated defender, and sees him as a sixth man. At the present time, we favor the second notion.

RICK'S RATINGS

Scoring: **A**   Defense: **A**
Shooting: **B**   Defensive Rebounding:
Free Throw Shooting: **D**   **AA**
Ball Handling: **B**   Intangibles: **A**
Passing: **B**   Overall: **A –**

——— Randolph Keys ———

Birthdate: April 19, 1966
Height: 6-7

Weight: 195
College: University of Southern Mississippi, Hattiesburg, Miss.
Drafted: Cleveland on first round, 1988 (22nd pick).
Position: Forward
Final 1989 Team: Cleveland Cavaliers
Final 1988–89 Statistics:

G	Fg	Fga	Fg%	Ft	Fta	Ft%	Orb	Reb	Ast	Stl	To	Blk	Pts	Ppg
42	74	172	.430	20	29	.690	23	56	19	12	21	6	169	4.0

Three-point goals: 1–10 (.100)   **TSP:** .433

SCORING

Playing only 7.9 minutes a game in 42 games as a rookie, Keys, a 6-7 small forward, didn't get to show much, but the word is he's a good face-up shooter from 20 feet and in. When he gets stronger (he only weighs 195), he'll eventually have three-point range (he was 1 of 10 last year). He has an extremely quick release and is best coming off picks, though at this stage, his ability to put the ball on the floor is limited. He has above-average jumping ability, but it remains to be seen whether he'll be a good offensive rebounder.

DEFENSE/DEFENSIVE REBOUNDING

Defensively, Keys proved to be better than Cleveland imagined. He has long arms and, with his quickness, can guard players on the perimeter. But his lack of strength is a drawback; he will have to get stronger to handle inside play. Keys averaged about seven rebounds a game in college as a center at Southern Mississippi but, again, his lack of bulk may hurt in the pros. In his limited minutes, he was, per minute, a below-average defensive rebounder.

THE FLOOR GAME

Keys is still learning the pro game—but he's a willing learner. He's also an adequate passer though, as mentioned, his dribbling needs work. He can get up and down the court.

INTANGIBLES

Keys has the right character traits: He's dedicated, coachable, a hard worker, and possesses a quiet pride. He has not made it into Cleveland's rotation but is willing to pay his dues.

IN SUM

Keys' big pluses are his touch and his athletic ability. As he matures, he'll get stronger. Of course, what he needs is quality minutes.

RICK'S RATINGS

Scoring: **B**   Defense: **B**
Shooting: **B**   Defensive Rebounding: **B**
Free Throw Shooting: **D**   Intangibles: **B**
Ball Handling: **C**   Overall: **B –**
Passing: **B**

Bernard King

Birthdate: December 4, 1956
Height: 6-7
Weight: 205
College: University of Tennessee, Knoxville, Tenn.
Drafted: New Jersey on first round as an undergraduate, 1977 (7th pick).
Position: Forward
Final 1989 Team: Washington Bullets
Final 1988–89 Statistics:

G	Fg	Fga	Fg%	Ft	Fta	Ft%	Orb	Reb	Ast	Stl	To	Blk	Pts	Ppg
81	654	1371	.477	361	441	.819	133	384	294	64	227	13	1674	20.7

Three-point goals: 5–30 (.167)   **TSP:** .479

SCORING

There was then, and there is now. Then was pre-March 6, 1985, when King, then a New York Knick, was the leading scorer in the league (he won the title in 1984–85 with 32.9 ppg) and was destroying opponents on a nightly basis with an unstoppable array of post-up moves, drives, and finishes on the fast break. He had been named to the All-NBA first team the year before and was to repeat the honor in 1984–85. But that fateful March night, his season—and many thought his career—ended when he tore his anterior cruciate ligament, basketball's most dreaded injury. King sat out the entire next season and played a mere six games in 1986–87. But King, a hard worker if there ever was one, came back and surprised a lot of people by averaging 17.2 in 1987–88. In 1988–89, he again surprised, nay, amazed, the basketball world by increasing his ppg to 20.7—a remarkable feat considering he's effectively playing on one leg. Still, the "new" King hardly resembles the King of old. Gone is the quickness, the explosiveness and the quick release that was his metier: his post up game is now a mere shadow of the healthy model. Now King relies on smarts—he's adept at receiving the ball in scoring position—and his perimeter shooting. He can still fill the lane—invariably on the left side—and went to the line a solid 5.4 times a game, only slightly below his career average of 6.4. And last year was the first time he ever shot over 80 percent from the stripe (.819), though his career average (.715) is misleading, because early on he was terrible (.662 after the first six years), but .782 in the last four.

DEFENSE/DEFENSIVE REBOUNDING

In bygone days, King's defense was predicated on the reasonable assumption that he would outscore his man. If his man scored 25—so what! King more than likely scored 30-plus. But as his average has dropped, it's pretty much a wash; he'll score 20 but his man can easily score the same. The problem is that his lateral movement is severely compromised by the injury. King was an awesome rebounder as a collegiate (Tennessee) and in his early years in the pros (9.5 a game in his rookie year). But these days, at 32 years old (33 in December), with a reconstructed knee, he's below-average (4.7 a game) for his position.

THE FLOOR GAME

King has never been a gunner; what has made his game so special is his ability to see the floor and make the tough pass. He's a student of the game and plays like it.

INTANGIBLES

King made the term "game face" part of the basketball lexicon. He is all business, a money player, who gives his all, though these days there's just not as much to give. He can still take over a game offensively, as he showed throughout the year.

IN SUM

Two-thirds of Bernard King is still one of the premier scorers in the league; last year he was one of 24 players to score 20 or more a game. That earned him a new two-year $3 million contract from the Bullets. Now the question is: Can he top or even equal last season's output? If Bernard King has taught us anything, it's to not underestimate him.

RICK'S RATINGS

Scoring: **AAA**	Defense: **C**
Shooting: **AA**	Defensive Rebounding: **C**
Free Throw Shooting: **A**	Intangibles: **AA**
Ball Handling: **A**	Overall: **A +**
Passing: **AAA**	

Greg Kite

Birthdate: August 5, 1961
Height: 6-11
Weight: 250
College: Brigham Young University, Provo, Utah
Drafted: Boston on first round, 1983 (21st pick).
Position: Center
Final 1989 Team: Charlotte Hornets
Final 1988–89 Statistics:

G	Fg	Fga	Fg%	Ft	Fta	Ft%	Orb	Reb	Ast	Stl	To	Blk	Pts	Ppg
70	65	151	.430	20	41	.488	81	243	36	27	58	54	150	2.1

Three-point goals: 0–0 (.000)   **TSP:** .430

SCORING

Per minute, Kite was the worst scoring center in the league last year (2.1 ppg in 13.5 minutes). If he had played the full 48, he would have averaged 7.6 ppg. Greg Dreiling (Greg Dreiling!) doubled Kite's scoring output on a per minute basis. He shot .488 (.488!) from the line and .430 from the field—remember, he's playing close to the basket. But in the occasionally wacky world of the NBA, Kite was a starter on two different teams—lousy teams (the Clippers, who waived him in March, and the Hornets, who signed him and where he finished the season), but a starter nonetheless. On those rare occasions when the ball actually goes through the net after leaving his hands, it's a putback (he's an average offensive rebounder), a left-handed hook (he's right-handed), or—and coaches cringe at this—a 15-footer from the foul line area.

DEFENSE/DEFENSIVE REBOUNDING

Kite is a banger, an extremely physical defender who pushes his man out of his operating area, and with decent timing, he even occasionally blocks a shot. He's an I've-got-six-fouls-to-give guy and has been known to get in foul trouble in a hurry. No, he doesn't jump well, but he's an average defensive rebounder who won't get any boards out of his jurisdiction.

THE FLOOR GAME

Poor ball handler, below-average passer, fair runner of the floor.

INTANGIBLES

He always works—on both ends of the floor. Has to, wouldn't be in the league, if he didn't. Kite is an overachiever of sorts.

IN SUM

Bob Ryan once called Kite the least talented player in the league, but he's been surpassed (here's one vote for Ben Gillery). But he's a survivor (six years in the NBA)—and he's done it with D, rebounding, and a relentless work ethic.

RICK'S RATINGS

Scoring: **D**
Shooting: **D**
Free Throw Shooting: **D**
Ball Handling: **C**
Passing: **C**

Defense: **B**
Defensive Rebounding: **B**
Shot Blocking: **B**
Intangibles: **A**
Overall: **C –**

Joe Kleine

Birthdate: January 4, 1962
Height: 7-0
Weight: 275
College: University of Arkansas, Fayetteville, Ark.
Drafted: Sacramento on first round, 1985 (6th pick).
Position: Center
Final 1989 Team: Boston Celtics
Final 1988–89 Statistics:

G	Fg	Fga	Fg%	Ft	Fta	Ft%	Orb	Reb	Ast	Stl	To	Blk	Pts	Ppg
75	175	432	.405	134	152	.882	124	378	67	33	104	23	484	6.5

Three-point goals: 0–2 (.000)   **TSP:** .405

SCORING

Kleine's major contribution to the Celtics is that he's not Mark Acres, Brad Lohaus, Greg Kite, or, for that matter, Artis Gilmore. Recall that the last time Boston won an NBA title (1985–86), they had a guy by the name of Bill Walton as backup center. The injury-plagued Walton played a remarkable (for him) 80 games that year, but then, as a result of an ankle problem, appeared in only 10 games in 1986–87 and hasn't played a game since. About Messrs. Kite, Gilmore, Lohaus, and Acres, who sought to fill Walton's shoes, you could say: They came, they tried, they failed. Enter Kleine, who arrived last February with Ed Pinckney in a trade that sent Danny Ainge and Lohaus to Sacramento. A Walton he is not, but at least he's a competitive NBA center with three years of (mostly) starting experience under his belt who can give 36-year-old starting center Robert Parish much-needed rest (in fact, Parish's minutes decreased with Kleine aboard). A career .456 shooter, the 7-foot Kleine shot a subpar .405 in 1988–89, but his problems were more in Sacramento (.383) rather than Boston (.457). He possesses an adequate turnaround jumper from the right block and a nice right-handed hook (his left-handed hook is not nearly as proficient). He can also spot up from 15 feet, but in the last couple of seasons he has not shown consistency from that distance. Part of the problem is his speed, or more precisely, the lack of it. His is a slow release and he can be bothered by quicker defenders. Throughout his career, Kleine's been an above-average offensive rebounder and last year was no exception (1.7 a game in 18.8 minutes). But he needs to expand his low-post repertoire. One of Kleine's big pluses is that he can be on the floor at the end of the game; he's one of the best foul shooters in the NBA (.882 last year, tied for sixth in the league).

DEFENSE/DEFENSIVE REBOUNDING

Kleine is a solid defensive rebounder (above-average for backup 5s, five total caroms a game). With his wide body, he blocks out well and defensively matches up well against "big" centers (in the West, players like Kevin Duckworth and James Donaldson). However, his lack of quickness hampers him against high-post centers. He is not a shot-blocking threat and has never had more than 60 rejections in a season.

THE FLOOR GAME

Kleine has a unique specialty: He sets one of the best picks in the league. At 275 (all muscle), he's a hulk, and when he sets the screen, he's an immovable force. He knows how and when to set screens and rarely gets called for head-hunting. But in Sacramento, the feeling was that he had bad hands and limited peripheral vision.

INTANGIBLES

Kleine will be outplayed, but he'll never be outworked or outhustled. However, in Sacramento, even with the effort there, the results, on a consistent basis, were not; Kleine rarely put together three good consecutive games. It's too soon to tell whether this will be the case in Boston.

IN SUM

As the sixth player picked in the 1985 draft, Kleine engendered high expectations but he didn't measure up as an NBA starting center. Now, he's with a team that recognizes and appreciates him for what he is—a decent backup center—no more, no less.

RICK'S RATINGS

Scoring: **C**
Shooting: **C**
Free Throw Shooting:
  AAA
Ball Handling: **C**
Passing: **B**

Defense: **B**
Defensive Rebounding: **A**
Shot Blocking: **D**
Intangibles: **A**
Overall: **B**

Jon Koncak

Birthdate: May 17, 1963

Height: 7-1
Weight: 260
College: Southern Methodist University, Dallas, Tex.
Drafted: Atlanta on first round, 1985 (5th pick).
Position: Center
Final 1989 Team: Atlanta Hawks
Final 1988–89 Statistics:

G	Fg	Fga	Fg%	Ft	Fta	Ft%	Orb	Reb	Ast	Stl	To	Blk	Pts	Ppg
74	141	269	.524	63	114	.553	147	453	56	54	60	98	345	4.7

Three-point goals: 0–3 (.000)   **TSP:** .524

SCORING

Despite an outstanding career-best shooting percentage, .524, in 1988–89, Koncak is neither a good shooter nor scorer. In fact, he's not offensive-minded at all. Last year, his 4.7 ppg (in 20.7 minutes) was compiled on less than four shots a game, and even if he had played the full 48, would barely have averaged 10 points a game. But note: In 16 games as a starter at the end of the season (the Hawks went 13-3 during this stretch), Koncak shot .693 (after shooting .303 in the 28 previous games), averaged 6.9 ppg, and continued his hot shooting during the playoff loss to the Bucks (.621 and 12.8 ppg). It turns out Koncak does have a few tools: an adequate 15-footer (which he, may, for example, get as the trailer on the break), some prowess on the offensive glass (2 a game in 1988–89), and the ability to get hoops off the pick-and-roll. But his most glaring deficiencies arise from his back-to-the-hoop game, which is basically nonexistent. He sorely needs a hook shot. And as a career .612 foul shooter (.553 last year), he really ought to put in some time at the foul line.

DEFENSE/DEFENSIVE REBOUNDING

Koncak's major contributions are here. At 7-1, with exceptionally long arms, he not only blocks shots (1.3 a game) but alters trajectories. He even comes away with steals (54 last year). While his lateral quickness is suspect, he's a fine defender because he positions well and understands defensive concepts. Another asset: he relieves the defensive pressure on Moses Malone (i.e., he can guard the Patrick Ewings, the Brad Daughertys). And he's an excellent defensive rebounder, who boxes out well.

THE FLOOR GAME

Koncak is part of the notorious Atlanta frontline that doesn't know from an assist. Consider: In his 1,073 minutes in 1987–88, he accumulated an amazing 19 assists. Last year, in 1,531 minutes, he was marginally (56 feeds) better. But he does run the floor.

INTANGIBLES

Koncak works hard on his conditioning; if only the same could be said about his basketball skills. By now, he should have mastered some semblance of a hook. His intensity level is also questionable.

IN SUM

One of Mike Fratello's best moves last year was inserting Koncak into the starting lineup. His performance indicated that he is, after all, a frontline player who can make major contributions defensively and on the boards. This year, he should play substantial minutes (though perhaps not as a starter if Kevin Willis is healthy). In time, when Malone retires, Koncak will start; by that time—or sooner—he should have advanced the level of his offensive skills.

RICK'S RATINGS

Scoring: **D**
Shooting: **C**
Free Throw Shooting: **D**
Ball Handling: **C**
Passing: **D**
Defense: **AA**

Defensive Rebounding: **AAA**
Shot Blocking: **A**
Intangibles: **C**
Overall: **B**

Larry Krystkowiak

Birthdate: September 23, 1964
Height: 6-9
Weight: 220
College: University of Montana, Missoula, Mont.
Drafted: Chicago on second round, 1986 (28th pick).
Position: Forward
Final 1989 Team: Milwaukee Bucks
Final 1988–89 Statistics:

G	Fg	Fga	Fg%	Ft	Fta	Ft%	Orb	Reb	Ast	Stl	To	Blk	Pts	Ppg
80	362	766	.473	289	351	.823	198	610	107	93	147	9	1017	12.7

Three-point goals: 4–12 (.333)   **TSP:** .475

SCORING

First things first. Krystkowiak suffered massive ligament damage to his left knee in last year's playoff series against the Pistons. The earliest he could play will be late this season, and there's a possibility he'll never play again. That said, in his first opportunity in a starting role, Krystkowiak averaged 12.7 in 1988–89, noteworthy because he has to manufacture his own points—Milwaukee doesn't run any plays for him. The 6-9 power forward runs the floor well, moves well without the ball, and has a deft touch around the basket (including an excellent left hand; he's right-handed). He does solid work, too, on the offensive glass (2.5 a game), where he bang, bang, bangs. Unlike most 4s, he can put the ball on the floor; he just needs consistency in hitting the jumper (range is 15 feet).

DEFENSE/DEFENSIVE REBOUNDING

Krystkowiak always guards the opposition's best forward, be it a 3 or a 4. His prowess is muscle, not finesse, and he is as physical a player (he loves the contact) as there is in the league, as close to an enforcer as Milwaukee has. His are the widely recognized short arms (he had the least blocked shots among starting power forwards; 9 in 2,472 minutes; Kiki Vandeweghe had more!) and he has only average lateral quickness. The short arms don't help on the defensive glass, where he's only average for his position.

THE FLOOR GAME

Krysto is a solid ball handler who can make the interior pass. His turnovers, per minute, were slightly below average.

INTANGIBLES

Krystkowiak plays with reckless abandon and never-ceasing hustle. A well-disciplined and conditioned athlete, he is where he is on the basis of his desire.

IN SUM

This last season, 1988–89, saw the emergence of Larry K. A fine defender, he also gets his share of hustle points. Krystkowiak is a consummate complementary player, whose brand of selflessness always seems to show up on winning teams. Unfortunately, his injury has put his career in jeopardy.

RICK'S RATINGS

Scoring: **B**
Shooting: **C**
Free Throw Shooting: **A**
Ball Handling: **B**
Passing: **B**

Defense: **A**
Defensive Rebounding: **B**
Shot Blocking: **D**
Intangibles: **AA**
Overall: **B**

Bill Laimbeer

Birthdate: May 19, 1957
Height: 6-11

Weight: 260
College: University of Notre Dame, Notre Dame, Ind.
Drafted: Cleveland on third round, 1979 (65th pick).
Position: Center
Final 1989 Team: Detroit Pistons
Final 1988–89 Statistics:

G	Fg	Fga	Fg%	Ft	Fta	Ft%	Orb	Reb	Ast	Stl	To	Blk	Pts	Ppg
81	449	900	.499	178	212	.840	138	776	177	51	129	100	1106	13.7

Three-point goals: 30–86 (.349)   **TSP:** .516

SCORING

Among centers, Laimbeer has few peers as a perimeter shooter (Jack Sikma is the only name that comes to mind). He can shoot it accurately (.499 last year; .502 lifetime), quickly (his "tippy-toe" release, while unusual, is effective), and with range—he's deadly from 15 to 18 feet, and last year he had his best year, .349, from three-point land; again, among 5s, only Sikma (.380 last year) rivals Laimbeer from that distance. For the Pistons, the advantage is that opposing centers have to come out to guard him, leaving the middle open for guard penetration and operating room for Mark Aguirre. Laimbeer is basically a standstill jump shooter, best on the catch, and can also score as well on the offensive glass (13.7 ppg), though his 1.7 offensive rebounds a game were the lowest, per minute, for starting centers. At 32, it turns out you can teach an old dog new tricks; last year he surfaced an occasional back-to-the-basket move (particularly when opponents tempted him by assigning a small forward to guard him), such as a turnaround jumper. Despite his solid overall year, Laimbeer shot poorly against the Bulls in the playoffs (.380) and was a minimal offensive force against the Lakers in the finals (just 8.0 ppg, though .545 from the field). An excellent foul shooter at .840 (he's been as high as .894).

DEFENSE/DEFENSIVE REBOUNDING

Figure this one out: he can't jump, he's not a hulk, he's not quick, but Laimbeer is one of the best defensive rebounders in the league. Last year, he was second in the league, per minute, to Akeem Olajuwon in defensive rebounds and averaged 9.6 total rebounds a game, tied for seventh in the league. This was the first time in six seasons he had *not* averaged 10 rebounds a game. His prowess can be explained by the fact that he's an astute, analytical player and studies where the ball is coming off the board. Defensively, Laimbeer makes opponents pay when they come down the lane; call it dirty, call it aggressive, your body is in danger when Laimbeer is around. And he uses every trick in the book to push his man out of the low block. He's not totally inconspicuous as a shot blocker (1.2 a game last year).

THE FLOOR GAME

Laimbeer has a solid sense of the five-man game. He's a great outlet passer and a competent passer in the Pistons' half-court offense. You don't want him dribbling the ball, and while he's not an ideal lane-filler on the break, he's

dangerous as a trailer. He sets a good hard pick and knows how to flare out for his jumper.

INTANGIBLES

One statistic is telling: Laimbeer has missed only four games (734 of 738) since his career began in 1980–81, included in which is a 685 consecutive game streak that was interrupted last year when he was suspended for one game for fighting with Cleveland's Brad Daugherty. He's a fierce competitor who hates to lose—at anything. A Bad Boy by virtue of his association with Rick Mahorn, Laimbeer may be the most universally hated player in the league, but so what? His reputation does little to detract from his game, though it may sway an official occasionally; Detroit coaches feel there are two sets of rules; one for Laimbeer and his former Bad Boy teammate, Mahorn, and one for the rest of the league. Note, for example, the offensive foul (where he stuck out his hip) with nine seconds left in the third game of the Chicago series—a call that is not ordinarily made at that juncture in a game.

IN SUM

You might not like him, but you have to respect his talent. Phenomenal defensive rebounder, still dangerous perimeter shooter, heady player, winner.

RICK'S RATINGS

Scoring: **B**	Defensive Rebounding:
Shooting: **AA**	**AAA**
Free Throw Shooting: **AA**	Shot Blocking: **C**
Ball Handling: **B**	Intangibles: **AAA**
Passing: **A**	Overall: **AA**
Defense: **B**	

Jerome Lane

Birthdate: December 4, 1966
Height: 6-6
Weight: 230
College: University of Pittsburgh, Pittsburgh, Pa.
Drafted: Denver on first round as an undergraduate, 1988 (23rd pick).
Positions: Guard, Forward
Final 1989 Team: Denver Nuggets

Final 1988–89 Statistics:

G	Fg	Fga	Fg%	Ft	Fta	Ft%	Orb	Reb	Ast	Stl	To	Blk	Pts	Ppg
54	109	256	.426	43	112	.384	87	200	60	20	50	4	261	4.8

Three-point goals: 0–7 (.000)   **TSP:** .426

SCORING

Players who can play two positions typically switch between 2 and 3, 4 and 5, and 1 and 2. Lane, the Nuggets first-round pick in 1988 (23rd overall), breaks the mold. He's a 1/3. Entering the league (he skipped his senior year at Pitt), it was projected that he would be a small forward to take advantage of his awesome rebounding skills—he led the country as a sophomore with 13.5 rpg and he's only 6-6. And in his rookie season, Lane lived up to his billing, leading the NBA, per minute, in offensive rebounds (a mighty 1.6 offensive caroms in a mere 10.2 minutes). But he also showed an ability to handle the ball as the middleman on the break. He'd take the ball off the board—he's also a superb defensive rebounder—and proved to be the Nuggets best passer in transition. His points came in the running game or off drives in half-court—he has a quick first step and can get to the basket. His offensive problems, however, begin when he moves away from the basket—both from the field and at the line. He has no range on his jumper, and some might even say he has no jumper at all. Didn't in college, either. And his foul shooting. Well, say this, it can only get better, an embarrassing .384.

DEFENSE/DEFENSIVE REBOUNDING

Early on, Lane was completely out of his element defensively. His effort was lacking, his footwork horrendous, and the Nuggets had their doubts. Coach Doug Moe wouldn't put him on the floor at the end of games because of his D. It didn't help that he had come to camp overweight—fat, really—and lacked stamina. But he lost weight during the season and with his good head for the game, started to pick up the defensive fundamentals. By the end of the year, he was an adequate defender. And even though he didn't always block out diligently, he put up excellent numbers on the defensive board.

THE FLOOR GAME

Lane's ball handling and passing surprised a lot of people. He has good court awareness; his advantage as a point guard, like Magic Johnson, is that he can see over opponents. His turnovers were too high, however.

INTANGIBLES

Predraft, scouts questioned Lane's work ethic (one reason, beside his problematic perimeter game, for his slipping to the 23rd pick), but he showed that he's willing to pay the price to be a player.

IN SUM

As he readied himself for his second season, Lane had two goals: lose more weight (he wanted to get down to 215). Good

idea. Second, look to score more. Another sound proposition—one which presupposes he has the weapons—i.e. an outside shot—to support it. Jerome should get in the gym and shoot jumpers until his arm gets weary. Once he develops some perimeter productivity, he has a big upside.

RICK'S RATINGS

Scoring: **B**
Shooting: **D**
Free Throw Shooting: **D**
Ball Handling: **A**
Passing: **A**
Defense: **C**

Defensive Rebounding: **AAA**
Playmaking: **A**
Intangibles: **B**
Overall: **B –**

Andrew Lang

Birthdate: June 28, 1966
Height: 6-11
Weight: 250
College: University of Arkansas, Fayetteville, Ark.
Drafted: Phoenix on second round, 1988 (28th pick).
Position: Center
Final 1989 Team: Phoenix Suns
Final 1988–89 Statistics:

G	Fg	Fga	Fg%	Ft	Fta	Ft%	Orb	Reb	Ast	Stl	To	Blk	Pts	Ppg
62	60	117	.513	39	60	.650	54	147	9	17	28	48	159	2.6

Three-point goals: 0–0 (.000)   **TSP:** .513

SCORING

The hope is that Lang, a 6-11, 250-pound center, who was a rookie in 1988–89, will eventually be able to score enough points that he could play significant minutes. He's not there yet (2.6 ppg in 8.5 minutes in 1988–89). In fact, he barely scored at Arkansas (6.9 ppg for his career). He doesn't know a good shot and has to learn to shoot. He's currently working on a hook and showed some ability—above average, per minute, for reserve 5s—on the offensive glass.

DEFENSE/DEFENSIVE REBOUNDING

If Lang sticks around, it will be on the strength of his defense and rebounding. He is an excellent shot blocker (and was throughout his college career) and is a big, strong body out there on defense. But like most rookies, he has to show he can play D without getting into foul trouble. His defensive rebounding numbers were above-the-norm. Lang started 25 games but was basically keeping the center spot warm for Mark West, then rarely reentering the game following West's appearance. Eventually, he was phased out of the rotation completely.

THE FLOOR GAME

Tree Rollins, you are not alone. Lang played 526 minutes, the equivalent of about 11 games, and garnered only nine assists. No, he's not a good ball handler or passer. But he will run the floor.

INTANGIBLES

Lang has a big heart and a large capacity for work, which has resulted in dramatic improvement in his game since training camp. He's cooperative and coachable as well.

IN SUM

Phoenix sees Lang as a younger West—a nonscorer who will rebound, defend, and block shots. He's a project, all right, but with his healthy work ethic, he'll likely get the time to see if he can cut it.

RICK'S RATINGS

Scoring: **D**	Defense: **B**
Shooting: **C**	Shot Blocking: **AAA**
Free Throw Shooting: **D**	Intangibles: **A**
Ball Handling: **C**	Overall: **C**
Passing: **D**	

Allen Leavell

Birthdate: May 27, 1957
Height: 6-2
Weight: 190
College: Oklahoma City University, Oklahoma City, Okla.
Drafted: Houston on fifth round, 1979 (104th pick).
Position: Guard
Final 1989 Team: Houston Rockets
Final 1988–89 Statistics:

G	Fg	Fga	Fg%	Ft	Fta	Ft%	Orb	Reb	Ast	Stl	To	Blk	Pts	Ppg
55	65	188	.346	44	60	.733	13	53	127	25	62	5	179	3.3

Three-point goals: 5–41 (.122)   **TSP:** .359

SCORING

Leavell, an erratic shooter throughout his career, put up some truly ugly numbers in 1988–89. Let's begin with his field goal percentage, .346, which was more than 10 percentage points lower than his .450 career mark. A lifetime .231 three-point shooter, he shot .122 (5 of 41) from out there. Most unusual was his foul shooting; a career .834 percenter coming in, he hit only .733 from the stripe. This poor performance can be explained at least in part by the fact that Leavell was in and out of the rotation (11.4 minutes a game). However, he's the type of player who, though he's missing, will continue to fire away—even though he's not a very good shooter to begin with. Primarily a jump shooter (he can create off the dribble), he's also pretty quick to the hole, though he goes right almost exclusively.

DEFENSE/DEFENSIVE REBOUNDING

Leavell has always had good hands—he was ninth in the league in steals in 1982–83—but he also takes chances. He's

---

still quick enough to keep up with most of the point guards in the league and is a smart veteran defender.

THE FLOOR GAME

In 1987–88 (he started 54 games) Leavell had a solid 3.12 assist-to-turnover ratio, significantly better than his career mark. But last year he reverted to his less-than-reliable ways, with a dismal 2.05 ATR.

INTANGIBLES

Leavell is tough as nails and plays his butt off. But his ball handling makes you nervous in crunch time.

IN SUM

Will this guy ever go away? He's a survivor who provides a shot of energy off the bench, some scoring, and aggressive defense.

RICK'S RATINGS

Scoring: **D**	Defense: **B**
Shooting: **D**	Defensive Rebounding: **B**
Free Throw Shooting: **C**	Playmaking: **C**
Ball Handling: **C**	Intangibles: **B**
Passing: **B**	Overall: **C –**

Eric Leckner

Birthdate: May 27, 1966
Height: 6-10
Weight: 265
College: University of Wyoming, Laramie, Wyo.
Drafted: Utah on first round, 1988 (17th pick).
Position: Center
Final 1989 Team: Utah Jazz
Final 1988–89 Statistics:

G	Fg	Fga	Fg%	Ft	Fta	Ft%	Orb	Reb	Ast	Stl	To	Blk	Pts	Ppg
75	120	220	.545	79	113	.699	48	199	16	8	69	22	319	4.3

Three-point goals: 0–0 (.000)   **TSP:** .545

SCORING

As a rookie in 1988–89, Leckner shot an eye-catching .545, which is precisely why the Jazz drafted him in the first round in the 1988 draft (17th pick overall). Leckner is a rare commodity—a 6-10 center with touch. It all starts with the hands—probably his biggest asset. In fact, they are huge and he can catch anything thrown his way. These mitts enable him, for example, to dunk in traffic. He can also shoot the turnaround jumper and the jump hook. While up and down the court slow, he has deceptively quick feet in the post, which provide the foundation for his ability to score there. (He averaged 4.3 ppg in 10.4 mpg, which is above average, per minute, for backup centers.) But both his foul shooting (.699) and his offensive rebounding (way below average for reserve 5s) need work. He's better as a trailer, rather than a finisher on the break.

DEFENSE/DEFENSIVE REBOUNDING

Some thought Leckner was soft coming into the league, but perhaps because he overcompensated, he showed an aggressiveness on D that resulted in an astounding number of fouls. If he played the full 48, he would have committed 10.7 fouls. He tends to let players get post position, is not a shot blocker, and needs to get stronger. Not a great rebounder in college, Leckner was above-average (for backup 5s) on a per minute basis for the Jazz, although there's room for improvement.

THE FLOOR GAME

Leckner had a miserable 0.24 assist-to-turnover ratio. Obviously, he has a scorer's mind-set; if he had logged 48 minutes a night, he'd have been credited with one assist per game.

INTANGIBLES

At draft time, NBA people questioned Leckner's desire, but he impressed doubters by signing early and playing with the Utah entry in the Southern California Summer Pro League. Starting out in incredibly bad shape—both overweight and flabby—he has lost a lot of body fat and is now on a weight program.

IN SUM

With the dearth of centers, and expansion creating a demand for same, the Jazz felt there would be few opportunities to sign a big man with Leckner's talent—in particular, one who could shoot the ball. His first season was encouraging.

RICK'S RATINGS

Scoring: **B**
Shooting: **A**
Free Throw Shooting: **D**
Ball Handling: **C**
Passing: **D**

Defense: **C**
Defensive Rebounding: **B**
Intangibles: **B**
Overall: **B –**

Keith Lee

Birthdate: December 28, 1962
Height: 6-10
Weight: 220

College: Memphis State University, Memphis, Tenn.
Drafted: Chicago on first round, 1985 (11th pick).
Positions: Forward, Center
Final 1989 Team: New Jersey Nets
Final 1988–89 Statistics:

G	Fg	Fga	Fg%	Ft	Fta	Ft%	Orb	Reb	Ast	Stl	To	Blk	Pts	Ppg
57	109	258	.422	53	71	.746	73	259	42	20	53	33	271	4.8

Three-point goals: 0–2 (.000)   **TSP:** .422

SCORING

Lee is a 25-year-old in a 50-year-old's body. The story of his career so far is a medical saga: He missed all of the 1987–88 season due to surgery to remove calcium deposits, and a significant portion of last year (he only played 57 games) with turf toe. If he ever stayed healthy, he might bring back memories that he once was a pretty good basketball player. Last year there were flashes of the old Keith Lee, the Lee who was one of the best college players in 1985 and the 11th pick overall that year. Everybody likes Lee's hands—and he has a deft touch facing the basket from 17 feet, though he hasn't displayed it (.422 in 1988–89 and .451 lifetime). He can also put the ball on the floor, and despite the fact that he barely jumps (he has long arms), he's an above-average offensive rebounder. This past summer he was sighted in Golden State's camp in New Hampshire.

DEFENSE/DEFENSIVE REBOUNDING

Those same physical tools are major assets on the defensive board. On a per minute basis, Lee was 7th in the league for defensive rebounding. And while only an average shot blocker, he's a smart defender, who helps out and plays with his hands up.

THE FLOOR GAME

Lee has a high basketball intelligence quotient. He sees the court and can make the play.

INTANGIBLES

Obviously, durability is the main concern in Lee's case. Because of the injuries, he's never really been in shape.

IN SUM

Assuming he's healthy—a huge if—Lee could be a significant contributor as a backup. He can shoot, pass, defend, and he knows the game.

RICK'S RATINGS

Scoring: **C**
Shooting: **D**
Free Throw Shooting: **C**
Ball Handling: **A**
Passing: **A**
Defense: **B**

Defensive Rebounding:
AAA
Shot Blocking: **B**
Intangibles: **C**
Overall: **C +**

Jim Les

Birthdate: August 18, 1963
Height: 5-10
Weight: 165
College: Bradley University, Peoria, Ill.
Drafted: Atlanta on third round, 1986 (70th pick).
Position: Guard
Final 1989 Team: Utah Jazz
Final 1988–89 Statistics:

G	Fg	Fga	Fg%	Ft	Fta	Ft%	Orb	Reb	Ast	Stl	To	Blk	Pts	Ppg
82	40	133	.301	57	73	.781	23	87	215	27	88	5	138	1.7

Three-point goals: 1–14 (.071)   **TSP:** .305

SCORING

Les, John Stockton's backup at the point (he played all 82 games; one of three reserves to do so) will have to do better than .301 (not a misprint) from the field if he's contemplating a future in the NBA. In his defense, he was a rookie last year (first-year players generally struggle) plus he shot the ball only 133 times, which makes it tough to develop any rhythm. At Bradley, he scored 14.2 ppg in his senior year and shot .475 for his career; and he was .781 from the line in 1988–89, so there are encouraging signs. His shots come on pull-up jumpers on the break or when Utah's big men are double-teamed (he shot 1 of 14 treys). When he goes to the hoop, he's looking to pass rather than finish.

DEFENSE/DEFENSIVE REBOUNDING

Almost by necessity—after all, he's only 5-11—Les is a pest. He has quick feet and can play pressure D full court. You'd think he'd be posted up a lot, but with Mark Eaton backing him up, that disadvantage is neutralized. An above-average defensive rebounder for the position in 1988–89.

THE FLOOR GAME

Stylistically, Les reminds you of Stockton—they're both small, true points, who can find the open man and who can push the ball. He demonstrated good leadership qualities and picked up Utah's offense quickly. But his assist-to-turnover ratio was only 2.44, though his assists on a per minute basis place him fourth among backup 1s.

INTANGIBLES

Les was Stockton's "caddy," if you will—a role that requires a firm grasp on reality. And that reality is that his role is to give Stockton a 10-minute breather, and no more. (But note he only played a total of five minutes—and Stockton averaged 46.3—in last year's three-game playoff loss to the Warriors.) Les is a hard worker who pays his dues during and after practice.

IN SUM

In a league in which point guards are becoming almost as

prized as centers, Les knows how to play the position. If he can up his shooting percentage, he could hang around for a while.

RICK'S RATINGS

Scoring: **D**	Defense: **B**
Shooting: **D**	Defensive Rebounding: **A**
Free Throw Shooting: **B**	Playmaking: **B**
Ball Handling: **B**	Intangibles: **A**
Passing: **A**	Overall: **C**

Fat Lever

Birthdate: August 18, 1960
Height: 6-3
Weight: 175
College: Arizona State University, Tempe, Ariz.
Drafted: Portland on first round, 1982 (11th pick).
Position: Guard
Final 1989 Team: Denver Nuggets
Final 1988–89 Statistics:

G	Fg	Fga	Fg%	Ft	Fta	Ft%	Orb	Reb	Ast	Stl	To	Blk	Pts	Ppg
71	558	1221	.457	270	344	.785	187	662	559	195	157	20	1409	19.8

Three-point goals: 23–66 (.348)   **TSP:** .466

SCORING

For Lever, the points come steadily—18.9 ppg the previous two seasons and 19.8 last year—if unspectacularly. No out-of-this-world stuff à la Michael Jordan. Few long-range missiles like teammate Michael Adams (Lever's 23 threes in 1988–89 constituted a career high). But like most good scorers, the diversity is there: jumpers off the dribble in transition or spotting up; drives to the basket for floaters in the lane; simple give-and-gos; finishes on the break, which he does extremely well; and offensive rebounds—a hefty 2.6 a game—third, per minute, among starting 2s (more on Lever's rebounding prowess below). If there's a crack in the 29-year-old's game, it's that he's not a pure shooter—his jumper can be streaky, as his .457 percentage in 1988–89 and lifetime mark of .453 (he's been under .447 four seasons out of seven) indicate. But, no doubt, Fat Lever can score.

DEFENSE/DEFENSIVE REBOUNDING

Pound for pound, literally, Lever is the best rebounder in the league. He's all of 6-3 and 175 pounds and averaged—do not blink—an astounding 9.3 rebounds a game. The Lever rebounding litany goes something like this: he's the first player 6-3 or under to have more than 600 rebounds in a season (which he's done for the last three); he's one of five guards to have averaged as many as nine rebounds a game (the others are Tom Gola, Jerry Sloan, Magic Johnson, Oscar Robertson); in 1988–89, Lever averaged more rebounds than Larry Nance, Brad Daugherty, Sam Perkins, and Patrick Ewing, all of whom are centers or power forwards and 6-9 or taller. You get the idea. Obviously Lever has a nose for the ball and the mind set to rebound. He's not a great leaper but his unsquelchable stamina provides the seemingly inexhaustible supply of energy to rebound and keep rebounding. Defensively, he's pretty special, too. A member of the All-Defensive second team in 1987–88, Lever's a superb thief, 2.7 a game last year, 4th in the league. And with his excellent lateral mobility, he can handle the quicker points, but at the same time is sufficiently tough and physical to take on the 2s.

THE FLOOR GAME

Lever has played both guard positions—in Denver's system it's sometimes difficult to distinguish any position—but on the fast break he doesn't push the ball well nor does he have much facility for controlling the tempo of a game. Which is why he is primarily a 2. However, he's a terrific passer—7.9 assists a game last year—and he doesn't the turn the ball over much.

INTANGIBLES

"Best practice habits in the league," said one coach. The type of player who runs sprints when everybody is breaking for water. A tireless worker, Lever was the picture of durability until the end of 1987–88 when a knee injury forced him to miss Denver's last four playoff games and last year he missed 11 games (he had missed only six regular season games in his first six years) and one of the three playoff games against the Suns.

IN SUM

There's been talk in Denver of trading Lever. But why? According to Pete Babcock, the Nuggets general manager, "If we traded Fat, we would be losing our leading rebounder, our leading assist man, our leader in steals and a 20-points-a-game scorer, not to mention all the intangibles he gives us." Duly noted. Why, then, did the Nuggets, who needed a backup point guard and a power forward, use their first two selections in the draft to pick Todd Lichti (first round) and Michael Cutright (second round)—both of whom are shooting guards?

RICK'S RATINGS

Scoring: **AA**
Shooting: **B**
Free Throw Shooting: **B**
Ball Handling: **B**
Passing: **A**

Defense: **AAA**
Defensive Rebounding: **AAA**
Intangibles: **AAA**
Overall: **AA**

Cliff Levingston

Birthdate: January 4, 1961
Height: 6-8
Weight: 220
College: Wichita State University, Wichita, Kan.
Drafted: Detroit on first round as an undergraduate, 1982 (9th pick).
Position: Forward
Final 1989 Team: Atlanta Hawks
Final 1988–89 Statistics:

G	Fg	Fga	Fg%	Ft	Fta	Ft%	Orb	Reb	Ast	Stl	To	Blk	Pts	Ppg
80	300	568	.528	133	191	.696	194	498	75	97	105	70	734	9.2

Three-point goals: 1–5 (.200)   TSP: .529

SCORING

Levingston is a lifetime .527 shooter (.528 last year), which is indicative of the fact that he scores the bulk of his points within close range of the hoop. He's a terrific athlete who can jump out of the building and run all day. Thus, he scores a lot of points filling the lane on the break and on put-backs. With a good nose for the ball, he has consistently been among the top offensive rebounders in the league on a per minute basis (2.4 a game last year). In the half-court setting, he gets garbage points when he moves without the ball. What he makes he has to earn, because Atlanta does not run plays for him. Levingston, who started 52 games at power forward (because Kevin Willis was injured and Antoine Carr couldn't hold the spot), can also shoot the turnaround jumper in the lane but has limited range (15 feet) and is only an average outside shooter. Nor does he put the ball on the floor well. Sources report he's currently trying to develop a left hand, which hasn't been part of his basketball vocabulary. A lousy foul shooter: .696 last year; .689 lifetime.

DEFENSE/DEFENSIVE REBOUNDING

With the ability to sky, Levingston is a decent defensive rebounder. Defensively, he has good speed, lateral quickness, anticipation, and at 6-8 can block some shots. But, with that size, and playing the 4 spot, he's often giving away several inches and pounds on a nightly basis, which takes its toll.

THE FLOOR GAME

Levingston is not a good ball handler or passer. He averaged less than 1 assist a game (in 27.3 minutes a game). However, he doesn't touch the ball much, which accounts for his few turnovers.

INTANGIBLES

They don't call him "Good News" for nothing. Levingston is upbeat, effervescent—a happy spirit who is good for any ball club. He'll do whatever it takes to win; he's a complete team player.

IN SUM

Levingston did a credible job as a starter but he's ideally suited to be a sixth man—providing superb rebounding on both boards and decent defense.

RICK'S RATINGS

Scoring: **C**	Defensive Rebounding:
Shooting: **C**	**AA**
Free Throw Shooting: **D**	Shot Blocking: **B**
Ball Handling: **C**	Intangibles: **AAA**
Passing: **C**	Overall: **A –**
Defense: **A**	

Ralph Lewis

Birthdate: March 28, 1963
Height: 6-6
Weight: 200
College: LaSalle College, Philadelphia, Pa.
Drafted: Boston on sixth round, 1985 (139th pick).
Positions: Guard, Forward
Final 1989 Team: Charlotte Hornets
Final 1988–89 Statistics:

G	Fg	Fga	Fg%	Ft	Fta	Ft%	Orb	Reb	Ast	Stl	To	Blk	Pts	Ppg
42	58	121	.479	19	39	.487	35	61	15	11	24	3	136	3.2

Three-point goals: 1–3 (.333)   **TSP:** .483

SCORING

Shooting guards who can't shoot don't, except in rare instances (T.R. Dunn comes to mind), last long in the NBA. Lewis, who can swing to the 3 spot (the position he played at LaSalle), has yet to display the kind of jumper that could ensure job security. Of course, we really don't know about his marksmanship since as a Piston in 1987–88 he sat behind Joe Dumars, Isiah Thomas, and Vinnie Johnson (playing all of 310 minutes) and didn't fare much better last year with the Hornets (336 minutes in 42 games as a backup to Robert Reid and Rex Chapman. Charlotte waived him on March 29). We do know Lewis is a good driver, can run the floor, and with his excellent spring, can be lobbed to.

DEFENSE/DEFENSIVE REBOUNDING

Right now, Lewis is making it on his defense. He is particularly effective in the half-court D, where he traps well. Strength, size (6-6), and a willingness to play defense are in his favor. And he rebounds well for a 2.

THE FLOOR GAME

As noted, Lewis can really run the court and has adequate ball handling skills.

INTANGIBLES

Lewis is what you want in an 11th or 12th man: He's a good practice player, team-oriented, gets along with everybody.

IN SUM

Lewis, at this stage, doesn't shoot well enough for a 2 and is too small to be an effective 3. He's a player who perennially will be on the bubble. This past summer, Lewis played on the Detroit Pistons' entry in the Southern California Summer Pro League.

RICK'S RATINGS

Scoring: **D**	Defense: **A**
Shooting: **D**	Defensive Rebounding: **A**
Free Throw Shooting: **D**	Intangibles: **B**
Ball Handling: **C**	Overall: **D**
Passing: **C**	

Reggie Lewis

Birthdate: November 21, 1965
Height: 6-7
Weight: 195
College: Northeastern University, Boston, Mass.
Drafted: Boston on first round, 1987 (22nd pick).
Positions: Forward, Guard
Final 1989 Team: Boston Celtics
Final 1988–89 Statistics:

G	Fg	Fga	Fg%	Ft	Fta	Ft%	Orb	Reb	Ast	Stl	To	Blk	Pts	Ppg
81	604	1242	.486	284	361	.787	116	377	218	124	142	72	1495	18.5

Three-point goals: 3–22 (.136)   **TSP:** .488

SCORING

If there was any trace of a silver lining to the absence of Larry Bird from the Celtics lineup last year, it was the emergence of Lewis, who two months into the season moved into Bird's 3 spot and proceeded to take the league by storm. He averaged 18.5 a game, shot .486 from the field, and was consistent throughout—hitting double figures in 47 consecutive games and scoring 20 or more over 37 times. Lewis, a two-year veteran, proved once again the axiom that playing time is the truest gauge of a player's abilities. As a rookie, Lewis didn't play significant minutes (8.3 a game), and while he showed flashes of brilliance, the jury was still out. But now the verdict is unanimous: Lewis will be a big-time scorer for a long time to come. With a multitude of weapons, Lewis is the prototypical scorer. Underlying it all is his athleticism. A wiry 6-7, he plays bigger because he can jump out of the gym. He also runs the floor exceptionally well and is extremely quick. He has a superb first step and can beat you off the dribble and then either jam it or make one of those soon to be patented runners in the lane. He also consistently drilled the face-up jumper from 16 to 18 feet—he can stop on a dime and loves to shoot it off the left-handed (he's a righty) dribble. He's only a fair offensive rebounder (1.4 a game) and a decent (.787) foul shooter. When Bird returns, Lewis is slated to move to the 2 spot.

DEFENSE/DEFENSIVE REBOUNDING

Lewis has a lot going for him defensively. He's quick, has long arms, moves his feet well, and can jump. He blocked 72 shots (per minute, that placed him in the top third among starting 3s) and had a team-high 124 steals. Twos going against Lewis have a tough time because of his size. But he's still in the developmental stage, defensively. He plays hard but his technique often comes up short. He's a below-average defensive rebounder for his position.

THE FLOOR GAME

Lewis is not the smoothest ball handler, but he doesn't hurt the Cs. There is some concern that, as a 2, he will have to handle more in transition, but, per minute, his turnovers were way below-average for starting small forwards. He moves well without the ball and, as noted, can fly on the break. He is the mainstay of the Celts' transition game.

INTANGIBLES

As a rookie, Lewis bided his time, never complained about his lack of minutes, and continued to work on his game, particularly his ball handling and shooting. The proof was in last year's pudding. He has a tremendous amount of self-confidence in his abilities.

IN SUM

A brilliant pick at No. 22, Lewis has arrived. He's a scorer, but with refinements in his defense, he has the potential to make a major contribution on both ends of the floor.

RICK'S RATINGS

Scoring: **AAA**   Defense: **A**
Shooting: **AA**   Defensive Rebounding: **C**
Free Throw Shooting: **B**   Intangibles: **A**
Ball Handling: **B**   Overall: **AA**
Passing: **B**

Alton Lister

Birthdate: October 1, 1958
Height: 7-0
Weight: 240
College: Arizona State University, Tempe, Ariz.
Drafted: Milwaukee on first round, 1981 (21st pick).
Position: Center
Final 1989 Team: Seattle Supersonics
Final 1988–89 Statistics:

G	Fg	Fga	Fg%	Ft	Fta	Ft%	Orb	Reb	Ast	Stl	To	Blk	Pts	Ppg
82	271	543	.499	115	178	.646	207	545	54	28	117	180	657	8.0

Three-point goals: 0–0 (.000)   **TSP:** .499

SCORING

Last season in Seattle's offense, the center played a limited role. Or was it that Lister, traded to the Warriors for a 1990 first-round pick, was the middleman, so the center made a minor offensive contribution? Whichever came first, the chicken or the egg, the fact is that Lister, in an eight-year career, has always been a bit player on offense, only once averaging more than 10 points a game, with a maximum of 9.2 shots from the field. His productivity has suffered because he's chronically in foul trouble and has averaged only 23.1 minutes a game for his career. As indicated by his shooting percentage, .499 in 1988–89 (first time he's been less than 50 percent), most of Lister's points come from territory close to the basket. He's been an above-average offensive rebounder for his career (on a per minute basis, fourth among starting centers last year), but he doesn't finish well. Baseline to baseline, Lister's one of the fastest centers in the league and can score on the break. Otherwise, besides a right-handed hook, his low post game has never developed, and he will sometimes take a jumper as a trailer on the break. He's an extremely poor foul shooter (.604 lifetime; .646 last year).

DEFENSE/DEFENSIVE REBOUNDING

Lister's major asset is his shot blocking (2.2 in 1988–89, ninth in the league). In its trapping schemes, Seattle funneled everything to the middle, to the hub of the defense: Lister. He has the ability to block a shot, recover, and then block a second attempt. He has the strength and size to bang, though he doesn't do it regularly. And then, of course, there's the foul trouble; despite his veteran status, he still can't get the calls. He has the capacity to be an awesome defensive rebounder (sixth best, per minute, historically, among centers), but last year his production dropped significantly with the arrival of Michael Cage.

THE FLOOR GAME

Lister doesn't have the best hands. When he comes down with a rebound, he's often stripped of the ball by opposing guards. However, he has improved his ability to catch the ball on the break, which had been an issue in the past. At best, he's an average passer.

INTANGIBLES

Lister has been Mr. Inconsistent. He whets your appetite with solid effort and then disappears. He tends to lose his concentration when the fouls go against him. But last season, he was much better on a night-in, night-out basis.

IN SUM

Lister does a couple things well: block shots and rebound. That wasn't enough for a near-championship contender like Seattle. With the Warriors, Lister (who previously played for Don Nelson in Milwaukee) will play both 4 and 5 and is a valuable insurance policy should Ralph Sampson not recuperate fully from his knee injury.

RICK'S RATINGS

Scoring: **C**   Defense: **A**
Shooting: **C**   Defensive Rebounding: **B**
Free Throw Shooting: **D**   Shot Blocking: **AAA**
Ball Handling: **C**   Intangibles: **C**
Passing: **B**   Overall: **B−**

Brad Lohaus

Birthdate: September 29, 1964
Height: 7-0
Weight: 235
College: University of Iowa, Iowa City Ia.
Drafted: Boston on second round, 1987 (45th pick).
Positions: Forward, Center
Final 1989 Team: Sacramento Kings
Final 1988–89 Statistics:

G	Fg	Fga	Fg%	Ft	Fta	Ft%	Orb	Reb	Ast	Stl	To	Blk	Pts	Ppg
77	210	486	.432	81	103	.786	84	256	66	30	77	56	502	6.5

Three-point goals: 1–11 (.091)   **TSP:** .433

SCORING

Is he a 3? A 4? A 5? All of the above? Or, as the Celtics evidently concluded, none of the above and traded him in February 1989 to Sacramento along with Danny Ainge for Ed Pinckney and Joe Kleine. But now he's with Minnesota, their fourth pick in the expansion draft.

If somebody could figure out what position Lohaus is best suited for—the Kings used him as a 4 and also at 5—maybe he'd settle down and become a quality NBA player. He is, however, a strange breed: a 7-footer who runs like a gazelle and has a terrific touch from the perimeter but is absolutely lost in terms of a back-to-the-basket game. With those credentials, his best position seemed to be 3, but he doesn't put the ball on the floor well and is vulnerable, quickness-wise, on defense. And last year he wasn't canning the jumper (only .432 after he shot .496 his rookie year). So now he's a 4, but he isn't strong (he bulked up in the summer of 1988, but he proceeded to lose all of the weight), and is not a good rebounder.

DEFENSE/DEFENSIVE REBOUNDING

Lohaus's defensive talents are best displayed in pressing situations, where he can use his agility and aggressiveness to deflect loose balls and block shots. But he loses his effectiveness in half court since he gets pushed around and simply doesn't understand how to be physical in the post. And his rebounding will have to improve if he wants substantial minutes as a power forward.

THE FLOOR GAME

Lohaus is a mistake player. He has the tools to be a good passer but his decision-making is questionable. He's an intelligent person but his basketball IQ often had Celtic coaches rolling their eyes.

INTANGIBLES

In Boston, Lohaus had a fragile ego and lost confidence easily. He lacked poise and is still learning how to play under control. In Boston, some questioned his work ethic but that definitely was not the case in Sacramento.

IN SUM

A huge disappointment in Boston, Lohaus is still a project, though the raw materials are promising. With Minnesota, Lohaus will get more minutes—on paper, he's their first frontcourt player off the bench—than he would with a more established team. He'll have time, in other words, to show whether he's anything more than a marginal support player.

RICK'S RATINGS

Scoring: **C**   Defense: **C**
Shooting: **C**   Defensive Rebounding: **C**
Free Throw Shooting: **B**   Shot Blocking: **A**
Ball Handling: **C**   Intangibles: **C**
Passing: **C**   Overall: **C**

Grant Long

Birthdate: March 12, 1966
Height: 6-8
Weight: 225
College: Eastern Michigan University, Ypsilanti, Mich.
Drafted: Miami on second round, 1988 (33rd pick).
Position: Forward
Final 1989 Team: Miami Heat
Final 1988–89 Statistics:

G	Fg	Fga	Fg%	Ft	Fta	Ft%	Orb	Reb	Ast	Stl	To	Blk	Pts	Ppg
82	336	692	.486	304	406	.749	240	546	149	122	201	48	976	11.9

Three-point goals: 0–5 (.000)   **TSP:** .486

SCORING

Long, a second-round pick in 1988, works hard for his points. He's a blue-collar player—not pretty, not flashy—who pounds the offensive boards (2.9 a game), runs the lanes well, and will hit the occasional turnaround jumper. Early on, his face-up game was nil, and he showed little consistency or even inclination to shoot the outside shot. But by season's end, he was shooting from the perimeter and also beating opponents off the dribble. Long's forte is getting to the line. At Eastern Michigan he averaged 23 points a game on just 14 field goal attempts and as an NBA rookie, he shot five free throws a game, which ranked him in the top third for starting 4s. One observer speculated that Long gets the calls because of his no-guff-to-the-refs attitude. He's an OK foul shooter (.749), and with his work ethic, will undoubtedly improve.

DEFENSE/DEFENSIVE REBOUNDING

Miami is pleased with Long's defense. In the post, Long is physical, accepts the defensive challenge, and understands team defense. He averaged 1.5 steals a game, way above average for 4s. Long doesn't block shots and is vulnerable to quicker players out on the floor. He can guard some 3s, 4s, and even smaller 5s. But while he gets the call on offense, the same can't be said for his defense: Long's 13 disqualifications were second in the league. At this point in his career, he's a better offensive rebounder than defensive rebounder (in the bottom third for starting 4s). An average jumper, he relies on positioning to get the ball.

THE FLOOR GAME

Long has a good knowledge of the game. He understands what Miami is trying to accomplish on both ends of the floor. His passing skills are adequate, though his turnovers were on the high side.

INTANGIBLES

Nobody outworks Long during games, in practice, or in the off-season. His desire to improve may be his biggest asset.

IN SUM

A superb pick as the 33rd player selected overall, Long is one of the mainstays of Miami's future. With his attitude, defensive skills, and hard-hat offense, he figures to have a long (pun intended) career in the league

RICK'S RATINGS

Scoring: **B**	Defense: **B**
Shooting: **B**	Defensive Rebounding: **D**
Free Throw Shooting: **C**	Shot Blocking: **C**
Ball Handling: **C**	Intangibles: **AAA**
Passing: **B**	Overall: **B**

John Long

Birthdate: August 28, 1956
Height: 6-5
Weight: 200
College: University of Detroit, Detroit, Mich.
Drafted: Detroit on second round, 1978 (29th pick).
Position: Guard
Final 1989 Team: Detroit Pistons
Final 1988–89 Statistics:

G	Fg	Fga	Fg%	Ft	Fta	Ft%	Orb	Reb	Ast	Stl	To	Blk	Pts	Ppg
68	147	359	.409	70	76	.921	18	77	80	29	57	3	372	5.5

Three-point goals: 8–20 (.400)   **TSP:** .421

SCORING

Long started the season with the Pacers but for both parties' benefit, the sooner he was out of Indianapolis, the better. He couldn't find the basket, shooting .401 in 44 games—curious since he has earned his NBA keep for 11 years as a shooter. Eventually, he was waived and picked up by Detroit where, in limited minutes (152), he shot better (.475; he's a .469 lifetime shooter). Overall, he averaged 5.5 ppg, the first time in his career he was under the 10-a-game mark (14.6 ppg lifetime). Long has always been a long distance threat, and the last two years he's positively scorched the nets from three-point land: an outstanding .442 in 1987–88 (34-for-77, third in the league) and .400 last year (8-for-20). He's better coming off of picks than creating off the dribble. Nor is he effective taking the ball to the hoop. But he is one of the league's best foul shooters (.921 last year on 70-for-76 shooting; .861 lifetime).

DEFENSE/DEFENSIVE REBOUNDING

Long is not the typical all-shoot, no-D, 2. He has a toughness about him and is a physical defender who fights over picks and takes pride in his defensive effort.

THE FLOOR GAME

Long is not a good ball handler, not a player you want breaking traps. But he's a smart veteran who doesn't hurt you when he's on the floor.

INTANGIBLES

Besides his abominable shooting, Indiana dispensed with Long because he was a disruptive force in the locker room—"cancerous," according to one source. But with Detroit, where he played from 1978–79 to 1985–86, he was a valuable insurance policy who gave some quality minutes when Isiah Thomas was suspended for two games for fighting in April.

IN SUM

Maybe one more year.

RICK'S RATINGS

Scoring: **B**   Passing: **B**
Shooting: **A**   Defense: **B**
Free Throw Shooting: Defensive Rebounding: **C**
  AAA   Intangibles: **C**
Ball Handling: **B**   Overall: **C**

John Lucas

Birthdate: October 31, 1953
Height: 6-3
Weight: 185
College: University of Maryland, College Park, Md.
Drafted: Houston on first round, 1976 (1st pick).
Position: Guard
Final 1989 Team: Seattle Supersonics
Final 1988–89 Statistics:

G	Fg	Fga	Fg%	Ft	Fta	Ft%	Orb	Reb	Ast	Stl	To	Blk	Pts	Ppg
74	119	299	.398	54	77	.701	22	79	260	60	66	1	310	4.2

Three-point goals: 18–68 (.265)   **TSP:** .425

SCORING

Lucas, a well-traveled point guard is heading back to Houston making it seven teams in fourteen seasons. He has always been able to score. As recently as 1986–87, while a Milwaukee Buck, he averaged 17.5. But the 36-year old veteran (he's the oldest guard in the league) has lost a step or two, and the result last year was a .398 shooting percentage, his career low. He also had a subpar year from three-point country, .265. More unusual, however, were his troubles from the line—he shot only .701, which was significantly below his .776 career mark. He shoots a set shot from afar and can also get into the lane and hang for the pretty floating one-hander.

DEFENSE/DEFENSIVE REBOUNDING

Lucas, never much of a defender, at least put forth the effort last year. Still, he'll hit a screen and stop, and doesn't contribute much in help situations. But he can steal the ball; on a per minute basis, he was ranked in the top quarter among backup point guards.

THE FLOOR GAME

Lucas's value is his leadership and ball handling. He can run the offense, is a fine push man on the break, and penetrates and dishes as well as anybody in the league. And he takes good care of the ball. When he's on the floor, he provides a steadying influence.

INTANGIBLES

Lucas is universally acknowledged as a leader. He's upbeat, with a great sense of humor, and he helps keep everybody loose.

IN SUM

Lucas's intangibles are the positive story here, a big plus on any team. He still has playing value, but his minutes have to be limited.

RICK'S RATINGS

Scoring: **C**   Defense: **C**
Shooting: **C**   Defensive Rebounding: **B**
Free Throw Shooting: **C**   Playmaking: **A**
Ball Handling: **A**   Intangibles: **AA**
Passing: **A**   Overall: **B –**

Rick Mahorn

Birthdate: September 21, 1958
Height: 6-10
Weight: 255
College: Hampton Institute, Hampton, Va.
Drafted: Washington on second round, 1980 (35th pick).
Position: Forward
Final 1989 Team: Detroit Pistons
Final 1988–89 Statistics:

G	Fg	Fga	Fg%	Ft	Fta	Ft%	Orb	Reb	Ast	Stl	To	Blk	Pts	Ppg
72	203	393	.517	116	155	.748	141	496	59	40	97	66	522	7.3

Three-point goals: 0–2 (.000)   **TSP:** .517

SCORING

Mahorn, a Bad Boy no more—he was Minnesota's first selection in the expansion draft—gets lots of attention for all that bruiser stuff, but the fact is he can also shoot the basketball. He possesses an accurate turnaround jumper from 15 feet and in (.517 last season, .574 in 1987–88, and .503 lifetime). His high percentages have a lot to do with his solid shot selection; he stays within his range and doesn't force his offense. He can shoot the jumper facing up or after posting up—with that big butt of his, he gets great low-post position. Otherwise, he scores on power moves inside—again, after setting himself in the blocks—and occasionally on offensive rebounds (2.0 a game in 24.9 minutes, though his numbers were below average for starting 4s). Mahorn was one of the least productive scorers among starting 4s (7.3 ppg), but note that the Pistons clearly define (and enforce!) roles, and scoring was not Mahorn's function. If he stays with Minnesota—he's attractive trade bait—look for him to be more offensive-minded.

DEFENSE/DEFENSIVE REBOUNDING

Don't try to tell Mahorn basketball is a non-contact sport. An ex-football player, he's expert at fighting—sometimes literally—the big guys (he can also guard small forwards; he did a superb job on the Lakers James Worthy during the NBA finals) for low-post position. A night against Mahorn is an accumulation of forearms in the neck, knees in the thigh—and whatever else he can get away with. He undoubtedly leads the league in gratuitous contact—opponents call it dirty, Detroit fans call it physical. Whatever it is, it's effective. Opponents who get "hot" often find themselves, for example, feeling the brunt of a hard Mahorn foul. That big behind also comes in handy on the defensive glass. He can't jump worth a damn—chronic back problems don't help matters—but he knows how to position himself and has a good pair of hands. Per minute, he outrebounded A.C. Green, Karl Malone, and Buck Williams last year. He can block a shot (almost one a game) but he's not a shot blocker, per se.

THE FLOOR GAME

Detroit, which can run with the best of them with Dennis Rodman and John Salley at forward, didn't have the same speed with Mahorn and Mark Aguirre up front. Mahorn's an adequate passer. And with that big body, he sets one of the meanest picks in the league, and runs an effective pick-and-roll.

INTANGIBLES

You can't overestimate the value of a big-time Enforcer. His opponents question his tactics but Mahorn's teammates relish the fact he's ready to mix it up in an instant. His master plan—don't doubt for a second that his methods aren't deliberate—centers in getting opponents to lose their cool (and thus their concentration). More often than not, it works. His back is a concern; in fact, Detroit GM Jack McCloskey cited it as a reason for leaving him unprotected in the expansion draft. Besides the muscle, the Pistons will dearly miss Mahorn's leadership in the locker room and on the floor.

IN SUM

The Bad Boys are dead, but Mahorn will, in spirit, remain a Bad Boy. But as one rival coach put it, "He's more than a thug." He can shoot, he can rebound, he can defend. And yes, he intimidates. On balance, that's a potent combination. Perhaps he'll now become the Minnesota Mauler.

RICK'S RATINGS

Scoring: **C**	Defensive Rebounding: **AA**
Shooting: **B**	Shot Blocking: **B**
Free Throw Shooting: **C**	Intangibles: **AA**
Ball Handling: **B**	Overall: **A**
Passing: **B**	
Defense: **AA**	

Dan Majerle

Birthdate: September 9, 1965

Height: 6-6
Weight: 215
College: Central Michigan University, Mt. Pleasant, Mich.
Drafted: Phoenix on first round, 1988 (14th pick).
Positions: Guard, Forward
Final 1989 Team: Phoenix Suns
Final 1988–89 Statistics:

G	Fg	Fga	Fg%	Ft	Fta	Ft%	Orb	Reb	Ast	Stl	To	Blk	Pts	Ppg
54	181	432	.419	78	127	.614	62	209	130	63	48	14	467	8.6

Three-point goals: 27–82 (.329)   TSP: .450

SCORING

Majerle (pronounced MAR-lee), a first-round selection (14th overall) and a member of the 1988 Olympic team, had typical first-year difficulties adjusting to the pro game. He had trouble finding a groove in terms of getting the shot he wanted or knowing when to take it, and he displayed a tendency to rush things. Result: He shot .419 from the field, though, curiously, he was comfortable from three-point range: .329. (During the playoffs, he was .438 from the field and .286 in threes). Part of his problem, if you want to call it that, is his strength; from the shorter distances, say mid-range jumpers, the rugged 6-6, 215-pound Majerle is almost too strong for his own good. Also, at Central Michigan, he was to a large extent an inside player (nicknamed "Thunder" for his tumultuous dunks). But in the NBA, he's a 2 (who can swing to the 3), so his game now is facing the basket. A slasher, he gets a lot of points on aggressive drives to the hoop. Early on, he had trouble finishing, but as the season progressed, he was knocking them down. Best way to defend him: Make him shoot the medium-distance jumper off the dribble going left.

DEFENSE/DEFENSIVE REBOUNDING

Majerle had an easier time playing defense, since so much of D is in the head. And this rookie showed that he has the requisite defensive mind-set. He's competitive, hard-nosed, and tenacious. He'll get in your jockstrap and stay all night, and he has the ability to guard 1s, 2s, or 3s. In the same vein, he does a nice job on the defensive boards (way above average for reserve shooting guards).

THE FLOOR GAME

Majerle is a careful ball handler. He's not a creator, but he doesn't turn the ball over, either; note his solid 2.71 assist-to-turnover ratio. But he needs to develop the ability to create off the dribble.

INTANGIBLES

Majerle's major assets are his toughness, fearlessness, and competitiveness. He knows only one way to play: All out. He missed 28 games last season with mononucleosis.

IN SUM

On draft day last June, Phoenix fans booed when the Suns announced they had selected Majerle. Now, he's a "favorite Sun." While he needs to improve his mid-range shooting and his ball handling, with his gung-ho attitude, defensive prowess, and ability to score, he'll be knocking around the NBA for a long time.

RICK'S RATINGS

Scoring: **B**	Defense: **AA**
Shooting: **C**	Defensive Rebounding:
Free Throw Shooting: **D**	**AAA**
Ball Handling: **A**	Intangibles: **A**
Passing: **B**	Overall: **B**

Jeff Malone

Birthdate: June 28, 1961
Height: 6-4
Weight: 205
College: Mississippi State University, Mississippi State, Miss.
Drafted: Washington on first round, 1983 (10th pick).
Position: Guard
Final 1989 Team: Washington Bullets
Final 1988–89 Statistics:

G	Fg	Fga	Fg%	Ft	Fta	Ft%	Orb	Reb	Ast	Stl	To	Blk	Pts	Ppg
76	677	1410	.480	296	340	.871	55	179	219	39	165	14	1651	21.7

Three-point goals: 1–19 (.053)   TSP: .480

SCORING

OK, everybody, get your cameras ready. Here comes Jeff Malone—two dribbles to his left, back arched, ball cocked, wrist snapped—the picture-perfect play. Malone has one of the prettiest jumpers in the league. Beyond its aesthetic pleasures, it's also a fairly accurate shot (.480 last year) though for a player known far and wide as a great shooter, Malone has had some curious seasons (.444 in 1983–84 and .457 in 1986–87). Consider, however, that Malone doesn't have the luxury of a Byron Scott, who can feast off of Magic Johnson's dishes or a Trent Tucker who can camp outside and wait for a Patrick Ewing pass. The Bullets have no inside threat from the post, so defenses can key on Malone, who for the last three of four seasons (21.7 ppg in 1988–89, 17th in the league) has been the Bullets' leading scorer. Malone is best from 15 to 19 feet; interestingly, he's a below-average three-point shooter (1–19 last year, .246

career). He's most effective coming off screens and shooting on the catch, or after a dribble or two. He's more a pure shooter than a scorer—he doesn't drive well and would rather pull up for the jumper than take it all the way to the hoop. Malone can draw fouls (4.5 attempts last year) and has consistently been one of the league's top foul shooters (.871 in 1988–89 and .868 career).

DEFENSE/DEFENSIVE REBOUNDING

Malone is a better defensive player than people give him credit for. He guards his man well and is willing to fight through picks, though he's not aggressive in help situations. He is known to rise to the occasion against stellar performers such as Michael Jordan. Malone doesn't jump well and is a poor rebounder (a mere 2.3 a game, tied with Mike McGee for the worst among starting 2s) for his position. And he virtually never steals the ball (.5 a game, worst among starting shooting guards).

THE FLOOR GAME

Malone has just average foot speed. Combine this with his lack of jumping ability, and the result is that he's not a real good finisher on the break. He's an adequate passer but his role is to score. Combine that with his unimpressive ball handling, and the result is a poor 1.33 assist-to-turnover ratio.

INTANGIBLES

Despite his shooting credentials, Malone once had a reputation for missing the clutch shot. His .408 shooting in the 1985–86 Bullet-76er playoff series and .370 bricksmanship in the 1986–87 Bullet-Piston series were two indications. But against Detroit in the 1987–88 playoffs, he dispelled the notion when he shot .515. However, he does occasionally have trouble getting his shot at the end of games because he can't easily manufacture his own offense.

IN SUM

Malone is one of the premier middle-distance shooters in the league. He plays a little defense but he's basically a one-dimensional player, which is why some think this two-time All-Star is overrated. On a more well-rounded offensive team, he'd be more effective.

RICK'S RATINGS

Scoring: **AAA**   Defense: **B**
Shooting: **AA**   Defensive Rebounding: **D**
Free Throw Shooting: **AA**   Intangibles: **A**
Ball Handling: **B**   Overall: **A**
Passing: **B**

Karl Malone

Birthdate: July 24, 1963
Height: 6-9
Weight: 260
College: Louisiana Tech University, Ruston, La.
Drafted: Utah on first round as an undergraduate, 1985 (13th pick).
Position: Forward
Final 1989 Team: Utah Jazz
Final 1988–89 Statistics:

G	Fg	Fga	Fg%	Ft	Fta	Ft%	Orb	Reb	Ast	Stl	To	Blk	Pts	Ppg
80	809	1559	.519	703	918	.766	259	853	219	144	285	70	2326	29.1

Three-point goals: 5–16 (.313)   **TSP:** .521

SCORING

The "Mailman"—the second-leading scorer in the league (29.1 ppg)—delivers over many routes. He can send it from the outside—he's developed into a dangerous perimeter shooter from 15 to 17 feet—or the inside, where he sets up shop (few can deny this he-man inside position) and shoots short turnaround jumpers, little jump hooks, and dribble drives to the basket (.519 from the field, tied for 16th in the league). He's solid as well on the offensive glass, grabbing 3.2 a game last year. On the break, Malone is one of the best—and from a defender's perspective—scariest finishers in the league. He'll grab a defensive rebound, find John Stockton on the outlet pass, and then come rip-roaring up the court—all 6-9, 260 well-chiseled pounds, and fill the lane. Then he'll either run over the defender (or the defender, wanting to preserve his body, will have already cleared out) for the jam. In the past, he was quite weak at the line; entering 1988–89 he was a .617 shooter. But last year, he finally achieved respectability from the stripe (.766), a critical improvement as he went to the line 11.5 times a game, by far the most in the NBA (he had a total of 918 attempts; no other player broke the 800 mark).

DEFENSE/DEFENSIVE REBOUNDING

Malone is a punishing defensive player, a physical defender who isn't afraid to put that massive body on his man. For his size, he moves well laterally and is quick. He also has great hands; his trademark is swiping the ball on the way up as the offensive player moves the ball to shooting position (1.8 steals a game, tops among power forwards). He knocks the ball away a lot but also gets called for a lot of fouls. How good a defender is Malone? He was named to the NBA All-Defensive team (second team) in 1987–88 and last year he received nine votes and just barely missed making the second team. With his strength, jumping ability, and size, he's a ferocious defensive rebounder. He finished fifth in the league in total rebounds (10.7 a game), one of just seven players with 10 or more rebounds per game.

THE FLOOR GAME

Malone runs the floor as well as any big man playing today and is likely the best runner at the 4 spot ever. First and foremost, he's basically a scorer: when the ball goes to Malone, you want and expect him to shoot. As a passer, Larry Bird he's not, but he's getting better at reading the double- and triple-teams he faces. He can put the ball on the floor in making moves to the basket, but otherwise you don't want him handling the ball (note his drab 0.77 assist-to-turnover ratio). But he was fifth among starting 4s, per minute, for assists.

INTANGIBLES

Malone has matured considerably in his four years in the league. Once a hothead—a child in a man's body, according to one coach—he's curbed his outbursts and now concentrates on playing the game. He's in extraordinary shape and has missed only three games in four years. His reputation as an enforcer is well-deserved, and he's been known to unnecessarily stick opponents with an elbow here or a forearm there.

IN SUM

If Stockton is the quintessential point guard, Malone is the quintessential power forward, unquestionably the best in the league at that position. He was the only unanimous choice for the All-NBA, first team last season. Say no more.

RICK'S RATINGS

Moses Malone

Birthdate: March 23, 1955

Height: 6-10
Weight: 250
College: None
Position: Center
Final 1989 Team: Atlanta Hawks
Final 1988–89 Statistics:

G	Fg	Fga	Fg%	Ft	Fta	Ft%	Orb	Reb	Ast	Stl	To	Blk	Pts	Ppg
81	538	1096	.491	561	711	.789	386	956	112	79	245	100	1637	20.2

Three-point goals: 0–12 (.000)   **TSP:** .491

SCORING

Thirteen years and still going strong. A slimmer, quicker Moses—he played last season at a svelte 250, down about 10 pounds from his Washington days—showed that he has a lot of basketball left in him, scoring over 20 (20.2) for the 11th consecutive year and averaging 11.8 rebounds a game, fourth in the league. Malone's game isn't complicated. He's a superstar who just outworks, outbangs, and outhustles his opponent. He is, of course, a master offensive rebounder (far and away the career leader in offensive caroms with 5,628; 4.8 a game last year, for second in the league). And for the few inches he's lost on his jump, he more than compensates for with his relentlessness and instinct for the ball. Then there's his post play. Smooth he is not, but Moses has a bundle of moves around the basket and knows how to get to the line (8.8 attempts in the 1988–89, tops among starting centers in the league; he's a fairly good foul shooter, .789 in 1988–89). In the last few years, he's added an accurate face-up jumper from 15 feet and in. And he's still one of the best running centers in the league and gets easy baskets by beating opponents up court.

DEFENSE/DEFENSIVE REBOUNDING

Malone's defensive rebounding numbers speak for themselves. Now that Kareem Abdul-Jabbar has retired, Moses is the NBA active career leader and last season pulled down seven defensive boards a game, 10th in the league. Defensively, he's never been much of a shot blocker (though his 100 blocks in 1988–89 was his best performance in the last four seasons), but he does an adequate job defending his own man, denying the ball, and fighting for low-post position. But he doesn't always change ends well and opposing centers get layups. Nor can you count on his defensive intensity every night.

THE FLOOR GAME

Malone has been criticized for not reading the double-team well, and the ball occasionally stops in his hands. He's been known to force shots with players draped all over him. Though he has improved his passing, he is not Abdul-Jabbar (only 1.4 assists a game) and his assist-to-turnover ratio was a poor 0.46.

INTANGIBLES

Malone is one of the true workhorses in the NBA; the term "comes to play" was invented to describe him. He leads by his work ethic, his competitiveness, and his ferocious desire to win.

IN SUM

Moses was the man who was going to lead the Hawks into the NBA's promised land. He said it himself: "I'm expecting a championship." So consider year one (Malone has a three-year contract) a failure. But it's hard to point the finger at Malone, who had a Moses-type year (he made the All-Star team) and performed to expectations. Still, his defensive inconsistency and his sporadic passing from the post are not the stuff of title-winning teams.

RICK'S RATINGS

Scoring: **AAA**
Shooting: **B**
Free Throw Shooting: **B**
Ball Handling: **C**
Passing: **C**
Defense: **B**

Defensive Rebounding: **AA**
Shot Blocking: **C**
Intangibles: **AA**
Overall: **AA**

Danny Manning

Birthdate: May 17, 1966
Height: 6-10
Weight: 240
College: University of Kansas, Lawrence, Kan.
Drafted: Los Angeles Clippers on first round, 1988 (1st pick).
Position: Forward
Final 1989 Team: Los Angeles Clippers
Final 1988–89 Statistics:

G	Fg	Fga	Fg%	Ft	Fta	Ft%	Orb	Reb	Ast	Stl	To	Blk	Pts	Ppg
26	177	358	.494	79	103	.767	70	171	81	44	93	25	434	16.7

Three-point goals: 1–5 (.200)　　**TSP:** .496

SCORING

It wasn't long before the debate was raging. Just how good was Danny Manning, the Clippers' well-credentialed (College Player of the Year, member of the 1988 Olympic Team, NCAA tourney MVP for winner Kansas) No. 1 pick (and first overall in the 1988 draft)? Was he an above-average NBA player, one blessed with multiple skills, but by no means an impact player? A notch above—a potential All-

Star? Or a down-the-road superstar, a franchise player, of the same ilk as a Magic Johnson, a Michael Jordan, a Larry Bird? Unfortunately, before any definitive answers to these questions could be offered, Manning—28 games into his rookie year (he had missed the first four in a contract dispute; he signed for a reported $10.5 million over five years)—suffered one of basketball's most horrid injuries in a game against Milwaukee on January 4: a torn anterior cruciate ligament (the so-called Bernard King/Mitch Kupchak injury; according to a Clipper source, an optimistic return date is the middle of this season). But Manning's absence did provide some tentative clues as to his NBA "station." The Clippers proceeded to lose 29 of their next 30 games, which would indicate, he's certainly an "impact" player; of course, it's too soon to tell whether he's a FRANCHISE. In his brief stint, Manning was difficult to pigeonhole; his game is an amalgam. At 6-10, 240, he can play the power forward slot and displayed some promising post-up skills, including a somewhat unusual looking half-hook. And he's a good, quick jumper who was extremely tough on the offensive glass (2.7 a game in 36.5 minutes). But he has (or perhaps, more accurately, had; players such as King and Kupchak who have come back from this type of injury invariably lose some agility and speed) the quickness, mobility, and running ability that enabled him to handle the 3 spot. He can put the ball on the floor from the perimeter—to take advantage of his superb ball handling and passing skills he was often used like a point forward—and showed an ability to hit the facing jumper from 15 feet and in. That, too, is a strange-looking shot—he has a low release point—and his growth as a player will come in his consistency from the outside. This variety is a strength, but could also be a weakness; he needs to develop a go-to move.

DEFENSE/DEFENSIVE REBOUNDING

The early signs were promising. While he still has some bad habits—such as reaching around his man—Manning has the tools to be an excellent defender. He anticipates well—an impressive 1.7 steals a game—can block a shot here and there (one a game), and will make the hustle play. A product of the "Larry Brown Defensive School," this is one multi-millionaire who is not afraid to get his knees skinned. So far, he's been more effective defending in the post (and he could use some more upper-body strength) than on the perimeter. An average defensive rebounder.

THE FLOOR GAME

Manning sees the floor exceptionally well and can make the tough pass. If he had a weakness, it's that the "colt" in him wanted to make the fancy pass over the workable one. He has a firm grasp on how to play.

INTANGIBLES

Manning is that rare player—and even rarer for a rookie—who made his teammates better. He carried Kansas to a national title, and in his short two-month stint with the Clippers, was beginning to assert his leadership. He's had low moments, basketball-wise—four points against Duke in the 1986 NCAA semi-final, no points against the Soviets in the 1988 Olympics—but no one doubts he's a winner.

IN SUM

At this stage, it's too difficult to speculate on his physical condition. But even a somewhat less athletic Manning—Clipper coach Don Casey has remarked that he may now be better suited for the 4—can make a significant contribution. As a power forward, any physical limitations he has will have less of an impact while his passing prowess, court awareness, and, most importantly, his heart will be unaffected.

RICK'S RATINGS

Scoring: **A**
Shooting: **B**
Free Throw Shooting: **B**
Ball Handling: **A**
Passing: **AA**

Defense: **A**
Defensive Rebounding: **B**
Intangibles: **AA**
Overall: **A**

Maurice Martin

Birthdate: July 2, 1964
Height: 6-6
Weight: 200
College: St. Joseph's University, Philadelphia, Pa
Drafted: Denver on first round, 1986 (16th pick).
Position: Guard
Final 1989 Team: None
Final 1988–89 Statistics: Did Not Play

SCORING

Martin, who was selected by the Minnesota Timberwolves in the expansion draft, has probably spent more time in physical therapy than on a basketball court since being drafted by the Nuggets in the first round in 1986. After a disappointing rookie season—he was a little-used bench player (286 minutes in 43 games) who shot .378, and didn't win any fans among the Denver coaching staff—Martin, slated to be a starter for the Nuggets in 1987–88, had arthroscopic surgery on his right knee before the start of that season and played only 26 games and 136 minutes. In August 1988, he again had arthroscopic surgery on the same knee, and when the knee didn't respond, he underwent reconstructive surgery in October 1988 and missed all of last year. Unfortunately, Martin has an anterior cruciate ligament problem (à la Mitch Kupchak, Bernard King, and Danny Manning); at the present time, his physical status is very much in the air. A shooting guard, Martin is (was?) a good jumper who can post up and thrives on picks. He's not a pure shooter; more of a scorer. He scored big in the Southern California Summer Pro League in 1987 so evidently the potential is there.

DEFENSE/DEFENSIVE REBOUNDING

In his short stint with the Nuggets, Martin paid little

attention to D, incurring coach Doug Moe's wrath. His defensive toughness was questioned, too.

THE FLOOR GAME

Martin is a good enough ball handler for a 2 and can get his own shot off the dribble. But he's not going to make his teammates better.

INTANGIBLES

Martin's health is obviously the big question. In Denver, too, he seemed to be coasting on what, most agree, is a considerable amount of natural ability.

IN SUM

In three years, Martin has played a total of 69 games, logged 422 minutes, shot .378 from the field, and averaged 3 points a game. Plus he's coming off major knee surgery. Not promising, not at all.

RICK'S RATINGS

Scoring: **B**
Shooting: **D**
Ball Handling: **B**
Passing: **B**

Defense: **C**
Defensive Rebounding: **B**
Intangibles: **C**
Overall: **C –**

Vernon Maxwell

Birthdate: September 12, 1965
Height: 6-4
Weight: 180
College: University of Florida, Gainesville, Fla.
Drafted: Denver on second round, 1988 (47th pick).
Position: Guard
Final 1989 Team: San Antonio Spurs
Final 1988–89 Statistics:

G	Fg	Fga	Fg%	Ft	Fta	Ft%	Orb	Reb	Ast	Stl	To	Blk	Pts	Ppg
79	357	827	.432	181	243	.745	49	202	301	86	178	8	927	11.7

Three-point goals: 32–129 (.248)   **TSP:** .451

SCORING

While his numbers were nothing to get excited about—.432 from the field, .248 from three-point land, and .745 from the line—Maxwell, a second round pick (47th overall; selected by Denver and then traded to the Spurs), showed that he is indeed an NBA-caliber scorer. His major asset is his athletic ability. An all-state halfback in high school, Maxwell is exceptionally fast and quick, which makes him most effective in transition where he fills the lanes well and often finishes with a resounding dunk. He's a fearless driver (though he needs to develop his left hand) and has a real knack for creating contact and getting to the line. Suffers from an inconsistent outside shot (in his senior year at Florida, he shot just .447).

DEFENSE/DEFENSIVE REBOUNDING

Maxwell's athleticism serves him well defensively. On the ball, he was San Antonio's best defender, using his potent combination of strength and quickness to pressure opponents. But he has yet to comprehend team defense and, despite his jumping ability, was a below-average defensive rebounder among starting point guards.

THE FLOOR GAME

Maxwell's natural position is the 2 spot, but with Johnny Dawkins out of the lineup for a significant portion of the year, Maxwell played the 1 and did a reasonably good job. In fact, he earned himself more minutes by his performance. But for the year, his assist-to-turnover ratio was 1.72, worst among starting point guards. He needs to play more under control.

INTANGIBLES

Maxwell raised question marks about himself when he announced that he had tested positive for cocaine in his senior year at Florida. On at least one occasion last year, he displayed a blasé attitude following a loss. And he missed a plane and was suspended for a game. But he has shown a willingness and ability to hit the big shot.

IN SUM

Maxwell has outstanding physical tools. If he shows more consistency in his outside shooting and learns to hone his talent, he can look forward to a long career in the NBA. But the character issues may loom large.

RICK'S RATINGS

Scoring: **B**	Defense: **A**
Shooting: **C**	Defensive Rebounding: **B**
Free Throw Shooting: **C**	Playmaking: **C**
Ball Handling: **C**	Intangibles: **C**
Passing: **C**	Overall: **C +**

Tim McCormick

Birthdate: March 10, 1962
Height: 7-0
Weight: 240

College: University of Michigan, Ann Arbor, Mich.
Drafted: Cleveland on first round as an undergraduate, 1984 (12th pick).
Positions: Forward, Center
Final 1989 Team: Houston Rockets
Final 1988–89 Statistics:

G	Fg	Fga	Fg%	Ft	Fta	Ft%	Orb	Reb	Ast	Stl	To	Blk	Pts	Ppg
81	169	351	.481	87	129	.674	87	261	54	18	68	24	425	5.2

Three-point goals: 0–4 (.000)   **TSP:** .481

SCORING

McCormick must be champing at the bit after last year. Consider: In 1987–88, with Philadelphia and then New Jersey, McCormick, a power forward/center, was a starter, averaging 30 minutes a game and 12 points (which followed a year where he scored 12.8 a game). And in preseason, he was the Nets leading scorer. But at the beginning of the 1988–89 season, he was shipped to Houston (along with Frankie Johnson, Lorenzo Romar, and Tony Brown for Joe Barry Carroll and Lester Conner). Which meant change on two fronts: First, he was slated to be a backup to both Akeem Olajuwon (center) and Otis Thorpe (power forward); second, Houston wanted to make him more a low-post player (since their offense was geared that way). McCormick did not adapt well. A career .541 shooter, he connected on only .481 of his attempts, his lifetime low and the first time in his five-year career he's been under 50 percent. The problem was that he was out of his element in the blocks, where he has a limited repertoire. He's better as a facing center where he can stick the 18-footer. He was inconsistent, never stringing together more than a couple good games. He's a poor free throw shooter (.674 in 1988–89, .704 lifetime).

DEFENSE/DEFENSIVE REBOUNDING

McCormick has some defensive weaknesses. For one, he lacks strength, particularly in his legs, and can be pushed around. For another, for a center McCormick is not at all a shot blocking threat (0.3 a game). And he doesn't always block out. Plus, he has below-average defensive rebounding numbers for a 5. On the other hand, he reads the scouting reports and has a handle on the strengths and weaknesses of opponents.

THE FLOOR GAME

One of McCormick's major assets is his passing. Houston runs plays through him; he's a fine high-to-low-post passer. Though he's not fast, he'll run the floor every time.

INTANGIBLES

A team player, McCormick nevertheless was unhappy with his reduced role. Overall, he's a hard worker who has maximized his talent.

IN SUM

McCormick is a reasonably solid player who can score and pass, but he's kidding himself if he thinks he's a starter on a good NBA team. Houston is the wrong team; he'd be better suited to a club where he can play the high post so he can shoot jumpers and hit cutters.

RICK'S RATINGS

Scoring: **C**
Shooting: **B**
Free Throw Shooting: **D**
Ball Handling: **A**
Passing: **A**

Defense: **C**
Defensive Rebounding: **D**
Shot Blocking: **D**
Intangibles: **B**
Overall: **C**

Rodney McCray

Birthdate: August 29, 1961
Height: 6-8
Weight: 235
College: University of Louisville, Louisville, Ky.
Drafted: Houston on first round, 1983 (3rd pick).
Position: Forward
Final 1989 Team: Sacramento Kings
Final 1988–89 Statistics:

G	Fg	Fga	Fg%	Ft	Fta	Ft%	Orb	Reb	Ast	Stl	To	Blk	Pts	Ppg
68	340	729	.466	169	234	.722	143	514	293	57	168	36	854	12.6

Three-point goals: 5–22 (.227)   **TSP:** .470

SCORING

When the Kings traded Reggie Theus (to Atlanta) and Otis Thorpe (to Houston, in exchange for McCray and Jim Peterson), they created a 43-points-a-game hole in their starting lineup. McCray, who had averaged just over nine shots a game and 12.5 ppg over his career, was supposed to take up some of the slack. It was hoped he would: (a) shoot more, (b) score more. But the Kings had their sights set on the wrong guy. McCray, who can pass, rebound, run, and defend with anybody in the league, has never been a big-time scorer. He has a beautiful game but it does not include outside shooting or the ability to create in the half-court offense (except on the drive). The result was that he averaged about 11 shots a game, 12.6 ppg, and shot .466 from the field, his career worst (including the year's singular lowliest night of bricksmanship, a 0–15 fiasco against Utah). It should be noted that McCray was hampered by a mysterious medical ailment (which turned out to be a nodule on his colon) which caused him to gain more than 20 pounds and miss 14 games. McCray's offensive strengths are in the transition game, where he can finish as well as anybody in the league or get offensive rebounds on missed break opportunities. And, as noted, he's a fine driver, with either hand, in the half-court structure.

DEFENSE/DEFENSIVE REBOUNDING

McCray's defensive honors speak for themselves. He was named to the All-Defensive team (second team) in 1986–87 and first team in 1987–88. His defensive assets are manifold: He's smart. He has a big wide body which enables him to push people out of the box. He plays defense with both hands. That his steals stats are only average (0.8 a game) shows that McCray is a conservative defender who doesn't get beat taking chances. He's not easily faked out. Then there's his rebounding. McCray has consistently rated among the leaders for small forwards in rebounding (6.8 a game lifetime; 7.6 a game last year). He virtually never mistimes a rebound, goes after every ball, and has a knack for coming up with long rebounds.

THE FLOOR GAME

Here's a small forward who can also play the point—he's that good a ball handler. Like his rebounding, McCray is year in, year out, in the upper echelon for assists among his small forward peers. While not fast, he runs the court exceptionally well and can dribble the ball at about the same speed as his running gait. McCray just knows how to play.

INTANGIBLES

McCray is the ultimate team player, so unselfish, in fact, that in Houston he was actually criticized for it (his detractors deemed he didn't shoot enough). He quickly became a leader on the Kings and is well-liked and well-respected by his teammates.

IN SUM

The Kings, a poor shooting team (at least until they acquired Danny Ainge and Wayman Tisdale) need scoring punch at the 3 spot. But McCray doesn't provide it. However, he more than makes up for this with his excellence in other areas. He's the type of player who can make others better; now that the Kings have some talent (for starters: Danny Ainge, Wayman Tisdale, Pervis Ellison, and Kenny Smith) that quality will be even more evident.

RICK'S RATINGS

Scoring: **C**
Shooting: **C**
Free Throw Shooting: **C**
Ball Handling: **AA**
Passing: **AAA**

Defense: **AA**
Defensive Rebounding:
   AAA
Intangibles: **AA**
Overall: **A**

Xavier McDaniel

Birthdate: June 4, 1963
Height: 6-7
Weight: 205
College: Wichita State University, Wichita, Kan.
Drafted: Seattle on first round, 1985 (4th pick).
Position: Forward
Final 1989 Team: Seattle Supersonics
Final 1988–89 Statistics:

G	Fg	Fga	Fg%	Ft	Fta	Ft%	Orb	Reb	Ast	Stl	To	Blk	Pts	Ppg
82	677	1385	.489	312	426	.732	177	433	134	84	210	40	1677	20.5

Three-point goals: 11–36 (.306)   **TSP:** .493

SCORING

With the need to get the talented Derrick McKey more minutes and the acquisition of Michael Cage from the Clippers, the X-Man, who made the All-Star team in 1987–88, was shifted to a sixth-man role. But the change benefited neither McDaniel nor the Sonics. For the first 72 games of the season, McDaniel shot .472 from the field (down from .488 in 1987–88), scored 19.1 ppg (down from 21.4, though more on a per minute basis) and the Sonics were 39–33. Overall, his play was extremely inconsistent; he never really adapted to the role. So when the Sonics went into a late season swoon, losing six straight games, McDaniel returned to the starting lineup. The results were dramatic: in 10 starts, he went for 30.5 ppg, shot .575 from the field, and the Sonics won eight of ten. However, ten games a season does not make and the X-Man cooled off during the playoffs (against the Rockets and the Lakers), hitting .403 from the field and averaging 18.8 points a game. The 6-7 small forward, who led the country in scoring and rebounding in 1985 at Wichita State, loves the corners. His best shot is the turnaround on the left side of the floor, where he'll catch and shoot (or catch, dribble once or twice and shoot) as he turns to the baseline. With his quickness and elevation (he once had a 42-inch vertical leap), he's usually in mid-air before his defender has a chance to get near him. He's also a relentless pounder of the offensive glass—2.2 a game—though his numbers were down last year (3.2 a game for his career; some suspect he may have lost a few inches on his leap as a result of an off-season knee operation). But McDaniel doesn't put the ball on the floor well, and his shot selection sometimes makes you wonder. He was a below-average three-point shooter in 1988–89 (.306; .273 lifetime) and the same applies to his foul shooting (.732; .708 lifetime)

DEFENSE/DEFENSIVE REBOUNDING

Defensively, McDaniel's assets are his aggressiveness and his willingness to bang with anybody. He's perfect for Seattle's trapping defenses and does an excellent job of smothering the ball and double-teaming. One-on-one, he's not as proficient, since he reaches too much and takes too many chances (one steal per game). Despite his rep as a great rebounder, he was below average, per minute, among backup 3s on the defensive glass.

THE FLOOR GAME

Ball handling is the weakest aspect of McDaniel's game. He's turnover-prone, and many of them come when he jukes and jives before he shoots (2.6 a game, with a poor 0.64 assist-to-turnover ratio). He also travels a lot, and the ball tends to stay in his hands for too long.

INTANGIBLES

McDaniel has been called the "fire and soul" of the Sonics, and indeed he plays the game at a high-pitched pace. But on a team in search of a leader, McDaniel, a candidate for the role, just doesn't consistently play with enough basketball smarts.

IN SUM

McDaniel is one of the linchpins of Seattle's championship plan. He's a potent scorer, an effective defender, and with his intensity, an inspiration to his teammates. If he improved his ball handling, he'd be even more valuable.

RICK'S RATINGS

Scoring: **AAA**   Defense: **B**
Shooting: **A**   Defensive Rebounding: **B**
Free Throw Shooting: **C**   Intangibles: **A**
Ball Handling: **C**   Overall: **A +**
Passing: **C**

Mike McGee

Birthdate: July 29, 1959

Height: 6-5
Weight: 207
College: University of Michigan, Ann Arbor, Mich.
Drafted: Los Angeles on first round, 1981 (19th pick).
Position: Guard
Final 1989 Team: New Jersey Nets
Final 1988–89 Statistics:

G	Fg	Fga	Fg%	Ft	Fta	Ft%	Orb	Reb	Ast	Stl	To	Blk	Pts	Ppg
80	434	917	.473	77	144	.535	73	189	116	80	124	12	1038	13.0

Three-point goals: 93–255 (.365)   **TSP:** .524

SCORING

McGee, a 6-5 shooting guard, has always been able to score—he's averaged about a point every two minutes for his career and is still the Big Ten's second all-time leading scorer. But he's been primarily a reserve throughout his pro career. Acquired from Sacramento just before the season started, he was thrust into the Nets' starting lineup and told to fire away. He started out the year on a high note—.504 after 18 games—but then ran into the problem that has plagued him throughout his career: inconsistency. It's 10–17 one night, 1–6 the next. Eventually, Dennis Hopson replaed him in the starting lineup in January. McGee's forte is the three-point shot—27.8 percent of his shots were trifectas of which he canned a respectable .365 percent (he's .349 in his career). But he's been criticized for shooting it too much or from too far out. McGee is also a strong driver and a fine finisher on the break (with the Lakers, he was third in the league in field goal percentage in 1983–84, .594, mostly layups). But he doesn't get to the line much (only 1.8 attempts last year), which may be a blessing in disguise, since he's an abominable foul shooter (.535 in 1988–89, .615 lifetime).

DEFENSE/DEFENSIVE REBOUNDING

McGee tries on D, but the results are disappointing. In the post, he'll bang, but on the perimeter, he consistently gets beaten off the dribble. He's also a far-below-average rebounder for his position.

THE FLOOR GAME

McGee is a suspect ball handler and dribbler; he had a negative (0.94) assist-to-turnover ratio. And he passed off for only 1.45 assists a game.

INTANGIBLES

McGee plays and practices hard. But inconsistency, his Achilles' heel, haunts him.

IN SUM

When he's on, McGee is a major asset. But when he's off, his other deficiencies can hurt a team. He's best as instant offense off the bench.

Kevin McHale

Birthdate: December 19, 1957
Height: 6-11
Weight: 225
College: University of Minnesota, Minneapolis, Minn.
Drafted: Boston on first round, 1980 (3rd pick).
Position: Forward
Final 1989 Team: Boston Celtics
Final 1988–89 Statistics:

G	Fg	Fga	Fg%	Ft	Fta	Ft%	Orb	Reb	Ast	Stl	To	Blk	Pts	Ppg
78	661	1211	.546	436	533	.818	223	637	172	26	196	97	1758	22.5

Three-point goals: 0–4 (.000)   **TSP:** .546

SCORING

Is there a better—has there *ever* been a better—low-post player? McHale is as sure a two points as there is in the NBA. He led the league in field goal percentage in 1986–87 and 1987–88 (.604 both years) and last year's .546 hovered right around his career mark (.565). McHale is a man of a million moves. To offer just a sampling, there's the jump hook on the right baseline, the turnaround jumper following the quick fakes, the step-through and the facing jump shot (range is limited to 12 feet). He has the rare ability to catch the ball, keep it high, never lowering arms, and then shoot it. He is unstoppable one-on-one, has no trouble splitting the double-team, and in Larry Bird's absence, was often triple-teamed, which is probably the most effective way to defend him. At 6-11, he's taller (and quicker) than most power forwards he's matched up against—and with those long arms, he plays like he's 7-2. He can also get to the line (6.8 times a game in 1988–89), and last season he had his second-best year from the stripe (.818). With no Bird, the expectation was that McHale would take up some of the scoring slack. But he averaged 22.5 ppg, about the same as 1987–88 (22.6). The fact is, he got 300 more shots last year, but he just didn't make as many; in Bird's and Danny

Ainge's absence (who was traded in February), defenses could key on McHale without worrying about being hurt from outside.

DEFENSE/DEFENSIVE REBOUNDING

McHale's defense has come under critical fire, which is ironic since he's been a member of the All-Defensive first team (1985–86, 1986–87, and 1987–88) and second team (1982–83), though many people felt that his selection in 1987–88 was particularly unwarranted. The criticism focuses on his lack of consistent defensive intensity, and indeed, McHale, who has averaged almost two blocks a game for his career, had only 1.2 a game last year (and 1.4 the year before). Not a physical player, he tends to let his man get low-post position and then contests him with those long arms. He generally guards (when Bird is around) the opposition's top-scoring forward (usually a 3), letting Bird be responsible for the less-potent 4s. Then there's McHale's defensive rebounding, another sore spot among Celtics aficionados. Last year he averaged 5.3 defensive rebounds (and 8.2 overall), close to his career norms (5 and 7.6 respectively). If Parish (whose rpg went from 8.5 in 1987–88 to 12.5 last year) could pick up the pace, why couldn't McHale?

THE FLOOR GAME

McHale also has been criticized for his black hole post play—but consider that his consistently 50-plus percent shot is one of the highest percentage shots around. And with Bird out of the lineup and Messrs. Shaw and Johnson in the backcourt (who shot .433 and .434 respectively), it made sense for McHale to think shot most of the time. He is not a natural runner, and the uptempo game does not bring out his best—for example, he doesn't have great hands in transition.

INTANGIBLES

With Bird sidelined, McHale, so went the expectations, was supposed to come forward and lead the team. But he's just not a take-charge guy. He will play hurt, as evidenced by his playing with a broken foot in 1987–88.

IN SUM

On the one hand, how can you complain about a guy who gets you 22 points a game, 8 rebounds, and opens up the perimeter game. On the other hand, McHale's defense is not night-in, night-out quality. Still, he's either the second best (Karl Malone is numero uno) or third best (Larry Nance?) power forward in the league.

RICK'S RATINGS

Scoring: **AAA**	Defense: **A**
Shooting: **AAA**	Defensive Rebounding: **C**
Free Throw Shooting: **A**	Shot Blocking: **A**
Ball Handling: **B**	Intangibles: **B**
Passing: **B**	Overall: **AAA**

Derrick McKey

Birthdate: October 10, 1966
Height: 6-10
Weight: 205
College: University of Alabama, University, Ala.
Drafted: Seattle on first round as an undergraduate, 1987 (9th pick).
Positions: Forward, Center
Final 1989 Team: Seattle Supersonics
Final 1988–89 Statistics:

G	Fg	Fga	Fg%	Ft	Fta	Ft%	Orb	Reb	Ast	Stl	To	Blk	Pts	Ppg
82	487	970	.502	301	375	.803	167	484	219	105	188	70	1305	15.9

Three-point goals: 30–89 (.337)   **TSP:** .518

SCORING

Multifaceted, diverse, varied, however you describe it, the 6-10 McKey has many gifts. He can drill the three-pointer (.337) or be on the receiving end of the alley-oop; he can put it on the floor with either hand and tomahawk-dunk the finish; or hurt you with his turnaround jumper. And he has the ability to run the floor and get it done on the offensive board. If he has a "weakness," it's that he hasn't discovered his bread-and-butter shot. McKey is that rare species who can play all five positions. Actually, he started most of last year at the 3 (until Xavier McDaniel moved into the starting lineup late in the season, and McKey swung to the 4), where he usually has a significant size advantage. When he moves to the 4 or 5, he's simply too quick and too mobile for them. One issue: He has a point guard's mentality and averaged only 11.8 shots a game (for 15.9 ppg) and occasionally will disappear on the offensive end. Note, for example, his meager 8.8 ppg output against Houston in the opening round of last year's playoffs.

DEFENSE/DEFENSIVE REBOUNDING

McKey is widely acknowledged as Seattle's best defender. Versatility is perhaps his major asset; he can guard anybody. Capable of flat out shutting down his man, he plays good fundamental defense. He blocks shots (70 last year), steals the ball (1.3 a game), denies, and fights his man for post position. More of a finesse rebounder (relying on jumping ability, he's slightly below-average for small forwards (if that's what he is).

THE FLOOR GAME

Superb passer, dribbles exceptionally well (though sometimes he overdribbles) for a player his size, sees the big picture—McKey is that unusual player: He makes his teammates better.

INTANGIBLES

McKey's talent is such that he merited a higher draft status than the ninth pick in the 1987 draft. The concern was that he was so young, so shy, and "didn't interview well." But Seattle was hiring a basketball player, not an orator, and there's no doubt about his ability to "articulate" on the basketball court—his game demonstrates the savvy of a 10-year veteran.

IN SUM

McKey is one of the NBA's promising up-and-comers. His full flowering may occur this year as he asserts himself more offensively.

RICK'S RATINGS

Scoring: **A**
Shooting: **A**
Free Throw Shooting: **A**
Ball Handling: **A**
Passing: **AA**

Defense: **AAA**
Defensive Rebounding: **B**
Intangibles: **B**
Overall: **A +**

Nate McMillan

Birthdate: August 3, 1964
Height: 6-5
Weight: 195
College: Carolina State University, Raleigh, N.C.
Drafted: Seattle on second round, 1986 (30th pick).
Position: Guard
Final 1989 Team: Seattle Supersonics
Final 1988–89 Statistics:

G	Fg	Fga	Fg%	Ft	Fta	Ft%	Orb	Reb	Ast	Stl	To	Blk	Pts	Ppg
75	199	485	.410	119	189	.630	143	388	696	156	211	42	532	7.1

Three-point goals: 15–70 (.214)   **TSP:** .426

SCORING

He doesn't shoot much (6.5 attempts, lowest for starting point guards); he doesn't score much, 7.1 a game (lowest for starting point guards); and he misses what he takes (.410 from the field, that's right, lowest among starting point guards). McMillan's jumper, which he seems to shoot a different way every time, gets no respect from opponents. But he is an excellent driver, though he'd be better off going more frequently. What stops him is the fact that opponents play him for the penetration (because he doesn't have the perimeter game) and he is not a good foul shooter (only .630 in 1988–89). At 6-5 and a good jumper, McMillan can also score on the offensive boards (1.9 a game, tops among starting 1s). Overall, alas, he has little confidence in his offensive abilities.

DEFENSE/DEFENSIVE REBOUNDING

With his height, McMillan matches up well with the bigger guards—the Magic Johnsons, the Terry Porters—and can guard 2s and 3s. He has good quickness (for his size) and plays the passing lanes well (2.1 steals a game, 14th in the league) but he's vulnerable to the little guys—the Michael Adamses, the Kevin Johnsons. An explosive jumper, McMillan's a superb defensive rebounder for his position, who can grab the ball in traffic.

THE FLOOR GAME

He never played the point at North Carolina State, but McMillan has nevertheless evolved into a solid playmaker. For starters, he sees the court well and is extremely unselfish—probably to a fault. He's a superior middleman on the break, can push the ball, and in half court can make the tough pass (9.3 assists a game, fifth in the league). He had an excellent 3.33 assist-to-turnover ratio last year. His one weakness may be that he has some trouble handling the ball against the smaller points.

INTANGIBLES

Quiet by nature, McMillan is not a take-charge type of guy, and Seattle may lack a little leadership at the key point position because of it. He plays hard but has not been consistent.

IN SUM

Above-average playmaker, way below-average scorer, above-average defender, so-so leader. The bottom line, however, is that if Seattle wants to go further, they may need a point guard who packs more wallop (enter Dana Barros).

RICK'S RATINGS

Scoring: **D**
Shooting: **D**
Free Throw Shooting: **D**
Ball Handling: **A**
Passing: **AAA**

Defense: **A**
Defensive Rebounding: **A**
Playmaking: **A**
Intangibles: **B**
Overall: **B**

Mark McNamara

Birthdate: June 8, 1959
Height: 6-11
Weight: 235
College: University of California, Berkeley, Calif.
Drafted: Philadelphia on first round, 1982 (22nd pick).
Position: Center
Final 1989 Team: Los Angeles Lakers
Final 1988–89 Statistics:

G	Fg	Fga	Fg%	Ft	Fta	Ft%	Orb	Reb	Ast	Stl	To	Blk	Pts	Ppg
39	32	64	.500	49	78	.628	38	100	10	4	24	3	113	2.9

Three-point goals: 0–0 (.000)   **TSP:** .500

SCORING

McNamara led the country in shooting percentage as a college senior (an absurd .702 at Berkeley). In 1983–84, while with the Spurs, he hit an amazing .621 from field (that was also the only year in his six-year career he played more than 600 minutes—1037). A great shooter? Not at all. McNamara, who was signed by the Lakers in October 1988, is anything but. In fact, he virtually has no range. His points come on layups and putbacks. Offensive rebounding is his most distinctive asset: for his career, he's second, per minute, among backup 5s.

DEFENSE/DEFENSIVE REBOUNDING

Slow, not a leaper, McNamara pushes people out of the block. Virtually nonexistent as a shot blocker and an adequate defensive rebounder.

THE FLOOR GAME

McNamara looks to make the play; a pretty fair passer for a center. He doesn't run the floor well.

INTANGIBLES

An unselfish player, an intelligent player. He has a ring (1982–83 76ers), so he understands winning.

IN SUM

A journeyman with limited skills, who is a third-stringer on a great team (the Lakers), same status on a good club, a backup on lesser teams.

RICK'S RATINGS

Scoring: **D**	Defense: **B**
Shooting: **D**	Defensive Rebounding: **B**
Free Throw Shooting: **D**	Shot Blocking: **D**
Ball Handling: **B**	Intangibles: **B**
Passing: **B**	Overall: **C –**

Reggie Miller

Birthdate: August 24, 1965
Height: 6-7
Weight: 190
College: University of California at Los Angeles, Los Angeles, Calif.
Drafted: Indiana on first round 1987 (11th pick).
Position: Forward
Final 1989 Team: Indiana Pacers
Final 1988–89 Statistics:

G	Fg	Fga	Fg%	Ft	Fta	Ft%	Orb	Reb	Ast	Stl	To	Blk	Pts	Ppg
74	398	831	.479	287	340	.844	73	292	227	93	143	29	1181	16.0

Three-point goals: 98–244 (.402)   **TSP:** .538

SCORING

Miller's calling card is and always has been the downtown game, the long-range shot. When he entered the league in 1987–88, he was hailed far and wide as a player with virtually limitless range. And in his first two years as a pro, he has done nothing to undermine that rep. He can shoot from way beyond the three-point line—and accurately: a superb .402 last year from three-point country (ninth in the league) for a true shooting percentage of .538. But if you play Miller tight, he's quick enough to get by you, and while he has a tendency to let his man recover, his size and jumping ability allow him to finish the play. And he can draw fouls (4.6 attempts a game) and is an excellent foul shooter (.844 last year). While he upped his average from 10 ppg in his rookie year to 16 in 1988–89, on a per minute basis he was in the bottom third among starting 2s, which reflects the fact that he only shot the ball 11.2 times a game. (Chuck Person, are you listening?)

DEFENSE/DEFENSIVE REBOUNDING

Miller has made major strides as a defender since his rookie year. The effort is there, and he's willing to be aggressive, to bang, though his pencil-thin build (6-7, 190) mitigates against that. However, he can still get stronger. With his long arms, he's effective in trapping situations, especially when combined with 6-5 backcourt partner Vern Fleming.

THE FLOOR GAME

Despite his rep as a long-range bomber, Miller is unselfish

(3.1 assists a game). He runs the floor and moves well without the ball. And he takes good care of the ball.

INTANGIBLES

Another rep that followed Miller into the pros was that he had an "attitude." Au contraire: He's coachable, a "good kid," with an unquestionable thirst to win—sometimes to a fault, since he'll try to do too much. Besides, how could anyone who grew up as Cheryl Miller's "kid" brother be anything but extremely competitive?

IN SUM

The Pacers are set at the 2 spot for the 1990s. Miller is an exceptional shooter, an improving defender, and a team player.

RICK'S RATINGS

Scoring: **A**   Defense: **A**
Shooting: **AAA**   Defensive Rebounding: **B**
Free Throw Shooting: **AA**   Intangibles: **A**
Ball Handling: **B**   Overall: **A**
Passing: **B**

Todd Mitchell

Birthdate: July 26, 1966
Height: 6-7
Weight: 205
College: Purdue University, West Lafayette, Ind.
Drafted: Denver on second round, 1988 (43rd pick).
Position: Forward
Final 1989 Team: San Antonio Spurs
Final 1988–89 Statistics:

G	Fg	Fga	Fg%	Ft	Fta	Ft%	Orb	Reb	Ast	Stl	To	Blk	Pts	Ppg
24	43	97	.443	37	64	.578	18	50	21	16	33	2	123	5.1

Three-point goals: 0–0 (.000)   **TSP:** .443

SCORING

Mitchell, a muscular 6-7 small forward, was drafted by Denver on the second round in 1988, cut by the Nuggets, played in the CBA, was picked up by Miami (22 games), returned to the CBA, and then had a two-game stint with the Spurs. He scored some in college (13.7 a game at Purdue). His strengths are running the floor and pounding the offensive glass; his weaknesses are that he's a streaky shooter and has limited range.

DEFENSE/DEFENSIVE REBOUNDING

Mitchell is a physical defender but must improve his ability to guard players on the perimeter. As a converted 4, he can do the job on the defensive glass.

THE FLOOR GAME

Good knowledge of the game; ball handling needs refinement.

INTANGIBLES

Mitchell competes well and knows his limitations.

IN SUM

Mitchell needs, as one coach put it, "the right situation." Another half-year in the CBA may be in order to hone his small forward skills.

RICK'S RATINGS

Scoring: **C**   Defense: **C**
Shooting: **C**   Defensive Rebounding: **B**
Free Throw Shooting: **D**   Intangibles: **B**
Ball Handling: **C**   Overall: **C –**
Passing: **C**

Paul Mokeski

Birthdate: January 3, 1957
Height: 7-0
Weight: 255
College: University of Kansas, Lawrence, Kan.
Drafted: Houston on second round, 1979 (42nd pick).
Position: Center
Final 1989 Team: Milwaukee Bucks
Final 1988–89 Statistics:

G	Fg	Fga	Fg%	Ft	Fta	Ft%	Orb	Reb	Ast	Stl	To	Blk	Pts	Ppg
74	59	164	.360	40	51	.784	63	187	36	29	35	21	165	2.2

Three-point goals: 7–26 (.269)   **TSP:** .381

SCORING

Mokeski hasn't lasted 10 years in the NBA on the strength of his scoring ability. As a backup (he was the No. 2 center in the Bucks' rotation, behind Jack Sikma), he's never averaged more than 7.1 ppg (last year, 2.2 on .360 shooting). He can, however, drill the 17-footer (and, in a new development, even shoot the three; he was 7-for-26 last year and previously had been a career 1-for-15) and has some power moves inside. But he just doesn't have a low-post game. He will hit the offensive board and even if he doesn't come up with ball, he taps it to a teammate.

DEFENSE/DEFENSIVE REBOUNDING

Mokeski's main function is to bang. He's 7-0, 255, and not afraid to put his body on people. While the fans love his physical game, the referees often have a different opinion, and he's still not getting the benefit of the doubt on calls.

THE FLOOR GAME

Mokeski does the little things—box out, set picks—that aren't revealed in stats. He gets up and down the court, but he's never been mistaken for Akeem Olajuwon.

INTANGIBLES

When Mokeski enters a game, he stirs things up: arousing the fans, his teammates, and even the opposition. He gets the juices rolling with his hustle and intensity. As he says, he's elevated the 10-minute stint (he averaged 9.3 mpg last year) to an "art form." He's a classic role player who knows his limitations and plays within himself.

IN SUM

Give the man credit. Mokeski has survived a decade with marginal athletic and basketball talent. An unrestricted free agent, he's a solid journeyman who could last for another season or two.

RICK'S RATINGS

Scoring: **D**	Defense: **B**
Shooting: **D**	Defensive Rebounding: **A**
Free Throw Shooting: **B**	Intangibles: **A**
Ball Handling: **B**	Overall: **B–**
Passing: **A**	

Sidney Moncrief

Birthdate: September 21, 1957
Height: 6-4
Weight: 180
College: University of Arkansas, Fayetteville, Ark.
Drafted: Milwaukee on first round, 1979 (5th pick).
Position: Guard
Final 1989 Team: Milwaukee Bucks
Final 1988–89 Statistics:

G	Fg	Fga	Fg%	Ft	Fta	Ft%	Orb	Reb	Ast	Stl	To	Blk	Pts	Ppg
62	261	532	.491	205	237	.865	46	172	188	65	94	13	752	12.1

Three-point goals: 25-73 (.342)   **TSP:** .514

SCORING

Vestiges remain. At least some of the skills that earned Moncrief a place on the All-NBA first team (once) and second team (four times; plus five All-Star selections) are still intact, though he definitely has lost a step. For the last three seasons, the 10-year veteran has been beset by injuries (missing 43, 26, and 20 games, respectively), and his knees are chronically bad. Last year, he averaged 12.1 ppg,

shot .491 from the floor, hit his usual solid percentage from the line (.865), and had his best year from three-point country (.342). These days, Moncrief doesn't jump well—he was once a top-notch offensive rebounder—but that just isn't his game anymore. Gone, too, is that unique explosiveness going to the hoop. Now he relies more on the jumper, which he gets off the catch—Moncrief moves exceptionally well without the ball—and he can also take it off the dribble. One of his bread and butter moves is the curl and fade. One of the greatest clutch players the league has known, Moncrief had trouble getting it done in the playoffs—his minutes, points (6.1), and shooting (.396) tailed off considerably from the regular season.

DEFENSE/DEFENSIVE REBOUNDING

Much of the quickness is gone, but Moncrief, whose defensive honors include Defensive Player of the Year twice (1982–83 and 1983–1984) and All-Defensive team first team (four times), can still be an effective defender. He knows the league like a coach, is rarely out of position, and is a superb weak side defender—one of the best in the business. Still, teams will go at him to take advantage of his fading quickness. Age (32) and injuries have curtailed his defensive rebounding.

THE FLOOR GAME

Moncrief is a careful ball handler who sees the court well but isn't overly creative. He can handle the ball against pressure and bring the ball up court. And he runs the floor relentlessly.

INTANGIBLES

Nobody has more respect from peers and coaches around the league. Rick Majerus, who was an assistant with the Bucks in 1986–87, offered a typical assessment: "Sid is the prototype pro. A terrific competitor, great heart, a consummate leader." Not surprisingly, Moncrief handled with aplomb his coming-off-the-bench role in the second part of the season. Unfortunately, you no longer can count on the injury-plagued Moncrief to play a full season.

IN SUM

Moncrief, an unrestricted free agent, who the Bucks elected not to resign (he was unsigned at press time), has been slowed, and he's probably better suited to a limited role off the bench. He can still give you some scoring, defense, and reliable floor play. But perhaps his prime contribution remains his leadership, which, as one coach says, "can't be measured." He'd like to play two more years.

RICK'S RATINGS

Scoring: **B**	Defense: **A**
Shooting: **B**	Defensive Rebounding: **B**
Free Throw Shooting: **AA**	Intangibles: **AAA**
Ball Handling: **B**	Overall: **B**
Passing: **B**	

Chris Morris

Birthdate: January 20, 1966
Height: 6-8
Weight: 210
College: Auburn University, Auburn, Ala.
Drafted: New Jersey on first round, 1988 (4th pick).
Position: Forward
Final 1989 Team: New Jersey Nets
Final 1988–89 Statistics:

G	Fg	Fga	Fg%	Ft	Fta	Ft%	Orb	Reb	Ast	Stl	To	Blk	Pts	Ppg
76	414	905	.457	182	254	.717	188	397	119	102	190	60	1074	14.1

Three-point goals: 64–175 (.366) **TSP:** .493

SCORING

Big things were expected from Chris Morris, the Nets' No. 1 draft choice in 1988 (fourth overall), and after an erratic start, big things he did deliver. With the departure of Orlando Woolridge (an unrestricted free agent who signed with the Lakers), the Nets had 16.4 points a game to replace at small forward. Morris was inserted into the starting lineup in January and it may be a long time before anybody shakes him from that spot. He averaged 14.1 ppg and was named to the All-Rookie second team. Morris has the whole package: a long-range game—he shot a decent .366 from three-point land; he's a superb driver, particularly in transition; and his biggest asset may be his work on the offensive glass (an outstanding 2.5 a game), where he's a quick and relentless jumper who often finishes with a spectacular dunk. His .717 foul shooting is deceiving as he improved as the year progressed (including 22 in a row). Only his shot selection needs work.

DEFENSE/DEFENSIVE REBOUNDING

Opposing 3s have great difficulty guarding Morris, but unfortunately, the reverse is also true. The physical skills are there; Morris just needs to increase his intensity and concentration. He tends to react rather than act, and veterans like Charles Barkley and Adrian Dantley took him to school. His defensive rebounding numbers are subpar, considering his athletic talent. Increased upper body strength is in order; he gets pushed around a lot.

THE FLOOR GAME

Major repair is also required in Morris' ball handling. He's a talented passer (dribbling needs work) but his judgment is questionable. As one source put it, he's a "daredevil" and his 0.63 assist-to-turnover ratio (worst among starting 3s) reflects it.

INTANGIBLES

Pre and post-draft, Morris' attitude and character were issues. He was a hothead in college, often giving a piece of his mind to teammates and officials. After a season in the pros, nothing much has changed. He listens to advice, but he does not hear. Right now, Morris only intermittently has his head in the game; he'll play within the team framework one night, go off on his own the next.

IN SUM

All-star and *superstar* are terms bandied about when Morris' name comes up. He clearly has the skills but talent is only one part of the pie. He needs discipline in his defense and decision-making and a more consistently cooperative spirit.

RICK'S RATINGS

Scoring: **AA**
Shooting: **B**
Free Throw Shooting: **C**
Ball Handling: **C**
Passing: **B**

Defense: **D**
Defensive Rebounding: **C**
Intangibles: **C**
Overall: **B**

Chris Mullin

Birthdate: July 30, 1963
Height: 6-7
Weight: 220
College: St. John's University, Jamaica, N.Y.
Drafted: Golden State on first round, 1985 (7th pick).
Position: Forward
Final 1989 Team: Golden State Warriors
Final 1988–89 Statistics:

G	Fg	Fga	Fg%	Ft	Fta	Ft%	Orb	Reb	Ast	Stl	To	Blk	Pts	Ppg
82	830	1630	.609	493	553	.892	152	483	415	176	296	39	2176	26.5

Three-point goals: 23–100 (.230) **TSP:** .516

SCORING

He *is* slow. He *isn't* quick. He *can't* jump. But as Mullin and Larry Bird and Alex English and even Magic Johnson have shown, speed and quickness and leaping ability aren't everything. There are other ingredients and in Mullin's case, he has two special qualities that separate him from the pack. Perhaps his most singular asset is his feel for the game; he just knows how to play. He sees the angles, knows how to get his shot off, moves well without the ball. And his pace, well, the bottom line is that it works. Then there are his hands, which account for the touch—he's as deadly an open shooter as there is in the league; the steals (with 2.2 a game, he was 12th in the league and first among forwards—he's a small forward); and the passes—besides Bird, who's a more proficient passer among frontcourt players? Last year Mullin was simply brilliant, emerging as the player many predicted he'd become after a storied college career at St. John's in which he was named the Player of the Year in 1985. He was named to the All-NBA second team. In his first seasons, Mullin had a rough time of it, averaging 14.0 and 15.1 ppg, respectively, but he wasn't an impact player. In 1987–88, after admitting himself to a alcoholic rehabilitation program during the season, he came back strong and averaged 20.6 ppg in the last 44 games. In the summer of 1988, he lost weight and got himself in the best shape of his career, which set the tone for 1988–89. Along with sensational rookie Mitch Richmond, Mullin was the focal point of the Warriors offense and averaged a career-best 26.5 ppg (fifth in the NBA) on .509 shooting. He is both a pure shooter and a scorer. His 15-footers are layups, but he also can get into the paint, create—he always seems to know where the defender is—and will draw the foul. And few are as accurate from the line as Mullin (.892 last year, fifth in the league).

DEFENSE/DEFENSIVE REBOUNDING

In the past, Mullin, who was a 2 until last year, was a compete liability on defense. In the past, he was also a lot heavier. Getting into shape helped his D. As the late Jack McMahon put it, "he gained a step." Then, too, guarding 3s, he could use the sideline or the baseline as allies (which you can't do when you're guarding 2s). Plus his good buddy, Manute Bol, the game's best shot blocker, covered for him when he chanced a steal. As one observer put it, he has "the *slowest* feet but the *quickest* hands" in the league.

THE FLOOR GAME

Mullin is an ideal player for Don Nelson's innovative point forward system, which relies on a small forward to make the entry pass that a point guard would ordinarily make. Mullin's decision-making is 1-like and he handles the ball well for his position. He will occasionally try to do too much with the ball; he'll force the action. Result: a hefty 3.6 turnovers a game. Surprisingly, despite the aforementioned lack of physical skills, he's a decent defensive rebounder.

INTANGIBLES

Last year, Mullin was at peace with himself (he seems to have effectively dealt with his alcoholism) and his surroundings (early in his career, he was homesick for his native New York). The measure of the major stars is their consistency, and Mullin got it done all year.

IN SUM

It's hard to imagine anyone having a better season than Mullin did in 1988–89. And there is no reason to believe he can't equal the effort (improving on it is almost asking too much), which in itself would be a considerable accomplishment.

RICK'S RATINGS

Scoring: **AAA**
Shooting: **AAA**
Free Throw Shooting: **AAA**
Ball Handling: **A**

Passing: **AA**
Defense: **B**
Defensive Rebounding: **B**
Intangibles: **A**
Overall: **AAA**

Pete Myers

Birthdate: September 15, 1963
Height: 6-6
Weight: 180
College: University of Arkansas at Little Rock, Little Rock, Ark.
Drafted: Chicago on sixth round, 1986 (120th pick).
Positions: Guard, Forward
Final 1989 Team: New York Knicks
Final 1988–89 Statistics:

G	Fg	Fga	Fg%	Ft	Fta	Ft%	Orb	Reb	Ast	Stl	To	Blk	Pts	Ppg
33	31	73	.425	33	48	.688	15	33	48	20	23	2	95	2.9

Three-point goals: 0–2 (.000)   **TSP:** .425

SCORING

Four teams in three years (Chicago, San Antonio, Philadelphia, and finally the Knicks, where Myers played 29 games in 1988–89) says something. Says this: Myers, a rangy 6-6, is destined for NBA marginality, the fringes, because (a) his outside shot is suspect, and (b) he doesn't really have a position. He's too small for the 3, doesn't have the artillery for a 2, and lacks the experience, skills, and mentality for the 1. He's a good athlete who runs the floor well and gets off the ground—he was third, per minute, among backups 1s for offensive rebounds. But he'll need more offensive weaponry if he wants steady NBA work.

DEFENSE/DEFENSIVE REBOUNDING

Myers does have NBA-level defensive skills. His aggressiveness, quickness, and long arms were well-suited for the Knicks' pressing, trapping schemes. And he was third, per minute, among backup points in steals. Also a fine defensive rebounder.

THE FLOOR GAME

Myers played backup 1 when Mark Jackson went down with a knee injury, but fortunately Jackson recovered quickly. There were two overriding problems: Myers had trouble getting the Knicks into their offense and he was vulnerable to pressure.

INTANGIBLES

Myers plays hard, and his versatility is probably his biggest asset.

IN SUM

A 10th, 11th, or 12th man, Myers' defense could keep him around for a while.

RICK'S RATINGS

Scoring: **C**	Defense: **A**
Shooting: **D**	Defensive Rebounding: **B**
Free Throw Shooting: **D**	Playmaking: **D**
Ball Handling: **C**	Intangibles: **B**
Passing: **C**	Overall: **C –**

Larry Nance

Birthdate: February 12, 1959
Height: 6-10
Weight: 215
College: Clemson University, Clemson, S.C.
Drafted: Phoenix on first round, 1981 (20th pick).
Position: Forward
Final 1989 Team: Cleveland Cavaliers
Final 1988–89 Statistics:

G	Fg	Fga	Fg%	Ft	Fta	Ft%	Orb	Reb	Ast	Stl	To	Blk	Pts	Ppg
73	496	920	.539	267	334	.799	156	581	159	57	117	206	1259	17.2

Three-point goals: 0–4 (.000)   **TSP:** .539

SCORING

Does anybody, except the fans in Cleveland and Phoenix (where he toiled for six seasons before being traded in 1988 with Mike Sanders for Mark West, Kevin Johnson, and Tyrone Corbin) realize how good Larry Nance is? Maybe if he performed in such media capitals as New York or Los Angeles he would get his due. But he has played in relative obscurity, accumulating a most impressive record: Among current players, he's ninth (.557) in career shooting percentage, year in, year out, he scores 17 to 20 a night, and he's one of the premier shot-swatters in the league. Nance plays above the rim as well as anybody in the game (he won the league's first Slam Dunk championship) and is one of the best alley-oopers in the league. At 6-10, quick and agile, Nance can explode to the hoop and jam it. With the threat of the drive, defenders give him room, which allows him the 10-to-14 foot jumper, a reliable shot (.539 from the floor in 1988–89). He can run all day, is a fair offensive rebounder (2.1 a game, he was much better earlier in his career), and in the last three years has become an above-average foul shooter (.799 last year).

DEFENSE/DEFENSIVE REBOUNDING

Nance has been the best shot-blocking forward in the NBA the last two years, rejecting 2.8 a game in 1988–89, fifth in the league. He consistently has been in the top ten in blocked shots (in five of his eight years) and last year blocked an amazing 11 shots in a game against the Knicks. He jumps high and quickly, and has a knack for being in the right place at the right time. He can guard both 3s and 4s and while he gives away something bulkwise to the power forwards, he compensates with his leaping ability and quickness. Nance has been a steady defensive rebounder throughout his career (7.8 total rebounds) and was in the same neighborhood last year (8.0 a game, and, above average, per minute, among starting 4s for defensive rebounds).

THE FLOOR GAME

Nance doesn't dazzle with his passing, but again, he's proven he's a solid performer who knows who's open and how to get him the ball. He's averaged 2.5 assists a game for his career (2.2 last year) and in 1988–89 had the best assist-to-turnover ratio among starting 4s. He reacts well to the constant double-teaming opponents throw at him.

INTANGIBLES

Nance is a classy pro, an inspiration to Cleveland's younger players. After being the head honcho in Phoenix, he demonstrated supreme adaptive skills and molded himself into Cleveland's system, which didn't feature any one player. The knock on Nance in Phoenix was that he disappeared in the fourth quarter, but that most definitely has not been the case in Cleveland. To wit: his solid playoff series against the Bulls (19.4 ppg, .551 from the field, 7.8 rpg, and 12 blocks).

IN SUM

Nance, who is recovering from ankle surgery and will not play until December at the earliest, made the All-Star team for the second time in 1988–89. He is that rare species: a complete player.

RICK'S RATINGS

Scoring: **AA**	Defense: **AAA**
Shooting: **A**	Defensive Rebounding: **B**
Free Throw Shooting: **B**	Shot Blocking: **AAA**
Ball Handling: **A**	Intangibles: **AA**
Passing: **A**	Overall: **AAA**

Craig Neal

Birthdate: February 16, 1964
Height: 6-5
Weight: 165
College: Georgia Tech, Atlanta, Ga.
Drafted: Portland on third round, 1988 (71st pick).
Position: Guard
Final 1989 Team: Miami Heat
Final 1988–89 Statistics:

G	Fg	Fga	Fg%	Ft	Fta	Ft%	Orb	Reb	Ast	Stl	To	Blk	Pts	Ppg
53	45	123	.366	14	23	.609	7	29	118	24	54	4	114	2.2

Three-point goals: 10–34 (.294)   **TSP:** .407

SCORING

Like most rookies (and rookie guards in particular), Neal, who was drafted by the Blazers on the third round, waived after playing 32 games, and then picked up by Miami, (he signed this summer with the Cavaliers) struggled with his shooting, bricking at a .366 clip. One reason: He rushed his shot. Another: While he's explosive with the ball and aggressive taking it to the hole, often once he got there he would bail out, perhaps because he's on the frail side (6-3, 165). Neal has three-point range (10 of 34 for .294) and is primarily a stationary jump shooter. The bottom line, however, is that Neal is not a scorer; in college, he averaged only 7.7 for his career. His role in the pros will be as a distributor rather than a maker of shots.

DEFENSE/DEFENSIVE REBOUNDING

Neal is a pesky, hard-nosed defender. While his lateral quickness is only fair—making it difficult for him to play a guy end line to end line—he'll do anything to bother his man. He needs to bulk up to avoid getting overpowered. His input on the defensive boards was negligible.

THE FLOOR GAME

Neal understands that his primary role—and the reason he's in the NBA—is to get the ball to other people. Both Portland and Miami's coaches were reasonably satisfied with his play-making though—and this was a big issue at Georgia Tech—he will play out of control for stretches. Eventually, when he learns to not force the issue, he'll be a good passer.

INTANGIBLES

Neal is coachable and understands his role as a point guard. He plays hard and with enthusiasm.

IN SUM

If he tones down his game, Neal stands a chance of being a role player in the league. He gives a team a nice energy boost off the bench and is a perfect fourth guard.

Ed Nealy

Birthdate: February 19, 1960
Height: 6-7
Weight: 238
College: Kansas State University, Manhattan, Kan.
Drafted: Kansas City on eighth round, 1982 (166th pick).
Position: Forward
Final 1989 Team: Phoenix Suns
Final 1988–89 Statistics:

G	Fg	Fga	Fg%	Ft	Fta	Ft%	Orb	Reb	Ast	Stl	To	Blk	Pts	Ppg
43	13	36	.361	4	9	.444	22	78	14	7	7	1	30	0.7

Three-point goals: 0–2 (.000)   **TSP:** .361

SCORING

In his rookie year, 1982–83, Nealy (traded to the Suns from Chicago for Craig Hodges in December) averaged 4.4 ppg—his career high. Scoring machines like Bob Thornton, Winston Crite, John Stroeder, and Ray Tolbert have outscored Nealy on a per minute basis throughout their careers. And last year, if he had played 48 minutes a game, he still wouldn't have averaged 10 a game. You get the idea: he can't score. His points come on putbacks—he's a banger on the offensive board—and an occasional 15 to 18 footer. In his first three seasons, Nealy was fairly accurate (over 50 percent each year) but has since slumped, shooting less than 46 percent the last three seasons. Actually, in 1988–89, he barely shot at all; he played 43 games, 258 minutes, and was 13-for-36 for the entire season. He once had three-point ambitions (firing up 31 treys in 1986–87) but after making just four, his long-range game has been on hold (four attempts in the last two years). A .671 foul shooter for his career.

DEFENSE/DEFENSIVE REBOUNDING

Rebounding is Nealy's strong suit. He's willing to mix it up and boxes out well, and his per minute numbers have consistently placed him in the top third among power forwards. He's an intelligent defender (though at 6-7, a bit short for a 4) who will not give up an easy layup—most players end up at the foul line when Nealy's around.

THE FLOOR GAME

Box scores will never reveal Nealy's contributions. He makes the "right" play—screens, gets the ball to the open man, boxes out his man on rebounds. For example, he's often been used as the inbounds passer at the end of games.

INTANGIBLES

A consummate team player, Nealy always gives his all. He's a perfect 12th man, a veteran who knows his role and understands the game.

IN SUM

Your classic journeyman, a marginal talent who has survived because he accepts his role and doesn't hurt the team.

RICK'S RATINGS

Scoring: **D**	Defense: **B**
Shooting: **C**	Defensive Rebounding: **A**
Free Throw Shooting: **D**	Intangibles: **A**
Ball Handling: **B**	Overall: **C**
Passing: **B**	

Chuck Nevitt

Birthdate: June 13, 1959
Height: 7-5
Weight: 237
College: North Carolina State University, Raleigh, N.C.
Drafted: Houston on third round, 1982 (63rd pick).
Position: Center
Final 1989 Team: Houston Rockets
Final 1988–89 Statistics:

G	Fg	Fga	Fg%	Ft	Fta	Ft%	Orb	Reb	Ast	Stl	To	Blk	Pts	Ppg
43	27	62	.435	11	16	.688	17	64	3	5	22	29	65	1.5

Three-point goals: 0–0 (.000)   **TSP:** .435

SCORING

Nevitt, 7-5, is a one-dimensional player, and that dimension most definitely is not scoring. If he could score, he'd play, because, after all, somebody that tall who could put points on the board would be a valuable player indeed. He does possesses a hook shot and a nice touch from 12 to 15 feet, and, of course, he can dunk if he gets it down low. But he has rarely gotten the chance to display these so-called weapons (5.3 minutes a game over a six-year career).

DEFENSE/DEFENSIVE REBOUNDING

Nevitt has been waived five times (four teams, including the Rockets; this is his second go-around with Houston), so hope evidently springs eternal that someday the rail-thin 237-pound Nevitt will develop into a Manute Bol or Mark Eaton-like disrupter. It hasn't happened yet, though last season there were at least hints of it (he was second among backup 5s, per minute, for blocked shots). The problem is he tends to foul when he blocks a shot. He needs strength and better footwork and somehow to avoid being pushed out of defensive position. He's been on weight programs with little effect; what he needs is a wholesale body makeover.

THE FLOOR GAME

Nevitt understands the game and can pass the ball. He can even run the floor.

INTANGIBLES

Nevitt is undoubtedly the world's largest cheerleader. His infectious team spirit has been an asset wherever he's played. He's constantly encouraging teammates and reinforcing his coaches' plans and advice.

IN SUM

Nevitt is a sixth-year pro but still a project. As Ben Gillery of the Sacramento Kings, a 7-footer himself, says, "You can't teach 7-foot," or, in this case, 7-5. An unrestricted free agent, the Rockets will not sign him. The feeling here is that the rest of the league will follow suit.

RICK'S RATINGS

Scoring: **D**	Defense: **B**
Shooting: **D**	Defensive Rebounding: **C**
Free Throw Shooting: **D**	Shot Blocking: **AA**
Ball Handling: **C**	Intangibles: **A**
Passing: **C**	Overall: **D**

Johnny Newman

Birthdate: November 28, 1963
Height: 6-7
Weight: 190
College: University of Richmond, Richmond, Va.
Drafted: Cleveland on second round, 1986 (29th pick).
Position: Forward
Final 1989 Team: New York Knicks
Final 1988–89 Statistics:

G	Fg	Fga	Fg%	Ft	Fta	Ft%	Orb	Reb	Ast	Stl	To	Blk	Pts	Ppg
81	455	957	.475	286	351	.815	93	206	162	111	153	23	1293	16.0

Three-point goals: 97–287 (.338)   **TSP:** .526

SCORING

Bombs away, said former Knick coach Rick Pitino, and Newman, along with his fellow bombardiers (primarily Mark Jackson, Gerald Wilkins, Rod Strickland, and Trent

Tucker), launched an NBA record 1,147 treys in 1988–89. The third-year small forward has a game well-suited for this innovative offense. He can shoot the trifecta with accuracy—a respectable .338 (though Knick fans cringe when they think of his last attempt of the year, a buzzer brick in the sixth game of the 4–2 playoff loss against Chicago)—so the defense must play him honest. Then, using ball fakes, quickness, and a superb first step, he'll take it to the hole, with either hand, for the jam or the layup. One of Newman's patented moves is going baseline with his left hand, much improved from a summer of hard work, and then using his explosive jumping ability to dunk on the trees. In bygone days, when he put it on the floor, Newman only considered a single option: to the hoop. These days, he'll occasionally pull up for the shot-range jumper. He's also a decent finisher on the fast break.

While his shooting percentage .475 was nothing to write home about, his true shooting percentage was an admirable .526. Still, he's a streaky shooter and he's capable of zero points one night and 23 the next, as he did in games 3 and 4 of the Bull playoff series.

DEFENSE/DEFENSIVE REBOUNDING

Newman is a *small* small forward (6-7, 190) but, surprisingly, he's a cagey low-post defender. It's his perimeter defense that needs work—his lateral speed is only average. In the press, he has good anticipation (1.4 steals a game), and his size, which might be a disadvantage in the half-court defense, is neutralized because the Knicks press and trap so much.

But Newman's a poor rebounder—period, the worst, per minute among starting small forwards. True, his frontcourt mates are Patrick Ewing and Charles Oakley, two major league window washers, but the fact is, the Knicks won't be a superior rebounding team until they get more productivity in this area from Newman. His tendency is to leak out—who wouldn't with Oakley and Ewing around—but he forgets to block out and opposition offensive rebounds are the result.

THE FLOOR GAME

There's work to be done. Newman has the typical 3 mind set—shoot first, pass later—but he needs to learn to dish off the drive. Without that option, he becomes somewhat predictable when he goes to the hoop. Plus, if he isn't scoring, he has to do other things (like rebound) to help the team. And he will occasionally play out of control—i.e., poor shot selection or forcing the drive when it's not there. He runs the floor pretty well, though he's not exceptionally fast.

INTANGIBLES

Newman has a lot of confidence in his ability to score, and just as importantly, so did his coach, who gave him the green light to fire away. He has worked hard on his game and the numbers (his 16 points a game were his career best) show the results.

IN SUM

You don't hear much about the Knicks' small forward woes anymore, what with Newman and Kiki Vandeweghe at the spot. Newman is a potent scorer and does a nice job in the press but doesn't give you much else. Vandeweghe is similarly one-dimensional, so the question is: who starts? The feeling here is that Kiki is both a better scorer and shooter and therefore should get the nod. Whether Newman could handle the demotion and be as effective as a sixth man is another matter.

RICK'S RATINGS

Scoring: **AA**
Shooting: **A**
Free Throw Shooting: **A**
Ball Handling: **B**
Passing: **C**

Defense: **B**
Defensive Rebounding: **D**
Intangibles: **B**
Overall: **B+**

Ken Norman

Birthdate: September 5, 1964
Height: 6-7
Weight: 215
College: University of Illinois, Champaign, Ill.
Drafted: Los Angeles Clippers on first round, 1987 (19th pick).
Position: Forward
Final 1989 Team: Los Angeles Clippers
Final 1988–89 Statistics:

G	Fg	Fga	Fg%	Ft	Fta	Ft%	Orb	Reb	Ast	Stl	To	Blk	Pts	Ppg
60	638	1271	.502	170	270	.630	245	667	277	106	206	66	1450	18.1

Three-point goals: 4–21 (.190)   **TSP:** .504

SCORING

Well, it's certainly not a science. Call it, rather, an inexact art—or, as one NBA scout put it, when you draft college players, "you're making an educated guess." Consider, for example, the Clippers first-round selections in 1987. No. 1, Reggie Williams (4th overall)—a can't-miss who has missed badly. No. 2, Joe Wolf (13th overall), who has also turned out to be a dud. But then there's Ken Norman, the Clippers No. 3 pick (19th overall), who has proven to be the best of the lot. As hard as it is to evaluate basketball talent, even more elusive is character and commitment. Norman, it turns out, has an ample supply of both. Coming into the league, the muscular 6-7 small forward was a slashing kind of post-up player who would run the floor and bang the offensive glass but was not a threat from outside. So in the summer of 1988, he took to the gym, shot 500 to 1,000 jumpers a day, and came back with a markedly improved perimeter attack. He's still not consistent out there, but it is at least a weapon. In fact, with coach Gene Shue's encouragement (fired in January 1989), Norman started to evolve into an "outside-in" player, rather than the other way around. One result: he rarely got to the line (just 3.4 times a game). The feeling among Clippers insiders is that Norman should look to put the ball on the floor more. Still, the combo of his jumper, his offensive rebounding (3.1 a game), occasional forays to the basket, and finishes on the break resulted in 18.1 ppg, a jump from 8.6 in his rookie year and a performance that earned him two votes for Most Improved Player in the League. Norman ought to apply the same diligence to his foul shooting; he shot .630 last season, better than his .512 in his rookie year, but still a long way to go.

DEFENSE/DEFENSIVE REBOUNDING

Norman has a toughness and aggressiveness that makes for a good defender; he takes the challenge. He moves his feet well—though he's had trouble with his first retreating step—and is often matched against the big 2s, such as Dale Ellis. He's also an excellent defensive rebounder—he's a power jumper. When you combine his work on both boards—you have one of the best rebounding small forwards in the league (an impressive 8.3 rebounds a game; only Charles Barkley and Tom Chambers had more among starting 3s).

THE FLOOR GAME

Like the rest of the game, Norman's ball handling showed marked improvement last year. He's an underrated passer, particularly good in transition off the dribble and does a nice job of keeping Benoit Benjamin happy in the post (3.5 assists a game). He moves exceptionally well without the ball, and while he doesn't have the grace of a Charles Smith, he's a fine runner of the floor.

INTANGIBLES

Norman has already shown a considerable drive to get better. He's unselfish, a great competitor, and has a lot of heart. He played mucho minutes last year (37.8 game) and held up well.

IN SUM

Norman needs a night-in, night-out jumper and more ventures to the hoop with the ball. But otherwise, his game is very solid in all phases. The Clippers didn't blow this pick.

RICK'S RATINGS

Scoring: **A**	Defense: **A**
Shooting: **B**	Defensive Rebounding:
Free Throw Shooting: **D**	**AA**
Ball Handling: **B**	Intangibles: **AA**
Passing: **A**	Overall: **A +**

Charles Oakley

Birthdate: December 18, 1963
Height: 6-9
Weight: 245
College: Virginia Union University, Richmond, Va.
Drafted: Cleveland on first round, 1985 (9th pick).
Position: Forward
Final 1989 Team: New York Knicks
Final 1988–89 Statistics:

G	Fg	Fga	Fg%	Ft	Fta	Ft%	Orb	Reb	Ast	Stl	To	Blk	Pts	Ppg
82	426	835	.510	197	255	.773	343	861	187	104	248	14	1061	12.9

Three-point goals: 12–48 (.250)   **TSP:** .517

SCORING

Oakley is one of the premier offensive rebounders in the league (4.2 a game in 1988–89; sixth in the league on a per minute basis). At 6-9, 245, he's the original wide body, a tower of strength who relentlessly pursues the ball. He'll miss an occasional conversion but night in, night out, he's in there banging. Besides putbacks, he'll score off penetration passes from the guards (12.9 ppg last year, right around his 12.4 career average). The rest of Oakley's offense is not as evolved. In Chiago, Oakley raised former coach Doug Collins' ire with his insistence on shooting the outside jumper. In New York, they want him to take the shot, but he has yet to prove he can hit it consistently. Oakley, a four-year veteran, needs a good summer of work on his back-to-the-basket game, which, at this stage, is virtually nonexistent. Once a terrible foul shooter (under 70 percent his first two years in the league), he made major strides last year and shot .773 (.710 career).

DEFENSE/DEFENSIVE REBOUNDING

Rebounding on both boards is Oakley's strength, his forte, his raison d'être. His numbers say it all: He was second in the league in 1986–87, ditto in 1987–88 and fifth last year (10.5 a game, one of seven players with 10 or more rebounds). In addition to his aforementioned strength and tenacity, Oakley gets excellent position, isn't afraid to put his body on people, and moves well laterally to get into position (though not high). He has the classic rebounder's mentality: Every missed shot is mine. With Oakley to worry about, opponents could no longer focus on Ewing, who, for the first time, averaged more than nine rebounds a game. Oakley's a fair defender in the low post, below-average on the perimeter (lousy footwork, below-average lateral quickness), but effective in the press (particularly on the inbounds passer) since he's so aggressive. He gets his hands on a lot of balls. But he is just not a shot blocker (a scant 14 blocks in 2,604 minutes last season) and he is foul and delay-of-game prone.

THE FLOOR GAME

Oakley fuels the Knicks running attack with defensive rebounding, outlet passes, and *inbound* passes after made baskets. He has few peers in these areas. With his strength and big hands, Oakley throws quarterback-like bullets, and the Knicks are off and running. He's also quite capable in the half-court offense, and with 2.3 assists a game, he was in the top 20 percent, on a per minutes basis, among power forwards—a notably non-passing group. The propensity to turn the ball over, a problem in Oakley's past, continued last season (three a game).

INTANGIBLES

His box score lines—3 for 7 from the field, 12 rebounds, 3 assists—are misleading. Oakley is a perfect example of the player whose contributions don't show up in the box score: there's the outlet and inbound passing, the heavy-duty picks, the intensity every night, the first-to-practice mentality, and the fact that, as one observer put it, "The Knicks feel safer with Oakley on the court."

IN SUM

Knicks' history evidently repeats itself. Twenty years ago, the Knicks were on the verge. They acquired a major league forward from a Midwestern team who turned out to be the final piece. His name was Dave DeBusschere. The Oakley trade has the same ring to it.

RICK'S RATINGS

Scoring: **B**
Shooting: **B**
Free Throw Shooting: **B**
Ball Handling: **B**
Passing: **AA**
Defense: **A**

Defensive Rebounding: **AAA**
Shot Blocking: **D**
Intangibles: **AAA**
Overall: **AA**

Akeem Olajuwon

Birthdate: January 21, 1963
Height: 7-0
Weight: 250
College: University of Houston, Houston, Tex.
Drafted: Houston on first round as an undergraduate, 1984 (1st pick).
Position: Center
Final 1989 Team: Houston Rockets
Final 1988–89 Statistics:

G	Fg	Fga	Fg%	Ft	Fta	Ft%	Orb	Reb	Ast	Stl	To	Blk	Pts	Ppg
82	790	1556	.508	454	652	.696	338	1105	149	213	275	282	2034	24.8

Three-point goals: 0–10 (.000)   **TSP:** .508

SCORING

"What separates the men from the boys," says Bob Cousy, "is speed and quickness," and Akeem the Dream is clearly a man among men. A 7-footer (some say he's more like 6-10), Olajuwon is blessed with the grace, agility, and quickness of a small forward—or is it a shooting guard? To a large extent, his edge is his ability to outphysical his opponent: outjump, outquick, outrun them. He also outworks them; his relentlessness—for example, his second and third jumps on the offensive glass—is unparalleled. All of this translates into an astonishing array of moves that continually leaves heads shaking. There's the "Dream Shake," where he posts up, fakes left, fakes right, and then splits the double-team. Or the baseline spin move—*pfff* and he's gone. Or the power dunks on the offensive glass—with his jumping ability and strength, he's tough to keep off the board (a superb 4.1 offensive rebounds a game). More mundanely, Olajuwon relies on a turnaround jumper—he has a soft, soft touch and the rare ability to change trajectories—face-up jumpers from 15 feet and in, and a potent jump hook. Then, too, he can beat opponents up court because he's the fastest center in the league. All of which added up to 24.8 points per game, 10th in the league and the fifth consecutive year he's been over 20 ppg. His only offensive weakness is foul shooting—a dreary .696 in 1988–89, lifetime .672.

DEFENSE/DEFENSIVE REBOUNDING

It's an anomaly: a center in the top 10 in steals (all others were guards; with 2.6 a game, he was sixth). Olajuwon has terrific anticipation. Less anomalous but equally impressive are his shot blocking stats (3.4 a game, fourth in the league) and his defensive rebounding (9.4 a game, which, *by itself* would have placed him ninth in the league in overall rebounds), and a league-leading 13.5 total rebounds. Defensively, his major problem has been foul trouble, but he's improving. He's beginning to realize that it's best to lay off an opponent (particularly in non-critical situations) than risk a third or fourth foul that might force him out of the game.

THE FLOOR GAME

Olajuwon is indefensible by one man and can often handle the double-team, so that leaves the triple-team. But he doesn't read it well: He has a tendency to force the shot or wait too long. For the amount of time the ball is in his hands, his 1.8 assists a game (none in the first seven games) is dreadful. He also had a miserable 3.4 turnovers a game (he'll beat his man, but defenders helping out will take it from him when he puts it on the floor). When Akeem really learns to pass, Houston will be a dangerous team. He's already an adequate outlet passer.

INTANGIBLES

You have to break Akeem's arm to beat him. He's an indomitable competitor who plays big in big games. He's a quick learner and has been happier in Don Chaney's reign.

IN SUM

Head to head with Patrick Ewing, Olajuwon made a resounding statement about who's the best center in the league. In two games, he outscored the Knick center 47 to 34 and outrebounded him 41 to 10. For the second year in a row, he was the only player to rank in the top 10 in four categories: rebounding, steals, blocked shots, and scoring—an unprecedented achievement. The only thing missing is the ability to make his teammates more effective, which will come when he improves his passing. My All-Pro team begins with Akeem.

RICK'S RATINGS

Scoring: **AAA**
Shooting: **AAA**
Free Throw Shooting: **D**
Ball Handling: **C**
Passing: **C**
Defense: **AAA**

Defensive Rebounding: **AAA**
Shot Blocking: **AAA**
Intangibles: **AAA**
Overall: **AAA**

Jose Ortiz

Birthdate: October 25, 1963
Height: 6-10
Weight: 225
College: Oregon State University, Corvallis, Ore.
Drafted: Utah on first round, 1987 (15th pick).
Position: Forward
Final 1989 Team: Utah Jazz
Final 1988–89 Statistics:

G	Fg	Fga	Fg%	Ft	Fta	Ft%	Orb	Reb	Ast	Stl	To	Blk	Pts	Ppg
51	55	125	.440	31	52	.596	30	58	11	8	36	7	141	2.8

Three-point goals: 0–1 (.000)   **TSP:** .440

SCORING

Early in the season, Ortiz, who came to the Jazz in an unusual deal that sent Mel Turpin ("Dinner Bell Mel") to a Spanish professional team, played the "Iavaroni" role: start, play a few minutes and then see little action thereafter. But eventually Iavaroni got his starting job back (only to lose it to Mike Brown), and Ortiz was, for the most part, limited to mop-up time. He simply didn't have the defensive and rebounding presence the role required. (He played only

327 minutes in 51 games.) Offensively, the most attractive part of his game is his running ability. A power forward/ center type at Oregon State, Ortiz is currently making the transition to small forward. He possesses a decent 15-footer but needs to learn to both shoot on the move and drive to the basket. Because of his college experience, he has an adequate low-post game, which includes hooks with either hand. But he hasn't shown much on the offensive glass.

DEFENSE/DEFENSIVE REBOUNDING

Ortiz played your basic rookie "what's-going-on-here?" defense. His biggest problem was getting pushed around; he needs toughening up. The weight program he's on should help. Because of his quickness and size (6-10), Ortiz has the potential to be a solid defender. A decent jumper, he needs to be more aggressive on the defensive glass.

THE FLOOR GAME

No complaints about Ortiz's passing skills, which are above-average. He has a reasonably good feel for the game.

INTANGIBLES

Ortiz, who played for the Puerto Rican National Team in the 1988 Olympic Games, has played basketball almost nonstop for two years. As last season progressed, it wore on him. He fits in well with the Jazz (Utah weeds out the bad apples) and has displayed a healthy work ethic.

IN SUM

There are few big guys who can run like Ortiz. But he needs to add grit to his rebounding and D to get quality minutes.

RICK'S RATINGS

Scoring: **C**
Shooting: **D**
Free Throw Shooting: **C**
Ball Handling: **B**
Passing: **A**

Defense: **C**
Defensive Rebounding: **D**
Intangibles: **B**
Overall: **C**

Robert Parish

Birthdate: August 30, 1953
Height: 7-0

145

Weight: 230
College: Centenary College, Shreveport, La.
Drafted: Golden State on first round, 1976 (8th pick).
Position: Center
Final 1989 Team: Boston Celtics
Final 1988–89 Statistics:

G	Fg	Fga	Fg%	Ft	Fta	Ft%	Orb	Reb	Ast	Stl	To	Blk	Pts	Ppg
80	596	1045	.570	294	409	.719	342	996	175	79	200	116	1486	18.6

Three-point goals: 0–0 (.000)   TSP: .570

SCORING

This past year (1988–89) was a year to sing the praises of Robert Parish, long an unsung hero. He had a spectacular season (18.6 ppg his best since 1983–84; .570 from the field, third in the league; and 12.5 rpg, his career best and also third in the league), which is all the more noteworthy considering he accomplished it at the ripe old age of 35 (he's now 36). The absence of a certain small forward (Larry Bird, for those who have been in Sri Lanka) and the Celtics' embracing of the running game were two reasons for Parish's preeminence. With Bird and his 22 shots a game out of the lineup, Parish was much more involved in the offense (13.1 shots a game, compared to 10.1 in 1987–88 when he averaged 14.3 ppg). Then, too, Boston's shift to the uptempo game maximized one of Parish's strengths—his ability to beat opposing centers up court for easy baskets. But the 13-year veteran also flourishes in the half-court game. He has that impossible-to-block, behind-the-ear turnaround (range is about 12 feet; anything farther is stretching it) and can also put it on the floor and spin around his man if he is crowded. And he turned in his best year (an awesome 4.3 a game) on the offensive glass; he has the uncanny ability to jump over people without fouling. He's a slightly below-average foul shooter, with his career .715 (.719 last year).

DEFENSE/DEFENSIVE REBOUNDING

Parish, always a quality defensive rebounder, outdid himself in 1988–89, averaging 8.2 defensive rebounds a game, his second-best outing ever. Again, the absence of Bird had an impact; the fact is, there were more rebounds to be had. Defensively, Parish can block shots (1.5 a game) and more than holds his own in the blocks, where he knows how to fight players for position, is an excellent weak side defender, and can even steal the ball (one a game).

THE FLOOR GAME

Parish is a decent outlet passer, reads the double-team well, and doesn't turn the ball over (though he does get called for traveling frequently). In keeping with the rest of his year, he had 175 assists, a career high. In 1988–89, he consistently made the "hustle" play.

INTANGIBLES

Parish has long lived in the enormous shadows of Bird and Kevin McHale, but you'll never hear him complaining about it; he prefers his relative anonymity. While he is, to a large extent, inaccessible to the press (and thus the public), his teammates love and respect him. He attributed his phenomenal season to being in the best shape he had been in in a long time (though he suffered at the end of the season with tendinitis in the elbow; his dreadful performance in the final playoff game against the Pistons showed the effects of the injury). Parish is a clutch player, particularly on the boards.

IN SUM

Parish didn't make the All-Star team, which was widely recognized as a glaring omission (no way Moses Malone was having a better year at the All-Star break). He is one of the few Celtics (Reggie Lewis is another) who actually raised his level of play with Bird out of the lineup. Even the leprechaun wouldn't have been able to help Boston had Parish not had the best year of his career.

RICK'S RATINGS

Scoring: **AA**
Shooting: **AAA**
Free Throw Shooting: **C**
Ball Handling: **A**
Passing: **A**
Defense: **A**

Defensive Rebounding: **AAA**
Shot Blocking: **B**
Intangibles: **AAA**
Overall: **AAA**

Jim Paxson

Birthdate: July 9, 1957
Height: 6-6
Weight: 210
College: University of Dayton, Dayton, O.
Drafted: Portland on first round, 1979 (12th pick).
Positions: Guard, Forward
Final 1989 Team: Boston Celtics
Final 1988–89 Statistics:

G	Fg	Fga	Fg%	Ft	Fta	Ft%	Orb	Reb	Ast	Stl	To	Blk	Pts	Ppg
57	202	445	.454	84	103	.816	18	74	107	38	57	8	492	8.6

Three-point goals: 4–24 (.167)   TSP: .458

SCORING

Paxson's name has long been synonymous with the phrase, "moving without the ball." Neither quick nor fast, he relies on a keen court awareness and the relentless rubbing of opponents off picks to get his 18-to-20-foot jumper, a reasonably reliable shot (.454 last year, though when he was in his prime in Portland, he shot 50 percent-plus for five consecutive years, 1981–85). He also is an adept driver because he sees the seams in the defense and has a knack for getting a guy on his hip. Layups, are also attained through his movement; and he has a delicate touch around the basket. But as a Celtic, he's been plagued by numerous injuries and hasn't been as productive as anticipated (playing only 57 games last year). Plus, those injuries, combined with age (he's 32), have slowed him a step and when the opposing defense digs in, he's at a significant disadvantage. Finally, Larry Bird's absence hurt Paxson as much as any Celtic, since he needs the ball at precisely the right moment, and, of course, nobody's better at delivering than Bird.

DEFENSE/DEFENSIVE REBOUNDING

Defensively, Paxson compensates for his lack of speed and quickness with experience and hard work. He is definitely vulnerable to the more athletic 2s. He can also be matched up against the smaller 3s (like Indiana's Mike Sanders) and in fact started briefly himself at the 3 spot. He's never produced on the defensive glass.

THE FLOOR GAME

One of Paxson's strong suits is his passing. He sees the court, can make the play, and doesn't turn the ball over. He handles it well enough for a 2. He reads game situations well.

INTANGIBLES

Paxson is strictly a team player, whose savvy and veteran qualities add stability to a now much younger Celtic team. But the key question is whether or not he can stay healthy for an entire season.

IN SUM

If he's OK physically—and that's a big if—Paxson can still provide some solid bench strength on certain teams.

RICK'S RATINGS

Scoring: **B**	Defense: **B**
Shooting: **B**	Defensive Rebounding: **D**
Free Throw Shooting: **A**	Intangibles: **A**
Ball Handling: **B**	Overall: **B –**
Passing: **A**	

John Paxson

Birthdate: September 29, 1960
Height: 6-2
Weight: 185
College: University of Notre Dame, Notre Dame, Ind.
Drafted: San Antonio on first round, 1983 (19th pick).
Position: Guard
Final 1989 Team: Chicago Bulls
Final 1988–89 Statistics:

G	Fg	Fga	Fg%	Ft	Fta	Ft%	Orb	Reb	Ast	Stl	To	Blk	Pts	Ppg
78	246	513	.480	31	36	.861	13	94	308	53	71	6	567	7.3

Three-point goals: 44–133 (.331)   **TSP:** .522

SCORING

Give Paxson room from the outside and he'll destroy you. He's an excellent jump shooter with three-point range (.331 from three-land in 1988–1989, .480 overall) who can shoot off the dribble or on the catch. And last year, when Chicago moved Michael Jordan to the point, Paxson, along with Craig Hodges and Scottie Pippen, got that room, and his game benefitted from it. While he lacks the explosiveness of other players his size, Paxson has a knack for finding the gaps in the defense and taking it all the way to the hoop. Curiously, he usually drives left, though he's right-handed. His foul shooting, a disappointing .733 in 1987–88 (though on only 45 attempts; he has never drawn many fouls), was back up to .861 in 1988–89, significantly better than his lifetime mark of .800.

DEFENSE/DEFENSIVE REBOUNDING

Paxson won't outquick people—he's vulnerable to high-speed guards such as Isiah Thomas—but he's a tough defender who relies on his strength and his smarts. His edge is his knowledge of opponents' tendencies and play sets, and his willingness to do the little things—take a charge here, dive for a ball there—that coaches preach. He's not going to get you many steals (fewest steals, per minute, among backup 1s last year) or rebounds (a mere 1.2 a game in 22.3 minutes).

THE FLOOR GAME

Paxson can play both guard positions and is comfortable in either role. A cautious, conservative ball handler, he is one of the most mistake-free players in the league; his assist-to-turnover ratio was an outstanding 4.34. As a point guard, Paxson is more effective in a half-court setting, since he lacks the breakaway speed to beat people off the dribble in the transition game.

INTANGIBLES

The key word here is *reliable*. Another is *steady*. Paxson accepts whatever is thrown at him—he'll score if needed or get others the ball. He's not a player coaches have to worry about in terms of being in shape or putting out in practice. In other words, he's a pro.

IN SUM

Paxson is a capable all-around player. He can score, play-make, play defense, won't turn the ball over, and is a solid citizen to boot. He's doesn't have the firepower to start, but he's an ideal backup.

RICK'S RATINGS

Scoring: **C**	Defense: **B**
Shooting: **AA**	Defensive Rebounding: **D**
Free Throw Shooting: **AA**	Playmaking: **B**
Ball Handling: **A**	Intangibles: **A**
Passing: **B**	Overall: **B**

Will Perdue

Birthdate: August 29, 1965
Height: 7-0
Weight: 240
College: Vanderbilt University, Nashville, Tenn.
Drafted: Chicago on first round, 1988 (11th pick).
Position: Center
Final 1989 Team: Chicago Bulls
Final 1988–89 Statistics:

G	Fg	Fga	Fg%	Ft	Fta	Ft%	Orb	Reb	Ast	Stl	To	Blk	Pts	Ppg
30	29	72	.403	8	14	.571	18	45	11	4	15	6	66	2.2

Three-point goals: 0–0 (.000)   **TSP:** .403

SCORING

Perdue, the Bulls first-round pick in 1988 (11th overall), has a nice touch for a seven-footer. In his senior year at Vanderbilt (he played only 190 minutes as a rookie, the least used of last year's first-rounders), he shot an outstanding .604, relying primarily on a turnaround jumper and a hook shot. His "soft" hands are a plus—he makes a big target and he can catch the ball. But at this stage, he lacks upper body strength (he has extremely narrow shoulders) and can be pushed easily out of the low post.

DEFENSE/DEFENSIVE REBOUNDING

Perdue led the SEC in rebounding as a college senior, but he's not a banger or a quick reactor to the ball and this will hamper him in the NBA. On the other hand, he *is* 7-0 and understands positioning, so he'll get his share of rebounds. Defensively, he can block shots in the post, but again strength is an issue; he has yet to show he can handle the trench warfare that is NBA post play.

THE FLOOR GAME

Perdue has better than average knowledge of the game, is a decent passer, and runs the court well for his size.

INTANGIBLES

With two experienced centers playing ahead of him (Dave Corzine and Bill Cartwright), 1988–89 was a no-pressure situation for Perdue, a learning year. But he seemed satisfied to be nursed along, rather than fighting for minutes on the floor. The question: Does he want it badly enough?

IN SUM

Many scouts felt that Perdue would not have an immediate impact. They were right. But with his touch and feel for the game he's more of a prospect than a project. He does, however, need toughening up, about 25 additional upper-body pounds, and most of all, minutes. The last should be forthcoming this season since the Bulls traded Corzine to Orlando and Stacey King will probably be used more in the 4 spot.

RICK'S RATINGS

Scoring: **C**	Defense: **C**
Shooting: **B**	Defensive Rebounding: **D**
Free Throw Shooting: **D**	Shot Blocking: **C**
Ball Handling: **B**	Intangibles: **C**
Passing: **A**	Overall: **C**

Sam Perkins

Birthdate: June 14, 1961
Height: 6-9
Weight: 260
College: University of North Carolina, Chapel Hill, N.C.
Drafted: Dallas on first round, 1984 (4th pick).
Position: Forward
Final 1989 Team: Dallas Mavericks

G	Fg	Fga	Fg%	Ft	Fta	Ft%	Orb	Reb	Ast	Stl	To	Blk	Pts	Ppg
78	445	959	.464	274	329	.833	235	688	127	76	141	92	1171	15.0

Three-point goals: 7–38 (.184)   **TSP:** .468

SCORING

On a different team, one without big-time scorers like Rolando Blackman, Adrian Dantley, Roy Tarpley, and even Derek Harper, Perkins might be more of an offensive force. Still, opponents can't ignore him: He consistently gets 15 a night (15.0 ppg last year, 14.1 career) and can score from inside and outside. His best shot is a left-handed hook sweeping across the lane, which I feel he should use more. He'll also shoot the turnaround after posting up. When he moves out, he's a standstill jump shooter (not good off the dribble) with three-point range, though his trifecta numbers (.184) and overall shooting percentage (.464)—both under his career averages: .267 and .474 respectively—indicate that he didn't have a good shooting year. Still, he should look for his shot more. Perkins has trouble putting the ball on the floor when he's away from the basket, so Dallas coaches have urged him to move closer for a one-dribble-and-up move. When he drives to the basket, he has a tendency to use his arms, rather than his body. Result: He gets fouled, but doesn't always get the calls. Inside, he's all left, and when opponents take away the hook, he has a tough time because he has no good moves to his right. A more varied arsenal of low-post maneuvers is in order. Perkins is a career .823 foul shooter, .833 last year.

DEFENSE/DEFENSIVE REBOUNDING

Perkins, offensively a 4, is that rare defender who can guard, with equal facility, a Michael Jordan or a Karl Malone. At one time or another, he's guarded players of all positions. At 6-9, he plays much taller (credit his exceptionally long arms). And his reach allows him to lay off his man, but still challenge him. In 1988–89, Perkins blocked 1.2 shots a game, slightly below average for starting 4s. He averaged 5.8 defensive rebounds a game (8.8 total rebounds), which was also slightly below average for power forwards on a per minute basis, and the feeling is he needs to be more aggressive on the defensive glass. Note, too, that Perkins has bulked up to 260 and is no longer giving away 25 pounds game in and game out.

THE FLOOR GAME

Perkins's outlet passing and perimeter passing are good, but he has trouble in the transition game due to poor peripheral vision; he simply doesn't always sees guys who are open. He doesn't run the floor well and tends to baby shots rather than making the aggressive dunk on the break.

INTANGIBLES

Perkins is a clutch player who consistently comes up with the big rebound or block. He plays hurt, is durable (15 missed games in five years), and doesn't understand anything but Ws. But while he rises to the occasion, Dallas coaches would like to see him do it earlier in games and do it more consistently.

IN SUM

Because good defense doesn't always show up in the box score (blocks and steals tell you just so much), Perkins's contribution often goes unnoticed, or at least unappreciated. While not a slouch on offense, he is nowhere near his potential and has the capability of advancing to another level if he works at expanding his repertoire.

RICK'S RATINGS

Scoring: **B**	Defense: **AAA**
Shooting: **B**	Defensive Rebounding: **B**
Free Throw Shooting: **B**	Shot Blocking: **B**
Ball Handling: **C**	Intangibles: **A**
Passing: **C**	Overall: **A**

Tim Perry

Birthdate: June 4, 1965
Height: 6-9
Weight: 200
College: Temple University, Philadelphia, Pa.
Drafted: Phoenix on first round, 1988 (7th pick).
Position: Forward
Final 1989 Team: Phoenix Suns
Final 1988–89 Statistics:

G	Fg	Fga	Fg%	Ft	Fta	Ft%	Orb	Reb	Ast	Stl	To	Blk	Pts	Ppg
62	108	201	.537	40	65	.615	61	132	18	19	37	32	257	4.1

Three-point goals: 1–4 (.250)   **TSP:** .540

SCORING

Perry, the seventh player picked in the 1988 draft, is converting from a power forward/center to a small forward, and the transition hasn't been easy. At Temple, he was basically a rebounding and defensive specialist with little scoring responsibility. But he turned many a scout's head at the Orlando All-Star Classic (a pre-draft camp, where he was named the MVP—his performance there was the major reason for his high draft status). He showed he has scoring ability: hooks, turnaround jumpers, and offensive rebounds—he's a superb jumper with exceptional quickness who can leap over opponents. But as a 3, he's just learning to put the ball on the floor and shoot the facing jumper. He's fast and can run the floor.

DEFENSE/DEFENSIVE REBOUNDING

With that live body, some see Perry as, potentially, a taller Dennis Rodman. In time, Perry could be a big-time shot blocker (among backup 3s, he was third, per minute, in blocks) and will get it done on the defensive glass. He's played the 4 and the 5 but is not physical enough to sustain high-quality play at those positions.

THE FLOOR GAME

As a small forward, Perry is now handling the ball more

than during his college days, and he needs lots of work. He's not used to dribbling or creating for himself off the dribble. He had the fewest assists, per minute, of all backup 3s who played at least three games.

INTANGIBLES

Perry has all the requisite physical tools, though he still doesn't quite understand what it takes to make it in the NBA. He needs to make significant off-season strides to move up to the next level.

IN SUM

Phoenix is stocked with forwards (Armon Gilliam, Tom Chambers, Eddie Johnson), so Perry is going to have to fight for minutes. But the Suns gave Perry a vote of confidence when they left Tyrone Corbin, who was a starter at the end of the season and in the playoffs, unprotected in the expansion draft (selected by Minnesota). The raw material is there, but Perry needs plenty of work to refine his small forward skills.

RICK'S RATINGS

Scoring: **C**   Defense: **B**
Shooting: **C**   Defensive Rebounding: **B**
Free Throw Shooting: **D**   Intangibles: **C**
Ball Handling: **C**   Overall: **C**
Passing: **C**

Chuck Person

Birthdate: June 27, 1964
Height: 6-8
Weight: 225
College: Auburn University, Auburn, Ala.
Drafted: Indiana on first round, 1986 (4th pick).
Position: Forward
Final 1989 Team: Indiana Pacers
Final 1988–89 Statistics:

G	Fg	Fga	Fg%	Ft	Fta	Ft%	Orb	Reb	Ast	Stl	To	Blk	Pts	Ppg
80	711	1453	.489	243	307	.792	144	516	289	83	308	18	1728	21.6

Three-point goals: 63–205 (.307)   **TSP:** .511

SCORING

For a shooter, the bottom line is getting the shots, and while

Person had a lot to complain about in 1988–89 (including his and his teammates' play), he had to be happy with Indiana's shot distribution. Post-housecleaning, when the Pacers waived John Long (picked up by Detroit) and traded Herb Williams (to Dallas) and Wayman Tisdale (to Sacramento), Person, more than ever, became the centerpiece of Indiana's offense. While his shots per game remained about the same, before and after the moves (overall 18.2 a game), he had seven games in the "after" period (compared to one before) when he launched an arm-wearying 25 or more shots a game. Of course, this strategy makes some sense since Person is one of the NBA's finest shooters. One result of all these shots was that he averaged 21.6 ppg, his best yet, and 18th in the league. With his strong wrists, he can stroke it with range, though he had a subpar year (for him) from trifecta country, .307 (coming in, he was .343 from that distance). He shot .489 overall and had a true shooting percentage of .511. Person can get his shot in any number of ways: off the dribble, posting up, or simply on the catch, though he needs to develop a pull-up jumper when he goes to the hoop. But he tends to rely on his outside game; for a prime-time scorer, he doesn't go to the line much, only 3.8 times a game. Though he doesn't always know a good shot, he has absolutely no reservations about wanting the ball in the clutch.

DEFENSE/DEFENSIVE REBOUNDING

As a rookie, Person won plaudits for his scoring *and* his defense. He was an aggressive, get-in-your-face defender. But in the last two seasons, his defensive intensity hasn't been consistent. For a small forward, he's an above-average defensive rebounder (6.4 total rebounds a game).

THE FLOOR GAME

Person is the designated scorer, but he is not entirely immune to passing. In fact, he sees the court well and averaged 3.8 assists a game. But he's extremely sloppy with the ball and averaged almost four turnovers per game. Nor does he steadily make the quick pass out of the double-team. He's only a fair runner of the floor.

INTANGIBLES

In the middle of last season, Person was named team captain. But is he the right man for the job? He has tended to lead with his lip (mouthing off against teammates such as Rik Smits, for example) rather than his actions. He wants to be a leader but hasn't shown the maturity to accomplish this goal. You'll see a slimmer, quicker Person this year; he lost 20 pounds over the summer.

IN SUM

No one doubts Person's talent. He's a big-time scorer, an excellent rebounder, can pass, and, when willing, will defend. But his immaturity has prevented him, and the Pacers, from maximizing their individual and collective potential.

Scoring: **AAA**
Shooting: **AA**
Free Throw Shooting: **B**
Ball Handling: **C**
Passing: **A**

Defense: **B**
Defensive Rebounding: **A**
Intangibles: **C**
Overall: **AA**

In 1988–89, Petersen was turnover-prone (he had significantly above-average turnovers per minute, for a starting center). One reason: he probably led the league in illegal picks. He'd stick his butt into the defender (to envision this, recall Bill Laimbeer's offensive foul with nine seconds to go in game three of the Chicago-Detroit playoff series) and the King attack would abort. He's an adequate ball handler who can make the routine play. On a scale of 1 to 10, he's a 4 when it comes to running the floor.

Jim Petersen

Birthdate: February 22, 1962
Height: 6-10
Weight: 235
College: University of Minnesota, Minneapolis, Minn.
Drafted: Houston on third round, 1984 (51st pick).
Positions: Center, Forward
Final 1989 Team: Sacramento Kings
Final 1988–89 Statistics:

G	Fg	Fga	Fg%	Ft	Fta	Ft%	Orb	Reb	Ast	Stl	To	Blk	Pts	Ppg
66	278	606	.459	115	154	.747	121	413	81	47	147	68	671	10.2

Three-point goals: 0–8 (.000)   **TSP:** .459

SCORING

Petersen, who was acquired from Houston in October 1988 (with Rodney McCray) for Otis Thorpe, started 40 games for the Kings and overall was a disappointment. He shot only .459, his career low, (he's a .490 lifetime shooter), and showed little offensive consistency. In his defense, he played—and started—a goodly portion of the year at center, but at 6-10, he is simply overmatched as an NBA starting center. He's more suited to the power forward or backup center role. The fact is, however, he's at best an average scorer. He'll shoot the half-hook or take the 15-to-17 foot spot-up jumper. A slightly below-average offensive rebounder with not much of a power game inside.

DEFENSE/DEFENSIVE REBOUNDING

As a starting 5, Petersen, while mobile for the position, was regularly overpowered. His opponents would push, and he'd push back—the result was foul trouble. Nor did he do a very good job of denying the lane—opponents would come rip-roaring into the paint and he'd neither take the charge nor block the shot. An average defensive rebounder, Petersen won't get rebounds beyond his area, but he does block out well.

INTANGIBLES

A team player, Petersen plays hard, and is coachable. But he's a little headstrong—he has his own ideas about things—and the concern is that he thinks he can solve everybody's problems while ignoring his own.

IN SUM

We know he's not a starting center. And the Kings, a bad team that has had trouble scoring (at least until Danny Ainge and Wayman Tisdale arrived), can't afford Petersen's minimal offensive contributions as a starting power forward. But he can be a contributing support player who rebounds some, defends some, scores some, but doesn't do anything particularly well.

Scoring: **C**
Shooting: **C**
Free Throw Shooting: **C**
Ball Handling: **C**
Passing: **B**

Defense: **B**
Defensive Rebounding: **A**
Shot Blocking: **B**
Intangibles: **B**
Overall: **B –**

Ricky Pierce

Birthdate: August 19, 1959
Height: 6-4
Weight: 220
College: Rice University, Houston, Tex.
Drafted: Detroit on first round, 1982 (18th pick).
Position: Guard
Final 1989 Team: Milwaukee Bucks

Final 1988–89 Statistics:

G	Fg	Fga	Fg%	Ft	Fta	Ft%	Orb	Reb	Ast	Stl	To	Blk	Pts	Ppg
75	527	1018	.518	255	297	.859	82	197	156	77	112	19	1317	17.6

Three-point goals: 8–36 (.222) **TSP:** .469

SCORING

Detroit has its "Microwave" (Vinnie Johnson); Milwaukee has Pierce, the "Laser Beam." On a point per minute basis, Pierce was third among backup 2s, averaging 17.6 in only 27.7 minutes of play. The seven-year veteran, who was named Sixth Man of the Year in 1986–87 (and received one vote last year), is one of the league's premier middle-distance shooters (but just .149, lifetime, from three-point range). What stands out is his 50 percent-plus shooting for the last five years (.518 in 1988–89), a feat unequaled by any guard in the NBA. While Pierce can shoot off the dribble, he is best coming off of screens or moving without the ball to get his shot. At 6-4, 220, he uses his strength to post up and shoots extremely well in traffic, making his accuracy all the more remarkable. The same ability to use his body comes in handy when he goes to the hoop, since he can take the contact and still make the shot. And he's a big-time foul shooter (.859 last year; .857 lifetime).

DEFENSE/DEFENSIVE REBOUNDING

Pierce's major weakness is defense. One-on-one, he sacrifices quickness and speed, and can't escape his scorer's mentality. But he's done an OK job within the framework of Milwaukee's sophisticated team defense. A below-average rebounder for his position.

THE FLOOR GAME

Lacking speed, Pierce is only a fair runner of the floor. Like former teammate Terry Cummings, he's improved his passing—that is, his willingness to get rid of the ball when he doesn't have a good shot. But his role, of course, is to score.

INTANGIBLES

"Intense competitor" is a phrase often used to describe Pierce. He takes a no-nonsense approach to games and practices and has great confidence in his ability to score. He will take—and consistently make—the money shot. With the Bucks decimated by injuries in last year's playoffs, Milwaukee looked for big production from Pierce and he came through handsomely—averaging 22.3 points per game on .546 shooting from the field and .871 from the line. Having finally settled his contractual situation—he sat out 42 games in 1987–88 in a money dispute—he was able to concentrate on basketball last season and it showed in his productivity.

IN SUM

Pierce is one of the best sixth men in the league. His game is scoring; few do it better or more consistently.

Ed Pinckney

Birthdate: March 27, 1963
Height: 6-9
Weight: 215
College: Villanova University, Villanova, Pa.
Drafted: Phoenix on first round, 1985 (10th pick).
Position: Forward
Final 1989 Team: Boston Celtics
Final 1988–89 Statistics:

G	Fg	Fga	Fg%	Ft	Fta	Ft%	Orb	Reb	Ast	Stl	To	Blk	Pts	Ppg
80	319	622	.513	280	350	.800	166	449	118	83	119	66	918	11.5

Three-point goals: 0–6 (.000) **TSP:** .513

SCORING

From Boston's point of view, the case for Pinckney, who didn't particularly distinguish himself in two previous stops (Phoenix and Sacramento—the Celtics acquired him in February from the Kings with Joe Kleine for Brad Lohaus and Danny Ainge), begins with the fact that he is a good athlete. As they move to an uptempo attack, the Celtics need "horses" who can run and jump, and Pinckney, a four-year veteran, who is mostly a 4, is a fine runner of the floor and can get up—and quickly. He does a lot of damage on the offensive glass (2.1 a game) and, in Cedric Maxwell fashion, with his squirmy moves down low, has the ability to get to the line (averaging 4.4 free throws a game in only 25.2 minutes). And he shot .800 in 1988–89, though he's only a career .744 from the stripe. As a collegian and as a pro, Pinckney has never shot less than 50 percent (.513 last year), which reflects the fact that he's primarily a close-to-the-basket player. But the Celtics see him spending some time as a 3, though he has yet to develop a consistent perimeter shot. Nor does he really have a go-to move in the post that he can bank on.

DEFENSE/DEFENSIVE REBOUNDING

From Sacramento's perspective, the case against Pinckney centered in the fact that, defensively, he lived up to his nickname: "Easy Ed." On the left coast, he lacked aggressiveness and, in effect, would ask his man where he wanted to catch the ball and let him set up shop. On the right coast, however, the Celtics were pleased with Pinckney's D and actually see him as a stopper, who does a good job of denying the ball and can play both 4s and 3s. For a backup 4, his defensive rebounding stats, per minute, were slightly below-average.

THE FLOOR GAME

Pinckney is a decent passer who doesn't turn the ball over and knows his limitations as a ball handler. But if he's going to play small forward, he's going to have to upgrade his handling skills.

INTANGIBLES

The fear in Boston was that Kevin McHale would go down with an injury and the Celts would be left with—banish the thought—Lohaus or Mark Acres playing the 4 spot. Pinckney provided quality backup relief and also allowed McHale to reduce his minutes. He's liked by his teammates, loved by the Celtic crowd, and comes from a winning program (he was on the Villanova team that beat Georgetown in the classic 1986 final). In Sacramento, however, according to one observer, Pinckney could be physically intimidated and lacked a feel for the game. Is his 3 of 12 shooting, five rebound (in three games) playoff performance against the "Bad Boy" Pistons a harbinger of things to come?

IN SUM

Boston is looking to Pinckney to provide 10 points, 6 to 7 rebounds a game, and solid defense off the bench. As long as that's the extent of the expectations, Pinckney ought to be able to deliver the goods. But, I wouldn't count on it being done from the 3 spot, unless it comes from post-up play.

RICK'S RATINGS

Scoring: **B**	Defense: **B**
Shooting: **B**	Defensive Rebounding: **C**
Free Throw Shooting: **A**	Shot Blocking: **B**
Ball Handling: **B**	Intangibles: **B**
Passing: **B**	Overall: **B**

Scottie Pippen

Birthdate: September 25, 1965
Height: 6-8
Weight: 210
College: University of Central Arkansas, Conway, Ark.
Drafted: Seattle on first round, 1987 (5th pick).
Position: Forward
Final 1989 Team: Chicago Bulls
Final 1988–89 Statistics:

G	Fg	Fga	Fg%	Ft	Fta	Ft%	Orb	Reb	Ast	Stl	To	Blk	Pts	Ppg
73	413	867	.476	201	301	.668	138	445	256	139	199	61	1048	14.4

Three-point goals: 21–77 (.273)   **TSP:** .488

SCORING

When the Bulls take the court, Michael Jordan's pyrotechnics are the focus of attention. But Scottie Pippen's game isn't exactly dull. Like his high-flying teammate, Pippen, a two-year veteran, also can do wonders in the air: finishing the break with a mighty jam, tip-dunking on the offensive glass (1.9 a game), creating all manner of layups off the drive. A reserve early in the year and inconsistent off the bench, Pippen replaced Brad Sellers at the 3 spot in December 1988 and it proved to be a change for the better, as he finished as Chicago's second-leading scorer with 14.4 ppg. Unlike his rookie year, where he was hesitant to shoot the jumper, Pippen last year started to show some confidence in his outside game, particularly from three-point land, where he shot a monstrous .393 during the playoffs (though just .276 during the regular season). What's missing is the mid-range game off the dribble. He's still a streaky shooter, but at least he's firing away—making defenses play him honest—which opens up the drive. From the line, Pippen shot an ugly .576 in his rookie year and followed that with a not-much-better .668 in 1988–89.

DEFENSE/DEFENSIVE REBOUNDING

Off the ball, Pippin is a dangerous defender. He anticipates extremely well—showing a passing lane and then coming out of nowhere to intercept the pass. His 1.9 steals a game (19th in the league) were second (to Chris Mullin) among small forwards. With his timing and long arms—he has the reach of a seven-footer—he can also block shots (61). Some liken his defensive talent to the Bucks' Paul Pressey's, but Pippen could do with some improvement in his foot quickness and defensive positioning (he tends to play erect) to reach that "stopper" level. On the defensive boards, he's very active and a great jumper, which resulted in an above-average 4.2 defensive rebounds a game (6.1 overall).

THE FLOOR GAME

Any coach has to love a guy who can play three positions with equal facility. The versatile Pippen can play point guard, shooting guard, and small forward—and the Bulls don't miss a beat. He's a superb passer (3.5 assists a game) with excellent court vision who's most effective in the open court, where he'll find people or take it all the way to the basket himself. Pippen is a free-wheeling ballplayer who takes chances; they don't always work, but they are mistakes a coach can live with.

INTANGIBLES

Is Pippen injury-prone? He was hurt in his rookie year (back, thumb) and had back surgery which kept him out of the first couple of weeks of the 1988–89 season. But he seems to have made a complete recovery. Some, however, question his willingness to play in pain. He's a fierce competitor whose high-energy style is a positive asset. He's also a "money-time" player.

IN SUM

Pippen is coming into his own. He has all the tools: speed, jumping ability, quickness, hands. With a consistent outside game and improved foul shooting, the sky's the limit.

RICK'S RATINGS

Scoring: **B**   Defense: **A**
Shooting: **B**   Defensive Rebounding: **A**
Free Throw Shooting: **D**   Intangibles: **B**
Ball Handling: **B**   Overall: **A –**
Passing: **A**

——— Olden Polynice ———

Birthdate: November 21, 1964
Height: 7-0
Weight: 220
College: University of Virginia, Charlottesville, Va.
Drafted: Chicago on first round as an undergraduate, 1987 (8th pick).
Position: Center
Final 1989 Team: Seattle Supersonics
Final 1988–89 Statistics:

G	Fg	Fga	Fg%	Ft	Fta	Ft%	Orb	Reb	Ast	Stl	To	Blk	Pts	Ppg
80	91	180	.506	51	86	.593	98	206	21	37	46	30	233	2.9

Three-point goals: 0–2 (.000)   **TSP:** .506

SCORING

Polynice, a 7-foot two-year veteran, tore up the California Summer League in 1988 and came into camp thinking he could take over Alton Lister's center job. But it didn't work

out that way. In fact, compared to his rookie year, he played less minutes (10.4 a game vs. 13.2), scored fewer points (2.9 ppg vs. 4.1), and continued his woes at the free throw line (.593 vs .639 in 1987–88). That said, Polynice, to some extent, salvaged his year with brilliant play during the two playoff series (against the Rockets and then the Lakers). Consider *these* numbers: In eight playoff games, he hit .610 from the field, averaged 7.1 points a game, and rebounded at an amazing 7.8 a game (in only 20.3 minutes per) pace, a performance that may have influenced Lister being traded to Golden State. Polynice's strength is his play on the offensive glass—he's quick, physical, and an excellent jumper (in the top 20 percent among backup 5s, per minute). He also runs the floor well, though his hands are suspect in transition. Otherwise, he hooks with either hand and has a rarely-displayed jump shot. With his poor foul shooting, it's hard to have him on the floor at the end of games.

DEFENSE/DEFENSIVE REBOUNDING

Polynice is a key man in the Sonics' pressing/trapping defenses. He guards the inbounds passer and has a knack for both deflecting and intercepting balls (second in steals, per minute, among reserve centers). He's that rare center who has the ability to guard players on the perimeter but is also physical enough inside. Despite his athleticism, he's inconspicuous by his absence as a shot blocker. He hammers the board, but his defensive rebounding, on a per minute basis, was below average.

THE FLOOR GAME

Polynice is an uncertain ball handler and dribbler: His assist-to-turnover ratio was a dreary 0.46.

INTANGIBLES

Polynice's role is to play defense and rebound but in his mind his agenda is scoring. There is an element of immaturity about him and he tends to get into tête-a-têtes with officials and opponents and loses concentration. His mental preparation for games is often lacking.

IN SUM

Second-year players are supposed to have ascending rather than, as in Polynice's case, descending numbers. But his playoff performance is perhaps a harbinger of good things to come. Obviously, the Sonics think so.

RICK'S RATINGS

Scoring: **D**   Defense: **B**
Shooting: **D**   Defensive Rebounding: **D**
Free Throw Shooting: **D**   Shot Blocking: **C**
Ball Handling: **C**   Intangibles: **C**
Passing: **C**   Overall: **C +**

Terry Porter

Birthdate: April 8, 1963
Height: 6-3
Weight: 195
College: University of Wisconsin at Stevens Point, Stevens Point, Wisc.
Drafted: Portland on first round, 1985 (24th pick).
Position: Guard
Final 1989 Team: Portland Trail Blazers
Final 1988–89 Statistics:

G	Fg	Fga	Fg%	Ft	Fta	Ft%	Orb	Reb	Ast	Stl	To	Blk	Pts	Ppg
81	540	1146	.471	272	324	.840	85	367	770	146	248	8	1431	17.7

Three-point goals: 79–219 (.361)   **TSP:** .506

SCORING

Quietly, with little fanfare, Porter has turned into one solid shooter. In 1987–88, he shot .519 (fourth among starting point guards), while connecting on .348 of his threes. But he was a somewhat reluctant marksman, managing to score almost 15 (14.9) a game on only 11 attempts per outing. A point guard who thinks pass first, Porter last year was encouraged to shoot more and he upped his shots to 14.1 a game, his average to 17.7, and had his best year from three-point land, .361. (Then he upped his numbers during the playoff loss to the Lakers: 22 ppg, 50 percent from the field, and .364 from three-point country.) While his overall percentage during the regular season dropped to .471, he did shoot 219 trifectas, more than he had launched in his entire career. His true shooting percentage was a very respectable .506. Porter is primarily a jump shooter who spots up well, can shoot off the dribble, and can drill the pull-up jumper off the break. Because of his shooting ability, he has also been effectively used at the 2 spot. He has good, though not great, speed and quickness and is a strong driver who can use either hand. He's an excellent foul shooter, .840 last year; .836 lifetime.

DEFENSE/DEFENSIVE REBOUNDING

Porter is a fine defender, combining strength, good hands, lateral quickness, and knowledge. For the last three years, he's averaged close to two steals a game. But he does have trouble with smaller, quicker guards like John Stockton or Michael Adams. However, he compensates with his physicality and his willingness to put his body on people in the half-court D. With his size, he does a nice job on the defensive boards (3.5 a game; 4.5 total rebounds).

THE FLOOR GAME

As a point guard, Porter has come a long way in a short time. When you take into account that he didn't play the point in college, and the role is one of the NBA's most difficult to learn, you must admit that Porter's progress is downright amazing. He is completely unselfish, and while not a fancy passer, makes the right pass—to the tune of 9.5 assists a game, placing him fourth in the league last year. In terms of his floor generalship—the ability to create tempo, to run the offense—there's been a learning curve, though it is apparent now that Porter is settling into the role.

INTANGIBLES

Porter was named captain of the Blazers, which is indicative of his leadership abilities. He, Jerome Kersey, and Kevin Duckworth constitute as hard working a trio as you'll find in the NBA. Porter is tough and doesn't shy from the big shot.

IN SUM

Porter plays on the same team as Clyde Drexler, who gets most of the ink. And he plays in Portland, not exactly the media capital of America. Nor does he create a lot of headlines. But he deserves to get his due. Porter is an underrated but no longer underpaid—he made $272,000 last year, but recently signed a six-year contract worth more than $2.5 million per year—player, skilled in all phases of the game, who is capable of directing a championship team.

RICK'S RATINGS

Scoring: **A**	Defense: **A**
Shooting: **AA**	Defensive Rebounding: **B**
Free Throw Shooting: **AA**	Playmaking: **AA**
Ball Handling: **A**	Intangibles: **AA**
Passing: **A**	Overall: **A+**

Paul Pressey

Birthdate: December 24, 1958
Height: 6-5
Weight: 205

College: University of Tulsa, Tulsa, Okla.
Drafted: Milwaukee on first round, 1982 (20th pick).
Positions: Guard, Forward
Final 1989 Team: Milwaukee Bucks
Final 1988–89 Statistics:

G	Fg	Fga	Fg%	Ft	Fta	Ft%	Orb	Reb	Ast	Stl	To	Blk	Pts	Ppg
67	307	648	.474	187	241	.776	73	262	439	119	184	44	813	12.1

Three-point goals: 12–55 (.218)   **TSP:** .483

SCORING

Pressey, who began his career as a 3 under Don Nelson and helped popularize the point forward, is now primarily a 1 who also swings to the 2 and 3 spot. He has usually shot for the good percentage (.492 career, though only .474 last season), which is not to say he is a good outside shooter. If anything, he's streaky from the perimeter. His high percentages are a result of his inside game. At 6-5, he's a good post-up player and generally has a height advantage against 1s. He's also an excellent driver (usually to his right), with a great first step who finishes well. Pressey thrives in the open floor and does a nice job on the offensive board (1.1 a game). One of his trademarks is his ability to shoot on the move: to drive into the lane, find the trees, and then shoot over them with the fade-away runner. He'd be more effective if he were more offensive-minded (only 9.7 shots a game for 12.1 ppg in 1988–89). A slightly below-average foul shooter for his career (.744) but better (.776) last year.

DEFENSE/DEFENSIVE REBOUNDING

Pressey's name, of course, is synonymous with defense. He's been named to the All-NBA Defensive first team twice and the second team once. He is, all agree, a stopper. His biggest assets are his long arms, which make it difficult to shoot over him and allow him to play "bigger." He also has great hands, above-average anticipation (1.8 steals a game), and is not easily picked. Pressey's similarly gifted away from the ball and has the versatility to guard three positions (the 1, 2, and 3). With his jumping ability and long arms, he's also an effective defensive rebounder.

THE FLOOR GAME

Is Pressey creative? Not particularly. A great passer? No. A top-notch ball handler? Not exactly. But Pressey sees the floor, has a point guard's mentality, makes good decisions in the open floor, and can make the interior pass to the low post from the top. His weaknesses include a penchant for the spectacular (reflected in a drab 2.39 assist-to-turnover ratio) and a vulnerability when facing quicker 1s. He's a better ball handler as a point forward, since 3s don't apply the same pressure as 1s.

INTANGIBLES

Pressey's teammates like him because he's an unselfish player. He's clutch, coachable, poised—in a word, a winner. And his leadership was sorely missed during the playoffs,

which he missed with a shoulder separation (he also missed the last 17 games of the regular season).

IN SUM

It's easy to take Pressey for granted, because he doesn't put up big numbers in the scoring column. But he's one of the game's best defenders, an excellent team player, and his versatility on both ends of the floor gives the Bucks the ability to use a variety of lineups. In a word, underrated.

RICK'S RATINGS

Scoring: **B**	Defense: **AAA**
Shooting: **C**	Defensive Rebounding: **B**
Free Throw Shooting: **B**	Intangibles: **A**
Ball Handling: **B**	Overall: **A**
Passing: **B**	

Harold Pressley

Birthdate: July 14, 1963
Height: 6-8
Weight: 210
College: Villanova University, Villanova, Pa.
Drafted: Sacramento on first round, 1986 (17th pick).
Positions: Guard, Forward
Final 1989 Team: Sacramento Kings
Final 1988–89 Statistics:

G	Fg	Fga	Fg%	Ft	Fta	Ft%	Orb	Reb	Ast	Stl	To	Blk	Pts	Ppg
80	383	873	.439	96	123	.780	216	485	174	93	124	76	981	12.3

Three-point goals: 119–295 (.403)   **TSP:** .507

SCORING

How do you explain these strange statistics? From three-point land, Pressley, who plays both shooting guard and small forward, shot .403 (eighth in the league) but his two point percentage, .439, was only slightly better. Pressley is basically a set shooter: He needs to have his feet firmly in place to be effective. From three-point country, he has time to do just that when he spots up. But when he ventures closer, he must put the ball on the floor and that's where he has trouble. Pressley can't get the mid-range jumper off the dribble, and when he takes it to the hoop, he's had trouble with shot selection and finishing, though he improved in these areas as the year progressed. Then, too, he rarely goes to the line; of players who played more than 2,000 minutes, only Rory Sparrow had fewer attempts from the line. Pressley's a fine offensive rebounder (2.7 a game) because he's quick to the ball, has long arms (he's 6-8 but plays bigger), and good timing.

DEFENSE/DEFENSIVE REBOUNDING

As a senior at Villanova (1986), Pressley was All-East Defensive Player of the Year, and defense continues to be his strong suit. He has great hands, deflects a lot of passes, and has a knack for coming up with loose balls. His steals (1.2 a game) placed him third among backup small forwards. With those long arms, he can bother shooters, particularly 2s, who are generally smaller than he is. At the 3 spot, though, he's sometimes overmatched against players like Thurl Bailey or James Worthy. He is only an adequate defensive rebounder.

THE FLOOR GAME

Pressley is a swingman, but he's probably better as a 2 than a 3, where he can use his height and reach. But for a shooting guard, his ball handling is shaky, at best. His decisions in the open floor leave something to be desired. When he penetrates he often gets caught up in the air with nowhere to go. He has only average foot speed.

INTANGIBLES

Pressley is coachable, liked by his teammates, and plays hurt. He has shown a desire to improve but it's not clear that he fully understands how much more he needs to move up. He has had trouble reacting to game situations, but he's getting better.

IN SUM

If you ran a profit and loss statement on Pressley at the end of the night, you'd show a net gain. His defense and three-point shooting are big assets, but he's not a player you want playing 35 minutes a game—or even 28.2 minutes (as he did last year). He could be a solid backup on a winning team in a more limited role.

RICK'S RATINGS

Scoring: **B**   Defense: **AA**
Shooting: **B**   Defensive Rebounding: **B**
Free Throw Shooting: **B**   Intangibles: **A**
Ball Handling: **C**   Overall: **B**
Passing: **C**

Mark Price

Birthdate: February 16, 1964
Height: 6-2
Weight: 175
College: Georgia Institute of Technology, Atlanta, Ga.
Drafted: Dallas on second round, 1986 (25th pick).

Position: Guard
Final 1989 Team: Cleveland Cavaliers
Final 1988–89 Statistics:

G	Fg	Fga	Fg%	Ft	Fta	Ft%	Orb	Reb	Ast	Stl	To	Blk	Pts	Ppg
75	529	1006	.526	263	292	.901	48	226	631	115	212	7	1414	18.9

Three-point goals: 93–211 (.441)   **TSP:** .572

SCORING

Price is an exceptional marksman, one of the best pure shooters in the league. He shoots consistently (.526 from the floor last year, 14th in the league, and third highest—behind John Stockon and Michael Jordan—for a guard) and with range (he led the NBA in three-point percentage in 1987–88, .486, a percentage many players would be happy with from two-point range) and shot .441 from three-point land in 1988–89, third in the league. Nor does he miss much from the foul line, (.901 last year, .880 career). Just one advantageous effect of Price's outside shooting is that it stretches opposing defenses out, leaving Cleveland's big men room to maneuver inside. He learned his textbook-form jumper from his father, who coached him in high school. But Price is not strictly a jump shooter. What makes him so tough to guard is that he mixes the drive with the jumper, beating opponents with quickness and smarts. He's a master at running the pick-and-roll, which may result in a shot, a drive, a pass, and or a draw-and-kick. He can also create his own shot off the dribble, going either way. Unfortunately, hampered by a groin pull, he had a severely "underpriced" playoff against the Bulls: .386 from the field.

DEFENSE/DEFENSIVE REBOUNDING

On D, Price, 6-2, makes up for his lack of size with quickness, anticipation and competitiveness. He knows how to beat his man to spots and make him take tough shots. He also plays good team defense and does a nice job of forcing opponents to the middle. His steals (1.5 a game) and defensive rebounds (2.4 per, and 3 overall) were subpar for starters at his position.

THE FLOOR GAME

When he came out of Georgia Tech, everybody knew that Price could shoot, but there were questions about his playmaking skills. He was considered too small for the 2 but didn't have the ball handling skills for the 1. (He was, as Price himself pointed out to *Sports Illustrated*, a 1.5). Under the wise tutelage of Lenny Wilkins, one of the consummate quarterbacks in NBA history, Price has grown into the role, last year maturing as a point guard. His 8.4 assists a game, seventh in the league, were his career high and his 2.98 assist-to-turnover ratio slightly better than the norm for starting points. The bottom line is that Price is a smart player who reads defenses well.

INTANGIBLES

The altar boy looks belie the fact that Price is a fiery competitor. Detractors said he was too slow; he proved them wrong. They said he couldn't play the 1—wrong again: He made the All-Star team as a point guard. He may not be a vocal leader like Magic Johnson, but Price, no question, runs the show in Cleveland.

IN SUM

Virtually everybody missed the boat on Price. Dallas drafted him on the second round and then traded him to Cleveland. When he signed a five-year $5 million contract prior to last season, critics claimed he was overpaid. But now the consensus is that, indeed, the Price was right. And based on last year's performance, you could argue the Cavs got a bargain!

RICK'S RATINGS

Scoring: **AAA**   Defense: **B**
Shooting: **AAA**   Defensive Rebounding: **C**
Free Throw Shooting: Playmaking: **A**
  AAA   Intangibles: **AAA**
Ball Handling: **A**   Overall: **AA**
Passing: **A**

Kurt Rambis

Birthdate: February 25, 1958
Height: 6-8
Weight: 213
College: University of Santa Clara, Santa Clara, Calif.
Drafted: New York on third round, 1980 (58th pick).
Position: Forward
Final 1989 Team: Charlotte Hornets
Final 1988–89 Statistics:

G	Fg	Fga	Fg%	Ft	Fta	Ft%	Orb	Reb	Ast	Stl	To	Blk	Pts	Ppg
75	325	627	.518	182	248	.734	269	703	159	100	148	57	832	11.1

Three-point goals: 0–3 (.000)   **TSP:** .518

SCORING

No, your eyes are not playing tricks on you. There's Kurt Rambis, shooting jump shots! From the baseline. From the elbows. This is not the same Kurt Rambis we know and love, not the Kurt Rambis who toiled seven years with the Lakers totally suppressing his scoring ego (averaging less than four shots a game, starting a goodly portion of the time). The Lakers version of Kurt Rambis had no offense beyond

putbacks and hustle points (accounting for his always hefty shooting percentages, .544 career). Well, Charlotte doesn't have personnel like Magic Johnson, Byron Scott, Kareem Abdul-Jabbar, or James Worthy, so Rambis took on some scoring responsibility. In 1988–89 with the Hornets, for the first time in his career, he averaged in double figures (11.1 ppg). In addition to his jumper, Rambis, pound for pound, is one of the best offensive rebounders in the league (3.6 a game). Not a great jumper, he does it through sheer force of will and concentration. Otherwise, he gets points on the break and even puts the ball on the floor occasionally.

DEFENSE/DEFENSIVE REBOUNDING

Rambis, a natural 4, can also play the 5 spot. Nobody battles for position better; he can push opponents out of the blocks even though, at 6-8, he's giving away inches to some 4s and to all 5s. He also used his smarts to come up with a healthy number of steals—100—second on the Hornets. Rambis is not a shot blocker, but he is a superb defensive rebounder (better than Karl Malone and Buck Williams last year on a per minute basis), and with 9.4 rebounds a game, one of 19 players to average more than nine rebounds a game. He uses positioning and effort to get the job done.

THE FLOOR GAME

Rambis leads the league in floor burns. Few players are as willing to give up their bodies to the hardwood as Rambis. While his wheels aren't what they used to be, he'll run the floor every time. Another skill that came to the fore this year was his passing. Rambis can thread the needle—he was fourth among starting power forwards in assists on a per minute basis.

INTANGIBLES

Rambis is the quintessential blue-collar player. His all-out hustle is contagious. And he doesn't save that intensity just for games. His practice MO is similar (which doesn't always please his teammates). As a veteran, he took on the expected leadership role. With four championships rings, *winner* is an apt word for Rambis.

IN SUM

As much as he loved the Lakers (and vice versa), Rambis wanted to play more: He played only 845 minutes in his last year with the Lakers (1987–88), so he signed with the Hornets. He gives them big-time defense and rebounding and also can score. And you can't put a number on his kind of attitude.

RICK'S RATINGS

Scoring: **C**   Defense: **A**
Shooting: **B**   Defensive Rebounding:
Free Throw Shooting: **C**   **AA**
Ball Handling: **B**   Shot Blocking: **B**
Passing: **A**   Intangibles: **AAA**
                          Overall: **A**

Blair Rasmussen

Birthdate: November 13, 1962
Height: 7-0
Weight: 250
College: University of Oregon, Eugene, Ore.
Drafted: Denver on first round, 1985 (15th pick).
Positions: Center, Forward
Final 1989 Team: Denver Nuggets
Final 1988–89 Statistics:

G	Fg	Fga	Fg%	Ft	Fta	Ft%	Orb	Reb	Ast	Stl	To	Blk	Pts	Ppg
77	257	577	.445	69	81	.852	105	287	49	29	49	41	583	7.6

Three-point goals: 0–0 (.000)   **TSP:** .445

SCORING

Rasmussen, a four-year veteran, had an off-year, and that's a nice way of putting it. Entering last season, the 7-0 center/power forward was coming off a fine 1987–88 campaign in which he averaged 12.7 ppg, shot .492 from the field, and played an integral role—both off the bench and in a starting role (he started the last 43 games) in Denver's 54-win season. He was, as one coach put it, "a player on the rise," who had shown significant improvement in each of his three seasons (for example, his scoring went from 3.2 to 9.5 to 12.7 while his shooting percentage jumped from .407 to .470 to .492). But due to a bulging disc in his back (an injury he suffered during the off-season), he missed most of training camp and never really got it going. He began the season on the bench, started only 22 games, averaged only 17 minutes, and played only four minutes in the 3–0 playoff loss to the Suns. His strong suit is shooting, but last year he shot an uninspiring .445; and when he's not shooting well, he's a liability because his defense is dubious. Primarily a facing center with good range (to 20 feet) who can also shoot the turnaround off the catch or with a dribble, Rasmussen will periodically shoot a jump hook (both hands) but does not put the ball on the floor to the basket at all. An average offensive rebounder for his position. One area in which he did show improvement last year was his foul shooting; his .852 was significantly better than his career .770.

DEFENSE/DEFENSIVE REBOUNDING

Rasmussen is a weak defensive link for two reasons. He lacks lateral mobility, and he's not physical. Soft best describes him. At 7-0, he'll block a few shots (41 in 1308 minutes; he's had as many as eight in a game) but he's not a fearsome presence in the lane. He's also a below-average defensive rebounder since he's a slow reactor to the ball and doesn't jump well.

THE FLOOR GAME

Nothing of note here. Rasmussen is a fair passer, an OK runner of the floor, with adequate hands. He doesn't turn the ball over much.

INTANGIBLES

While he was unhappy with his diminished playing time—and has asked for a trade—Rasmussen maintained his professionalism. He worked hard, kept his head in the game, and remained, according to one coach, "a good guy to have around."

IN SUM

Rasmussen went from being one of Denver's most valued players—a talent at the top of their protected list for the 1988 expansion draft—to a trade commodity. And at 7-0, with a touch, he does definitely have value. But because of his defensive and rebounding limitations, his role should be as an off-the-bench scorer.

RICK'S RATINGS

Scoring: **B**	Defense: **D**
Shooting: **B**	Defensive Rebounding: **C**
Free Throw Shooting: **AA**	Shot Blocking: **B**
Ball Handling: **B**	Intangibles: **B**
Passing: **B**	Overall: **C +**

Robert Reid

Birthdate: August 30, 1955
Height: 6-8
Weight: 215
College: St. Mary's University, San Antonio, Tex.
Drafted: Houston on second round, 1977 (40th pick).
Positions: Guard, Forward
Final 1989 Team: Charlotte Hornets
Final 1988–89 Statistics:

G	Fg	Fga	Fg%	Ft	Fta	Ft%	Orb	Reb	Ast	Stl	To	Blk	Pts	Ppg
82	519	1214	.428	152	196	.776	82	302	153	53	106	20	1207	14.7

Three-point goals: 17–52 (.327)   **TSP:** .435

SCORING

Reid can thank expansion for reviving a career that was fading fast. In 1987–88, in his tenth year with Houston, Reid had become a bit player, suffering career lows in minutes (15.8 a game), shots attempted (5.7), and points per game (6.3). At season's end, he was 33, and the prognosis was not promising. But in July 1988, Reid was traded (for Bernard Thompson and a 1990 second-round pick) to the Hornets and the change in scenery made all the difference in the world. Reid won a starting role, played all 82 games, averaged 26.2 minutes, and earned career "second bests" in scoring (14.7 a game), three-point shooting (.327, which he had reached once previously), and free throw shooting (.776). Reid is a streak shooter—his .428 from the field was a career "second worst"—who relies almost exclusively on the jumper to score. He is one of the most effective players in the league coming off screens and shooting on the catch; occasionally, he'll bounce it a few times, but creating off the dribble is not his forte. Defending him is a matter of getting him to put it on the floor. He rarely gets to the line (only 2.4 times a game) and is not a good finisher. He never saw a shot he didn't like.

DEFENSE/DEFENSIVE REBOUNDING

Reid has lost a step and is vulnerable to quicker opponents. He played at both the 2 and 3; at 6-8 and with long arms, his size is an advantage against guards and his dimensions allow him to match up with most 3s. He's always been a solid defensive rebounder (in the top quarter for starting 2s on a per minute basis last year), relying on toughness and positioning.

THE FLOOR GAME

Reid's role was to score, and he has somewhat of a one-track mind. He averaged a scant 1.9 assists a game, but on the other hand, he rarely turns it over (only 1.3 a game). At his age, he doesn't run the floor consistently, harboring his energy. He's a smart player.

INTANGIBLES

Without a guaranteed contract, Reid came into camp in great shape, and his enthusiasm and leadership played a big role in the Hornets' early success. Charlotte coaches were pleasantly surprised by his overall play.

IN SUM

Clearly, Reid is on the downside of his career. But he's finishing on a resoundingly positive note.

RICK'S RATINGS

Scoring: **A**	Defense: **C**
Shooting: **C**	Defensive Rebounding:
Free Throw Shooting: **B**	**AA**
Ball Handling: **B**	Intangibles: **A**
Passing: **C**	Overall: **B**

Jerry Reynolds

Birthdate: December 23, 1962
Height: 6-8
Weight: 206
College: Louisiana State University, Baton Rouge, La.
Drafted: Milwaukee on first round as an undergraduate. 1985 (22nd pick).
Positions: Forward, Guard
Final 1989 Team: Seattle Supersonics
Final 1988–89 Statistics:

G	Fg	Fga	Fg%	Ft	Fta	Ft%	Orb	Reb	Ast	Stl	To	Blk	Pts	Ppg
56	149	357	.417	127	167	.760	49	100	62	53	57	26	428	7.6

Three-point goals: 3–15 (.200)   **TSP:** .422

SCORING

Reynolds, who was acquired from Milwaukee (where he had played the first three years of his career) for a second-round draft pick at the beginning of the 1988–89 season, never quite fit in the Bucks half-court oriented offense. It was hoped that Seattle's running game would be better suited to his open-court athleticism. Unfortunately, the fit in the Great Northwest wasn't much better. Reynolds, who can swing between the 2 and the 3, was a .427 career shooter coming in, continued to struggle with .417. Part of the problem was that he was in and out of the rotation. He can shoot the pull-up jumper in transition (18-foot range), but also can slash to the basket and make the unorthodox playground shot. And despite his slightness of build (6-8, 206), he will go to the offensive glass. He was a non-factor during the playoffs (40 minutes of playing time in two series). Not surprisingly, he was left exposed in the expansion draft and selected by Orlando.

DEFENSE/DEFENSIVE REBOUNDING

Reynolds has superb anticipation; on a per minute basis, he was tops among backup 3s for steals, but he is not yet a consistent one-on-one defender and tends to lose concentration in help situations. He does very little on the defensive boards.

THE FLOOR GAME

Reynolds often tries to create something that is not there—he will, for example, drive into the lane and either get the ball stripped or blocked—his turnovers on a per minute basis were high. He wants to make the career pass rather than the safe play.

INTANGIBLES

Despite his four-year tenure in the league, Reynolds isn't brimming with self-confidence. He may not have the mental toughness to ever be much more than a backup player.

IN SUM

Reynolds has shown that he can play in the NBA but he has nowhere near approached his potential. The physical tools are there, but he's still treading water.

Scoring: **A**
Shooting: **D**
Free Throw Shooting: **B**
Ball Handling: **C**
Passing: **C**

Defense: **C**
Defensive Rebounding: **D**
Intangibles: **C**
Overall: **C**

Mitch Richmond

Birthdate: June 30, 1965
Height: 6-5
Weight: 215
College: Kansas State University, Manhattan, Kan.
Drafted: Golden State on first round, 1988 (5th pick).
Position: Guard
Final 1989 Team: Golden State Warriors
Final 1988–89 Statistics:

G	Fg	Fga	Fg%	Ft	Fta	Ft%	Orb	Reb	Ast	Stl	To	Blk	Pts	Ppg
79	649	1386	.468	410	506	.810	158	468	334	82	269	13	1741	22.0

Three-point goals: 33–90 (.367)   **TSP:** .480

SCORING

Frank Layden said it best: "There's only one guy in history who could walk on water. Mitch Richmond can do everything else." The near unanimous Rookie of the Year (80 of 85 votes), the 6-5 Richmond is indeed a complete offensive player. Incredibly strong and rock-hard at 6-5, 215—it's not difficult to imagine him in the 49ers backfield alongside Ronnie Lott—Richmond is a "power guard." With that big butt and huge thighs, he has few peers as a post-up player among the league's backcourt players. Inside, he's also an explosive jumper and did heavy damage on the offensive glass (two a game). Move him outside and he'll drill the trifecta (a solid .367 from three-land). If there's a weakness in his game, and you can hardly call it that, it's that he's not yet a deadeye shooter—like, say, Dale Ellis (overall shooting percentage in 1988–89 was .468). And then there's his driving ability. Richmond hath no fear going to the hoop and will take it to anybody, though he did pick up a lot of charges. But at the same time, he can draw the foul and he shot .810 from the line. Because of his extraordinary one-on-one abilities, Richmond was often isolated in crucial situations—a rare scenario in Don Nelson-coached teams where rookies get no respect—and he produced. He played big in big games. At 22 a game, Richmond was the leading scorer among rookies in the league (15th overall).

DEFENSE/DEFENSIVE REBOUNDING

Sure, Golden State liked Richmond's offense, but they never would have drafted him unless he played D. And the consensus is that Richmond has the potential to be a stopper. He's aggressive, takes a challenge, thinks defense, and has deceptive quickness. And he's an excellent defensive rebounder who can grab the ball in traffic (only Fat Lever and Michael Jordan had more defensive rebounds, per minute, among starting 2s). His improvement will come in becoming a better help defender. He's not a ballhawk (one steal a game).

THE FLOOR GAME

More plaudits: Richmond is unselfish, a superb passer in the open court, and can take the ball end to end. In half court, however, he's prone to getting caught up in the air on the drive and trying to do too much (a lousy 1.24 assist-to-turnover ratio and above-average turnovers per minute).

INTANGIBLES

Richmond has that swagger, that walk, that says, "I can play." As the late Jack McMahon, the Warriors former player personnel director, put it, he's "good cocky," and he was a star from the get-go. He has a tremendous desire to excel.

IN SUM

Richmond didn't make the All-Star team last year, but you could make a sound case that he deserved to be named. But no doubt he will be a perennial All-Star for years to come. One of the marquee players for the 1990s, Richmond is the best rookie guard to come into the league since Michael Jordan (who, for an all-star team excluding himself, selected Richmond for *first team* All-NBA).

Scoring: **AAA**
Shooting: **A**
Free Throw Shooting: **A**
Ball Handling: **A**
Passing: **A**

Defense: **A**
Defensive Rebounding: **AAA**
Intangibles: **AAA**
Overall: **AAA**

David Rivers

Birthdate: January 20, 1965
Height: 6-0
Weight: 170
College: University of Notre Dame, Notre Dame, Ind.
Drafted: Los Angeles Lakers on first round, 1988 (25th pick).
Position: Guard
Final 1989 Team: Los Angeles Lakers
Final 1988–89 Statistics:

G	Fg	Fga	Fg%	Ft	Fta	Ft%	Orb	Reb	Ast	Stl	To	Blk	Pts	Ppg
47	49	122	.402	35	42	.833	13	43	106	23	61	9	134	2.9

Three-point goals: 1–6 (.167)   **TSP:** .406

SCORING

He was a rookie, he didn't get many or consistent minutes (he played in 47 games, 9.4 minutes per), he was in the high-expectations environment of back-to-back NBA champions, and he was playing behind the game's premier point guard, and, of course, he suffered by comparison. Was it any surprise, then, that Rivers, the Lakers No. 1 draft pick in 1988 (25th overall) who was selected by the Timberwolves in the expansion draft, did not have a particularly good year? He didn't shoot the ball well (.402), but even at Notre Dame he was only a .442 shooter. The difference is he did score in the college game (17.4)—much of it on drives—but in the NBA, he's had trouble finishing the play. Size, he's only 6-0, was one reason; weak decision-making—when he got into the lane, he'd pass up good shots and shoot when he should have dished off—was another. The book on Rivers was to make him hit the 18-footer, which he hasn't yet shown he can do consistently. He did, however, show occasional signs of brilliance—he's very fast with the ball and can beat the defense in transition. And he's a fine foul shooter at .833.

DEFENSE/DEFENSIVE REBOUNDING

Entering the league, Rivers' strength was questioned, but he worked hard on the weights last year and got much stronger. His defensive assets include quick hands and a nose for the ball—he has a way with long rebounds. His improvement will come in being more aggressive on the ball. Of course, he's small, but these days NBA teams have a way of neutralizing that disadvantage.

THE FLOOR GAME

The Lakers had envisioned Rivers as a player who would bring an uptempo element to their gradually slowing (Showtime has become more and more half-court time) attack. The idea was to move Michael Cooper—who had backed up Magic Johnson—back to his more natural positions, 2 and 3. But Rivers had trouble playing fast under control—his turnovers were way above average for backup 1s—and curiously, he often *slowed* the pace because he walked the ball instead of running.

INTANGIBLES

There are few questions about Rivers' character. He survived a near-fatal car accident in 1987, endured an exhaustive rehabilitation program, and worked his game back to make the pros. He's coachable and has a mind for the game.

IN SUM

Compare Rivers' situation in Minnesota: He'll have an NBA season under his belt, he'll likely get substantial minutes and possibly even start (though he'll have stiff competition from Pooh Richardson, the T-Wolves's No. 1 draft pick), the expectations will be minimal, and Johnson won't be looking over his shoulder. His speed and quickness and feel for the game are his biggest assets; he'll have to prove he can consistently hit the jumper, play under control, and run a team.

RICK'S RATINGS

Scoring: **C**
Shooting: **C**
Free Throw Shooting: **A**
Ball Handling: **A**
Passing: **A**

Defense: **B**
Defensive Rebounding: **B**
Playmaking: **C**
Intangibles: **A**
Overall: **C**

Doc Rivers

Birthdate: October 13, 1961
Height: 6-5
Weight: 185
College: Marquette University, Milwaukee, Wis.
Drafted: Atlanta on second round as an undergraduate, 1983 (31st pick).
Position: Guard
Final 1989 Team: Atlanta Hawks
Final 1988–89 Statistics:

G	Fg	Fga	Fg%	Ft	Fta	Ft%	Orb	Reb	Ast	Stl	To	Blk	Pts	Ppg
76	371	816	.455	247	287	.861	89	286	525	181	158	40	1032	13.6

Three-point goals: 43–124 (.347)   **TSP:** .481

SCORING

Penetrate, penetrate, penetrate. Rivers, a point guard, goes to the hoop as well as anybody in the league. A strong and athletic 6-5, he'll fight you off as he slashes his way to the hoop—usually to his right (he needs work on his left hand). When he gets there, good things happen: either a foul, or a basket—Rivers is an excellent finisher who can dunk on you. And last year, in keeping with the overall improvement in his game, he had his best year (.861) from the stripe. While his jump shot has never struck fear in the hearts of opposing coaches (.455 from the floor last year and .460 lifetime), it's good enough to keep defenses honest. And in 1988–89, for the first time he made major—and effective—use of the three point shot, canning trifectas at a decent .347 pace (and attempting more and making more than he had in his entire career). And his size and jumping ability are a plus on the offensive glass where he garnered 1.2 a game.

DEFENSE/DEFENSIVE REBOUNDING

Rivers has the tools to be an outstanding defensive player—strength, superb anticipation (2.4 steals a game, 7th in the league), lateral quickness, size—but he doesn't do it night in, night out. He has a tendency to slack off against non-scoring point guards, though sometimes this is a result of a strategy to double-team low. On the other hand, Rivers will rise to the occasion and get you a stop when you need it. An average defensive rebounder for his position.

THE FLOOR GAME

Rivers, who never played point guard at Marquette nor in his first two years in the NBA, has gotten his fair share of criticism as a 1, but he has evolved into a better-than-average playmaker. Last year, he subjugated his scoring (to wit, his ppg dropped from 14.2 ppg in 1987–88 to 13.6 in 1988–89) to get everybody involved (with Reggie Theus, Moses Malone, and Dominique Wilkins as teammates, this made sense). He does what a point guard should do: runs the offense (he has a thorough mastery of Atlanta's system), gets the ball to players when they need it, and runs the break. He's not a big-time creator, just a careful, solid ballhandler (a 3.32 assist-to-turnover ratio, fifth among starting point guards).

INTANGIBLES

Early in the season, Rivers was a little awed by his new teammates (Mssrs. Malone and Theus—now an ex-teammate) but as the season progressed he gained confidence in himself—and his fellow Hawks returned the favor. His most notable intangible, according to one coach, is that he is an outstanding person—widely respected by fans, teammates, coaches, and the community.

IN SUM

Rivers was an All-Star in 1987–88 and though his numbers were down slightly last year, he is clearly an upper-echelon point guard. He doesn't have to score to be effective but if he shot better, he'd be top rung. Look for him to be a more aggressive leader this year.

RICK'S RATINGS

Scoring: **B**	Defense: **A**
Shooting: **B**	Defensive Rebounding: **B**
Free Throw Shooting: **AA**	Playmaking: **A**
Ball Handling: **A**	Intangibles: **AA**
Passing: **A**	Overall: **A +**

Fred Roberts

Birthdate: August 14, 1960
Height: 6-10
Weight: 220
College: Brigham Young University, Provo, Utah
Drafted: Milwaukee on second round, 1982 (27th pick).
Position: Forward
Final 1989 Team: Milwaukee Bucks
Final 1988–89 Statistics:

G	Fg	Fga	Fg%	Ft	Fta	Ft%	Orb	Reb	Ast	Stl	To	Blk	Pts	Ppg
71	155	319	.486	104	129	.806	68	209	66	36	80	23	417	5.9

Three-point goals: 3–14 (.214)   TSP: .491

SCORING

There was the regular season: Roberts, a journeyman small forward (San Antonio, Utah, Boston, and Milwaukee in six years), played his usual utility role, averaging 17.6 minutes a game and 5.9 points a game, and giving no indication that he was capable of much more. He was average or below average in virtually all offensive and defensive categories. But come playoff time, while it was the same gruesome haircut, the same wiry 6-10, 220-pound frame, a different Fred Roberts emerged. With Terry Cummings sidelined for much of the time with an ankle injury, Roberts got big minutes against Atlanta and Detroit (leading the Bucks with 38.3 mpg), and he responded. It turns out he can do a few things. Like score, including a career-high 33 against the Pistons, one of the NBA's toughest defensive teams (and 14.7 ppg for the entire playoffs). His strength is running the floor, and he gets easy baskets because he beats opponents down court, though occasionally he has trouble finishing. He likes the 15-foot baseline jumper and he can be a fairly accurate shooter when he has confidence (which was certainly the case during the playoffs). Otherwise, he puts it on the floor, usually to the baseline, going to his right, is adequate on the offensive glass, and is a fine foul shooter (.806 last year).

DEFENSE/DEFENSIVE REBOUNDING

Roberts, who can also play the 4, does a nice job defensively. He defends the post well, studies the scouting reports, and boxes out. But he is vulnerable to opponents out on the floor and has never been a good defensive rebounder.

THE FLOOR GAME

Roberts is a smart player who doesn't make a lot of mistakes. He handles the ball and passes well for his position.

INTANGIBLES

Roberts works as hard in practice as he does in games. He does the little things, like diving for loose balls, and boxing out, that win games—and win over coaches.

IN SUM

Until the playoffs, the line on Roberts was that the numbers were not a gauge of his value. He pushed people in practice, played with his head, and defended well. Now, he's added the wrinkle of scoring, and his stock has risen accordingly. Once thought of as a ninth to twelfth man in a rotation, he showed he's perfectly capable as a seventh or eighth man, and even as a spot starter.

RICK'S RATINGS

Scoring: **C**
Shooting: **C**
Free Throw Shooting: **A**
Ball Handling: **B**
Passing: **B**

Defense: **B**
Defensive Rebounding: **D**
Intangibles: **B**
Overall: **B**

Alvin Robertson

Birthdate: July 22, 1962
Height: 6-4
Weight: 190
College: University of Arkansas, Fayetteville, Ark.
Drafted: San Antonio on first round, 1984 (7th pick).
Position: Guard
Final 1989 Team: San Antonio Spurs
Final 1988–89 Statistics:

G	Fg	Fga	Fg%	Ft	Fta	Ft%	Orb	Reb	Ast	Stl	To	Blk	Pts	Ppg
65	465	962	.483	183	253	.723	157	384	393	197	231	36	1122	17.3

Three-point goals: 9–45 (.200)   **TSP:** .488

SCORING

Shooting guards come in two basic models. There's the classic variety: the Byron Scotts, the Dale Ellises, the Rolando Blackmans—jump shooters extraordinaire. Then there are the Clyde Drexlers and Alvin Robertsons of the world: players whose jumpers are only good enough to keep defenses honest but who rely on their abilities in transition, on the drive, and on their defense for offense. Robertson is a streaky outside shooter at best, but has twice led the NBA in steals (1985–86 and 1986–87) and gets a lot of easy buckets as a result of his thievery. He's also an aggressive driver and a ferocious dunker. Then, too, he's an opportunity scorer who gets a lot of his points simply by hustle; in particular on the offensive board (2.4 a game, third among starting 2s), though he often leaves his team exposed defensively when he goes to the glass. He'll shoot the three, but it's not his shot (9 of 45 last year; .268 lifetime). With the exception of his rookie year (9.2), he's been a steady high teens scorer for his career (17.3 last year).

DEFENSE/DEFENSIVE REBOUNDING

In his five pro seasons, Robertson has accumulated a batch of defensive honors. In 1985–86, he was named Defensive Player of the Year and has been named to the NBA All-Defensive first team (1986–87) and second team (1985–86 and 1987–88). His rep is founded, to a large extent, on the fact that you can never relax when he's around; he's one of the most dangerous ball thiefs in the league, the NBA record holder for steals (301 in 1985–86) in a season, and second in the league last year (with 3.0 a game, to John Stockton's 3.2). On the other hand, the consensus is that he takes too many chances, often leaving the defense vulnerable when he gambles. On the ball, he wants to guard everybody except his own man. Then, too, he's foul-prone, leading all starting 2s, per minute, and many of those fouls come at the wrong time. Strong, a good jumper, and persistent, he's consistently been one of the top defensive rebounders among guards in the NBA (almost six total rebounds a game in 1988–89).

THE FLOOR GAME

Robertson sees the court and can make the play in both half-court and in transition (six assists a game last year). But the turnovers—oh my, the turnovers. Per minute, Robertson was second highest among starting 2s. These, too, often come at inopportune moments. He frequently makes poor decisions as the middleman on the break, and doesn't know when to pull up for the 8-footer or take it all the way.

INTANGIBLES

Nobody, repeat, nobody, plays harder than Alvin Robertson. But he tends to play with his heart rather than his head. He wants to win badly, but he doesn't always know how to go about it. One of the highlights last year—if you want to call it that—was the gradual mellowing between Robertson and Coach Larry Brown who early on did not exactly see eye to eye. Obviously, it wasn't enough since Robertson has been traded to Milwaukee.

IN SUM

We are talking about a three-time All-Star. Robertson accumulates big totals in points, rebounds, and assists—and there's no way to measure intensity. But then there are the turnovers and the inconsistent outside shooting. Is he overrated, a talented basketball player who doesn't help you win games (San Antonio was 156–254 during his five-year tenure)? The jury is still out. Now it's up to Del Harris to maximize Alvin's potential.

RICK'S RATINGS

Scoring: **A**
Shooting: **B**
Free Throw Shooting: **C**
Ball Handling: **B**
Passing: **A**

Defense: **A**
Defensive Rebounding: **A**
Playmaking: **B**
Intangibles: **A**
Overall: **A**

Cliff Robinson

Birthdate: March 13, 1960
Height: 6-10
Weight: 240
College: University of Southern California, Los Angeles, Calif.
Drafted: New Jersey on first round as an undergraduate, 1979 (11th pick).
Position: Forward
Final 1989 Team: Philadelphia 76ers
Final 1988–89 Statistics:

G	Fg	Fga	Fg%	Ft	Fta	Ft%	Orb	Reb	Ast	Stl	To	Blk	Pts	Ppg
14	90	187	.481	32	44	.727	19	75	32	17	34	2	212	15.1

Three-point goals: 0–1 (.000)   **TSP:** .481

SCORING

Mark down Robinson for 16, 17, 18 points a game. For 10 years, the 6-10 forward (he can play 3 and 4) has been a consistent mid-teen scorer (lowest average: 13.6, rookie year; highest, 19.5 in 1980–81; last year, 15.1, but he played in only 14 games due to an early season knee injury). His best shot is the facing jumper, 15 to 18 feet from the basket, which he takes off the dribble or on the catch. He also likes the turnaround, which if you're a coach, is often one of those "Oh no, oh no, good shot!" affairs; Robinson's shot selection often leaves something to be desired. He will also shoot a right-handed hook coming across the lane and occasionally put the ball on the floor, but neither is his forte. He runs the floor well, but 76er coaches would like him to finish stronger. A historically poor foul shooter (.722).

DEFENSE/DEFENSIVE REBOUNDING

At one time, Robinson was one of the premier defensive rebounders for his position in the league (8.6 defensive rebounds per game and 11.1 overall in 1982–83). But those days are long past, and Robinson is now below the norm (only 5.4 a game overall in 1988–89). Of course, a lot of that has to do with position. Robinson usually guards the opposition's 3 (leaving Barkley on the 4), so he's often out on the floor and not in position for the carom. On a night-in, night-out basis, Robinson is not a good defender. Like many scorers, his mind tends to wander on D. He can guard people on the perimeter and does a fine job of denying the ball and making his man catch the ball farther out than he'd like,

but he gives away position too easily in the post. He does have a knack for steals (for a power forward), 1.2 per game.

THE FLOOR GAME

Like his shot selection, Robinson's passing decisions often make his coaches wince. He'd rather thread the needle than make the simple play. He has had big problems in the open floor, opting to dribble the ball after a rebound instead of throwing the quick outlet pass. But he's a fine interior passer and, per minute, he was tops among starting 4s for assists.

INTANGIBLES

You can't count on Robinson to play a full season. He has missed large chunks of the last three seasons, and his career has been an unending succession of injuries. He has played in as many as 70 games in just four out of 10 years.

IN SUM

Just when you think Robinson is the answer, he goes down with an injury. He's an excellent talent but he hasn't been able to beat the injury bug. An unrestricted free agent, he will likely not be with the 76ers this year.

RICK'S RATINGS

Scoring: **AA**	Defense: **C**
Shooting: **A**	Defensive Rebounding: **C**
Free Throw Shooting: **C**	Shot Blocking: **D**
Ball Handling: **B**	Intangibles: **C**
Passing: **B**	Overall: **B**

David Robinson

Birthdate: August 6, 1965
Height: 7-1
Weight: 235
College: U.S. Naval Academy, Annapolis, Md.
Drafted: San Antonio on first round, 1987 (1st pick).
Position: Center
Final 1989 Team: None
Final 1988–89 Statistics: Did Not Play.

SCORING

The David Robinson era is at hand in San Antonio and the

timing couldn't be better. The Spurs, after all, are coming off their worst season in the franchise's 22-year history (21–61) and if anybody's a franchise player, it's the big midshipman, the Spurs' No. 1 pick in 1987, who is entering the league after two years of service in the Navy. It's nice to know, for example, that your anchor in the middle is, unlike some of the other players the Spurs have marched out to the 5 spot recently (Frank Brickowski and the now-departed Cadillac Anderson), a true center—Robinson is 7-1, 235. And unlike some of the parties that jumped center last year for San Antonio (how about Mike Smrek and Jerome Whitehead), Robinson is a first-rate talent. Let's begin with what most agree is his superior athletic ability: the quickness, the speed, the jumping (both high and quickly) and the ability to change direction. The only physical attribute he seems to lack at this point is strength. His shoulders are big and wide, but the frame around his derrière is not, and the concern is that he can be moved around. While he's just beginning to scratch the surface of his offensive potential—recall that he played only one year of high school ball and spurted seven inches following his entrance to the Naval Academy—Robinson scored big in college (28.4 a game, fourth in the country in his senior year), relying on offensive rebounds (which he converts to dunks), turnaround jumpers from either baseline, and a left-handed hook. Then, too, he has superb speed and can run the floor and finish the play. Robinson shot an astounding .613 from the field at Navy, but unfortunately, his free throw percentage was only slightly (.627) higher.

DEFENSE/DEFENSIVE REBOUNDING

If the Spurs are excited about Robinson's offensive capabilities, they are downright ecstatic about his defensive potential. Simply stated, Robinson is the greatest shot blocker in the history of college basketball. He holds the NCAA record for most blocks in a game (14), in a season (207), and for a career (327). In his senior year, he led the nation in blocks with 4.5 a game. He has the potential to be the next Bill Russell of shot blocking. Robinson, however, does have several areas in which he can improve defensively. One is his defense before his man catches the ball; he'll have to force him to receive the ball farther out in the blocks. Then, too, despite his huge college rebounding numbers (there was no one else in the conference his size), he'll have to become more aggressive on the defensive board.

THE FLOOR GAME

Robinson can handle the ball, but he's still learning, for example, to pass the ball under pressure. As noted, he can run the floor but he accumulated only 87 assists in 127 college games. (Of course, if you're shooting over 60 percent, it makes sense to look to the hoop.)

INTANGIBLES

Denizens of Los Angeles know that laid back is a high form of being. But on the basketball court, that same quality is frowned upon. Since the game has seemingly come so easy for him, Robinson has been criticized for his occasional lackluster effort; he's not a player who inspires a gushy, "He loves to play." However, when challenged, such as against the Soviets in the 1988 Olympics, he has no trouble generating enthusiasm. Will he be able to sustain his intensity against the Greg Kites and Dave Hoppens of the NBA world? How, too, will he handle the inevitable microscopic evaluation of his performance?

IN SUM

Robinson is frequently likened to Bill Russell, the most dominating defensive player ever. But unlike the Celtic center, Robinson, say his supporters, is also a commanding offensive presence. But not having played a lot of quality basketball, David needs to work hard to become the star everyone expects.

Dennis Rodman

Birthdate: May 13, 1961
Height: 6-8
Weight: 210
College: Southeastern Oklahoma State University, Durant, Okla.
Drafted: Detroit on second round, 1986 (27th pick).
Position: Forward
Final 1989 Team: Detroit Pistons
Final 1988–89 Statistics:

G	Fg	Fga	Fg%	Ft	Fta	Ft%	Orb	Reb	Ast	Stl	To	Blk	Pts	Ppg
82	316	531	.595	97	155	.626	327	772	99	55	126	76	735	9.0

Three-point goals: 6–26 (.231)   **TSP:** .601

SCORING

At .595, Rodman led the league in field goal percentage last year, but don't get the impression he can shoot. He can't. What he *can* do is go to the offensive glass better than anybody in the league (well, just about anybody; per minute, he was second to the Nuggets' Jerome Lane, but Lane logged only 550 minutes, while Rodman played 2,208). The original live body, the lithe, 6-8 third-year man nicknamed the "Worm" jumps high, jumps quickly, and averaged an amazing four offensive rebounds a game in just 26.9 minutes. Then, too, he's a speed merchant—few players can keep up with Rodman baseline to baseline—and he's an excellent finisher on the fast break. So the points come on layups and dunks. Dunks and layups. Occasionally, he'll post up and shoot the turnaround jumper, but that's not the shot the Pistons want. He even attempted 26 threes last year, but that's not his shot either (he made six and is a lifetime .250 from trifecta country). And Rodman's foul shooting? Consider it an accomplishment of sorts that in 1988–89, his free throw percentage, .626, was higher than his field goal percentage (unlike 1987–88, when he shot .535 from the line and .561 from the field). But he's still a terrible foul shooter.

DEFENSE/DEFENSIVE REBOUNDING

Stopper. Rodman has been called the best defensive player in the league (he was All-Defensive Team, first team last season and third in the voting for Defensive Player of the Year), and you'll get few arguments from this quarter. He has the whole package: quickness, tenacity, jumping ability, lateral mobility. He can deny, block shots, take a charge, scoop up loose balls. And he can guard anybody. He's also just as potent on the defensive board as he is offensively— only Lane had more defensive boards per minute among small forwards than Rodman (he averaged 9.4 rebounds a game, tied for eighth in the league). So aggressive is Rodman on the boards that he not infrequently snatches rebounds from teammates!

THE FLOOR GAME

You don't want Rodman handling the ball in pressure situations. He's only a fair passer but has begun to show some ability to put the ball on the floor. His strength, as noted, is running the floor.

INTANGIBLES

To the world at large, the name Rodman is synonymous with *hot dog*. While his fist-thrusting, cheerleading antics may incite rival fans and opponents, they simply reflect Rodman's high-level intensity and enthusiasm for the game. As one source put it, "Rodman just loves being in the league." Along with Vinnie Johnson, John Salley, and James Edwards, he is part of the vaunted Piston second unit (he was third in the balloting for Sixth Man of the Year), a "team" that could make the playoffs on its own. Despite suffering from season long back spasms, he didn't sit out a single game last year.

IN SUM

The beauty of Dennis Rodman is that he could never score (he averaged nine a game) and still be one of the most valuable players in the league. Defense wins championships and so does rebounding, and Rodman is an awesome presence in both domains. Can you imagine if he had a jump shot?

RICK'S RATINGS

Scoring: **C**	Defense: **AAA**
Shooting: **C**	Defensive Rebounding:
Free Throw Shooting: **D**	**AAA**
Ball Handling: **B**	Intangibles: **AAA**
Passing: **B**	Overall: **AA**

Wayne "Tree" Rollins

Birthdate: June 16, 1955
Height: 7-1
Weight: 240
College: Clemson University, Clemson, S.C.
Drafted: Atlanta on first round, 1977 (14th pick).
Position: Center
Final 1989 Team: Cleveland Cavaliers
Final 1988–89 Statistics:

G	Fg	Fga	Fg%	Ft	Fta	Ft%	Orb	Reb	Ast	Stl	To	Blk	Pts	Ppg
60	62	138	.449	12	19	.632	38	139	19	11	22	38	136	2.3

Three-point goals: 0–1 (.000)   **TSP:** .449

SCORING

Rollins, of course, is the classic good-field, no-hit center. In 11 seasons with the Atlanta Hawks, he never averaged over 9.0 points a game or seven shots a game, and while Cleveland wanted him to look for his shot more, old habits die hard and he shot about as infrequently as he ever did. When he does score, it's generally off offensive rebounds or his jump hook. He surfaced a jumper from 10 to 12 feet last season, though it's not a shot the Cavs want him taking in crunch time.

DEFENSE/DEFENSIVE REBOUNDING

Rollins' speciality is shot blocking. He's second in the league (with Kareem Abdul-Jabbar's retirement, Mark Eaton is now first) in career blocks, but three knee operations have robbed him of a great deal of mobility; nevertheless, his long arms and plain old basketball sense make him a threat in the middle. The same goes for his one-on-one defense, where he uses savvy and physicality to get the job done.

THE FLOOR GAME

Rollins has some incredibly scant assist numbers. In 1987–88, for example, he garnered an assist every 88.2 minutes. Last year was better: one every 30.7 minutes. In his defense, it must be pointed out that Tree has rarely been part of the offense. Actually, he's an adequate passer (but not dribbler) on those rare occasions when he does get to touch the ball.

INTANGIBLES

You can't put a number on what Rollins does for a ballclub. He provides leadership, stability, maturity—all those good veteran traits. He worked well with Cleveland's young centers (Brad Daugherty and Chris Dudley), and though he certainly would have liked to see more minutes (only 9.7 a game), he didn't whine about it.

IN SUM

Rollins got those extra minutes, come playoff time. With Daugherty playing poorly, Rollins logged 14.8 mpg and played his role to a T: good defense (seven blocks), few mistakes (one turnover), and a bucket here and there (15 points in five games). He's 34 and has one more year left on his contract. So Tree has at least one more go-around.

RICK'S RATINGS

Scoring: **D**
Shooting: **C**
Free Throw Shooting: **D**
Ball Handling: **B**
Passing: **D**

Defense: **AA**
Defensive Rebounding: **B**
Shot Blocking: **AA**
Intangibles: **A**
Overall: **B**

Scott Roth

Birthdate: June 3, 1963
Height: 6-7
Weight: 212
College: University of Wisconsin, Madison, Wis.
Drafted: San Antonio on fourth round, 1985 (82nd pick).
Positions: Forward, Guard
Final 1989 Team: San Antonio Spurs
Final 1988–89 Statistics:

G	Fg	Fga	Fg%	Ft	Fta	Ft%	Orb	Reb	Ast	Stl	To	Blk	Pts	Ppg
63	59	167	.353	60	87	.690	20	64	55	24	40	5	181	2.9

Three-point goals: 3–16 (.188)   **TSP:** .362

SCORING

We know Roth, who played for Utah and San Antonio last year and was selected by Minnesota in the expansion draft can shoot—in the CBA. For example, during the 1987–1988 season, with the Albany Patroons, he shot .529, including 50 percent from trifecta country. Nice numbers. But while he reportedly drills them in practice, in his two seasons in the NBA, the 6-7 swingman has logged in at a chilly .369 pace, including a tepid .353 last season. OK, he hasn't gotten the shots (only 241 in two years), but it's imperative that he shoot well, since the rest of his game doesn't offer much. Slow afoot and not quick, he arrived in San Antonio from Utah woefully out of shape, which compounded his misery. He's not a shake-and-baker, not at all; he can't get his shot himself. Needs a pick or will spot up.

DEFENSE/DEFENSIVE REBOUNDING

Nightly, Roth guards the heavy artillery, the 2s and the 3s, and his lack of speed and quickness puts him at a distinct disadvantage. On the other hand, he knows what he's doing. The feeling is that he could be a more aggressive defensive rebounder.

THE FLOOR GAME

Roth will run the floor, but let's put it this way: James Worthy will not be usurped. He handles the ball well enough.

INTANGIBLES

A hard worker, team-oriented, Roth will have to get himself in better shape.

IN SUM

Maybe he should go back to Turkey, where he was a national hero, of sorts, a few years ago. Or the CBA, where he definitely would see substantial playing time. As long as Roth's jumper is on vacation, the NBA—even an expansion team—is a stretch.

RICK'S RATINGS

Scoring: **C**
Shooting: **A**
Free Throw Shooting: **D**
Ball Handling: **B**
Passing: **B**

Defense: **C**
Defensive Rebounding: **D**
Intangibles: **B**
Overall: **D**

Brian Rowsom

Birthdate: October 23, 1965
Height: 6-9
Weight: 220
College: University of North Carolina at Wilmington, Wilmington, N.C.
Drafted: Indiana on second round, 1987 (34th pick).
Position: Forward
Final 1989 Team: Charlotte Hornets
Final 1988–89 Statistics:

G	Fg	Fga	Fg%	Ft	Fta	Ft%	Orb	Reb	Ast	Stl	To	Blk	Pts	Ppg
34	80	162	.494	65	81	.802	56	137	24	10	18	12	226	6.6

Three-point goals: 1–1 (1.000)   **TSP:** .497

SCORING

Though only getting a glimpse of Rowsom in 1988–89 (he broke his hand in November and played just 34 games), the feeling is that with more playing time, he could develop into a credible scorer—in the 12-to-15 points a game range—as a starter. On a per minute basis, he was in the top quarter among backup 4s in scoring. He can run the court, possesses good jumping ability and aggressiveness on the offensive board (1.6 a game), and has a nice touch from about 15 feet and out. Encouraging is the fact that he shot .802 from the line.

DEFENSE/DEFENSIVE REBOUNDING

The early reviews are favorable in this category as well. Rowsom has a nose for the ball and desire to do the dirty work of rebounding. On D, he's quick and willing to bang, though at 6-9, 220, he could use a little more muscle.

THE FLOOR GAME

Rowsom is an average passer, but he's not a player you want to put the ball on the floor for more than a dribble or two.

INTANGIBLES

Another plus: Rowsom wants to become a better player. A quiet but intense kid, he plays extremely hard.

IN SUM

Rowsom could turn out to be a real find. As a second-round draft pick of Indiana's in 1987–88 (34th pick overall), he lasted all of four games as a Pacer. His scoring, rebounding, defense, and hustle are promising.

RICK'S RATINGS

Scoring: **B**

Shooting: **B**

Free Throw Shooting: **A**

Ball Handling: **C**

Passing: **B**

Defense: **B**

Defensive Rebounding: **B**

Shot Blocking: **B**

Intangibles: **B**

Overall: **C +**

John Salley

Birthdate: May 16, 1964

Height: 7-0

Weight: 230

College: Georgia Institute of Technology, Atlanta, Ga.

Drafted: Detroit on first round, 1986 (11th pick).

Positions: Forward, Center

Final 1989 Team: Detroit Pistons

Final 1988–89 Statistics:

G	Fg	Fga	Fg%	Ft	Fta	Ft%	Orb	Reb	Ast	Stl	To	Blk	Pts	Ppg
67	166	333	.498	135	195	.692	134	335	75	40	100	72	467	7.0

Three-point goals: 0–2 (.000)   **TSP:** .498

SCORING

Last year, his third, Salley started to fill what had been a rather bare offensive cupboard. In his first two years in the league, he shot .562 and .566, respectively—his offense consisted almost entirely of dunks and layups off fast breaks and offensive rebounds. But in 1988–89, while his shooting percentage (.498) was dropping, his game was expanding—in particular, he was beginning to show confidence in a 10-to-15-foot jumper. Still, his bread and butter remains the transition basket—with Dennis Rodman, he forms one of the best running combos in the league—and his work on the offensive glass (two a game in 20.1 minutes and way above average among backup power forwards). Early in his career, Salley had a tendency to be "cute" with the ball, but now he's slam dunking at will. His minutes (21.8) and offensive output (7 ppg) might have been higher last year had he not

been plagued by foul trouble. And his troubles continued at the line; after making marked improvement there since his rookie year (.614 to .709), he dropped to .692 in 1988–89.

DEFENSE/DEFENSIVE REBOUNDING

"Spider" is an apt nickname. "Cat" might be another. With his long arms and quickness, Salley is an excellent defender who can play both center and power forward. He's a superb shot blocker (1.1 a game) and alters the trajectory of umpteen others. He's mobile for a guy 7-0 and is tough in help situations. It's not often that a team has *two* stoppers (Salley and Rodman) *coming off the bench*—twin linchpins of the vaunted Detroit D. But, as noted, he tends to clutch and grab and foul too much. Once skinny as a rail, Salley has bulked up considerably though he could do well to add more strength, as he is, after all, primarily a power forward. His absence of beef hurts on the defensive glass, where he was below average, per minute, among backup 4s.

THE FLOOR GAME

Salley runs the floor as well as any power forward in the league. Among Detroit's frontcourt passers, he's clearly the best; he can make the judgment pass in key situations. He has a real feel for the game.

INTANGIBLES

Witty and upbeat, Salley is a boon to the Pistons' collective psyche and is well liked by both his teammates and his coaches. What's holding him back is inconsistency; he just doesn't get it done every night.

IN SUM

As a backup, Salley provides major league shotblocking and big-time running. Now that Rick Mahorn is gone to expansion (Minnesota), Salley would seem to be the natural candidate for Detroit's starting 4 spot. But Piston coach Chuck Daly has recently said that Salley isn't physical enough to be a starter. Whether those words were forwarded as a motivational tool, it's clear that Salley must get stronger and play with more consistency.

RICK'S RATINGS

Scoring: **C**

Shooting: **B**

Free Throw Shooting: **D**

Ball Handling: **B**

Passing: **A**

Defense: **AAA**

Defensive Rebounding: **C**

Shot Blocking: **AAA**

Intangibles: **B**

Overall: **B +**

Ralph Sampson

Birthdate: July 7, 1960
Height: 7-4
Weight: 230
College: University of Virginia, Charlottesville, Va.
Drafted: Houston on first round, 1983 (1st pick).
Position: Center
Final 1989 Team: Golden State Warriors
Final 1988–89 Statistics:

G	Fg	Fga	Fg%	Ft	Fta	Ft%	Orb	Reb	Ast	Stl	To	Blk	Pts	Ppg
61	164	365	.449	62	95	.653	105	307	77	31	90	65	393	6.4

Three-point goals: 3–8 (.375)   **TSP:** .453

SCORING

Say hello to Ralph Sampson: role player, bench warmer, fallen star. One of the most intriguing stories of the 1988–89 season was the Sampson saga, a grim tale, but one that is still evolving and may in fact ultimately have a happy ending. Our account begins on December 12, 1987, when, in one of the most talked about transactions in NBA history, Sampson, along with Steve Harris, is dealt to the Warriors from the Rockets for Sleepy Floyd and Joe Barry Carroll. Instantly, Sampson becomes the centerpiece of a bad team, the potential salvation of a floundering franchise (to that point, one playoff appearance in 10 years). But in 29 games, Sampson's play is pretty ordinary: shooting .438 from the field, averaging 15.4 ppg. On March 10, 1988, his season ends early when he undergoes arthroscopic surgery on his *right* knee. Chapter two begins during the exhibition season last year. In training camp, Warrior coach Don Nelson says: "I haven't seen his talent yet." Rumor has it that Sampson is being shopped. And the first game of the season is a harbinger of things to come. Sampson plays just 17 minutes, shoots 2–9, and scores 4 points. After 24 games he's shooting .397, averaging 8.3 ppg, and everybody's asking: "What's wrong with Ralph? What's wrong with Ralph is very clear: his *left* knee, upon which he had arthroscopic surgery during the 1986–87 season, is killing him. So he goes under the knife in December and misses a month. In the meantime, Golden State has moved to their now vaunted "small" lineup and are doing the unexpected: winning (in 1988–89, the Warriors went from 20 wins to 43 wins—the fourth best turnaround in league history). Sampson returns in late January but never even becomes part of the rotation. For the year, he shoots .449 and averages 6.4 ppg. When he does play, even though the knee has been declared OK medically, the reality is that Sampson is a mere shadow of his former self. His strength offensively which, of course, had been his mobility, his jumping, and his running now is neutralized, and with the knee not fully recovered, he's effectively playing on one leg. Before, he could be on the receiving end of an alley-oop, or he'd run the lanes, or hit the offensive glass. But now he just can't do it physically. And in the half-court setting, it turns out he's not the dominant low-post player the Warriors had imagined. He'll shoot the sky hook, but he hasn't mastered its technique. Or he'll fire turnarounds that make him look like he's never played the game. Sampson's basketball mission, if you will, has been to be known as a complete player—unfortunately, that goal has been pursued at the expense of developing a go-to move such as a hook or a jumper.

DEFENSE/DEFENSIVE REBOUNDING

A healthy Sampson has been an excellent defensive rebounder throughout his career (he averaged 10 total rebounds in his 29 games with the Warriors in 1987–88 and has 'bounded at a 9.6 game pace for his career). His height (7-4), jumping ability, and anticipation are the reasons why. And defensively, he can be a force in the middle—Sampson has averaged 1.8 blocks a game for his six-year career.

THE FLOOR GAME

Scratch a center, find a point guard, but for most big men, the dream is illusory. Not Ralph. Is there a more incredible sight than the 7-4 Sampson taking the ball upcourt? He's a fine passer from either the high post or the low post and is not particularly turnover-prone.

INTANGIBLES

Before writing off Sampson, you have to take into consideration his medical history: prior to his most recent surgery, he wasn't healthy—and he wasn't much better afterwards, either. There are two schools of thought on the issue. Either, his knees are shot and he's damaged goods, or he just needs a summer to fully rehabilitate. To his credit, Sampson endured his ordeal with a great deal of class. Even when he was sitting, he practiced hard and was ready to play. And word has it, he worked very hard this summer.

IN SUM

Our happy ending would go something like this: Sampson gets back to full strength and forms with Chris Mullin and Mitch Richmond the type of three-man core that championships are made of. Of course, Sampson, might come back healthy and not hold his own. His career, after all, has been marked by unmet expectations: he's never won a championship, not in college, not in the pros. He has never become the dominant player—a Bill Russell, a Wilt Chamberlain—that the pundits predicted. And last year, he wasn't even Ralph Sampson, who, even when healthy, has never scored enough, rebounded enough, or won enough to satisfy anyone.

Scoring: **A** Defense: **A**
Shooting: **B** Defensive Rebounding: **A**
Free Throw Shooting: **D** Shot Blocking: **A**
Ball Handling: **A** Intangibles: **C**
Passing: **A** Overall: **B**

Mike Sanders

Birthdate: May 7, 1960
Height: 6-6
Weight: 210
College: University of California at Los Angeles, Los Angeles, Calif.
Drafted: Kansas City on fourth round, 1982 (74th pick).
Position: Forward
Final 1989 Team: Cleveland Cavaliers
Final 1988–89 Statistics:

G	Fg	Fga	Fg%	Ft	Fta	Ft%	Orb	Reb	Ast	Stl	To	Blk	Pts	Ppg
82	332	733	.453	97	135	.719	98	307	133	89	104	32	764	9.3

Three-point goals: 3–10 (.300) **TSP:** .455

SCORING

Sanders is a different breed of small forward. Unlike other starting 3s, whose ranks include the likes of such high-powered scorers as Mark Aguirre, Dominique Wilkins, and Alex English, in Cleveland's system, Sanders wasn't expected to shoulder much of the scoring burden. In fact, he was really the fifth option (Larry Nance, Brad Daugherty, Mark Price, and Ron Harper take precedence) in the Cavs' offense. His major responsibility is to keep opposing defenses honest by hitting the jumper. For that role, Sanders is ideally suited because he moves well without the ball and knows how to situate himself to get his shot. However, he didn't have a good year from the field, shooting .453, his career worst. (He's a lifetime .487 shooter and had never been under .478.) Sanders started slowly and never developed any consistency. He's primarily a spot-up jump shooter (18-foot range) with an occasional foray to the basket. He will hit the pressure free throw, though overall he had a lousy year (.719) from the line.

DEFENSE/DEFENSIVE REBOUNDING

Sanders is a strong, hard-working defender who sacrifices a little quickness to the small forwards. He works well within a team's defensive framework. He's a good jumper but only a so-so defensive rebounder.

THE FLOOR GAME

Sanders knows the game. He's a decent passer who takes care of the ball. And he runs pretty well.

INTANGIBLES

Winning teams always seem to have players like Sanders: selfless types who know their roles and don't need the ball. A veteran of the CBA and twice waived (by Kansas City and San Antonio), Sanders, now with the Pacers, is in the league by dint of his work ethic and positive attitude.

IN SUM

Sanders was the "other guy" in the blockbuster trade with Phoenix that brought Nance to Cleveland (for Kevin Johnson, Mark West, and Tyrone Corbin plus draft picks). But he surprised everybody by earning a starting role and then keeping it. His numbers were nothing to write home about, but his intelligence, his defense, and the threat of his outside shot worked well within Cleveland's system. After all, the Cavs did win 57 games with Sanders in the starting lineup. However, by not signing Sanders, the Cavaliers have opted to go with their more talented small forward, John Williams.

Scoring: **C** Defense: **B**
Shooting: **C** Defensive Rebounding: **C**
Free Throw Shooting: **C** Intangibles: **A**
Ball Handling: **B** Overall: **B**
Passing: **B**

Danny Schayes

Birthdate: May 10, 1959
Height: 6-11
Weight: 245
College: Syracuse University, Syracuse N.Y.
Drafted: Utah on first round, 1981 (13th pick).
Position: Center
Final 1989 Team: Denver Nuggets

Final 1988–89 Statistics:

G	Fg	Fga	Fg%	Ft	Fta	Ft%	Orb	Reb	Ast	Stl	To	Blk	Pts	Ppg
76	317	607	.522	332	402	.826	142	500	105	42	160	81	969	12.8

Three-point goals: 3–9 (.333)   **TSP:** .525

SCORING

For Schayes, an eight-year pro, 1987–88 was a banner year, hitting career highs in points (13.9 ppg), rebounds (8.2 rpg), and shooting percentage (.540). An unrestricted free agent, he then signed a six-year $8.7 million contract—this, mind you, for a player who at the time of signing had averaged 8.9 points per game for his career. Those big dollars typically invite more careful scrutiny, and while his 1988–89 numbers—12.8 ppg and 6.6 rpg—compare favorably with his career averages (9.3 ppg and 5.9 rpg respectively), the more relevant yardstick was the 1987–88 season. By that standard, his performance just didn't measure up. Part of the problem was that the veteran Schayes was burdened by "rookie" calls—his constant foul trouble made it difficult to develop any rhythm on offense. Then, too, Schayes, who is not a good jumper and doesn't elevate well to the basket, missed a lot of layups. In Denver's motion offense, he's frequently positioned at the top of the key, where he can drill the 20 footer. He gets the same shot—perhaps a little closer in—as the trailer on the break, but he's not a guy who fills the lane well. He also scores—as most Denver players do—on hard cuts to the basket in their passing game. In the process, he gets fouled frequently (5.3 attempts a game); only Moses Malone, Brad Daugherty, Akeem Olajuwon, and Patrick Ewing shot more free throws among starting centers. And befitting a young man of his lineage (his father, Dolph, led the NBA in free throw percentage three times), Danny's a good (.826 last year; .799 lifetime) foul shooter.

DEFENSE/DEFENSIVE REBOUNDING

Schayes is a workhouse on D. He's very physical, does a decent job of denying position, though he's just a fair shot blocker (1.1 a game in 25.2 minutes). But, as noted, he had a big problem with foul trouble, leading the Nuggets with eight disqualifications. And his defensive rebounding numbers dropped, on a per minute basis, from way above average in 1987–88 to slightly above average last year. He relies on positioning and blocking out rather than leaping ability.

THE FLOOR GAME

Schayes is prone to thoughtless turnovers and sloppy passes, which is reflected in his high turnover per minute rate. He doesn't have the best hands, or for that matter, the quickest feet.

INTANGIBLES

Early in his career, Schayes lacked aggressiveness, and there were questions about his work ethic. Neither is an issue these days, and even though he had the big contract in hand, he worked even harder in the summer of 1988 to get ready for the season. It's taken a while, but he's matured as a person and a player.

IN SUM

Schayes' game is ideal for Denver's system. If he had to play as a "true" center in a more patterned offense, he'd be lost. Despite his down season, he's a decent center—way beneath a Patrick Ewing or an Akeem Olajuwon, but just a notch below a Mike Gminski or a Kevin Duckworth.

RICK'S RATINGS

Scoring: **B**
Shooting: **B**
Free Throw Shooting: **A**
Ball Handling: **C**
Passing: **B**

Defense: **A**
Defensive Rebounding: **B**
Shot Blocking: **B**
Intangibles: **A**
Overall: **B +**

═══ Detlef Schrempf ═══

Birthdate: January 21, 1963
Height: 6-10
Weight: 214
College: University of Washington, Seattle, Wash.
Drafted: Dallas on first round, 1985 (8th pick).
Positions: Forward, Guard
Final 1989 Team: Indiana Pacers
Final 1988–89 Statistics:

G	Fg	Fga	Fg%	Ft	Fta	Ft%	Orb	Reb	Ast	Stl	To	Blk	Pts	Ppg
69	274	578	.474	273	350	.780	126	395	179	53	133	19	828	12.0

Three-point goals: 7–35 (.200)   **TSP:** .480

SCORING

It's the old story about playing time. Player sits on the bench, never getting a chance to strut his stuff. Finally, he gets an opportunity—voilá—a ballplayer emerges. It's not as if Schrempf, who was traded to Indiana from Dallas for Herb Williams in February 1989, collected splinters in Dallas. He did, after all, average 22.8 minutes a game last year with the Mavs, but sitting behind Mark Aguirre he wasn't getting near the starter time (31.4 mpg) he enjoyed with Indiana. Result: With the Pacers he shot over 50 percent for the first time in his four-year career (.514), averaged double-figures (14.8—also a career high), and most importantly, was on the floor at the end of the game—and proved to be a consistently productive prime-time performer. Versatility is the key word here. Schrempf can play three positions (big guard, small forward, and power forward) and can score in a variety of ways. He has three-point range—he's a career .336 from that distance—but in the last couple of years (.156 in 1987–88 and .200 last year) he hasn't been able to find the basket from afar. So he's been staying inside, where he loves to post up, head fake his man into the paratrooper club, and get fouled. (His 5.1 free throw attempts a game was third among backup 3s; he shot .780 from the line.) Because of his leaping ability, Schrempf can also complete the alley-oop, and he's aggressive (1.8 a game) on the offensive boards. He can run all day and finishes well.

DEFENSE/DEFENSIVE REBOUNDING

Quicker 3s and 2s give Schrempf trouble, but his ability to play several positions is a big advantage. The problem is he's overly aggressive and often gets into foul trouble. He's an above-average defensive rebounder, whether you call him a 2, 3, or 4.

THE FLOOR GAME

Schrempf is a solid passer (2.6 assists a game) and an OK ball handler, but he takes too many chances (almost two turnovers per game). If he stayed away from the spectacular pass, he could improve his rather ordinary 1.35 assist-to-turnover ratio. He's a terrific athlete, who, as noted, runs the court well.

INTANGIBLES

Schrempf is tireless, coachable, and loves to play. With Dallas, in limited minutes, he was inconsistent and often his own worst enemy. But with regular minutes in Indiana, he was not only consistent but clutch, making numerous key plays in several games.

IN SUM

In Dallas, Schrempf encountered the same problem a former Mav, Dale Ellis (now with Seattle), did a few seasons back: They sat behind an All-Star, Mark Aguirre. Ellis, of course, has made the most of his opportunity with the Sonics and is now an All-Star himself. Based on his 32 games with the Pacers, it looks like Schrempf's career is headed in the same positive direction.

RICK'S RATINGS

Scoring: **B**	Defense: **B**
Shooting: **B**	Defensive Rebounding:
Free Throw Shooting: **B**	**AA**
Ball Handling: **B**	Intangibles: **B**
Passing: **B**	Overall: **B +**

Byron Scott

Birthdate: March 28, 1961
Height: 6-4
Weight: 195
College: Arizona State University, Tempe, Ariz.
Drafted: San Diego on first round as an undergraduate, 1983 (4th pick).
Position: Guard
Final 1989 Team: Los Angeles Lakers
Final 1988–89 Statistics:

G	Fg	Fga	Fg%	Ft	Fta	Ft%	Orb	Reb	Ast	Stl	To	Blk	Pts	Ppg
74	588	1198	.491	195	226	.863	72	302	231	114	157	27	1448	19.6

Three-point goals: 77–193 (.399)   **TSP:** .523

SCORING

When you score 19.6 a game, shoot .863 from the line, drill almost 40 percent of your threes (.399, tied for 10th in the league), and hit .491 overall, it's hard to fathom how you could possibly be accused of having an off-year! But recall that Scott, the Lakers starting shooting guard, was coming off a 1987–88 campaign in which he had established a career high in scoring (21.7 ppg), a career second-best in shooting percentage (.527), displayed a season-long consistency, and was considered one of the Lakers' top defensive players. So with his 1987–88 effort as the benchmark, the feeling was that the 1988–89 Scott was not the same player. Inconsistency—a knock on "B" throughout his career—raised its nasty head again and his shooting as well as his defense were erratic. In his defense, Scott could read his naysayers his medical report—at least a summer's worth of reading—which details his litany of physical troubles including back spasms, a urological disorder, a bruised wrist (his shooting hand), and a sprained ankle, but most painfully—figuratively, if not literally—a partially torn muscle in his left hamstring that kept him out of the NBA finals against the Pistons. (He was shooting .494 from the field and averaging 19.9 during the playoffs when he went down.) The more cynical among us might add that 1987–88 was Scott's contract year—which always seems to bring out the best in NBA players. Still his 1988–89 numbers represent some pretty fine shooting and the fact remains that Scott is one of the premier pure shooters in the league; you'd be hard-pressed to name a GM who wouldn't grab him as fast as you can say "Norm Nixon" (who is the player, now retired from the NBA, the Lakers exchanged to get Scott from the Clippers in 1983) if he were available. He has no peers, we can say confidently, as a pull-up jump shooter in transition. He'll dribble to the spot, look down at the opponent's feet, and elevate—he gets up high, his jumper displaying the textbook two-part motion: jump . . . shoot. For the Lakers, those transition hoops are "easy baskets," baskets they don't have to grind out in their half-court offense. Scott works hand-in-glove with the estimable Magic Johnson in the backcourt and knows how to position himself for the "magic" pass. Sure, Magic makes him better but Scott makes Magic look good, too, because he hits his shots. Scott is less proficient with the ball—i.e., creating for himself off the dribble—but he has become more effective taking it to the hole than he was early in his career (though he went to the line only 3.1 times a game last year). With his quickness, speed, and jumping ability, he can blow by people and dunk it home.

DEFENSE/DEFENSIVE REBOUNDING

Defensively, Scott is often matched against the 1s, while Magic covers a power forward or even a center and Worthy handles the 2s. Scott has the ability to contain his man on the perimeter—he moves his feet well—but last year Lakers coaches were mystified that his man would just as likely eat him alive; his concentration and intensity were often lacking. But his defense was sorely missed in the finals as the Pistons guards lit up the scoreboard.

THE FLOOR GAME

Scott, a true Laker greyhound on the break (along with Worthy, A.C. Green, and Orlando Woolridge), can sky for the slam-dunk finish. As a 2, and with Johnson his backcourt partner, he doesn't handle the ball much but he makes few mistakes.

INTANGIBLES

As a player who early on acquired a reputation for disappearing in big games (his playoff troubles in Boston Garden are almost legendary), Scott may always have a residue of doubt about his ability. But he has also, to a large extent, dispelled the notion that he's not a clutch performer; consider, for example, his solid work in the 1987–88 finals against Detroit. And until last season, he was durable, having missed only 16 games in his first five seasons.

IN SUM

Scott has been a starter and one of the central pieces in the Laker puzzle that won three out of the last seven NBA championships (and, but for his and Johnson's hamstring injuries had an excellent chance to make it four rings last year). When other teams look to emulate that record, they would do well to study Scott, the prototype 2, who is now in the prime of his career.

Scoring: **AA**
Shooting: **AAA**
Free Throw Shooting: **AA**
Ball Handling: **B**
Passing: **B**

Defense: **B**
Defensive Rebounding: **B**
Intangibles: **A**
Overall: **AA**

Rony Seikaly

Birthdate: May 10, 1965
Height: 7-0
Weight: 240
College: Syracuse University, Syracuse, N.Y.
Drafted: Miami on first round, 1988 (9th pick).
Position: Center
Final 1989 Team: Miami Heat
Final 1988–89 Statistics:

G	Fg	Fga	Fg%	Ft	Fta	Ft%	Orb	Reb	Ast	Stl	To	Blk	Pts	Ppg
78	333	744	.448	181	354	.511	204	549	55	46	200	96	848	10.9

Three-point goals: 1–4 (.250)   **TSP:** .448

SCORING

The tools are there—quickness, speed, jumping ability, touch—but Seikaly is, in a word, raw. His rookie year was only his fifth year playing organized basketball in the United States (he's Lebanese-born and went to high school in Greece) and his inexperience showed. In the low post, for example, he doesn't know how to use his body for leverage. Seikaly has a bunch of moves near the basket but wastes a lot of motion; he'll fake, juke, jive (to avoid contact), instead of powering the ball to the basket. However, as the season progressed, he developed more economy of movement. Facing the basket, he can put the ball on the floor and shoot the 15-footer (though anything beyond 15 feet is out of his range). He'll also shoot a turnaround jumper and a jump-hook from the blocks. In his first year, offensive rebounding was his strongest suit. He finished in the top third among starting centers (2.6 a game) on a per minute basis. One reason: He keeps his hands over his head so he can often grab the ball while his opponent is still gathering for his jump. He runs the floor extremely well—often scoring as the trailer on the break—but he doesn't run it consistently. And then there's his foul shooting, which is indeed foul. He was horrible as a collegian (.576), *worse* (.511) as a pro.

DEFENSE/DEFENSIVE REBOUNDING

So far, Seikaly is a better offensive rebounder than a defensive rebounder (in the bottom third among starting centers; seven total rebounds a game). He needs work on blocking out and improving his anticipation of where the ball is going. But with his long arms, quickness, and jumping ability, he'll eventually get the job done on the defensive boards. Defensively, he played soft. He's 7-0, 240, but was put on a weight program this past summer. He isn't accustomed to physical post play and is just learning how to use his body, his hands, and his elbows, to deny position. He can block shots (1.2 a game) but has a tendency to try to block every one, and, as a result, was in constant foul trouble.

THE FLOOR GAME

When the ball goes in to Seikaly, it usually doesn't come out. He averaged a miniscule 0.7 assists a game (for every 13.5 shots, he had one assist). Miami wants him to shoot it, not pass it. He handles the ball OK, but not in traffic, and he had the highest turnovers, per minute, among starting centers.

INTANGIBLES

Seikaly came out of Syracuse thinking he could play with the big boys, but he soon discovered he wasn't the hotshot he imagined he was. His work habits have been erratic, but he's learning, albeit slowly, that he will have to pay some dues. He definitely wants to improve—he worked exceptionally hard this past summer—and is now beginning to understand what it takes to do so. With his dearth of experience, he lacks the instinctual feel for the game of American players.

IN SUM

Seikaly has potential, plenty of it. He needs to bulk up, improve his foul shooting, hone his inside moves, learn to play defense—you got it, he's still a basketball babe. But the only thing that can stop him is himself.

RICK'S RATINGS

Scoring: **B**	Defense: **C**
Shooting: **C**	Defensive Rebounding: **C**
Free Throw Shooting: **D**	Shot Blocking: **B**
Ball Handling: **D**	Intangibles: **C**
Passing: **D**	Overall: **C +**

Brad Sellers

Birthdate: December 17, 1962
Height: 7-0
Weight: 210
College: Ohio State University, Columbus, O.
Drafted: Chicago on first round, 1986 (9th pick).

Position: Forward
Final 1989 Team: Chicago Bulls
Final 1988–89 Statistics:

G	Fg	Fga	Fg%	Ft	Fta	Ft%	Orb	Reb	Ast	Stl	To	Blk	Pts	Ppg
80	231	476	.485	86	101	.851	85	227	99	35	72	69	551	6.9

Three-point goals: 3–6 (.500)   TSP: .488

SCORING

A center at Ohio State, Sellers, who was traded by the Bulls in June to the Sonics for a 1989 first-round pick (which became B.J. Armstrong), has struggled in his first three years in the NBA (.464 career from the field) making the transition to the small forward spot. (Small forward, in this case, is obviously a misnomer: Sellers is 7-0.) That two-position switch is a difficult adjustment, as the experience of a player like the Knicks' Kenny Walker attests. Early last season, Sellers found his comfort zone and his touch: shooting .528 for the first 19 games of the season and averaging about 11 points a game. But there were too many nights when he disappeared, and in late December, he lost his starting spot to Scottie Pippen, who had been inconsistent as a reserve. Off the bench, Sellers was inconspicuous, ineffective, and unhappy, finishing the year with 6.9 ppg and shooting .485 from the field. The playoffs were worse: .375 from the floor and 3.2 points a game. He's primarily a stationary jump shooter with 18-foot range, who shoots it on the catch. But he needs to develop other small forward skills, such as putting the ball on the floor and creating his shot off the dribble. And at 7-0, he could easily post up inside but prefers the perimeter game. He runs the floor well but doesn't always finish, often "babying" the ball instead of dunking. Despite his size, he's a way below average offensive rebounder—in part because he was designated to get back on D when Michael Jordan drove; in part because he doesn't like to bang.

DEFENSE/DEFENSIVE REBOUNDING

Early on last season, Sellers played well defensively—at one point, he was in the top 10 in blocks—but as his minutes dropped, so did his numbers (he finished with 0.9 a game, third, per minute, among backup 3s). He can block shots because he's usually three to five inches taller than his opponents, and he's learned to use that to his advantage: He can play a couple of steps off his man and still be effective because of his long arms, timing, and jumping ability.

How do you figure it? Sellers led the nation in rebounding as a college senior but in 1987–88 he was the worst defensive rebounder among starting small forwards. His stats last season were similarly depressed and he finished in the bottom third, per minute, among backup 3s for defensive rebounding. He's a "fringe" player—he hangs out on the outskirts where there is no contact—and Bull coaches would have liked to see him get his fingernails and his game a little dirtier.

THE FLOOR GAME

Sellers has good speed and can get up and down the court. He's a fair passer—though by no means a creator—but when he touches the ball, it's usually to shoot it. His turnovers are on the low side, again reflecting the absence of ball handling.

INTANGIBLES

From day one, Sellers had it rough in Chi-town. In the 1986 draft, the "people's choice" was Duke's Johnny Dawkins (now with the 76ers; nice backcourt, Jordan and Dawkins) but Sellers got the nod and he was the guy Chicago fans loved to hate. Unfortunately, Sellers merited the rough treatment: he lost confidence and has yet to show he can give quality minutes on a consistent basis.

IN SUM

Is Sellers (a) a star waiting to happen or (b) an adequate backup player who can score occasionally and play defense? At the three-year mark, the answer is b. Perhaps Seattle will be a better venue for him to explore the first possibility.

RICK'S RATINGS

Scoring: **C**   Defense: **B**
Shooting: **A**   Defensive Rebounding: **D**
Free Throw Shooting: **AA**   Intangibles: **C**
Ball Handling: **B**   Overall: **C**
Passing: **C**

Charles Shackleford

Birthdate: April 22, 1966
Height: 6-10
Weight: 225
College: North Carolina State University, Raleigh, N.C.
Drafted: New Jersey on second round as an undergraduate, 1988 (32nd pick).
Position: Center
Final 1989 Team: New Jersey Nets
Final 1988–89 Statistics:

G	Fg	Fga	Fg%	Ft	Fta	Ft%	Orb	Reb	Ast	Stl	To	Blk	Pts	Ppg
60	83	168	.494	21	42	.500	50	153	21	15	27	18	187	3.1

Three-point goals: 0-1 (.000)   **TSP:** .494

SCORING

The shots are mainstream—a turnaround jumper and a jump hook—but for Shackleford, a 6-10 center who is entering his second year with the Nets, the problem is when to shoot. His shot selection is, to be polite, unorthodox. He'll take the jump shot when the hook shot is more appropriate and vice versa. He also has an annoying tendency of putting offensive rebounds on the floor, which verifies the fact that "Shack" is a raw rookie, who came out a year early (undoubtedly too early) from North Carolina State. His strength, at this stage, is his athleticism: Strong, quick, and an excellent jumper, he can run the floor and will finish with a monster dunk. A back-to-the-basket center.

DEFENSE/DEFENSIVE REBOUNDING

Those physical assets are a bonus on the defensive board; on a per minute basis, he was tenth in the league, quite a feat considering he relies almost exclusively on his jumping ability rather than blocking out his man. But defense is foreign to Shackleford, though he does have shot blocking potential.

THE FLOOR GAME

He can run but his ball handling falls far below the norm.

INTANGIBLES

Shackleford has a fuzzy concept of the game. It's going to take a while.

IN SUM

A project. But with his physical tools, probably a worthwhile investment for a couple of years.

RICK'S RATINGS

Scoring: **C**   Defensive Rebounding:
Shooting: **D**   **AAA**
Free Throw Shooting: **D**   Shotblocking: **A**
Ball Handling: **C**   Intangibles: **C**
Passing: **C**   Overall: **D**
Defense: **B**

John Shasky

Birthdate: July 31, 1964
Height: 6-11
Weight: 240
College: University of Minnesota, Minneapolis, Minn.
Drafted: Utah on third round, 1986 (61st pick).
Position: Center
Final 1989 Team: Miami Heat
Final 1988–89 Statistics:

G	Fg	Fga	Fg%	Ft	Fta	Ft%	Orb	Reb	Ast	Stl	To	Blk	Pts	Ppg
65	121	248	.488	115	167	.689	96	232	22	14	46	13	357	5.5

Three-point goals: 0–2 (.000)   **TSP:** .488

SCORING

No team, not even an expansion club like Miami, will look to Shasky to score a bunch of points. He was a modest scorer in college (9.6 career average), a modest scorer in the CBA (7.9 ppg in 1987–88), and yes, a modest scorer in his rookie year (5.5 a game in 14.5 mpg though, curiously, slightly above average on a per minute basis for backup centers). While he's not a good jumper, Shasky's prime weapon is his aibility on the offensive glass, where he fared better than three-quarters of his reserve peers. He also relies on a turnaround jumper (range is 12 feet), but his low-post moves are raw. He shot an unacceptable .689 from the line.

DEFENSE/DEFENSIVE REBOUNDING

Shasky, a seven-footer, weighed in at 225, which is much too lean to be an effective post defender. He needs to bulk up and get some experience. He does not block shots; his major defensive tool is knowledge. But he is a hard worker, blocks out well, and has the potential to be an adequate defensive rebounder.

THE FLOOR GAME

Shasky runs well and consistently—he does not pick and choose his spots. He's an OK passer who plays within his limitations and has a good feel for the game.

INTANGIBLES

Shasky will come to practice early, and never be late for the bus. Likeable and coachable, he's just happy to be in the league.

IN SUM

Shasky is a backup center—nothing more. He should survive in the league, at least for a while, on smarts and his healthy work ethic. Until, that is, someone with a comparable attitude and work capacity but just a smidgen more talent comes along.

RICK'S RATINGS

Scoring: **B**
Shooting: **C**
Free Throw Shooting: **D**
Ball Handling: **B**
Passing: **B**

Defense: **C**
Defensive Rebounding: **C**
Intangibles: **B**
Overall: **C –**

Purvis Short

Birthdate: July 2, 1957
Height: 6-7
Weight: 220
College: Jackson State University, Jackson, Miss.
Drafted: Golden State on first round, 1978 (5th pick).
Position: Forward
Final 1989 Team: Houston Rockets
Final 1988–89 Statistics:

G	Fg	Fga	Fg%	Ft	Fta	Ft%	Orb	Reb	Ast	Stl	To	Blk	Pts	Ppg
65	198	480	.413	77	89	.865	65	179	107	44	70	13	482	7.4

Three-point goals: 9–33 (.273)   **TSP:** .422

SCORING

Forty-one percent (.413) from the field? Purvis Short? Did one of the league's finest pure shooters (career .476) suddenly lose his touch? Not exactly. Short started last season on the wrong foot—rather hamstring, he tore his right one—and slowed by the injury (he missed most of the preseason), got off to a horrendous start (.357 in his first 16

games). Then, when Buck Johnson went down with a thigh injury, Short got the starting nod at the 3 spot and his shooting improved (.441 in 16 starts), but he still wasn't a model of consistency. He's always been a streaky shooter who can wear you out one night (he has scored over 50 twice) and not be able to find the basket the next. Short's bread and butter is that patented rainbow jumper (he loves the baselines), which, curiously, he likes to shoot with players crowding him. He's best coming off a pick and has never been one to create a shot or a drive for himself. Best way to defend him: keep the ball out of his hands and double him when he puts it on the floor. He has excellent range (though only .273 from three-point land last year and .282 lifetime).

DEFENSE/DEFENSIVE REBOUNDING

At 32, and not the quickest guy in the league, teams constantly go after Short on the defensive end. His effort is there, but he lacks lateral quickness. He's a fair defensive rebounder for his position.

THE FLOOR GAME

Short, because he dribbles high, is vulnerable to defensive pressure. Befitting a player who has lived off his scoring, his passing remains just so-so.

INTANGIBLES

A big question at this stage in Short's career is durability; he's missed 84 games over the past four seasons. A starter for most of his career, he's nevertheless comfortable coming off the bench.

IN SUM

Houston looked to Short to give them instant offense, but he never got it going. And they have elected not to sign Short, an unrestricted free agent. A healthy Short has a few miles left, but not much.

RICK'S RATINGS

Scoring: **B**
Shooting: **B**
Free Throw Shooting: **AA**
Ball Handling: **C**
Passing: **C**

Defense: **C**
Defensive Rebounding: **D**
Intangibles: **B**
Overall: **C**

Jerry Sichting

Birthdate: November 29, 1956
Height: 6-2
Weight: 180
College: Purdue University, West Lafayette, Ind.
Drafted: Golden State on fourth round, 1979 (82nd pick).
Position: Guard

Final 1989 Team: Portland Trail Blazers
Final 1988–89 Statistics:

G	Fg	Fga	Fg%	Ft	Fta	Ft%	Orb	Reb	Ast	Stl	To	Blk	Pts	Ppg
25	46	104	.442	7	8	.875	9	29	59	15	25	0	102	4.1

Three-point goals: 3-12 (.250)   **TSP:** .457

SCORING

Don't let last year's .442 from the field fool you. Sichting is as pure a shooter as there is in the NBA. He is one of two guards among current players (Ricky Pierce is the other) who has shot over 50 percent for five consecutive seasons (1983–1988). In 1985–86, playing 1,596 minutes for the Celtics, he shot an astounding .570. And he's a career .511 shooter. But in 1988–89, beset by a series of injuries, he played in only 25 games and shot the ball just 104 times. Those lofty percentages have a lot to do with the fact that Sichting knows a good shot and is basically a spot-up shooter, whose shots come when he has room. He plays the kick-in, kick-out game well, though he's just a fair three-point shooter (.273 lifetime). Sichting's game is on the perimeter; for his career, he's averaged 21.7 minutes a game but has gone to the line a mere one time per game (though he's an excellent foul shooter, .858 lifetime). He can bury the pressure shot.

DEFENSE/DEFENSIVE REBOUNDING

Sichting, who can play the 1 or the 2, is a tough, hard-nosed defender who understands position defense. Of course, at 6-2, he matches up better against the points, though quicker 1s and larger 2s give him problems. He contributes little on the defensive glass.

THE FLOOR GAME

Sichting can provide a team spot duty at the 1, but since he's only an adequate ball handler, you don't want to keep him there long. However, he doesn't make many mistakes with the ball and can run an offense. He picked up Portland's system quickly.

INTANGIBLES

Sichting plays hard. He's not a whiner and is a good role model for younger players. He has a ring; he knows how to win.

IN SUM

Sichting is not going to beat you with speed, quickness, or jumping ability. He can give you outside shooting and tenacious D off the bench, and his attitude is terrific. But he's a 33-year-old guard. One more season? Portland waived him in July.

RICK'S RATINGS

Scoring: **C**	Defense: **B**
Shooting: **A**	Defensive Rebounding: **D**
Free Throw Shooting: **AA**	Playmaking: **B**
Ball Handling: **B**	Intangibles: **A**
Passing: **B**	Overall: **C**

Jack Sikma

Birthdate: November 14, 1955
Height: 7-0
Weight: 260
College: Illinois Wesleyan University, Bloomington, Ill.
Drafted: Seattle on first round, 1977 (8th pick).
Position: Center
Final 1989 Team: Milwaukee Bucks
Final 1988–89 Statistics:

G	Fg	Fga	Fg%	Ft	Fta	Ft%	Orb	Reb	Ast	Stl	To	Blk	Pts	Ppg
80	360	835	.431	266	294	.905	141	623	289	85	145	61	1068	13.4

Three-point goals: 82–216 (.380)   **TSP:** .480

SCORING

Sikma has long been one of the league's most dangerous outside-shooting big men. His trademark, of course, is the vaunted Sikma move, where he takes the ball in the blocks, back to the basket, steps back, puts the ball high over his head, and fires away (a move, like Kareem Abdul-Jabbar's skyhook, widely admired but rarely copied—and, in fact, now infrequently used by Sikma himself). For almost overnight, the 12-year veteran has changed the complexion of his offense; these days his major weapon is the trey. Thus in 1988–89, Sikma more than tripled both the number of attempts and his percentage for his entire *career* (he was 7-for-68, .103, coming in), drilling them at a superb .380 pace (82-for-216). More than one-fourth of his shots were trifectas, which is one reason his overall percentage, .431, was the worst of his career. Since opponents play him for the jumper, he's wily enough to ball fake and take it to the hole. And you can virtually bank on it when he goes to the line. In 1987–88, he was the first center ever to lead the league in free-throw percentage (.922), and last year shot .905, second in the league. (But who can forget his missed free throw in the fourth playoff game against Atlanta last season that would have sealed the victory. Atlanta went on to win in overtime.) His low-post game is thin nor does he give you much on the offensive board. And at 34 and never quick to begin with, Sikma is clearly slowing down and is vulnerable to the younger, more athletic players, a fact most evident during the playoffs when he shot .394 and a dreadful .293 against the Pistons. He was, he admitted later, worn down.

DEFENSE/DEFENSIVE REBOUNDING

Historically, Sikma has been one of the league's premier

defensive rebounders, averaging as many as 9.9 defensive rebounds *per game* and 12.7 overall (1981–82 with Seattle). Last year, however, he had his worst season on the boards, averaging 7.8 total rebounds and putting up slightly below-average numbers on the defensive glass. And his production tailed off considerably (only 5.6 rebounds per game) during the playoffs. Not a leaper, he relies instead on boxing out and positioning. Defensively, Sikma uses his smarts, size, and physicality. He's never been a shot blocker (only one season did he get more than 100 blocks), but he can steal the ball (1.1 a game, last year) and the effort is always there. His perimeter shooting takes opposing centers away from the board, which improves the Bucks' team rebounding. He is foul-prone and had six disqualifications in 1988–89.

THE FLOOR GAME

Sikma has consistently ranked as one of the top passing centers in the league (tops, per minute, among starting 5s in 1988–89 with 3.6 a game). He reads the double-team well as well as makes the right transfer passes in Milwaukee's set offense. And he takes good care of the ball; this is one smart veteran. He even runs the floor, though his speed is below-average.

INTANGIBLES

Sikma is Mr. Durable. He once had a 283-straight-games streak going and has missed an amazing 25 games out of a possible 984. He is also one of the hardest working practice players in the league. A classy veteran.

IN SUM

Sikma is in the "maintenance" stage of his career. But the game he maintains still has considerable impact: the shot, the passing, the smarts, the attitude. He's signed for another three years.

RICK'S RATINGS

Scoring: **B**	Defense: **B**
Shooting: **A**	Defensive Rebounding: **B**
Free Throw Shooting:	Shot Blocking: **D**
AAA	Intangibles: **AA**
Ball Handling: **A**	Overall: **A –**
Passing: **AAA**	

Scott Skiles

Birthdate: March 5, 1964
Height: 6-2
Weight: 200
College: Michigan State University, East Lansing, Mich.
Drafted: Milwaukee on first round, 1986 (22nd pick).
Position: Guard
Final 1989 Team: Indiana Pacers

Final 1988–89 Statistics:

G	Fg	Fga	Fg%	Ft	Fta	Ft%	Orb	Reb	Ast	Stl	To	Blk	Pts	Ppg
80	198	442	.448	130	144	.903	21	149	390	64	177	2	546	6.8

Three-point goals: 20–75 (.267) **TSP:** .471

SCORING

Skiles, a three-year veteran who played with the Pacers last year and was selected by the Magic in the expansion draft, was a big-time scorer in college (27.4 in his senior year at Michigan State, second in the nation), but his role in the pros has been as a pure point. The result is that he's averaged only 5.7 ppg (6.8 last year) on 5 attempts a game. He's a legitimate three-point threat but has yet to shoot for attractive percentages from either three-land (.267 in 1988–89) or overall (.448 last year). Unlike his college days, when he scored a lot on drives, Skiles has had trouble finishing; he has a bad habit of challenging the big guys and getting it back in his face. His major drawback, both offensively and defensively, is his lack of quickness. While he weighed in about 15 pounds lighter last year, he still doesn't have blow-by ability, so he's confined primarily to the perimeter game, which he gets on spot-up shots or off the dribble. At .903 last year, he was third in the league in foul shooting.

DEFENSE/DEFENSIVE REBOUNDING

His lack of quickness also hurts him defensively, and it explains why he's destined to be a backup guard. Most of the 1s in the league can get by him or shoot over him (he's a small 6-2). But despite his size, Skiles has a good nose for the ball and has been an above-average defensive rebounder for his position. He's tough, will dive for loose balls, and doesn't back down from anybody (he must lead the league in minor scrapes, pushing and shoving matches, and finger-pointing exchanges).

THE FLOOR GAME

Skiles sees the floor as well as anybody in the league and knows how to deliver the ball. He has that rare ability to anticipate what happens before it develops. His limitations are, again, quickness—he doesn't penetrate that well—and a penchant for the pizzazz over the prosaic pass. (His assist-to-turnover ratio was a mediocre 2.20.) He is a floor leader to the point of being bossy, which at times has alienated some of his teammates.

INTANGIBLES

Skiles's competitive fire is such that he actually quit the Pacers briefly in mid-season because he couldn't stand losing. He is, pound for pound, one of the most hard-nosed players in the NBA. Sometimes his têtes-a-têtes with opponents distract him from the game.

IN SUM

Discussions about Skiles invariably use the word "if." As in if he were only quicker. But alas, Skiles is Skiles, a competent backup who can run a team, is weak defensively, and can score from the outside.

Scoring: **C**

Shooting: **C**

Free Throw Shooting:
  AAA

Ball Handling: **B**

Passing: **A**

Defense: **C**

Defensive Rebounding: **A**

Playmaking: **A**

Intangibles: **A**

Overall: **B –**

Charles Smith

Birthdate: July 16, 1965
Height: 6-10
Weight: 230
College: University of Pittsburgh, Pittsburgh, Pa.
Drafted: Philadelphia on first round, 1988 (3rd pick).
Position: Forward
Final 1989 Team: Los Angeles Clippers
Final 1988–89 Statistics:

G	Fg	Fga	Fg%	Ft	Fta	Ft%	Orb	Reb	Ast	Stl	To	Blk	Pts	Ppg
71	435	878	.495	285	393	.725	173	465	103	68	146	89	1155	16.3

Three-point goals: 0–3 (.000)   **TSP:** .495

SCORING

Throughout their checkered history, the Los Angeles Clippers have made—let's pull no punches—a lot of dumb moves. How about the 1984 deal that sent Terry Cummings (All-Star in 1988–89), Craig Hodges (current valuable member of the Bulls), and Ricky Pierce (sixth man extraordinaire) to Milwaukee for Junior Bridgeman (retired), Harvey Catchings (retired), and Marques Johnson (retired)? Or when in 1983, they traded the draft rights to Byron Scott, a premier shooting guard, to the Lakers for Norm Nixon (retired from the NBA—he finished last season in Italy)? But the Clippers will catch little, if any flak, for the complicated three-way transaction that brought Charles Smith, the third player picked overall in the 1988 draft, to Los Angeles. (The deal also involved the 76ers and the Sonics and resulted in Hersey Hawkins winding up in Philadelphia, Michael Cage in Seattle, and Gary Grant with the Clippers.) Smith is one of the veritable harvest of first-round picks the Clippers have accumulated recently, and he bore immediate fruit, averaging 16.3 ppg, making the All-Rookie first team, and giving every indication that, along with Danny Manning and Kenny Norman, the Clippers have a competitive frontcourt for the 1990s. Imagine what potential they would have had if Danny Ferry, their No. 1 pick in 1989,

had not gone to Italy. Smith brings to the mix some impressive physical tools: he's quick, jumps well, has marvelous agility for a 6-10 player, a long wingspan, and runs the court like a gazelle. It's not clear whether he's a 3 or a 4; he played both positions last year. Favoring the former designation is the fact that he likes to shoot 15-foot jumpers and doesn't have the bulk of the classic power forward. Whatever he is, Smith is already a prime time post-up player with a barrelful of inside moves, including turnarounds, spins to the baseline, and power stuff where he'll pump fake his man several times and draw the foul (he went to the line a hefty 5.5 times), though at .725 his foul shooting will have to improve. But, as noted, he can play the facing game; his offensive growth will come in learning how to catch the ball in better scoring position. His range is limited—15 feet—though he tended to shoot beyond it. A fair offensive rebounder.

DEFENSE/DEFENSIVE REBOUNDING

Smith has the tools to be a quality defender, but being offensive-minded, he will coast on D. Despite his size, he has quick feet and can guard 3s on the perimeter. And with that reach, he has above-average shot blocking ability (1.3 a game in 30.4 minutes). One knock on Smith, though, is that he's soft and doesn't rebound commensurate with his size and leaping ability. Indeed, if you consider him a 4 his defensive rebounding numbers were pitiful; only Grant Long, Terry Teagle (who played out of position last year), and Cliff Robinson were worse. But compared to 3s, he's way above average!

THE FLOOR GAME

Smith needs to improve his ball handling and passing. The raw skills are there; his judgment is questionable. His teammates would appreciate, at least occasionally, being on the receiving end of a Smith pass. He averaged just 1.5 assists a game; it's not clear whether it's selfishness or an inability to make the play. Smith also has a little Ralph Sampson in him; he wants to do too much with the ball on the perimeter.

INTANGIBLES

Coachable, mature, poised, competitive. One issue: Is Charles Smith just out for Charles Smith? Bears watching.

IN SUM

A big upside and he's already established the roots. Should score in the high teens or low 20s for a long time to come. Once his rebounding (which improved in the final third of the season) and passing come around, Smith's a potential All-Star.

Scoring: **AA**

Shooting: **B**

Free Throw Shooting: **C**

Ball Handling: **B**

Passing: **C**

Defense: **B**

Defensive Rebounding: **C**

Shot Blocking: **A**

Intangibles: **B**

Overall: **A**

Derek Smith

Birthdate: November 1, 1961
Height: 6-6
Weight: 218
College: University of Louisville, Louisville, Ky.
Drafted: Golden State on second round, 1982 (35th pick).
Position: Forward
Final 1989 Team: Philadelphia 76ers
Final 1988–89 Statistics:

G	Fg	Fga	Fg%	Ft	Fta	Ft%	Orb	Reb	Ast	Stl	To	Blk	Pts	Ppg
65	216	496	.435	129	188	.686	61	167	128	43	88	23	568	8.7

Three-point goals: 7–31 (.226) **TSP:** .443

SCORING

The Derek Smith story—in three chapters. Chapter One: In 1984–85, Smith, then with the Los Angeles Clippers, was at the peak of his then considerable offensive powers. That year he averaged 22.1 ppg, shot .537, and pulled down five rebounds a game. He was a superstar in the making, an unstoppable machine who could play the post-up game, jump over people, get by you in a moment, or drill jumpers from outside. Chapter Two: Nine games into the next season, again on a torrid pace, he tore cartilage in his left knee; he's never been the same since. He played 11 games in 1985–86 (and was traded to Sacramento in August 1986), 52 in 1986–87, 35 in 1987–88. Early last season, he became a persona non grata in Sacramento. The Kings were of the opinion that his game was going, going, gone. They felt he had lost his quickness and his explosiveness and that he would not (or could not) land on his left knee, which makes life tough for a right-handed player. Eventually, they waived him on February 7. Chapter Three: With Cliff Robinson out for the season and the 76ers hurting at the 3 spot, the 76ers sign Smith on February 13. Smith played 36 games for Phillie (18 as a starter) and, while he didn't remind anybody of the Clipper Smith, he also was not the has-been the Kings had depicted. He can still attack the basket, make the occasional jumper, but on the 76ers, he was not a primary scoring option.

DEFENSE/DEFENSIVE REBOUNDING

Smith was always a smart and tenacious defender, but now he can't escape his physical deficiencies. His lateral movement and quickness are limited and he's a little bit helpless against quicker 3s. But he's a physical post defender, and gives good hard fouls. His defensive rebounding numbers were way below average.

THE FLOOR GAME

Smith is an OK ball handler. In years past, the ball often stopped in his hands, but his role has changed now. He can't run the floor.

INTANGIBLES

His health, of course, is a major question mark. If he plays substantial minutes (which he didn't do very often), he can't handle the physical demands of playing consecutive nights. The 76ers were impressed with his professionalism, his come-to-work-every-night attitude.

IN SUM

Smith, an unrestricted free agent, has a little left and the 76ers will likely sign him. He offers quality minutes—"veteran stability" was how one source described it—off the bench. Sad to say, he's only 28.

RICK'S RATINGS

Scoring: **B**
Shooting: **B**
Free Throw Shooting: **D**
Ball Handling: **B**
Passing: **B**

Defense: **C**
Defensive Rebounding: **D**
Intangibles: **C**
Overall: **C**

Kenny Smith

Birthdate: March 8, 1965
Height: 6-3
Weight: 170
College: University of North Carolina, Chapel Hill, N.C.
Drafted: Sacramento on first round, 1987 (6th pick).
Position: Guard
Final 1989 Team: Sacramento Kings
Final 1988–89 Statistics:

G	Fg	Fga	Fg%	Ft	Fta	Ft%	Orb	Reb	Ast	Stl	To	Blk	Pts	Ppg
81	547	1183	.462	263	357	.737	49	226	621	102	249	7	1403	17.3

Three-point goals: 46–128 (.359) **TSP:** .482

SCORING

While there are dramatic stylistic differences among the seven teams that won 50 or more games last year (Detroit, L.A. Lakers, Cleveland, New York, Phoenix, Atlanta, and Utah)—compare, for example, the get-'em-up-Suns with the hold-'em-down-Jazz—there is at least one common thread: All have a point guard who can score. Besides their considerable playmaking abilities, Magic Johnson (22.5 ppg), Kevin Johnson (20.4), Mark Price (18.9), Isiah Thomas (18.2), John Stockton (17.1), Mark Jackson (16.9), and Glenn Rivers (13.6) all know where the hoop is. Thus Sacramento, which barely won half of 50 games in 1988–89 (27 to be exact), is at least headed in the right direction with Smith, a 1 with a scorer's mentality who was the club's third leading scorer at 17.3, just barely behind Danny Ainge and Wayman Tisdale (both at 17.5 overall; they averaged 20.3 and 19.8, respectively with the Kings). Smith's forte is the jumper off the dribble from 15 to 20 feet. He can also shoot the trey; he upped his percentage from his rookie year's .308 to a tidy .359 last year. Speedy and exceptionally quick, Smith gets by people at will but still misses a lot of layups. With the arrival of Danny Ainge from Boston in February, Smith had the luxury of occasionally playing the 2 and having his backcourt mate consistently find him for the open jumper. Never below 80 percent from the stripe in college and in the pros, Smith mysteriously sank to .737 in 1988–89.

DEFENSE/DEFENSIVE REBOUNDING

With his speed, quickness, and background (four years under Dean Smith at North Carolina), Smith has what it takes to be a quality defender. But he has yet to develop a consistent defensive mind-set; he'll play good D for stretches and then cruise. At this stage, he's probably a better trapper than one-on-one defender. Nor does he make many steals (1.3 a game) or grab many rebounds (2.8 a game; he's 6-3 but slight at 170)—which puts him in the bottom third in both categories among starting point guards.

THE FLOOR GAME

Early on, Sacramento insiders admitted some disappointment in Smith's helmsmanship. For one, the 2 in him didn't always look to create. For another, his decisions on the break and play-calling often came up short. But he showed marked improvement as the year progressed, though his assist-to-turnover ratio only improved fractionally from a poor 2.36 in 1987–88 to a still-lousy 2.49 last year.

INTANGIBLES

Smith has never lacked confidence, but some say his opinion of himself didn't quite measure up with his performance on the floor. But that was his rookie year. In 1988–89, he seemed to recognize that there was room for improvement, and he was putting in the extra time. Ainge's professionalism and work habits have rubbed off on Smith.

IN SUM

Smith is part of the solution, not the problem, in the Kings' scheme of things. He has the athletic tools to be in the upper echelon of point guards. But he's at least a year away.

RICK'S RATINGS

Scoring: **A**	Defense: **C**
Shooting: **A**	Defensive Rebounding: **D**
Free Throw Shooting: **C**	Playmaking: **B**
Ball Handling: **B**	Intangibles: **B**
Passing: **B**	Overall: **B +**

Larry Smith

Birthdate: January 18, 1958
Height: 6-8
Weight: 235
College: Alcorn State University, Lorman, Miss.
Drafted: Golden State on second round, 1980 (24th pick).
Position: Center
Final 1989 Team: Golden State Warriors
Final 1988–89 Statistics:

G	Fg	Fga	Fg%	Ft	Fta	Ft%	Orb	Reb	Ast	Stl	To	Blk	Pts	Ppg
80	219	397	.552	18	58	.310	272	652	118	61	110	54	456	5.7

Three-point goals: 0–0 (.000)   **TSP:** .552

SCORING

Broadly speaking, one stat succinctly summarizes Smith's game. The 11-year veteran, who signed with the Rockets as an unrestricted free agent, has only once (1984–85) totaled more points than rebounds. He's always been a rebounding machine (10.4 rpg lifetime)—the Warriors' designated rebounder (a designation, by the way, he doesn't particularly care for)—but he'd love to get more scoring opportunities, certainly more than the five shots he averaged last year (6.6 for his career). But these are not forthcoming for a good reason: Smith doesn't have a low-post game or, for that matter, a high-post game. When he scores, it's because he's working hard on the offensive glass. He is one of the league's best offensive rebounders, garnering an outstanding 3.4 a game in just 23.7 minutes. Rarely will you see a close-in jumper or hook. He'll also get a few points off of guard penetration. But he virtually never goes to the line—58 times in 1897 minutes, which is fortunate, since he's an absurdly bad foul shooter—.310 in 1988–89 and .539 lifetime.

DEFENSE/DEFENSIVE REBOUNDING

The 31-year-old Smith is slowing a bit—per minute, his rebounding numbers in 1988–89 were down from his career average—but he's still a legitimate big-league defensive rebounder. Not a great leaper nor particularly big at 6-8, Smith succeeds by consistently blocking out his man and sheer force of will. He wants the ball, takes pride in his "Rs," and well understands that his board work is what's kept him in the league. Defensively, he'll bang and deny position, but he's not much of shot blocker.

THE FLOOR GAME

Coach Nelson made a pleasant discovery: Smith is a better than average passer from the high post. Per minute, he was in the top third among starting centers for assists. He's an average runner of the floor.

INTANGIBLES

From the old school. Mr. Mean (as he is known) is one of the ultimate hard hat players in the league, a tremendous competitor who does the dirty work. He was the Warriors' captain last season, but he didn't win any friends among Warrior coaches by grumbling about his lack of offensive involvement.

IN SUM

The Warriors will sorely miss Smith's toughness and work ethic, qualities which don't exactly grow on trees around the league. With the Rockets, Smith will back up both Akeem Olajuwon and Otis Thorpe. But there will be occasions when the three are on the floor at the same time, comprising one of the most awesome rebounding trios in the history of the NBA.

RICK'S RATINGS

Scoring: **D**	Defensive Rebounding:
Shooting: **D**	**AA**
Free Throw Shooting: **D**	Shot Blocking: **A**
Ball Handling: **B**	Intangibles: **A**
Passing: **A**	Overall: **B +**
Defense: **A**	

Otis Smith

Birthdate: January 30, 1964
Height: 6-5
Weight: 210
College: Jacksonville University, Jacksonville, Fla.
Drafted: Denver on second round, 1986 (41st pick).
Positions: Guard, Forward
Final 1989 Team: Golden State Warriors
Final 1988–89 Statistics:

G	Fg	Fga	Fg%	Ft	Fta	Ft%	Orb	Reb	Ast	Stl	To	Blk	Pts	Ppg
80	311	715	.435	174	218	.798	128	330	140	88	129	40	803	10.0

Three-point goals: 7–37 (.189)   **TSP:** .440

SCORING

In 1988–89 Otis Smith, who split his first three years between Denver and Golden State (he was acquired by the Warriors on December 22, 1987), was going to emerge—to move from "potential" to "there." One of the best pure athletes in the league—he was a contestant in the Slam Dunk championship in 1988—Smith was coming off a fine 1987–88 season, where, in 57 games with the Warriors (he also played 15 with Denver), he averaged 13.1 ppg and shot .506 from the field. But he shot a dreary .435 in 1988–89, which is one reason he was left unprotected in the expansion draft and was selected by the Orlando Magic. Nor, compared to the previous year (.317) could he find the basket from three-point range (just .189 beyond the arc). That type of shooting is usually associated with the term "streaky," and indeed Smith is not a perimeter player. His strength is his explosive quickness to the hoop, where he can finish with a flourish. That skying ability also serves him well on the offensive glass, where he garnered a solid 1.6 rebounds in just 20 minutes per contest. And he can run, too; either as a trailer or the wingman, he has a knack for getting open on the break. When you watch Smith, who can swing between the 2 and the 3 and has even played some 1, it's often hard to figure out whether he's right-handed or left-handed (he's the former); he is one of the most ambidextrous players in the league and has been known to shoot short jumpers with his left hand. However, it's not clear whether his two-handedness adds any real effectiveness to his game.

DEFENSE/DEFENSIVE REBOUNDING

The jury is out on Smith's defense. The tools are there—the speed, the strength, the quickness—but he hasn't shown much defensive consistency. Primarily an offensive-minded player, Smith hasn't disciplined himself to be a good defender. He suffers mental lapses, for example, following his opponent into the paint rather than denying the pass, and he often got lost in coach Don Nelson's sophisticated defensive schemes. But he did the job on the defensive glass; per minute, he was third among backup 2s.

THE FLOOR GAME

For a 2, Smith's an above-average ball handler. For a 1, he's suspect. One problem: when he takes it all the way to the bucket, he has tunnel vision—the little handoff pass to the big guys is not part of his repertoire. But he likes the ball in his hands and is a better passer than you might expect.

INTANGIBLES

Accolades abound. Smith wants to improve and is coachable and unselfish. But he just doesn't have a real feel for the game and his concentration level is not what it should be.

IN SUM

With Chris Mullin and Mitch Richmond in place at the 2 and 3, and with the addition of Sarunas Marciulionis, the first Soviet signed to play in the NBA, Smith was expendable. Orlando is another opportunity to reestablish himself. He's a quality talent for an expansion team but needs to improve his outside shooting and defensive intensity to make a bigger dent.

RICK'S RATINGS

Scoring: **B**   Defense: **C**
Shooting: **C**   Defensive Rebounding:
Free Throw Shooting: **B**   **AAA**
Ball Handling: **A**   Intangibles: **C**
Passing: **B**   Overall: **C**

Rik Smits

Birthdate: August 23, 1966
Height: 7-4
Weight: 250
College: Marist College, Poughkeepsie, N.Y.
Drafted: Indiana on first round, 1988 (2nd pick).
Position: Center
Final 1989 Team: Indiana Pacers
Final 1988–89 Statistics:

G	Fg	Fga	Fg%	Ft	Fta	Ft%	Orb	Reb	Ast	Stl	To	Blk	Pts	Ppg
82	386	746	.517	184	255	.722	185	500	70	37	130	151	956	11.7

Three-point goals: 0–1 (.000)   **TSP:** .517

SCORING

The Pacers had planned to bring Smits, a 7-4 center and the second player picked in the 1988 draft, along slowly but an injury to Steve Stipanovich thrust him into a starting role. (Stuart Gray and Greg Dreiling, Indiana's other centers, were not realistic prospects though Dreiling did start four games.) But the "Dunking Dutchman" (he was born and bred in Holland) acquitted himself quite well, scoring 11.7 a game, shooting .517 from the field, and eliciting a collective sigh of relief in the Pacer front office that they hadn't made a BIG mistake. What's most distinctive about Smits is the fact that he's so tall but has such a good touch. He has superb hands—he has no trouble catching the ball on the break, and he finishes well—and runs the court as well as anybody his size (or even near his size). Right now, he's most comfortable shooting the turnaround jumper from 15 and in; his growth will come in expanding his arsenal. For example, he shot the hook in college but he seemingly had

it under wraps in the first pro year. He showed potential as an offensive rebounder (2.3 a game and slightly above average on a per minute basis) but needs to improve his foul shooting (.722). His scoring production would have been better had he not been plagued by foul troubles—a lot of "rookie calls" according to one source. As it were, on a per minute basis, he scored more than Bill Cartwright, Jack Sikma, and Joe Barry Carroll.

DEFENSE/DEFENSIVE REBOUNDING

Smits's foul trouble stemmed from a tendency to put his opposite hand on his man when he went up to block a shot. Once he learns to go straight up, with both hands, he could be a big-time shot blocker; his 1.8 blocks a game were, on a per minute basis, better than such major league swatters as Mark West and James Donaldson. But he needs major work in the weight room (which is what he did this past summer), because he's easily pushed out of the blocks. His leg strength is fine but his upper body needs significant chiseling. He needs to become a better defensive rebounder; last year, non-boarders like Bill Cartwright and Charles Jones outrebounded him on a per minute basis on the defensive glass.

THE FLOOR GAME

For somebody who has been playing since he was 15, Smits has a pretty good feel for the game of basketball. But his passing and ball handling (less than 1 assist a game) need work.

INTANGIBLES

Early on, there was some question about Smits's intensity level, but he competed well enough last season. He has displayed a healthy work ethic, which he'll need to rise to the next level(s).

IN SUM

A comer. One of the few bright points in Indiana's dreary year. Smits, who made the All-Rookie first team, has a promising future. Most of all, he needs upper body strength and experience.

RICK'S RATINGS

Scoring: **B**   Defense: **B**
Shooting: **A**   Defensive Rebounding: **D**
Free Throw Shooting: **C**   Shot Blocking: **A**
Ball Handling: **C**   Intangibles: **B**
Passing: **C**   Overall: **B +**

Rory Sparrow

Birthdate: June 12, 1958
Height: 6-2
Weight: 175
College: Villanova University, Villanova, Pa.

Drafted: New Jersey on fourth round, 1980 (75th pick).
Position: Guard
Final 1989 Team: Miami Heat
Final 1988–89 Statistics:

G	Fg	Fga	Fg%	Ft	Fta	Ft%	Orb	Reb	Ast	Stl	To	Blk	Pts	Ppg
80	444	982	.452	94	107	.879	55	216	429	103	204	17	1000	12.5

Three-point goals: 18–74 (.243)   **TSP:** .461

SCORING

The NBA Comeback Player of the Year award has been discontinued, but if it were still being awarded, Rory Sparrow would have been a leading candidate for the 1988–89 season. In 1987–88, as a reserve guard with the Bulls and the Knicks, Sparrow shot .399, a career low, averaged only 4.5 ppg (his lowest since his rookie year in 1980–81), and even shot poorly from the line (.727). At 30 (he's now 31), Sparrow's basketball future didn't loom bright. There he was, contemplating his future outside of the game, when the Miami Heat called. He signed two days before the season started, was in the starting lineup on opening night—and stayed there for the entire year. (He played 80 games and started 79). He was the Heat's second-leading scorer, averaged 12.5 a game (his career best), and raised his free throw percentage to .879, also a lifetime high. Sparrow relies primarily on a 15 to 17-footer which, when he's open and squared, is a reasonably accurate shot. He drives occasionally—in fact, he's rather fearless going to the bucket—and is not reluctant to take (he made several buzzer beaters that won games for the Heat)—the clutch shot.

DEFENSE/DEFENSIVE REBOUNDING

Sparrow is a solid all-around defender. He will hound his man full court and is cognizant of the strengths and weaknesses of his opponents. He also understands help defense and reads offensive allignments well. At 6-2, Sparrow's on the small side and is a below-average rebounder for his position.

THE FLOOR GAME

Sparrow's playmaking won't make any highlight films, but then he doesn't make many mistakes, either. He sees the passing opportunities he should see and runs the offense, but he's not an improviser. In other words, he gets the job done. While his assist-to-turnover ratio was way below-average, keep in mind that Miami was the worst-scoring team in the league (the only team that averaged less than 100: 97.8), that Sparrow had major scoring responsibilities, and his poor ratio was more a matter of too few assists than too many turnovers.

INTANGIBLES

Sparrow is a positive influence on any team. He is the consummate veteran: providing leadership and a willingness to share his knowledge. And he is a model citizen (as exemplified, for one, by his extensive work with charities).

IN SUM

Sparrow revived his career with a great season. A solid scorer, playmaker, and defender, he'd be a backup on a good team, but Miami had no complaints about his play as a starter.

RICK'S RATINGS

Scoring: **B**	Defense: **B**
Shooting: **B**	Defensive Rebounding: **D**
Free Throw Shooting: **AA**	Playmaking: **B**
Ball Handling: **B**	Intangibles: **AA**
Passing: **B**	Overall: **B**

John Starks

Birthdate: August 10, 1965
Height: 6-3
Weight: 180
College: Oklahoma State University, Stillwater, Okla.
Drafted: Free Agent
Position: Guard
Final 1989 Team: Golden State Warriors
Final 1988–89 Statistics:

G	Fg	Fga	Fg%	Ft	Fta	Ft%	Orb	Reb	Ast	Stl	To	Blk	Pts	Ppg
36	51	125	.408	34	52	.654	15	41	27	23	39	3	146	4.1

Three-point goals: 10–26 (.385)   **TSP:** .448

SCORING

Starks came out of nowhere—he wasn't drafted—to make the Warriors as a backup 1, ahead of such players as Indiana's Keith Smart. He made it on his athleticism and his defense—the 6-4 Starks is a big-time leaper with excellent quickness. His offense consists primarily of aggressive drives to the hoop (finishing with a dunk), offensive rebounds—per minute, he was in the top 20 percent for backup 1s—and three-pointers (a solid .385 on 10-for-26 shooting). Classic rookie-guard inconsistent shooting, .408 from the field. But his three-point shooting was promising.

DEFENSE/DEFENSIVE REBOUNDING

Starks reminds some of Alvin Robertson on D—an aggressive defender who can steal the ball (above average for his position), and who isn't afraid to get in his man's face. In fact, his college coach, Leonard Robinson, noted that Starks loves to play deny defense. Also like Robertson, he can get the ball off the board.

THE FLOOR GAME

Starks is a "tweener" of sorts—he really doesn't have a position—but the Warriors were force-feeding him the 1 spot. BIG adjustment, and while he made the effort, the results were not encouraging. Starks had the worst assist-to-turnover ratio among backup points and was turnover-prone. But he didn't play much (36 games and 316 minutes). His speed and quickness and jumping ability best fit in an up tempo game.

INTANGIBLES

Starks is hungry and competitive, but he hasn't played a lot of ball (he didn't play in high school) and was severely underexperienced as a 1.

IN SUM

After the season, the Warriors did not make Starks a qualifying offer, which allowed him to negotiate with any team. His defense, his range, and his physical skills will ensure that GMs at least take a serious look at his game as they fill their rosters.

RICK'S RATINGS

Scoring: **C**   Defense: **A**
Shooting: **C**   Playmaking: **D**
Free Throw Shooting: **D**   Intangibles: **B**
Ball Handling: **C**   Overall: **C −**
Passing: **C**

Everette Stephens

Birthdate: October 21, 1966
Height: 6-2
Weight: 175
College: Purdue University, West Lafayette, Ind.
Drafted: Philadelphia on second round, 1988 (31st pick).
Position: Guard
Final 1989 Team: Indiana Pacers
Final 1988–89 Statistics:

G	Fg	Fga	Fg%	Ft	Fta	Ft%	Orb	Reb	Ast	Stl	To	Blk	Pts	Ppg
35	23	72	.319	17	22	.773	11	23	37	9	29	4	65	1.9

Three-point goals: 2-10 (.200)   **TSP:** .333

SCORING

Stephens came to Indiana from Philadelphia for Ron Anderson in what turned out to be the most lopsided trade of the year. While Anderson was the 76ers third-leading scorer (16.2 ppg), Stephens, a rookie out of Purdue, languished on Indiana's pine, averaging about six minutes a game and 1.9 ppg. He's a point guard with great athletic talent—running, jumping (he'll dunk on the break)—who possesses a decent medium-range jumper.

DEFENSE/DEFENSIVE REBOUNDING

Stephens will hound you defensively, but he's a slight 6-2, 175, and must become more physical.

THE FLOOR GAME

Stephens, at this stage, has major limitations as a point. At his size, he will have to be a 1, but he doesn't make good decisions nor handle the ball well.

INTANGIBLES

"Nice kid, works hard," said one observer.

IN SUM

Stephens's inefficiencies as a ball handler may be fatal. Of course, he hasn't played, but the early prognosis isn't promising.

RICK'S RATINGS

Scoring: **C**   Defense: **B**
Shooting: **D**   Defensive Rebounding: **C**
Free Throw Shooting: **B**   Playmaking: **D**
Ball Handling: **C**   Intangibles: **B**
Passing: **C**   Overall: **D**

Brook Steppe

Birthdate: November 7, 1959
Height: 6-5
Weight: 195
College: Georgia Institute of Technology, Atlanta, Ga.
Drafted: Kansas City on first round, 1982 (17th pick).
Position: Guard
Final 1989 Team: Portland Trail Blazers
Final 1988–89 Statistics:

G	Fg	Fga	Fg%	Ft	Fta	Ft%	Orb	Reb	Ast	Stl	To	Blk	Pts	Ppg
27	33	78	.423	32	37	.865	13	32	16	11	13	1	103	3.8

Three-point goals: 5-9 (.556)   **TSP:** .455

SCORING

If Steppe is in the league this year—and underline the word *if*—chances are he'll be somewhere besides Portland. After all, he wouldn't want to ruin his pattern: a new team each year. Five years and five teams (Kansas City, Indiana, Detroit, Sacramento, and in 1988–89, Portland). Of course, he's also spent a lot of time in the CBA, which some observers feel is a more appropriate place of employment. Why? He's a 2 guard with minimal firepower—always a precarious situation. A fair shooter (.469 lifetime) with decent range (five-for-nine from three last year), he'll pull up for the jumper in transition but doesn't manufacture his shot with any facility. He'll also barrel his way to the hole and make the foul shots (.820 lifetime).

DEFENSE/DEFENSIVE REBOUNDING

NBA teams keep calling because Steppe has a toughness about him. He's a physical defender who is not above antagonizing opponents with verbal taunts. Then, again, with only fair lateral quickness, he gets taken off the dribble.

THE FLOOR GAME

You don't hang around like Steppe has without knowing how to play.

INTANGIBLES

On the other hand, he might have extended his stay(s) if he weren't so abrasive; he rubs opponents *and* teammates the wrong way. Won't win any popularity contests. "Uncoachable," said one ex-CBA coach.

IN SUM

Just hangin' on. Maybe we'll see him this year, maybe we won't. Team fortunes will not sway one way or the other.

RICK'S RATINGS

Scoring: **C**	Defense: **B**
Shooting: **C**	Defensive Rebounding: **B**
Free Throw Shooting: **AA**	Intangibles: **D**
Ball Handling: **B**	Overall: **D**
Passing: **B**	

Steve Stipanovich

Birthdate: November 17, 1960
Height: 6-10
Weight: 250
College: University of Missouri, Columbia, Mo.
Drafted: Indiana on first round, 1983 (2nd pick).
Position: Center
Final 1989 Team: None
Final 1988–89 Statistics: Did Not Play

SCORING

Stipanovich, who missed the entire 1988–89 season with a knee injury, is from the "facing" school of centers—Bill Laimbeer, Dave Corzine, Danny Schayes—whose strength is the perimeter jumper (range is 15 to 18 feet). Actually at 6-10 and not overwhelmingly strong, he's probably better suited to the power forward position but in the absence of Pacer centers, he's had to play the 5 spot. Now that Indiana has a bona fide big man in Rik Smits, "Stipo" should log significant time this year as a 4. Besides his outside game, he can put the ball on the floor, runs the court well, rarely takes a bad shot, and is a clutch shooter. He has less confidence in his low-post game, which consists of spin moves and an occasional hook. For a center, he's a slightly above-average (1.9 a game throughout his career) offensive

rebounder. He's been a remarkably steady performer in his five years in the league, averaging 12 ppg in his rookie and in the "13s" for the next four. He's a career .484 from the field and .796 from the line.

DEFENSE/DEFENSIVE REBOUNDING

One of Stipo's biggest assets defensively is his willingness to help out—when there's penetration, he's there, even though he may be a step slow. He's not much of a shot blocker for a center (about one a game, lifetime), but those stats are decent for a power forward. He follows defensive game plans to the letter; if fronting, or three-quartering his man is called for, he does it. His numbers are average as a defensive rebounder (7.7 total rebounds a game for his career), but what the statistics don't reveal is that his man doesn't get to the offensive glass; for Stipanovich is conscientious about blocking his man out. And if the ball is on the floor, Stipanovich will put his body to the hardwood—a rare sight indeed for a center.

THE FLOOR GAME

Stipanovich has excellent court awareness. He sees plays develop, reads the double-team, and has averaged a solid (for a center) 2.3 assists a game for his career. Also, he doesn't make many mistakes. He's a fundamentally sound basketball player.

INTANGIBLES

Until last year, Stipo had been a model of durability, missing only seven games in five years. He's a team player who couldn't care less about his own stats. He is not the most gifted basketball player, but he has maximized what he does have through hard work. He plays with a lot of heart.

IN SUM

Indiana sorely missed Stipanovich's consistency: his 13 points, 8 rebounds, every-night intensity, and unselfish play. He may never be an All-Star, but at 29 (in November), he's in his prime and could be a starting forward or center on a contending team. At press time, it was still uncertain whether Stipanovich's knee was healthy enough to allow him to play this year.

RICK'S RATINGS

Scoring: **B**	Defense: **A**
Shooting: **A**	Defensive Rebounding: **A**
Free Throw Shooting: **B**	Shot Blocking: **C**
Ball Handling: **B**	Intangibles: **AA**
Passing: **A**	Overall: **A**

John Stockton

Birthdate: March 26, 1962
Height: 6-1
Weight: 175
College: Gonzaga University, Spokane, Wash.
Drafted: Utah on first round, 1984 (16th pick).
Position: Guard
Final 1989 Team: Utah Jazz
Final 1988–89 Statistics:

G	Fg	Fga	Fg%	Ft	Fta	Ft%	Orb	Reb	Ast	Stl	To	Blk	Pts	Ppg
82	497	923	.538	390	452	.863	83	248	1118	263	308	14	1400	17.1

Three-point goals: 16–66 (.242)   **TSP:** .547

SCORING

Stockton does so many things well—no, make that brilliantly, and shooting is no exception. For starters, he's remarkably accurate. After shooting an astounding .574 in 1987–88, he proved it wasn't a fluke last year, singeing the nets at a .538 pace (he and Michael Jordan, who also shot .538, were the only guards in the top 10 in field goal percentage). This is, mind you, the percentage of a player barely over 6-0 (he's listed at 6-1, but that's pushing it) who is consistently guarded by players several inches taller. But what Stockton lacks in size, he more than makes up for in versatility, deception, quickness, savvy, and touch. What makes him so tough to guard is that he has the jumper from outside—he shoots the 15-to-17-foot jumper off Eaton or Malone-set picks—and the move to the hoop with which he simply beats his man off the dribble. Utah clears the left side for the five-year veteran, and he can take it either way to the goal. His only offensive deficiency is his three-point shot, .242 last year and .259 lifetime. Of course, he's an excellent foul shooter, with .863 in 1988–89. Opinion poll: How did Stockton miss six straight uncontested jumpers in the fourth quarter of the second playoff game (at home) against the Warriors last spring? We can't figure it out. (Fatigue? Slightly beyond his range?) Send your answers to the publisher.

DEFENSE/DEFENSIVE REBOUNDING

Stockton is a pickpocket. In 1988–89, he led the league in steals (3.2 a game), employing a great pair of hands and you-can't-teach-it anticipation. He has a sixth sense for the ball and plays the passing lanes as well as anybody in the league. He's also a solid team defender, with many of his steals coming in help situations. But he's vulnerable, height-wise, to bigger guards, such as the Lakers' Byron Scott who can shoot jumpers over him.

THE FLOOR GAME

Stockton is the prototype point guard, a consummate artist of the think-pass-first school of playmaking. He has few peers as a passer, both in the half-court offense and on the break. Nothing fancy, just gets the job done—to the tune of a league-leading 13.6 a game (for the second year in a row; in 1987–88 he set the NBA record for most assists in a season with 1,128). His court awareness is superb—he's an expert at knowing when to push the break and when to set up the half-court offense—and is up there with the Birds, the Magics, the Oscars, the Cousys, in terms of being able to see the whole court. It helps, too, that he's on a team with several players who run the floor well and can fill the lane: Mssrs. Malone and Bailey. His 3.63 assist-to-turnover ratio was second to Maurice Cheeks among starting point guards. And he was the winner of the "Good Hands" award, which ranks players according to steals, assists, and turnovers.

INTANGIBLES

At Jack and Dan's Bar, a Spokane, Washington watering hole owned by Jack Stockton, John's father, there are pictures all over the wall: Karl Malone, Mark Eaton, and other Jazz members. But not John Stockton. If Jack is one not to toot his son's horn, John is the same way, a self-effacing fellow who hasn't let his success go to his head. Instead, he has become a fiery leader, if a quiet one. As much as any player in the league, John Stockton makes his teammates better. He can run all day and hasn't missed a game yet (410 straight).

IN SUM

Stockton made the All-Star team for the first time last year and started when Magic Johnson got hurt. Many feel he's the second-best point guard (Kevin Johnson is also getting some votes) in the league, behind the Magic man. Utah is indeed in good hands well into the 1990s with Stockton at the helm.

RICK'S RATINGS

Scoring: **A**	Defense: **AA**
Shooting: **AAA**	Defensive Rebounding: **D**
Free Throw Shooting: **AA**	Playmaking: **AAA**
Ball Handling: **AAA**	Intangibles: **AAA**
Passing: **AAA**	Overall: **AAA**

Rod Strickland

Birthdate: July 11, 1966
Height: 6-3
Weight: 180
College: DePaul University, Chicago, Ill.
Drafted: New York on first round as an undergraduate, 1988 (19th pick).
Position: Guard
Final 1989 Team: New York Knicks
Final 1988–89 Statistics:

G	Fg	Fga	Fg%	Ft	Fta	Ft%	Orb	Reb	Ast	Stl	To	Blk	Pts	Ppg
81	265	587	.467	172	231	.745	51	160	319	98	148	3	721	8.9

Three-point goals: 19–59 (.322)   **TSP:** .484

SCORING

Strickland can do it all offensively: shoot effectively from long range (.322 from three-land), from mid-range, and take it to the hole. On a per minute basis, he led all backup point guards in points per game and was even a more efficient scorer than Mark Jackson, whom he played behind. Very quick, very fast, and completely ambidextrous, Strickland has no trouble getting into the lane, where he reminds you of Jackson with his ability to create his own shot amidst the behemoths. Early on, the rookie would force a few, but by the end of the year, he'd pick and choose his spots better. He can shoot the stationary jump shot or take it off the dribble going either direction. His .467 is OK vis à vis the league, terrific considering he was a rookie. A slightly below-average foul shooter at .745.

DEFENSE/DEFENSIVE REBOUNDING

Quickness and out-of-this-world anticipation make Strickland a dangerous defender. He had an outstanding 1.2 steals a game (in just 16.8 minutes), in the top 20 percent of all guards (and significantly more than Jackson on a per minute basis). He's particularly effective in the Knicks' pressing/trapping schemes. Once he learns about weak side help, he has the potential to be a devastating all-around defensive player. An above-average defensive rebounder for his position.

THE FLOOR GAME

As backup to one of the consummate floor generals in the NBA, the comparisons are inevitable, but Strickland simply doesn't have Jackson's take-charge ability. Off the court, he's shy and quiet, and on the court he's not as assertive as he should be. He's not a pure point guard and his growth will come from better distribution—and care (he had an unimpressive 2.17 assist-to-turnover ratio)—of the basketball. But he's a superb dribbler and can do just about anything he wants to with the ball.

INTANGIBLES

Much ink has been expended on Strickland's various incidents—a missed practice, late for others, his "Joe Cool" attitude (as former Knick coach Rick Pitino labeled it)—but it's basically much ado about nothing. He needs a little maturing, a little discipline and he'll be fine. He's not lazy, but he's never been confused with being a hard worker. His lack of stamina is also an issue.

IN SUM

Why, asked the critics, would the Knicks draft Strickland, a point guard, when they already had Jackson, one of best at the position? Strickland demonstrated why—and how! He's an extremely talented basketball player who not only maintained the status quo when he subbed for Jackson, but presented, with his speed, quickness, and scoring ability, a brand-new set of problems for the defense. He could undoubtedly start for a goodly number of the teams in the league (and acquitted himself admirably in his 10 starts, when Jackson went down with a knee injury). The question: How long will Strickland willingly tolerate limited minutes? The answer: He won't. Either he starts (in place of Wilkins), gets major minutes off the bench, or becomes valuable trade material.

RICK'S RATINGS

Scoring: **AA**	Defense: **A**
Shooting: **B**	Defensive Rebounding: **A**
Free Throw Shooting: **C**	Playmaking: **B**
Ball Handling: **A**	Intangibles: **C**
Passing: **A**	Overall: **A –**

Jon Sundvold

Birthdate: July 2, 1961
Height: 6-2

Weight: 170
College: University of Missouri, Columbia, Mo.
Drafted: Seattle on first round, 1983 (16th pick).
Position: Guard
Final 1989 Team: Miami Heat
Final 1988–89 Statistics:

G	Fg	Fga	Fg%	Ft	Fta	Ft%	Orb	Reb	Ast	Stl	To	Blk	Pts	Ppg
68	307	675	.455	47	57	.825	18	87	137	27	87	1	709	10.4

Three-point goals: 48–92 (.522)   **TSP:** .490

SCORING

A pure shooter: One who hits nothing-but-net jumpers from anywhere on the floor; one who needs help—a pick—to get his shot. That's Jon Sundvold, who, employing textbook mechanics, has survived six years in the NBA on the strength of his perimeter shooting. In 1988–89, he shot an NBA record .522 (48 of 92) from three-point land and is an outside threat from any distance. But he is not a complete offensive player. He has trouble creating a shot for himself (which is one reason he only shot .455 overall; he was one of ten players in 1988–89 whose three-point percentage was higher than their regular field goal percentage; he was, however, the only one with more than 20 trey attempts) and though an excellent foul shooter (never under 80 percent, .825 last year), rarely gets to the line (less than one attempt a game for his career). When he drives, he dishes rather than finishes. On a per minute basis, he was in the top quarter among backup 2s for scoring.

DEFENSE/DEFENSIVE REBOUNDING

Sundvold, who can play both guard positions (though the Heat used him mostly at the 2), is a defensive liability. He's a step behind the 1s, and too small for the 2s. With his lack of quickness and speed, he's not effective pressuring players. Rebounding-wise, he was the least productive backup 2 in the league in 1988–89.

THE FLOOR GAME

When used as a 1, Sundvold is a heady floor leader, a coach on the floor. He can run an offense and knows how to hit the hot man. He doesn't force the action and gets his points within the flow of the game.

INTANGIBLES

Sundvold is not a rah-rah type; he leads by example. Besides his shooting, his evolved court sense is another reason he's stuck around. He was one of Miami's best clutch players last year.

IN SUM

Sundvold can shoot the heck out of the ball and gives the green Heat (they used 10 rookies last year) a steadying influence in the backcourt. Don't be surprised if he lasts another five years. Great shooters are a rare commodity, especially ones with range.

Roy Tarpley

Birthdate: November 28, 1964
Height: 7-0
Weight: 240
College: University of Michigan, Ann Arbor, Mich.
Drafted: Dallas on first round, 1986 (7th pick).
Positions: Center, Forward
Final 1989 Team: Dallas Mavericks
Final 1988–89 Statistics:

G	Fg	Fga	Fg%	Ft	Fta	Ft%	Orb	Reb	Ast	Stl	To	Blk	Pts	Ppg
19	131	242	.541	66	96	.688	77	218	17	28	45	30	328	17.3

Three-point goals: 0–1 (.000)   **TSP:** .541

SCORING

Tenacity plus size plus arm length plus hands plus positioning plus quickness: Tarpley is one of the league's major-domos on the offensive boards. (On a per minute basis, he was first in 1987–1988; last season, 8th, though he played just 19 games. He missed four weeks early in the season after knee surgery on November 16. And for failing to adhere to the NBA's drug aftercare program, spent most of the season at the NBA's drug rehab center in Van Nuys, California.) He plays both power forward and center; he's too big for the forwards and too quick for the centers. And Tarpley can run, too, scoring healthy numbers on transition dunks and follow ups. But otherwise—surprise, surprise—he's primarily a perimeter player who can knock down the 16-footer with regularity (usually off a pick or because his man lays off him, figuring Tarpley, 7-0, won't shoot it). Imagine how good he's going to be when he develops confidence in his low-post game, which is still in its infancy. He has a jump hook, but it isn't reliable. The best way to defend him is to make him put the ball on the floor from the outside with his left hand and be sure to block him off the boards.

DEFENSE/DEFENSIVE REBOUNDING

Tarpley is not the chairman of the Defensive Boards (last season that honor belonged to Akeem Olajuwon) but he was on the "board" (pun intended) of directors. Per minute, he was third in the NBA (behind Olajuwon and Bill Laimbeer) and in 1987–88, he was the only non-starter ever to finish in the top ten in rebounding. Defensively, Tarpley is an unfinished product. At this point, his best assets are his hands; like Olajuwon, he deflects and steals (1.5 a game in 31.1 minutes in 1988–89) a lot of balls. With his timing, size, and quickness, he has the potential to be a major shot blocker but he has yet to get it all together (1.6 last season, slightly above average for backup centers). Tarpley will fight his man for position (and just plain fight, too; he's as quick to the draw as any player in the league), but he's not a physical player of the same ilk as Charles Oakley or Rick Mahorn. He could easily handle an additional 15 upper-body pounds.

THE FLOOR GAME

Tarpley often plays defense on the other teams' center, and power forward on offense. That suits him just fine as he's a better defensive rebounder from the center position and feels more comfortable in the 4 spot offensively. He's a good passer in the half-court offense though his judgment on when (he tends to dribble too much) and how to handle the ball (around the back is not uncommon) is questionable.

INTANGIBLES

Tarpley now has two strikes against him, and under the NBA's drug policy, another will result in an automatic dismissal from the league for at least two years. How much did Dallas miss Tarpley? With him (and James Donaldson) in the lineup in 1987–88, the Mavs took the Lakers to a seventh game in the Western Conference finals. Last season, with Tarpley out for most of the year (and Donaldson the final six weeks of the season), Dallas failed to make the playoffs and finished at 38–44. At best, they are a mediocre team without Tarpley. Though Tarpley practices hard, he's not a gym rat. He's enormously talented but also a bit on the lazy side and needs constant prodding to progress to the things that will take him to the next level: All-Star. Assuming Donaldson is not available, Tarpley, who won the Sixth Man of the Year award in 1987–88, will be Dallas' starting center this year.

IN SUM

As Tarpley goes, so go the Mavericks. Dallas' title hopes rest on his continued improvement—and sobriety.

RICK'S RATINGS

Scoring: **AA**	Defensive Rebounding: **AAA**
Shooting: **A**	
Free Throw Shooting: **D**	Shot Blocking: **AA**
Ball Handling: **C**	Intangibles: **C**
Passing: **B**	Overall: **AA**
Defense: **A**	

Terry Teagle

Birthdate: April 10, 1960
Height: 6-5
Weight: 195
College: Baylor University, Waco, Tex.
Drafted: Houston on first round, 1982 (16th pick).
Position: Forward
Final 1989 Team: Golden State Warriors
Final 1988–89 Statistics:

G	Fg	Fga	Fg%	Ft	Fta	Ft%	Orb	Reb	Ast	Stl	To	Blk	Pts	Ppg
66	409	859	.476	182	225	.809	110	263	96	79	116	17	1002	15.2

Three-point goals: 2–12 (.167)   **TSP:** .477

SCORING

Terry Teagle's New Year's resolution did not include having the best scoring year of his career. Huh? Let's go back to the first week of 1989, the morning of January 7, to be exact. At this point, Teagle, who had been to basketball purgatory previously (40 games in the CBA during 1984–85, following two seasons in the NBA), is facing one of the toughest tests of his eight-year career. He's healthy, he's ready, but he's not getting the time. It's not a matter of enough minutes; he's not playing at all—hasn't since December 2 (13 consecutive DNP–CDs). Trade talk is swirling. He plays two minutes on January 7, sits out another two games, and he's back in the rotation in a reserve role for the next two games. Then, as fast as you can say Don Nelson, Teagle's inserted in the starting lineup on January 16—as a 6-5, 195-pound power forward! In one of the great non-decisions of the 1988–89 season (i.e., they didn't trade him), the Warriors stuck with Teagle and it paid off handsomely. For the year, he averaged 15.2, shot .476 from the field, and was one of the primary cogs in the Warriors' astounding turnaround (from 20 wins in 1987–88 to 43 last year). While he's actually a 2, playing up front suits him well. For one, he loves to post up. With his extraordinary leaping ability, he can take a bigger guy into the blocks and simply elevate over him for the turnaround. For another, he's deadly from the corners, where he shoots the fadeaway. He's been known to hit a backboard or two with that shot (he's often close to the baseline when he fires); Teagle's shot selection is not his strong point. He is, by all accounts, a streaky shooter, but when he's on, he has the rare ability to take over a game offensively. While beating opponents off the dribble is not his game—he's a terrible ball handler—it was not uncommon to see Teagle getting by the slower 4s he was matched up against. While he'll dunk it on the break, he doesn't have the ability to jam in traffic on the drive; instead, he's developed a one-handed runner in the lane.

DEFENSE/DEFENSIVE REBOUNDING

Defense has never been a priority with Teagle, but give him credit, he made the effort last year. Of course, he was often guarding power forwards and was simply overmatched. One thing he does well is play the passing lanes (1.2 steals a game). An average defensive rebounder for a 2, way below average—no surprise—for a 4.

THE FLOOR GAME

Teagle is a "nervous time" ball handler. The only time you want him dribbling the ball—and no more than a couple times—is to get his shot. When he's hot, he'll get into that "zone," and the nine other players might as well watch.

INTANGIBLES

Teagle, for the most part, didn't gripe and moan when he was buried on the bench; he wasn't disruptive at all. You like a guy who, after sitting for so long, comes into the lineup and then explodes. He has fine work habits.

IN SUM

Don Nelson did some incredible things last year and the exhuming of Terry Teagle was a case in point. He scored, which was expected, but he also became a better all-around player. For the long haul, he's obviously not a starting power forward. Better as a sixth man; kind of a poor man's Ricky Pierce.

RICK'S RATINGS

Scoring: **AA**   Defense: **C**
Shooting: **A**   Defensive Rebounding: **C**
Free Throw Shooting: **A**   Intangibles: **B**
Ball Handling: **D**   Overall: **B+**
Passing: **C**

Reggie Theus

Birthdate: October 13, 1957
Height: 6-7

Weight: 213
College: University of Nevada at Las Vegas, Las Vegas, Nev.
Drafted: Chicago on first round as an undergraduate, 1978 (9th pick).
Position: Guard
Final 1989 Team: Atlanta Hawks
Final 1988–89 Statistics:

G	Fg	Fga	Fg%	Ft	Fta	Ft%	Orb	Reb	Ast	Stl	To	Blk	Pts	Ppg
82	497	1067	.466	285	335	.851	86	242	387	108	194	16	1296	15.8

Three-point goals: 17–58 (.293)   **TSP:** .474

SCORING

The problem was Atlanta's lack of scoring punch—in particular, outside shooting—from its 2 spot. The answer, it was hoped, was Reggie Theus. With Randy Wittman, the starting shooting guard, scoring only 10 a game and reluctant to shoot, at the end of the 1987–88 season the Hawks went shopping for a proven scorer. In exchange for Wittman and a first-round pick (who became Ricky Berry), they came up with Theus, who on the face of it, fit the bill. In his 10 years in the league (Chicago, Kansas City, and Sacramento), he had averaged 18.8 and was coming off a season in which he had hit for a career second-best of 21.6 a game. Theus had been the go-to guy in Sacramento, with a rep as a player who never saw a shot he didn't like. The Hawks, so went the refrain, would need three basketballs: one for Reggie, one for Moses Malone, who had been acquired from the Bullets, and one for Dominique Wilkins, the Hawks leading scorer. While Wilkins and Malone had their usual productive years, Theus had a tough time of it. Although his numbers were in the neighborhood of his career averages (15.8 and .466—he's a lifetime .475 shooter), his play was inconsistent, most notably in the playoff loss to the Bucks, where he shot a paltry .368. He started out well—19.4 ppg and .502 after 16 games—but he couldn't sustain it. It wasn't just that he was no longer the majordomo; more likely it was because in Atlanta, Theus had to play defense, and exerting on both ends of the floor took away from his stamina and hurt his offense. He's primarily an on-the-catch jump shooter with good range (he had his best year, a not-at-all impressive .293, from three-point country). He can also put the ball on the floor, but he doesn't always finish strongly—eschewing the dunk for the finger roll. An excellent foul shooter (.851 last year, .822 lifetime). Theus' sub par performance earned him a trip to Disney World—Orlando really—he was the second player picked by the Magic in the expansion draft.

DEFENSE/DEFENSIVE REBOUNDING

With the Kings, Theus didn't pay much attention to defense. In Atlanta he had no choice, and while he showed that he was willing to work hard and came equipped with the size, quickness and foot speed to get it done defensively . . . he didn't get it done defensively. His problems were numerous and varied: He lacks strength, doesn't cover well for teammates who are double-teaming, and probably most significantly, thought what he was doing was what coach Mike Fratello wanted done when the facts were otherwise. A below-average rebounder for his position.

THE FLOOR GAME

Theus is that rare 2 guard who has true point guard skills; in fact, he played the 1 for a significant portion of his career, averaging 6.5 assists a game (career) and 4.7 (last year). With the Kings, Theus was a player people paid to see; if there was a choice between a safe pass and an ooh-aaher, he invariably chose the latter. But in Atlanta, Reggie's carelessness was cause for concern and the source of friction between Theus and Fratello. He's a thread-the-needle passer when playing under control.

INTANGIBLES

Theus, the 11-year veteran, had to learn some new tricks in 1988–89; and it wasn't easy. No longer was he the machine but a mere cog in an unfamiliar system. He bore the brunt of much of Fratello's criticism, and Theus, a sensitive, introspective sort, didn't always hold up well. When the going got tough, said his critics, Reggie didn't get going (case in point: the playoffs).

IN SUM

Theus was supposed to be a big part of the solution, but instead turned out to be the problem—or at least one of the many—as the made-for-championship Hawks went quietly in the first round of the playoffs. Atlanta and Reggie Theus were not cut out for each other. Unfortunately, he's now back where he started: with a loser. But expansion teams need scorers and Reggie will undoubtedly put big numbers on the board. He'd rather have a ring.

RICK'S RATINGS

Scoring: **A**   Defense: **C**
Shooting: **B**   Defensive Rebounding: **D**
Free Throw Shooting: **AA**   Intangibles: **C**
Ball Handling: **A**   Overall: **B +**
Passing: **A**

Isiah Thomas

Birthdate: April 30, 1961
Height: 6-1
Weight: 185
College: Indiana University, Bloomington, Ind.

Drafted: Detroit on first round as an undergraduate, 1981 (2nd pick).
Position: Guard
Final 1989 Team: Detroit Pistons
Final 1988–89 Statistics:

G	Fg	Fga	Fg%	Ft	Fta	Ft%	Orb	Reb	Ast	Stl	To	Blk	Pts	Ppg
80	569	1227	.464	287	351	.818	49	273	663	133	298	20	1458	18.2

Three-point goals: 33–121 (.273)   **TSP:** .477

SCORING

"It's not about going out and trying to get numbers," Thomas told the *Washington Post* earlier this year. But last season, Thomas, as usual, went out and got the numbers: 18.2 a game, right around his career mark of 20.3 ppg (and 18.2 during the playoffs). His point, however, spoken like the champion he now is (the Pistons, of course, swept the Lakers in four), is that statistics mislead, and that the real story is team and winning. Case in point: Isiah Thomas! Item one—Thomas shoots an abysmal .333 against the Celtics in the Pistons' 3–0 playoff win. Third game, Pistons are down nine midway through the third quarter. Result: Thomas scores 22 second-half points and the Pistons win 102–95. Item 2—Chicago playoff series. Thomas again shoots under 40 percent (.390) for the series. But he explodes for 33 points in game 2, 27 in game 4, and 33 in game 6 and the Pistons win all three games and the series, 4–2. And Thomas continued the good work and shot better (.485) as the Piston guards (Thomas, Joe Dumars, and Vinnie Johnson) averaged almost 50 a game among themselves in the finals against the Lakers. Thomas' performance(s) highlighted what is the most salient fact about his game: he's a crunch-time guy, a go-to player who demands the ball in the fourth quarter and produces. So intent was he on winning the NBA title—"Don't ever let me get this obsessed about anything ever again," he said to the *Detroit Free Press*—that he seemed to raise his play to new heights throughout last season's playoffs as he uncannily and consistently got the Pistons a hoop when they needed it. And he has a lot of shots to choose from. Underlying his wide repertoire is his extraordinary quickness. One of the best dribblers in the league, Thomas gets by opponents at will and explodes to the hoop. Or he can pull up and shoot the stop-on-a-dime jumper. He's also expert coming off screens and firing the jumper. There's still some Chicago playground in him (where he grew up) and he can shake and bake with the best of 'em, making near-impossible shots in a crowd (though Thomas has regularly been criticized for trying to do too much and taking the occasional bad shot). He's not a pure shooter—only once over 48 percent (.463 lifetime), nor does he have any kind of consistent three-pointer (.273 last year, .278 lifetime) but when he's on a roll, he takes over the game. (Recall game 6, 1987–88 NBA finals, when he scored 25 points in the third quarter in a 43-point effort against the Lakers.) He's a .761 career foul shooter, and his .818 last season was his high mark in an eight-year career.

DEFENSE/DEFENSIVE REBOUNDING

Thomas is not a shut-you-down defender but he's a dangerous one; as with his offense, he has explosive spurts on

D—steals, deflections, forcing turnovers—which can turn a game. He has excellent anticipation—1.7 steals a game in 1988–89 (and 2.1 a game for his career)—and his seemingly omnipresent hands are distracting for his opponent. He also does a good job in Detroit's help defense schemes, though he's not consistent in getting through screens. A slightly below-average defensive rebounder.

THE FLOOR GAME

There is some bad news, but there's mostly good news. First, the bad news: The turnovers—Thomas commits a lot of them (3.7 a game last season); he tries to do too much. And remember, he often plays the 2 and isn't handling the whole time. Now, for the good news: his decision-making over the years has improved and while previously he was assailed for shooting too much, now occasionally he is criticized for not shooting enough (i.e. Games 1 and 3 of the Chicago series when he only scored a total of 14 points and the Pistons lost both games). These days, he's much more attuned to the flow of the game and what he has to do, as playmaker, to allow the Pistons to win. He's a marvelous passer—particularly effective off the dribble with either hand—and can run the break with anybody (he averaged 8.3 assists a game in 1988–89) and led the league in assists in 1984–85.

INTANGIBLES

Thomas broke his left hand last April 7 in a fight with the Bulls' Bill Cartwright. Doctors figured he'd miss three weeks. He missed only two games (he was suspended for the two games). Typical Thomas; as much as any player in the league, Zeke, as he is nicknamed, plays in pain. Another now famous example: game 7 of the 1987–88 NBA finals when Thomas played with a severely sprained ankle. Captain of the Pistons, he's their inspirational leader.

IN SUM

After three first-team All-NBA selections (1983–84, 1984–85, 1985–86) and two second-team appearances, Thomas' name hasn't appeared on an All-NBA team the last two years. But no matter to him; he's been the driving force behind the Pistons, now clearly first among all NBA teams.

RICK'S RATINGS

Scoring: **AA**	Defense: **A**
Shooting: **B**	Defensive Rebounding: **B**
Free Throw Shooting: **A**	Playmaking: **A**
Ball Handling: **AAA**	Intangibles: **AAA**
Passing: **AA**	Overall: **AAA**

Bernard Thompson

Birthdate: August 30, 1962
Height: 6-6
Weight: 210
College: Fresno State University, Fresno, Calif.
Drafted: Portland on first round, 1984 (19th pick).
Positions: Guard, Forward
Final 1989 Team: Houston Rockets
Final 1988–89 Statistics:

G	Fg	Fga	Fg%	Ft	Fta	Ft%	Orb	Reb	Ast	Stl	To	Blk	Pts	Ppg
23	20	59	.339	22	26	.846	9	28	13	13	19	1	62	2.7

Three-point goals: 0–2 (.000)   **TSP:** .339

SCORING

Except for one year (1985–86, when he played 21 minutes a game for Phoenix), Thompson has been a fringe player during his five-year career. The reason is simple: There's no flame to his game, no firepower. When released by Houston in February, he was shooting all of .339, his career worst, but that's not surprising since he's a career .439 shooter. He has limited range on his jumper (15 feet) and can take it to the hole.

DEFENSE/DEFENSIVE REBOUNDING

You can't teach height but you can teach defense, and Thompson learned his lessons well at Fresno State, a school with a reputation for turning out quality defenders. And, of course, the reason he lasted this long is that he plays tough, physical, fundamentally sound D. He can guard both 2s and 3s. He also does a nice job on the defensive glass.

THE FLOOR GAME

Thompson's a conservative ball handler who doesn't take many chances and has adequate foot speed for the transition game.

INTANGIBLES

Thompson understands his limited role and makes the best of it.

IN SUM

Thompson's value is defense. He can slow down the big guns,

at least for a while, and doesn't make a lot of mistakes. The Bulls gave him a look this past summer when he played for their team in the Southern California Summer Pro League.

Billy Thompson

Birthdate: December 1, 1963

Height: 6-7

Weight: 215

College: University of Louisville, Louisville, Ky.

Drafted: Atlanta on first round, 1986 (19th pick).

Position: Forward

Final 1989 Team: Miami Heat

Final 1988–89 Statistics:

G	Fg	Fga	Fg%	Ft	Fta	Ft%	Orb	Reb	Ast	Stl	To	Blk	Pts	Ppg
79	349	716	.487	156	224	.696	241	572	176	56	189	105	854	10.8

Three-point goals: 0–4 (.000)   **TSP:** .487

SCORING

Thompson's got the body—6-7 and wiry strong at 215—the bounce (he can jump out of the gym), and the background (an NCAA championship and two NBA titles with the Lakers). But the Lakers left him unprotected in the 1988 expansion draft (he had bench-warmed with L.A., playing only 800 minutes in two years, including a 1987–88 season in which, because of a knee injury, he played in just nine games). So last year was the first time he got to display his wares on a full-time basis and the results were fairly encouraging. He's not a "scoring 3," per minute, his 10.8 ppg placed him in the bottom 20 percent among starting small forwards—but he does have a few tools. Best is his ability on the offensive glass (3 a game); he can jump over people. He also runs the floor well and can dunk with a flourish. Less certain are his medium-range jumper and his ability to put the ball on the floor. And his foul shooting (.696) is inexcusable.

DEFENSE/DEFENSIVE REBOUNDING

Thompson's ability to sky, plus his long arms, make for a big league shot blocker, tops (1.3 a game) among starting small forwards. Those same assets help on the defensive glass, where he pulled down 4.2 rebounds a game and 7.2 'bounds overall, both way above-average for starting 3s. He does a more-than-adequate job defending players in the post (his strength here is a major asset), but he often loses his concentration in team defense.

THE FLOOR GAME

Thompson's ball handling skills are fair. He sees people and will make the pass but his turnovers, per minute, are on the high side. Nor is he a good dribbler.

INTANGIBLES

Thompson isn't a problem player, but he is not, as one observer put, "a totally dedicated basketball player." It remains to be seen how much he wants to exploit his considerable talent.

IN SUM

Despite his laid-back approach to the game, Thompson showed some signs that he might grow into his potential. He needs to improve his outside shot and his ball handling skills, but his rebounding and shot blocking are already big time.

LaSalle Thompson

Birthdate: June 23, 1961

Height: 6-10

Weight: 240

College: University of Texas, Austin, Tex.

Drafted: Kansas City on first round as an undergraduate, 1982 (5th pick).

Positions: Forward, Center

Final 1989 Team: Indiana Pacers

Final 1988–89 Statistics:

G	Fg	Fga	Fg%	Ft	Fta	Ft%	Orb	Reb	Ast	Stl	To	Blk	Pts	Ppg
76	416	850	.489	227	281	.808	224	718	81	79	179	94	1059	13.9

Three-point goals: 0–1 (.000)   **TSP:** .489

SCORING

In 1988–89, Thompson, a seven-year veteran who was traded in February (with Randy Wittman for Wayman Tisdale) from Sacramento to Indiana, enjoyed his best offensive output as a pro. He averaged 13.9 a game (after seeing his average drop in the previous three years from 12.8 to 11.1 to 8.0), shot .808 from the line (he had never been above .737), and while with Indiana, shot a career-best .538 (and .489 overall). It helped that Thompson, who has played most of his career at center, logged a good part of the season (and virtually all of his time with the Pacers) at power forward, which is his natural position and where, at 6-10, 240, he matches up better with opponents. He's an above-average offensive rebounder (2.9 a game in 1988–89) with terrific hands; if he gets his mitts on a rebound, it's his. Thompson also scores with jumpers from 17 feet and in and a right-handed hook in the lane. His low-post moves are minimal.

DEFENSE/DEFENSIVE REBOUNDING

Thompson's got the great hands. Also, he virtually never mistimes the ball and he blocks out well. The result: Thompson, on a per minute basis, is one of the top defensive rebounders in the league; he finished 11th among players who played more than 100 minutes. Not surprising, considering he led the nation in rebounding in 1982 while at the University of Texas. A physical defender, he's a fearless competitor who's not afraid to put his body on people and can guard 4s on the perimeter or the post. But when it comes to defending centers, he has major problems: size, for one, as he's more like 6-9 than the listed 6-10; he's simply no match for players like Akeem Olajuwon. For another, he doesn't jump well and is not a shot-blocking threat (only 1.2 blocks a game), but those numbers are impressive for a 4.

THE FLOOR GAME

Thompson runs the floor hard but not fast. He also sets some of the meanest picks in the league. While he can handle the ball, his judgment is poor. He tries to make the impossible play, and his assist-to-turnover ratio was bad news: 0.45.

INTANGIBLES

In the macho Central Division, Thompson brings a toughness to the Pacers that was previously missing. One observer called him a "Rick Mahorn who can score" though, unlike Mahorn, he is rarely involved in altercations; players around the league know not to mess with "Tank", as Thompson is nicknamed.

IN SUM

Following a poor 1987–88 season (his 8 ppg and 4.2 rebounds a game were his lowest totals since his rookie year), for which his effort was questioned, Thompson showed it was an aberration and came back with his finest year ever as a pro. He's a more-than-adequate starting power forward who can score, rebound in a big way, and play the enforcer role in a quiet sort of way. He can also provide quality minutes as a starting or backup center.

RICK'S RATINGS

Scoring: **B**
Shooting: **B**
Free Throw Shooting: **A**
Ball Handling: **C**
Passing: **C**
Defense: **B**

Defensive Rebounding: **AAA**
Shot Blocking: **B**
Intangibles: **A**
Overall: **A**

Mychal Thompson

Birthdate: January 30, 1955
Height: 6-10
Weight: 235
College: University of Minnesota, Minneapolis, Minn.
Drafted: Portland on first round, 1978 (1st pick).
Position: Center
Final 1989 Team: Los Angeles Lakers
Final 1988–89 Statistics:

G	Fg	Fga	Fg%	Ft	Fta	Ft%	Orb	Reb	Ast	Stl	To	Blk	Pts	Ppg
80	291	521	.559	156	230	.678	157	467	48	58	97	59	738	9.2

Three-point goals: 0–1 (.000)   **TSP:** .559

SCORING

He's been in the background—a vital cog, perhaps even the missing piece in the puzzle—and that's suited him just fine. But now, with the retirement of Kareem Abdul-Jabbar (sounds strange, doesn't it?), the spotlight is shifting towards Mychal Thompson. Since being acquired from San Antonio in February 1987,—one of Laker GM Jerry West's most savvy moves—Thompson has been everything you want in a backup center (the term is used loosely; Thompson played more minutes than Kareem last year): solid defender, consistent rebounder, clutch performer, and occasional scorer. But now, as a starter, Thompson will be asked to pick it up offensively. (This assumes, of course that (a) the Lakers don't acquire a starting center—we wouldn't put it past

West—or (b) their backup center can score like Thompson has (9.6 ppg last season). If so, Thompson could, as a starter, maintain the same pace, 10.1 ppg, that Kareem did in his last year and the Lakers still would have almost 20 points a game from the center spot. Can Vlade Divac, their Yugoslavian No. 1 pick, score at that rate? It's an interesting question). Another interesting question is whether Thompson could score at a 15-to-17-a-game clip? It's likely. Recall that in his pre-Laker days (with Portland and San Antonio) he was a starter and a majordomo on offense, and had averaged just over 16 points a game. Yes, he can score though he doesn't have a classic post-up game. He has that funny-looking jumper, and that awkward-looking hook, but, hey, he's effective (.559 from the field in 1988–89). With Magic Johnson, he's perfected the pick-and-roll (on the roll, he catches the ball; he has terrific hands). Look to see him extending his range and shooting the 15-foot jumper from the corners. He also runs the floor well and is a better-than-average offensive rebounder (two a game in 24.9 minutes last season). One concern is his foul shooting (.678 last season; .650 lifetime).

DEFENSE/DEFENSIVE REBOUNDING

One of the major reasons the Lakers originally acquired Thompson was that he was reputed to be one of the few players in the league who could defend Kevin McHale. Indeed, his D on the Celtic power forward was a key element in the Lakers' victory over the Celts in the 1986–87 finals. He's a top-notch post defender, who consistently pushes his man out of the block and makes it tough for him to receive the ball in scoring position. He's only a fair shot blocker, and in 1988–89, his defensive rebounding numbers were slightly below average.

THE FLOOR GAME

A solid passer, though so far his role hasn't required him to handle it with any frequency. But note Thompson's assist history: he's averaged as many as 4.8 assists (1982–83) a game.

INTANGIBLES

One of the smartest players in the league, he's always there in big games. He has, as one coach put it, "a lightening effect in the locker room." That is, he adds levity to the proceedings with his wit, his charm, his savoir faire. He was second team, All-Interview (there is such a team).

IN SUM

A consummate backup, can Thompson—and the Lakers—handle his transition to starting center? Can they, in other words, win a championship with Thompson in the middle? To a large extent, as recent history has shown, the answer will depend on the quality of the backup center. To wit, until they lost to the Pistons last year, the Lakers had not lost a playoff series with Mychal Thompson aboard. And the Pistons, since James Edwards has backed up Bill Laimbeer, have also only lost one playoff series (the 1987–88 final).

How fast Divac, an undisputed talent, but untested in NBA waters (and making a major cultural adjustment besides), comes around—if at all—will tell us a lot. But in the absence of a decent backup, the 34-year-old Thompson (in January) will have to log a lot of minutes and he'll be feeling it, come playoff time.

RICK'S RATINGS

Scoring: **B**
Shooting: **A**
Free Throw Shooting: **D**
Ball Handling: **B**
Passing: **A**

Defense: **AAA**
Defensive Rebounding: **B**
Shot Blocking: **C**
Intangibles: **A**
Overall: **A**

Bob Thornton

Birthdate: July 10, 1962
Height: 6-10
Weight: 225
College: University of California at Irvine, Irvine, Calif.
Drafted: New York on fourth round, 1984 (87th pick).
Positions: Forward, Center
Final 1989 Team: Philadelphia 76ers
Final 1988–89 Statistics:

G	Fg	Fga	Fg%	Ft	Fta	Ft%	Orb	Reb	Ast	Stl	To	Blk	Pts	Ppg
54	47	111	.423	32	60	.533	36	92	15	8	23	7	127	2.4

Three-point goals: 1–3 (.333) **TSP:** .428

SCORING

Thornton is your basic Betty Crocker scorer: Anything he gets is icing on the cake. In 1988–89, non-scorers like Chris Dudley, Jack Haley, and Charles Shackleford outscored him on a per minute basis. Which is no surprise, since even in college, he was far from a threat (highest collegiate scoring average: 12.7 ppg). Thornton's points come on the offensive board—he's a banger—and on power moves, bullying his way to the hoop. He's a terrible foul shooter at .533 in 1988–89 and .556 career. Evidently he has a jump shot (15-foot range), but he rarely displays it and has little confidence in it.

DEFENSE/DEFENSIVE REBOUNDING

Were it not for his defense, Thornton would not be in the NBA. He's capable of guarding 3s, 4s, and 5s; he's physical enough to handle the big guys and quick enough to guard players on the perimeter. But he's often overly aggressive and gets in foul trouble in a hurry. Despite his size and aggressiveness, his defensive rebounding numbers are below average.

THE FLOOR GAME

Thornton will run the floor, but it isn't a pretty sight. This is not a player who is going to make the scoring pass. But he's not turnover-prone.

INTANGIBLES

Thornton only knows one speed: full-blast. Nobody works harder, but he doesn't get much accomplished. There's better talent in the CBA, but Thornton has the good sense to accept his role and practice hard.

IN SUM

A troubled team is a team that has to play Thornton a lot of minutes. Philadelphia used him for only 8.3 a game, which is about right. Thornton will bang and practice hard and that's about it. As one scout put it, "Persistence is sometimes better than talent, but persistence plus talent is always better than persistence alone." Unfortunately, Thornton is simply a case of persistence.

RICK'S RATINGS

Scoring: **D**	Defense: **B**
Shooting: **D**	Defensive Rebounding: **D**
Free Throw Shooting: **D**	Playmaking: **D**
Ball Handling: **C**	Intangibles: **A**
Passing: **C**	Overall: **D**

Otis Thorpe

Birthdate: August 5, 1962
Height: 6-10
Weight: 249
College: Providence College, Providence, R.I.
Drafted: Kansas City on first round, 1984 (9th pick).
Position: Forward
Final 1989 Team: Houston Rockets
Final 1988–89 Statistics:

G	Fg	Fga	Fg%	Ft	Fta	Ft%	Orb	Reb	Ast	Stl	To	Blk	Pts	Ppg
82	521	961	.542	328	450	.729	272	787	202	82	225	37	1370	16.7

Three-point goals: 0–2 (.000)   **TSP:** .542

SCORING

When the Rockets acquired Thorpe in the summer of 1988 from Sacramento (for Rodney McCray and Jim Peterson), they were looking to shore up their 4 spot, left punchless by the December 1987 trade of Ralph Sampson to Golden State. In 1987–88, neither Jim Peterson, a career 8.1 scorer, nor Joe Barry Carroll, a center who wasn't comfortable playing power forward, were the answer. But Thorpe, who was coming off a year in which he averaged 20.8 ppg and 10.2 rpg (one of four players to be over 20 points and 10 rebounds a game), seemed to be just what the doctor ordered. He looked like the perfect fit stylistically, because under coach Don Chaney, Houston was going to run, and the 6-10, 249-pound, five-year veteran has few equals (Karl Malone, for one) among power forwards who can run the floor. Plus, he was an inside force who could relieve the pressure on teammate Akeem Olajuwon. For the most part, Thorpe lived up to expectations, averaging 16.7 points a game and 9.6 rebounds a game. While his moves are somewhat mechanical, he's awfully strong and can power his way to the basket. And his limited offensive arsenal is expanding—he's learning a jump hook and taking the turnaround 12-footer. Then, too, he bangs the offensive board (a solid 3.3 a game). He's even showing signs of being able to put the ball on the floor. A slightly below-average foul shooter (.729 last year, .718 career).

DEFENSE/DEFENSIVE REBOUNDING

Thorpe came to the Rockets with a reputation of being a less-than-stellar defender but has made major strides in terms of moving his feet, boxing out, and putting his body on people. He is not now, nor may ever be, a shot blocker, which is strange, considering his size and explosive jumping ability (but then look at his short arms). He is, however, a decent defensive rebounder and one of 10 players to average more than 9.5 total rebounds a game last year.

THE FLOOR GAME

In Sacramento, Thorpe was the focus of the offense; passing was an afterthought. But in Houston, no longer the first option, he took less shots and showed that he's a solid passer as well. With his huge hands, he can rifle the ball the length of the court (2.5 assists a game, sixth among power forwards on a per minute basis) and does an excellent job of passing out of the double-team.

INTANGIBLES

When asked about Thorpe, 76er Derek Smith once said: "Someday Otis could become a great player, but it will depend on this," and he pointed to his heart. In Houston, however, Thorpe pretty much delivered the goods all year, though his playoff rebounding numbers against Seattle (Houston lost 3–1)—five rebounds per and a high of seven—were disturbing.

IN SUM

Thorpe gets the Rockets 16 points and almost 10 rebounds a night in a league where only 17 players averaged double figures in points and rebounds. Houston gave up a lot to get him, but based on his 1988–89 effort, they received equivalent value.

Scoring: **A**
Shooting: **A**
Free Throw Shooting: **C**
Ball Handling: **B**
Passing: **A**

Defense: **B**
Defensive Rebounding: **B**
Shot Blocking: **D**
Intangibles: **A**
Overall: **A**

Sedale Threatt

Birthdate: September 10, 1961
Height: 6-2
Weight: 177
College: West Virginia Institute of Technology, Montgomery, W. Va.
Drafted: Philadelphia on sixth round, 1983 (139th pick).
Position: Guard
Final 1989 Team: Seattle Supersonics
Final 1988–89 Statistics:

G	Fg	Fga	Fg%	Ft	Fta	Ft%	Orb	Reb	Ast	Stl	To	Blk	Pts	Ppg
63	235	476	.494	63	77	.818	31	117	238	83	77	4	544	8.6

Three-point goals: 11–30 (.367)   **TSP:** .505

SCORING

For Threatt, it was a matter of finding the right team, the right system, the right coach. After a brief and unhappy sojourn in Chicago (December 1986 to February 1988, which followed a little more than three years with the 76ers), the six-year veteran, a sixth-round draft pick in 1983, thrived in the run-and-gun offense/pressure defense style fashioned by Seattle coach Bernie Bickerstaff. A backup 1 or 2, Threatt is an excellent jump shooter (an eye-catching .494 from the field in 1988–89; compared to his lifetime .466) who can pull up on the break, spot up, come off screens, or create off the dribble. Then, too, Threatt, blessed with superb speed and quickness, creates offense with his ball-hawking defense (he was tied, with Pearl Washington for most steals, per minute, among backup 2s—1.3 steals a game in just 19.4 minutes). A consistent performer throughout the season, Threatt saved his best for the playoffs, scorching the Rockets for 22 points, a season-high, in the first game of the Houston-Seattle series. And he came back with 16 in the next game (Seattle won both games and the series). Though he is a good foul shooter (.818 last year; .798 lifetime), his one offensive limitation is that his scoring is limited almost exclusively to the perimeter. A terrible three-point shooter entering the year (.142 on 16-for-113), he hit a respectable .367 last season.

DEFENSE/DEFENSIVE REBOUNDING

On a team noted for its tenacious D, Threatt may be the most relentless of the lot. Simply put, he's a superb defender, a lethal combination of quick hands, lateral mobility, and aggressiveness. Those traits appear on the job description for the Sonics' pressing/trapping schemes. Threatt is in the man's jockstrap for 94 feet, gets through picks, and can pressure the smaller points. If there's a negative, it's that at 6-2 he doesn't match up with the taller off-guards. A below-average rebounder for his position.

THE FLOOR GAME

Threatt's role is to uptempo the Sonic attack, which he does effectively both on defense and offense, because he can push the ball. In Chicago, he was an erratic ball handler whose decision-making drove former Bull coach Doug Collins crazy. But in Seattle, he settled down and had a fine 3.09 assist-to-turnover ratio and 3.5 assists a game.

INTANGIBLES

Threatt plays at a consistently high intensity level. The key here is that he was unhappy playing for Collins (the feeling was mutual) and feels very much at home with Bickerstaff.

IN SUM

Versatile, a first-rate shooter, an accomplished defender—Threatt has about everything you want in a backup guard.

RICK'S RATINGS

Scoring: **B**
Shooting: **A**
Free Throw Shooting: **A**
Ball Handling: **B**
Passing: **B**

Defense: **A**
Defensive Rebounding: **C**
Intangibles: **A**
Overall: **B+**

Wayman Tisdale

Birthdate: June 9, 1964
Height: 6-8
Weight: 240

College: University of Oklahoma, Norman, Okla.
Drafted: Indiana on first round as an undergraduate, 1985 (2nd pick).
Position: Forward
Final 1989 Team: Sacramento Kings
Final 1988–89 Statistics:

G	Fg	Fga	Fg%	Ft	Fta	Ft%	Orb	Reb	Ast	Stl	To	Blk	Pts	Ppg
79	532	1036	.514	317	410	.773	187	609	128	55	172	52	1381	17.5

Three-point goals: 0–4 (.000)   **TSP:** .514

SCORING

Tisdale, who was traded to Sacramento from Indiana (for Randy Wittman and LaSalle Thompson) in February 1989, was a most unhappy camper with the Pacers. Two major complaints: He didn't start (27.6 minutes off the bench in 1988–89) and he didn't get the ball enough (read: enough shots—only 12 a game for 16 ppg). Sacramento, however, desperately needed a low-post player who could score. And that was Tisdale to a "T." In 31 games (he started all but one) with the Kings, he logged 35.7 minutes a game, shot the ball 15 times a game and averaged 19.8 ppg—and he would have scored more had he not frequently been in foul trouble. Tisdale's métier is the post-up game, where he can flat out score in the low blocks, relying, for the most part, on a quick turnaround jumper. He can also shoot the facing jumper from 17 feet, a shot he has improved significantly since he first entered the league in 1985. And he will occasionally put the ball on the floor, but that's not his strength. A decent offensive rebounder with the Pacers (2 a game), he picked up the pace with the Kings (2.8 a game). He also did a better job of running the floor.

DEFENSE/DEFENSIVE REBOUNDING

With Indiana, Tisdale was not a consistently tenacious defender. With Sacramento, at least he played aggressively (accounting for the foul trouble), though he's still weak in this area. Playing the 4 spot, he's frequently outsized—listed at 6-8 in the Pacers media guide, the feeling is that he's at least an inch smaller. He does, however, possess decent quickness so there is hope. Encouraging, however, was his work on the defensive glass. An average defensive rebounder with the Pacers, he improved considerably in Sacramento (more on a per minute basis, and a potent 9.6 rebounds overall).

THE FLOOR GAME

Tisdale's role is to score; to be effective, he needs the ball. Because he draws a crowd, he opens up the outside game (Sacramento's offense features the three-pointer), and he did an adequate job—he could get a lot better—of passing out of the double-team.

INTANGIBLES

In Indiana, there were a lot of negatives surrounding Tisdale's play. His work ethic, particularly on defense, was suspect. He seemed more concerned with Wayman Tisdale's point totals than the team. He could "get you to the point of winning, but you couldn't win with him," said one source. But Sacramento seems to be an ideal situation: He's starting, he's one of the go-to guys on offense, and as a result, his rebounding and defensive intensity have improved.

IN SUM

Tisdale's challenge will be to maintain the same level of productivity in scoring (no problem), and in rebounding (harder), and to improve his defense (the most difficult task of all). But based on his short time in Sacramento, he's beginning to become the player many thought he would be when he was the second player picked in the 1985 draft.

RICK'S RATINGS

Scoring: **AAA**	Defense: **C**
Shooting: **A**	Defensive Rebounding: **B**
Free Throw Shooting: **B**	Shot Blocking: **C**
Ball Handling: **B**	Intangibles: **B**
Passing: **C**	Overall: **A +**

Ray Tolbert

Birthdate: September 10, 1958
Height: 6-9
Weight: 225
College: Indiana University, Bloomington, Ind.
Drafted: New Jersey on first round, 1981 (18th pick).
Positions: Forward, Center
Final 1989 Team: Atlanta Hawks
Final 1988–89 Statistics:

G	Fg	Fga	Fg%	Ft	Fta	Ft%	Orb	Reb	Ast	Stl	To	Blk	Pts	Ppg
50	40	94	.426	23	37	.622	31	88	16	13	35	13	103	2.1

Three-point goals: 0–0 (.000)   **TSP:** .426

SCORING

Is he still around? Tolbert has changed jerseys six times since he was drafted in 1981 in the first round by the Nets. Thrice waived. Twice traded. Two years in the CBA. Last year he ended up in Atlanta where he played his usual fringe role, averaging 2.1 points a game in 341 minutes. Tolbert, a 6-9 power forward who can also play center, is fairly quick for his size and has a decent back-to-the-basket game, including a hook shot. He will also bang the offensive board; career-wise, he's slightly above average for power forwards on a per minute basis. And he can also put the ball on the floor. But his jumper is suspect, and the description of his foul shooting (.544 career) is unprintable.

DEFENSE/DEFENSIVE REBOUNDING

Tolbert does just what you'd expect from a journeyman: He bangs, he works hard, but he's not a shot blocker. And his defensive rebounding numbers are below average.

THE FLOOR GAME

Tolbert's assist-to-turnover ratios over the last two years have been, in a word, lousy. But he will run the floor.

INTANGIBLES

Tolbert seems, as one coach put it, to have "gotten in his own way" and never really panned out. Despite his marginal talent, he moaned and groaned about lack of playing time.

IN SUM

With Kevin Willis due back on Atlanta's roster this year, Tolbert's days with Atlanta are numbered. It wouldn't be surprising if his NBA career suffered a similar fate, but then again, why not seven NBA lives?

RICK'S RATINGS

Scoring: **D**	Defense: **B**
Shooting: **D**	Defensive Rebounding: **A**
Free Throw Shooting: **D**	Shot Blocking: **A**
Ball Handling: **D**	Intangibles: **B**
Passing: **C**	Overall: **D**

Kelly Tripucka

Birthdate: February 16, 1959
Height: 6-6
Weight: 225
College: University of Notre Dame, Notre Dame, Ind.
Drafted: Detroit on first round, 1981 (12th pick).
Position: Forward
Final 1989 Team: Charlotte Hornets
Final 1988–89 Statistics:

G	Fg	Fga	Fg%	Ft	Fta	Ft%	Orb	Reb	Ast	Stl	To	Blk	Pts	Ppg
71	568	1215	.467	440	508	.866	79	267	224	88	236	16	1606	22.6

Three-point goals: 30–84 (.357)   **TSP:** .480

SCORING

1988–89 marked the second coming of Kelly Tripucka. After virtually disappearing from the face of the NBA earth in Utah (resulting from a combo of injuries and Frank Lay-

den's mysterious "Did Not Play-Coach's Decisioning" him), Tripucka reappeared in his former Piston guise: a 20-plus-a-game scorer, finishing at 22.6 ppg (in his five seasons with Detroit, he was over 20 ppg four times, 19.1 the other year). Possessor of one of the best strokes in the league, Tripucka is a master at utilizing picks, setting up his man, and then getting free; with his quick release, he needs only a glimmer of an opening. He can shoot from anywhere on the court, including three-point territory (where he shot .357, right around his .364 career average). But Tripucka is not simply a pure shooter. While his first step is just average, using his smarts he can get by players, take it to the hole, and get fouled. And he doesn't miss many foul shots (.866 last year; .842 lifetime). On the break, with his average foot speed, he's only a fair finisher.

DEFENSE/DEFENSIVE REBOUNDING

No secret. Tripucka does not play D. He is, on a given night, outquicked, outsized, or outmuscled. He has it in his head that he can't play defense and, indeed, he doesn't. But he does play the passing lanes well (1.2 steals a game). His input on the defensive glass (1.1 a game and 3.8 total rebounds a game) is minimal.

THE FLOOR GAME

Words like savvy and intelligent frequently pop up in describing Tripucka's game. He has a thorough grasp of Charlotte's numerous sets and knows how to utilize it to his best advantage. Surprisingly, he's a pretty good passer (3.2 assists a game), but he tends to hold the ball too long in the double-team, which explains his unimpressive 0.95 assist-to-turnover ratio.

INTANGIBLES

Tripucka was Charlotte's main go-to guy, a player who, as one coach put it, "allowed the Hornets to win games." He plays hard—at least on the offensive end.

IN SUM

If they still gave the award, Tripucka would have been a leading candidate for the Comeback Player of the Year. He basically took two years off, so he's a young 30 and should have a number of productive years ahead of him.

RICK'S RATINGS

Scoring: **AAA**	Defense: **D**
Shooting: **AA**	Defensive Rebounding: **D**
Free Throw Shooting: **AA**	Intangibles: **A**
Ball Handling: **C**	Overall: **A**
Passing: **A**	

Trent Tucker

Birthdate: December 20, 1959
Height: 6-5
Weight: 193
College: University of Minnesota, Minneapolis, Minn.
Drafted: New York on first round, 1982 (6th pick).
Position: Guard
Final 1989 Team: New York Knicks
Final 1988–89 Statistics:

G	Fg	Fga	Fg%	Ft	Fta	Ft%	Orb	Reb	Ast	Stl	To	Blk	Pts	Ppg
81	263	579	.454	43	55	.782	55	176	132	88	59	6	687	8.5

Three-point goals: 118–296 (.399)   **TSP:** .556

SCORING

Few can shoot the trey better: Entering the year, Tucker was the NBA career leader in three-point percentage—and now, after a .399 mark last season (which included a dreadful late-season slump), he's third (.414), behind Mark Price (.438) and Hersey Hawkins (.428). While he's never been the leader in three-point percentage for any single season, the seven-year veteran has been under 40 percent just twice (last year and a 6-for-16, .375 in 1983–84). And he sizzled during the playoffs with .469 (including a buzzer-beater against Philly and a four-point play in the sixth game against the Bulls, which, but for Michael Jordan's heroics, would have been the shot heard 'round the world in 1989). In other words, the man can shoot and shoot with range. But until recently, that's about all Tucker could do on the offensive end. His mid-range game was minimal because, lacking quickness, he had trouble creating his own shot and appeared to have an aversion to taking the ball to the hoop (lifetime, in 22.1 minutes a game, he's averaged a paltry 0.9 foul shots a game). He relied primarily on spotting up to get the long-range jumper. With a little push from the Knicks coaching staff, however, Tucker has varied his attack. Now, at least on occasion, he'll put it on the floor, which means the defense can't crowd his jumper (though he still doesn't get to the line, just 0.7 attempts in 22.5 mpg in 1988–89). And when he plays the two-man game with teammate Patrick Ewing, the defense has to honor his shot, preventing his man from doubling on the big guy.

DEFENSE/DEFENSIVE REBOUNDING

Tucker is pigeonholed as a shooter, but actually he is an underrated defensive player—the best one-on-one defender on the Knicks. He plays sound fundamental defense—he doesn't gamble (though he managed 1.1 steals)—and he takes pride in his defensive effort. Tucker knows the strengths and weaknesses of opponents and is willing to put his body on people. A slightly below-average defensive rebounder for his position.

THE FLOOR GAME

Tucker knows the value of the ball. He rarely commits turnovers—less than one a game—and his assist-to-turnover ratio was an excellent 2.24. He doesn't try to do too much with the ball and he's a solid passer, though not an imaginative one. He doesn't run the court well but is adept at positioning himself to get his shot.

INTANGIBLES

Tucker, the longest standing member of the Knicks, has assumed a leadership role on the team. And he had added credibility last season, when, for a change, he came to training camp in shape and got off to a scintillating start (.554 from three-land after 19 games).

IN SUM

After an abominable 1987–88 season, when he shot .424, Tucker came back strong, and his fine all-around play was an essential ingredient in the Knicks' 14-win (from 38 to 52) improvement. Though he started 24 games, his skill level is better suited for a reserve. Great shooter, plays D, team player—what else do you want in a backup?

RICK'S RATINGS

Scoring: **B**
Shooting: **AA**
Free Throw Shooting: **B**
Ball Handling: **A**
Passing: **B**

Defense: **A**
Defensive Rebounding: **C**
Intangibles: **A**
Overall: **B +**

Elston Turner

Birthdate: June 10, 1959
Height: 6-5
Weight: 200
College: University of Mississippi, University, Miss.
Drafted: Dallas on second round, 1981 (43rd pick).
Positions: Guard, Forward
Final 1989 Team: Denver Nuggets
Final 1988–89 Statistics:

G	Fg	Fga	Fg%	Ft	Fta	Ft%	Orb	Reb	Ast	Stl	To	Blk	Pts	Ppg
78	151	353	.428	33	56	.589	109	287	144	90	60	8	337	4.3

Three-point goals: 2–7 (.286)   **TSP:** .431

SCORING

When the Nuggets didn't resign T.R. Dunn for the 1988–89 season (he played for Phoenix last year), they needed somebody to take on the "stopper" role that he had performed so admirably for eight years. Turner, who had previously played for the Nuggets (1984–85 and 1985–86), is a veritable Dunn clone. Both are 2s, both are punishing, physical defenders, and both, shall we say, keep a low profile on the offensive end of things. In 1988–89, two backup shooting guards would not have even averaged 10 points a game playing the full 48. Right. T.R. Dunn and Elston Turner. Neither has any facility for putting the ball on the floor. Neither has any range. Neither is a very good shooter; Dunn's a lifetime .436 while Turner's a .432, including last year's .428. Because his man often double-teams the ball, Turner often gets open for the standstill jumper or sneaks in for the offensive rebound.

DEFENSE/DEFENSIVE REBOUNDING

Turner's defensive assets run the gamut: he's not easily faked out, he's versatile (can guard 1s, 2s, 3s, and even some 4s), strong (at 6-5, 200, built like a strong safety), has good hands (1.2 steals a game in 22.4 minutes), and he takes pride in his work. He jumps well, which explains why he is an above-average defensive rebounder.

THE FLOOR GAME

Turner is not clever with the ball, but he does take good care of it (less than one turnover a game). He's an average passer and a fair dribbler, who will run the court and moves well without the ball.

INTANGIBLES

In the NBA—actually in any league—having a player who doesn't worry about his shots and scoring is always an asset. Turner is a nice element in the Nuggets' chemistry.

IN SUM

Turner does the dirty work—defense and rebounding—without complaining. That's why he's stuck around for eight years. A classic role player, who may be more effective playing slightly fewer minutes. With rookie 2s Todd Lichti and Michael Cutright in camp, Turner has keen competition for a job.

RICK'S RATINGS

Scoring: **D**	Defense: **AA**
Shooting: **D**	Defensive Rebounding:
Free Throw Shooting: **D**	**AA**
Ball Handling: **B**	Intangibles: **A**
Passing: **B**	Overall: **B –**

Kelvin Upshaw

Birthdate: January 24, 1963
Height: 6-2
Weight: 180

College: University of Utah, Salt Lake City, Utah
Drafted: Free Agent
Position: Guard
Final 1989 Team: Boston Celtics
Final 1988–89 Statistics:

G	Fg	Fga	Fg%	Ft	Fta	Ft%	Orb	Reb	Ast	Stl	To	Blk	Pts	Ppg
32	99	212	.467	18	26	.692	10	49	117	26	55	3	219	6.8

Three-point goals: 3–15 (.200)   **TSP:** .474

SCORING

It's K-e-l-v-i-n, Kelvin. Not Calvin. Or Kevin. If it's an unfamiliar name, that's because Mr. Upshaw, until last season, had been toiling in basketball's boondocks. First, there was a stint at Northeastern Junior College in Oklahoma. Then two years at the University of Utah. Passed over by every NBA club in the 1986 draft, he apprenticed in the United States Basketball League and then moved, in 1986, into the CBA, where he played for four clubs until he finally made it to the "Big Show" last season with the Heat where he lasted all of two 10-day contracts (and nine games). Finally, when Dennis Johnson and Jim Paxson went down with injuries, the Celtics signed Upshaw in March. In an auspicious debut on national television against the Nuggets, the 6-2, 180-pound point guard went four-for-four with four assists in 13 minutes, which augured well for his future prospects. Indeed, Boston liked what it saw in the 26-year-old waterbug. While he showed he could score in the CBA (15 a game with Albany 1987–88), Upshaw's place in the Cs' offense was to uptempo their attack and distribute the ball. Though he was the last option, he did a nice job of taking it all the way to the hole in transition and knocking down the open jumper. His comfort zone is 18 feet (just three-for-15 from beyond the arc).

DEFENSE/DEFENSIVE REBOUNDING

The Celtics had few complaints with Upshaw's D, which was surprising considering that that end of things was not a prominent section on his resume. He performed more than adequately, employing his quickness and aggressiveness, playing pressure defense, full court.

THE FLOOR GAME

Upshaw's uptempo abilities were precisely what the Celtics needed. In their new push attack, he's a solid push-man who made pretty good decisions on the break and ably quarterbacked in the half-court game. But Upshaw was slightly turnover-prone and his 2.13 assist-to-turnover ratio was anything but exemplary.

INTANGIBLES

Upshaw, it seems, had what amounts to a character transformation once he got his first taste of the NBA with Miami. Until then, the book on him was that he was a hothead, with a chip on his shoulder the size of a basketball. But with the Celtics, this dark side was not evident and he made it his business to find out what coach Jimmy Rodgers wanted and quickly picked up the Celtic system.

IN SUM

A nice little NBA success story. Upshaw may not do anything particularly well, but the sum of it certainly makes him employable in a backup role for a spell.

Kiki Vandeweghe

Birthdate: August 1, 1958

Height: 6-8

Weight: 220

College: University of California at Los Angeles, Los Angeles, Calif.

Drafted: Dallas on first round, 1980 (11th pick).

Position: Forward

Final 1989 Team: New York Knicks

Final 1988–89 Statistics:

G	Fg	Fga	Fg%	Ft	Fta	Ft%	Orb	Reb	Ast	Stl	To	Blk	Pts	Ppg
45	200	426	.469	80	89	.899	26	71	69	19	41	11	499	11.1

Three-point goals: 19-48 (.396)   **TSP:** .492

SCORING

As a bald, one-eyed wacko from New Jersey might say: "He can flat out shoot the rock." Vandeweghe, a much bally-hooed acquisition (from the Trail Blazers for a 1989 first round draft pick, right before last season's trading deadline), has been lighting people up for years. The formula is classic. Part I: Shoot the jumper accurately, from anywhere. Vandeweghe, entering his 10th NBA campaign, is a career .532 shooter, has averaged 22.8 a game, and led the NBA in three-point percentage in 1986–87 (he's a career .362 from three-point territory). Part II: If denied the jumper, drive to the hoop. He has one of the best first steps in the league (the patented "Kiki" move) and gets by people and then, with his big hands, can control the ball for a slam with either hand. Part III: Get to the line and make the foul shots (a career .870 foul shooter and .899 last year). Impressive credentials indeed, and the theory was that Vandeweghe's

perimeter preeminence was the missing piece—since playoff basketball equals half-court basketball—in the Knicks' championship puzzle. But unfortunately, the practice was otherwise. In New York's equal-opportunity offense, Vandeweghe simply didn't get the ball enough or at the right time. Compare, for example, Phoenix's Eddie Johnson, the winner of the Sixth Man Award, who fired away once every 1.6 minutes while Kiki was limited to a shot every 2.4 minutes. Compounding the problem was his lack of minutes (20.8 per game). The result was that his shooting was up and down and his .469 represented his worst year from the field since his rookie year, .426 (the only time he's been under 50 percent). If you're going to have Vandeweghe on your team, you have to go to him, and go to him frequently. Otherwise, why have him around?

DEFENSE/DEFENSIVE REBOUNDING

Certainly not for his defense. Or his rebounding. Vandeweghe makes the effort defensively but he's usually overmatched quickness-wise. If you play good team defense, his defensive liabilities can be camouflaged. Look it up: He once was a decent defensive rebounder (3.8 defensive caroms a game in 1981–82 and 1982–83), but no more.

THE FLOOR GAME

Vandeweghe doesn't turn the ball over and he swings the ball when the defense rotates, but you don't want to put him in situations where he has to create for somebody else. When he gets the ball, the Knicks want him to shoot it. He runs the floor fairly well.

INTANGIBLES

Vandeweghe hurt his back during the 1987–88 season, which caused him to miss a substantial portion of that year (he played only 37 games). Regarding the current status of his back, depending on who you talk to, his injury is (a) an ongoing medical problem which could flare-up at any time or (b) was a ruse to get him out of Portland. The proof obviously will be in how healthy he is this year.

IN SUM

Vandeweghe, 31, can still fill it up with the best of them. With a training camp under his belt, both he and the Knicks should do a better job of getting him what he needs most: shots. More shots means more minutes and one of Coach Stu Jackson's biggest challenges will be balancing Kiki's and Johnny Newman's playing time.

Jay Vincent

Birthdate: June 10, 1959
Height: 6-7
Weight: 220
College: Michigan State University, East Lansing, Mich.
Drafted: Dallas on second round, 1981 (24th pick).
Position: Forward
Final 1989 Team: San Antonio Spurs
Final 1988–89 Statistics:

G	Fg	Fga	Fg%	Ft	Fta	Ft%	Orb	Reb	Ast	Stl	To	Blk	Pts	Ppg
29	104	257	.405	40	60	.667	38	110	27	6	42	4	249	8.6

Three-point goals: 1–3 (.333)   TSP: .407

SCORING

Vincent had a most forgettable season. It began in Denver, with a bitter and well-publicized contract dispute with Nugget management. Vincent, making $400,000 per year, felt he was underpaid which, considering his talent, was true. He wanted a fatter deal, but because of salary cap restrictions, the Nuggets couldn't accommodate him—but we'll beg off further comment on this imbroglio. With Denver, he was on the injured list twice, played just 5 games, and finally on January 28 was shipped to San Antonio (along with Calvin Natt for David Greenwood and Darwin Cook). After all was said and done, Vincent put up career-worst numbers in games played (29), shooting percentage (.405), scoring (8.6), and free throw percentage (.667)—among other categories. This, of course, was atypical Vincent. When he is healthy and has his mind in the game (more on his "head" problems below), Vincent is a big-time scorer and a dangerous sixth man. With Denver in 1987–88, for example, he averaged 15.4 a game, was their second-leading scorer (17.5 a game) in the playoffs, and even the Nugget's media guide claims he was the best sixth man in the franchise's history. The 6-7 small forward, while not a pure shooter, can put points on the board in a variety of ways—mid-range jumpers off the dribble or on the catch (he's not a good three-point shooter, 3-for-25 lifetime), drives to the basket (he's very creative around the hoop), and by running the floor. His point-producing ability is the key reason the 76ers—who were hurting for firepower from the 3 spot last year—acquired him from the Spurs in August.

DEFENSE/DEFENSIVE REBOUNDING

It's not as if Vincent lacks skills as a defender or a rebounder. It's just that the Big E, effort, is frequently lacking. He's been an above-average defensive rebounder for his career but to play good D, he needs to be in shape—he tends to the heavy side—because he's not that quick.

THE FLOOR GAME

Vincent can run the floor, sees the court, handles the ball well, and is not turnover-prone.

INTANGIBLES

As one observer put it, "Vincent doesn't have many weaknesses—from the shoulders down." Upstairs, his troubles center on the fact that he hates to practice and has a low threshold for pain. One coach noted that Vincent gets as little out of his potential as any player in the league.

IN SUM

Maybe Jimmy Lynam can get to him (Doug Moe did, for a while, and he was an integral part of the Nuggets success in 1987–88). He's a superb scorer, who, with a modicum of commitment, could also contribute defensively and on the boards. But will he make the effort? Who knows? Even Jay Vincent may not know for sure.

RICK'S RATINGS

Scoring: **AA**
Shooting: **A**
Free Throw Shooting: **D**
Ball Handling: **B**
Passing: **B**

Defense: **D**
Defensive Rebounding: **A**
Intangibles: **D**
Overall: **C +**

Sam Vincent

Birthdate: May 18, 1963
Height: 6-2
Weight: 185
College: Michigan State University, Lansing, Mich.
Drafted: Boston on first round, 1985 (20th pick).
Position: Guard
Final 1989 Team: Chicago Bulls
Final 1988–89 Statistics:

G	Fg	Fga	Fg%	Ft	Fta	Ft%	Orb	Reb	Ast	Stl	To	Blk	Pts	Ppg
70	274	566	.484	106	129	.822	34	190	335	53	142	10	656	9.4

Three-point goals: 2–17 (.118)   TSP: .486

SCORING

Vincent's bread and butter is the stop-and-pop jumper—he has a quick release—from 15 to 18 feet. The four-year veteran, who was the fourth player picked (from Chicago; he had previously been with Seattle and Boston) by the Magic in the expansion draft, can create off the dribble (right-handed, he's very good going to his left) but also gets shots in transition, and, with the Bulls, he'd position himself to receive passes from his sometimes backcourt mate, Michael Jordan, who was inevitably double-teamed. Until last year, Vincent was, at best, a streaky shooter (.433 career before 1988–89), but note that it wasn't until February 1988 (when the Bulls acquired him from Seattle for Sedale Threatt) that he became a full-time player. In 1988–89, he started 56 games, and his shooting percentage (.484) was the better for it. He's a good driver in transition, where he uses his exceptional speed to get by defenders; but in the half-court setting he won't beat people off the dribble. Vincent doesn't get to the line much (1.8 attempts a game in 1988–89), but he's a top-notch foul shooter (.872 career, .822 last year).

DEFENSE/DEFENSIVE REBOUNDING

Vincent is only a fair defender. He's not aggressive, doesn't pressure the ball well, and gets lost on picks. His anticipation is also below average, as his steals (0.8 a game) indicate. But he's a pretty good rebounder, above-average for a starting 1, quite an accomplishment, considering he's only 6-2.

THE FLOOR GAME

Vincent pushes the ball well on the fast break, which was the major reason why the Bulls acquired him: to quicken the tempo of their running game. But his limitations as a floor general cost him his starting job last March, and Michael Jordan took over. Vincent went from being the starting point guard to effectively the fourth guard (behind Jordan, Craig Hodges, and John Paxson) in the rotation. Basically, he's still learning how to create tempo, to get shots for teammates, and when to shoot himself—in other words, how to run a team. Note his shabby 2.34 assist-to-turnover ratio. He's more of a one-pass-to-get-the-offense-going playmaker than a penetrator/creator.

INTANGIBLES

Vincent competes well enough, but he is not yet a day-in, day-out performer. His ability to handle pressure is questionable. Even when he started, John Paxson, then his backup, was often on the floor at the end of the game.

IN SUM

Ex-Chicago coach Doug Collins recognized that Vincent's deficiencies on D and as a floor leader were holding the Bulls back, that Chicago couldn't win (or come close to winning) a championship with him at the point. Vincent's better as a backup 1 or even 2, since he's more naturally a shooting guard. With the lowered expectations of an expansion team Vincent, on his fourth team in five years, may finally establish himself.

RICK'S RATINGS

Scoring: **B**
Shooting: **B**
Free Throw Shooting: **A**
Ball Handling: **C**
Passing: **B**

Defense: **C**
Defensive Rebounding: **D**
Intangibles: **C**
Overall: **C**

Darrell Walker

Birthdate: March 9, 1961
Height: 6-4
Weight: 180
College: University of Arkansas, Fayetteville, Ark.
Drafted: New York on first round, 1983 (12th pick).
Position: Guard
Final 1989 Team: Washington Bullets
Final 1988–89 Statistics:

G	Fg	Fga	Fg%	Ft	Fta	Ft%	Orb	Reb	Ast	Stl	To	Blk	Pts	Ppg
79	286	681	.420	142	184	.772	135	507	496	155	184	23	714	9.0

Three-point goals: 0–9 (.000) **TSP:** .420

SCORING

Walker is another one of those "if-he-only-had-a-jumper" players. The dismal numbers: In 1988–89 he shot .420 from the field; in a six-year career he has been above 44 percent only once; and the last time he made a three was in Ronald Reagan's first term (1983–84). He has no range or consistency in his outside game. But Walker *can* score. Using his great jumping ability and willingness to mix it up, he was the second-best offensive rebounder in 1988–89 (1.7 a game) among point guards. He can drive with either hand, finishes well, and his long arms give him an edge when he posts smaller guards and shoots turnarounds. Walker is probably best suited to a running game, and much of his scoring are "opportunity" points in transition. He's been OK from the foul line the last two years (.781 and .772, respectively), after shooting a below-average .729 in his first four years.

DEFENSE/DEFENSIVE REBOUNDING

Walker has the entire defensive package: quickness, long arms, lateral quickness, feistiness, jumping ability. He's a stopper who may be the best defender never named to the All-Defensive team. He can pick your pocket (almost 2 a game, 16th in the league) and he's a superb defensive rebounder for his position, finishing with 4.7 a game (6.4 total rebounds, including 14 in one game thrice), second to Magic Johnson.

THE FLOOR GAME

So is he a 1? Or a 2? Walker is not your classic model point guard. He's an average passer and a fair dribbler, but at the 2 he has no outside game that commands respect. In other words, he's a guard—period. Walker had only 6.3 assists a game, which reflects his lack of creativity, but then he doesn't turn the ball over much. Unlike the great point guards, Walker can't break down defenses with the dribble.

INTANGIBLES

Walker will scratch and claw and do anything to beat you. He's a tough guy, doesn't back down from anybody, and comes to play every night. Even if he isn't contributing offensively, he'll always play the D and rebound. All of which explains why coach Wes Unseld named Walker captain of the Bullets.

IN SUM

At the end of a typical night's work, Walker will have contributed 9 or 10 points, 5 assists, 7 rebounds, and played his heart out. But he's not going to beat anybody with his jumper.

RICK'S RATINGS

Scoring: **C**
Shooting: **D**
Free Throw Shooting: **B**
Ball Handling: **B**
Passing: **B**
Defense: **AAA**

Defensive Rebounding: **AAA**
Playmaking: **B**
Intangibles: **AA**
Overall: **B+**

Kenny Walker

Birthdate: August 18, 1964
Height: 6-8
Weight: 210
College: University of Kentucky, Lexington, Ky.
Drafted: New York on first round, 1986 (5th pick).
Position: Forward
Final 1989 Team: New York Knicks
Final 1988–89 Statistics:

G	Fg	Fga	Fg%	Ft	Fta	Ft%	Orb	Reb	Ast	Stl	To	Blk	Pts	Ppg
79	174	356	.489	66	85	.776	101	230	36	41	44	45	419	5.3

Three-point goals: 5-20 (.250)   **TSP:** .496

SCORING

Simply put, small forwards are supposed to score, but Walker, who mostly plays the 3, simply isn't much of a scorer. In fact, he's a strange incarnation of a small forward: He excels at skills often absent among 3s—such as offensive rebounding and defense—but he lacks most of their standard repertoire: the ability to put the ball on the floor, to shoot the jumper with consistency, and to create his own shot. Which is why Johnny Newman took Walker's starting job in 1987–88 and, relegated him to backup duty again last year. Walker, 6-8, 210 pounds, is really a 4 in a 3's body, and when Kiki Vandeweghe arrived last February, Walker played substantial minutes at power forward. With the departure of Sidney Green to Orlando, he's scheduled to log most of his minutes as Charles Oakley's backup at the 4. He's an erratic jump shooter, and in his first two years in the league, his confidence took a beating as Knicks fans mercilessly booed his masonry. But last year, he was more comfortable shooting the ball (in his three seasons, he's been steady from the field: .491, .473, and .489) and even had the green light to shoot the trey (5-for-20). Now a Garden favorite, the New York crowd loves Walker's hustle on the offensive glass, which is his main offensive weapon. Nicknamed "Sky," Walker can do just that and isn't afraid to mix it up. On a per minute basis, he was in the top third, per minute, among backup 3s for offensive rebounding (1.3 a game in just 14.7 mpg). He's also the beneficiary of Mark Jackson's (or Rod Strickland's) largesse on the break, since he runs and dunks with the best of 'em (he came out of nowhere to win the 1989 Slam Dunk Championship on All-Star Saturday).

DEFENSE/DEFENSIVE REBOUNDING

Walker is an active, aggressive defender who is effective in the Knicks' trap. He gets his hands on a lot of balls and, with his jumping ability, is capable of blocking shots (fourth, per minute, among backup small forwards). His defensive rebounding numbers are slightly below average among his small forward peers.

THE FLOOR GAME

Walker was a center in college, which helps explain why he can't dribble the ball. His passing isn't much better. But he does get out on the break well and, baseline-to-baseline, is one of the fastest Knicks.

INTANGIBLES

Walker hustles his butt off. He's a team player who will do whatever it takes to win. Once a starter, now a backup, he has accepted his new role without complaining. He is, said one coach, "a coach's dream."

IN SUM

As the fifth player picked in the 1986 draft, and playing in a town in dire need of basketball success, Walker has had a heavy load to bear. He was supposed to take up the slack for the departed Bernard King, but, unfortunately, Bernard King or Chuck Person (who was picked fourth in the same draft), he is not. As the Knicks found out in 1987–88, Walker's not even a starter. What he is, though, is a solid role player who can (and should) play 15 to 20 minutes, bang the boards, play tough defense, and get a bucket here and there.

Scoring: **C**   Defense: **A**
Shooting: **B**   Defensive Rebounding: **B**
Free Throw Shooting: **B**   Intangibles: **AAA**
Ball Handling: **C**   Overall: **B**
Passing: **C**

Pearl Washington

Birthdate: January 6, 1964
Height: 6-2
Weight: 195
College: Syracuse University, Syracuse, N.Y.
Drafted: New Jersey on first round as an undergraduate, 1986 (13th pick).
Position: Guard
Final 1989 Team: Miami Heat
Final 1988–89 Statistics:

G	Fg	Fga	Fg%	Ft	Fta	Ft%	Orb	Reb	Ast	Stl	To	Blk	Pts	Ppg
54	164	387	.424	82	104	.788	49	123	226	73	122	4	411	7.6

Three-point goals: 1–14 (.071)   **TSP:** .425

SCORING

With the Nets, the Pearl played primarily at the point and was, by all accounts, a bust. He never could find that happy medium between playmaking and creating his own offense. When push came to shove, he'd take it one-on-three and throw up a weird off-balance shot. He has the uncanny ability to make bad shots, so he never saw the error of his ways. Miami, (who selected him from the Nets in the 1988 expansion draft) switched him to shooting guard to take advantage of his scorer's mentality; now, all he had to concern himself with was his own points. But unlike most 2s, Washington's missing a major piece of weaponry: a consistent outside shot. True, coming off screens, with his feet set, no farther out than 15 to 17 feet, he is a decent shooter. But when he tries to create on his own (which is often the case) or move out beyond 17 feet, it's a different story. His shooting percentage, .424, tells all. No, Washington isn't anybody's definition of a shooter, though you can't *give* him the jumper. He's a scorer who can get into the paint (usually going left, though he is right-handed and readily beats people off the dribble), where he shoots well in traffic and draws fouls. His shot selection, previously ulcerous, is now simply irritating.

DEFENSE/DEFENSIVE REBOUNDING

Washington, who occasionally plays point, is better guarding 2s than 1s. That's because he's more alert when his man is about to receive the ball (which is what guarding 2s is all about), but he tends to lose concentration after his man gives up the ball (2s generally shoot when they get it; 1s pass). For his size (6-2), Washington has surprising strength and quickness. He gets more than his share of steals (1.3 a game and tops—tied with Sedale Threatt—among backup 2s on a per minute basis), but he takes too many chances and his gambling hurts the team. His defensive rebounding numbers are average.

THE FLOOR GAME

You can't take the playground out of the player and Pearl often gets lost in the structured offense. If he's running the team, and option one breaks down, he panics and tries to force the action. An excellent dribbler, he has a tendency to penetrate, regardless of the situation. His assist-to-turnover ratio improved from a shabby 1.47 in 1987–1988 to an OK 1.85 last year.

INTANGIBLES

Remember Maynard G. Krebs on Dobie Gillis? For those of you too young to remember, every time he heard the word "work," he'd flinch. In his first two years in the league, Washington had a lot of Maynard in him. He was overweight and had no idea what it took to be an NBA player. But after two years of pitiful play and seeing his rep sink to an all-time low, he began to get the message. In 1988–89, for the first time in his career, he played at least part of the season under 200. But then his weight flared up while he was on the injured list with a groin injury—incurring coach Ron Rothstein's wrath—which slowed him considerably.

IN SUM

The luster is off the Pearl. If he can't make it as a backup guard with an expansion team—and last year's performance didn't cut it—he may be, sad to say, history.

Scoring: **B**   Defense: **C**
Shooting: **D**   Defensive Rebounding: **C**
Free Throw Shooting: **B**   Playmaking: **C**
Ball Handling: **B**   Intangibles: **D**
Passing: **B**   Overall: **D**

Spud Webb

Birthdate: July 13, 1963
Height: 5-7

Weight: 135
College: North Carolina State University, Raleigh, N.C.
Drafted: Detroit on fourth round, 1985 (87th pick).
Position: Guard
Final 1989 Team: Atlanta Hawks
Final 1988–89 Statistics:

G	Fg	Fga	Fg%	Ft	Fta	Ft%	Orb	Reb	Ast	Stl	To	Blk	Pts	Ppg
81	133	290	.459	52	60	.867	21	123	264	70	83	6	319	3.9

Three-point goals: 1–22 (.045)   TSP: .460

SCORING

It was a rough year for Spud Webb. The Spudster got off to a horrible start—after making five of six in the season opener, he proceeded to make a total of two baskets in the next six games. He spent most of the year shooting in the high 30s and low 40s (.424 after 58 games) but managed to finish at .459 (he's a career .469) on a late-season spurt. But his 3.9 ppg was a career low. We're seeing a different Webb these days, a former Slam Dunk champion who doesn't dunk in games and, until he developed a fadeaway on the drive, had trouble finishing the play. He's made himself into a fairly decent outside shooter, but he has limited range (1 of 22! from three-point land). But he did have his best year from the line (.867); for his career, he's .797.

DEFENSE/DEFENSIVE REBOUNDING

As with all mighty mites, Webb's D is a double-edged sword. On the one hand, he is vulnerable to posting up and has trouble harassing the shooter and passer. On the other hand, he can get in your jock, harass you full court, and make the ball handler turn his back (his steals, per minute, were slightly above-average for backup 1s). And he's always been (yes, he's 5-7) an above-the-norm defensive rebounder.

THE FLOOR GAME

Nobody accelerates with the ball better than the Spudman. His essence is up-tempoing the attack. He's a superb passer in transition and also does a decent job of getting the ball to the open man in half-court. But he's vulnerable to traps and presses because he has trouble seeing around people. His 1988–89 assist-to-turnover ratio was a superb 3.42.

INTANGIBLES

Webb is one tough hombre. He works hard at his game, and his teammates and the Atlanta citizenry love him. But, as one observer said, a little of the "sparkle" has gone out of his game. And he feels he should be playing 30 minutes a night rather than the 15 a game he logged last year.

IN SUM

Webb's strength is igniting the Hawks' break. But when he's not hitting the shot or even dunking on people, his value is reduced—and that was the case last year. With the drafting of Haywoode Workman, a 1, the Hawks acknowledged the fact their backup point position is up for grabs.

RICK'S RATINGS

Scoring: **D**
Shooting: **C**
Free Throw Shooting: **AA**
Ball Handling: **A**
Passing: **A**
Defense: **C**
Defensive Rebounding: **AA**
Playmaking: **A**
Intangibles: **B**
Overall: **B–**

Christian Welp

Birthdate: January 2, 1964
Height: 7-0
Weight: 245
College: University of Washington, Seattle, Wash.
Drafted: Philadelphia on first round, 1987 (16th pick).
Position: Center
Final 1989 Team: Philadelphia 76ers
Final 1988–89 Statistics:

G	Fg	Fga	Fg%	Ft	Fta	Ft%	Orb	Reb	Ast	Stl	To	Blk	Pts	Ppg
72	99	222	.446	48	73	.658	59	193	29	23	42	41	246	3.4

Three-point goals: 0–1 (.000)   TSP: .446

SCORING

Welp, a 7-0 backup center, is not simply a space eater. He has a nice little repertoire of shots: a good touch from 16 feet, a step-back jumper, a baby hook, and he even can go to the basket (after ball-faking his man). But he's been gun-shy, averaging only 3.1 shots in 11.7 minutes a game (which didn't accomplish much: 4.2 ppg on .446 shooting). Welp, who was acquired by the Spurs in August, needs to look for his shot more to open up his drive. He never was much of a jumper and coming off basketball's worst knee injury (he missed most of the 1987–88 season with a ruptured anterior cruciate ligament) hasn't helped matters. So, don't expect much from him on the offensive glass. He continues to feel most comfortable playing the high post, his college days' territory.

DEFENSE/DEFENSIVE REBOUNDING

Welp will never block a tremendous number of shots, but with his intelligence, defensive knowledge, and positioning, he's an adequate defender. While quicker centers give him trouble, he holds his own against the "seconds" around the league. He diligently blocks his man out, has a good pair of hands, and his defensive rebounding numbers were close to the norm for backup centers.

THE FLOOR GAME

Despite the knee injury, Welp runs the floor fairly well. He sees the court and does a good job of making the entry pass from the high post. He doesn't commit a lot of turnovers.

INTANGIBLES

Since he only played 10 games in 1987–88, last season was effectively Welp's rookie year and he played like it. He hasn't fully grasped what it takes to be a quality NBA player. He needs to be more "selfish" on the offensive end.

IN SUM

Until he plays significant minutes, it's hard to tell if Welp is a frontline center, a quality backup, or just another big body. On paper, he figures to be David Robinson's backup.

RICK'S RATINGS

Scoring: **D**
Shooting: **D**
Free Throw Shooting: **D**
Ball Handling: **B**
Passing: **B**

Defense: **B**
Defensive Rebounding: **B**
Playmaking: **B**
Intangibles: **B**
Overall: **C +**

Bill Wennington

Birthdate: December 26, 1964
Height: 7-0
Weight: 245
College: St. John's University, Jamaica, N.Y.
Drafted: Dallas on first round, 1985 (16th pick).
Positions: Center, Forward
Final 1989 Team: Dallas Mavericks
Final 1988–89 Statistics:

G	Fg	Fga	Fg%	Ft	Fta	Ft%	Orb	Reb	Ast	Stl	To	Blk	Pts	Ppg
65	119	275	.433	61	82	.744	82	286	46	16	54	35	300	4.6

Three-point goals: 1–9 (.111)   TSP: .435

SCORING

Wennington is not a productive scorer, never has been. On a per minute basis, he finished in the bottom third among backup centers; even in college he never averaged more than 12.5 a game. But then Dallas doesn't look to the four-year veteran for scoring punch. Wennington can drain the face-up jumper from about 15 feet and has a turnaround from the corners. But he has no low-post game to speak of (though he is working on it), nor can he drive to the basket. An exceptionally active player, Wennington does run the court well, gets points in transition, and also can score on the offensive glass.

DEFENSE/DEFENSIVE REBOUNDING

Wennington is an average defender, but like most big men,

he has trouble guarding players away from the basket. With his quickness, he's an excellent shot blocker from the weak side but his over-exuberance often gets him into foul trouble. While he's a good leaper, he needs what amounts to a running start to get up, which hurts him on the defensive glass. Plus, he's not strong and can be pushed out of position.

THE FLOOR GAME

Wennington can play both power forward and center. An adequate passer with decent hands, he sometimes tries to do too much, which results in unnecessary turnovers. He moves well without the ball.

INTANGIBLES

Despite his dearth of playing time (11.1 minutes a game for his career), Wennington's been a positive force on the Mavs with his team spirit, even though he's given up the towel waving. With the opportunity to play, he's currently working harder on his game than he did in the past.

IN SUM

After a career-low 125 minutes in 1987–88, Wennington got his chance last year. With Tarpley out of the lineup for most of the year (knee, rehab center), Wennington was no longer an insurance policy but a key member of the rotation. He's a competent backup but he needs to get stronger and add a few low-post moves to his currently limited supply.

RICK'S RATINGS

Scoring: **C**
Shooting: **D**
Free Throw Shooting: **C**
Ball Handling: **B**
Passing: **B**

Defense: **B**
Defensive Rebounding: **B**
Shot Blocking: **B**
Intangibles: **A**
Overall: **B –**

Mark West

Birthdate: November 5, 1960
Height: 6-10
Weight: 230
College: Old Dominion University, Norfolk, Va.
Drafted: Dallas on second round, 1983 (30th pick).

Position: Forward
Final 1989 Team: Phoenix Suns
Final 1988–89 Statistics:

G	Fg	Fga	Fg%	Ft	Fta	Ft%	Orb	Reb	Ast	Stl	To	Blk	Pts	Ppg
82	243	372	.653	108	202	.535	167	551	39	35	103	187	594	7.2

Three-point goals: 0–0 (.000)   **TSP:** .653

SCORING

Despite his gaudy shooting percentage, .653 (which would have led the league had he had enough attempts), West plays a minor role (4.5 shots a game and 7.2 ppg) in Phoenix's offensive scheme. His role is to defend and block shots; whatever points he gets are gravy. Because his scoring comes close to the basket—short hooks with either hand, putbacks (he's an average offensive rebounder), and dunks off guard penetration—he's consistently been a high percentage shooter (.565 career). The same cannot be said for his foul shooting, an abominable .535 last year and .540 lifetime—he's never been above 60 percent. The less seen of West's jumper, the better.

DEFENSE/DEFENSIVE REBOUNDING

West, who led all Division I players in blocked shots in 1981 and 1982, has continued his swatting ways as a pro. He was eighth in the league last year (2.3 a game), relying on quickness, anticipation, and a keen understanding of when to help (most of his blocks are from the weak side). As a one-on-one defender, he's physical and can't be intimidated. He's an OK defensive rebounder—leading the Suns on a per minute basis—though only average in the league for the position. His one weakness defensively has been his penchant for silly fouls—which is why he's frequently used as a sub (he started just 32 games last season).

THE FLOOR GAME

West is an uncertain ball handler, averaging a scant 0.5 assists a game (in 24.6 minutes per) with a terrible 0.38 assist-to-turnover ratio. He gets called for traveling a lot and has particular trouble when he puts the ball on the floor in traffic (though his turnovers, per minute, were below the norm).

INTANGIBLES

West's absence of scoring ego is a plus (and a necessity!) on a team that features such scorers as Eddie Johnson, Kevin Johnson, and Tom Chambers. He accepts his role and works hard it at. He'll play hurt, has improved each year he's been in the league, and is a quality citizen off the court as well.

IN SUM

West is Phoenix's pillar of strength and anchors the Suns defense. He's an ideal role player, one of Phoenix's solid supporting cast that includes Jeff Hornacek, Dan Majerle, and T.R. Dunn.

RICK'S RATINGS

Scoring: **D**
Shooting: **C**
Free Throw Shooting: **D**
Ball Handling: **D**
Passing: **D**

Defense: **A**
Defensive Rebounding: **B**
Shot Blocking: **AAA**
Intangibles: **A**
Overall: **B**

Clinton Wheeler

Birthdate: October 27, 1959
Height: 6-1
Weight: 185
College: William Paterson College, Wayne, N.J.
Drafted: Kansas City on seventh round, 1981 (150th pick).
Position: Guard
Final 1989 Team: Portland Trail Blazers
Final 1988–89 Statistics:

G	Fg	Fga	Fg%	Ft	Fta	Ft%	Orb	Reb	Ast	Stl	To	Blk	Pts	Ppg
28	45	87	.517	15	20	.750	17	31	54	27	24	0	105	3.8

Three-point goals: 0–1 (.000)   **TSP:** .517

SCORING

What are we to conclude from the fact that Wheeler, a CBA journeyman point guard who made two NBA stops last year (Miami and then Portland; in 1987–88, he played 59 games with Indiana), hit .517 of his shots last season, tops among backup 1s? That he's a *great* shooter? A *good* shooter? Can't shoot at all? Since he played only 28 games and shot the ball 87 times, we might hesitate to offer any conclusions. But we know this: his shooting is not so proficient as to keep him in the NBA. He has scored and shot well in the CBA, where he played for four seasons, but Portland sources weren't impressed by his firepower, and it's unlikely he'll be with the Blazers this year. He did can the open 18-footer last season but he wasn't adept at finishing the play.

DEFENSE/DEFENSIVE PLAYER

But Wheeler, who thrice has been named to the CBA All-Defensive first team, clearly has NBA-level defensive skills. He's small (6-1), but he's strong, has quick hands (1 steal a game in just 12.3 minutes), and will go nose-to-nose with his man, full court. Nothing special on the defensive glass.

THE FLOOR GAME

While he does a decent job of pushing the ball in transition and making good decisions on the break, in half court, he's an adequate penetrator, at best. Lacks explosiveness.

INTANGIBLES

Wheeler is an intelligent player with an unimpeachable work ethic.

IN SUM

Nobody's knocking down doors for this 30-year-old veteran. A roster filler.

RICK'S RATINGS

Scoring: **D**
Shooting: **B**
Free Throw Shooting: **B**
Ball Handling: **C**
Passing: **C**

Defense: **A**
Defensive Rebounding: **D**
Playmaking: **C**
Intangibles: **B**
Overall: **C −**

Eric White

Birthdate: December 30, 1965
Height: 6-7
Weight: 200
College: Pepperdine University, Malibu, Calif.
Drafted: Detroit on third round, 1987 (65th pick).
Position: Forward
Final 1989 Team: Los Angeles Clippers
Final 1988–89 Statistics:

G	Fg	Fga	Fg%	Ft	Fta	Ft%	Orb	Reb	Ast	Stl	To	Blk	Pts	Ppg
38	62	120	.517	34	42	.810	34	70	17	10	26	1	158	4.2

Three-point goals: 0–0 (.000)   TSP: .517

SCORING

White's resume reads: shooter. A small forward, the 6-7 Pepperdine graduate has shuttled between the CBA and the Clippers during the last two seasons and was selected by Minnesota in the expansion draft. He put up some nice numbers in the big leagues in limited minutes. In his first stint, in 1987–88, he averaged 10.1 ppg in 17 games. Last year, he played fewer minutes per game and scored less (4.2 ppg) but in both years he's hit more than 50 percent of his shots (.532 and .517, respectively). Not real quick, White needs time to get his jumper off, but with his long wing span he can shoot the jumper over his defender from 15 feet. Two other assets: he runs the floor well and finesses his way in for offensive boards.

DEFENSE/DEFENSIVE REBOUNDING

Not surprisingly, White's resume doesn't mention defense or rebounding. He's a way below-average defensive rebounder—the weight program he was on this past summer should help—and doesn't do a good job containing quicker 3s on the perimeter.

THE FLOOR GAME

An average passer, you don't want White putting the ball on the floor for any length of time. Nor does he create well off the dribble.

INTANGIBLES

Nice kid, coachable, but one CBA source said he needs

toughening, needs to adopt a more hard-nosed attitude. He also needs to improve his overall consistency on both ends of the floor.

IN SUM

A finesse player who can shoot the ball, White has to make big strides on D and the boards. Now that he's showed he can play in the league, he ought to be working harder to solidify his position on a team. We'll see if he's any better than a marginal player with longer stretches of minutes, which he will only come by if he plays better defense for coach Bill Musselman.

RICK'S RATINGS

Scoring: **C**
Shooting: **A**
Free Throw Shooting: **A**
Ball Handling: **C**
Passing: **B**

Defense: **C**
Defensive Rebounding: **D**
Intangibles: **B**
Overall: **C −**

Jerome Whitehead

Birthdate: September 30, 1956
Height: 6-10
Weight: 225
College: Marquette University, Milwaukee, Wis.
Drafted: Buffalo on second round, 1978 (41st pick).
Position: Center
Final 1989 Team: San Antonio Spurs
Final 1988–89 Statistics:

G	Fg	Fga	Fg%	Ft	Fta	Ft%	Orb	Reb	Ast	Stl	To	Blk	Pts	Ppg
57	72	182	.396	31	47	.660	49	134	19	23	24	4	175	3.1

Three-point goals: 0–0 (.000)   TSP: .396

SCORING

The peripatetic Whitehead (San Diego, Utah, Dallas, Cleveland, back to San Diego, Golden State, and last year San Antonio) has fashioned an 11-year career with modest offensive talents. Acquired from Golden State for Shelton Jones at the beginning of the 1988–89 season (when Mike Smrek and Peter Gudmundsson went down with injuries), Whitehead has been a backup center virtually everywhere (except for Golden State and San Diego) and, as expected, has a limited repertoire. He relies on a left-handed hook (he's right-handed) and will bang the offensive boards. He is not comfortable facing the basket.

DEFENSE/DEFENSIVE REBOUNDING

Whitehead's longevity rests on his willingness to bang bodies, to play physical defense. His strong legs enable him to prevent players from camping in the blocks. He jumps fairly well but he is not what you'd call a shot blocker, though he does get the job done on the defensive glass.

THE FLOOR GAME

Whitehead is another one of these centers who never

accumulates many assists because he's not involved in the offense. Never a speedster, he's now downright slow.

INTANGIBLES

Whitehead is a quiet, go-about-his-business type. You don't last as long as he has making waves. The downside is that his knees hurt and he can't practice all the time.

IN SUM

A journeyman center who bangs and rebounds, Whitehead may have made his last stop.

RICK'S RATINGS

Scoring: **D**
Shooting: **D**
Free Throw Shooting: **D**
Ball Handling: **C**
Passing: **C**

Defense: **B**
Defensive Rebounding: **D**
Shot Blocking: **D**
Intangibles: **B**
Overall: **C**

Morlon Wiley

Birthdate: September 24, 1966
Height: 6-4
Weight: 185
College: California State University at Long Beach, Long Beach, Calif.
Drafted: Dallas on second round, 1988 (46th pick).
Position: Guard
Final 1989 Team: Dallas Mavericks
Final 1988–89 Statistics:

G	Fg	Fga	Fg%	Ft	Fta	Ft%	Orb	Reb	Ast	Stl	To	Blk	Pts	Ppg
51	46	114	.404	13	16	.813	13	47	76	25	34	6	111	2.2

Three-point goals: 6–24 (.250)   **TSP:** .430

SCORING

Wiley, a Dallas Maverick last season, had a typical rookie, typical backup-1 (who collectively shot about 44 percent in 1988–89) shooting year, making a measly .404. But then again he only averaged eight minutes a game (and less than three shots), so it's difficult to gauge whether he's an NBA-caliber marksman. We should get a better fix on his shooting ability now that he's a member of the expansion Magic, since he'll likely get some quality time. But at Long Beach State, he played both guard positions and showed, at least in his senior year (51 percent), that he can shoot the ball. Wiley has three-point range (though he made just 6 of 24 trifectas for 25 percent last year) but is particularly adept at getting into the paint and shooting the 8-foot jumper over the big guys. He needs to work on getting to the rim.

DEFENSE/DEFENSIVE REBOUNDING

Unlike many rookies, Wiley came into the pros as a fairly accomplished defender. He possesses many of the same assets as former teammate Derek Harper: good hands, long arms, quickness, and above-average anticipation. But he needs to reduce his gambling, to play better position defense, and also to show he can apply pressure for long stretches.

THE FLOOR GAME

While he can swing to the 2, Wiley is being penciled in as a point guard. He sees the floor, makes good decisions on the break, and is a creative passer. But his leadership ability is still untested and he needs, more than anything, a heavy dose of major minutes.

INTANGIBLES

From day one, Wiley has demonstrated that he belongs—despite the fact that he was the 46th player picked in the draft and a definite long shot to make the Mavericks. He is a quick learner and has exemplary practice habits.

IN SUM

In the future, Morlon Wiley will be the answer to a great trivia question: What rookie guard beat out Steve Alford for the fourth guard spot on the 1988–89 Mavericks? With improvements in his shooting and defense and some much needed experience, he also figures be an integral member of Orlando's rotation.

RICK'S RATINGS

Scoring: **D**
Shooting: **C**
Free Throw Shooting: **A**
Ball Handling: **A**
Passing: **AA**
Defense: **B**

Defensive Rebounding:
  AA
Playmaking: **B**
Intangibles: **A**
Overall: **B –**

Dominique Wilkins

Birthdate: January 12, 1960
Height: 6-8
Weight: 200
College: University of Georgia, Athens, Ga.
Drafted: Utah on first round as an undergraduate, 1982 (3rd pick).

Position: Forward
Final 1989 Team: Atlanta Hawks
Final 1988–89 Statistics:

G	Fg	Fga	Fg%	Ft	Fta	Ft%	Orb	Reb	Ast	Stl	To	Blk	Pts	Ppg
80	814	1756	.464	442	524	.844	256	553	211	117	181	52	2099	26.2

Three-point goals: 29–105 (.276)   **TSP:** .472

SCORING

Since Wilkins scores every which way, let's review the checklist:

—How good is his jump shot? A look at the numbers reveals he shot .464 in 1988–89 (.448 during the playoff loss to the Bucks) and he's a career .467 shooter. In other words, Wilkins is not a pure shooter; but he's undeniably a potent scorer (he led the league in scoring in 1985–86 with 30.3 a game and his 26 a game is seventh among current NBA players). Nobody's giving Dominique so much as an inch to shoot, because he's liable to hit—he loves to use the backboard—6, 7, 8 in a row. He is, at all times, dangerous from the perimeter. But he's a streak shooter.

—Can he create off the dribble? As well as anybody in the league. Atlanta will isolate Wilkins on the left side, where he takes a hard dribble and rises for the jumper, or spins and takes it to the hole for a Human Highlight Film finish. (If he had a left hand, he'd be even more dangerous.)

—Does he have three-point range? Yes, though he's never shot well from that distance (.276 in 1988–89, .269 career). If he's going to beat you, then let him do it from three-point country.

—How about his offensive rebounding? One of the best for his position—3.2 a game—many of them coming from following his own missed shots.

—Can he finish on the break? Besides James Worthy and Karl Malone, who's better?

—Does he take bad shots? Yes.

—Too many shots? Yes. Atlanta would be a better team with more offensive balance.

—Is he a good foul shooter? Yes, and he's shown steady progress: from .682 in his rookie year (1982–83) to .844 last year.

—Is he a clutch shooter? See Boston vs. Atlanta, seventh game, 1987–88 playoff series, Boston Garden.

DEFENSE/DEFENSIVE REBOUNDING

When you shoot 22 times a night, who has the energy to play D? If Wilkins needs a breather, he takes it on the defensive end. He'll get after guys, but the effort is not consistent, and he tends to get lost on picks. With his jumping ability, he's a decent defensive rebounder, but he's better utilized filling the lanes than pounding the glass (6.9 total rebounds a game).

THE FLOOR GAME

Wilkins has improved his ball handling and passing in the last couple of seasons—for example, he more readily passes out of the double-team—but he still holds the ball too long, too frequently. He averaged only 2.6 assists a game, a small

number (and below average for starting 3s), considering the number of times he handles the ball. The rap is that he doesn't make his teammates better, which is true; but then again the Hawks would be a mediocre team (and certainly wouldn't have won at least 50 games four years in a row) without him.

INTANGIBLES

A sampling of opinions: "Indefatigible." "Never takes a night off." "Extraordinary competitor." "Nicest superstar in the league." "You can jump on his shoulders, and he will carry you." "A warrior."

IN SUM

Dominique has an NBA scoring title, has made the All-NBA first team (and second team, twice), and been selected to the All-Star team four times. What's missing, of course, is a ring. For that to happen, Wilkins, *for his part,* will have to: tone down his game—i.e., learn to take better shots; become a more adept passer out of the double-team; be more consistent on the defensive end.

RICK'S RATINGS

Scoring: **AAA**
Shooting: **B**
Free Throw Shooting: **AA**
Ball Handling: **B**
Passing: **B**

Defense: **C**
Defensive Rebounding: **C**
Intangibles: **AAA**
Overall: **AA +**

Eddie Lee Wilkins

Birthdate: May 7, 1962
Height: 6-10
Weight: 220
College: Gardner-Webb College, Boiling Springs, N.C.
Drafted: New York on sixth round, 1984 (133rd pick).
Position: Center
Final 1989 Team: New York Knicks
Final 1988–89 Statistics:

G	Fg	Fga	Fg%	Ft	Fta	Ft%	Orb	Reb	Ast	Stl	To	Blk	Pts	Ppg
71	114	245	.465	61	111	.550	72	148	7	10	56	16	289	4.1

Three-point goals: 0–1 (.000)   **TSP:** .465

SCORING

Few question Wilkins' ability to score. He did it in the CBA in 1987–88 (22.8 ppg), in the Princeton Summer League in the summer of 1988 (26.4 ppg), and in limited minutes with the Knicks in 1988–89 (4.1 ppg in 8.2 mpg; third, per minute, among backup 5s). He's primarily a back-to-the-basket player with a nice jump hook, and a decent turn-around jumper from the baseline and the blocks. He was also a way above-average offensive rebounder last year. Wilkins has a scorer's mentality: catch and shoot, catch and shoot, but at least he takes good shots.

DEFENSE/DEFENSIVE REBOUNDING

Wilkins lacks what you might call "defensive presence." He's not a shot blocker, he can't keep up with the quicker centers, and, while he reacts well in spurts, he doesn't maintain it. He rebounded well in the CBA (9.1), but he hasn't shown the same prowess on the defensive boards with the Knicks.

THE FLOOR GAME

Wilkins can run the court but stamina remains an all too real issue. His ball handling is below average, and he's a well, a bottomless pit, a black hole . . . seven assists in 584 minutes.

INTANGIBLES

To a large extent, Wilkins is in the league on sheer guts and determination. After one year with the Knicks (1984–85 season), he blew out his knee in the summer of 1985. As a bit player, his chances of making it back to the NBA were slim and none. He sat out a year, went through an arduous rehabilitation, played in Europe, played in the CBA, played for the Knicks, was sent back to the CBA, and finally, started and finished the 1988–89 season with New York. Yes, he is a hard worker.

IN SUM

"And now, starting at center, for the Knicks, Eddie Lee Wilkins." Fortunately, Knicks fans were, except on two occasions, spared those words last season as Patrick Ewing stayed healthy for the second straight season. In fact, when Kiki Vandeweghe was acquired, Sidney Green moved over to the backup 5, squeezing Eddie Lee's minutes. Wilkins tries, but he's strictly a scorer—and a limited one at that. However, with Green an expansion casualty (Orlando), he now becomes a member of the rotation as Ewing's backup. Considering that big-time backup centers have recently been an essential element of the championship equation, the Knicks enter the fray lacking a key component of the formula.

RICK'S RATINGS

Scoring: **A**   Defense: **C**
Shooting: **C**   Defensive Rebounding: **D**
Free Throw Shooting: **D**   Shot Blocking: **C**
Ball Handling: **C**   Intangibles: **B**
Passing: **D**   Overall: **C**

Gerald Wilkins

Birthdate: September 11, 1963
Height: 6-6
Weight: 190
College: University of Tennessee-Chattanooga, Chattanooga, Tenn.
Drafted: New York on second round, 1985 (47th pick).
Positions: Guard, Forward
Final 1989 Team: New York Knicks
Final 1988–89 Statistics:

G	Fg	Fga	Fg%	Ft	Fta	Ft%	Orb	Reb	Ast	Stl	To	Blk	Pts	Ppg
81	462	1025	.451	186	246	.756	95	244	274	115	169	22	1161	14.3

Three-point goals: 51–172 (.297)   **TSP:** .476

SCORING

It's got to be in the genes. Like his older brother, the high-flying Dominique of the Hawks, Gerald Wilkins has exceptional quickness and leaping ability, and a smorgasbord of ways to score. Gerald's repertoire, to give only a sampling, includes mid-range jumpers off the dribble, three-point bombs (.297 last year), baseline drives on the left side, floating leaners in the lane (after his patented crossover dribble, from right to left), and much more. With his quickness and great first step, Wilkins gets to the basket and gets there in a hurry; once there, he will dunk on you all night—with either hand. His "rising" finishes are something to behold. He's the Knicks' best one-on-one player in the half-court offense. But Wilkins is most effective in the transition game, where he can use his devastating speed and quickness to its best advantage. The knock on Gerald, who was in, out, and then back in the starting lineup again (58 starts), has been twofold: He doesn't shoot the jumper consistently and he occasionally plays out of control. Indeed his numbers indicate he's more a scorer than a pure shooter. He shot .451 in 1988–89, which was right around his career mark of .463. He averaged 14.3 ppg in 1988–89 but has the ability to explode for 30 on a given night. His foul shooting has improved dramatically from .557 as a rookie to .756 in 1988–89.

DEFENSE/DEFENSIVE REBOUNDING

Wilkins has what it takes—speed, strength, mobility—to be a good defensive player, but he's not there yet. For example, he must become more active on the weak side. and he's a way below-average defensive rebounder for his position, which reflects his tendency to leak out when the ball is shot. On the other hand, his steals (1.4 a game, his best year yet), indicate he's starting to put his quickness to better use on D.

THE FLOOR GAME

Since his rookie year (1985–86), Wilkins has made major strides in his overall court awareness. In 1988–89, he had a healthy 3.4 assists a game, and he can penetrate and dish. He has also improved his passing to the post. On the break, he has a tendency to give the ball up at the wrong time (but, more often than not, he *will* give it up). Wilkins can run all day and works hand-in-glove with Jackson in the half-court offense.

INTANGIBLES

Wilkins is a fierce competitor. One of he Knicks' hardest workers, his game has improved considerably in four years. Once strictly a scorer, he now better understands the team concept. He is not afraid to take the big shot and his shooting was crucial in several Knicks' victories last year. He's a fun guy to have around and keeps his teammates loose.

IN SUM

New York is a tough nut to crack, and the expectations have ben high for this four-year pro. Considering he was the 47th player (2nd round) picked in the 1985 draft, he's done quite well. But he needs consistency in his outside shooting and more assertiveness, both defensively and on the boards, to move up a notch. He was extremely productive off the bench and may in fact be better suited for the sixth man role.

RICK'S RATINGS

Scoring: **A**	Defense: **B**
Shooting: **C**	Defensive Rebounding: **D**
Free Throw Shooting: **B**	Intangibles: **B**
Ball Handling: **B**	Overall: **B**
Passing: **B**	

———— Buck Williams ————

Birthdate: March 8, 1960
Height: 6-8

Weight: 235
College: University of Maryland, College Park, Md.
Drafted: New Jersey on first round as an undergraduate, 1981 (3rd pick).
Position: Forward
Final 1989 Team: New Jersey Nets
Final 1988–89 Statistics:

G	Fg	Fga	Fg%	Ft	Fta	Ft%	Orb	Reb	Ast	Stl	To	Blk	Pts	Ppg
74	373	702	.531	213	320	.666	249	696	78	61	142	36	959	13.0

Three-point goals: 0–3 (.000)   **TSP:** .531

SCORING

Williams is a long-standing member of the NBA's all-lunch-pail team. The eight-year veteran, who was traded to the Trail Blazers in June, brings his hard hat every night and goes to work: scoring on putbacks (he's consistently been one of top offensive rebounders in the league, 3.4 a game in 1988–89), running the fast break (he gets up and down the court well for a muscular 6-8, 235 power forward), powering his way into the lane for close-in hoops. He also possesses a nice hook (either hand) and has recently added a face-up jumper, which he can hit from 10 to 12 feet. But Williams, whose career average is 16.4 ppg (he's never gone under .523 from the field and has been as high as .582), has never had a big scoring ego. And with the emergence of scorers such as Dennis Hopson and Chris Morris, and the addition of Joe Barry Carroll, Williams last year had his lowest point production as a pro, 13 ppg, which reflected his fewer attempts from the field (a career-low 702; he had never shot less than 832 previously) and his reduced minutes (33.1 a game, also a lifetime low). He has diligently worked on his foul shooing—to no avail (.666 last year; .649 career).

DEFENSE/DEFENSIVE REBOUNDING

Williams' name has always been synonymous with rebounding. Until last year, he had never been lower than fifth in the league in rebounding and only once had averaged less than 12 rebounds a game (11.9). But in 1988–89, he suffered through a series of nagging injuries and his production sagged considerably as he finished with *only* 9.4 boards a game (13th in the league). His assets: quickness, relentlessness, strength, going for rebounds with both hands, and a focus that says, "I will get every rebound." He's also a premier defender. He'll bang his man for position, knows the league, and even has the quickness to guard 3s. Early in his career, Williams was an effective shot blocker (more than 100 blocks a season from 1983 to 1985), but last year he swatted away a career-low 36 shots.

THE FLOOR GAME

This is undoubtedly the weakest part of Williams's game. He is not a good passer (just over one assist a game last year), has bad hands in transition (but, curiously, not when rebounding the ball in traffic), and is turnover-prone, though many come on "energy" plays such as charges or going over the top on offensive rebounds.

INTANGIBLES

Williams is also a lifetime member of the all-solid-citizen team. He's consistent, incredibly hard-working, and tough. Every team should be blessed with a Buck Williams. Remarkably durable for most of his career (no missed games due to injury for the first six and a half years) he has missed 20 games in the last two years as a result of injury.

IN SUM

For what he does, defense and rebounding, Williams is as good as they come. At 29, he may be wearing down a bit, but the Trail Blazers are set at power forward for the next several years. If anybody deserves to play for a contender, it's Buck Williams.

RICK'S RATINGS

Scoring: **B**
Shooting: **B**
Free Throw Shooting: **D**
Ball Handling: **C**
Passing: **C**

Defense: **AAA**
Defensive Rebounding: **A**
Shot Blocking: **D**
Intangibles: **AAA**
Overall: **A**

Herb Williams

Birthdate: February 16, 1958
Height: 6-11
Weight: 242
College: Ohio State University, Columbus, O.
Drafted: Indiana on first round, 1981 (14th pick).
Positions: Forward, Center
Final 1989 Team: Dallas Mavericks
Final 1988–89 Statistics:

G	Fg	Fga	Fg%	Ft	Fta	Ft%	Orb	Reb	Ast	Stl	To	Blk	Pts	Ppg
76	322	739	.436	133	194	.686	135	593	124	46	149	134	777	10.2

Three-point goals: 0–5 (.000)   **TSP:** .436

SCORING

Williams, who was traded to Dallas for Detlef Schrempf in February 1989, has not shot the ball well over the last couple of years. Coming off a 1987–1988 when he shot a career-low .425 (he had never previously been below .475), the 31-year-old veteran was in the same zone last year with .436 (including a mere .396 in his stint with Dallas) and was

wildly inconsistent, juxtaposing 9–14 nights with 1–7 disappearing acts. His base is either block, where he'll shoot the turnaround jumper (he uses the glass a lot) or an occasional hook with the right hand. He also has a facing jumper, but his range—please, Herbie, no more than 15 feet—is limited. He needs to expand his low-post moves. Williams can score on the offensive glass (1.8 caroms a game) but vis-à-vis starting 4s, his numbers are poor.

DEFENSE/DEFENSIVE REBOUNDING

Williams has consistently been a prime-time shot blocker, averaging almost two a game for his career and he finished 11th in the league last year with 1.8 a game. He not only blocks shots but, with his long arms (he's 6-11), changes directions on countless others. He is one of the best weak side defenders in the league and will help out, even though his man scores layup after layup (some players are reluctant to rotate because their man gets the deuce). He gives you flexibility defensively because he can also play center but: (a) he doesn't like to and (b) he is overmatched physically at the position. While on the skinny side, he doesn't mind contact and is a solid defensive rebounder, above average for starting power forwards.

THE FLOOR GAME

Williams, as one wag put it, "has a body of stone, including his hands." Nor does he handle or pass well. Enough said.

INTANGIBLES

Williams is an intelligent veteran, but the feeling in Indiana was that he was a disruptive force in the locker room. Some question his commitment to basketball and feel he has a low tolerance for pain.

IN SUM

Williams started 20 games for Dallas at center, but his role in the Mavs' future will be as a backup 4, and in a pinch, a 5. With his shot blocking ability, he can cover up a team's weaknesses defensively, but his scoring and intensity remain question marks.

RICK'S RATINGS

Scoring: **C**
Shooting: **D**
Free Throw Shooting: **D**
Ball Handling: **C**
Passing: **C**

Defense: **AA**
Defensive Rebounding: **A**
Shot Blocking: **AAA**
Intangibles: **C**
Overall: **B**

John "Hot Rod" Williams

Birthdate: August 9, 1961
Height: 6-10
Weight: 230
College: Tulane University, New Orleans, La.
Drafted: Cleveland on second round, 1985 (45th pick).
Position: Forward
Final 1989 Team: Cleveland Cavaliers
Final 1988–89 Statistics:

G	Fg	Fga	Fg%	Ft	Fta	Ft%	Orb	Reb	Ast	Stl	To	Blk	Pts	Ppg
82	356	700	.509	235	314	.748	173	477	108	77	102	134	948	11.6

Three-point goals: 1–4 (.250)   **TSP:** .509

SCORING

For a player his size, Hot Rod, a 6-10, 230 pound power forward/small forward, has as good a move to the basket as anybody in the league. From the right baseline (he doesn't go left well), he explodes to the basket with a quick first step and slams it home. He sets up the drive with a ball fake and the threat of the 10 to 12 footer, which he can knock down consistently (.509 from the floor in 1988–89). The remainder of his points come on the break—he runs extremely well—and the offensive glass, where his 2.1 offensive boards a game were above average for backup 3s. Offensively, Williams's major assets are his quickness and mobility, particularly since he's often matched up against slower, less-mobile 4s.

DEFENSE/DEFENSIVE REBOUNDING

Combine those aforementioned assets with his long arms and jumping ability and it adds up to a big-time shot blocker (1.6 a game, 12th in the league). Plus, Hot Rod makes it difficult for players to shoot over him. He's a hard-working defender who fights his man for position, though he gives away a bunch of pounds every night. His defensive rebounding numbers, per minute, are above average for a 3, below average for a 4, though a concern is that he grabbed 43 fewer in 1988–89 than the previous year in about the same number of minutes.

THE FLOOR GAME

Williams's ball handling skills are OK (a mere 1.3 assists per). As far as his knowledge of the game, he's still in the learning stage.

INTANGIBLES

Bothered by a foot injury, Williams had a disappointing year in 1987–88 and his numbers were down in minutes, rebounds, points, and blocked shots. By the time he was healthy, he had lost his starting job to Mike Sanders. But he made the most of the situation, finished the year respectably, and continued along that path in 1988–89. He accepted his sixth-man role graciously, but with Sanders signing with Indiana, he'll now be starting.

IN SUM

Williams's shot blocking, running ability, and scoring off the bench made him one of the league's most valuable sixth men. Major areas of improvement: defensive rebounding, ball handling. He'll thrive as a starter.

RICK'S RATINGS

Scoring: **B**	Defense: **AA**
Shooting: **B**	Defensive Rebounding: **B**
Free Throw Shooting: **C**	Shot Blocking: **AAA**
Ball Handling: **C**	Intangibles: **A**
Passing: **C**	Overall: **A**

John Williams

Birthdate: October 26, 1966
Height: 6-9
Weight: 235
College: Louisiana State University, Baton Rouge, La.
Drafted: Washington on first round as an undergraduate, 1986 (12th pick).
Position: Forward
Final 1989 Team: Washington Bullets
Final 1988–89 Statistics:

G	Fg	Fga	Fg%	Ft	Fta	Ft%	Orb	Reb	Ast	Stl	To	Blk	Pts	Ppg
82	438	940	.466	225	290	.776	158	573	356	142	157	70	1120	13.7

Three-point goals: 19–71 (.268)   **TSP:** .476

SCORING

At 6-9, 235, Williams has a 4's body, the moves and grace of a 3, and the mind-set of a 1. He's probably a natural small forward but has played all of the frontcourt positions, and even the point is not out of the question. Scoring-wise (he averaged

13.7) this translates to a post-up game, the ability to put the ball on the floor with either hand (he has a marvelous touch around the basket), and a somewhat reluctant attitude towards shooting: Like a playmaker, Williams looks for others before taking it himself. Despite his bulk, he also runs the floor well. Williams is adept at driving, faking his frustrated defenders with Adrian Dantley-like head fakes, and drawing the foul. But he tends to look for the drive because he lacks—and it's the only missing link in his repertoire—a consistent perimeter game (he's not a very good three-point shooter, .268 in 1988–89, .221 lifetime). He's picked up his foul shooting (.776) after .693 in his first two years.

DEFENSE/DEFENSIVE REBOUNDING

What a pair of hands! Williams was fourth among all forwards with 1.7 steals a game and has few peers for stripping the ball or slapping it away, often at critical moments. He also has quick feet, the muscle to body people, and he knows how to deny the ball. He also possesses the versatility to guard 3s, 4s, and 5s. He can block shots (70 last year) and he's consistently been an above-average defensive rebounder (7 total rebounds a game in 1988–89).

THE FLOOR GAME

Players with bodies like Williams's are invariably poor passers. That's what makes him so intriguing. It's not inconceivable—if he lost a few pounds—that Williams could play the point. He can make the play both in the open court and in the half-court. Simply put: Williams sees people and is willing to give it up. Excluding Larry Bird (who played only six games last year), Williams was tops among all forwards, per minute, for assists.

INTANGIBLES

Williams, a three-year veteran, came out of LSU after his sophomore year so last year would have been his rookie year. He's only 23, still maturing as a ballplayer, and beginning to assert his leadership. But he hasn't been driven to improve his jumper. And the feeling is that he could afford to lose 10 to 15 pounds.

IN SUM

Williams is the cornerstone of the Bullets' future, an all-around talent who led Washington in rebounding, was second in assists, blocks and steals, and third in scoring. If he can develop a consistent outside game, he's All-Star caliber. Otherwise, he's an above-average player in all categories except shooting. And the combination is greater than the sum of its parts.

RICK'S RATINGS

Scoring: **A**	Defense: **A**
Shooting: **A**	Defensive Rebounding:
Free Throw Shooting: **B**	**AAA**
Ball Handling: **AA**	Intangibles: **A**
Passing: **AAA**	Overall: **A**

Kevin Williams

Birthdate: September 11, 1961
Height: 6-2
Weight: 180
College: St. John's University, Jamaica, N.Y.
Drafted: San Antonio on second round, 1983 (46th pick).
Position: Guard
Final 1989 Team: Los Angeles Clippers
Final 1988–89 Statistics:

G	Fg	Fga	Fg%	Ft	Fta	Ft%	Orb	Reb	Ast	Stl	To	Blk	Pts	Ppg
50	81	200	.405	46	59	.780	28	70	53	30	52	11	209	4.2

Three-point goals: 1–6 (.167)   **TSP:** .408

SCORING

Despite putting up some awesome numbers—30.8 points a game in the CBA in 1985–86—Williams, who started the year with Nets and finished with the Clippers, has yet to show he can score in any meaningful way in the NBA. Of course, he hasn't played much, averaging only 11.3 minutes a game for his career. But he's been an inconsistent offensive player who has never shot over .446, bottoming out last year with .405. He's a jump shooter—with that distinctive jackknife style—who doesn't put the ball on the floor well and doesn't have a feel for a good shot.

DEFENSIVE/DEFENSIVE REBOUNDING

Williams has a rep for being a good defender; he is hard working, gets in your face, and hounds you. On the other hand, while the work ethic is there, he sometimes ends up chasing his man instead of keeping between him and the basket.

THE FLOOR GAME

Williams' handling skills (he's a 1/2) make coaches nervous. You never quite know what he is going to do with the ball.

INTANGIBLES

Five teams (San Antonio, Cleveland, Seattle, plus the Nets and Clippers) in five seasons and, more often than not, Williams has been an unhappy camper. In Miami, for example (Miami selected him in the 1988 expansion draft from Seattle), he claimed he didn't make the club because of racism. Perhaps his biggest problem is that he doesn't recognize he's a limited talent who is destined to be a marginal player. He is a superbly conditioned athlete.

IN SUM

Williams give you aggressive defense, but the rest of his game is suspect. He's hanging by a thread.

RICK'S RATINGS

Scoring: **C**	Free Throw Shooting: **B**
Shooting: **D**	Ball Handling: **C**

Passing: **B**
Defense: **B**
Defensive Rebounding: **B**

Playmaking: **D**
Intangibles: **C**
Overall: **C –**

Michael Williams

Birthdate: July 23, 1966
Height: 6-2
Weight: 175
College: Baylor University, Waco, Tex.
Drafted: Detroit on second round, 1988 (48th pick).
Position: Guard
Final 1989 Team: Detroit Pistons
Final 1988–89 Statistics:

G	Fg	Fga	Fg%	Ft	Fta	Ft%	Orb	Reb	Ast	Stl	To	Blk	Pts	Ppg
49	47	129	.364	31	47	.660	9	27	70	13	42	3	127	2.6

Three-point goals: 2–9 (.222)   **TSP:** .372

SCORING

Williams, the Pistons second-round draft pick in 1988, seemed to be a promising candidate: he tore up the Southern California Summer Pro League in 1988 and continued to impress in training camp. All of which earned the quick point guard some time on the pine; Williams was the fourth guard in the league's most impregnable rotation: Isiah Thomas, Joe Dumars, and Vinnie Johnson. He did manage some quality time when Dumars went down with a broken hand in January, but he was, in a word, erratic: from the field (.364), with the ball (a miserable 1.67 assist-to-turnover ratio), and on defense. When Dumars recovered, he resumed his sitting—he averaged just 7.3 minutes—and at the end of the season was traded to Phoenix, along with Kenny Battle, the Piston's No. 1 draft pick, in exchange for Anthony Cook. Let's give Williams the benefit of the doubt. He played just sparingly, and the feeling is he has some skills: he's dazzlingly quick, exceptionally fast, a good jumper and displayed his scoring ability in college, in the summer league, and in preseason. He has a medium-range jumper, though there is some question whether he can get it himself or is better as a spot-up shooter.

DEFENSE/DEFENSIVE REBOUNDING

What hurt Williams was his lack of concentration on defense. For example, he'd score and then forget all about playing D. His toughness has also been questioned. But his quickness and ability to pressure the ball remain in his favor.

THE FLOOR GAME

Some sources feel Williams is more of a scoring 2 than a pure point—which is precisely what Kevin Johnson is, the man he'll be backing up. Williams has said he's looking forward to playing in the Suns' open-court game, and indeed his speed and quickness may be best utilized in the running game. He is an excellent middleman on the break, though

he must break his habit of picking up the dribble too soon in the half-court offense. Another issue: Can he go left?

INTANGIBLES

Williams played like he belonged from the start. He doesn't lack for confidence.

IN SUM

Williams is penciled in as the backup to Kevin Johnson, who Phoenix would like to see play less minutes this year (he averaged 39.1 a game and clearly was tired during the playoffs). With steady minutes, Williams ought to be able to work out the kinks in his game, and we venture to say that eventually he'll be a vital part of the Suns' rotation.

RICK'S RATINGS

Scoring: **C**
Shooting: **C**
Free Throw Shooting: **D**
Ball Handling: **B**
Passing: **B**

Defense: **C**
Defensive Rebounding: **B**
Playmaking: **B**
Intangibles: **A**
Overall: **C +**

Reggie Williams

Birthdate: March 5, 1964
Height: 6-7
Weight: 190
College: Georgetown University, Washington, D.C.
Drafted: Los Angeles Clippers on first round, 1987 (4th pick).
Position: Guard
Final 1989 Team: Los Angeles Clippers
Final 1988–89 Statistics:

G	Fg	Fga	Fg%	Ft	Fta	Ft%	Orb	Reb	Ast	Stl	To	Blk	Pts	Ppg
63	260	594	.438	92	122	.754	70	179	103	81	114	29	642	10.2

Three-point goals: 30–104 (.288)   **TSP:** .463

SCORING

In L.A. they are still searching for explanations. Trying to understand the why and how of the disaster (so far) known as Reggie Williams. The fourth pick in the 1987 draft, Williams was as close as you can come to a sure thing. He could shoot, he could defend, and as a John Thompson/

Georgetown product, there were few doubts about his toughness. If not a franchise turner, Williams would certainly be an instant contributor, an impact player. But his rookie year was a nightmare. Plagued by injuries, he played in only 35 games, shot a horrendous and league-low .356, and for much of the year played out of position as a small forward. Last season, now a 2, he earned the starting off-guard position, but 11 games into the season lost it to Quintin Dailey. Of course, Williams didn't play that badly (he was shooting 45 percent through 11 games), but Dailey was playing exceptional ball. Still, Williams's game didn't exactly inspire confidence among the Clipper coaching staff. His problems, scoring-wise, have been manifold. One: he has trouble creating off the dribble—he's only a fair ball handler. Two: he doesn't get easy shots; Williams hasn't learned how to use screens to get open. Three: even when he's open, he hasn't knocked them down consistently. His performance varies not only game to game, but *within* a game—from period to period, a reflection of the fact that his confidence is shot. He does have good range—he shot .288 from three-point land and last year was the Clippers only threat from that distance—and has shown some ability to finish the play in transition. In fact, with the more up-tempo style favored by coach Don Casey (compared to Gene Shue's slow-down game) Williams's open court talents may finally be exploited. However, there's a serious question of whether Williams is a good shooter. Note: he shot only .482 as a senior at Georgetown. An adequate foul shooter at .754 in 1988–89.

DEFENSE/DEFENSIVE REBOUNDING

Williams has rarely shown the type of in-your-face defense he displayed at Georgetown. Where is that intensity? One explanation—he's been plagued by foul trouble, so he backs off. He's particularly pitiful getting around picks, and his lack of strength (he's on a weight program) is a disadvantage. He does have good hands (1.3 steals in 20.7 minutes), can block an occasional shot, and is a good leaper and defensive rebounder.

THE FLOOR GAME

As a rookie, Williams befuddled the Clippers with his lack of passing, his selfish play. Last year, he looked to make the play more, but his ball handling makes all involved a little nervous. He runs the floor well.

INTANGIBLES

Williams is both physically and mentally fragile. He needs to somehow regain his confidence. He's been a nine-to-five player; when practice is over, he's out the door.

IN SUM

Still too soon to write Williams off. Third-year players have a way of emerging. He hasn't consistently gotten substantial minutes. We suspect, however, that he's not the major league talent the Clippers thought they drafted.

Kevin Willis

Birthdate: September 6, 1962
Height: 7-0
Weight: 235
College: Michigan State University, East Lansing, Mich.
Drafted: Atlanta on first round, 1984 (11th pick).
Positions: Forward, Center
Final 1989 Team: Atlanta Hawks
Final 1988–89 Statistics: Did Not Play

SCORING

Which Kevin Willis will it be in 1989–90? Will it be the Willis who averaged 16.1 points a game and 10.5 rebounds during the 1986–87 season and gave every indication that he was emerging as one of the league's premier power forwards? Or the Willis who saw his scoring average plummet to 11.6 a game and his rebounds to 7.3 per in 1987–88? Or the Willis who didn't play at all in 1988–89 (broken foot) and was suspended by the Hawks for failing to adhere to his rehabilitation program and for not attending games? Whichever Willis shows up will be an immensely talented 7-0 athlete who can run the court as well as any big guy in the league. Willis is also an excellent jumper and a way above-average offensive rebounder (3.1 a game for his career). He has a decent post-up game, which includes a fine jump-hook, but he needs to diversify his repertoire. A big weakness is his foul shooting (.671 career).

DEFENSE/DEFENSIVE REBOUNDING

Because of his athleticism and his size, Willis is a solid defender; his short arms, however, stop him from being a shot blocker (only 42 blocks in 2,091 minutes in 1987–88). And Willis has been prone to foul trouble. He should be a better defensive rebounder, considering, again, his height and physicality (below average, per minute, for starting 4s over their careers).

THE FLOOR GAME

A remarkable statistic: In 2,091 minutes in 1987–88, Willis accumulated all of 28 assists, which works out to roughly an assist every one and a half games. His basketball IQ is adequate.

INTANGIBLES

While he keeps himself in superb shape, Willis needs to take more time to refine his basketball skills. In the past, he's been distracted by off-court issues and hasn't fully focused on his trade. He made himself a persona non grata last year and his maturity has been questioned.

IN SUM

An oft-repeated refrain last year was, "If the Hawks only had Willis." What they missed is an exceptionally mobile power forward who thrives in the transition game, has a better-than-adequate post-up game, and can defend and rebound. If he set his mind to it, Willis could be an All-Star, but he has yet to display the concentration needed to get there.

RICK'S RATINGS

Scoring: **B**
Shooting: **B**
Free Throw Shooting: **D**
Ball Handling: **C**
Passing: **D**

Defense: **A**
Defensive Rebounding: **B**
Shot Blocking: **D**
Intangibles: **B**
Overall: **B +**

David Wingate

Birthdate: December 15, 1963
Height: 6-5
Weight: 185
College: Georgetown University, Washington, D.C.
Drafted: Philadelphia on second round, 1986 (44th pick).
Position: Guard
Final 1989 Team: Philadelphia 76ers
Final 1988–89 Statistics:

G	Fg	Fga	Fg%	Ft	Fta	Ft%	Orb	Reb	Ast	Stl	To	Blk	Pts	Ppg
33	54	115	.470	27	34	.794	12	37	73	9	35	2	137	4.2

Three-point goals: 2–6 (.333)   **TSP:** .478

SCORING

Wingate went from a career-threatening 40 percent in 1987–88 to a more presentable .470 last season, an improvement that reflected his: (a) better shot selection, (b) improved jump shot, and (c) eschewing the jumper in favor of taking it to the hole, which is his finest offensive weapon. He can really attack the basket and elevate over people. Still, his jumper is suspect—he shoots a different way each time—it will have to improve if he wants to stick around.

Traded to the Spurs in August in the deal that sent Maurice Cheeks and Christian Welp to San Antonio for Johnny Dawkins and Jay Vincent.

DEFENSE/DEFENSIVE REBOUNDING

Wingate is a stopper, and you can't say that about too many players. He combines lateral quickness, good hands, excellent speed, determination, and knowledge about the game. In a trapping defense, you want David Wingate on the floor. He is an average defensive rebounder for his position.

THE FLOOR GAME

Wingate, who spent the final two months of the season on the injured list (knee), can play both guard positions but spent most of last year at the point. When Maurice Cheeks was injured, Wingate started six games. Otherwise, he was basically the third 1 in the rotation (behind Cheeks and Scott Brooks) and in the same slot as a 2 (behind Hersey Hawkins and Gerald Henderson). He is still learning the point, is slightly turnover-prone, but can handle the ball against pressure.

INTANGIBLES

Wingate has yet to find his niche as an NBA player. He lacks confidence in his overall abilities and hasn't figured out how to match his abilities to the NBA game.

IN SUM

Wingate must improve his outside shooting and his floor generalship. Strictly as a defender, he won't last long. But the Spurs lack depth in the backcourt, so he's on the right team.

RICK'S RATINGS

Scoring: **C**
Shooting: **C**
Free Throw Shooting: **B**
Ball Handling: **C**
Passing: **C**

Defense: **A**
Defensive Rebounding: **C**
Intangibles: **C**
Overall: **C –**

Randy Wittman

Birthdate: October 28, 1959
Height: 6-6
Weight: 210
College: Indiana University, Bloomington, Ind.
Drafted: Washington on first round, 1983 (22nd pick).
Position: Guard
Final 1989 Team: Indiana Pacers
Final 1988–89 Statistics:

G	Fg	Fga	Fg%	Ft	Fta	Ft%	Orb	Reb	Ast	Stl	To	Blk	Pts	Ppg
64	130	286	.455	28	41	.683	26	80	111	23	32	2	291	4.5

Three-point goals: 3–6 (.500)   **TSP:** .460

SCORING

In Sacramento, where he began the season, the reports of Wittman's decline were *not* greatly exaggerated. This once deadeye marskman—a career .507 shooter entering the year—had seemingly lost it. The change in scenery—Wittman had been traded in June 1988 to the Kings from Atlanta for Reggie Theus and the Hawks No. 1 pick in 1988 (which became Ricky Berry)—was a change for the worse. In Atlanta, he made a living getting open when Dominique Wilkins was double-teamed; in Sacramento, where there was no one to double-team, Wittman was forced, for the most part, to rely on his own, rather limited devices. He never could create a shot for himself and doesn't drive to the basket (throughout his career, he has averaged 25.4 minutes a game and an incredible 1.1 foul shots a game). So most of his offense comes from moving off screens, but he just couldn't find the basket, shooting .427 coming off the bench. Fortunately, he was traded in February to the Pacers with LaSalle Thompson for Wayman Tisdale. In Indiana, Wittman shot much better, but take note, Coach Versace: only in a starting role. In 11 starts, Wittman singed the nets at a .552 pace; as a reserve he shot a paltry .370. With Reggie Miller ensconced at the starting 2 spot, Wittman is going have to adapt to his backup role.

DEFENSE/DEFENSIVE REBOUNDING

Bobby Knight-schooled, Wittman is a smart defender who relies on positioning, rather than quickness, to get the job done. He's not a player who can apply a lot of pressure, but he won't hurt you on the defensive end. His contribution on the defensive boards is virtually nonexistent—on a per minute basis, his output was the lowest among backup 2s who played at least five games.

THE FLOOR GAME

Wittman is a fine passer who doesn't make mistakes. He was second among backup shooting guards with an outstanding 3.47 assist-to-turnover ratio. He moves well without the ball, as well as moving the ball to beat double-teams.

INTANGIBLES

Wittman is a team player. For example, in Sacramento, despite his own problems, he remained a positive influence on the team and actively encouraged his teammates.

IN SUM

The challenge for Wittman is to show that he can consistently stick the jumper off the bench. If not, he doesn't give you enough otherwise to make it worthwhile having him around.

RICK'S RATINGS

Scoring: **D**	Defense: **B**
Shooting: **C**	Defensive Rebounding: **D**
Free Throw Shooting: **D**	Intangibles: **B**
Ball Handling: **A**	Overall: **C –**
Passing: **A**	

Joe Wolf

Birthdate: December 17, 1964
Height: 6-10
Weight: 230
College: University of North Carolina, Chapel Hill, N.C.
Drafted: Los Angeles Clippers on first round, 1987 (13th pick).
Positions: Forward, Center
Final 1989 Team: Los Angeles Clippers
Final 1988–89 Statistics:

G	Fg	Fga	Fg%	Ft	Fta	Ft%	Orb	Reb	Ast	Stl	To	Blk	Pts	Ppg
66	170	402	.423	44	64	.688	83	271	113	32	94	16	386	5.8

Three-point goals: 2–14 (.143) **TSP:** .425

SCORING

Bob Thornton? Mike Brown? Ron Grandison? All of these players—none of whom you could confuse with offensive threats—outscored Wolf on a per minute basis last year. He shot a dreary .423 from the field (which followed his rookie year's .407) and just .688 from the line. He averaged 5.8 points a game, got to the line a mere one time a game (in 22 minutes per), and he seems unable to string together three good consecutive games. But the irony is that Wolf, at least on paper, has some NBA-level scoring ability. The 6-10 North Carolina grad, who has played the 3, the 4, and the 5, has a good-looking shot with range (20 feet), though he's not going to create it himself and has trouble getting it off when he's matched against quicker 3s. Which is why his niche in the league will likely be as a 4, who will give him less trouble when he's out on the floor. And he can also post up, using either hand to shoot the hook. One problem, perhaps a vestige from his Tar Heel days, where offensive expression tends to be submerged (you've heard the line: only one person has been able to stop Michael Jordan—Dean Smith), is that Wolf tends to be too unselfish; he needs to be more assertive offensively, to both look for his shot more (only 6.1 shots a game) and bang the offensive glass more consistently (1.3 offensive caroms).

DEFENSE/DEFENSIVE REBOUNDING

Wolf works hard defensively and understands help defense, but as a 4, he got pushed around a lot (he's a step slow for the 3s). Big priority: hit the weights and gain 15 to 20 pounds. Not a good jumper, Wolf doesn't block shots. Nor is he a good defensive rebounder (he relies on positioning); his numbers were way below average for backup 4s.

THE FLOOR GAME

If there are question marks about the rest of his game, there are few doubts about Wolf's passing. He can feed the post, makes the tough pass, and frequently handles the ball from the high post. As noted, he will give it up—to a fault.

INTANGIBLES

Wolf's confidence has taken a beating in his first two NBA seasons. Call it finesse, call it soft, his play has been passive, and he tends to disappear. He's shown flashes but simply hasn't competed with sufficient ferocity on a night-to-night basis.

IN SUM

While he's not exceptionally talented, Wolf has some skills—the touch, the passing, the court awareness—but hasn't come close to putting it all together. As one coach described it: "He needs to stand up and establish himself." But even an evolved Wolf is no better than a role player.

RICK'S RATINGS

Scoring: **D**	Defense: **B**
Shooting: **C**	Defensive Rebounding: **D**
Free Throw Shooting: **D**	Shot Blocking: **D**
Ball Handling: **A**	Intangibles: **C**
Passing: **A**	Overall: **C**

Mike Woodson

Birthdate: March 24, 1958
Height: 6-5
Weight: 198
College: Indiana University, Bloomington, Ind.
Drafted: New York on first round, 1980 (12th pick).
Position: Guard
Final 1989 Team: Houston Rockets
Final 1988–89 Statistics:

G	Fg	Fga	Fg%	Ft	Fta	Ft%	Orb	Reb	Ast	Stl	To	Blk	Pts	Ppg
81	410	936	.438	195	237	.823	51	194	206	89	136	18	1046	12.9

Three-point goals: 31–89 (.348)   **TSP:** .455

SCORING

To keep defenses from sagging on Akeem Olajuwon, Houston paid big dollars in the summer of 1988 for Woodson (then an unrestricted free agent) to provide a consistent perimeter game. With the later acquisition of Otis Thorpe, the need to establish an outside threat was reiterated. Woodson seemed like a good bet: He was a career .475 shooter, had scored wherever he played (New York, Kansas City/Sacramento, and the Los Angeles Clippers), and had a reputation for being an excellent outside shooter. But unfortunately, Woodson, never 100 percent physically last season (bad knee), had a miserable year, shooting .438 from the field (including .347 in the 3–1 playoff loss to Seattle) and never showed signs of consistency. It's not as if opponents were giving him the shot—so, to an extent, the idea of keeping defenses honest worked—he just wasn't hitting it, though. Curiously, Woodson had his best year from three-point land (.348). He is best coming off picks but is not a strictly catch-and-shoot man; once he gets it, he can bounce it a few times and create. One of his favorite moves is the fall-away baseline jumper. He's always been a good foul shooter, last year (.823).

DEFENSE/DEFENSIVE REBOUNDING

Woodson, a nine-year veteran, has lost a step, which hurts the Rockets because he's up against explosive 2s every night (in his conference alone, for example: Rolando Blackman, "Fat" Lever, and Byron Scott). But he works at it, and after a while adapted well to Chaney's defensive schemes. He's always been a below-average defensive rebounder.

THE FLOOR GAME

Woodson runs the floor intelligently, even though he's not known for his speed. His role is to shoot; he's never accumulated many assists. But he doesn't turn the ball over much.

INTANGIBLES

A class act is the widely held consensus. Woodson is a team player and follows the game plan well.

IN SUM

Woodson was a dud. He was obtained to provide consistent outside shooting and he simply didn't deliver. Considering that he has shot .437, .445, and .438 the last three years, what evidence is there that the 31-year-old will be better from hereon in?

RICK'S RATINGS

Scoring: **A**	Defense: **C**
Shooting: **C**	Defensive Rebounding: **C**
Free Throw Shooting: **A**	Intangibles: **B**
Ball Handling: **B**	Overall: **B –**
Passing: **C**	

Orlando Woolridge

Birthdate: December 16, 1959
Height: 6-9
Weight: 215
College: University of Notre Dame, Notre Dame, Ind.
Drafted: Chicago on first round, 1981 (6th pick).
Position: Forward
Final 1989 Team: Los Angeles Lakers
Final 1988–89 Statistics:

G	Fg	Fga	Fg%	Ft	Fta	Ft%	Orb	Reb	Ast	Stl	To	Blk	Pts	Ppg
74	231	494	.468	253	343	.738	81	270	58	30	103	65	715	9.7

Three-point goals: 0–1 (.000)   **TSP:** .468

SCORING

Woolridge, who was signed by the Lakers as an unrestricted free agent in August 1988 (because of injuries and time spent in a drug rehab center, Woolridge played only 19 games for the Nets during the 1987–88 season), came to L.A. with a reputation as a big-time scorer. Indeed, in the three seasons prior to 1987–88, he had averaged more than 20 ppg each year (one with the Nets, two with the Bulls), and he's averaged 16.7 ppg over his career. But the Lakers, with Magic (Johnson), Byron (Scott), James (Worthy), and Kareem (Abdul-Jabbar) providing the points, had other plans for "O." For one, they were going to convert him, a career small forward, to the big-forward spot (Woolridge effectively was taking Kurt Rambis' place, who signed with Charlotte). For another, they wanted him to focus on both boards and defense—particularly shot blocking, where they were needy. Then, too, Woolridge, a starter for most of his career, was slated to come off the bench. These multiple adjustments proved to be too much for the 30-year-old (in December) Woolridge to handle. While he played well in spots (such as against the Suns in the playoffs), for the most part "O" was a zero. His defense and rebounding were subpar, and his offensive output was insignificant. A career .522 shooter, he shot just .468. Some players need lots of minutes and lots of shots to get it going, but in Woolridge's case, neither was forthcoming. He averaged 6.7 shots in 20.1 minutes, down from 11.9 shots and 29.1 for his career. With limited shot opportunities, Woolridge tended to stick to what he does best: take the ball on the left wing, drive into the paint (he covers a lot of territory with each stride), and dunk it with either hand. It's a good move but, alas, it was just about his only move. After a while, everybody in the building knew what was coming when he got the ball. Opponents would give him room to shoot the jumper saying—"Orlando, if you're going to beat us, you'll have to do it from outside." But his jumper was on an extended vacation—he evidently had no confidence in it—and he continued to take it to the hole. At least he managed to get fouled a lot (4.6 attempts a game); though he's only a fair (.738 last year; .742 lifetime) foul shooter. Otherwise, he can be alley-ooped to—he's a phenomenal jumper—but his low-post game is underdeveloped. And despite his hulk of a physique and jumping ability, he's inconspicuous on the offensive glass (just 1.1 a game).

DEFENSE/DEFENSIVE REBOUNDING

Give Woolridge credit: a career nondefender, he made the effort on D. But he's not a good perimeter defender, and stamina was an issue. It's interesting that the Lakers thought they could get boards from Woolridge, because he's never been a good defensive rebounder. And indeed, per minute, his numbers were poor among backup 4s—Joe Wolf, Russ Schoene, and Blair Rasmussen all outrebounded him. Same thing for shot blocking. He's been just a so-so shot blocker throughout his career, and the pattern continued last year (0.9 a game in 1988–89).

THE FLOOR GAME

The impression was that Woolridge was turnover-prone—he got the ball stripped frequently and had a penchant for miscues in crucial situations—but per minute, his numbers were average. However, clearly, he is not a good ball handler or passer. While he has great end-to-end speed, he was often out of sync filling the lanes on the break.

INTANGIBLES

Woolridge had an extremely frustrating season, but he continued to play hard and made no waves. He's a recovering drug addict, and his rehabilitation takes effort—energy which is not available for the mental and physical demands of the NBA. For the Lakers, he's a critical insurance policy should Worthy's tendinitis (knee)—a chronic problem—become worse.

IN SUM

With Kareem gone, a logical place to look for more points is Woolridge. He—and the Lakers—will be better off if he's more than just an afterthought in the offense. He needs to regain confidence in his jumper.

RICK'S RATINGS

Scoring: **A**	Defense: **B**
Shooting: **C**	Defensive Rebounding: **D**
Free Throw Shooting: **C**	Shot Blocking: **B**
Ball Handling: **C**	Intangibles: **B**
Passing: **C**	Overall: **B –**

James Worthy

Birthdate: February 27, 1961
Height: 6-9
Weight: 235
College: University of North Carolina, Chapel Hill, N.C.
Drafted: Los Angeles on first round as an undergraduate, 1982 (1st pick).
Position: Forward
Final 1989 Team: Los Angeles Lakers
Final 1988–89 Statistics:

G	Fg	Fga	Fg%	Ft	Fta	Ft%	Orb	Reb	Ast	Stl	To	Blk	Pts	Ppg
81	702	1282	.548	251	321	.782	169	489	288	108	182	58	1657	20.5

Three-point goals: 2–23 (.087)   **TSP:** .548

SCORING

Worthy is your basic unstoppable small forward. (His brethren include the likes of Dominique Wilkins, Chris Mullin, Charles Barkley, Alex English, and Larry Bird.) Within 12 feet of the basket, he's as dangerous as anybody in the league. His best and brightest assets: an explosive first step, quickness, ambidexterity, and the ability to receive the ball in scoring position. For example, Worthy, whose 20.5 ppg in 1988–89 was his career best, will post up on the right block and utilizing that deadly first step, spin to the baseline for a dunk or his patented (actually, Julius Erving has the patent) arm-extended, one-hand-on-the-ball fingerroll. Or, in the same position, he'll fake to the baseline, and reverse and finish the play with his left hand. Worthy can also play facing the basket. He'll flash to the middle, receive the ball—with his huge hands, he catches everything—and with the quick release, shoot the 12-to-15 footer (his range, extended in recent years, is to 18 feet but he's best within 12 feet of the basket. Note his shooting percentage: .548 last season; .556 lifetime). His ability to turn either way *and* shoot the jumper accurately is what makes him so tough to guard. And, of course, the Lakers are fortunate to have both the league's best delivery man (Magic Johnson) and finisher (Worthy) on the break. And in half court, the tandem is just as dangerous. Worthy moves well without the ball, and Magic needs only a crack in the defense and, boom, Worthy has a layup. His foul shooting (.782 last year, .756 lifetime) doesn't quite jibe with the rest of his offensive excellence.

DEFENSE/DEFENSIVE REBOUNDING

He's not a stopper but Worthy is a solid, even underrated defender. He plays good position defense, anticipates well (1.3 steals a game), and has the versatility to guard 3s and even some 2s. Against the shooting guards, his advantage is size, though he's better against a Dale Ellis (a catch-and-shoot guy) than a Joe Dumars (who uses the dribble and took Worthy—and everybody else the Lakers put on him—apart in the NBA finals). For his career and last season (six total rebounds a game in 1988–89), Worthy has been an average defensive rebounder; of course, he's caught in the classic tradeoff between defensive rebounds and getting out on the break. As one source said, if he's going to be effective running the lane, "He needs to be leaning away from the board." But when needed, he will 'bound—case in point, the seventh game of the 1988 finals when he had his first triple double (16 rebounds, 36 points, and 10 assists).

THE FLOOR GAME

Worthy is the consummate wingman. He's fast, catches the ball, and never stops running. He can finish the break from either side, though being right-handed, he prefers that side. He's a decent passer (3.6 assists a game) who takes good care of the ball.

INTANGIBLES

Playoff time is Worthy Time. The measure of the man is the fact that he has consistently upgraded the level of his regular season play (and he's been on the All-Star team four times) during the playoffs. Last year, he was his usual prime-time self, scoring 24.8 a game (his best yet in the playoffs) and shooting .567 (he had just two off-games—games 1 and 2 in the finals against the Pistons). On most other teams, Worthy would be THE MAN; but with Magic and Kareem as teammates, he's played third fiddle. But the soft-spoken North Carolinian has never complained and seems comfortable with his low profile.

IN SUM

In 1985–86, after the Lakers had ignominiously lost to Houston in the second round of the playoffs, trade rumors swirled: Worthy was going to Dallas for Mark Aguirre (then with the Mavericks). Laker general manager Jerry West, resisting the prevailing winds, threatened to resign if the trade were consummated. Laker fans can thank West for his foresight. Worthy, along with Magic Johnson, has well earned the status "untouchable."

RICK'S RATINGS

Scoring: **AAA**	Defense: **A**
Shooting: **AA**	Defensive Rebounding: **B**
Free Throw Shooting: **B**	Intangibles: **AAA**
Ball Handling: **B**	Overall: **AAA**
Passing: **A**	

Danny Young

Birthdate: July 26, 1962
Height: 6-4
Weight: 175
College: Wake Forest University, Winston-Salem, N.C.
Drafted: Seattle on second round, 1984 (39th pick).
Position: Guard
Final 1989 Team: Portland Trail Blazers
Final 1988–89 Statistics:

G	Fg	Fga	Fg%	Ft	Fta	Ft%	Orb	Reb	Ast	Stl	To	Blk	Pts	Ppg
48	115	250	.460	50	64	.781	17	74	123	55	45	3	297	6.2

Three-point goals: 17–50 (.340)   **TSP:** .494

SCORING

Young, who was signed by the Blazers at the beginning of last year after Seattle waived him (he had played with the Sonics for four years), is a true point guard and, consequently, looks to distribute rather than to shoot. But Portland would like him to do more of the latter since he's a pretty fair marksman. In his best year, 1985–86, he shot .506, and while he hit only .460 in 1988–89, he's a fine three-point shooter (.340 last year and .327 lifetime). He's basically a standstill jump shooter who spots up to get his shot and will occasionally take it all the way to the hole. He doesn't hurt you from the foul line, either—.781 last year (.823 lifetime) and he makes the clutch free throws.

DEFENSE/DEFENSIVE REBOUNDING

Young plays fundamentally sound defense. He's not exceptionally quick but he moves his feet well, gets around screens, and does a good job of keeping his man away from the basket. His size, 6-4, but only 175, may explain his slightly below-average defensive rebounding numbers.

THE FLOOR GAME

Young is a careful ball handler who rarely loses the ball. In 1987–88 he led all guards with an incredible 6.10 assist-to-turnover ratio. Last year, he was down to an ordinary 2.73, though he was in the top 20 percent for fewest turnovers per minute among backup 1s. He's a conservative ball handler and doesn't take many chances. He can penetrate and dish, and does a nice job of getting the ball to Portland's big guns.

INTANGIBLES

His nickname is "Cool Breeze," so named for his ability to deal with pressure. A reliable point, he plays a solid all-around floor game.

IN SUM

Young is a dependable backup whose major assets include his hustling on defense and his ability to stay clear of making mistakes. On the other hand, he's not going to give you much in the way of scoring or creativity.

RICK'S RATINGS

Scoring: **C**
Shooting: **B**
Free Throw Shooting: **B**
Ball Handling: **A**
Passing: **A**

Defense: **B**
Defensive Rebounding: **C**
Playmaking: **B**
Intangibles: **B**
Overall: **B –**

The 54 Draft Picks and Others to Watch Out For

In 1988–89, for the first time, the NBA draft consisted of only two rounds. What follows is a *composite* evaluation of the draft picks (excluding Danny Ferry and Anthony Cook, who have signed to play in Italy) derived from interviews with NBA scouts and college coaches. Besides numerous viewings (both in person and on tape) of a player in regular season play and in the NCAA tournament (or NAIA tournament), three postseason events—the Portsmouth (Virginia) Invitational Tournament, the Orlando All-Star Classic, and the NBA Pre-Draft Instructional Camp in Chicago—play a major role in drafting decisions. These are referred to as Portsmouth, Orlando, and Chicago in the text.

With the draft reduced to two rounds, several players were not selected who would have been in years past (the draft was three rounds in 1987–88, seven in 1986–87, and ten in 1983–84). Players who are not drafted are free to negotiate with any team, though their chances of making it are slim. For example, only five of the 25 third-rounders in the 1987–88 draft (the undrafted players last season are, in effect, third rounders or worse) made NBA rosters in 1988–89, while 11 of the 324 players on opening rosters for 1988–89 were free agents who had not been drafted. Of course, with the two new expansion teams (the Orlando Magic and the Minnesota Timberwolves) there are an additional 24 jobs available this year.

Following the analysis of the draft picks, we discuss some of the leading undrafted college players who have either signed with a team or have been or are likely to be invited to a tryout camp. In the section titled "OTHERS," we discuss players who played in the CBA, abroad, or did not play at all last year who have a shot at making an NBA team. Included here are profiles of four foreign players—Drazen Petrovic of the Trail Blazers, Sarunas Marciulionis of the Warriors, Alexsandr Volkov of the Hawks, and Zarko Paspalj of the Spurs.

Pervis Ellison

Team: Sacramento Kings
Round: First
Overall: 1st
HW: 6-9, 201
College: Louisville

ANALYSIS

A franchise? ... No ... How about a complete player who will score in the mid-teens, average 8 to 9 rebounds a night, block a couple of shots, and make all the right passes? ... Not the people's choice—Sean Elliot was much preferred—but he can't guard NBA centers ... Nor can Wayman Tisdale or Jim Peterson, the only players the Kings have who even resemble centers (they are 4s) ... So Ellison makes a lot of sense from a defensive standpoint ... With his long wingspan, he's a seven-footer in a 6-9 body ... And he's a big-time shot blocker who can swat them with either hand ... Notion is that King GM Bill Russell drafted him because Ellison reminds Russell of himself ... But Russell was nowhere near the offensive player Ellison can be ... Does it with back-to-the-basket and quick power moves and half-hooks, or facing the basket from 13 feet and in ... Scenario has Ellison playing the 4 offensively with Tisdale at the 5, causing matchup problems (i.e., quickness) for opposition ... Great jumper (38-inch vertical leap) ... Kings think he's in Danny Ferry's class as a passer ... Weight, strength an issue ... Will have to get stronger ... His "coolness" also a concern ... But they said the same thing about Kareem Abdul-Jabbar (then Lew Alcindor) 20 years ago.

Sean Elliot

Team: San Antonio Spurs
Round: First
Overall: 3rd
HW: 6-8, 198
College: Arizona

ANALYSIS

Does it all ... Takes it to the bucket and finishes ... Takes it to the bucket and pulls up ... Takes it to the bucket and dishes ... Shoots the 20-footer (.437 from college three but doesn't have NBA three-point range) ... Posts up ... Sees the floor ... Creates for other people, particularly on penetration ... Rebounds well for his size (excellent jumper) ... Shoots free throws (.841 last season) ... Plays defense, though not all scouts convinced of his lateral quickness ... Handles well enough to play the 2, but he'll be the Spurs' starting 3 with Terry Cummings at the 4 and Willie Anderson at the 2 ... He and Anderson will occasionally exchange positions, giving San Antonio flexibility ... Spurs figure he's a better defender at the 3 than

Anderson . . . Also think he can be more effective exploiting 3s in half-court offense than Willie A . . . Explosive first step . . . Doubts about old knee injury may have scared off Clippers from drafting him at No. 2 . . . A finesse player who "overreacts to contact," according to one scout . . . Smart player . . . Does he have killer instinct? . . . Character and commitment in ample supply.

Glen Rice

Team: Miami Heat
Round: First
Overall: 4th
HW: 6-7, 210
College: Michigan

ANALYSIS

Can't miss, sure thing, etc. . . . Best pure shooter to come down the pike in a long time . . . And what range! . . . Downtown guy . . . Shot .516 from college three . . . No one doubts he'll be a premier trifecta shooter in the NBA . . . Will be big-time scorer for next decade . . . Particularly since he's playing for punchless (formerly punchless, that is) Heat . . . A 3/2 who runs the floor exceptionally well and has terrific hands . . . Dunks with the best of them . . . Skies . . . Underrated passer . . . Prime-time abilities confirmed by unforgettable NCAA tourney performance (30.7 a game) leading Michigan to title . . . Needs work on ball handling from the perimeter . . . Mentioned in same breath as Dale Ellis since both are catch-and-shoot guys . . . Can post up like Ellis, too . . . Knows how to use screens . . . He rebounds, too . . . Outstanding work ethic . . . Will help immediately.

J.R. Reid

Team: Charlotte Hornets
Round: First
Overall: 5th
HW: 6-9, 256
College: North Carolina

ANALYSIS

Was he fifth best player in draft? . . . Maybe not . . . But Charlotte owner George Shinn, mindful of his market, couldn't live with possibility that North Carolina grad Reid would "turn out to be a great player" with another team . . . Fell out of favor with many scouts because of sub-par junior year (he's an early entry) due to injury, reduced playing time, and reputed conflicts with Carolina coach Dean Smith . . . But consensus is that, like other Tar Heel alums (Michael Jordan, James Worthy, and Brad Daugherty to name three prominent examples), will be a better pro than collegian . . . "How can you not like him," said one scout, "He's huge, quick, and has great hands" . . . A 4, who may be Charlotte's starting 5 . . . Thrives in the low block . . . How effective will he be? . . . "I've seen players who don't have half his power or moves score in the NBA," said one scout . . . "He will get to the line a lot," said another . . . Questions have centered on his shooting ability facing the basket . . . Opinions run the gamut from he's a good, OK, or below-average shooter . . . Range is limited (12–14 feet) but he is a 4, after all . . . Fine runner of the floor . . . Physical player who hasn't been consistently aggressive, particularly on the boards . . . If he puts his mind to it, quickness could be a big edge guarding 4s. . . . Body is mature but may still have some growing up to do.

Stacey King

Team: Chicago Bulls
Round: First
Overall: 6th
HW: 6-10½, 240
College: Oklahoma

ANALYSIS

Smiles all around Chi-town when King was still available at No. 6 . . . Bulls lacked go-to guy with Michael Jordan out of the game . . . Bottom line on King: He finds a way to score . . . Averaged more than 26 a game in his senior year . . . Bread and butter is a turnaround in the blocks . . . Can also shoot the jump hook and runs the floor well for his size . . . Quick . . . Needs to develop more of a power game in the blocks and more deception down low . . . "He'll get his shot blocked initially," said one scout . . . A 4, but Bulls like knowing he can also play backup 5 . . . Particularly since Bill Cartwright is getting on in years (32) and nobody knows about Will Perdue . . . Many think he should be a better rebounder but he's not a slouch on the boards (10.2 per game last season but there were a lot of missed shots in Oklahoma's offense) . . . All-time Big Eight leader in blocked shots but there are doubts about his true shot-blocking skills . . . Has the frame to put on more weight . . . So-so toughness . . . Fair passer . . . Defensive intensity not consistent . . . Wants to improve and is willing to work . . . Scouts loved the fact that he showed in Orlando even though he had little to gain.

George McCloud

Team: Indiana Pacers
Round: First
Overall: 7th
HW: 6-7, 205
College: Florida State

ANALYSIS

The Pacers insist he is a point guard . . . A considerable body of opinion thinks otherwise . . . Indiana is understandably sensitive about the issue since its most glaring need is for a big-time 1 . . . And it would indeed be strange if they used the seventh pick to draft a player who doesn't really meet the job requirements . . . Better description: He's just a guard," said one scout . . . Pacers intend to play him at the 1 and the 2 so we'll find out soon enough whether he is a 1/2, 2/1, plain 1, or plain 2 . . . Maybe he's a 3, where he played a couple of years at Florida State . . . We do know a few things for sure . . . He is a *big* guard . . . He can score (22.8 ppg last season) . . . He "effortlessly" shoots the NBA three (.439 from the college three last year, though only .448 overall; shot selection is questionable at times) . . . He has superb vision and passing skills . . . Doesn't give defense a second thought . . . Could also be a much better rebounder . . . Has STAR written all over him if he increases his intensity and concentration level.

Randy White

Team: Dallas Mavericks
Round: First
Overall: 8th
HW: 6-7½, 240
College: Louisiana Tech

ANALYSIS

White's name, at least for now, mentioned in same breath as Karl Malone . . . Both are muscular power forwards from Louisiana Tech . . . Mavs made admitted mistake in passing on Utah's Malone in 1985 draft (selecting Detlef Schrempf instead) . . . Hoping their selection of White reaps same dividends as Jazz's choice of Mailman . . . They are similar players but White is *not* a Malone clone . . . Both excel at power game inside but White is better perimeter player (.447 from college three last season on 17-for-38) while Malone more gifted athlete . . . White's advantage will be taking 4s out on the floor . . . Mavs went from being best rebounding team in 1987–88 to second-worst last season (as a result of the absence of Roy Tarpley for most of the year and James Donaldson for last six weeks of season) . . . Tarpley one strike away under NBA's drug policy and Donaldson's knee iffy so White's potential to be a big-time rebounder (10.5 rpg last season) may be critical . . . Polished low-post player who can take opponents up with him . . . So-so ball handler . . . Extraordinary work ethic . . . All eyes on Dallas coach John MacLeod who hasn't had much success in handling young players.

Tom Hammonds

Team: Washington Bullets
Round: First
Overall: 9th
HW: 6-8, 220
College: Georgia Tech

ANALYSIS

'Tweener size. . . . A college 5 converting to the 3 and the 4 . . . Needs work on perimeter game . . . Doesn't handle the ball well . . . Live body . . . Can dunk in traffic . . . Impeccable intangibles . . . Description sound familiar? . . . Hammonds, according to one Eastern Conference scout, might be another Kenny Walker . . . But Bullets are hoping Hammonds amounts to more than the Knick forward, who has found his niche as a role player . . . Strength is inside, post-up game . . . Possesses deadly turnaround on the baseline from 7 to 10 feet . . . Small forward skills underdeveloped . . . Needs to extend range, learn to face the basket, and put the ball on the floor for more than a bounce or two . . . Not a dominating 'bounder but "can get NBA rebounds," was how one scout described it . . . Should play substantial minutes; may start (Terry Catledge, Bullets' starting 4 last year, selected in expansion by Orlando) . . . Quality person with big-time work ethic.

Pooh Richardson

Team: Minnesota Timberwolves
Round: First
Overall: 10th
HW: 6-2, 183
College: UCLA

ANALYSIS

In T-Wolves' mind, "truest" of point guards in draft . . . Equally adept running half-court offense or break . . . Makes good decisions and in senior year had an outstanding 3.3 assist-to-turnover ratio . . . Court awareness and passing skills are top-notch . . . He's not a blur but has above-average speed and quickness . . . Knock has been inconsistency as outside shooter, but quieted some critics with .555 senior year, including .495 from three-point country . . . But same critics point to his still-abominable foul shooting (.562 last season) . . . Gets after you defensively . . . Loves to play . . . Extremely coachable . . . Wants to be a leader . . . Minnesota felt it vital to fill critical point guard slot first.

Nick Anderson

Team: Orlando Magic
Round: First
Overall: 11th
HW: 6-4½, 205
College: Illinois

ANALYSIS

Think a young Bernard King . . . Same quick release on the way up and ability to explode over opponents . . . Same game face . . . Same scorer's mentality . . . King had more range and was better shooter early on . . . Anderson most comfortable from 12 feet and in (though he shot .364 from college three last season) . . . Quite a physical specimen . . . Great jumper, long arms, strong . . . Runs, can dunk on you in traffic, post up, fill the lanes, or hit the offensive glass . . . A 3 for now but he's only 6-4½ (he had been listed at 6-6) so eventually will move to the 2 spot . . . But has little experience in the backcourt . . . Decent passer and ball handler . . . "His best is in front of him," said one scout . . . Came out a year early to help family with medical bills.

Mookie Blaylock

Team: New Jersey Nets
Round: First
Overall: 12th
HW: 6-1, 185
College: Oklahoma

ANALYSIS

How desperate were Nets for point guard? . . . N.J-Portland deal which sent three-time All-Star Buck Williams to Portland for Blazers' pick at 12 (which became Blaylock) and oft-injured Sam Bowie can be viewed as Williams-for-Blaylock swap, with ultra-risky Bowie a throw in . . . Is Mookie that good? . . . Great defender—steals the ball, creates turnovers, wears down opposition—but so is Lester Conner, Nets' quarterback last year . . . Offensively, best asset is pushing the ball, foul line to foul line . . . "He moves the basketball," said one scout . . . Creates 3 on 2s and 2 on 1s . . . May not be as effective running a half-court offense . . . Exceptional quickness with explosive first step . . . Scouts wonder how well he creates for others . . . Perimeter shooting has been questioned (only .454 overall and just .650 from the line last season) but did can .371 of college trifectas in 1988–89 . . . Good rebounder for his position . . . Can run all day. . . . Orlando no-show perceived negatively by scouts but redeemed himself with fine Chicago play . . . First NCAA player to have two consecutive 200-assists, 100-steals seasons.

Michael Smith

Team: Boston Celtics
Round: First
Overall: 13th
HW: 6-10, 225
College: Brigham Young

ANALYSIS

Consider what Red Auerbach said after the draft . . . "He plays like Larry (Bird). I hope" . . . Two meanings gleaned . . . One, Smith is insurance policy should Bird not return to old self . . . Two, Smith's game in fact has elements of the master's . . . Both are three-point shooters, both are ambidextrous, both thread the needle from the forward spot . . . Like Bird, Smith is both scorer and shooter . . . Besides the long-range game, can also post up and is clever around the hoop . . . And again like Larry, doesn't miss foul shots (.925 last year) . . . Can put it on the floor . . . Runs the floor OK . . . Defense is a word he'll have to look up. . . . Didn't play it in college . . . Age (24—he was Mormon missionary for two years in Argentina) considered a plus . . . Not totally inconspicuous as a rebounder, either (8.6 a game in senior year) . . . May play a little 4, but is basically L.B.'s backup at 3.

Tim Hardaway

Team: Golden State Warriors
Round: First
Overall: 14th
HW: 5-10, 175
College: UTEP

ANALYSIS

Was the rage of Orlando and MVP at Portsmouth . . . Postseason play elevated him to point guard elite . . . Warriors felt he was most creative of this year's crop (B.J. Armstrong, Mookie Blaylock, Pooh Richardson, Sherman Douglas, Dana Barros, George McCloud) . . . Wonderful feel for the game . . . Fine penetrator and disher . . . "He knows how to get people the ball," said one scout . . . Small and chunky and strong . . . No doubts about his toughness, one of his major assets . . . His shot isn't pretty but he was .364 from three-land last year and averaged 22 a game . . . Readily beats opponents off the dribble . . . Has knack for shooting over people . . . Excellent speed and quickness . . . Since he was drafted by Don Nelson, no surprise he plays defense . . . A Hardaway/Mitch Richmond/Chris Mullin combo is going to drive opponents nuts.

Todd Lichti

Team: Denver Nuggets
Round: First
Overall: 15th
HW: 6-5½, 210
College: Stanford

ANALYSIS

Nuggets were looking point guard or power forward, but none to their liking were left, so took best player available . . . Lichti, a 2, has a lot going for him . . . Fearless driver who is completely ambidextrous and doesn't shy from contact . . . Best in the open court, so will mesh in Denver's system . . . "Better end-to-end than side-to-side," as one player personnel director described his play . . . Fine athlete with pro body (legs are major asset) who jumps extremely well . . . Strong defender who can guard 2s, some 1s, and an occasional 3 . . . Only superlatives for his intangibles . . . Plays exceptionally hard . . . Wants to succeed . . . Coachable . . . Question marks center in fact he is only "capable shooter—overrated," doesn't manufacture shot well off dribble, has moderately slow release, and suspect midrange game, though he can shoot the three (.434 from three-point range last year) . . . Just adequate ball handler . . . Might not be a star, but "he'll be as good as he's capable of becoming," said one scout.

Dana Barros

Team: Seattle Supersonics
Round: First
Overall: 16th
HW: 5-10, 170
College: Boston College

ANALYSIS

All of the 50-or-more win teams last season had one . . . A point guard who can score . . . Seattle won 47 games without one (Nate McMillian is worst scorer among starting 1s) . . . Enter Barros, a man who can spread defenses with his three-point bombs . . . Led Big East in scoring the last two seasons (21.9 ppg and 23.9 ppg) . . . Shot .429 from trifecta land in his senior year . . . Pure shooter who needs work on taking it to the hoop . . . But if experts question whether George McCloud is a 1, you have to ask the same question about Barros, who was basically a 2 at BC . . . Mind-set is geared toward shooting, so will have to make adjustment . . . Pushes ball well on break, though doesn't have blow-by ability in half court . . . Plays under control . . . Tough and durable . . . Didn't miss a game in four years of college ball . . . Pretty fair defender who will pressure the ball in backcourt . . . Quiet, shy type who will have to lead by example . . . In the Mark Price mold.

Shawn Kemp

Team: Seattle Supersonics
Round: First
Overall: 17th
HW: 6-10, 240
College: None

ANALYSIS

Sonics weren't only team drooling over this rawest of talents . . . Pistons, Lakers, Pacers all seriously interested

. . . More than one scout mentioned James Worthy as "reminds me of" for 19 year old who hasn't played organized ball since high school . . . Enrolled at Kentucky last year, was Proposition 48 casualty, then left school after pawning a necklace which teammate said was stolen from him . . . Trinity Valley Community College in Texas was next stop but he didn't play there . . . Then declared for draft . . . Tremendous athlete . . . Exceptional leaper, quick, good hands, fast, mobile . . . "Unbelievable skills and natural ability," said one very interested scout . . . He's more instinctual than knowledgeable about how to play . . . A 3/4 who can block shots, run the break, shoot the three . . . He didn't play center for his high school team! . . . Sees the floor . . . More of a perimeter player. . . . Obviously not ready for NBA combat . . . A lot of work ahead . . . But Sonics are willing to make a long term commitment . . . Seattle stocked with frontcourt players (Xavier McDaniel, Derrick McKey, Brad Sellers, Olden Polynice, Michael Cage) so won't be thrown to the wolves . . . A no pressure situation . . . Two years ago, was ranked third-best (behind Alonzo Mourning and Billy Owens) high school player in U.S. by some scouting services . . . Biggest needs: Grow up, play.

B.J. Armstrong

Team: Chicago Bulls
Round: First
Overall: 18th
HW: 6-2, 165
College: Iowa

ANALYSIS

With M.A. (Air) Jordan likely to spend time at the 2, Bulls needed a point guard . . . But one with a specific talent . . . Ability to bury open jumper when M.A. is double teamed . . . B.J., in Bulls' estimation, was most proficient outside shooter among points available in draft . . . Better as a spot-up shooter than creator of his own so fit is right . . . Shot .397 in treys in his senior year, and feeling is he has NBA three-point range . . . More of a scoring point than pure, though some feel penetrating and creating ability underrated . . . Others contend "not as quick as people think," . . . Everybody loves his off-the-court intangibles: "The kid you'd like your daughter to marry," etc. . . . But may be "too nice" . . . A little soft, defensively? . . . Then, again, he held his own in the rugged Big Ten . . . "Second-rounder" said one scout from a team that needed a point guard but opted not to take Armstrong in the first round . . . Shot .831 from the line for his college career.

Kenny Payne

Team: Philadelphia 76ers
Round: First

Overall: 19th
HW: 6-8, 225
College: Louisville

ANALYSIS

Philly surprised a few people with this pick . . . Early line had 76ers going for shot blocker or point guard . . . What they got was a pure shooter . . . Payne fills gaping hole at 3 spot, where Sixers had no point production after Cliff Robinson hurt his knee in December . . . Great open shooter with three-point range who one observer called second-best marksman in draft, after Glen Rice . . . Shot .429 from college three in senior year . . . A catch-and-shoot guy who doesn't put the ball on the floor to the hoop that well . . . Or create much off the dribble . . . Decent passer . . . Good, strong body . . . Will be vulnerable guarding quick 3s out on the floor . . . Good enough rebounder (5.7 a game as a senior).

Jeff Sanders

Team: Chicago Bulls
Round: First
Overall: 20th
HW: 6-9, 225
College: Georgia Southern

ANALYSIS

Conventional wisdom has it Bulls made great strides in draft . . . With a No. 6 pick (Stacey King), it's almost a given that team will get impact player . . . Real question is how good are other two picks, No. 18 (B.J. Armstrong) and No. 20, Sanders . . . Fact that he is a well-coordinated 6-9 who can score from the low post (excellent one-on-one ability) and has deft touch from 15 whets scouts' appetites . . . And runs the floor . . . And can rebound . . . And can put it on the floor . . . Before annointing him, however, note that he played the 4 and the 5 in college and will be a 3/4 in the NBA . . . Adjustment means ball handling and passing need to improve . . . So does strength; he's not a physical player . . . Needs 10 more pounds to be a viable 4 . . . Played at small Division I school and tended to coast . . . Didn't show consistent intensity, particularly on defense . . . Not soft but will have to show he can compete at NBA level . . . Will be fighting for minutes, since a Horace Grant-Scottie Pippen-King frontline rotation seems most likely . . . Many scouts had him as high second-rounder . . . Play in Chicago may have propelled him into first round . . . In body, reminds Chicago GM Jerry Krause of a young Cornbread Maxwell—flexible, loose-limbed, floppy kind of runner . . . "Lots of potential, may take some time," concluded one scout.

Blue Edwards

Team: Utah Jazz

Round: First
Overall: 21st
HW: 6-5, 225
College: East Carolina

ANALYSIS

Jazz's 2s didn't have good seasons (Darrell Griffith, 31, and aging; and Bobby Hansen, injury-plagued in 1988–89) . . . Need more punch, and Edwards is a long-term solution . . . Unheralded out of a small school, calling card is scoring ability . . . Fifth-leading point producer in nation with 26.7 a game . . . Can shoot with range (.490 last year from three) . . . Has fine first step to the hoop . . . Played some 3 in college but will be a 2 in the NBA . . . Can post up . . . Athlete: fast, quick, good jumper . . . Solidly built and ideal size . . . Rebounds too (almost seven a game in senior year) . . . Can he get his jumper with a man on him? . . . Intense . . . Play in Portsmouth and Chicago moved him up in draft . . . Utah considers him a project in the best sense of the term.

Byron Irvin

Team: Portland Trail Blazers
Round: First
Overall: 22nd
HW: 6-6, 191
College: Missouri

ANALYSIS

May never be a superstar but . . . Has good all-around skills . . . Shoots well (.348 from college three in 1988–89) but isn't major-league shooter Portland needs . . . He can score (19.1 ppg as senior) . . . Likes to pull up in transition . . . Pretty good driver, though some feel he lacks explosiveness . . . Rugged, hard-working defender . . . Oft-noted is "better basketball player than athlete" . . . Not extremely quick or great leaper . . . Unselfish . . . Good range—at least 20 feet . . . Shoots well off screens . . . Comes to play every night . . . Shot .826 from free throw line in senior year.

Roy Marble

Team: Atlanta Hawks
Round: First
Overall: 23rd
HW: 6-6, 190
College: Iowa

ANALYSIS

With departure of Reggie Theus (to Orlando), Hawks needed a shooter at the 2 spot . . . So why Marble, whose jumper leaves a little to be desired? . . . But he has improved . . . Did can .396 of his college trifectas in senior year . . . A decent (.761 in his senior year) foul shooter . . . Hawks sold on his athleticism . . . Toughness . . . Game is to the hoop . . . Loves to drive, draw contact, jump over people . . . Wiry strong . . . Skywalker . . . Hard to contain around the basket . . . Good defender on the ball . . . Adequate ball handler . . . Played the 2 only his senior year.

John Morton

Team: Cleveland Cavaliers
Round: First
Overall: 25th
HW: 6-3, 180
College: Seton Hall

ANALYSIS

Cavs need perimeter shooting and backup point guard . . . Rolled into one with Morton . . . He can play both guard positions, though is not a pure point . . . A scoring 1 . . . He'll shoot you in or he'll shoot you out . . . Streaky . . . Note his senior-year .436 shooting percentage . . . But who can forget his 35-point explosion against Michigan in the NCAA final? . . . Game didn't hurt his draft standing, not at all . . . Hard-nosed . . . Good quickness . . . Long arms . . . Can both drive it and shoot from distance . . . Orlando play also in his favor . . . NBA three-point range . . . More than adequate defender . . . New York street-tough, which the Cavs could use.

Vlade Divac

Team: Los Angeles Lakers
Round: First
Overall: 26th
HW: 7-1, 243
Previous Team: Partizan Belgrade

ANALYSIS

By all accounts, a major-league talent . . . Would have gone top 10 but for fact he speaks no English and doesn't always play hard . . . He can play 3 through 5 . . . Not a true center . . . But not strictly a perimeter player, either . . . Has range of offensive skills . . . Handles exceptionally for a guy his size . . . Actually brings the ball up court . . . Sees the court . . . Puts it on the floor to the hoop . . . Decent shooter with facing jumper from 15 to 18 feet . . . Lakers like his fluidity, unusual for tall European players . . . "Reminds me of Larry Nance," said one scout . . . Will have trouble defensively . . . Tends to stand erect . . . Will have to get better on the defensive glass . . . How good? Who knows? But, said one source, "Hard for him to *fail* since he's so tall, so skilled."

Kenny Battle

Team: Phoenix Suns (drafted by Detroit and acquired by trade along with Michael Williams for Anthony Cook)
Round: First
Overall: 27th
HW: 6-6, 211
College: Illinois

ANALYSIS

If he only had a jump shot . . . Perimeter game is suspect . . . Still, picked in first round which says something about the rest of his game . . . A lot to recommend . . . Intangibles loom large . . . Tough, enthusiastic, hard-nosed competitor . . . Exceptional runner of the floor . . . Scores on leaners and runners in the lane and by following his own missed shots . . . He can score . . . 18.2 ppg for his college career . . . All left . . . Needs a transition game to survive, so Suns may be right team . . . Will play D, too . . . Pro body . . . Jumps out of the gym.

Sherman Douglas

Team: Miami Heat
Round: Second
Overall: 28th
HW: 6-0, 180
College: Syracuse

ANALYSIS

Questions abound . . . And he didn't answer them—and lowered his stock—by not playing in Orlando or Chicago . . . Penetrates but can he finish? . . . Runs the break, but how about a half-court offense? . . . Will and can he play defense? ("He didn't play defense his senior year," said one scout) . . . Then, too, outside shooting and foul shooting (.632 last year) are both suspect . . . But, hey, didn't he make AP's All-American first team last year? . . . He *does* have some assets . . . Speed and quickness, for two examples . . . Has the patent on the alley-oop pass . . . Makes the big shot, the big steal, the big pass . . . "He produces," said one player personnel director . . . Competitiveness mentioned by several scouts as most distinctive trait . . . Rory Sparrow won't be around forever, so he'll get his opportunity with the Heat . . . Reunited with Syracuse teammate, Rony Seikely.

Dyron Nix

Team: Indiana Pacers (drafted by Charlotte and then traded for Stuart Gray)
Round: Second

Overall: 29th
HW: 6-7, 210
College: Tennessee

ANALYSIS

First word out of everybody's mouth: athlete... Above average jumping ability, floor speed... Small forward (nothing but) but at Orlando some 3 skills were in short supply... Like putting the ball on the floor... And a consistent jumper (range is limited—say 18 feet)... One scout: "Not a bad standstill shooter"... Others say range and shooting ability have improved... Fine post-up player... Solid rebounder on both boards (averaged as many as 10.7 rebounds a game for the Vols)... Not a good ball handler... Will venture to say he can beat out Anthony Frederick... Stock was much higher in junior year... Despite big numbers last season (21.6 ppg and 9.4 ppg) not perceived to have had good year... "Great guy to gamble on," said one player personnel director.

Frank Kornet

Team: Milwaukee Bucks
Round: Second
Overall: 30th
HW: 6-9, 235
College: Vanderbilt

ANALYSIS

Bucks' 1988–89 starting frontcourt, Terry Cummings and Larry Krystkowiak gone... Cummings to Spurs, Larry K. to career-threatening knee injury... Replacements include Greg Anderson (acquired from Spurs) and Kornet, a hustler/banger type... Like so many Milwaukee players, is versatile... A 4/3... Works hard on D... Hits the offensive glass... Big heart, plays smart... Biggest asset may be ability to run the floor... Has medium-range jumper... Limited one-on-one skills... Fundamentally sound... Play in Chicago pushed him higher in the draft than most expected.

Jeff Martin

Team: Los Angeles Clippers
Round: Second
Overall: 31st
HW: 6-6, 195
College: Murray State

ANALYSIS

Pure shooter... Shot .496 from college three in his senior year... Scored in college (25.7 ppg)... A small forward making the switch to the shooting guard... Therein lies some potential problems... Some feel he has trouble creating off the dribble... Others think he'll have a tough time of it defensively... Runs the floor well and is a good athlete... Was big fish in little pond (Ohio Valley Conference)... Can he adjust to being littler fish in bigger pond and compete against NBA 2s?... Clippers weak at 2 spot so will get careful look.

Stanley Brundy

Team: New Jersey Nets
Round: Second
Overall: 32nd
HW: 6-6½, 205
College: Depaul

ANALYSIS

A poorman's Dennis Rodman?... Extremely active on both boards... Nose for the ball... Live body... Sleek body... Runs the court well... Not a good shooter though showed in postseason tourneys that he has a little outside game... Very good athlete... Aggressive... Wouldn't have been drafted but impressed in Portsmouth and Chicago... A small 4 and that's a problem... With Buck Williams gone, Nets need rebounding and Stan may be the man—off the bench... "Gets a lot done," said one scout... Abominable foul shooter (.486 in his senior year).

Jay Edwards

Team: Los Angeles Clippers
Round: Second
Overall: 33rd
HW: 6-3½, 185
College: Indiana

ANALYSIS

Was MQP of the draft—Most Questionable Player... Numerous off-court problems have raised major questions regarding his attitude and maturity... Came to Chicago and did absolutely nothing to dispel doubts!... Looks like he's loafing when he plays—is quite fluid—but in fact was loafing in Chi... Listlessness cost him possible first-round selection... All that said, the man can shoot the ball... Shot an outstanding .448 from three-land in college and definitely has NBA three-point range... Some question whether he'll be able to get his shot against good NBA defenders... Not that quick... Handles it well enough... Last year's Big Ten Player of the Year as a sophomore... Came out early... Too early according to naysayers... If he gets his act together, can give Clippers the legitimate three-point threat they've lacked.

Gary Leonard

Team: Minnesota Timberwolves
Round: Second
Overall: 34th
HW: 7-1, 233
College: Missouri

ANALYSIS

Best true center available, so why did he drop to the second round? . . . If all you have to show for your first-round pick is a backup center, why bother? . . . Definitely a project . . . Unimpressive college numbers but he had an OK senior year . . . Game seems to be on the upswing . . . He is not a clod . . . Runs the floor . . . Catches and passes the ball . . . Has developed a jump hook but moves are mechanical . . . Should stay away from jump shot . . . Needs to get stronger . . . A back-to-the-basket player . . . Desire remains the big question mark . . . Will have time to develop with the T-Wolves.

Pat Durham

Team: Dallas Mavericks
Round: Second
Overall: 35th
HW: 6-7½, 206
College: Colorado State

ANALYSIS

Scouts liked his play in Orlando . . . Showed that he can play facing the basket and shoot it from outside . . . Pivot man in college so wasn't clear where he would play . . . He will be a 3 . . . He can also post up . . . More of a scorer, than a pure shooter . . . Goes to the offensive glass . . . Runs the court well . . . Not afraid of contact . . . Can be lobbed to . . . A Boyd Grant product at Colorado State so knows how to play D . . . Tough . . . Has shot blocking ability . . . High intensity . . . Still learning the 3 spot. . . . He'll back up Adrian Dantley.

Cliff Robinson

Team: Portland Trailblazers
Round: Second
Overall: 36th
HW: 6-11, 225
College: Connecticut

ANALYSIS

Draft position doesn't reflect talent level . . . Many thought he'd go in mid or late first round . . . Has all-around skills but intensity is a big issue . . . So is consistency, or more precisely, the lack of it . . . Played some center in college, but is 3/4 in the NBA . . . A Thurl Bailey 3 . . . Runs the court extremely well . . . Can score inside and outside, facing and back-to-the-basket . . . Adequate rebounder . . . Can block shots . . . Needs to improve strength and stamina . . . He might not make it but, on the other hand, he could be a very good player . . . Fact that Portland is looking to bolster its bench, helps his chances.

Michael Ansley

Team: Orlando Magic
Round: Second
Overall: 37th
HW: 6-8, 225
College: Alabama

ANALYSIS

Bruiser who will eventually be a 3, but for now is a 4 . . . Scouts worry about his size for the latter . . . However, he's a strong, physical player who likes to throw his body around . . . Relentless pounder of the offensive glass . . . Averaged 9.2 rebounds and 20.3 points in his senior year . . . Played well in Orlando Classic . . . Low-block mentality but does have ability—and confidence is growing—in 15 footer . . . Many thought he'd go higher than 37 . . . Others thought he was out of shape . . . Brings his hard hat every night . . . Does not match up well defensively with 3s on the perimeter . . . Plays a little out of control on occasion.

Doug West

Team: Minnesota Timberwolves
Round: Second
Overall: 38th
HW: 6-6, 200
College: Villanova

ANALYSIS

Terrific size for a 2 . . . Long wingspan . . . Has plenty of skills and is a fine athlete, too . . . Question marks about his shooting . . . Had lousy senior year, shooting just .459 . . . Looks like he should make every jumper . . . Didn't win many converts in Orlando . . . Can run the floor, good leaper, quick . . . Competes . . . Needs work on ball handling and passing but he's improved in those areas . . . Has to develop ability to create off dribble and better moves to hoop . . . Has the tools to be a quality defender . . . If he shoots consistently, great pick at 38.

Ed Horton

Team: Washington Bullets
Round: Second
Overall: 39th
HW: 6-8, 258
College: Iowa

ANALYSIS

Bullets went "large" in draft and Horton was case in point . . . (Other picks were 6-9 Tom Hammonds and 6-11¾ Doug Roth) . . . Has the classic bulk of a 4 but, for many tastes, it's a little much . . . Overweight in postseason competition . . . Played well in Orlando, but didn't play in Chicago which hurt his draft standing . . . So did his admission to drug rehab center in summer of 1988 . . . Has bunch of moves around the basket . . . Physical player who will pound both boards (11 rpg in his senior year) . . . Runs the floor well for his size . . . Good inside defender but not out on the floor . . . Not smooth . . . Can surprise with his quickness . . . With Terry Catledge's departure, figures to stick.

Dino Radja

Team: Boston Celtics
Round: Second
Overall: 40th
HT: 6-11
Last team: Yugoslavian national team

ANALYSIS

Can play the 4 and even some 5 . . . Post-up player who also can run the floor . . . In his favor: speaks English . . . Doesn't back down from anybody . . . "Will be a plodder in our league," said one scout . . . Mechanical . . . A blue-collar type who works hard on both ends . . . A backup player all the way . . . Sets good picks . . . Potentially a good rebounder . . . 22 years old.

Doug Roth

Team: Washington Bullets
Round: Second
Overall: 41st
HW: 6-11¾, 255
College: Tennessee

ANALYSIS

Was a consensus choice *not* to get drafted . . . Why, then? . . . Bullets aren't teeming with large bodies . . . Roth is almost seven foot . . . Few like his game . . . Is legally blind in one eye . . . Peripheral vision? . . . Needs something to hang his hat on besides size . . . Is just OK in all other categories though some think he's a good shooter from 12 to 15 feet . . . But just 7.4 ppg for his career and .471 from the field . . . Rebounds well enough, passes well enough . . . Coachable . . . A long shot.

Michael Cutright

Team: Denver Nuggets
Round: Second
Overall: 42nd
HW: 6-3½, 219
College: McNeese State

ANALYSIS

Never heard of him? . . . Well, when he entered the league, you probably never heard of the last guy to make it in the NBA from McNeese State, either . . . Fellow by the name of Joe Dumars . . . Actually, reminds some of Dumars' teammate Vinnie Johnson . . . A muscular 2 who can create his own shot, has great strength, is capable of making off-balance shots . . . Roly-poly looking, tends to the heavy side . . . When slimmer, has NBA body . . . A scorer and a shooter . . . Effective in transition and can shoot the three-pointer . . . Intensity level is suspect; plays hard intermittedly . . . Street-tough . . . Extra weight hurts him defensively . . . Does he have the dedication and discipline? . . . Nuggets chose him because he was best player available at 42.

Chucky Brown

Team: Cleveland Cavaliers
Round: Second
Overall: 43rd
HW: 6-8, 211
College: North Carolina State

ANALYSIS

Plays a 4's game in a 3's body . . . Rebounds well (nine a game as a senior). . . . Played inside in college . . . Will have to move out to the perimeter—i.e., a pro 3 . . . Can he develop consistency in his face-up jumper? . . . Decent post-up game . . . Adequate ball handling skills . . . Wiry strong . . . Active around the glass . . . Possesses good speed and quickness . . . Can run the floor . . . Tough . . . Plays hard . . . But sometimes disappears . . . Pretty fair defender . . . With Larry Nance out until at least December (recovering from ankle surgery), likely to make squad . . . Role player in the NBA.

Reggie Cross

Team: Philadelphia 76ers
Round: Second
Overall: 44th
HW: 6-8, 243
College: Hawaii

ANALYSIS

Banger . . . Loves contact . . . Undersized 4 or 'tweener who thrives inside . . . Can post up and score on larger players . . . "You have to like his intensity," said one scout . . . A center type in college but showed a 15-foot facing jumper in post-season play . . . Not a great leaper but gets more rebounds than he should with his wide body and big effort (8.1 rpg as a college senior) . . . 76ers are hoping he'll push veterans such as Ben Coleman . . . Work ethic is a big plus . . . Doesn't put the ball on the floor.

Scott Haffner

Team: Miami Heat
Round: Second
Overall: 45th
HW: 6-3½, 185
College: Evansville

ANALYSIS

No doubt, he can shoot . . . And Miami, lowest-scoring team in the league, needs players who can fill it up . . . Once scored 65 points in a college game . . . Averaged 24.5 as a college senior . . . Excellent three-point shooter (.458 in 1988–89) who will be able to shoot the pro 3 . . . His skinny body scared some . . . "He will get punished," said one scout . . . A "2 in a 1's body," said another . . . In fact, may have to play 1 to have a chance . . . Definitely needs to bulk up . . . He works hard defensively . . . Could have trouble putting the ball on the floor and scoring . . . Heady . . . Overachiever . . . Well-coached . . . Some think he'll have hard time sticking . . . May need CBA apprenticeship.

Ricky Blanton

Team: Phoenix Suns
Round: Second
Overall: 46th
HW: 6-7, 215
College: LSU

ANALYSIS

"He competes so well," said former Vanderbilt coach C.M.

Newton . . . And that appears to be the consensus . . . Has Bobby Hansen/Bill Hanzlik toughness about him . . . 2/3 swingman . . . Scored 20.3 a game in senior year . . . Can rebound . . . Though a solid .404 from three-point country in senior year, isn't considered a great shooter . . . Solid passer who sees the court . . . Aggressive defender . . . Cerebral player who is dedicated to game . . . Lacks quickness but compensates with hard work . . . Knows his limitations . . . Would have been drafted higher but hurt his knee in Orlando and subsequently underwent arthroscopic surgery in July . . . In the rotation but perhaps not a starter.

Reggie Turner

Team: Denver Nuggets
Round: Second
Overall: 47th
HW: 6-8½, 240
College: Alabama-Birmingham

ANALYSIS

Versatility is biggest plus . . . A 3/4 . . . Inside/out player . . . Big and strong enough to go inside . . . Also possesses nice shooting touch from 15 . . . Excellent foul shooter (.868 in his senior year) . . . Standstill jump shooter who doesn't create much off the dribble . . . Catch and shoot, catch and shoot . . . Some scouts feel that's all he does . . . Nuggets think he's a more than adequate rebounder . . . Fine body . . . Had good second half of senior year and played well in postseason, which helped his prospects . . . Coachable . . . Physical enough for a 4?

Junie Lewis

Team: Utah Jazz
Round: Second
Overall: 48th
HW: 6-2, 185
College: South Alabama

ANALYSIS

Jazz looking for backup to John Stockton, and Lewis may be the answer . . . Athleticism is major selling point . . . Exceptional leaper (40-inch vertical jump) . . . Strong . . . "Tough kid" . . . Played a lot of 2 at South Alabama, but last year was mostly point . . . Utah thinks he'll be a quality defender . . . And they like his unselfishness . . . Excellent one-on-one skills to the hole, but consistency and range on spot-up jumper suspect (just 1-for-13 from college three-point line) . . . But good mechanics . . . Rebounds on both boards . . . Understands the game . . . May be better as a middleman on the break than in half-court offense.

Haywoode Workman

Team: Atlanta Hawks
Round: Second
Overall: 49th
HW: 6-2½, 180
College: Oral Roberts

ANALYSIS

Could be a steal as the 49th pick . . . Was a 2/3 in college but will play the point in the NBA . . . Showed tremendous leadership abilities in Chicago . . . Shot decently from three-point in college (.366) but doesn't have NBA three-range . . . Strong . . . Likes the pull-up jumper in transition . . . Can create his own shot . . . Drives well . . . Very good rebounder for his position . . . Hawks looking to get tougher and Workman is ex-football player . . . Tenacious defender . . . Many scouts thought he would go in the 30–35 range.

Brian Quinnett

Team: New York Knicks
Round: Second
Overall: 50th
HW: 6-9, 236
College: Washington State

ANALYSIS

Can really stroke it . . . That's why he was drafted . . . Played the 4 and the 5 in college but will move to the 3 in the pros . . . Likes to pull up in transition . . . Also possesses a turnaround fadeaway and jump hook from the blocks . . . Has NBA three-point range. . . . Shot .364 from trifecta-land in college . . . Runs the court better than you'd think . . . Played in slow-down college attack but when unleashed, scored big—45 against Loyola Marymount . . . Put-the-ball-on-the-floor skills are OK . . . Decent passer . . . Not real physical defensively . . . Will have trouble guarding 3s . . . Better find a small 4 for him to match up with . . . Played well in postseason competition . . . Knick coach Stu Jackson was assistant coach at Washington State when he was a freshman.

Mike Morrison

Team: Phoenix Suns
Round: Second
Overall: 51st
HW: 6-4, 195
College: Loyola (Maryland)

ANALYSIS

Exceptional athlete . . . Jumping ability, quickness, speed—all there. . . . Played some 3 in college but wouldn't be anything but a 2 in the NBA . . . Strong for a guard . . . Averaged 21.8 ppg as a senior . . . Excellent driver and finisher. . . . Has good range . . . An improving jump shooter . . . But can he hit it consistently? . . . Defense needs work but he is athletic enough to stay with NBA 2s . . . Outstanding work ethic . . . "Has a chance," said one scout.

Greg Grant

Team: Phoenix Suns
Round: Second
Overall: 52nd
HW: 5-7, 145
College: Trenton State

ANALYSIS

A Spud Webb who can score . . . Led Division III in scoring with 32.6 a game . . . A jet . . . Exceptional quickness . . . He *is* tiny . . . Good shooter who hit the college trey but may have trouble with the NBA trifecta . . . Will uptempo an attack . . . Stock rose as a result of play in Portsmouth and Orlando . . . Very good passer . . . Knows how to play . . . Quick hands. . . . A *delight* to watch . . . Suns needed a backup for Kevin Johnson . . . Will have to beat out recently acquired (from Detroit) Michael Williams . . . Loves to play.

Jeff Hodge

Team: Dallas Mavericks
Round: Second
Overall: 53rd
HW: 6-3, 168
College: South Alabama

ANALYSIS

Lower echelon second-round pick, next-to-last selection . . . Says something about his chances . . . Not good . . . Major issue: played the 2 in college but will be converting to the 1 . . . Doesn't really have point skills . . . Was unimpressive in Orlando, and quick 1s took it from him in Chicago . . . But overall speed and quickness is good . . . Definitely can shoot the ball. . . . Another concern: whether thin body can take the pounding . . . Simply doesn't have size or strength for the 2 spot . . . Intangibles all check out . . . A head for the game . . . Solid work ethic . . . Winner.

Toney Mack

Team: Philadelphia 76ers
Round: Second
Overall: 54th
HW: 6-5, 220
College: Georgia

ANALYSIS

And, finally . . . The last player picked . . . A 3 converting to the 2 . . . Philly was looking for a scorer and they found one . . . Led country in scoring (41.3 ppg) as a high school senior . . . But career at Georgia was disappointing . . . Played only 12 games as a sophomore and missed all of senior year because of academic ineligibility . . . Overweight in his junior year . . . Streaky outside shooter with excellent range . . . Attacks the basket from the perimeter . . . Two questions: can he shoot well enough to be a backup guard (he'll be competing for a spot behind Hersey Hawkins)? . . . Can he get his shot off against NBA competition? . . . Has all the athletic skills but is "better athlete than basketball player," according to one scout . . . Plays hard.

Undrafted Rookies

KATO ARMSTRONG

College: SMU
HW: 6-1, 160
ANALYSIS: Super quick point guard . . . Scouts liked his work in Chicago . . . Previously thought too selfish . . . Showed he can distribute . . . Was academically ineligible after playing 12 games in senior year.

STEVE BABIARZ

College: State University of New York, at Potsdam
HW: 6-0, 165
ANALYSIS: Signed by New York Knicks . . . He can shoot from way out . . . Shot .444 in college trifectas in 1988–89 . . . Can make the play . . . NBA is big step from Division 3.

STEVE BUCKNALL

College: North Carolina
HW: 6-5½, 226
ANALYSIS: Jury out on NBA prospects . . . Was overweight in Chicago . . . In Chi, "played like he had a job outside of basketball," said one scout . . . Others like his body and think he can score in NBA.

JAY BURSON

College: Ohio State
HW: 6-0, 165
ANALYSIS: Health (he broke neck in February) obviously big issue . . . He's too small, too fragile, etc . . . But "he'll find a way to be on somebody's team," said one scout . . . Tremendous competitor . . . Fearless driver . . . Decent outside shooter . . . Will have to be a point guard . . . Signed by the Rockets.

ADRIAN CALDWELL

College: Lamar
HW: 6-8½, 263
ANALYSIS: Pro body . . . Potentially a good position rebounder . . . Offensive repertoire is virtually nil . . . Has the "touch of a blacksmith," said one scout . . . Needs to lose 10 to 15 pounds . . . "Could be a very good European player," opined one observer . . . NBA project . . . Signed by the Rockets.

CHRIS CHILDS

College: Boise State
HW: 6-2, 190
ANALYSIS: Has a point mentality . . . Plays hard . . . Fine defender . . . Surprised some that he didn't get drafted . . . Hit the college three-pointer at .437 pace.

LANARD COPELAND

College: Georgia State
HW: 6-6, 185
ANALYSIS: Scintillating performance (.645 from the field) in Southern California Summer Pro League piqued interest . . . 76ers signed him for guaranteed money . . . Previously considered CBA material . . . A 2 who is an excellent athlete . . . Didn't play high school ball . . . "Diamond-in-the-rough," was how one player personnel director described him.

TONY DAWSON

College: Florida State
HW: 6-6, 203
ANALYSIS: A scorer all the way . . . A 3 who could also play 2 . . . In Orlando, some felt he was a gunner . . . One leg shorter than the other, but doesn't seem to affect game.

BYRON DINKINS

College: UNC Charlotte
HW: 6-2, 167
ANALYSIS: Fact is will have tough time making team since Rockets have signed John Lucas and Anthony Bowie, who both play 1 . . . Didn't have a good senior year . . . Note his weight: strength is an issue—can he take the contact? . . . A scoring point but will have to think more like a pure point to survive . . . Tremendously quick . . . Hard worker . . . Can he shoot consistently?

TERRY DOZIER

College: South Carolina
HW: 6-9, 205
ANALYSIS: A skinny 3 . . . Jump shot is not consistent . . . Active defender . . . Bad sign: scoring average dropped in his last two collegiate seasons . . . Didn't impress in Orlando . . . Played well for Spurs in Southern California Summer Pro League.

KENNY DRUMMOND

College: High Point
HW: 5-8, 160
ANALYSIS: Fesity point guard who plays with a lot of confidence . . . Impressive in summer league play with Charlotte's team, but signed by Miami . . . Excellent quickness . . . Thrives in the open floor . . . Fearless driver who goes right at you . . . Can penetrate and dish . . . Shoots with range . . . Started college career at Sacramento City College, then a year at North Carolina State, and finished up at High Point . . . Will have to beat out Sherman Douglas.

CEDRIC GLOVER

College: Cincinnati
HW: 6-7½, 239
ANALYSIS: Had lousy senior year . . . His body is a big plus . . . Not much of an offensive player . . . Was college center but can he convert to the 4? . . . Was injured during season and in postseason.

PAUL (SNOOPY) GRAHAM

College: Ohio University
HW: 6-6, 206
ANALYSIS: A college small forward who will play shooting guard . . . Scorer and shooter . . . Not an overabundance of speed, quickness.

LOWELL HAMILTON

College: Illinois
HW: 6-7, 213
ANALYSIS: Good athlete . . . Runs, jumps, quick . . . But that's not enough . . . Small for a 4 but he has a 4's game. . . . Doesn't shoot or handle it well for a 3.

GERALD HAYWARD

College: Loyola (Illinois)
HW: 6-5, 220
ANALYSIS: A 2/3 who can really score . . . Led country in scoring as junior but only played 10 games last season due to academic ineligibility . . . Never been in great shape.

HUBERT HENDERSON

College: Southwest Missouri State
HW: 6-9, 215
ANALYSIS: Easily could have been drafted . . . A small forward who runs well and shoots well . . . Plays defense, too.

RANDY HENRY

College: Middle Tennessee State
HW: 6-9, 215
ANALYSIS: Several teams interested in this 3 who is a fine marksman . . . A little skinny. . . . Runs the court . . . Averaged 19.5 ppg last season.

RICHARD HOLLIS

College: Houston
HW: 6-5, 212
ANALYSIS: A physical 2 who can run, play D, and jumps well . . . Streaky shooter but has good range . . . Averaged 8.4 rebounds as senior.

MARK HUGHES

College: Michigan
HW: 6-8, 235
ANALYSIS: Signed by the Pistons after solid performance in Southern California Summer Pro League . . . Played center on NCAA champion Wolverines but is a 4 all the way in the NBA . . . With departure of Rick Mahorn, Pistons looking to shore up power forward slot . . . Fundamentally sound . . . Smart, heady player . . . Sets excellent picks . . . Decent rebounder . . . Shot well in summer league play.

JARREN JACKSON

College: Georgetown
HW: 6-4, 190
ANALYSIS: A pleasant surprise to some observers of Southern California Pro Summer League . . . A 2 with excellent quickness . . . A John Thompson product: defense may be what gets him a job . . . Hard-nosed . . . Adequate ball handler . . . His .439 from the field for his college career doesn't excite but note his .365 from three-point land . . . Can he get his own shot?

TRENT JACKSON

College: Wisconsin
HW: 6-0, 192
ANALYSIS: Played 2 in college but must be 1 in the NBA . . . Good shooter who is physically strong . . . Works hard on D.

WALLY LANCASTER

College: Virginia Tech
HW: 6-5, 216
ANALYSIS: Strictly a shooter, say many scouts . . . Can get his own shot . . . Shot .324 from college three . . . Defense? Passing?

JEFF LEBO

College: North Carolina
HW: 6-1½, 195
ANALYSIS: Knows how to play . . . Problem is he's too small for the 2, not quick, fast enough for 1 . . . Inconsistent shooter.

CLIFFORD LETT

College: Florida
HW: 6-3, 176
ANALYSIS: Quick guard who can play both the 1 and

2 . . . Shot well in Southern California Summer Pro League . . . Big-time jumper who rebounds well for his position . . . Doesn't excel at any one skill but has nice all-around game . . . One scout said biggest asset may be his work ethic . . . "Good person," said another.

ROB LOEFFEL

College: New Mexico
HW: 7-0, 299
ANALYSIS: 7-0 individuals have way of finding jobs in NBA . . . Hardly played last year as he backed up future NBAer Luc Longley . . . Has some shooting skills but he is overweight.

MEL McCANTS

College: Purdue
HW: 6-8¾, 256
ANALYSIS: Nice post-up game . . . Could afford to lose weight . . . Some scouts liked him in Orlando, some didn't.

MITCH McMULLEN

College: San Diego State
HW: 6-10½, 250
ANALYSIS: Few centers in draft, but still didn't get picked . . . Scores strictly within 5 feet of basket . . . Mechanical . . . Doesn't have real feel for game . . . Physical player who doesn't mind banging.

KEN (MOUSE) McFADDEN

College: Cleveland State
HW: 6-1, 178
ANALYSIS: Had his moments in Orlando but not enough to get drafted . . . A point guard who may look for his own too much . . . Speed and quickness are A–OK . . . Smart player.

BRENT McNEAL

College: Western Kentucky
HW: 6-3, 177
ANALYSIS: Quick, left-hander who is a converted 2, playing the point . . . Pretty fair defender . . . Can shoot the ball.

DARRYL OWENS

College: Nevada Reno
HW: 6-0, 200
ANALYSIS: A point guard who can fly . . . Shoots from outside but can also finish the play . . . Good defender . . . Powerful for his size.

RAMON RAMOS

College: Seton Hall
HW: 6-9½, 240
ANALYSIS: Signed by Portland . . . Big, strong NBA body

. . . Works hard . . . 10–12 foot range . . . Played center in college but would have to be a 4 in pros. . . . Defends well in low post.

CHARLES SMITH

College: Georgetown
HW: 6-1, 155
ANALYSIS: Biggest "name player" who wasn't drafted . . . Was major disappointment in Orlando and Chicago . . . One, he has scrawny body that may not be equipped for NBA pounding . . . Two, not a true point . . . He "sits on the ball too much," said one scout . . . Makes flashy play when safe one will do . . . Tough, a winner, clutch . . . Gets the ball up court in a hurry . . . He may be a Celtic.

JAY TAYLOR

College: Eastern Illinois
HW: 6-3, 190
ANALYSIS: Signed by Nets after lighting up Southern California Pro Summer League . . . Borderline pure shooter . . . Once scored 47 in college game . . . Can get his own shot and can shoot from NBA three-point territory (.375 for his college career from trifecta-land) . . . Consistent intensity . . . Physical, can take a pounding . . . Ball handling good enough that he could play some 1 . . . Nets weak at 2, so may get minutes.

LEONARD TAYLOR

College: University of California, at Berkeley
HW: 6-8, 225
ANALYSIS: Signed with Golden State Warriors . . . Great stroke . . . A 3, maybe a 4 . . . Injury-plagued college career may have scared some teams . . . Will rebound . . . Strong . . . Doesn't put the ball on the floor well.

CHARLIE THOMAS

College: New Mexico
HW: 6-7, 220
ANALYSIS: 'Tweener . . . Plays more like 4 but is small for position . . . Doesn't have a lot of range on jumper . . . Powerful player who runs floor well . . . Effective around the basket . . . hard worker.

JEFF TIMBERLAKE

College: Boston University
HW: 6-2, 205
ANALYSIS: Point guard with feel for game . . . Intensity, tenacity big plusses . . . Not a very good shooter (.421 last year).

KEITH WILSON

College: Arkansas
HW: 6-3, 175
ANALYSIS: D is strong suit . . . A 2 who has a good body and can score.

Others

RANDY ALLEN

College: Florida State
Final 1989 Team: Sacramento Kings
HW: 6-8, 230
ANALYSIS: Played seven games with Kings last season ... Big-time leaper who is an excellent rebounder ... Was fourth (11 a game) in CBA in rebounding in 1988–89 ... Particularly effective on offensive glass ... Runs the floor well ... Some feel he is a 'tweener, others say he is strictly a 4 ... Can block shots, too—eighth in the CBA last year, though tries to swat everything ... Must improve post moves ... OK shooter from 15 ... "Belongs in league but will never play," said one coach ... Has signed with Sacramento.

GENE BANKS

College: Duke
Final 1989 Team: Played in Italy
HW: 6-7, 215
ANALYSIS: Missed all of 1987–88 with torn achilles and played in Italy last year ... Member of Charlotte's summer league team this past summer ... Hornets looking for backup 3 ... Unlike incumbent starter, Kelly Tripucka, Banks plays D ... Fine post defender, but didn't shoot the ball well in summer league play ... The body has slowed a bit, though still can run the floor ... Gives you solid veteran presence.

KEN BANNISTER

College: St. Augustine's
Final 1989 Team: Los Angeles Clippers
HW: 6-9, 240
ANALYSIS: "The Animal" ... Apt nickname for prototype banger ... Main assets include ability to defend in low post and rebound on both boards ... Played most of 1988–89 in CBA and ended season with nine-game stint with Clippers ... Figures to be Benoit Benjamin's backup ... Carried excess baggage in CBA but lost weight this past summer ... Limited offensive repertoire but knows limitations ... Played with Knicks in 1984–85 and 1985–86 ... Terrible foul shooter (.510 lifetime).

WINSTON BENNETT

College: Kentucky
Final 1989 Team: Pensacola Tornados (CBA)

HW: 6-7, 210
ANALYSIS: Uncanny offensive rebounder ... Small forward converting from 4 spot ... Must improve his outside shooting ... Hard worker ... Aggressive defender ... Role player all the way ... Averaged 13.8 ppg and 11.1 rpg in CBA last season ... Signed by Cleveland.

LARRY DREW

College: Missouri
Final 1989 Team: Played in Italy
HW: 6-2, 190
ANALYSIS: Signed with the Lakers in August ... Lakers see him as a "third" guard who can play both positions ... Some feel he is a 2 in a 1's body ... Indeed, as point, is more a scorer than creator ... Quick ... Gets to the basket but can also shoot it from a distance, though not good three-point shooter (.247 lifetime) ... In 1987–88, per minute, had fewest steals and rebounds of starting points ... Streaky from perimeter ... Defense is questionable ... Never has played full 82-game season and missed 30 games in last two NBA seasons ... 31 years old ... Veteran who savors chance to play for winner.

DEAN GARRETT

College: Indiana
Final 1989 Team: Did Not Play
HW: 6-10, 220
ANALYSIS: Missed all of 1988–89 with fractured foot ... Can play center and power forward ... Shot blocking and defensive rebounding are biggest assets ... Post-up game is underdeveloped ... Good turnaround jump shot ... Lacks lateral quickness ... Spot player ... Good attitude ... Property of Phoenix.

DERRICK GERVIN

College: University of Texas-San Antonio
Final 1989 Team: Played in Spain
HW: 6-8, 215
ANALYSIS: George's brother ... Birthright is scoring ability ... A 3/2 who runs the floor well and has great nose for the ball on the offensive glass ... Excellent spring ... Streaky shooter ... Average defender ... Needs a running game to thrive ... Signed by Clippers in August following good performance for them in Southern California Summer Pro League.

STEVE HARRIS

College: University of Tulsa
Final 1989 Team: Albany Patroons (CBA)
HW: 6-5, 195
ANALYSIS: A 2 who can really stroke it . . . Range is 16 to 18 feet . . . Doesn't create that well for himself . . . Decent anticipation on D . . . Played three games with the Pistons last year and 10 with CBA's Albany Patroons . . . Lacks speed so is destined for NBA fringes . . . Has spent bulk of four-year career with Houston Rockets.

KEVIN HOLMES

College: DePaul
Final 1989 Team: Played in Switzerland
HW: 6-8, 225
ANALYSIS: Originally drafted by 76ers on fifth round in 1986 . . . Has played in Switzerland the last three seasons . . . Consensus is he's much better player now than when Philly drafted him . . . A 3/4 who jumps and defends well . . . Offensive skills limited . . . Averaged 7.6 ppg for his college career but 25 a game last year . . . 76ers will give him a shot.

LEWIS LLOYD

College: Drake
Final 1989 Team: Cedar Rapids Silver Bullets (CBA)
HW: 6-6, 205
ANALYSIS: Readmitted to NBA after being banned for violating league's anti-drug rules in January 1987 . . . Saw limited action in CBA last season . . . One of the premier open-court talents in the league . . . He'll get you two on the break . . . Has never shot less than 50 percent but has limited range on his jumper and is only a fair outside shooter . . . Game is strong around the basket—can finish in traffic . . . Defense is not high on list of priorities . . . Instinctual player . . . Likes to leak out or, as they say on the playground, cherry pick . . . Houston could use his help.

SIDNEY LOWE

College: North Carolina State
Final 1989 Team: Charlotte Hornets
HW: 6-0, 195
ANALYSIS: Played 14 games with the Hornets last season but signed with Minnesota . . . Not surprising, as Coach Musselman, who coached him in the CBA, is one of his biggest fans . . . Has genius-level basketball IQ . . . A coach on the floor who can run a complicated offense and plays the point role to a T . . . In 250 minutes with Charlotte, had best assist-to-turnover ratio in league . . . Is not a scoring threat and doesn't look for shot . . . Will play D, but the years (he's 29) are starting to show.

SARUNAS MARCIULIONIS

Final 1989 Team: Soviet National Team
HW: 6-4, 190
ANALYSIS: First Soviet player signed to play in the NBA (he is Lithuanian, not Russian) . . . Went with Warriors because he was sold on Coach Don Nelson . . . Left-handed 2 who can also play the point . . . Excellent driver who can dunk with either hand . . . Decent outside shooter with 20-foot range . . . Sees the floor and handles it well . . . Quicker than most foreign players . . . Penetrates and finishes or penetrates and dishes . . . Competitive and physical . . . Plays hard every night . . . May get into foul trouble since he's so aggressive on D . . . Understands some English but speaks little . . . Good hands, quick feet . . . Work ethic is beyond reproach . . . Gail Goodrich is one name that comes to mind.

ANTHONY MASON

College: Tennessee State
Final 1989 Team: Turkish Professional League
HW: 6-8, 240
ANALYSIS: Played in Turkey last season and doesn't want to go back . . . Was on Nets team in Southern California Summer Pro League . . . N.J. could use his big body since Buck Williams is gone to Portland . . . Problem: What position does he play? . . . Played some 2 in college but ball handling skills are not the greatest, lacks quickness for 3, and is a small 4 . . . Has three-point range but also will bang on the offensive board . . . Power player.

CARLTON McKINNEY

College: SMU
Final 1989 Team: Played in Philippines after beginning season with Topeka Sizzlers (CBA)
HW: 6-4, 200
ANALYSIS: Strong performance in Southern California Summer Pro League earned him a contract with Clippers . . . A 2/3 who can put points on the board . . . Was third-leading scorer in CBA last year (23.3 ppg) . . . Good athlete . . . Can get his shot off over big guys . . . Runs the floor well . . . Needs improvement in ball handling skills . . . Has quickness to play D but doesn't apply himself consistently.

SAM MITCHELL

College: Mercer (Georgia)
Final 1989 Team: Played in France
HW: 6-7, 210
ANALYSIS: Signed by Minnesota . . . Played for T-Wolves coach Musselman in CBA in 1986–87 . . . A 4/3 who is quality rebounder on both boards . . . Scorer rather than shooter who runs the floor well . . . Averaged 28.5 ppg last season in France . . . Hard worker who gets job done defensively . . . Knows his limitations . . . Likes the open floor . . . Versatility a big plus.

TOD MURPHY

College: University of California-Irvine
Final 1989 Team: Played in Spain
HW: 6-9, 230
ANALYSIS: A 4/5 who runs the floor well and shoots

effectively facing the basket . . . Played in Spain last year after stint with Minnesota coach Musselman in CBA in 1987–88 . . . "Underrated," said one coach . . . "Hasn't gotten a chance," said another . . . Well-drilled defender . . . Good work ethic and accepts any role . . . Will get his shot with Minnesota.

JAWANN OLDHAM

College: Seattle University
Final 1989 Team: Did Not Play
HW: 7-0, 215
ANALYSIS: Missed all of 1988–89 due to knee injury (anterior cruciate ligament) . . . Strengths are defense and shot blocking . . . Has thrice averaged more than two blocks a game in eight-year career . . . Runs the floor well but otherwise has limited offensive skills (half-hook is best shot) . . . Problem is he has high opinion of self not shared by others . . . If accepts backup role (he better since first-round pick Pervis Ellison will start), Kings have themselves a competent reserve center.

ZARKO PASPALJ

Final 1989 Team: Partizan Belgrade
HW: 6-9, 215
ANALYSIS: One of four Yugoslavian players (others are Vlade Divac of Lakers, Drazan Petrovic of Trail Blazers, and Dino Radja of Celtics) signed by NBA teams this season . . . Small forward with decent offensive skills . . . "He can shoot, pass, and dribble," summarized one coach . . . Understands the game . . . Has a lot to learn on D . . . Reasonably fluid for a European player . . . Needs to get stronger . . . Speaks limited English but comprehends fairly well . . . Signed by Spurs.

DRAZEN PETROVIC

Final 1989 Team: Real Madrid
HW: 6-5, 190
ANALYSIS: One of the most celebrated European players . . . Can flat out shoot the ball . . . Has NBA three-point range . . . A 2 who could also play 1 . . . Had been some concern that he only thought shot but has markedly improved ability to create for others . . . Could have some trouble creating for himself off the dribble but would thrive in the kick-in, kick-out game since is great spot-up shooter . . . Speaks English . . . Speed and quickness average by American standards . . . Excellent ball handler . . . Never heard of defense . . . Will he be happy playing reserve role after being majordomo abroad? . . . He says he savors the challenge of making it here . . . Reminds some of Pistol Pete Maravich . . . Signed by Portland.

DAREN QUEENAN

College: Lehigh
Final 1989 Team: Charleston Gunners (CBA)
HW: 6-5, 190
ANALYSIS: Last season was second-leading scorer (tied with Ron Rowan at 24.7) and Rookie of the Year in CBA

. . . A 2 with Terry Teagle-like elevation on jumper . . . Converting from small forward and hasn't shown much ability to put it on the floor . . . Excellent range (shot .392 from three-point country in CBA) though tends to be streaky . . . Everybody loves his attitude . . . Physical tools—speed, strength, quickness—are NBA caliber . . . Signed by the Pistons.

JIM ROWINSKI

College: Purdue
Final 1989 Team: Philadelphia 76ers
HW: 6-8, 260
ANALYSIS: With departure of Christian Welp to Spurs, could be 76ers backup center . . . Can also play 4 . . . Weightlifter physique . . . Plays hard . . . Can make 16 to 18 foot shot and get to the line off drive . . . Sets terrific picks . . . Lateral quickness is suspect . . . Limited role player.

DONALD ROYAL

College: Notre Dame
Final 1989 Team: Cedar Rapids Silver Bullets (CBA)
HW: 6-8, 210
ANALYSIS: Signed by Timberwolves after impressive showings in summer league play . . . A small forward who gets to the basket and gets to the line . . . Hard-working defender . . . Above-average quickness . . . Solid all-around player . . . Big question is can he hit the outside shot consistently?

JIM THOMAS

College: Indiana
Final 1989 Team: Rapid City Thrillers (CBA)
HW: 6-3, 190
ANALYSIS: Signed by Timberwolves . . . Steady guard who can play 1 or 2, though likely stronger at the latter . . . Plays under control . . . Fine passer . . . A Bobby Knight product: tough defender . . . Doesn't excel in any one area but doesn't have any major weaknesses . . . Averaged 8.6 ppg in three NBA campaigns with Indiana (1983–84 and 1984–85) and Los Angeles Clippers (1985–86).

JEFF TURNER

College: Vanderbilt
Final 1989 Team: Played in Italy
HW: 6-9, 240
ANALYSIS: Has played the last two years in Italy . . . Played three seasons (1984–1987) with the Nets with little impact . . . Then was a step slow for the 3s and not physical enough for the 4s . . . Now says he feels more comfortable being in NBA . . . Shooting is major asset . . . Didn't have three-point range when he left; does now . . . Runs the floor well . . . Smart player . . . Orlando sees him as another first-round pick.

MEL TURPIN

College: Kentucky

Final 1989 Team: Played in Spain
HW: 6-11, 275
ANALYSIS: Bullets signed appropriately nicknamed "Dinner Bell Mel" in July . . . Back for a second helping of NBA after playing last year in Spain . . . In first go-around, ate himself out of the league . . . In Utah (1987–88), his last stop before going abroad, was fined significant chunk of salary for surpassing weight limits but continued to gorge . . . Previously played for Cavaliers (1984–1987) where had best season in 1985–86, when he averaged 13.7 ppg and 7 rpg . . . Shame of it is that he's a talent . . . A center with a fine touch to 17 feet . . . When in shape, can run the floor and is quick reactor to the ball on boards . . . If anybody can whip him into form, it's Wes Unseld.

ALEKSANDR VOLKOV

Final 1989 Team: Soviet National Team
HW: 6-10, 220
ANALYSIS: One of two Soviet players (Sarunas Marciulionis of the Warriors is the other) in the league . . . Unlike his countryman, Volkov isn't expected to be impact player . . . Hawks signed him to three-year deal in August . . . A slashing 3/4 who runs the floor well and passes adeptly for a big man . . . Can put it on the floor but needs to drastically improve his outside shot . . . Would have preferred another team besides Hawks who are stocked with talented forwards . . . Very determined . . . Has a feel for the game . . . Understands some English but will take a while before he can comprehend instructions about sophisticated NBA offenses and defenses.

MITCHELL WIGGINS

College: Florida State
Final 1989 Team: Did Not Play
HW: 6-4, 185
ANALYSIS: Missed two and two-thirds seasons after being disqualified under league's Anti-Drug Program in January 1987 . . . Rockets will be a better team if he's what he used to be . . . A quality defender . . . Dangerous offensive rebounder . . . Tough . . . Outside shot is suspect . . . Handles adequately for a 2 . . . Did not play organized ball last season.